GLOBAL GOLIATHS

GLOBAL GOLIATHS

MULTINATIONAL CORPORATIONS IN THE 21ST CENTURY ECONOMY

Edited by

C. FRITZ FOLEY
JAMES R. HINES JR.
DAVID WESSEL

BROOKINGS INSTITUTION PRESS
Washington, D.C.

1775 Massachusetts Avenue, N.W.
Washington, D.C. 20036
www.brookings.edu

The Brookings Institution is a private nonprofit organization devoted to research, education, and publication on important issues of domestic and foreign policy. Its principal purpose is to bring the highest quality independent research and analysis to bear on current and emerging policy problems. Interpretations or conclusions in Brookings publications should be understood to be solely those of the authors.

Library of Congress Control Number: 2021932886

ISBN 9780815738558 (pbk)
ISBN 9780815738565 (ebook)

9 8 7 6 5 4 3 2 1

Typeset in Minion Pro

Composition by Elliott Beard

CONTENTS

ACKNOWLEDGMENTS

The editors thank Stephanie Cencula, Haowen Chen, Jeffrey Cheng, Manuel Alcala Kovalski, and Jessica McCloskey. This work was supported by the Smith Richardson Foundation, the European Tax Policy Forum, and the Hutchins Center on Fiscal and Monetary Policy at the Brookings Institution, but does not represent their views. The views expressed here are those of the authors and do not necessarily represent the U.S. Bureau of Economic Analysis or the U.S. Department of Commerce. Foley thanks the Division of Research of the Harvard Business School for financial support.

1

Multinational Activity in the Modern World

C. FRITZ FOLEY
JAMES R. HINES JR.
RAYMOND J. MATALONI JR.
DAVID WESSEL

> "The multinational corporation has become one of the most controversial economic and political institutions of our time. What international investment does to jobs, exports, prices, income distribution, access to raw materials, taxes, and market power is debated in host and home countries alike. To some observers, multinationals threaten the international economic and political system; to others, they stabilize international relations. In one view, they are engines of progress; in another, agents of exploitation."
>
> —From the foreword to *American Multinationals and American Interests* (1978)[1]

Multinational corporations are the global goliaths of modern times. These entities collectively are responsible for large portions of world production, employment, investment, international trade, research, and innovation. Although their economic impact is most pronounced in high-income countries, where their activities have been concentrated historically, their reach increasingly extends to every corner of the world. Decisions made by these firms affect not only those who work for them, buy from them, do business with them, and compete with them, but also communities and countries in which they are located. As a result, their operations and activities are subjects of considerable interest and heated speculation.

To some, multinational firms are highly problematic. From this vantage point, these firms seek to monopolize markets, exploit foreign and domestic labor, avoid paying taxes, dodge government regulations, manage innovation inappropriately, and exploit their financial positions to the detriment of other companies. Large multinational firms are uniquely capable of deploying their market positions and influence over government to solidify their control, obtaining outsized profits with actions that undermine the public interest. "Huge multinational companies often act as if the rules we all live by don't apply to them. They use loopholes to claim they don't owe tax and cynically push their workers to the limit," the former head of Britain's Labor Party, Jeremy Corbyn, has said.[2] Lawrence Summers, a former U.S. Treasury secretary, adds: "There is no gap in the architecture of globalization more serious than the failure of nations to prevent global companies and wealthy individuals from escaping taxation through tax havens, accounting devices, and pressure to bring down business tax rates."[3]

To others, multinational firms are the epitome of modern capitalism, producing many of the benefits of economic life that many take for granted. The McKinsey Global Institute, an arm of the consultancy, offers that multinational corporations (MNCs) "contribute disproportionately to the U.S. economy's growth and health" and are responsible for more than 40 percent of all the gains in U.S. labor productivity since 1990.[4] And Matthew J. Slaughter, dean of the Tuck School of Business at Dartmouth, challenges the view—espoused by many pundits—that U.S. multinationals export American jobs. "[W]hen U.S. multinationals hire more people at their overseas affiliates, it does not come at the expense of American jobs," he writes. "How can this be? Large firms need workers of many different skills and occupations, and the jobs done by employees abroad are often complements to, not substitutes for, those done by workers at home. Manufacturing abroad, for example, can allow workers in the United States to focus on higher value-added tasks such as research and development, marketing, and general management."[5]

Differing views of multinational corporations carry implications not only for understanding today's world economy but also for government policies. Governments contract with multinational corporations, tax them, and regulate them. Diplomatic negotiations, international treaties and economic agreements, and even military interventions are of central concern to international investors. Furthermore, governments offer multinational firms tax concessions and other inducements to attract and retain their activities. These interactions are premised on views of the nature of the multinational enterprise, and its role in the modern economy, over which there is considerable difference of opinion.

This book offers fact-based analysis of the activities of multinational corporations. For this purpose, we apply the definition used in foreign direct investment statistics: multinationals are business entities with one or more foreign affiliates in which the parent company holds at least a 10 percent ownership stake, although most foreign affiliates are 100 percent–owned by their parents.[6] Thoughtful consideration of the evidence can augment our understanding of multinational firms, contributing to informed public discussion and better public policies. This chapter puts the modern multinational enterprise in historical and global context and identifies important patterns that appear in publicly available data. Subsequent chapters, written by distinguished scholars with relevant expertise, assemble the best available evidence to address some of the key questions about multinationals that arise in public debates: Do U.S. multinationals export jobs? Do they exploit foreign workers? What drives multinationals to look beyond home-country borders? Do they shift profits to tax havens to the detriment of other countries? Where do they conduct R&D, and why? Does the rise of the digital economy allow multinationals to dominate their markets, or does it challenge their market power? Do multinational corporations have an edge over other firms in raising money? How important are cross-border takeovers, and what drives them? How have U.S., European, and Japanese multinationals responded to the remarkable rise of Asia—China, in particular?

This book was largely completed prior to the outbreak of the COVID-19 pandemic, which—in addition to killing people all over the world—led to a deep global recession and disrupted global trade flows and supply chains. As of this writing, we do not know how long it will take the global economy to recover, or how the behavior of multinational corporations and national governments will change as a result. Even before the pandemic, global trade measured as the sum of global imports and exports as a share of Gross Domestic Product was falling for the first time since World War II, a development that leads trade historian Douglas Irwin to declare that globalization is in retreat.[7] The pandemic, Irwin says, adds momentum to the deglobalization trend. The rise of protectionist political leaders, animosity toward foreigners and immigrants, redefinitions of "national security" to extend to public health, attacks on multinational institutions such as the WTO, and the rethinking of global supply chains and the virtues of keeping more production at home undoubtedly will shape decisions made by multinational corporations and by governments. We do not attempt to predict what multinationals and governments will decide or how these decisions will affect the trends that this book documents, but we recognize this time may prove to be an inflection point in the history of globalization. As William Baldwin and Eiichi Tomiura warn: "There is a danger of permanent damage to the trade system driven by policy and firms' reactions. The combination of the United States' ongoing trade war against all of its trading partners (but especially China) and the supply-chain disruptions that are likely to be caused by COVID-19 could lead to a push to repatriate supply chains. Since the supply chains were internationalized to improve productivity, their undoing would do the opposite."[8]

Concerns about the role of multinational corporations in the economy and society are not new, and this is not the first time that their activities have been subject to comprehensive examination. In 1978, C. Fred Bergsten, Thomas Horst, and Theodore Moran published *American Multinationals and American Interests*, a volume that synthesized the state of knowledge and captured the worries of the era over the growing size and power of multinational corporations. In the late 1970s, the U.S. economy still exhibited its postwar economic preeminence, as symbolized by large U.S. multinational corporations that seemingly controlled the industries and markets in which they operated and appeared able to keep foreign competitors and governments at bay. Bergsten, Horst, and Moran catalogued the growth, size, and influence of U.S. multinational firms, noting the benefits that size and market leadership conferred, and posed the question of to what extent governments and private competitors would be able to limit the power of large U.S. multinationals in the future.

A lot has changed since then. Between 1978 and 2020, Asian economies rapidly expanded while economic growth in the West decelerated. China, in particular, established itself as one of the world's largest economies and a formidable competitor to the United States. Other emerging markets also have become major economic players. The Berlin Wall fell—and, with it, Soviet domination of Eastern Europe. Nineteen European countries surrendered their national currencies to join the eurozone. Central banks around the world now wrestle not with too much inflation, but too little. The internet has changed almost every aspect of business and daily life. The average share of workers in manufacturing in OECD countries fell from 22.5 percent in 1978 to 13.5 percent in 2019, with corresponding increases in shares of workers in services.[9] Labor's share of national income appears to have fallen around the world, declining by about four percentage points in advanced economies since the 1970s.[10] Global supply chains stretched around the world as trade barriers fell, China and other developing economies matured, and technology advanced. By one recent estimate, more than two-thirds of world trade now goes through global value chains, in which production crosses at least one, and typically several, borders before final assembly.[11] Exports of goods and services, measured as a share of global GDP, nearly doubled between 1978 and 2008, but have plateaued since.[12]

These changes in the global business environment have been associated with the foreign expansion of many firms. For U.S. multinationals, one big change has been the growth of their foreign activities and workforces. In 1982, about one-fifth of all their employees were outside the United States, and this fraction rose to one-third by 2011 but has leveled off since. Foreign multinational corporations operating in the United States account for small, but steadily growing, shares of total U.S. economic activity and employment. Cross-border merger and acquisition activity has surged, with numbers of annual transactions more than tripling between 2001 and 2017 (see chapter 4 of this volume by Chari).

The identities of leading multinational corporations also have changed, with multinationals based in the United States and Europe no longer dominating the league tables as they once did. When *Fortune* magazine began ranking companies globally in 1988, nine of the fifteen largest were U.S.-based, five were European, and one was Japanese.[13] No Chinese company made the top fifty. In 2020, seven of the top fifteen were U.S. based, three were European, three were Chinese, and there was one each from Japan and Saudi Arabia. Twelve of the top fifty were Chinese. Notably, half the top fifty companies in 2020 did not exist in their present forms in 1978.

Despite considerable change in the world economy and in multinational activity, current concerns about the nature of multinational corporations and their likely effect on the future course of society bear striking resemblance to concerns prevalent in 1978. At the time, it seemed that the profits generated by multinational activity, together with the advantages of scale and scope that make integrated international operations highly cost-effective, meant that multinational firms would inevitably dominate the competition and ultimately even challenge governments. These dominant positions would make it feasible, and profitable, for multinational firms increasingly to exploit low-cost foreign labor at the expense of domestic workers, and thereby erode the social contract in the high-income countries in which they were based. Furthermore, multinational firms would be able to maintain and augment their market positions by exploiting low-cost finance to acquire competitors and outperform others in research and development. Due to the political power of multinational corporations, and their abilities to relocate their valuable activities, governments would be unwilling or unable to effectively tax or regulate them in the public interest.

These concerns are understandable, given the circumstances of 1978 and the associated uncertainty over the future course of the world economy. While subsequent events brought some of these concerns into sharp relief, and offered new reasons to worry about the behavior of multinational firms, the dire versions of the predictions of the 1970s have not materialized. Concerns that multinational firms, particularly those based in the United States, would overcome any constraints on their behavior seem in retrospect to have been premised on visions of the future that did not reckon with large changes in the world economy. While multinationals are large enough to have considerable influence, they are subject to limits imposed by competitors, financial markets, and governments. There are constraints on their abilities to control labor and product markets, largely because they compete with each other and with smaller, and often nimbler, upstarts. Multinationals seeking to minimize labor costs can choose to locate production in countries with low prevailing wages, and many do, thereby reducing their demand for lower-skilled workers elsewhere, including in their home countries; but these firms also typically maintain large workforces of highly skilled workers in high-income countries where output per worker is higher. Multinational employers tend to offer above-average compensation to their workers. Multinational firms dominate the market for private research and development, but the resulting innovation, in addition to augmenting the profits of the innovators, has widespread benefits. And while governments struggle to make multinational firms pay the taxes that they appear to owe on crafty or contested transactions, the governments nonetheless find ways to collect significant taxes from other aspects of the firms' operations. All that said, however, multinational firms remain extremely important, and in some cases dominant, players in certain markets, with the ability to exert the influence that comes with market dominance.

Differences in business settings and the complicated reality of multinational operations make it easy to mischaracterize the activities of these firms. To correct misunderstandings, it is helpful to consider the available information about the activities of multinational corporations. The following chapters consider several important aspects of current multinational business practice, evaluating the available evidence in light of prevailing theories.

In this introductory chapter, we frame the discussion with a description of the current scope of multinational activity and how practice has evolved over recent decades. Since the United States collects much of the world's high-quality information about multinational firms, and these data cover U.S.-based multinationals and U.S. operations of foreign-based multinationals, this review of multinational activity focuses largely on U.S. evidence, augmented, when possible, with information on firms based in other countries.

THE SCALE OF MULTINATIONAL ENTERPRISE

By any measure, multinational corporations are major participants in the U.S. economy, as figure 1-1 illustrates. The vertical axis measures the fractions of U.S. totals accounted for by multinationals—both those headquartered in the United States and U.S. affiliates of foreign-headquartered firms.

In 2017, U.S.-headquartered multinationals accounted for 20.1 percent of all U.S. private sector employment, and foreign-headquartered firms accounted for another 6.4 percent. Of course, their direct employment figures capture only part of the effect of multinationals on the U.S. labor market, as firms employing the remainder of the American private sector workforce include suppliers, customers, and competitors of the multinationals. Jobs at multinationals tend to pay more, on average, than others, so multinationals account for a larger share of total labor compensation than their share of workers, as figure 1-1 shows. This wage premium, in part, reflects a skill premium, in that multinationals tend to employ a more highly skilled workforce than their industry peers. Multinationals play a particularly large role in manufacturing: U.S.-based multinationals accounted for 51.6 percent of U.S. manufacturing employment in 2017, and the U.S. operations of foreign-based multinational firms employed an additional 21 percent of the U.S. manufacturing workforce. And the multinational share of total manufacturing compensation is even greater: more than 80 percent of all wages paid to U.S. manufacturing workers come from multinational firms. Multinational firms also accounted for more than half of all non-residential capital expenditures and more than 80 percent of all industrial R&D done in the United States. Not surprisingly, given their global reach and prominence in manufacturing, multinationals account for a large share of U.S. trade of goods and services—more than 60 percent all of U.S. exports and more than 50 percent of U.S. imports are attributable to multinationals, U.S.- and foreign-based combined.

FIGURE 1-1. Multinationals' Share of U.S. Economic Activity in 2017

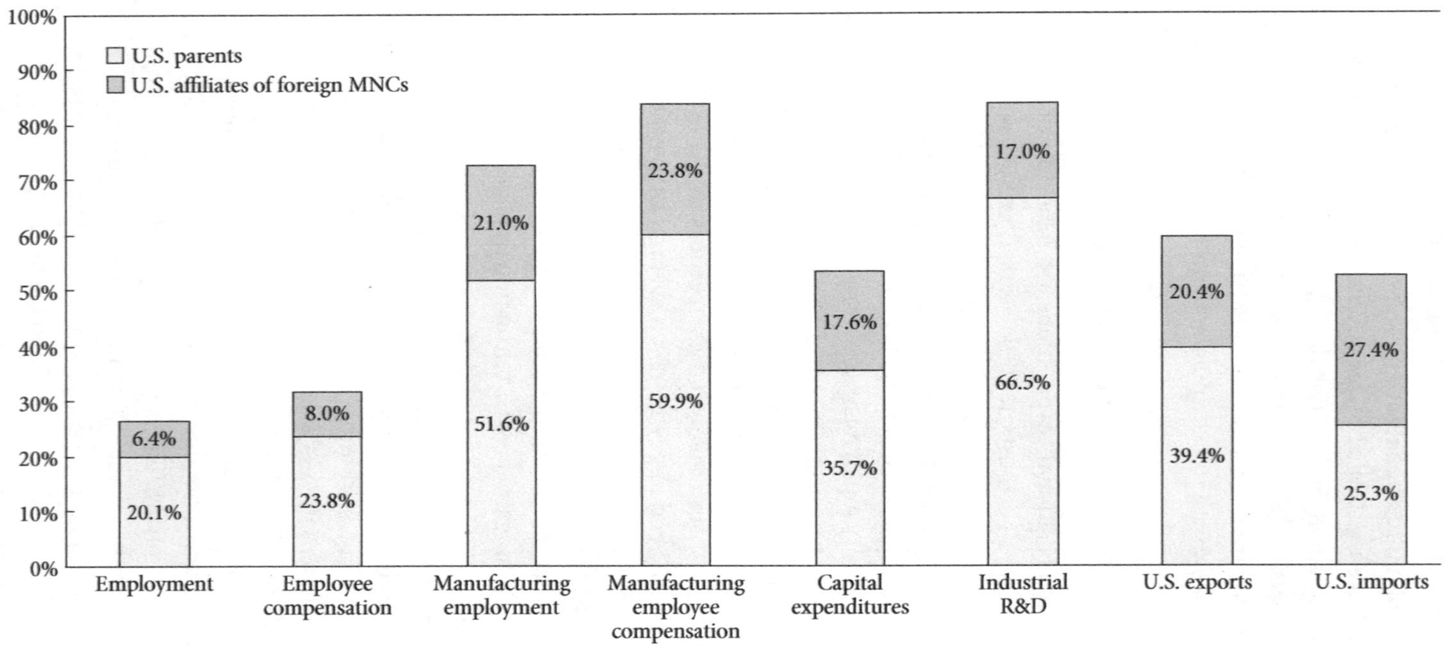

Note: This figure displays the share of U.S. economic activity accounted for by multinational firms. The lighter-shaded section of each bar represents the share accounted for by the parent operations of U.S. multinationals. The darker-shaded section represents the share accounted for by the U.S. affiliates of foreign multinationals. U.S. parents that are majority foreign-owned are accounted for as U.S. affiliates in the shaded sections. The all-U.S.-companies totals for manufacturing are not strictly comparable with the totals for U.S. parents and U.S. affiliates, because the former are based on the industry of establishment, but the latter are based on the industry of enterprise. Data are drawn from the BEA, the Census Bureau, and the National Science Foundation.

THE LOCATION AND NATURE OF MULTINATIONAL ACTIVITY

Data on the geographic distribution of multinational activity sheds light on its nature. To the extent that firms are motivated to operate in foreign countries to employ low-cost labor and avoid costly regulations, one would expect to see high levels of multinational activity in developing economies with low-cost labor and light regulation. This is the basis of theories of *vertical* foreign direct investment. These theories emphasize the ability of firms to locate different stages of production in places where they can be performed at lowest cost. An alternative view holds that multinational firms perform similar activities in different locations so they can be close to their customers; this is known as *horizontal* foreign direct investment. The available data suggest that horizontal foreign direct investment is dominant: most of those who work for multinational corporations do so in relatively high-income countries, not in low-wage, low-income countries, though the rising share of multinational activity in middle-income countries (such as Brazil and China) may portend a change.

Figure 1-2 displays shares of U.S. multinational firm employment accounted for by their affiliates located in countries with different levels of per capita income as classified by the World Bank as of October 2006, a year chosen somewhat arbitrarily to avoid distorting the data by countries moving among income categories over time. Figure 1-2 shows that the fraction of foreign employees of U.S. multinationals employed by affiliates in high-income countries declined between 1982 and 2017. By 2017, employees of affiliates in high-income countries still represented close to half of the foreign workforces of U.S. firms, but this represents a significant decline from the three-quarters in the 1980s. Over the same time span, the share of foreign employment by affiliates located in lower-middle-income countries (including Brazil, China, and India) rose by almost as much as the high-income share declined, and the share of employment by affiliates in low-income countries did not budge. While the data show a movement in the direction of low-cost operations, if U.S. multinational firms were motivated primarily by a quest for low-wage, lightly regulated locations, one would have expected an even sharper decline in high-income employment, and at least some growth in the employment share of affiliates in low-income countries.

More generally, the operations of multinational firms reflect the locus of world economic activity. Historically, much of the world's foreign direct in-

FIGURE 1-2. The Share of U.S. MNC Foreign Affiliate Employment by Host Country Income

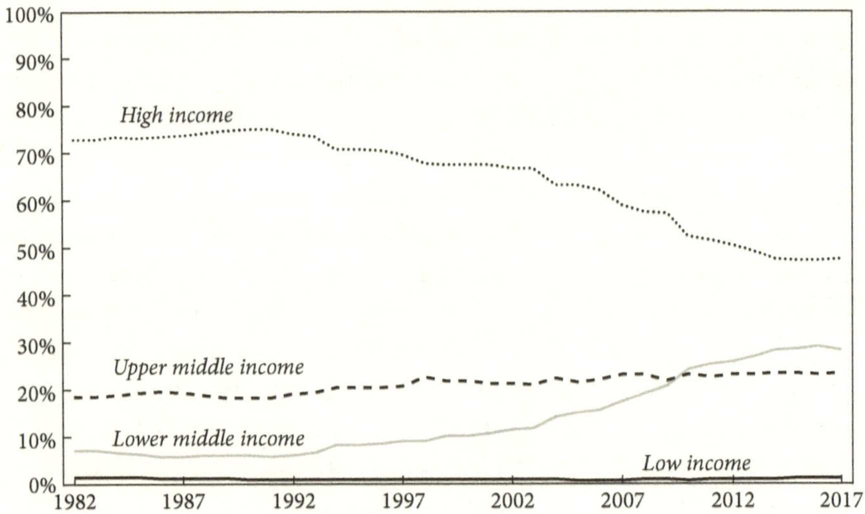

Note: This figure displays the share of U.S. multinational firm foreign affiliate employment accounted for by affiliates located in countries with different income classifications. The income classifications are the ones issued by the World Bank as of October 2006. The income levels of countries are classified in the following four tiers on the basis of their annual per capita gross national income in 2005 dollars: high-income countries, in which income is US$10,726 or more; upper-middle-income countries, in which income ranges from US$3,466 to US$10,725; lower-middle-income countries, in which income ranges from US$876 to US$3,465; and low-income countries, in which income is US$875 or less. Data are drawn from the BEA.

vestment consisted of investments by firms from large wealthy countries in affiliates located in other wealthy countries. However, as the share of global economic activity in developing countries has grown, so has multinational activity in those countries. The share of the stock of outward foreign direct investment (FDI) from countries classified as developing by the United Nations Conference on Trade and Development (UNCTAD)[14] (including China, South Korea, Taiwan, and other Asian economies, plus all of Latin America and Africa) has increased from 12 percent in 1982 to 22 percent in 2017. Developing countries long have been the recipients of FDI and attracted nearly a third of it in 2017. Changes in multinational activity also reflect Asia's rising share of world economic activity. Figure 1-3 displays the falling shares of total worldwide sales of U.S. multinationals' foreign affiliates that are accounted for by affiliates located in Europe and in Canada. It also shows that the share of sales from their Asian affiliates doubled from 14 percent in 1982 to 28 percent in 2017. As figure 1-4 illustrates, the same

FIGURE 1-3. The Share of U.S. MNC Foreign Affiliate Sales, by Affiliate Location

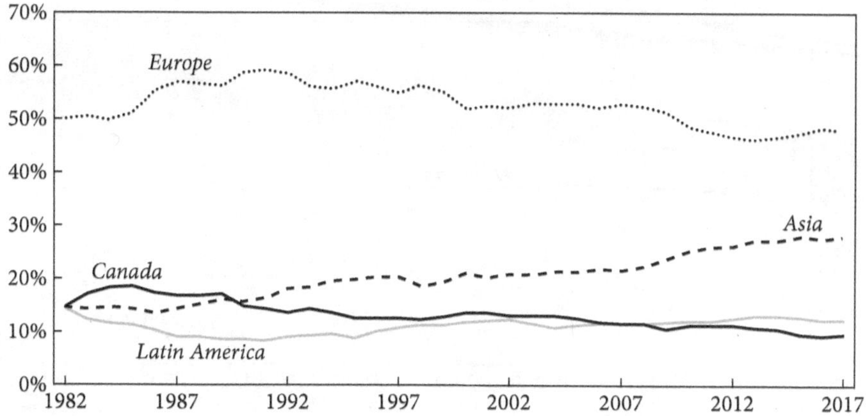

Note: This figure displays the share of U.S. multinational firm foreign affiliate sales accounted for by affiliates located in different regions. The data cover majority-owned foreign affiliates. Data are drawn from the BEA.

FIGURE 1-4. The Share of Japanese MNC Foreign Affiliate Sales, by Affiliate Location

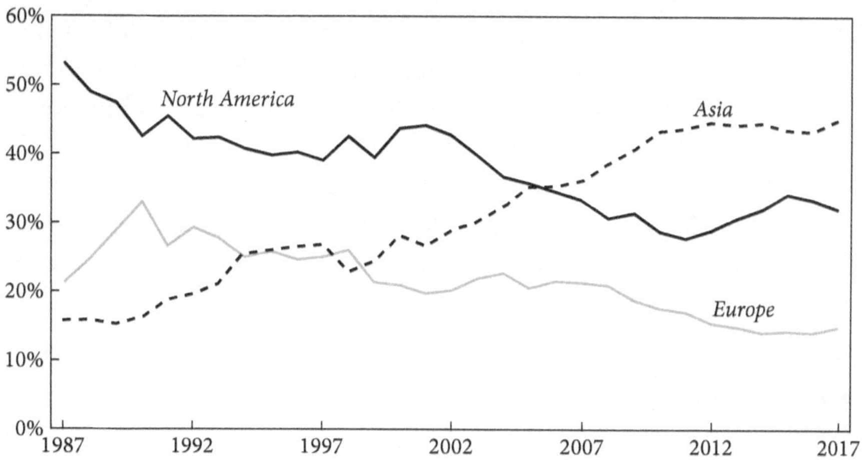

Note: This figure provides information about the sales of overseas affiliates of Japanese multinational firms. The dark solid line illustrates the share of total overseas affiliate sales accounted for by affiliates based in North America. The dark dashed line illustrates the share for affiliates based in Asia, and the gray line illustrates the share for affiliates based in Europe. Data are drawn from the Ministry of Economy, Trade, and Industry Survey on Overseas Business Activity.

FIGURE 1-5. The Share of European MNC Foreign Affiliate Sales, by Affiliate Location

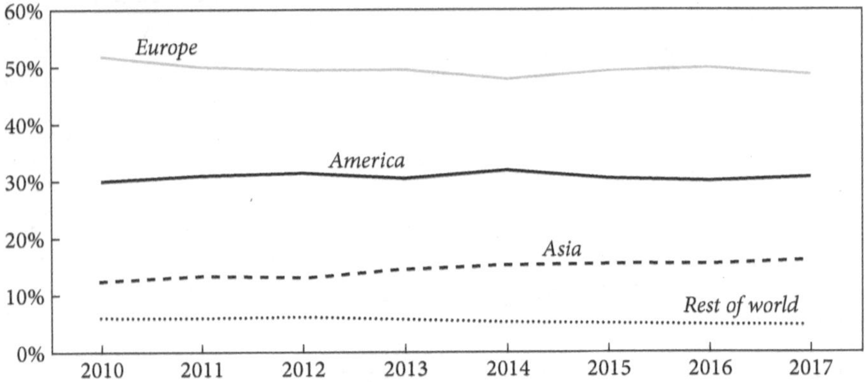

Note: This figure is based on data on the sales of the foreign affiliates of multinational firms from six selected European countries: Austria, Belgium, Finland, France, Germany, and Portugal. Each line illustrates the share of aggregated sales that are generated by foreign affiliates located in a particular region. Data are drawn from the Organisation for Economic Co-Operation and Development.

pattern applies to the overseas affiliates of Japanese multinationals. In 1987, North American and European affiliates of Japanese multinational firms collectively accounted for 74 percent of total sales by Japanese overseas affiliates that year, whereas their Asian affiliates accounted for just 16 percent. Three decades later, in 2017, North American and European affiliates were responsible for 47 percent of total sales by foreign affiliates, and Asian affiliates 45 percent. And as figure 1-5 illustrates, European multinationals have also experienced disproportionately high growth recently among their Asian affiliates. The figure presents data for 2010–2017, and over this period, the share of sales by their foreign affiliates in Europe declined from 52 to 49 percent while the share of sales by their Asian affiliates increased from 12 to 16 percent.

GROWTH OVER TIME

Rapidly declining trade, transportation, and communications costs supported a marked globalization of the world economy in recent decades—at least until recently. These trends raise questions about how multinationals have responded. Have the domestic operations of multinationals become a larger share of their economies? Has foreign affiliate activity grown faster than parent and host country activity? Data on U.S. multinationals and on U.S. affiliates of foreign multinationals shed light on these questions.

U.S. multinational parent firms in aggregate have grown at roughly the same pace as the rest of the U.S. economy. Shares of total U.S. private sector employment and capital expenditures accounted for by the parent companies of U.S. multinationals have changed little since the early 1980s. Figure 1-6 shows that U.S. multinational parent companies employed 24 percent of the U.S. private sector workforce in 1982 and 22 percent in 2017. In between, the fraction of U.S. workers employed by these firms fluctuated, declining during the economic expansions of the 1990s and 2000s, bottoming at 18 percent in 2008 as other firms expanded, and rising during the Great Recession as multinational firms proved to be more stable than other employers. The U.S. multinational parent company share of annual U.S. private capital expenditures fluctuated between roughly 30 and 40 percent over the years 1982–2017.

Other evidence indicates that multinationals have extended their foreign reach at rates that are high relative to parent and host country growth. The foreign activities of U.S.-based firms and the U.S. activities of foreign-based firms grew much faster than did the domestic activities of U.S. multinationals. Figure 1-7 illustrates that majority-owned foreign affiliates accounted for 21 percent of total employment in U.S. multinational firms in 1982, and 34 percent in 2017. The aggregate activity of the U.S. affili-

FIGURE 1-6. U.S. MNC Parent Share of U.S. Activity

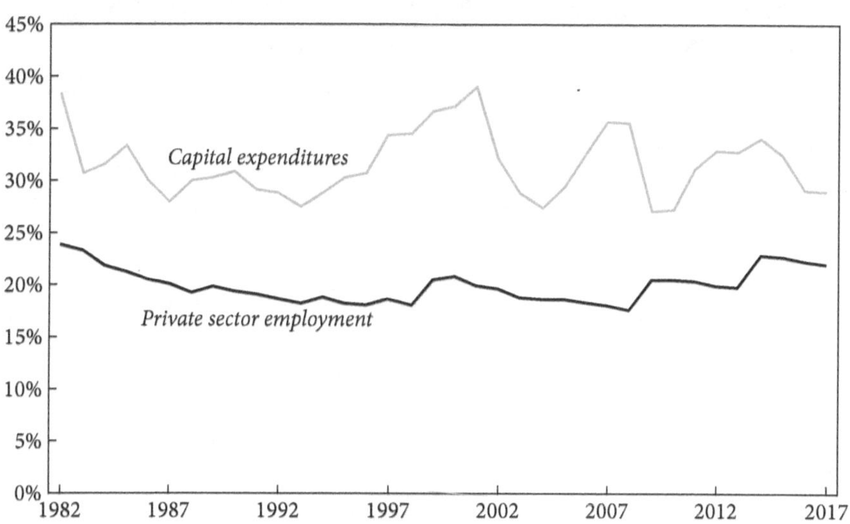

Note: This figure shows the U.S. MNC parent share of U.S. private sector employment and capital expenditures. Data are drawn from the BEA.

ates of foreign multinationals has grown considerably faster than the U.S. economy. The share of U.S. private sector workers employed by U.S. affiliates of foreign-headquartered multinationals doubled, albeit from a low level of 3 percent in 1982 to 6 percent in 2017, as shown in figure 1-8.

FIGURE 1-7. Share of U.S. Multinational Employment Accounted for by Foreign Affiliates

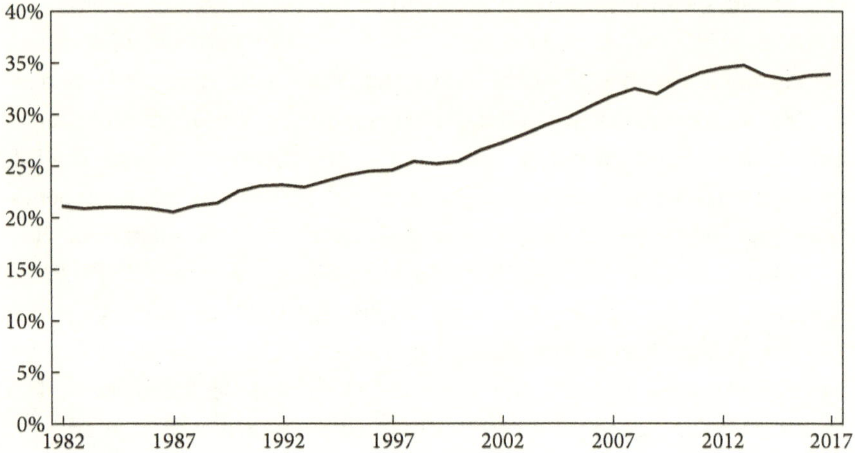

Note: This figure illustrates the extent to which U.S. multinational firms' employment is located outside of the United States. Data are drawn from the BEA.

FIGURE 1-8. Share of U.S. Employment Accounted for by U.S. Affiliates of Foreign MNCs

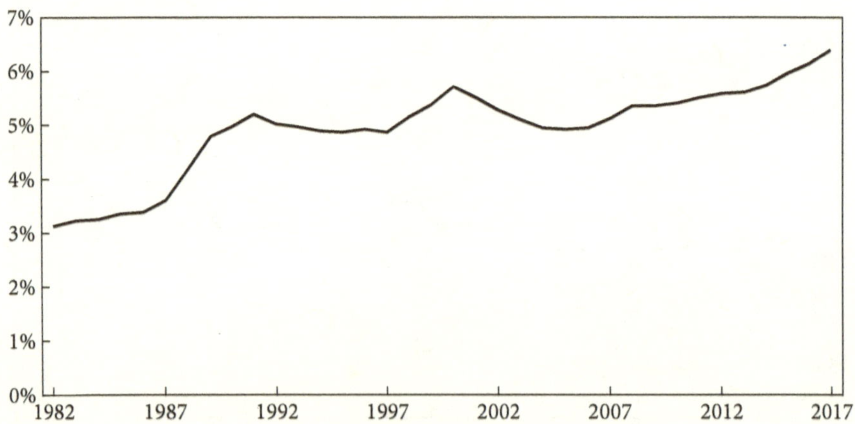

Note: This figure shows the share of U.S. private sector employment accounted for by U.S. affiliates of foreign MNCs. Data are drawn from the BEA.

MULTINATIONALS AND LABOR

Given their scale and flexibility regarding where to locate activity, multinational firms have the ability to organize production in ways that reduce their labor costs, typically by putting labor-intensive operations in low-wage locations. Concern over this possibility is responsible for the common refrain in high-income, high-wage countries that multinational firms export jobs, and more generally, that they undermine worker interests. The data paint a rather more complicated picture. Wages of U.S. workers employed by multinationals are consistently higher than average wages in the U.S. economy—in part, due to the industries in which multinationals are most active and the occupations of the workers they employ. Figure 1-9 compares average compensation per employee—unadjusted for inflation—for the entire U.S. private sector to the average compensations of U.S. workers employed by U.S.-based multinational firms and those employed by U.S. affiliates of foreign firms. The gap between compensation of workers employed by multinationals has persisted over the last few decades. These patterns are provocative, but hardly extensive or conclusive.

On the question of whether and to what extent multinationals export jobs from high-wage countries, there clearly are cases of U.S. firms substi-

FIGURE 1-9. Compensation per Employee

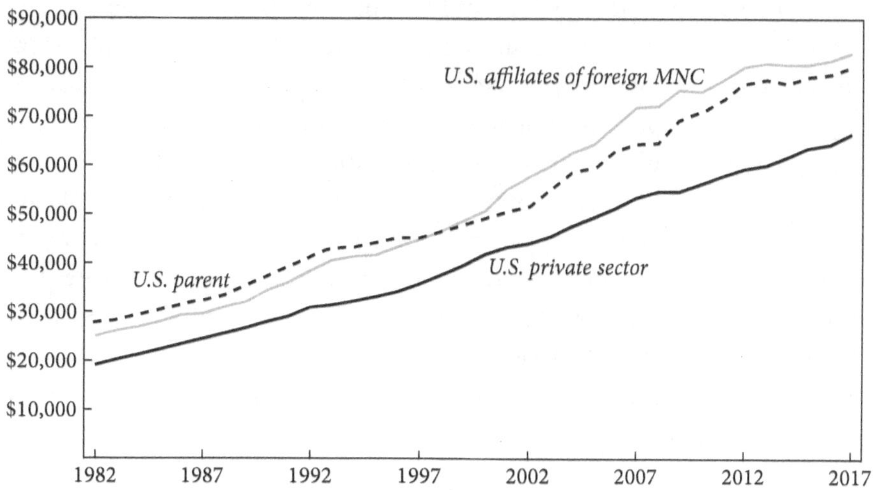

Note: This figure displays the average annual nominal compensation per employee for the U.S. private sector, the U.S. parents of U.S. multinationals, and the U.S. affiliates of foreign multinationals. Data are drawn from the BEA.

FIGURE 1-10. Changes in Domestic and Foreign Employment by a Matched Sample of 1,687 U.S. Multinationals, 2004–2014

	Decrease in foreign employment	Increase in foreign employment
Increase in U.S. employment	293	704
Decrease in U.S. employment	336	354

Note: This figure presents number counts of firms that experienced different changes in U.S. and foreign affiliate employment over the 2004–2014 period. These counts were produced using BEA data.

tuting low-wage foreign employment for higher-wage U.S. employment, though aggregate data suggest that this type of substitution may be offset by job creation. Between 1982 and 2017, U.S. multinational corporations added almost exactly the same number of workers (9.4 million) to their payrolls in the United States as they added abroad—and while this fact does not identify the net effect of foreign employment on U.S. jobs, it suggests that foreign expansion did not entirely supplant U.S. job creation. Figure 1-10 provides further evidence.[15] Between 2004 and 2014, 1,687 U.S. multinational firms expanded their foreign workforces; of these, roughly two-thirds (704) contemporaneously expanded their U.S. employment. Over the same time period, 629 U.S. multinational firms reduced their foreign workforces, and of these, about half (336) also reduced their employment in the United States. The prevalent pattern is U.S. multinationals that increase their foreign employment also increase their domestic employment. Such changes would occur if foreign operations increased the productivity of domestic activities, thereby stimulating demand for domestic labor. Of course, these aggregate patterns mask considerable heterogeneity at the levels of firms and labor markets, so any substitution effects of greater foreign expansions can cause significant hardships for sectors of labor markets in high-wage countries, with lower-skilled workers likely most at risk. But a complete analysis of the job market effects of multinational firms includes consideration of their effects on job creation as well as job destruction.

THE RISE OF SERVICES

One striking economic trend of modern times is the decline of manufacturing as a fraction of economic activity, particularly among high-income countries. Throughout the modern era, multinational firms have been more manufacturing-intensive than economies as a whole, as the cost savings and market access advantages of integrated worldwide production are generally more pronounced in manufacturing than in other industries. As a result, manufacturing firms are the most willing and able to incur the costs and bear the risks associated with foreign investment. Other industries, such as construction, retail trade, transportation, and mining and other extractive industries, also tended to be overrepresented among multinational firms, as foreign locations presented special opportunities for integrated international operations. But the provision of services often requires deep local knowledge, so the rising importance of services in foreign economies has the potential to put multinationals at disadvantages relative to local firms.

Their potential cost disadvantages do not appear to have prevented the international expansion of U.S.-based services firms, as indicated in figure 1-11.

FIGURE 1-11. The Share of Services in U.S. Parent Sales, Foreign Affiliates Sales, and U.S. GDP

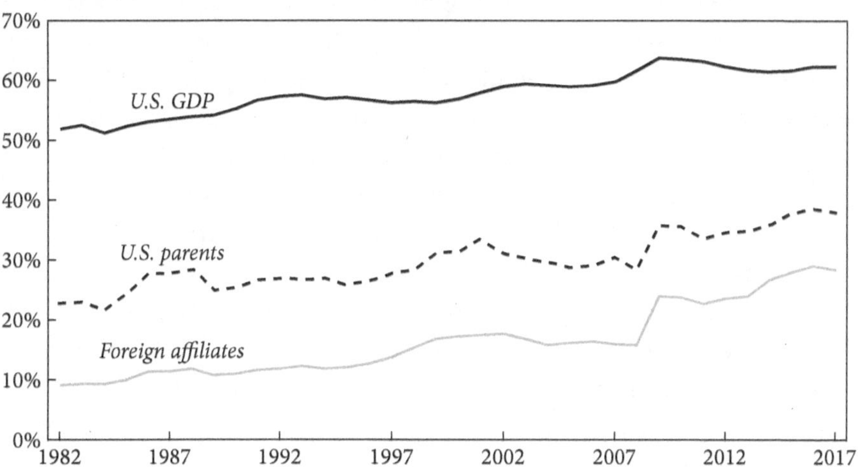

Note: This figure displays the importance of services in the sales of U.S. multinationals and the U.S. economy. The dark line depicts the share of U.S. GDP accounted for by services, including government services. The dashed line illustrates the share of U.S. parent sales that are sales of services, and the lighter line illustrates the share of foreign affiliate sales that are sales of services. Data are drawn from the BEA.

In 1982, 52 percent of the output of the U.S. economy was in services, and 23 percent of the sales of U.S. multinational parent companies represented services. By 2017, the U.S. economy was 62 percent services, and 38 percent of the sales of U.S. parent companies were in services. Over the same time period the foreign sales of U.S. multinationals moved even more dramatically in the direction of services: in 1982, just 9 percent of the sales of U.S. majority-owned foreign affiliates were in services; by 2017, 28 percent were. Furthermore, other measures of activity indicate that the foreign operations of U.S. multinational firms were even more concentrated in services.

INNOVATION

Despite the popular fascination with the innovative activities of small start-up firms, multinational firms account for a large fraction of total research and development expenditures. Prevailing theories of the multinational enterprise hold that integrated international operations are best able to exploit sources of value in intangible assets. Once a firm develops a novel product or process, the incompleteness of market contracts compels managers to deploy such innovations within the firm, since the alternative of licensing the intangible asset to another party yields lower returns and the prospect of fostering unwelcome competition or imitation. These incentives are particularly strong for international opportunities, and thus encourage innovative firms to establish multinational operations. Innovation requires and begets scale and scope: larger and more internationally oriented firms have the greatest ability to exploit new innovations, and have access to the resources necessary for large-scale modern research projects.

To the extent that international opportunities created by important innovations are most effectively exploited by multinational firms, it follows that firms with established multinational operations have the strongest incentives to produce internationally profitable innovations. They also typically have the resources necessary to finance the development of such innovations. It is no surprise, then, that multinational firms are highly active researchers. Figure 1-12 indicates that research and development spending in the United States by U.S.-based multinationals in 2017 accounted for a large fraction of the total performed by all U.S. businesses. This has been true consistently over the last three decades, and figure 1-12 shows the fraction of U.S. private sector R&D accounted for by U.S.-based multinationals hovering in the neighborhood of 70 percent every year since 1989.[16] Certain

FIGURE 1-12. U.S. Parent Share of U.S. Business R&D

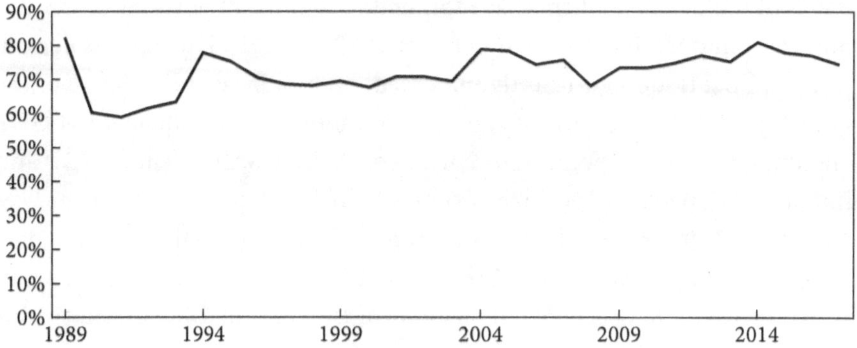

Note: This figure shows the extent to which business R&D in the United States is performed by the parents of U.S. multinational firms. Data are drawn from the BEA and the National Science Foundation.

aspects of the multinational research landscape have changed, however, as multinationals perform increasing portions of their research and development outside their home countries. U.S.-based firms did 9 percent of their total R&D spending outside the United States in 1989, a share that grew to 16 percent by 2017. This is not the product of any decline in total research expenditures by U.S. parent companies, whose aggregate R&D spending increased at a compound nominal annual growth rate of 4.7 percent, while R&D spending by their foreign affiliates grew at a faster compound annual growth rate of 7.3 percent.

INTEGRATED OPERATIONS OF MULTINATIONAL FIRMS

How integrated are the operations of multinationals? What fraction of international trade is intrafirm trade? How has that fraction changed as trade, transport, and communication costs have fallen? The answers to these questions reveal features of the structure of global supply chains and mechanisms that propagate shocks across countries. One of the cost advantages afforded by the multinational mode of production is that integrated operations permit firms to avoid arm's-length market transactions that may be costly or difficult to tailor to individual firm circumstances, that may entail relinquishing control over production processes, and that can make it difficult to prevent subsequent diffusion of firm-specific intellectual capital. Multinational firms can sidestep these problems by arranging foreign purchases and sales through foreign affiliates they own.

The evidence displayed in figure 1-13 indicates that the intrafirm trade in goods of multinational firms has represented significant portions of U.S. exports and imports in every year between 1982 and 2017. During this period, international trade significantly increased, even as measured relative to the growing U.S. economy. In 1982, total U.S. exports were 6.3 percent of GDP and imports were 7.4 percent; in 2017, exports were 8.0 percent of GDP and imports 12.1 percent. Intrafirm exports, which include exports from U.S. parents to their foreign affiliates and from U.S. affiliates to their foreign parents, were roughly one-third of the total value of U.S. exports in 1982 and constituted an almost identical fraction of the total in 2017. Similarly, intrafirm imports were 37 percent of total U.S. exports in 1982, and 39 percent of U.S. imports in 2017. As the figure illustrates, these fractions have fluctuated over time, albeit in rather narrow bands, always constituting significant fractions of U.S. international trade, but never as much as half. It is noteworthy that the global expansion of multinational enterprise and the opportunities afforded by greater international trade have not translated into a rising share of intrafirm trade, nor has intrafirm trade been supplanted by trade

FIGURE 1-13. Related-Party Share of U.S. Exports and U.S. Imports of Goods

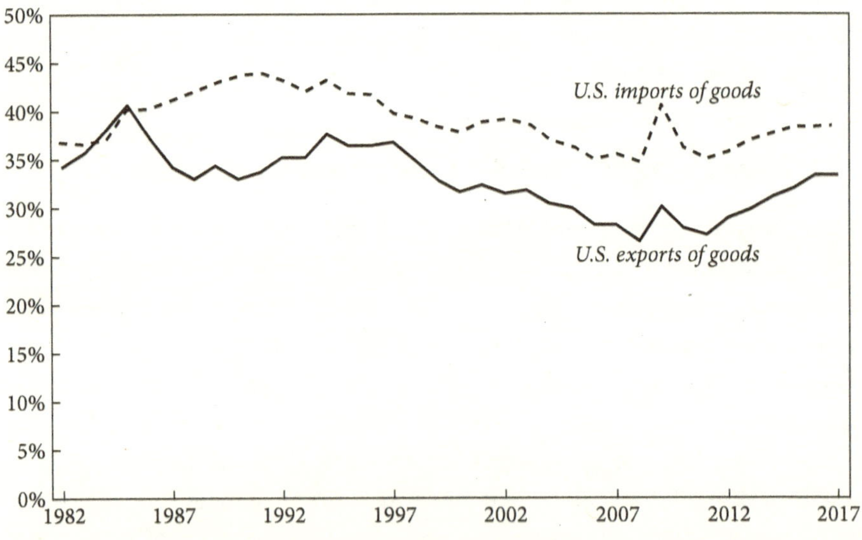

Note: This figure illustrates the extent to which U.S. trade in goods occurs between related parties. Related party trade includes trade between a U.S. parent and its foreign affiliates as well as trade between a U.S. affiliate of a foreign multinational and its foreign parent group. Data are drawn from the BEA and the Census Bureau.

between unrelated parties. In short, there appear to be important limits to the benefits of structuring international transactions between related parties. Unfortunately, there are no comprehensive data that capture the widely reported increase in cross-border contract manufacturing, an arrangement in which multinational firms hire foreign firms in which they have no equity stakes to make and assemble products.[17] These arrangements are common in several industries, including apparel and electronics.

FOREIGN PROFITABILITY OF MULTINATIONAL FIRMS

Foreign operations are increasingly important sources of value for multinational firms, reflecting the growing scale and profitability of their foreign activities. Given the available data and inherent ambiguity in the origin of profits, estimates of foreign profitability shares are imprecise. Figure 1-14 presents U.S. firms' direct investment income on equity investments abroad, after taxes, as a share of U.S. firms' total pretax income from current production. These data, drawn from the U.S. national income and product accounts, indicate that profits from overseas represent a growing share of U.S. firms' global profits—the share was 14 percent in 1982 and 23 percent in 2017. The foreign share of profits tends to rise during U.S. recessions, particularly evident in 2008, because of the relative decline of profitability in the United States.

Another approach to measuring the foreign profit shares of U.S. firms uses data on total and foreign pretax income reported by U.S.-based publicly listed firms and compiled by Compustat. As illustrated in figure 1-15, the reported foreign share of total profits of these companies has risen from 23 percent in 1989 to 34 percent in 2017. These data likewise show that the foreign share of profits rises when the U.S. economy is weak; indeed, the measure exceeds 100 percent in 2008, when many large listed financial services firms reported significant losses. These data must be interpreted carefully, since the total number of publicly listed firms has declined precipitously over time, so those that remain listed tend to be larger on average than was previously the case. With that caveat, it is noteworthy that 19 percent of listed firms reported earning pretax foreign income in 1989, whereas 38 percent did so in 2017. One question raised by these measures is the extent to which multinationals shift profits from one location to another because of tax and other incentives.

FIGURE 1-14. U.S. Direct Investment Abroad Equity Income Share of U.S. Worldwide Corporate Profits

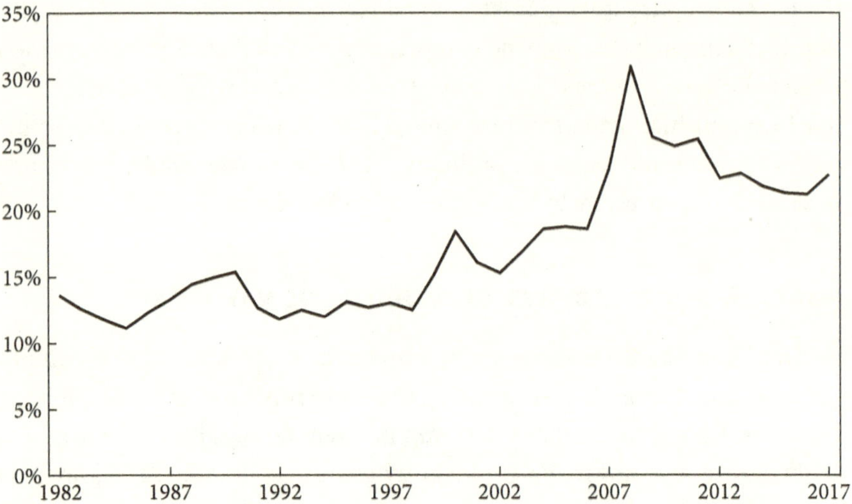

Note: This figure presents a measure of the extent to which U.S. firms earn profits outside of the United States. This measure is a ratio. The numerator is direct investment income on equity, and it represents parents' share in the net income of their affiliates, after provision for income taxes and excluding extraordinary gains and losses. The denominator captures the portion of total income earned, before deducting income taxes, from current production by U.S. corporations.

FIGURE 1-15. Foreign Pretax Income as a Share of Total Pretax Income

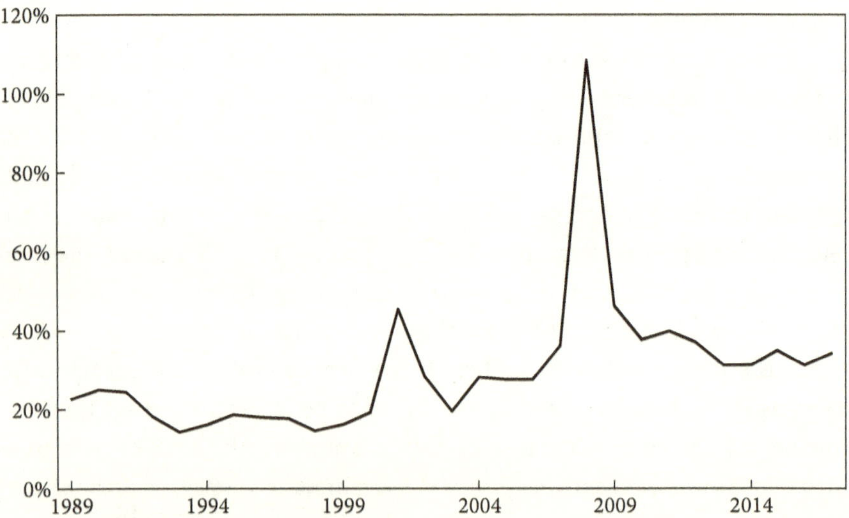

Note: This figure presents an alternative measure of the extent to which U.S. firms earn profits outside the United States. It is created using Compustat data on firms incorporated in the United States and publicly traded on U.S. exchanges. The line plots the ratio of aggregate foreign pretax income to aggregate pretax income.

MULTINATIONAL FIRMS AND INTERNATIONAL TAXATION

Multinational firms owe taxes to the countries in which they earn income, and in addition, their foreign incomes are also potentially subject to taxation in their home countries. Tax rates and tax burdens differ significantly across locations, offering multinational firms opportunities to arrange their investments, operations, and financial affairs in ways that minimize their taxable incomes in high-tax countries. There is considerable evidence that firms respond to these tax incentives: multinational investment, operations, foreign employment, and income levels are lower in high-tax locations, and higher in low-tax locations, than would otherwise be predicted on the basis of the characteristics of these economies. One common concern about the reported growth and rising share of foreign profits among U.S. multinational firms is that this growth reflects behavior aimed at avoiding U.S. tax obligations, as firms report that income was earned in low-tax foreign countries rather than the United States. Similar concerns are expressed about the behavior of multinationals based in other high-tax countries. Widely publicized examples of companies using complicated financial transactions to avoid tax obligations, together with rising fractions of reported profitability in low-tax foreign locations, suggests to many that high-tax countries are increasingly unable to prevent multinational firms from shifting significant portions of their profits away from the places in which those profits were actually earned.

The impact of low tax rates on firm operations and tax avoidance behavior is evident from the experience of tax haven countries, which are those with very low tax rates, business-friendly regulations, and other features intended to attract foreign business investment. The tax havens identified by Hines Jr. (2010) in 2016 had just 0.9 percent of the non-U.S. world population, and 3.2 percent of non-U.S. world GDP, but nonetheless accounted for 13.5 percent of the foreign property, plants, and equipment of U.S. multinational firms, 9.1 percent of their foreign employee compensation, and 5 percent of their foreign employment (see chapter 11 in this volume by Dharmapala, table 11-1). In addition to the economically disproportionate concentration of investment and employment in tax haven countries, firms reported large portions of their total foreign incomes to have been earned there; though the nature of accounting data and the use of tax haven holding companies make these income figures notoriously difficult to interpret. It is nonetheless clear that low-tax jurisdictions such as tax havens draw considerable portions of the taxable incomes of multinational firms, thereby reducing the firms' total tax obligations.

Figure 1-16 illustrates the use of tax haven affiliates by U.S. multinational firms. In 1982, 41 percent of U.S. multinational firms had one or more affiliates in tax haven countries, a ratio that increased to 50 percent by 2014. Since the small economic footprints of these jurisdictions make them very unlikely to attract so many multinational firms in the absence of tax incentives, the high and rising fraction of U.S. multinational firms with tax haven affiliates is consistent with other evidence of increasing tax avoidance. Still, it is noteworthy that even by 2014 only half of U.S. multinationals have any tax haven affiliates at all, suggesting that the other half has decided that they are either unwilling or unable to shift taxable income into those locations. Despite the concentration of multinational investment in high-income countries that also tend to have high tax rates, statistical evidence consistently indicates that countries with high tax rates receive significantly lower levels of multinational investment than would otherwise be predicted based on economic determinants.[18] This pattern is consistent with firms having limited capacity to shift income into low-tax countries, since in the absence of impediments, these firms could earn income in high-tax countries and

FIGURE 1-16. Share of U.S. Multinational Parent Firms with Affiliates in Tax Havens

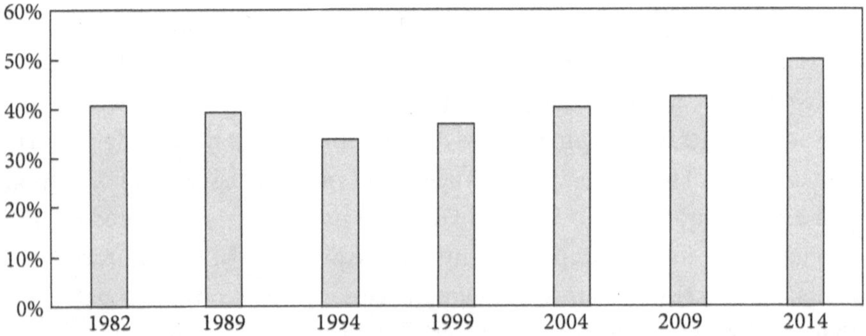

Note: This figure illustrates the share of U.S. multinational parent firms that have at least one affiliate in a tax haven country. Data are drawn from the BEA. Tax haven countries are those identified in Hines Jr., James R., "Treasure Islands," *Journal of Economic Perspectives*, 24/4 (2010): 103–26, with the exception of the Cook Islands, the U.K. Channel Islands, and Niue, which cannot be separately identified in the BEA data. The 2014 parents are restricted to those that match 2013, because in 2014, the BEA made a concerted effort to improve its coverage of FDI by U.S. private equity firms, which added thousands of new private equity U.S. parents that cannot be separately identified.

simply report it in low-tax countries, and there would be no need to limit investment in high-tax countries.

The average rates of taxes paid by multinational firms have gradually fallen over time. At least in part, this reflects changes in government policies, as corporate tax rates have steadily declined over the last forty years. Tax rate reductions have been most pronounced among middle-income and developing countries, so, to the extent that multinational firm operations have grown in these parts of the world, the average tax rates of multinational firms may decline as a result. Furthermore, the tendency of multinational firms to seek locations with low tax rates accelerates this trend. Of course, it is possible for taxpayers to seek tax reductions without relocating, either by appealing to governments for rate reductions or by engaging in self-help tax reductions through complicated financial maneuvers. Through a combination of factors, the average tax rates paid by U.S. multinationals, and the multinationals headquartered in other countries, have steadily declined over time, provoking concern for government finances and tax fairness, and political ire, particularly in many parts of the high-tax world.

THE PAST AND FUTURE OF MULTINATIONAL ACTIVITY

The available information offers a rich picture of multinational activity in the modern world. In the foreword to the 1978 volume, it was noted that, at that time, answering policy-relevant questions about multinationals was frustrated by inadequate data, inappropriate theories and analytical methods, and complex interactions between the economics and politics of foreign investment. Since that time, the expanded availability of data on multinational companies from surveys conducted by the U.S. Bureau of Economic Analysis and other national statistical agencies, access to the underlying microdata, and the resulting academic research has brought to light many important findings, including many of those summarized in this volume.

Multinational firms are large, and they are important contributors to modern economies. The same was true in 1978, and it is instructive to consider why it is that over the course of the intervening years multinational firms neither expanded to occupy all of the space in the economy nor shrank under the weight of their own costs. It seems that the costs and benefits of multinational operations make them properly suited for certain types of business activities and not others. These activities are focused in manufacturing, mining, and trade-related industries, and in those that rely heavily on intellectual property produced by research and development. While the scale and profitability of multinational firms makes them ferocious potential competitors in factor markets, for other firms, and even for national governments, the history of recent decades is that dire predictions of unwanted consequences of their actions largely have not come true.

THE REMAINDER OF THE VOLUME

Each of the subsequent eleven chapters focuses on a specific aspect of multinational corporations, while the final chapter uses this evidence to draw implications for public policy.

Multinational firms use wide varieties of organizational forms, including international joint ventures, creative supply chains, and market-based arrangements strategically introduced in what otherwise might have been within-firm production relationships. Chapter 2, by Davies and Markusen, identifies factors such as labor market conditions, the availability of capital, and tax considerations that explain the use of different organizational forms. The chapter also discusses the relative importance of the two leading models of multinational activities—horizontal investment, in which firms undertake similar activities in multiple locations, and vertical investment, in which firms perform different steps of production processes in different locations. Although there is evidence of vertical investment, the data suggest that horizontal investments are more prevalent. The chapter concludes that a significant share of the activity of multinational firms is replicative, occurs between wealthy countries, and is geared toward serving local final consumers and nearby businesses.

Chapter 3, by Thomas and Bernard, explores motivations for corporations to expand across borders and their choices between acquisitions and greenfield investments, with particular attention to decisions that Western European companies made after the fall of the Berlin Wall opened up Eastern Europe. The chapter finds that while bilateral factors explain little of the variation in MNC activity across countries within the region, or the motives for entry via acquisition rather than greenfield investment, much of the foreign direct investment in the region as a whole appears to be factor-seeking by parent firms in nearby Western European countries. Firm-level factors—as opposed to investments by peer MNCs from the same home country—play important roles in shaping entry decisions.

Chapter 4, by Chari, documents the growth of cross-border mergers and acquisitions (M&A), which accounted for nearly half of foreign direct investment since the global financial crisis of 2008–2009. The chapter observes that M&A activities are concentrated in the United States and a small number of European countries, examines the incentives for foreign acquisitions, and considers post-acquisition outcomes. The chapter cites three reasons for firms to acquire control of foreign firms: to increase valuation by improving governance and protecting intellectual property, especially in emerging markets; to access cheaper capital or exploit cheaper valuations of targets; and to exercise control over foreign affiliates rather than rely on contracts with unrelated parties. The chapter shows that cross-border M&A improves productivity and increases returns. Acquiring firms tend to restructure target firms, with adjustments to employment and capital investment, which is consistent with post-acquisition improvements in firm-level efficiency. But such policy considerations as national security and market concentration must be weighed against any efficiency gains from increased foreign direct investment.

Chapter 5, by Erel, Jang, and Weisbach, explores the question of whether being a multinational corporation confers advantages in financing. Among other things, the chapter finds that multinational firms have better access to capital markets outside their home countries than do other publicly held firms, but that multinationals also face costs—both country risk and foreign exchange risk—that domestic firms do not. U.S. multinationals were likely to hold larger percentages of their assets in cash (possibly because of pre-2018 tax incentives to maintain profits overseas rather than repatriate them) than other publicly held firms. They were also less likely to borrow, but when they did, they relied less on banks and more on capital markets, often with foreign lenders. The chapter finds that when firms are geographically diverse, they generally face lower borrowing rates. Evidence on whether multinationality matters for the cost of equity is inconclusive.

Chapter 6, by Oldenski, seeks to answer a popular question: Do multinational firms export jobs? The answer is a definite yes, but the chapter notes that multinationals also import jobs, and in many cases, offshoring enables that job creation at home. Overall, the net effect of MNC offshoring on domestic jobs and wages is close to zero or possibly a small positive. That net effect, however, masks the fact that some workers are hurt by offshoring while others gain. In general, less educated workers and those who perform routine tasks are more likely to experience job losses and reduced wages as a result of offshoring, while more highly educated workers gain. Measuring value added by U.S.-owned firms in each host country, the chapter finds that of the top ten offshoring destinations for U.S. firms, only two, Mexico and China, are developing countries, and together they account for only 14 percent of aggregate value added in those top ten locations. The chapter draws attention to evidence suggesting that worker training can help mitigate some of the negative effects of offshoring without sacrificing the benefits.

Chapter 7, by Aisbett, Harrison, Levine, Scorse, and Silver, considers whether MNCs exploit workers in poor countries, based on three definitions of exploitation: paying below market wages, failing to compensate employees with a fair share of surplus, and violating human rights. The chapter finds almost no evidence of exploitation based on the market definitions. Compared to domestic firms, MNCs offer slightly better wages and conditions, and they generally increase the demand for workers in high-paying occupations. The chapter finds no direct evidence that MNCs fail to share their surpluses with their poor-country workers, although it argues that MNCs may be responsible for some negative effects on the labor market and a declining labor share of national income. Aspects of this argument, however, rely on macroeconomic patterns rather than firm-level data, making it difficult to draw causal conclusions. The chapter reports evidence that MNCs violate basic human rights in poor nations—including discrimination against women and migrant workers, suppression of the right to organize, and poor health and safety conditions. The chapter suggests that broad policy changes and activism, such as increasing labor productivity and improving the enforcement of labor standards, can have larger effects on the well-being of workers in poor nations than focusing solely on multinationals specifically.

Chapter 8, by Branstetter, Glennon, and Jensen, shows that over the past two decades, U.S. MNCs have moved increasing amounts of R&D overseas—doing so for efficiency reasons and thereby creating a division of labor akin to that more commonly documented in the production of goods. Combining MNCs' innovation experience with talent around the world, including from developing countries, may revive and sustain innovation and improve productivity growth. The rise in the number of patents from inventor teams with addresses both inside and outside the United States suggests that fears that U.S. expertise is being hollowed out may be overstated. New hubs of foreign R&D activity, such as China, India, and Israel, have highly educated workers and significant technological domains. The chapter indicates that several challenges might limit the benefits of the globalization of R&D, including the rise of economic nationalism, aggressive use of tariffs, global efforts to restrict or tax international data flows, opposition to immigration, and U.S.-China trade tensions.

Chapter 9, by Edelman, examines forces that have contributed to the rise of digital MNCs, as well as the challenges that these firms face. The chapter observes that the digital economy is more centralized than might have been expected. Successful firms, such as Facebook, evolved quickly into multinationals that provide global services from a centralized location. They have benefited from software standardization—such as the internet and Unicode characters for languages—which disproportionately emanates from the United States. As a result, software is cost-effective, and it is easily scalable for free, instant, and reliable deployment around the world. This allows firms to grow rapidly. Digital MNCs that have become behemoths have the scale and resources to withstand pressure from local competitors and national governments. The chapter finds that MNCs increase local employment in response to competition, nuances in knowledge, and privacy concerns, but they face increasing questions related to regulation and taxes. Governments invoke traditional law enforcement and have developed new multifaceted strategies to regulate digital MNCs.

Addressing the controversial issue of taxation, chapter 10, by Dyreng and Hanlon, notes that MNCs pay substantial taxes, both direct and indirect, but also reports evidence of rising tax avoidance, including cross-jurisdictional income shifting and tax-sensitive location of investment, debt, and employment. The paper identifies circumstances in which tax avoidance entails significant adjustments to firms' real activities. While there is evidence of firms shifting taxable income to low-tax locations, the literature is far from settled on the extent to which it occurs. Non-tax factors, including reputational incentives and financial accounting considerations, may influence the magnitude of tax avoidance. Although evidence suggests that tax avoidance by one firm begets tax avoidance by others, it is too early to assess the effects of recent tax-regime changes on levels of aggregate avoidance.

Chapter 11, by Dharmapala, addresses MNCs' use of tax havens, a topic that has attracted increasing attention and scrutiny in recent years, and is the focus of recent proposals to set minimum taxes on MNC profits. The chapter cites empirical evidence that is consistent with MNCs' disproportionate use of tax havens as locations for holding companies, intellectual property, and financial activities, but also considerable evidence of limits on MNCs' use of havens. Challenging the standard view that tax havens are parasitical on other countries, the chapter argues that MNCs' use of tax havens relies crucially on forbearance or active facilitation by these non-havens, which have available a variety of powerful legal and economic instruments to neutralize the effect of MNCs' use of havens. The chapter speculates that the failure to deploy these instruments fully is a deliberate policy choice, due either to collective action problems among non-havens or to the possibility that, in certain circumstances, MNCs' use of havens increases the welfare of non-haven countries.

Multinational corporations play significant roles in shaping the global economy, but there are few rigorous examinations of their *political* influence on foreign policymaking. Chapter 12, by Kim and Milner, argues that MNCs' economic dominance reduces the relative cost of engaging in political activities, while their large-scale transnational activities increase the marginal benefits of influencing policymaking individually. To examine this empirically, they deploy a novel dataset encompassing lobbying activities of all U.S. public firms from 1999 to 2019, using a difference-in-differences identification strategy to estimate the effect of MNC status on lobbying. They find strong evidence that lobbying expenditures increase when firms become multinationals. They also find that MNCs tend to lobby on more diverse sets of foreign policy issues than do other firms.

And chapter 13, by Foley, Hines Jr., and Wessel, offers some principles for policy drawn from the evidence and discussion in this volume.

NOTES

1. Bruce K. McLaury, "Forward" in C. Fred Bergsten, Thomas Horst, and Theodore Moran, *American Multinationals and American Interests* (Brookings Institution Press, 1978), vii.

2. "U.K.'s Labour Vows Action on 'Tax and Wage Cheat' Multinationals," Reuters, November 22, 2019.

3. Lawrence H. Summers, "Corporations Are Cheating the Global Tax System. World Leaders Can't Afford to Ignore It," *Washington Post,* April 10, 2019.

4. Jonathan Cummings and others, *Growth and Competitiveness in the United States: The Role of Its Multinational Companies,* www.mckinsey.com/featured-insights/americas/growth-and-competitiveness-in-us.

5. Matthew J. Slaughter, "The 'Exporting Jobs' Canard," *Wall Street Journal,* June 14, 2017.

6. For this reason, and because more data are available for majority-owned foreign affiliates, most of the calculations here focus on majority-owned affiliates.

7. Douglas A. Irwin, "Globalization Is in Retreat for the First Time since the Second World War," Peterson Institute for International Economics (PIIE), April 23, 2020, www.piie.com/research/piie-charts/globalization-retreat-first-time-second-world-war; and Chad P. Brown, "COVID-19 Could Bring Down the Trading System," *Foreign Affairs,* April 28, 2020.

8. Richard Baldwin and Eiichi Tomiura, "Thinking Ahead about the Trade Impact of COVID-19," in Richard Baldwin and Beatrice Weder di Mauro, *Economics in the Time of COVID-19* (London: Centre for Economic Policy Research Press, 2020), www.primo-europe.eu/wp-content/uploads/2020/03/ecointhetimesofcovid19.pdf#page=66.

9. OECD, *Short-Term Labour Market Statistics,* https://stats.oecd.org/viewhtml.aspx?datasetcode=STLABOUR&lang=en#.

10. Mai Chi Dao and others, "Drivers of Declining Labor Share of Income," *IMFBlog,* April 12, 2017, https://blogs.imf.org/2017/04/12/drivers-of-declining-labor-share-of-income/.

11. *Technological Innovation, Supply Chain Trade, and Workers in a Globalized World,* edited by David Dollar and others (Geneva: World Trade Organization, 2019), http://documents.worldbank.org/curated/en/384161555079173489/pdf/Global-Value-Chain-Development-Report-2019-Technological-Innovation-Supply-Chain-Trade-and-Workers-in-a-Globalized-World.pdf.

12. World Bank and OECD, *Exports of Goods and Services (% of GDP),* https://data.worldbank.org/indicator/ne.exp.gnfs.zs.

13. Fortune Global 500, *Fortune,* Aug. 1, 1988.

14. "Classifications," in *2019 e-Handbook of Statistics* (Geneva, Development Statistics and Information Branch, UNCTAD, 2019), https://stats.unctad.org/handbook/Annexes/Classifications.html.

15. The data for this figure are drawn from table 6-1 of chapter 6 of this volume, written by Lindsay Oldenski. The U.S. MNCs in this comparison accounted for more than two-thirds of total U.S. parent employment in 2014.

16. The U.S.-based multinationals whose foreign R&D activities are presented in figure 1-11 and discussed in this section include both U.S.-based companies and the

U.S. affiliates of foreign-based companies if those U.S. affiliates themselves own foreign affiliates.

17. For an example of the data on global supply chains that does exist, see www.wto.org/english/res_e/booksp_e/gvc_dev_report_2019_e.pdf.

18. See, for example, Mihir A. Desai, C. Fritz Foley, and James R. Hines Jr., "Foreign Direct Investment in a World of Multiple Taxes," *Journal of Public Economics*, 88/12 (December 2004), 2727–44; Shafik Hebous, Martin Ruf, and Alfons J. Weichenrieder, "The Effects of Taxation on the Location Decision of Multinational Firms: M&A Versus Greenfield Investments," *National Tax Journal*, 64/3 (September 2011), 817–38; Johannes Becker, Clemens Fuest, and Nadine Riedel, "Corporate Tax Effects on the Quality and Quantity of FDI," *European Economic Review*, 56/8 (2012), 1495–1511.

2

The Structure of Multinational Firms' International Activities

RONALD B. DAVIES
JAMES R. MARKUSEN

When one thinks about multinational enterprises (MNEs), several questions come to mind, including why some firms become multinationals, how policies influence a country's attractiveness to firms, and how MNEs affect both the home countries from which they come and the host countries where they go. Central to the answers to these questions is how multinationals structure their global activities. One way to envision that structure is as a snake. Each part of the snake performs a separate activity, all of which adds up to a well-functioning whole. The head decides where to go, the mouth swallows food, and the spine twists for movement. Similarly, a firm may organize itself so that different affiliates perform different activities that combine together to produce a finished output.

Alternatively, the structure can be more like an octopus. Each of the octopus's arms does essentially the same thing, with its head coordinating the movements. Here, the MNE's various affiliates replicate each other with guidance from the home headquarters. Thus, just as animals can be structured in different ways, so, too, can firms.

Understanding the firm's structure helps explain why the bulk of activity is in developed countries, why trade policy can have conflicting effects on investment, why some firms (but not all) die when an affiliate runs into trouble, and how increased foreign direct investment (FDI) potentially affects labor markets.

In this chapter, we provide a broad framework describing how different parts of an MNE fit into one another and what the data suggest about the relative importance of alternative structures. This exercise points toward a particularly important role for horizontal FDI, an octopus-like structure in which the MNE performs a roughly similar activity in its different affiliates—that is, it replicates its activities across borders. Knowing that can then help explain all sorts of key issues, such as why, despite decades of warnings, a negative link between outbound FDI and home wages is not generally evident.

This chapter begins with definitions, concepts, and clarifications of some basic terms. First, a multinational firm has equity interests in establishments, such as plants or offices, in foreign countries. The key here is ownership, with a standard definition of ownership as when a single individual owns at least 10 percent or more of the equity. When that owner is in a different country than the establishment, this counts as FDI. Some large firms have extensive business with foreign customers and suppliers via contracts and other arrangements, but do not actually own those activities. As such, they are not normally defined as MNEs and—importantly—they are not included in the multinational data sets that are the focus in this chapter.

Abstracting from the considerable heterogeneity among firms, the most primal form of an MNE consists of a headquarters (parent) in the home country and at least one foreign affiliate in a host country. A key aspect of this relationship is that the parent generally supplies intangible assets and other services (for example, management, technology, intellectual property, marketing, and finance) to the foreign affiliate. The firm's headquarters is a net exporter of these intangibles and services to affiliates, and those affiliates are net suppliers of goods (final or intermediate) or services (for example, legal, accounting, advertising, and so on) to customers. Profits, or the returns to intangibles and other services, flow from affiliates to parents. Thus, much intra-firm trade is not in physical intermediate or final goods.

These service flows are often or even typically poorly measured and documented, confounding attempts to fully understand the functioning of multinationals. The headquarters can, of course, also produce goods or services that it sells at home and/or exports to affiliates or third parties.[1] Affiliates produce goods and/or services and occasionally conduct some of their own research and development (R&D). Many affiliates are exclusively in service industries, though their services tend to be more customer-oriented than are headquarter services. This, however, is a description of what the different parts of the firm do, not how they relate or compare to one another—in other words, the structure of the MNE's global activities.

Four characteristics help define the structure of a multinational firm. The first is the geographic distribution of a firm's establishments. The second is the activities performed by the various establishments, including their value added and whether outputs are final or intermediate goods and services. A third is where the foreign affiliate sells its outputs (locally in the host market, exported to the home country, and/or exported to third countries) and from where it purchases inputs. A final characteristic is the interactions among establishments—that is, the intra-firm flows of goods, services, and intangibles. The first goal of this chapter is to bring these together into a handful of archetypes that provide a lens for viewing the data. Doing so generates two main MNE structures: the snake-like vertical MNE (where different affiliates do different things) and the octopus-like horizontal MNE (where affiliates replicate activities).

The second aim is assembling and analyzing broad quantitative and qualitative data on these two structures for U.S. MNEs and their foreign affiliates. Although we focus on U.S. data, both because of data quality and to simplify exposition, it includes the experience of other nations, as appropriate, to show that what is found for the United States is true for the other major sources of FDI. In doing this, we identify general characteristics and patterns rather than emphasize the specific experience of individual firms, industries, or countries. Our goal is to highlight which general concepts are most important to the data (including beliefs perhaps widely held but not supported by data) as well as areas where the data are as yet underdeveloped. The data analysis, therefore, operates on a more aggregate level than is done with case studies in order to arrive at this broad vision. When doing so, the bulk of the evidence suggests horizontal FDI plays a dominant role in the aggregate data.

Finally, in focusing on the structure and patterns of multinational activity, we do not consider several other important firm decisions. These could be characterized as earlier-stage firm choices. Specifically, we do not examine the firm's choice of whether to produce at home or abroad, generally referred to as the offshoring decision. We also set aside the ownership decision, also known as outsourcing versus vertical integration, which concerns whether to own the foreign affiliate or contract with local firms for the work. These topics are dealt with elsewhere in this volume. Further, we do not explore the choice of where to locate foreign affiliates in detail except insofar as it relates to the central discussion of MNE structure. Therefore, issues such as the role of tax policy in the location decision are omitted.

The next section lays out two main MNE structures: horizontal (activity is replicated across borders) and vertical (the production process is fragmented). It also discusses some of their more prominent offshoots and develops a set of predictions for which patterns in the data are most consistent with one structure or another. The third section analyzes primarily U.S. data to gain an insight into which structure appears to dominate the FDI landscape, finding that most FDI is horizontal. The fourth section introduces a new approach based on global value chains (GVC), which supports and extends the insights of the third section. The fifth section focuses on the issue of intangible assets in order to point to the limitations of the current data and the need for future research. The final section concludes by suggesting how understanding these structures is likely important for policy.

STRUCTURAL ARCHETYPES AND PREDICTIONS

Two main structures for MNE activity have been developed over the past forty years: horizontal and vertical FDI.[2] The fundamental difference between the two is one of differentiation versus replication. Most people's initial instinct is to imagine that an MNE is vertical (a snake), performing different activities across its different affiliates, fragmenting its production process. The classic example of a vertical MNE is an apparel company such as Nike. It designs apparel in the United States, produces it in countries like China or Vietnam, and then ships it to a Nike-owned store in Europe for sale to consumers. This vertical structure is a natural embodiment of the GVC, with each step in the process contributing to a final good. The key to this structure is that each stage of the GVC performs a different activity, with the different stages located in different countries.

In contrast, a horizontal MNE (an octopus) replicates key parts of its production process across borders. For example, Toyota may design its car in Japan and use this blueprint to produce cars in Japan, the United States, and the United Kingdom. While the cars are designed in one location, and thus there is still an element of a supply chain in the firm's structure, the major part of its activities—here, the manufacturing of the cars—is repeated in different countries.

In addition to manufacturing industries, such as autos, cement, and chemicals, many service firms and industries closely fit the horizontal structure. Fast-food restaurants, hotels, accounting, and consulting and legal services all perform roughly the same activities in many countries as well as within countries. Indeed, replication is a key attraction of chain fast-food; its familiarity appeals to customers even when the chain is foreign-owned. As an example, in 2018, there were 5,910 KFC outlets (Xinhua, 2019) and 2,700 McDonald's (Ross, 2020) in China. Vertical examples include the *maquiladoras* factories in Mexico, where parts, components, and other intermediates are assembled and the final output exported. Domestic value added is about 15 percent of output, imported intermediates are about 80 percent to 90 percent of all intermediates used by these plants, and virtually all output is exported. Business-process outsourcing is an example of vertical production in services. Industries ranging from banks to airlines can locate routine white-collar activities, from payroll to data entry to call centers, in places like India, the Philippines, or Ireland.[3]

While this distinction may initially seem minor, it has fundamental implications for what would be expected in the data. There are three differences between the two structures: relative input costs in the home and host countries, the location of sales, and the relationship between FDI in one host and FDI in other hosts. The first two build from the same question: why choose FDI rather than simply produce at home? That last is more relevant to why the firm has invested in a particular host as distinct from another one.

Why do firms choose to become multinationals in the first place? The answer is somewhat different for horizontal and vertical MNEs. A common assumption is that firms choose to become MNEs because labor is cheaper overseas than at home. This idea naturally extends to any inputs the firm uses in its production process (including raw materials), but the intuition is the same: an input is cheaper in the foreign country than at home. If this were true for the entire production process, the firm might be best off entirely relocating to that foreign location. But then it would not be an MNE, since it would entirely operate in the host, without cross-border ownership. Instead, for FDI to make sense, it must be that *some* inputs are cheaper at home while *other* inputs are cheaper in the host. Put differently, firms locate different stages of the production process in various countries because each location is the least expensive for that particular stage of production. Thus, differences in costs across borders drive vertical FDI.

If cost differences are indeed a driving force, then vertical FDI makes sense only when countries are different from one another. The classic example, Helpman (1984), is when a firm in a highly skilled developed country invests in a host country where low-skilled labor is abundant. In this case, the developed country serves as the home, since its abundance of high-skilled workers makes it the natural place to focus on innovative activity, including the development of intangible assets. Assembly workers in the less developed country, meanwhile, earn low wages, making it the natural location to produce the finished good. Thus, vertical FDI will flow from developed to developing countries, since this allows the firm to fragment its GVC and take advantage of the production-cost differentials across borders. The output can then be sold wherever consumers are located. In particular, given the relative wealth in the home country, a good deal of MNE output would be exported from the host back to the home country. This structure then closely fits the example of Nike.

Note that these cost savings are driven by production costs. A second source of costs is delivering output to consumers. In some cases, these costs can be quite daunting. One example is when the good is very difficult to transport because of its weight (for example, concrete) or its delicacy (such as fresh foods). Another example of trade costs is policy barriers such as quotas or tariffs. For example, when the United States imposed severe trade restrictions on Japanese auto imports in the 1980s, many Japanese firms jumped the tariff wall and began producing in the United States for U.S. consumers rather than continuing to import from elsewhere. Third, it may be that to effectively compete in a market, a firm must have a local presence to read the market's desires and effectively distribute its product to local consumers.

In each of these cases, even if producing in the host does not bring cost savings, there can be significant savings in terms of serving the market. Just as these savings encourage production in the host, they likewise encourage production at home since it would be comparably costly to serve the home market from a distance. These factors then result in a horizontal MNE structure where the firm produces its final product in both home and host with each production location's output geared toward local sales. This replication is the trademark of the horizontal MNE. In addition, the parent of the MNE generates intangibles, such as designs or trademarks, and uses this joint input across the two affiliates (where the jointness refers to its use in multiple locations at once). Since the parent produces both output and the joint input, the affiliate is not a carbon copy of the parent. Instead, the horizontal MNE is marked by a significant overlap in the activities of the parent and affiliate, with similar activities being carried out across borders.

As with the vertical MNE, this pattern generates two predictions for where horizontal FDI is most likely to thrive. Vertical FDI, in which different production processes occur in different countries, works best between developed and developing countries, that is, when countries differ from one another. Horizontal FDI, however, replicates processes across borders. This makes sense when costs are *not* very different across countries. Thus, horizontal FDI should be found when the home and host are similar to one another. This is one of the key insights of Markusen (1984), who shows that horizontal FDI can even happen when the two countries are identical to one another. Further, given the importance of developing intangible assets—a skill-intensive endeavor—horizontal FDI tends to be found between developed countries. In addition, there is a clear difference in where affiliate output is sold. In vertical FDI, a sizable share of output is shipped back to the rich home consumers. In contrast, horizontal affiliate output is sold locally, since the desire to access those consumers is the entire point of this MNE structure.

There are, thus, two ways to distinguish between the horizontal and vertical structures in the data: a comparison of the costs between the home and host country (often proxied by differences in skill levels or other measures of the development of the home and host) and analysis of whether affiliate output is sold locally or exported to home.

Up to this point, these two archetypes have focused on a setting with only two countries: the home and host. This is obviously a simplification, and one which, when relaxed, offers a third way to distinguish between vertical differentiation and horizontal replication. When opening the model to third countries, vertical FDI can be broadened by introducing further fragmentation of the GVC. It is most natural to think about linear GVCs, for example, where silicon is converted into computer chips, which are then exported to a factory, where they are installed on motherboards that are then shipped to another facility for assembly into a laptop. Another possibility is that the chips and motherboards are produced separately and then the installation and assembly happen in a central location.

Baldwin and Venables (2013) discuss these alternative vertical structures, labeling the first, linear structure a "snake" and the second, hub-and-spoke approach, a "spider." The spider differs from a horizontal MNE, since, in a spider, the intermediates flow to the central "body," whereas in the horizontal GVC, intermediates flow from the central parent to the affiliates. In any case, both complex vertical structures are, again, based on differentiation, since each affiliate performs a different part of the overall process, which is brought together through international trade.[4]

Opening the basic horizontal structure to third countries means gaining access to more consumers.[5] These additional consumers can be served by not only exporting from the parent or producing in this new third country, but also by exporting from an affiliate in a nearby host. For example, a U.S. firm operating in Ireland has access to Irish consumers but also, and perhaps more important, consumers in the European Union who can be served by the Irish affiliate without being troubled by the tariffs and quotas that apply to imports from non-member countries. Thus, this export-platform investment is attracted not only by the host's consumers but by those in nearby countries, what is sometimes referred to as surrounding market potential.

For example, as detailed by Barry (2004), U.S. software firms, including Microsoft, have affiliates in Ireland that duplicate and package software, provided by the parent firm, with that output destined for the European market.[6] Likewise, to achieve "just in time" manufacturing, Dell has located affiliates in the United States, Ireland, China, and other countries so it can assemble the same computers near regional consumers. Nevertheless, the central feature of export-platform FDI is the same as in the simpler horizontal structure—the replication of key activities across barriers. In the Microsoft example, it is still the case that the Irish affiliate is designed to replicate U.S. production for overseas consumers. This, then, fits well with the octopus analogy, in which the central head guides the activities of the arms, all of which are capable of essentially the same thing.[7]

Together, these extended versions of the horizontal and vertical models provide two additional predictions for the data. The first relates to the substitutability or complementarity of investment across hosts (as opposed to between a given host and the home country). If an MNE has a complex vertical structure, it is integrated via trade between its affiliates (either from one link to the next in a snake structure or from various links to the central node in the spider structure). This works best when trade barriers are low between hosts, suggesting that investment in one host makes the most sense if there is also investment in other nearby hosts. This results in a complimentary relationship in FDI across hosts. If an MNE has an export-platform structure, FDI in one host is a substitute for FDI in another nearby host. The reason is that the consumers in one country can be served reasonably well by the affiliate in the proximate host. Thus, examining the complementarity or substitutability of FDI across hosts offers another way of judging whether FDI structures fragment the GVC or replicate it. In addition, since the export-platform structure is again geared for local sales (where "local" now refers to the host's region), then significant sales in third countries provide a further clue to the nature of MNE structures.

The next section develops a set of stylized facts that provide insight into which of the two core structures—vertical fragmentation or horizontal replication—dominates FDI activity. It is important to recall that the flow of intangibles is a critical aspect of the overall integration of a firm. In the vertical MNE, the parent firm often provides services to the next link in its GVC. The same is true for the horizontal firm, with the difference being that in the horizontal MNE those services are used jointly across affiliates. Thus, neither of these models require actual physical exports by the parent to its affiliates, nor do they contradict the description of the prototypical MNE. Both structures, however, do suggest a critical role in the export of intangibles from the parent to the affiliate, which the fifth section addresses.[8]

USING U.S. DATA TO DISTINGUISH STRUCTURES

This section discusses, in turn, three methods of distinguishing across FDI structures—differences between the home and host, the destinations of affiliate sales, and the substitutability or complementarity of affiliate activity.

The early work attempting to distinguish horizontal from vertical FDI often relied on differences in factor endowments, such as land, labor, and capital, as a proxy for cost differences. This work predicted that horizontal investment should be more common between developed countries whereas vertical FDI should be prevalent from developed to developing countries. Even a brief look at the data finds that the bulk of FDI is between developed countries, consistent with horizontal FDI. Figure 2-1 presents the United Nations Conference on Trade and Development (UNCTAD) data on U.S. stocks of inbound and outbound FDI, decomposed between developed and developing countries.[9] From this, two things are readily apparent. First, most U.S. investment comes from and goes to other developed countries, strongly suggestive of horizontal FDI. Second, although the United States does invest a growing amount in developing countries, showing that vertical FDI is important, FDI in the United States from developing countries remains negligible. This is consistent with the idea the vertical FDI should primarily originate in skill-abundant developed countries but be hosted by developing nations.

FIGURE 2-1. U.S. FDI Stocks by Country Group

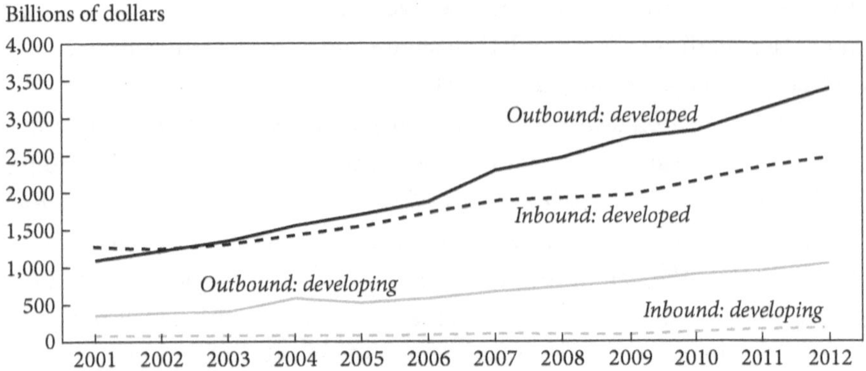

Further, these patterns are not only evident in the U.S. data. Figure 2-2 also uses UNCTAD data, but looks at inbound and outbound FDI stocks by country group. This figure is unable to break the investment down by origin (for inbound) or destination (for outbound) investment, since the bulk of FDI comes from and goes to developed countries. But the figure shows that MNEs operate primarily between developed countries. While simple data analysis such as this can mask other underlying forces, these same patterns are found in econometric analyses that specifically control for other factors, such as the wealth of consumers and the geographic distribution of developed countries.

Studies building from the integrated horizontal and vertical analysis of Markusen (2002) find that the bulk of investment is between countries with similar shares of skilled labor (see, for example, Markusen and Maskus (1999) or Blonigen, Davies, and Head (2003)). While evidence of vertical FDI can be found by using this approach (for example, Davies (2008)), the empirical evidence strongly suggests FDI is primarily between the skilled countries, a result most consistent with horizontal FDI as the dominant structure for MNE activity.

The second approach to distinguishing horizontal from vertical is via affiliate sales. Tables 2-1 through 2-3, which use publicly available data drawn and condensed from the U.S. Department of Commerce's Bureau of Economic Analysis (BEA), provide some evidence and answers.[10] The data are for majority-owned foreign affiliates—that is, for U.S.-outbound FDI. The BEA data also provide a quick perspective on the importance of foreign-affiliate production in total. The upper right panel of table 2-1 shows the

FIGURE 2-2. Total FDI Stocks by Country Group

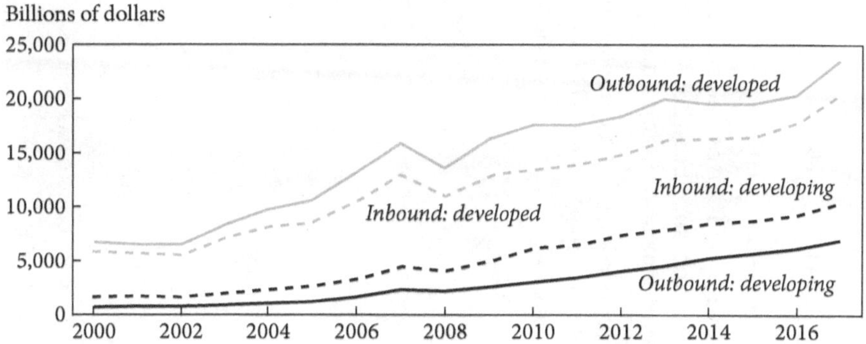

value of U.S. foreign affiliate supply of goods and services as a proportion of total U.S. exports of goods and services, respectively. The supply of goods from U.S. majority-owned foreign affiliates is about 2.8 times the total value of U.S. exports, and the supply of services by foreign affiliates is about 2.3 times the value of U.S. exports. Some affiliate sales embody imports from the United States, so there is some double counting, but affiliate imports from the United States are small and, conversely, some foreign content is embodied in U.S. goods exports.

Table 2-1 presents data on the destination of affiliate sales in the top left panel. Sales to the host country market are about 60 percent of total affiliate sales, with the share for goods lower and the share for services higher. While this means a large proportion of sales (about 40 percent) is exported, the second and third columns of table 2-1 show that most of the exports go to third countries, not back to the United States. Sales back to the United States account for only about 11 percent of total sales. Detailed statistics on intra-firm trade are not reported, but the available data show that both intra-firm imports and exports of goods by affiliates are a very small proportion of total affiliate goods sales. Exports of goods from parents to affiliates are only 5.6 percent of total affiliate-goods sales, while exports of goods from affiliates to parents are only 8.5 percent of affiliate-goods sales.[11] These numbers on intra-firm trade and total affiliate exports likely are smaller than what many would guess. In any case, the primary market for U.S. affiliates abroad clearly is not the United States, as the vertical model would suggest.

The bottom panel of table 2-1 digs deeper by showing the relative importance of goods versus services in affiliate production. The motivation for in-

TABLE 2-1. Goods and Services Supplied by Foreign Affiliates of U.S. MNEs

Destination of affiliate sales [2014 BEA benchmark survey, Table II.E.1 abridged]

	Share host country	Share other foreign	Share U.S.
Shares	0.594	0.297	0.109
Goods	0.562	0.331	0.107
Services	0.676	0.209	0.115

Importance of goods versus services—foreign affiliates [2014 BEA benchmark survey, Table II.E, F, G abridged]

	Share of sales	Share of value added	Share of employment
Goods**	0.723	0.516	0.406
Services**	0.277	0.484	0.594

Goods and services supplied by affiliates relative to total U.S. exports of goods and services [2014 BEA benchmark survey, BEA international trade data]

	As proportion of total U.S. exports of goods	As proportion of total U.S. exports of services
Affiliate supply of goods	2.761	
Affiliate supply of services		2.339

** "Goods" includes mining; "services" includes some that are arguably not services: agriculture, forestry, fishing (very small numbers), construction, utilities.

cluding this is that many international economists, perhaps because of data availability, continue to focus empirical analysis on goods—specifically, manufacturing. But that focus has distorted the view of MNE activity. The bottom panel shows that goods account for 72 percent of affiliate sales. That said, goods production uses many more purchased intermediate inputs than services do. This is why the second column reveals that, measured by value added, the value of goods and services are about the same. This suggests a "double counting" of sales in goods, because of trade in intermediates. Indeed, this double counting of trade is one reason why trade fell so sharply following the economic crisis of 2007 (Behms, Johnson, and Yi (2011)), even though services trade did not fall sharply (Ariu (2016)). Finally, services are more labor intensive than goods (the authors' interpretation), and the third column shows that, measured by affiliate employment, services are much more important than goods. So, focusing on trade in goods misses a crucial aspect of MNE activity.

Table 2-2 provides more detail on the destination of affiliate sales by dividing the world into six regions. The first row gives the world total for reference and is the same as the first row in table 2-1. The first column of table 2-2 emphasizes that U.S. affiliate production abroad is a first-world phenomenon. Furthermore, sales are highly concentrated in the rich regions of the world.[12] This is generally interpreted as another hint that foreign affiliates are likely dominated by horizontal affiliates that are producing goods and services similar to those produced in the (rich) United States.

The second column of table 2-2 shows the local (host country) share of sales in each region. These numbers are similar across the regions. The share for Europe is low, but the third column, which lists the share sold to third countries, reveals the cause. Much European production is sold to third countries, a result suggestive of export-platform FDI and something examined more in table 2-3 below. The fourth column shows the share exported back to the United States (including all U.S. customers, not just intra-firm exports). These numbers are also consistently small and continue to tell the same story: multinational affiliates are not primarily created for low-cost production to ship back home.

The biggest share for exports back to the United States is for Canada (at 20 percent), which is not surprising. Economists have emphasized the importance of within-plant specialization between the United States and Canada, with, for example, plants in the auto industry dedicated to limited numbers of models and parts that are then freely traded across the border

TABLE 2-2. Regional Concentration of Affiliate Activity; Shares of Affiliate Sales
(Millions of dollars, 2014 BEA benchmark survey, Table II.E.1 abridged)

Region	Share of total world affiliate sales	Of regional total, share to host country	Of regional total, share to third countries	Of regional total, share to United States
World	1.00	0.59	0.30	0.11
Europe	0.47	0.51	0.40	0.09
Asia-Pacific	0.27	0.63	0.28	0.09
Canada	0.11	0.77	0.03	0.20
Latin America, other Western Hem.	0.12	0.68	0.17	0.15
Africa	0.02	0.57	0.28	0.14
Middle East	0.01	0.57	0.27	0.16
World (2014)		0.59	0.30	0.11
World (2004)		0.62	0.27	0.11
World (1994)		0.67	0.23	0.10
World (1984)		0.64	0.24	0.12

(a fairly horizontal structure). It is worth noting that this share of U.S. sales outstrips that of Latin America, where the lower wages would be the most fertile ground for vertical investment. Thus, again the sales data suggest horizontal dominance.

The lower panel of table 2-2 provides some historical perspective on the shares of affiliate sales. What is interesting and important is that these shares have changed little in thirty years. In particular, the share of sales back to the United States has remained at 10 percent to 12 percent over the entire period. The local share of sales has declined some, but this has been offset by sales to third countries. A conjecture is that falling trade barriers and transport costs have allowed firms to more easily serve nearby countries from a single plant or office in one country (that is, export-platform FDI).

The data in this lower panel of table 2-2 belie an expectation—from discussions among economists and in the business press about growing fragmentation and global value chains—that cross-border trade by multinationals has grown considerably. However, even if all the increase in sales to third countries is part of complex vertical FDI, table 2-2 confirms that serving local and regional markets remains the principal task of foreign affiliates. Thus, even as technological and policy changes have made vertical FDI easier, the data indicate that horizontal FDI's importance has held steady for a very long time.[13]

Table 2-3 sheds light on third-country sales by foreign affiliates, which account for about 30 percent of total sales. Here Canada, where third-country sales are understandably very small, is excluded, so we could concentrate on own-region third-country sales. The first column of table 2-3 lists the share of third-country sales that are generated in each region and shows that the overwhelming portion of third-country sales are by affiliates in Europe and the Asia-Pacific region. Together, these two regions account for 90 percent of total third-country sales by U.S. affiliates, considerably larger than their proportion of total sales (74 percent).

The real insight of table 2-3, however, is in the second column, which shows that most of these third-country sales are intra-regional—that is, what is produced in Europe is sold in Europe. Overall, 75 percent of world third-country sales stay in the same region. For Europe and Asia-Pacific, the figure is 80 percent. This is, again, indicative of export-platform investment, particularly in wealthy Europe (which, as illustrated by figure 2-1, is a major destination for U.S. FDI).

Although the BEA data do not identify the specific country that is the

TABLE 2-3. Sales by Affiliates to Countries Other than the Host Country

(Third-country sales are largely intra-regional or to other high-income countries)

(Share values, 2014 BEA benchmark survey, Table II.D.5 abridged)

	Proportion of total world third-country sales by U.S. affiliates	Proportion of region's third-country sales that are intra-regional
World	1.00	0.75
European affiliates' third-country sales	0.64	0.80
Asia-Pacific affiliates' third-country sales*	0.26	0.80
Latin America, Western Hemisphere affiliates' third-country sales	0.07	0.43
African affiliates' third-country sales	0.02	0.17
Middle East affiliates' third-country sales	0.01	0.22
Proportion of world third-country sales that are intra-European or intra-Asia-Pacific	0.72	

*Asia-Pacific data consists of high- and middle-income countries only; no observations for the poorest.

destination of third-country sales, the regional numbers point toward U.S. MNEs establishing affiliates in one country to serve all of Europe—that is, export-platform FDI. Firms determine which specific country (or countries) based on cost and other considerations. These could include centrality, labor costs, taxes, and so forth. While some business leaders argue that tax issues are second-order considerations, three European countries are particularly export platform–oriented, as shown in the table that follows.

	Local share (%)	Third-country share (%)
Ireland	18	61
Netherlands	40	52
Switzerland	24	67

All three countries have low taxes, with Tørsløv, Wier, and Zucman (2018) counting them among the top ten tax havens. As discussed elsewhere in this volume, their tax structure has the potential for distorting the value of sales. Nevertheless, the source of revenues clearly remains local. Similar results could potentially be found for the Asia-Pacific, with multinationals choosing a specific location such as Singapore, Hong Kong, or Taiwan to serve the much-larger region. Indeed, third-country sales are 59 percent of Singapore's total, compared with local sales of 34 percent (and much of the local total likely is sales to other local downstream firms for further processing and export). Overall, the data again suggest that horizontal motives for foreign investment seem to dominate vertical ones.

Finally, extending the basic horizontal and vertical models to multiple host countries yields a third way of distinguishing between replication and fragmentation, namely, by looking at whether FDI in nearby countries is a substitute for (consistent with export platform and replication) or a complement to (consistent with complex vertical fragmentation) FDI in a given host. Blonigen and others (2007), using spatial econometric techniques for U.S. outbound FDI, find some variation. U.S. FDI in Europe, in particular, is characterized by substitution of FDI across borders. They also find a positive effect for surrounding market potential. These two patterns are strongly indicative of export-platform FDI, further supporting the notion that MNEs are replicating their activities across countries to gain access to consumers. Comparable results can be found for other parent countries in the results of Baltagi, Egger, and Pfaffermayr (2007), Garretsen and Peters (2009), and others.

Thus, building from the various methods the models of FDI suggest, the data consistently point to a major role for horizontal investment in which most FDI takes place between wealthy, developed nations to better compete for local consumers by replicating key activities. The next section presents an additional method for examining MNEs and their place in global value chains.

FDI AND GLOBAL VALUE CHAINS

This section presents a new way of differentiating between horizontal and vertical FDI by using data on global value chains. The idea is that whereas vertical FDI is explicitly designed around intra-firm trade, horizontal FDI, by the nature of its replication, relies less on intra-firm trading of intermediate inputs. Thus, the two MNE structures use GVCs differently. This section offers a new window on FDI's strong horizontal aspect by examining how FDI fits into GVCs. It uses two measures of GVC participation: the Output Index (which measures the inputs an industry in a given country provides to other firms) and the Input Index (which measures how much the country-industry pair relies on inputs from the GVC). We find that FDI in developed countries is concentrated in industries where these measures are relatively small compared with FDI in developing countries. This is consistent with the notion that developed countries (which are the major hosts) attract mostly horizontal investment while developing countries host more vertical FDI.

For vertical FDI, the MNE's GVC is evident, since the snake-like structure of this type of MNE is designed to fragment the production process across borders. The parent and affiliate are obviously links in a GVC. Horizontal firms' GVC is less obvious, but is still present in the form of joint input produced in the headquarters and used across various production affiliates. Both vertical and horizontal GVCs, however, are internal and do not describe how MNE activity fits into the production of other firms.

In the early models of FDI, such as Helpman (1984) and Markusen (1984), production technologies were simplified so that only MNEs used intermediate inputs, and those inputs were made by the MNE itself. In practice, many MNEs purchase intermediate inputs from other firms. Further, those inputs can originate in the home, host, or third countries. In addition, although the early models of FDI described the foreign affiliates' customers as being end-use consumers, this does not have to be true. Instead, the multinational's output can serve as an input into the production activities of other firms. That said, the location of unrelated purchasers would still vary across MNE structures: that is, at home (vertical), in the host (horizontal), or to firms in third countries (export platform). While, as discussed in box 2-1, the distinction between intermediate and final goods is somewhat hazy in practice, the intuitive difference and what it means for describing GVCs is clear.

With that in mind, the location of parents and affiliates in GVCs can help explain the structure of MNE activities. Although data on intra-firm GVCs is unavailable, industry data developed by Antràs and Chor (2018), which positions an industry in a given country in the global GVC, can be used. Their work explicitly recognizes that the production of a final good can involve many stages across industries and countries. Their industry data can be used to construct two measures: one capturing how much an industry feeds into GVCs by supporting the production of others and one measuring how much the industry draws its inputs from GVCs. Both measures

BOX 2-1. The Final Word on Final Goods

Despite the importance of defining what is an intermediate and what is a final good, the distinction is blurred, to say the least. By definition, a final good is one sold to the ultimate consumer—that is, the person who uses the output without producing anything else that is provided for another's use. While this may seem straightforward, it is not. Some products, such as gasoline, can easily be a finished good (when sold to a private driver) or an intermediate (when sold to a taxi driver). When one pushes the point, what might seem like a finished good (a steak eaten by a hungry worker) can be thought of as an input (into the production of muscle strength by that worker). All of this is to say nothing of the issue of aggregation where the "automobile" sector includes minivans (relatively on the final good end of the spectrum) and tour buses (more on the intermediate end). Therefore, when approaching the data, the interpretation of the share of final goods in sales should be taken as an overall guide of the relative degree to which final users consume a product rather than as a hard and fast definition.

are constructed for an industry as a whole.[14] Thus, for a given country, they combine the local production of domestically owned MNEs, foreign-owned MNEs, and purely domestic firms.

That said, MNEs feature heavily in the construction of the Antràs and Chor (2018) measures. Roughly one-third of global output, two-thirds of worldwide exports, and half of imports are attributable to MNEs (OECD, 2018).[15] Thus, MNEs undoubtedly form a major part of their construction, particularly when it is focused on the cross-border aspects of GVCs. Further, the inclusion of non-MNEs is potentially advantageous since MNEs can both buy and sell intermediates with unrelated firms.[16] Thus, the inclusion of all firms rather than just MNEs may be necessary to accurately describe GVCs' operation.

The *Output Index* captures the degree to which an industry's sales contribute to the production process of other firms.[17] One way to do this is to simply measure the percentage of an industry's sales that are intermediates. This method, however, misses the chain part of the GVC, since it ignores what happens beyond the next link in the chain. As a result, it would understate the industry's contribution to the GVC.

For example, consider the aluminum industry in three hypothetical countries. In Country A, the industry produces aluminum that is sold directly to final consumers as aluminum foil. Thus, for Country A's aluminum industry, there is no subsequent link in the GVC. Country B's aluminum industry, meanwhile, produces aluminum for beverage companies, which turn it into cans that are then filled and sold to final consumers. In comparison, Country C's aluminum industry sells to a screw manufacturer, which, in turn, sells its screws to an airline company, which uses them to make planes, which are delivered to final consumers. Unlike Country A's industry, both Country B and Country C producers have subsequent links—one link for Country B and two for Country C. Obviously, the GVC that the Country A sector feeds into is the shortest—there is one step between it and the final consumer. This would then get the lowest value for the Output Index among the three. Even if both the Country B and Country C industries sell the same share of their output as intermediates, Country B's Output Index value would lie between Country A's and Country C's, because the value chain for the Country B sector is shorter (two steps away from the final consumer).

Thus, the Output Index accounts for the number of steps between an industry's production and the final consumer.[18] In addition, as detailed in box 2-2, it controls for the varying shares of output sold as intermediates in each link in the GVC. In broad strokes, the Output Index is higher when a country-industry sells more as intermediates itself and when its customers sell more as intermediates to a longer GVC chain. Thus, the higher the Output Index for a nation's industry, the more it contributes to GVCs.[19] As discussed in box 2-2, some industries, such as mining, contribute heavily to GVCs, whereas others (for example, real estate) contribute little.

In contrast to the Output Index, which measures contribution, the *Input Index* measures a country-industry's reliance upon the GVC—that is, the degree to which the GVC contributes to its own output. One simple way of doing so would be to measure the cost of purchased intermediates relative to output. However, just as using only the share of output sold as intermediates understates the contribution to the GVC, doing this would understate the reliance on the GVC, since a given country-industry's suppliers may themselves purchase intermediates from links further back in the chain. The Input Index accounts for this by decomposing a country-industry's value added across the various links in the GVC.

As an example, consider the electronics industry in three hypothetical countries: Country D, Country E, and Country F. Country D electronics use no inputs other than their own labor.[20] Because it uses nothing from the rest of the GVC, its Input Index would be low. Country E's electronics industry, on the other hand, purchases wiring from suppliers, which it uses to make components that go into its electronics. It, therefore, has one link before it in the GVC. Finally, Country F's computer industry purchases its components from a supplier that, itself, purchases the wires from a third firm—that is, it has two links before it in the GVC.[21]

Comparable to the Output Index, an industry drawing from a longer GVC would have a higher Input Index score—that is, Country F's score is greater than Country E's, which is greater than Country D's. Further, as detailed in box 2-2, the Input Index also accounts for variation in the amount of purchased intermediates. Thus, the more that a country's industry relies on the GVC for producing its output, the higher its Input Index. As discussed in box 2-2, reliance on GVCs varies considerably across countries and industries. The electrical equipment and transport equipment industries are especially reliant on GVCs. Real estate, as was true in the Output Index, is fairly self-contained.

Together, the Input and Output Indices provide a method of describing how a foreign affiliate fits in to the GVC and with the pattern varying across MNE structures. To visualize this, a part of the multinational (either parent

BOX 2-2. Details on the Output and Input Indices

For our Output and Input Indices, we utilize the data provided by Antràs and Chor (2018). Although we refer readers to their study (as well as the seminal papers of Fally (2012) and Antràs and Chor (2013)) for details, here we provide a brief overview of the technical construction of the measures and their underlying data.

For both of these, the starting point is the 2013 version of the World Input-Output Database.[a] This lists the sales and purchases for thirty-five sectors (indexed by *s*) across forty countries (indexed by *j*), as well as the value added of each country-industry.[b] For a sector *r* in country *i*, denote Y_i^r its gross output, F_i^r the value of gross output sold to final consumers, and Z_{ij}^{rs} the dollar value of sales sold as an intermediate to sector *s* in country *j*. Thus, $Y_i^r = F_i^r + \sum_s \sum_j Z_{ij}^{rs}$—that is, the sum of what is sold to final consumers and other producers. In addition, denote $\alpha_{ij}^{rs} = \frac{Z_{ij}^{rs}}{Y_j^s}$, which is the cost of inputs that sector *s* in country *j* needs from sector *r* in country *i* to produce one dollar of its own output. This can be used to rewrite output in industry *r* in country *i* as:

$$Y_i^r = F_i^r + \sum_s \sum_j \alpha_{ij}^{rs} F_j^s + \sum_s \sum_j \sum_t \sum_k \alpha_{ij}^{rs}\, \alpha_{jk}^{st} F_k^t + \dots$$

The first term is one stage from the final consumer, the second is two stages away (that is, *ri* sells to another industry, which then sells to the final consumer), the third is three stages away, and so forth. Then, multiplying each of these terms by the number of stages away from the consumer and normalizing by gross output, we obtain a measure of how much *ri* contributes to the GVC:

a. This can be found at www.wiod.org/home.

b. It does so from 1995–2011, however, we ignore the time dimension and only use the 2011 values.

$$U_i^r = \frac{F_i^r}{Y_i^r} + 2\frac{\sum_s \sum_j \alpha_{ij}^{rs} F_j^s}{Y_i^r} + 3\frac{\sum_s \sum_j \sum_t \sum_k \alpha_{ij}^{rs}\, \alpha_{jk}^{st} F_k^t}{Y_i^r} + \cdots \geq 1$$

In this, firms that sell more as inputs (have higher α_{ij}^{rs}s), which are used in processes further removed from the final consumers, will have a higher value. Our Output Index takes this U_i^r and normalizes it so that it runs from 0 to 1.

There is considerable variation both across industries within a single country and across countries within a single industry. Figure 1B plots the values of the Output Index for several countries, with the U.S. values in the final group. From this, three things can be seen. First, within a country, there is a range of values for the Output Index (that is, within a group, there is variation in the vertical dimension). Second, the average value for a given country varies nation to nation (that is, the within-group center varies horizontally). Globally, the average value is 0.32. For the United States, the average is 0.26. China, mean-

FIGURE 1B. Output Index within Countries

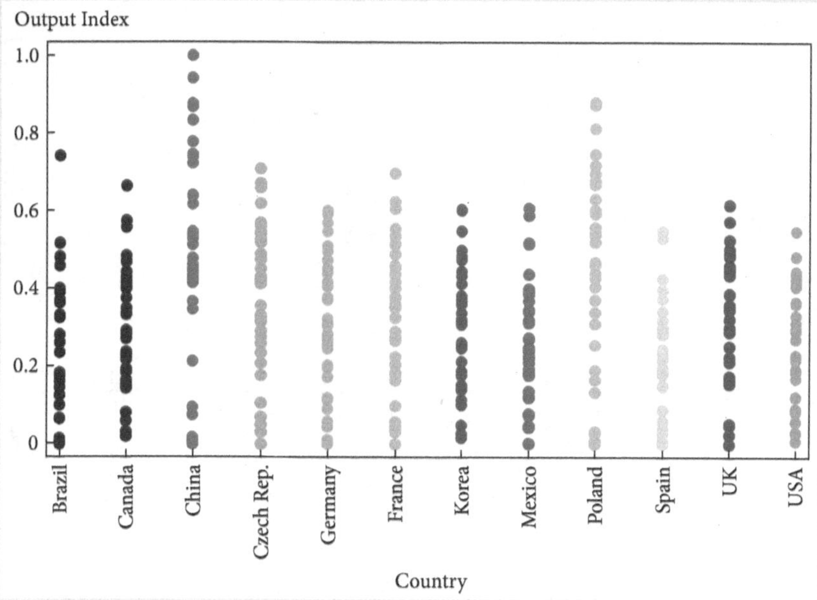

while, has an average of 0.49. This means that the average U.S. industry contributes less to GVCs than the average industry globally, which itself contributes less than the average Chinese industry. Third, the range of values also varies across countries. Whereas the standard deviation for the United States is 0.15, the standard deviation for China is 0.28.

This should not be taken to mean that the only variation is across countries. In Figure 2B, we illustrate the values across countries within a given industry. As one might expect, there are clear differences in the average value of the Output Index across industries. However, this figure also shows that there is considerable variation within an industry but across countries (again, the vertical variation within a group). Thus, although some industries on average contribute more to GVCs than others, the extent to which this occurs depends highly on the country in question. There are two sources of the variation in

FIGURE 2B. Output Index within Industries

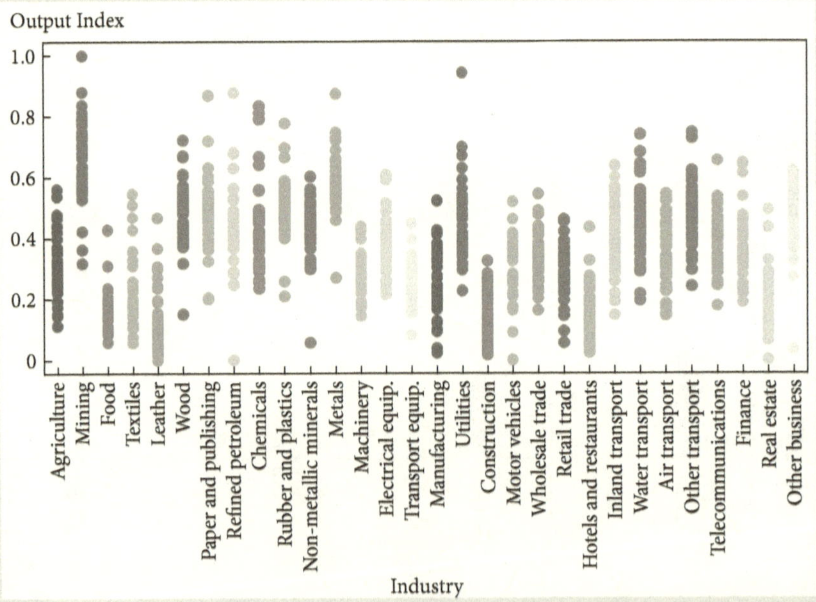

these two figures. First, there is the share of a country-industry's output sold as an intermediate where higher shares lead to a higher Output Index. Second, there is the matter of who buys those intermediates, since selling to another industry that itself sells intermediates links to a longer GVC and generates a higher Output Index. As these two figures show, there is a great deal of heterogeneity across industries and countries.

For the Input Index, define $b_{ji}^{sr} = \frac{z_{ji}^{sr}}{Y_j^s}$, which is share of *sj*'s output used as an input by industry *ri*.[c] With this, gross output can be written as $Y_i^r = VA_i^r + \sum_s \sum_j b_{ji}^{sr} Y_j^s$—that is, gross output for *ri* equals its value added and the sum of its expenditures on non-processed factors of production and on intermediate inputs. Expanding this, we see that:

$$Y_i^r = VA_i^r + \sum_s \sum_j b_{ji}^{sr} VA_j^s + \sum_s \sum_j \sum_t \sum_k b_{kj}^{ts} b_{ji}^{sr} VA_k^t + \ldots$$

—that is, output is the sum of value added along the different links in the production chain feeding into *ri*'s output. The first term is one step before *ri*'s output—that is, what it does itself. The second term is the value added coming from the intermediates *ri* uses, making that value added two steps away from output; the third term is three steps away and so on. Multiplying each stage by the number of links in the chain before it reaches *ri*'s output and dividing by the value of output, we obtain

$$D_i^r = \frac{VA_i^r}{Y_i^r} + 2\frac{\sum_s \sum_j b_{ji}^{sr} VA_j^s}{Y_i^r} + 3\frac{\sum_s \sum_j \sum_t \sum_k b_{kj}^{ts} b_{ji}^{sr} VA_k^t}{Y_i^r} + \cdots \geq 1$$

where again, the greater the importance of inputs (higher b_{ji}^{sr}s) and the more links before output, the higher this score. To arrive at our Input Index, we normalize this value so that it runs from 0 to 1.

As with the Output Index, the Input Index varies within a

---

c. The difference between α and *b* is that the first is what *ri* sells to *sj* as an input while the second is what *ri* buys from *sj* as an input.

country across industries and within an industry across countries. Figure 3B is the counterpart to Figure 1B, except it uses the Input Index. Globally, the average industry has an Input Index of 0.42, with different countries having different within-country averages. As with the Output Index, the United States is somewhat below this average at 0.26 and China is somewhat higher, with an average of 0.63. Further, as shown in Figure 4B, there is again variation both across industries (the average for each of the groupings varies across them) and within an industry but across countries (the vertical variation). As with the Output Index, this variation is generated by the use of intermediates and where those intermediates come from (that is, the length of the GVC that is tapped into).

FIGURE 3B. Input Index within Countries

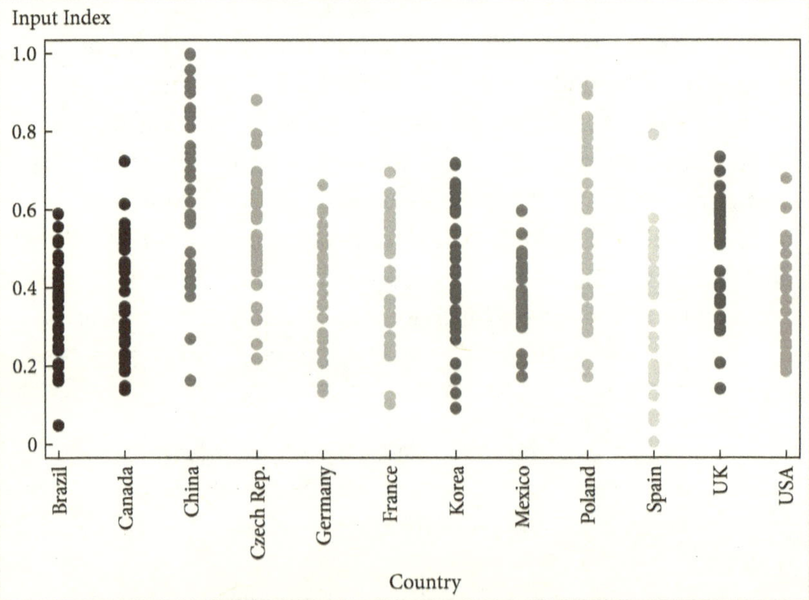

FIGURE 4B. Input Index within Industries

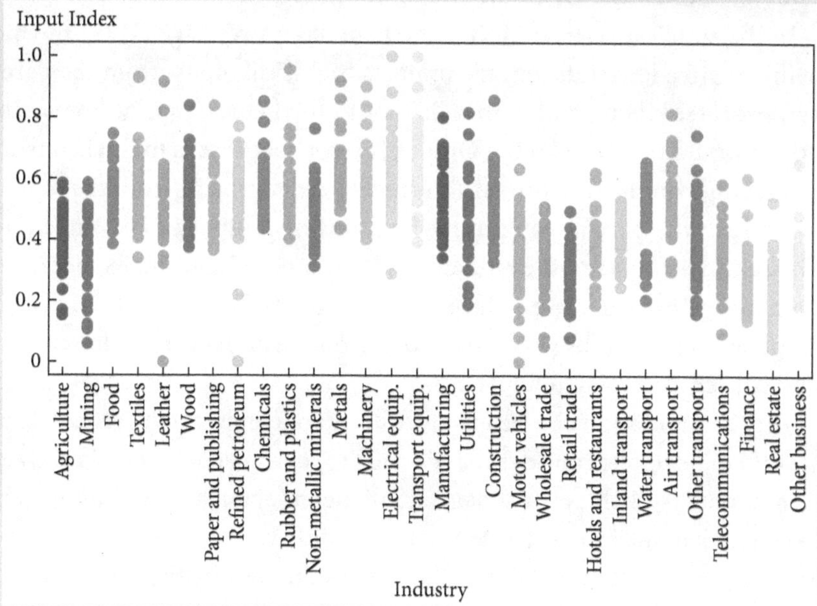

or affiliate) is located in the GVC box in figure 2-3. The box is constructed so that the higher a part of the MNE's Output Index score (contributions to the GVC) the closer to the top of the box it is, and the higher its Input Index score (reliance on the GVC) the farther to the right it is.

In the simplest vertical MNEs, the firm has a two-stage GVC, in which an affiliate in a low-skill country imports high-skill inputs from the parent firm, processes them, and then sells that to final consumers at home. This affiliate would rank low on the Output Index (since it sells to final consumers) and high on the Input Index (due to its need for inputs from the parent). In contrast, the parent would rank high on the Output Index, since most of its sales are inputs to the affiliate, and low on the Input Index, because it purchases no intermediates. The parent part of the firm would then place in the top left corner of the GVC box and the foreign affiliate in the lower right-hand corner, as shown in figure 2-3.

This configuration can be extended to more complicated vertical structures.[22] For example, consider the iPhone. It is designed in the United States, its components, such as the screen, are made in Japan, and the components are assembled in China.[23] The U.S. parent would rank highly on the Output Index, since its output (the design) is used exclusively by the other stages in the iPhone production line. In addition, the Japanese affiliate's sale of inputs to China further boosts the parent's Output Index score. The Japanese affiliate also exclusively sells intermediates; however, since it is closer to the

FIGURE 2-3. FDI in the GVC Box

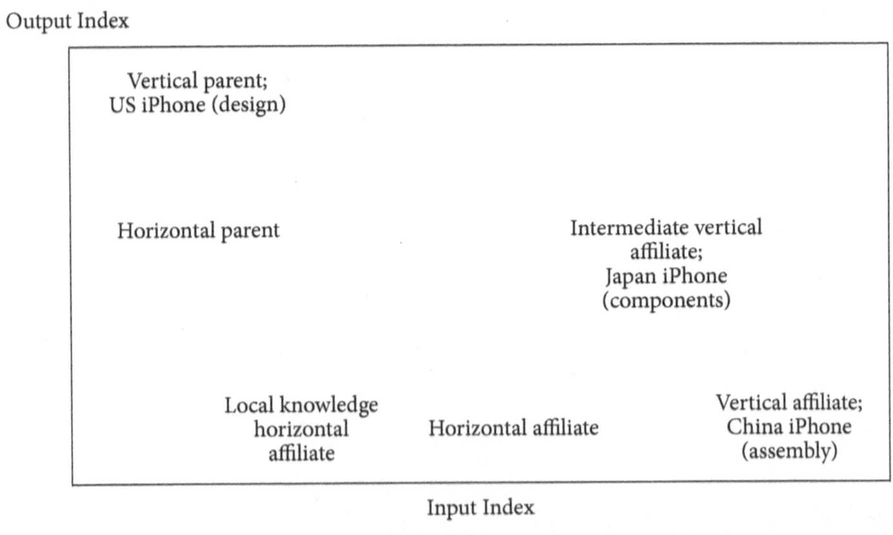

end of the GVC (only the Chinese assembly remains), it would have a more moderate Output Index score.[24] The Chinese affiliate, meanwhile, is at the end of the chain and would have a low Output Index score.

For the Input Index, the reverse ordering holds. The U.S. affiliate is essentially self-contained and does not use inputs from the GVC. Both the Japanese and Chinese affiliates, however, are very reliant on the United States for the value added (60 percent of profits are attributable to the U.S. affiliate, as discussed in table 2-8). Therefore, both would rank fairly high on the Input Index, with the Chinese value somewhat higher because it has two links in the chain before its stage in the production process. As figure 2-3 illustrates, this would then show the beginning and end of the iPhone GVC matching the simple vertical MNE, with the middle link in between.

For a simple horizontal structure, the parent produces the joint input used in production both locally and in the foreign affiliate, with all output going to final consumers (some at home, others abroad). As with the vertical foreign affiliate, the horizontal foreign affiliate sells no output as an intermediate and ranks low on the Output Index. Unlike the vertical parent, the horizontal parent sells both intermediates and final goods. Therefore, although it has an Output Index score higher than its affiliate, it is not as high as the exclusively intermediate-selling vertical parent.

On the Input Index side, as with the vertical parent, the horizontal parent purchases no intermediate inputs and has a low score. The foreign horizontal affiliate, meanwhile, does purchase intermediate inputs (the joint input from the parent). In contrast to the vertical affiliate in a low-skill developing country, however, the horizontal affiliate is located in a high-skill abundant country and carries out significant skill-intensive production tasks (tasks that replicate some of those in the parent). Thus, while the horizontal affiliate relies on the inputs supplied by the parent, it provides more of the final product's value than a low skill–intensive vertical affiliate does. Together, these factors would tend to place the two parts of the simple horizontal MNE in the lower left corner of the box when compared with a vertical MNE.

This simple horizontal baseline can also be extended. One way to do so is to assume that the affiliate sells its output as an intermediate to an unrelated firm rather than a final consumer (for example, the MNE's various affiliates produce concrete, which is sold to local construction firms). This added link in the GVC, after the affiliate's production stage, would increase the Output Index score both for the affiliate and its parent (who is now linked to a longer GVC). It would still be the case, however, that the parent part of the firm would have a higher Output Index than the affiliate, because of the joint input the parent provides to its affiliates. In a similar way, additional intermediates can be added to the replicated production stage. This would increase the Input Index for the parent and all of its affiliates, since they all engage in this activity. In contrast, incorporating intermediates into the development of the joint input (for example, technical machinery needed for the R&D behind the design) would increase the Input Index for the parent directly and then indirectly for its affiliates as they are tied to a longer-input GVC.

Finally, one can alter the importance of the inputs obtained from the parent. For example, suppose that knowledge of local consumer desires is important to producing in each country. As the importance of local knowledge rises, the value generated by the affiliate would grow, lowering its Input Index. For the parent, where the joint input and distribution are done locally, this shift in value generation from the joint input to distribution would net out, leading to no change.

Analyzing where parents and affiliates are located in the GVC box can then provide yet another indication of the structure of MNE activities. FDI concentrated in the top-left (home) and right-hand side (host) of the box would generally be vertical FDI. FDI in the middle and bottom-right of the box would indicate horizontal investment. In practice, since both horizontal and vertical FDI exist (and have much more complex possibilities than the stereotypical models), this distinction will be less clear-cut. However, comparing the index placement in developed and developing countries reveals some suggestive patterns.

Figure 2-4 positions inbound and outbound U.S. investment for different industries in the GVC box. It uses affiliate sales data so that the size of a blue circle corresponds to the relative size of sales by foreign affiliates in the United States. Similarly, the size of the red circles indicate the relative value of sales by U.S.-owned affiliates abroad.[25] To position each of these in the GVC box, the industry's Output and Input Indices for the United States are used, since the sales data do not distinguish between the origin of inbound FDI or the destination of outbound investment.

As discussed in box 2-2, compared to the global average, the average U.S. industry is both less reliant on GVCs (with a mean across industries of 0.36 relative to the global mean of 0.42) and contributes less to them (the U.S. industry average is 0.26 whereas the global average is 0.32). This would

FIGURE 2-4. Total U.S. FDI in the GVC Box

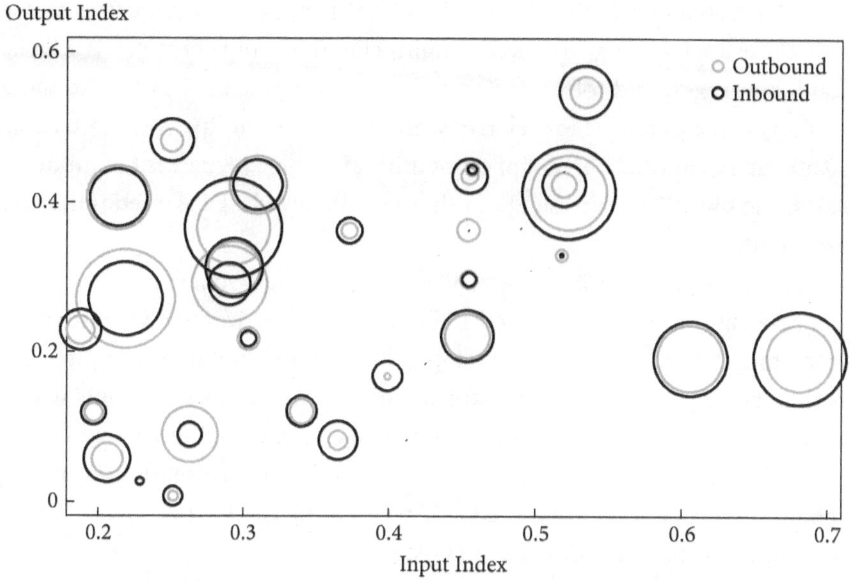

Note: A higher Input Index score indicates more reliance on GVCs. A higher Output Index score indicates more contribution to GVCs. The size of the bubble indicates the relative size of the industry in affiliate sales.

place U.S. industries toward the lower-left corner of the GVC box, compared to the global average. This is also the region of the box where horizontal FDI is most likely to be found. Given the large role that U.S. inbound and outbound FDI plays in global FDI, this pattern provides additional support to the conclusion that the horizontal FDI plays a considerable role in overall FDI activity.

The figure itself shows two things. First, the sizes of the blue inbound and red outbound circles are similar.[26] This indicates that, for the United States, the major outbound FDI industries are also its major inbound ones. This pattern, again, suggests replication—that is, horizontal FDI—in the data, since vertical investment should move primarily in one direction or the other, not both. The second feature in figure 2-4 is that, even accounting for the fact that overall U.S. activity skews toward the lower-left corner, the bulk of FDI (the larger circles) tends toward the middle left of the GVC box. Thus, compared to the United States as a whole, more FDI is found in those industries that require relatively few inputs from GVCs and yet contribute in a fair way to them. This pattern, again, fits the horizontal notion illustrated in figure 2-3. That said, there are three notable exceptions to this pattern illustrated by the three large circles with Input Index measures above 0.5. These are (moving from left to right) chemicals and chemical products; food, beverages, and tobacco; and transport equipment. All of these seem to suggest the potential for relatively more vertical activity. Although these sectors make up 16.2 percent of outbound sales and 32.8 percent of inbound sales, the overall picture suggests that U.S.-involved FDI is predominately horizontal.

The dominance of horizontal FDI in the United States, however, does not rule out the existence of vertical FDI. Instead, vertical FDI is more likely to be found in relatively less developed hosts. One limitation of figure 2-4 is that it does not use bilateral information—that is, it does not show where investment into the U.S. originates, or the location of U.S.-owned affiliates. As such, it uses the U.S. values of the two indices for its outbound investment and does not contrast the GVC positioning of U.S. outbound FDI to developed hosts versus developing hosts.

A different dataset from the BEA does provide such bilateral information, albeit for a limited number of countries and industries. Figure 2-5 plots U.S. outbound investment, unlike figure 2-4, using the Input and Output Index values of the host rather than the United States. In addition, it differentiates between two broad groups: developing hosts (Brazil, Mexico, and China) and developed hosts (Canada, France, Germany, the United Kingdom, the Netherlands, Australia, Japan, and Switzerland).

Distinguishing between developing and developed hosts is important, because they have significant differences in the GVC patterns, as illustrated in the lower part of table 2-4. Developed countries have an average Input Index score of 0.44 and an average Output Index score of 0.34. Both scores are lower, but only slightly, than the average of the three developing countries. However, when weighting by the relative share of U.S. FDI of an industry within each group of countries, the differences become more pronounced. The developing countries' Input Index is 56 percent higher and the Output Index is 23 percent higher than the comparable averages for the developed countries. Put simply, the U.S. FDI in developing countries is directed much more toward industries that are both more reliant upon GVCs and feed more into them.

This pattern can also be seen in figure 2-5. Even after accounting for the fact that the developing countries overall tend toward the right-hand side of the box, their FDI-dominated industries have higher Input Indices than the

FIGURE 2-5. U.S. Outbound FDI Using Host GVC Indices

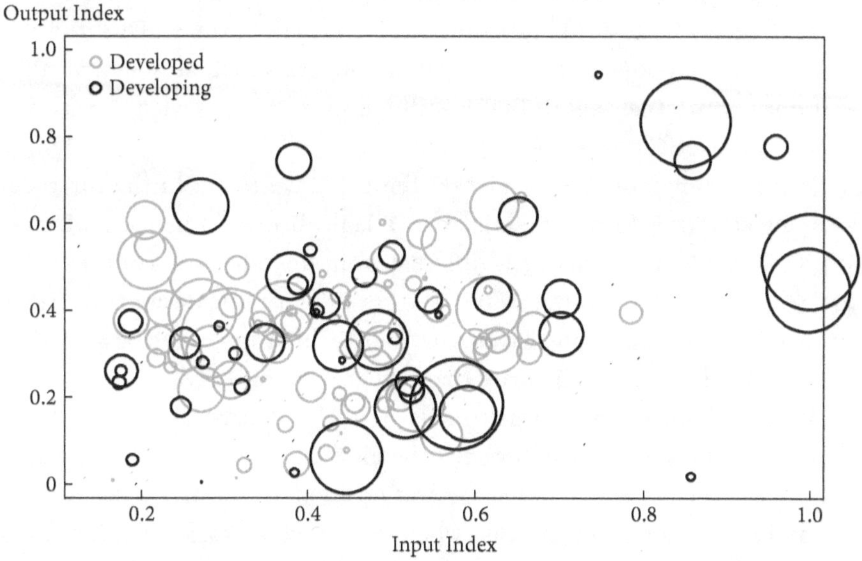

Note: A higher Input Index score indicates more reliance on GVCs. A higher Output Index score indicates more contribution to GVCs. The size of the bubble indicates the relative size of the industry in affiliate sales.

TABLE 2-4. Input and Output Indices

	Input index	Output index
Unweighted		
All countries	0.427	0.320
U.S.A.	0.365	0.260
Major U.S. hosts		
Unweighted		
Developed	0.443	0.347
Developing	0.474	0.365
% difference (developing versus developed)	7.0%	5.2%
Weighted by industry FDI share		
Developed	0.410	0.335
Developing	0.642	0.413
% difference (developing versus developed)	56.7%	23.1%

Note: Weights are the share of FDI for this country-industry within the group of countries. The developed and developing country subsets are those used in figure 2-5.

country-specific average. If outbound FDI to developing countries is more vertical, this is what would be expected. Nevertheless, since FDI activity is larger in the developed hosts, this pattern suggests that, although vertical FDI does occur, the bulk of FDI is still found in the lower-left, horizontal region of the GVC box.

Figure 2-6 focuses specifically on the U.S. investment in the three developing countries for which data are available: Brazil, China, and Mexico. While there is overlap, China is different from the other two countries due to its high Input and Output values (see box 2-2 for more discussion). Thus, even among these emerging nations, U.S. FDI China appears to be an outlier in that it tends to be in industries that rely heavily on GVCs.

While this chapter has largely focused on U.S. data because of availability, it is worthwhile to try to broaden the picture, because the United States may be a special case due to its size and position as the largest destination for, and recipient of, FDI, at least when measured as stocks of FDI (China currently is first in FDI inflows and the United States second). With this in mind, data from the Organization for Economic Cooperation and Development (OECD) provides information on total inbound and outbound FDI

FIGURE 2-6. U.S. Outbound FDI to Brazil, Mexico, and China

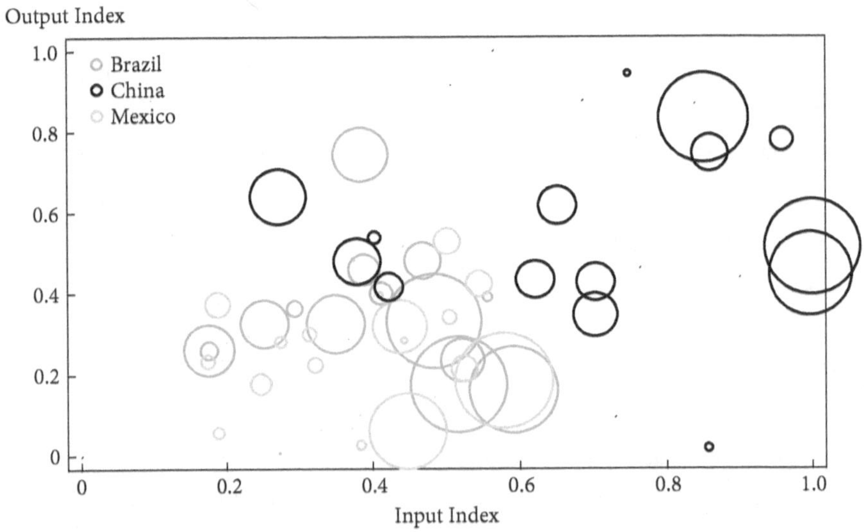

Note: A higher Input Index score indicates more reliance on GVCs. A higher Output Index score indicates more contribution to GVCs. The size of the bubble indicates the relative size of the industry in affiliate sales.

stocks in 2011, where, just as in figure 2-4, these data lack bilateral information.[27] Despite switching the measure of FDI from affiliate sales to FDI stocks, as shown in figure 2-7, the U.S. picture in the OECD data looks similar to the 2014 BEA sales data in figure 2-4. Thus, the lessons learned for the United States from the BEA data likely carry over to the OECD data and vice versa. The purpose of switching datasets, however, is not to compare different FDI measures but to look at the experience of other countries.

Figure 2-8, as with figures 2-6 and 2-7, focuses on inbound FDI and uses the host country Input and Output Index values to compare the United States with four other major OECD FDI hosts: the United Kingdom, Germany, Canada, and France—collectively, "the Big Five." To ease comparison to the U.S. baseline, the U.S. values are denoted by Xs rather than circles. This comparison reveals two features. First, these countries' industries are generally found in the same lower-left corner of the box as the U.S. industries. Second, even within a country, more FDI is found in the lower-left region of the box than in the top right. This suggests that the strong horizontal flavor of U.S. FDI extends to the rest of the Big Five.

FIGURE 2-7. U.S. Stocks of FDI in the GVC Box

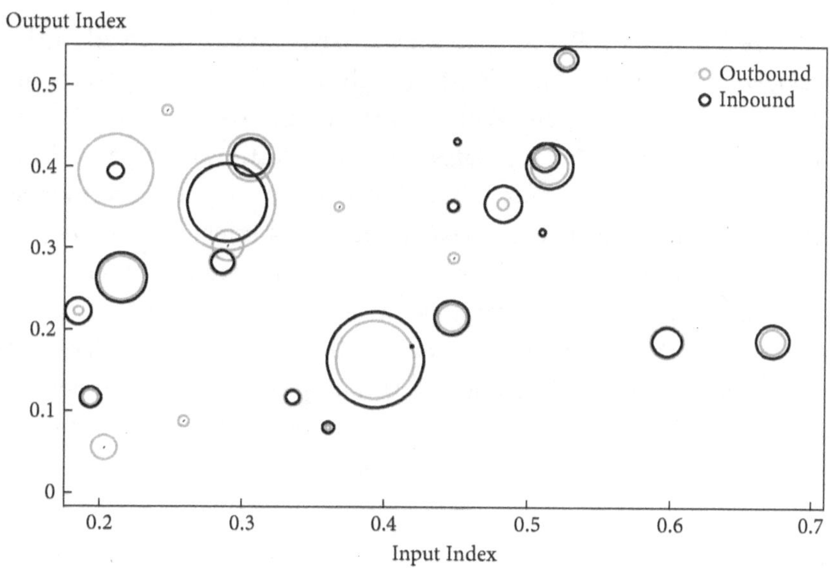

Note: A higher Input Index score indicates more reliance on GVCs. A higher Output Index score indicates more contribution to GVCs. The size of the bubble indicates the relative size of the industry in affiliate FDI stock.

FIGURE 2-8. Inbound FDI of the Big Five in the GVC Box

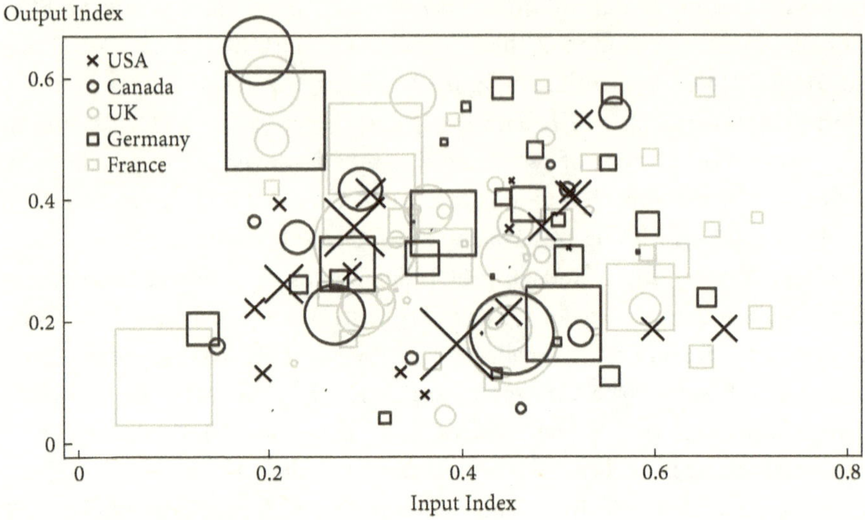

Note: A higher Input Index score indicates more reliance on GVCs. A higher Output Index score indicates more contribution to GVCs. The size of the bubble indicates the relative size of the industry in affiliate FDI stock.

Figure 2-9, meanwhile, compares the U.S. baseline to four relatively less developed OECD host countries (the Czech Republic, Korea, Poland, and Spain). As in figure 2-5, these relatively developing hosts are situated further to the right than is the United States—that is, industries in these countries rely more on GVCs than those in the United States. Furthermore, even accounting for this difference, we see that their most important FDI-hosting industries have higher Input Index scores than the country-specific average. As in figure 2-6, this pattern suggests that, as the level of development lags, vertical FDI becomes more important. The GVC box approach of these figures—and the fact that the Big Five are both the sources of and destinations for a significant share of global FDI—further supports that the dominant structure of FDI activity is horizontal.[28]

FIGURE 2-9. Inbound FDI of Developing OECD in the GVC Box

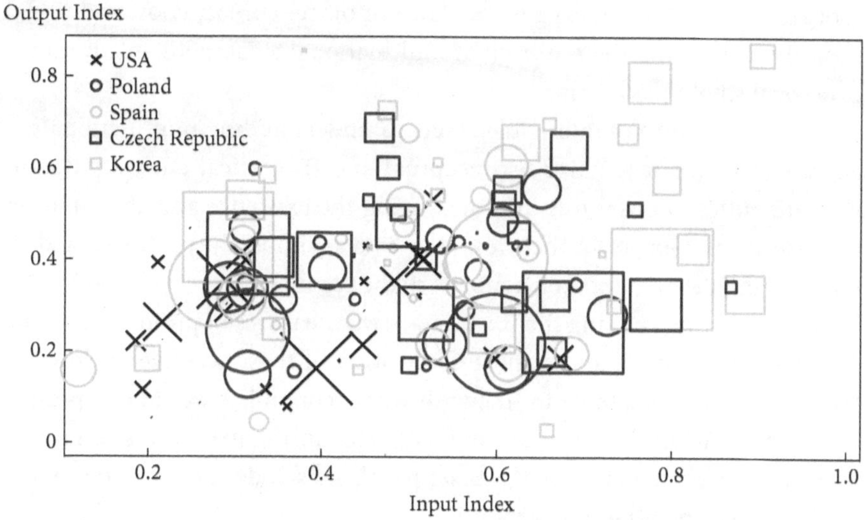

Note: A higher Input Index score indicates more reliance on GVCs. A higher Output Index score indicates more contribution to GVCs. The size of the bubble indicates the relative size of the industry in affiliate FDI stock.

EVALUATING INTANGIBLE ASSETS AND OTHER SERVICE FLOWS

As we note in the introduction, intangible and other services supplied by parent firms to affiliates are generally unobserved and unmeasured. Multinational supplies of management, technology, R&D, intellectual property, marketing, and finance to affiliates are believed to be large and a crucial part of MNE activity. International business literature emphasizes them, and they are a cornerstone of theoretical models of multinational firms as embodied in the idea of the horizontal model's joint input. Thus, data on these services are all the more crucial.

In theoretical models, intangibles, particularly those that are knowledge-based, are assumed to possess a "joint," or non-rivaled, nature that is not found in physical capital such as plant, equipment, and property. A knowledge-based asset, a blueprint, for example, can be used in multiple locations without reducing its value in any one location. In other words, intangibles and specifically knowledge-based assets create firm-level scale economies as opposed to or in addition to any plant-level economies of scale. These firm-level scale economies give the multinational a powerful tool and incentive for adding more plants or offices abroad at low additional cost, thereby giving the multi-plant multinational a competitive advantage over local single-plant firms.

The importance of intangible assets to understanding multinationals is acknowledged, but remains a conceptual and theoretical curiosity due to the difficulties in observing and measuring the existence and contribution of these assets. Generally, their role shows up as simply the profits earned by foreign affiliates rather than payments to the parent for its services. Table 2-5 makes this point by using the BEA data. Two measures of profits or income are given in the data, and a short description of these are given below the table. "Profits" tends to be in line with what economists would call profits, while "Net Income" is more in line with accounting definitions of profits. For example, profit here includes taxes paid but excludes capital gains, while net income is the other way around.

The second column of table 2-5 shows that profits and net income are significant but not especially large relative to total affiliate sales. Column 3, however, shows that profits and net income are a large share of value added. Unfortunately, comparable numbers for the U.S. corporate sectors as a whole are not available. The BEA reports profits as a share of revenues as 3.4 percent in 2018, while Federal Reserve data shows the share as 10 percent to 12 percent of value added (Federal Reserve Bank of Saint Louis (2020)). But it is not clear whether this Federal Reserve number is closer to the (economic) definition of profits in table 2-5 or to the (accounting) definition of net income. In addition, the Federal Reserve figures are for complete corporations, while table 2-5 (BEA data) gives only numbers for affiliates. Thus, a statement to the effect that foreign affiliates are, as a whole, highly profitable cannot be supported.

Nevertheless, profit and net income as shares of sales, and especially value added, are included for two reasons. First, these high numbers are often quoted by critics of multinational firms, who assert the firms earn excessive monopoly profits, move jobs abroad, and are not repatriating profits. Second, and regardless of whether these figures are significantly higher than the U.S. corporate averages, this chapter will argue that they are likely much inflated by failing to take into account the value of knowledge-based and other intangible assets.

One obvious approach to evaluating the importance of intangibles is to look at royalties, fees, and R&D figures for affiliates and parents. While

BEA data provide these numbers for affiliates, it does not provide figures for parents and corporations as a whole. Thus, that data cannot shed light on whether multinational corporations are R&D- and intellectual property–intensive compared with the corporate sector as a whole (though all researchers are confident that this is true). Second, reported royalties and fees for intellectual property are only a small part of intangible assets and services. Management and engineering services, marketing, finance, and brand values may, in total, reduce formal licensing fees to a small part of this unmeasured capital.

Rows 5–7 of table 2-5 report figures from BEA data. Royalties received and paid by affiliates and R&D performed by them are quite small, though not trivial, shares of value added. A second concern about using reported fees and royalties (and, for that matter, profits on an individual country basis) is that they can be affected by income shifting and double counting. This chapter concentrates on real production and supply decisions, and it is beyond its scope to discuss financial and accounting questions.

That said, the lower panel of table 2-5, which gives statistics for Irish affiliates of U.S. multinationals, illustrates the issue. As is widely known, U.S. multinationals establish subsidiaries in Ireland to serve the whole EU (recall its earlier noted high levels of third-country sales). While Ireland has many advantages for U.S. firms, including an English-speaking and skilled labor force, favorable land prices, and modest regulation, it also has highly advantageous tax policies for U.S. firms. For perspective, Ireland's population is about 0.06 percent of the world's population, yet Irish affiliates of U.S. firms account for about 6 percent of all U.S. foreign affiliate sales, 5 percent of affiliates' value added and R&D, though a modest 1 percent of affiliates' employment worldwide.

These numbers are not surprising, given Ireland's status as an export platform. But table 2-5 shows that Irish affiliates' share of all U.S. affiliates' profits worldwide is 11 percent, double Ireland's share of sales and value added, suggesting profit shifting to this low-tax jurisdiction. However, the truly impressive numbers in table 2-5 are that Irish affiliates receive a full 50 percent of all fees and royalties received by U.S. foreign affiliates and pay 42 percent of all fees and royalties paid by U.S. affiliates. This is partly because of Irish affiliates' industry composition, which is heavily weighted toward computer hardware and software and pharmaceuticals. Still, it likely also suggests financial and accounting maneuvers. Although these issues are beyond the scope of this chapter, the data on profits and income are im-

TABLE 2-5. Foreign Affiliates of U.S. MNEs: Sales, Value Added, Profits, and Net Income

(2014 BEA benchmark survey, Table II. D, F, I abridged)

	Total million US$	As a share of total sales	As a share of value added
Sales (1)	6,504,909		
Value added (2)	1,490,153	0.229	
Profit (3)	554,226	0.085	0.372
Net income (4)	1,166,223	0.179	0.783
Royalties and fees received (5)	67,786	0.010	0.045
Royalties and fees paid (6)	107,096	0.016	0.072
R&D performed by affiliates (7)	55,278	0.008	0.037
Ireland (affiliate activity as a proportion of U.S. affiliates worldwide)			
Royalties and fees received (5)	0.507		
Royalties and fees paid (6)	0.415		
Affiliate sales (1)	0.057		
Value added (2)	0.053		
R&D performed by affiliates (7)	0.051		
Employment (8)	0.009		
Profit (3)	0.110		

(1) Sales from Table II.D.1

(2) Value added from Table II.F.1

(3) Profit from Table II.F.7

Profit-type return is an economic accounting measure of profits from current production. Unlike net income, it is gross of foreign income taxes; excludes capital gains and losses and income from equity investments; and reflects certain other adjustments needed to convert profits from a financial accounting basis to an economic accounting basis.

(4) Net income from Table II.D.1

Net income receipts include not just sales from production, but also (unlike profits) income from equity investments in affiliates; from other equity investments; capital gains and losses and other income; and (unlike profits) subtracts foreign taxes paid.

(5) Royalties and fees received from Table II.I.8

(6) Royalties and fees paid from Table II.I.8

(7) R&D performed by affiliates from Table II.I.1

(8) Employment from Table II.G.1

portant insofar as they lead into the next issue, which is the overestimation of affiliate profits due to the omission of intangibles.

A promising new approach is to measure intangibles in GVCs as a residual difference between values of final goods and payments for all tangibles. This is found in a recent analysis by Chen, Los, and Timmer (2019). As they discuss, the World Input-Output Database (WIOD), as is typical of all input-output tables, lumps many things into one item simply called payments to "capital."[29] This is, in part, a residual balancing item that includes actual payments to capital but also pure profits, possible types of Ricardian rents, and so forth. The authors, independently of the input-output capital number, construct a traditional measure of physical and tangible capital such as property, plant, and equipment. They then calculate the difference between their measure of tangible capital and the WIOD number to determine a residual value that they label intangible capital. They are careful to emphasize that this is a residual measure, and thus can, of course, include some income that is not a return to intangibles. One advantage of their methodology is that all returns from all countries are included, and thus their measure is immune to profit shifting and other accounting maneuvers by multinationals.

Table 2-6 shows results from their working paper. They divide world factor income into payments to labor, tangible capital, and intangible capital. The share they attribute to intangible capital is very large at 30.7 percent of total factor payments, which is 1.7 times the share of payments to tangible capital. The second row of the upper panel shows the changes in the three shares from 2000 to 2014. As the authors state, the fall in labor share has been well documented and is widely known. What has not been identified, however, is that much of the share growth in capital has been in the share of intangible capital.

The lower panel of table 2-6 divides the share of intangible capital into stages of production. The biggest share is found in upstream production stages, which is assumed to include many headquarter services, as well as parts and components often more skill-intensive than final assembly and distribution. Not only do these upstream stages account for the largest share of intangible capital income, but that share has grown significantly between 2000 and 2014, while the shares to both labor and tangible capital have shrunk. While the data in table 2-6 are for all industries in all countries aggregated and by no means specific to multinational firms, they suggest a high level and growing importance of intangible capital in the world economy.

TABLE 2-6. The Role of Intangibles in Global Value Chains
(Chen, Los, and Timmer, NBER WP 25242)

Shares of factor income in global value chains of manufactured goods (2014)	Labor share	Tangible capital share	Intangible capital share	Ratio of intangible to tangible
Factor shares	51.2	18.1	30.7	1.7
Percentage point change (2000–2014)	–5.2	2.3	2.9	

Shares of stages of production in intangible capital income (2014)	Distribution stage	Final production stage	Upstream production stages
Share of intangible capital	27.0	26.6	46.4
Percentage point change (2000–2014)	–1.3	–4.2	5.5

Attempts to document and measure intangible service flows within multinational firms are scarce, and the Chen, Los, and Timmer study estimates the contribution of intangible capital as a residual value for the world economy as a whole. Nevertheless, their numbers are large enough that they surely motivate more research specifically on MNEs. Several attempts make some progress at a restrictive level, either looking at a particular intangible or at a single firm. Tables 2-7 and 2-8 provide results in this vein.

Table 2-7, with information from the website of a consulting firm, shows brand value for large firms.[30] While the data are for 2009, making some rankings out of date, they nevertheless provide a feel for the size of the asset values involved. The elements that go into brand value are listed on the right side of table 2-7. Although the firm's precise methodology is somewhat obscure, these numbers are impressive. Coca-Cola tops the list at US$69 billion followed by IBM at US$60 billion. While some of these totals surely just reflect the accumulated effects of many years of advertising, the list also suggests large amounts of reputation capital for product quality, reliability, and

TABLE 2-7. Brand Value as an Example of Intangible Assets

Name	Brand value (US$ billion) 2009 survey	Name	Brand value (US$ billion) 2009 survey
Coca-Cola	69	Hewlett-Packard	24
IBM	60	Mercedes-Benz	24
Microsoft	57	Gillette	23
GE	48	Cisco	22
Nokia	45	BMW	22
McDonald's	32	Louis Vuitton	21
Google	32	Marlboro	19
Toyota	31	Honda	18
Intel	31	Samsung	18
Disney	28	Apple	15

Source: Paul Hague, "Measuring Brand Value: How Much Are Brands Worth?" B2B International, www.b2binternational.com/publications/value-of-brands/. This B2B International study assesses brand value on a variety of issues, such as strategic brand management, marketing budget allocation, marketing ROI, portfolio management, brand extensions, M&A, balance sheet recognition, licensing, transfer pricing, and investor relations.

sophistication. These intangible brand values have almost assuredly grown considerably since their publication.

Table 2-8 gives data for a specific product, an Apple iPhone 4, taken from Brennan and Rakhmatullin (2015).[31] Some critics love to hate these numbers, either because they believe they show excess profits or because they believe U.S. content is too low. We disagree with both of these views. The first numbers in table 2-8 are a cost breakdown of the physical components in the phone plus assembly costs, which total US$194. Then distribution and miscellaneous is added, to arrive at a total cost of US$324. The U.S. content

TABLE 2-8. Apple iPhone Breakdown

Unmeasured services and intangibles, mislabeled as simply "profit"

Physical components and assembly	
Korea	80.05
Germany	16.08
France	3.25
Japan	0.70
Other	62.79
U.S.A.	24.63
China VA	6.54
Factory gate price	194.04
Distribution	90.00
Misc.	45.95
Total "cost"	**329.99**
Retail price	**600.00**
Apple "profit" (45% of retail price)	**270.01**

Services and intangibles (Apple "profit"):

- software
- management
- marketing
- finance
- R&D and intellectual property
- brand value and goodwill
- contracts and customer lists
- trained and assembled workforces

Source: Louis Brennan and Rakhmatullin Ruslan, "Global Value Chains and Smart Specialisation Strategy. Thematic Work on the Understanding of Global Value Chains and Their Analysis within the Context of Smart Specialisation," European Commission, December 2015, www.researchgate.net/publication/303523378.

measured in this way is rather small, even if most of the distribution and miscellaneous costs are U.S. content. The iPhone sells for US$600, leaving a residual "profit" of US$270 per phone.

However, many items are missing from this breakdown. For example, it does not include the software in the phone—a significant omission, as Apple is as much a software company as a hardware firm. Further, the iOS ecosystem (including iTunes) is one of the major attractions of Apple products. On the right-hand side of table 2-8, we have provided a list of just some of the long-term firm investments that are contributing to this "profit." This is our list, not Brennan's and Rakhmatullin's. Their decomposition makes no attempt to value any of the items on the list. Assuming that Apple makes just a "normal" return on investment, it could be argued that the contribution of intangible assets is as much as 45 percent of the retail price. Further, it seems likely that most of this value is American content, since the parent firm produces intangible services while foreigners make parts and assemble them.

While there is a need for more work in this area, a recent working paper from the World Bank Group by Ayyagari, Demirguc-Kunt, and Maksimovic (2019) makes substantial progress in estimating the value of intangible capital more directly. It does not focus on multinational firms specifically, but instead uses a sample of large U.S. firms. This working paper, in turn, builds on the methodology and empirical results of Peters and Taylor (2017). At issue is the oft-documented high returns on invested capital (ROIC) for the most successful firms, with a particular run-up starting around 1990.

The authors show that these high measured profits are largely caused by the mismeasurement—or, rather, non-measurement—of intangible capital in the denominator of standard ROIC calculations. To correct this, they calculate intangible capital as the sum of two measures: knowledge capital and organizational capital. The methodology they use to calculate both knowledge capital and organizational capital is similar to the perpetual inventory method used to calculate physical capital stocks. Past investments in R&D and other measures for knowledge capital are summed and depreciated to measure knowledge capital, and a portion of selling, general, and administrative expenses are summed and depreciated to measure organizational capital.

Table 2-9 shows some of their results. The top two rows show the conventional measure of ROIC and the corrected measure, which accounts for intangible capital in the denominator of the measure (it also affects the numerator but that effect is small). The right-hand column gives the percentage point difference between the conventional measure and the corrected measure for firms in the ninetieth percentile and up. Accounting for intangible capital lowers the ROIC by 29 percentage points for the top firms.

They then divide the industries into those with high and low levels of routine manual labor in their workforces (RMAN) and industries with high and low levels of intangible capital (ICAP). Industries with low labor-force shares of routine labor (and therefore more cognitive skill requirements) have higher ROIC returns with and without the correction (table 2-9, rows 3–6). Within each group, the correction lowers the measured ROIC much more in the low-RMAN industries: 49 percentage points for the low-RMAN industries, 22 percentage points for the high-RMAN industries.

Rows 7–10 of table 2-9 show similar figures for high- and low-ICAP industries. The high-ICAP industries (which may overlap a lot with low-RMAN industries) have substantially higher returns than the low-ICAP industries. The correction for intangible capital lowers the ROIC considerably—by 41 percentage points—for the ninetieth percentile of firms.

Table 2-9 illustrates two main points that underscore the sizable role of intangibles. First, the more successful firms have high returns on invested capital, and the correction for intangible capital lowers those returns much more than for less successful firms. Second, among the most successful firms, the intangible correction lowers returns much more for those with a low share of routine manual labor and those with a high share of intangible capital.

The work of Chen and others (2019) and Ayyagari and others (2019) does not distinguish between multinational and non-multinational firms. But a lot of work, summarized and extended most recently in Bernard, Jensen, Redding, and Schott (2018), consistently and convincingly shows that the most internationally engaged firms are the highest productivity firms, and the most profitable. The top decile of firms account for a very large share of international trade and production. While the current state of knowledge does not allow for a definitive statement, there likely is a substantial overlap between the top decile of firms in Bernard and others and the top decile of firms in Ayyagari and others. Thus, the low-RMAN and high-ICAP firms in the Ayyagari and others' paper likely are dominated by multinationals. This, in turn, suggests that the high returns to multinational affiliates discussed in connection with tables 2-5, 2-8, and 2-9 may be due to mismeasurement, with some of the value of U.S.-generated intangibles misallocated to affiliate profits.

Assuming a high correlation between multinationality and intangible

TABLE 2-9. Return on Invested Capital (ROIC), Conventional and Corrected for Intangible Capital *(RMAN—routine manual labor, ICAP—intangible capital) from Ayyagari, Demirguc-Kunt, and Maksimovic (2019).*

Return on invested capital, 1990–2015	25th percentile	median	75th percentile	90th percentile	90th percentile: percentage point difference: conventional minus corrected
ROIC as conventionally measured	9.3	19.9	36.9	69.1	
ROIC corrected for intangible capital	1.6	11.9	23.3	40.3	–28.8
ROIC conventional low RMAN industries	9.0	21.8	45.1	98.1	
ROIC corrected low RMAN industries	1.9	13.2	27.6	48.9	–49.2
ROIC conventional high RMAN industries	9.5	19.1	33.1	55.7	
ROIC corrected high RMAN industries	1.5	11.2	20.8	33.9	–21.8
ROIC conventional low ICAP industries	7.0	14.8	25.6	41.9	
ROIC corrected low ICAP industries	2.1	11.1	20.6	34.5	–7.4
ROIC conventional high ICAP industries	11.4	23.8	44.1	85.7	
ROIC corrected high ICAP industries	0.9	12.4	25.0	45.3	–40.5

capital, several important policy conclusions follow. First, overseas affiliates are probably less profitable than they currently appear. Second, the U.S. content of foreign affiliate production likely is much higher than has been asserted by some politicians and business journalists, and claimed in case studies such as the iPhone example. Accounting for intangible capital and its supply from parents to affiliates potentially shifts the location of measured activity and profits from the affiliates and host country to the parents and parent country. That said, this is about re-judging the importance of joint inputs. Even reallocating the value of production toward the parent firm is unlikely to overturn the understanding that FDI is a developed-country phenomenon and therefore has a strong replicative, horizontal nature.

CONCLUSIONS

When discussing foreign direct investment, several hot button issues arise, including its effect on labor markets, technology spillovers, and its implications for competition with domestic firms. Addressing these issues, however, requires an understanding of the structure of multinational activity. This chapter has provided a framework based on theory that divides investment structures into those that replicate activity across borders (the octopus-like horizontal MNE) and those that fragment the production process into different stages in different countries (the snake-like vertical MNE). These two structures and their more recent expansions all suggest patterns in the data that can help differentiate between the two. As shown in table 2-10, the different structures generate very different predictions on where MNEs operate, sell their output, and how they connect to their supply chains. The first two columns show the predictions of the horizontal model and the vertical model, while the third column reflects the data.

The data point toward a dominant role for horizontal investment. This conclusion arises from both the identities of major parent and host countries (and the comparison across the two), the location of affiliate sales, and the interaction of affiliates with parent firms and other affiliates. In addition to these techniques, which academic literature has explored, this chapter introduces a new methodology based on positioning within global value chains. In each case, although evidence of vertical-style investment can be found, the bulk of the data suggests the horizontal motive. This indi-

TABLE 2-10

	Horizontal (replication)	Vertical (different)	Data
Country pairs	Developed-developed	Developed-developing	Developed-developed
Sales	Regional	Global	Regional
GVC	Self-contained	Long	Self-contained
Parent intangibles	Joint input	First link in GVC	Important but need more data

cates that a significant share of MNE activity is replicative, occurs between wealthy countries, and is in no small part geared toward servicing local consumers and nearby countries, both final customers and customers who use intermediates purchased to produce for other customers. Many of these findings differ from the common public perception of FDI.

Recognizing that MNEs have both internal and external GVCs means that policies aimed at FDI can affect both the local and overseas firms connected in GVCs. These effects are far from hypothetical. Starting in 2017, the Committee on Foreign Investment in the United States (an interagency body of the U.S. government with the power to halt investment) significantly increased its examination of inbound investment. In 2018, the number of investments scrutinized was 40 percent higher than in 2016.[32] Among the investments it blocked was Singaporean Broadcom's acquisition of Qualcomm, a U.S. manufacturer of computer chips. This acquisition would have been horizontal (as Broadcom affiliates produce chips globally—that is, replication) and would have involved the sale of intermediates to local purchasers. In 2018, Qualcomm sold US$603 million of its output in the United States (Wagner (2019)). Thus, if this acquisition would have increased efficiency and lowered chip costs, blocking the investment may well have negatively affected other U.S. firms.

These effects extend to other countries as well. When Qualcomm chips sold in the United States contribute to the assembly of smartphones in China, blocking Broadcom's investment and halting the cost reductions that may have resulted can negatively affect Chinese production. This effect can occur even when the assembly plants in China are unrelated to either Broadcom or Qualcomm. Thus, it is possible for FDI policy in a host country to spill over to third nations with consequent political effects. Indeed, since Qualcomm had sales of more than US$15 billion in China in 2018, the U.S. decision to block the investment from Singapore might have had more to do with China than Singapore itself.

The value of understanding the structure of MNE activity extends beyond just understanding individual firms. For example, the fact that a significant share of FDI is replicating skill-intensive activities across skill-abundant countries suggests that offshoring via FDI may be less about eliminating the low-skill domestic workforce and more about gaining access to new markets. Thus, the notion that outbound FDI ships production jobs overseas may not be as well-founded as the typical political rhetoric would suggest. In addition, just as an octopus can survive after losing an arm, a horizontal MNE may be fairly resilient to local events that negatively affect one of its subsidiaries.

Vertical MNEs are less likely to be resilient to local events since, just as the whole snake will die if you cut out a short middle part of its length, losing a key affiliate can have significant implications across the entire vertical MNE. Indeed, Davies and Studnicka (2018) link changes in the stock market valuations of British firms following the Brexit referendum to their vertical GVCs. An additional example from early 2020 was the effect of the novel coronavirus. When Apple's iPhone suppliers were shuttered for health concerns, it sent ripple effects across Apple's whole GVC (Feiner, 2020). Thus, understanding an MNE's risks may require understanding its overall structure.

However, it is important to acknowledge that limitations on the data can affect our ability to draw conclusions. In particular, challenges in measuring intra-firm intangible assets affect the data on FDI since these assets are hard to quantify and quite mobile for tax and other purposes. New papers by Chen, Los, and Timmer (2019) and Ayyagari, Demirguc-Kunt, and Maksimovic (2019), while not about multinational firms per se, make a very strong case that unmeasured intangible capital is of major importance, particularly for large and successful companies. Reporting unmeasured intangible services as "profits" skews the measured and reported U.S. content of foreign production downward. That potentially throws off the understanding of multinationals and the resulting public policy debates. More work on intangibles is therefore most welcome.

NOTES

1. When we say "production," we mean the production of goods and/or services, unless otherwise noted.

2. The seminal horizontal model was laid out in Markusen (1984), while the vertical model was formalized in Helpman (1984). Since then, numerous extensions and variants have been developed, too many to adequately cover here, except the main updates to the models discussed below.

3. For many cases of both horizontal and vertical international production, firms do not actually own the foreign production partner. Some fast-food restaurants and hotels are franchises. Many firms outsource relatively simple and low-skilled production and final assembly to independent contractors or licensees. This includes manufacturers of clothing and footwear as well as the assembly of sophisticated electronic goods such as smartphones. When the multinational does not have an equity interest in the foreign producer, that activity is not in the foreign affiliate data we exploit in this paper, and there is no obvious way to measure it.

4. See the work of Bergstrand and Egger (2007) for a complete treatment of complex vertical FDI.

5. For a full discussion, see the work of Ekholm, Forslid, and Markusen (2007).

6. He notes a similar strategy for pharmaceutical companies, including Pfizer and Merck.

7. Indeed, since affiliates generally operate with a fair degree of autonomy, the giant Pacific octopus is especially relevant, since it has nine brains: one central and one for each of the somewhat autonomous arms.

8. This flow refers to where the intangible is generated, not where it is "located" for tax purposes, an issue at the heart of the taxation of FDI taken up elsewhere in this volume.

9. These data come from https://unctad.org. Stocks measure the value of foreign-owned equity, retained earnings, and net loans, at their historical cost value. While this can roughly be considered the "capital" of the MNE, it should be taken as an approximation, because of depreciation. In addition, it is only a rough approximation of the value of investment, since the productivity and intensity of capital can vary across countries and industries. These issues do not arise for affiliate sales, however, which are potentially more prone to year-on-year fluctuations relative to more stable FDI stocks. The two give fairly similar pictures of FDI, although as discussed by Davies (2008), the stocks may give more prominence to investment in developing countries.

10. These can be found at www.bea.gov/data/intl-trade-investment.

11. In French data, Davies and others (2018) find that, even when there is an affiliate in a destination country, one-third of MNEs engage in no intra-firm trade to those countries and export only at arm's length.

12. It should be noted that the Asia-Pacific data do not have information for most of the poorer countries of Southeast, South, and Central Asia, with Indonesia being the lowest-income country in the data.

13. Just in case you were interested, the first octopuses appeared on Earth roughly 500 million years ago; snakes arrived on the scene only 100 million years ago.

14. This is because the input-output data that are available combines all firms within an industry.

15. This is particularly impressive, since they only account for 23 percent of global employment (OECD, 2018).

16. For U.S. firms, Ramando, Rappaport, and Ruhl (2016) find that intra-firm trade may be the exception rather than the rule.

17. In the World Input-Output Database (WIOD) data used by Antràs and Chor (2018), sales are precisely that, and as such combine the contributions of labor, capital, intellectual property, and intermediates (which are at the heart of the GVC measures). The WIOD data also break down the sales into the contributions of labor, capital, and intermediates. Recent work by Chen, Los, and Timmer (2019) suggests that this may misallocate the importance of intellectual property to capital. This is further discussed in the section "Evaluating Intangible Asset and Other Service Flows" in this chapter.

18. These steps include reaching consumers themselves—that is, the distribution network. The WIOD database builds from supply-use tables based on national accounts data. Using wholesale and retail trade data, margins for these activities are constructed and gathered into two industries: wholesale services and retail services. These are then treated as an industry in and of themselves, with the share of purchases/sales linked to another industry based on relative purchase/sale levels. In the iPhone example of table 2-8, this stage in the GVC is worth US$90, which, when combined with the physical components and miscellaneous costs, amounts to a total "cost" of US$329.99.

19. It is not necessary that the output be sold to another country-industry for further processing. Instead, it is certainly possible that the output is sold to another firm (including a related affiliate) in the same industry in the same country. Thus, this is specifically not a measure of internal/external transactions, but rather a measure of how the output is used.

20. As such, their value added would equal their sales.

21. Since a country-industry can sell intermediates to itself, so, too, can it purchase inputs from itself, something relevant in this specific example, since electronics and electronic components are combined into a single industry.

22. In addition to this three-stage production process, as with the horizontal model, adding more intermediate inputs to parent or affiliate production can increase the Input Index.

23. For details on iPhone production, see www.lifewire.com/where-is-the-iphone-made-1999503.

24. Indeed, this would be true for any affiliate selling intermediates, including the final one in the MNE's production chain.

25. These are all foreign affiliates (some U.S.-owned and some not), not the parent part of the MNE.

26. Since the coordinates for both inbound and outbound FDI are those for the U.S. industry, the circles by definition have the same location in the GVC box.

27. These can be found at https://data.oecd.org/fdi/fdi-flows.htm. Due to data availability, here we use stocks, not sales, and information for 2011 rather than 2014. One issue with using stocks of FDI is that it increases the relative importance of capital-intensive industries. Further, when comparing across countries, Davies (2008) finds that vertical hosts of FDI seem to be more capital-intensive than horizontal hosts. Finally, the industry breakdown is less fine in these data, and therefore fewer data points per country are shown.

28. Although they do not control for the size of investment, Davies, Desbordes, and Ray (2018) analyze the number of affiliates established from 2003 to 2010. Using this, the Big Five countries account for 38.3 percent of outbound cross-border mergers and acquisitions and 32.6 percent of inbound M&A. In terms of greenfield investment, which is more often found hosted by developing countries, the Big Five are the home for 50.2 percent of new affiliates and host to 21.1 percent of them. Thus, both as home and hosts, these five nations make up a substantial portion of FDI activity.

29. These can be downloaded from www.wiod.org/home. The WIOD data also form the basis for the data used for this chapter's Input and Output Indices.

30. These come from www.b2binternational.com/publications/value-of-brands/.

31. Several analogous case studies seem to come up with roughly similar stories, both for Apple and other products.

32. See Sherman (2018) for discussion.

REFERENCES

Antràs, Pol and Davin Chor (2018). On the Measurement of Upstreamness and Downstreamness in Global Value Chains. NBER Working Paper No. 24185.

Ariu, Andrea (2016). "Crisis-Proof Services: Why Trade in Services Did Not Suffer during the 2008–09 Collapse," *Journal of International Economics*, 98 (1), 138–49.

Ayyagari, Meghana, Asli Demirguc-Kunt, and Vojislav Maksimovic (2019). "The Rise of Star Firms: Intangible Capital and Competition," World Bank Group working paper.

Baltagi, Badi H., Peter Egger, and Michael Pfaffermayr (2007). "Estimating Models of Complex FDI: Are There Third-Country Effects?" *Journal of Econometrics*, 140 (1), 260–81.

Barry, Frank (2004). "Export-Platform Foreign Direct Investment: The Irish Experience," EIB Papers 6/2004, European Investment Bank, Economics Department.

Bems, Rudolfs, Robert C. Johnson, and Kei-Mu Yi (2011). "Vertical Linkages and the Collapse of Global Trade," *American Economic Review*, 101 (3), 308–12.

Bergstrand, Jeffrey H. and Peter Egger (2007). "A Knowledge-and-Physical-Capital Model of International Trade Flows, Foreign Direct Investment, and Multinational Enterprises," *Journal of International Economics*, 73 (2), 278–308.

Bernard, Andrew B., J. Bradford Jensen, Stephen J. Redding, and Peter K. Schott (2018). "Global Firms," *Journal of Economic Literature*, 56 (2), 565–619.

Blonigen, Bruce A., Ronald B. Davies, and Keith Head (2003). "Estimating the Knowledge-Capital Model of the Multinational Enterprise: Comment," *American Economic Review* 93 (3), 980–94.

Blonigen, Bruce A., Ronald B. Davies, Glen R. Waddell, and Helen Naughton (2007). "FDI in Space: Spatial Autoregressive Relationships in Foreign Direct Investment," *European Economic Review*, 51 (5), 1303–25.

Brennan, Louis and Ruslan Rakhmatullin (2015). Global Value Chains and Smart Specialization Strategy, JRC technical paper JCR 98014.

Bureau of Economic Analysis (2014), www.bea.gov/international/usdia2014r.

Carr, David, James R. Markusen, and Keith E. Maskus (2001). "Estimating the Knowledge-Capital Model of the Multinational Enterprise," *American Economic Review*, 91, 693–708.

Chen, Wen, Bart Los, and Marcel P. Timmer (2018). "Factor Incomes in the Global Value Chains: The Role of Intangibles," NBER Working Paper No. 25242.

Davies, Ronald B., Julien Martin, Mathieu Parenti, and Farid Toubal (2018). "Knocking on Tax Haven's Door: Multinational Firms and Transfer Pricing," *Review of Economics and Statistics*, 100 (1), 120–34.

Davies, Ronald B. (2008). "Hunting High and Low for Vertical FDI," *Review of International Economics*, 16 (2), 250–67.

Davies, Ronald B., Rodolphe Desbordes, and Anna Ray (2018). "Greenfield vs. Merger and Acquisition FDI: Same Wine, Different Bottles?" *Canadian Journal of Economics*, 51 (4), 1151–90.

Davies, Ronald B. and Zuzanna Studnicka (2018). "The Heterogeneous Impact of Brexit: Early Indications from the FTSE," *European Economic Review*, 110, 1–17.

Ekholm, Karolina, Rikard Forslid, and James R. Markusen (2007). "Export-Platform Foreign Direct Investment," *Journal of the European Economic Association*, 5 (4), 776–95.

Federal Reserve Bank of Saint Louis (2020). "Profit per Unit of Real Gross Value Added of Non-financial Corporate Business," https://fred.stlouisfed.org/series/A466RD3Q052SBEA.

Feiner, Lauren (2020). "iPhone Manufacturing in China Is in Limbo amid Coronavirus Outbreak," CNBC online, February 10, 2020. Garretsen, H. and J. Peeters (2009). "FDI and the Relevance of Spatial Linkages: Do Third-Country Effects Matter for Dutch FDI?" *Review of World Economics*, 145 (2), 319–38.

Helpman, Elhanan (1984). "A Simple Theory of International Trade with Multinational Corporations," *Journal of Political Economy*, 94 (3), 451–71.

Markusen, James R. (1984). "Multinationals, Multi-Plant Economies, and the Gains from Trade," *Journal of International Economics*, 16 (3/4), 205–26.

Markusen, James R. and Keith E. Maskus (2001). "Multinational Firms: Reconciling Theory and Evidence," in *Topics in Empirical International Economics: A Festschrift in Honor of Robert E. Lipsey*, edited by Magnus Blomstrom and Linda Goldberg (University of Chicago Press, 2001), 71–98.

Markusen, James R. and Maskus, Keith E (2002). "Discriminating among Alternative Theories of the Multinational Enterprise," *Review of International Economics*, 10, 694–707.

Markusen, James R. (2002). *Multinational Firms and the Theory of International Trade* (MIT Press, 2002).

OECD (2018). *Multinationals in the Global Economy*, policy note.

Peters, Ryan H. and Lucian A. Taylor (2017). "Intangible Capital and the Investment-q Relation," *Journal of Financial Economics*, 123 (2), 251–72.

Ramondo, Natalia, Veronica Rappoport, and Kim J. Ruhl (2016). "Intrafirm Trade and Vertical Fragmentation in U.S. Multinational Corporations," *Journal of International Economics*, 98, 51–59.

Ross, Sean (2020). "Ten Countries with the Most McDonald's Locations," Investopedia.com, March 2, 2020.

Sherman, Natalie (2018). "U.S. Weighs Plans to Curb Chinese Investment," BBC News Online, May 21, 2018. Thomas R. Tørsløv, Ludvig S. Wier, Gabriel Zucman (2018). "The Missing Profits of Nations," NBER Working Paper No. 24701.

Xinhua News Agency (2019). "Chinese Market Drives Sales Growth of U.S. Fast Food Company in 2018," ChinaDaily.com.cn, September 2, 2019.

Wagner, I. (2018). "Qualcomm's Revenue in FY 2018," Statistica, November 8, 2018, www.statista.com/statistics/737844/revenue-of-qualcomm-by-region/.

3

Multinational Firms' Market Entry and Expansion, with Evidence from Eastern Europe

CATHERINE THOMAS
ANDREW B. BERNARD

Multinational corporations (MNCs) are organizations that have in common only that they operate in at least two countries (Caves, 2007). They differ from each other in many more dimensions, such as in the activities undertaken by each production and non-production establishment within the organization, and in the relationships between establishments. The determinants of any one MNC's global reach are similarly varied, and are reflected in the cumulative market entry and expansion decisions made by the firm. This chapter focuses on how firms make these decisions.

An MNC chooses to establish or expand operations in a country when the new affiliate is expected to contribute to the value of the overall organization and the chosen destination is preferred to available alternatives. Second, the MNC must have a good reason to prefer to own a foreign affiliate in the chosen location rather than interact with a separate entity there via arm's-length contracts. Related to the first two aspects of the decision, the MNC chooses how to enter, either by acquiring part or complete ownership of existing operations in the country or by building operations from scratch—greenfield investment. These three features of the entry or expansion decision are often interdependent because of value-creating complementarities between host country characteristics, ownership, and the assets available for acquisition. To add further complexity, the expected contribution of any new affiliate will also depend on attributes of the parent firm, including their current activities and existing global footprint.

Prevailing theories of MNC entry and expansion are, collectively, broad enough to offer predictions related to all these margins of variation. However, it is rare to find theories that tackle them all at the same time. A useful starting point is to pin down the reason for operating in a given host country in the first place. As reviewed in chapter 2, by Davies and Markusen, in this volume, the research literature has developed two main motives. One rationale is that producing in a local market allows firms to access the consumers in that market more profitably than by exporting. Customer-seeking affiliates are referred to as "horizontal," and these affiliates may replicate the activities performed elsewhere in the organization. However, replication of the entire production process in a given market is not the only way to access those customers. MNC affiliates may perform only a share of downstream activities in a local market, such as processing imported intermediates, or even just final distribution, while conducting more upstream production activities in other locations.

The second main reason to operate in another country is to access the factor markets in that country. Locally provided factors could serve as inputs at any point in the firm's overall value chain. The new country may offer natural resources, labor, or technologies that can be combined with other factors owned by the firm. Investments in affiliates for the purpose of accessing local factors are referred to as "vertical" investments. The local output can then be exported elsewhere, back to the parent firm's country or to other countries.

Once an MNC has identified a final market or factor market opportunity in a foreign country, and decided that owning local operations rather than trading relationships is the best way to access that opportunity, it decides whether to enter via greenfield or acquisition, and makes the capital investment necessary to establish the affiliate. As long as the parent firm owns at least 10 percent of the foreign entity, it will be recorded in national statistics as a foreign direct investment (FDI). Data about such FDI flows, aggregated to the year-industry level, are readily available from sources such as CEPII (Centre d'Etudes Prospectives et d'Informations Internationales).

The information that becomes available about affiliate activities often depends on the reporting requirements in the affiliate's host country and in the parent firm's country. In many cases, data from financial statements reveal revenues, employee numbers, and some balance sheet information. The main activity of the affiliate, in terms of industry classification, may also be available. Less frequently, researchers outside the firm may be able to access data on the relationships among the various affiliates of a given MNC, or can infer the relationships by careful combination of several datasets.

The data on FDI flows and on affiliate activities provide clues about MNC entry motives. This chapter begins, as does much of the literature, by considering the role of variation in location attributes. Hanson and others (2001) review this literature and examine the relative volume of U.S. MNC affiliate activity across different host markets. They comment that early work observed U.S. affiliates had greater sales in large and developed economies. This implied that, on average, U.S. MNC affiliates were horizontal, existing to access relatively high-income foreign consumers. Hanson and others (2001) go on to show that other data on affiliate activity suggest U.S. affiliates often serve as platforms for exports to nearby markets, or are engaged only in local distribution activities rather than in local manufacturing for local consumers.

Other cuts of the data point toward vertical motives. Bernard and others (2005) observe that imports from overseas affiliates make up nearly one half of U.S. imports by value, which strongly suggests U.S. parent firms are sourcing intermediate inputs abroad from within firm boundaries. Some work finds evidence that supports vertical motivations for FDI activity in host country–industry variation. Entry for the purpose of accessing local factor markets is more appealing when local factor costs are relatively low and in activities where production can be fragmented across locations in a global value chain. Alfaro and Charlton (2009) show that defining an affiliate as horizontal or vertical depends on the level of available detail about its activities, since much affiliate activity takes place within the closely related industries that provide inputs to the production activities of other parts of the firm.

Considering data about the home country of the parent firm also helps distinguish between entry motives. Bilateral trade costs and distance are positively associated with horizontal affiliate activity because, at higher levels of both, local investment becomes an attractive substitute for accessing consumers via exports. The same features are negatively associated with vertical affiliate activity, because importing and exporting intermediate products across country borders complements local investment in this case. Yeaple (2003) points out that the same MNC may have horizontal affiliates in some host countries and vertical affiliates in others.

The second aspect of the entry decision—namely, why MNCs decide to access customers or factors via investment rather than via arm's-length contracts, has become better understood in recent decades. Antràs and Yeaple (2014) provide an overview of these theories, which hold that MNCs exist because some aspect of the environment makes contracting incomplete. Transaction costs could be significant, or relationship-specific investments could be required when contracts cannot guarantee that the investing parties will enjoy the full marginal return on their investments. Firm boundaries are hence drawn to mitigate inefficiencies in joint production. Since ownership creates investment incentives, the relative value of each party's investment in the production process is an important consideration. The parent firm typically provides capital or knowledge inputs, and vertical integration is therefore expected in stages of production that are capital- or R&D-intensive. In these cases, ownership of the affiliate helps mitigate the parent's under-provision of capital or R&D to production activities in the host country.

The relative appeal of integration versus arm's-length transactions has also been shown to be related to information flows. When setting up a foreign affiliate, MNCs take on the challenge of coordinating and managing activities across country borders. Head and Ries (2008) argue that monitoring costs within firm boundaries shape the relative appeal of operating affiliates in a given country, depending on the location of the parent firm. They explain variation in bilateral FDI flows as a consequence of a competitive market for corporate control of globally distributed productive assets, where monitoring costs increase with geographic distance. This model provides micro-foundations for the well-known empirical pattern of "gravity" in FDI flows—that is, the volume of FDI flows decreases with distance, controlling for source- and host country–fixed effects.

What can be learned from an MNC's decision to enter via acquisition or greenfield in a given location? Antràs and Yeaple (2014) note that MNC entry via acquisition is far more common, especially for FDI flows between developed economies. Theories of entry mode often assume that this preference is related to the nature of MNC production and it is perhaps likely that the assets available for acquisition in more developed economies have greater productive potential. Nocke and Yeaple (2007) model how the most productive parent firms tend to enter via greenfield because they prefer to employ their own productive assets across country borders at some cost rather than utilize the assets that exist locally in potential acquisition targets. Data on the entry modes chosen by U.S. MNCs support this rationale, but there is little other empirical work studying entry-mode variation.[1]

Researchers have asked what these theories imply for which local firms will be acquired by entering MNCs. One line of reasoning is that if the MNC combines its own productive assets with the assets of a local firm, and productivity is a public good within firm boundaries, the productivity of the local firm is irrelevant to its value as an affiliate. If unproductive local firms can be acquired at a lower cost, the prediction is that MNCs will acquire the least productive local firms. Alternatively, if the MNC production function involves a complementarity between the inputs from both the local affiliate and the parent firm, parents will seek to acquire the most productive local firms. Guadalupe and others (2012) show evidence of this second pattern in MNC acquisitions in Spain after its accession to the European Union (EU), although they do not compare the subsequent productivity of MNC greenfield versus acquired affiliates.

The rest of this chapter is divided into three sections that review the different ways in which various observable factors shape MNCs' entry and expansion motives. The factors are: host country characteristics, bilateral host-source country characteristics, and then the less well-studied idea that there are information frictions in the market for corporate control. Each section comments on the main theoretical predictions, documents some key empirical findings, and discusses some remaining research challenges.

To illustrate how the data are often used, the chapter asks how the factors discussed in each section explain MNCs' entry and expansion in a newly collected dataset on FDI in ten Eastern European Union countries in the years since their EU accession.[2] The data include entries via acquisition and greenfield from 116 source countries, and the ten host countries vary in size and income levels. Since all ten are in the single EU market, and have low wage levels relative to other EU countries located nearby, the theory predicts that they are attractive locations for vertical FDI from Western Europe. At the same time, the theory predicts they are attractive locations for horizontal FDI from MNCs in the rest of the world to access consumers with growing incomes. MNCs from Germany and other Western European countries make up the lion's share of Eastern European affiliate owners, but there are interesting exceptions. For example, Asian manufacturing firms have invested significantly in the region, particularly in the automotive sector. This appears to be vertical FDI from outside the EU single-tariff area, and reflects the high degree of production fragmentation typical in this industry (Head and Mayer (2019)).

The data from Eastern Europe permit an investigation of how one aspect of across-parent-firm variation relates to entry decisions. When MNCs are new to this region, they are more likely to invest in countries that already host more investment from the same parent country. This fact has been documented in other settings and described as herding or agglomeration in MNC entry decisions, as discussed in Navaretti and others (2006). In Eastern Europe, however, this relationship is limited to MNCs making their first entry to the region. It is therefore unlikely to be related to the challenges parent firms from the same location face in operating affiliates in a given host country. The relationship is also unlikely to be related to costs or benefits arising from any unobserved factor, such as agglomeration externalities, that makes affiliate activities more valuable for MNCs from a given country. It is more likely related to frictions that hamper entry itself. One possibility is that MNCs without a presence in the region nonetheless have access to information about countries in the region from other firms from the same source country that do have investments there. Information from same source–country firms then becomes less important once MNCs have information from their own local presence in the region.

While it is now clear that MNCs choose to enter or expand in a given location for a variety of complex reasons, it is also well known that their presence has a large impact on the host country. Multinational parents tend to be the largest and most productive firms in their home economy (Helpman and others (2004)), and their overseas affiliates are larger and more productive than local firms (Navaretti and others (2006)). This second fact is shown to also hold true in the Eastern European data studied in this chapter. Further, several studies show that when entry occurs via acquisition, acquired affiliates become more productive than they were under domestic ownership (Arnold and Javorcik (2009); Guadalupe and others (2012)).

MNCs' overall local impact depends on the range of activities that they undertake in the local market. The inputs that they employ are likely to see increases in their factor prices, which may affect income distribution in the local economy, while purely horizontal affiliates are less likely to have redistributional effects. These affiliates may well generate consumption gains from variety in local markets. On the production side, affiliates are known to produce knowledge that spills over to local competing firms and affect demand and productivity in local supplier industries (Javorcik and Spatareanu (2008), Alfaro-Urena and others (2019)).

One consequence of the fact that FDI flows follow FDI stocks, as illustrated here for Eastern Europe, is that affiliates from any one source country are increasingly unevenly and differently distributed across host countries in the region. Because whether a host country receives FDI from a high- or low-income country shapes the resulting productivity gains from FDI (see, for example, Bloom and others (2012)), frictions in entry and expansion decisions are likely to have a persistent impact on host economies.

THE ROLE OF HOST COUNTRY CHARACTERISTICS

Early general equilibrium models of multinationals featured two symmetric countries, and showed that multinationals can exist even in contexts where wages are equal across countries and without barriers to trade if firms' average costs are lower when producing across multiple plants.[3] In Markusen (1984), production requires an input that can be used as a public good within firm boundaries across plants. Multinationals can exist as a substitute or as a complement to trade when the firm locates different production activities in each country.

With asymmetric countries, the two main reasons why MNCs enter new markets give contrasting predictions for which attributes of the local workers and consumers have greatest appeal. Researchers have, hence, used variation in the size and incomes of the local population to understand MNCs' decisions. Simply put, does the local market offer an MNC many high-income consumers, favoring horizontal affiliates, or low-cost labor, favoring vertical FDI? Because it is unlikely that a single market offers both, relative variation across potential location choices together with location decisions helps categorize new FDI into being either market- or factor-seeking.

While the base-case model in Markusen (1984) assumes no trade costs, in a model extension, trade costs make multi-plant horizontal MNCs relatively more profitable for the firm. This line of thought raises the idea that country-specific barriers to trade, such as tariffs and other non-tariff obstacles, play a large role in shaping MNC entry motives. A country that offers a large, high-income consumer market yet has high import tariffs is an appealing location for horizontal FDI, especially in industries where transport costs are high. A country with a low-wage workforce and low import tariffs is an attractive destination for vertical FDI, especially in industries where production can be fragmented into stages that differ in labor intensity and where the costs of transporting intermediate goods are low.

Brainard (1997) addresses many of these country-level sources of variation, together with production-function variation across industries, in exploring the "proximity-concentration" hypothesis, which predicts that firms should expand horizontally across borders whenever the advantages of access to the destination market outweigh the advantages from production-scale economies. The results show that firms are more likely to expand production horizontally across borders when transport costs and trade barriers are high. They are also more likely to expand horizontally across borders when investment barriers and scale economies at the plant level relative to the corporate level are low. Because of these relationships, a large part of the variation across countries in U.S. affiliate sales relative to total U.S. sales in a destination can be explained by a combination of host country and industry fixed effects.

Much of the empirical work that uses data to uncover what MNC affiliates are actually doing in foreign markets adopts an approach that is similar to Brainard (1997). The motives for investment are inferred by relating variation in the extent of affiliate activities to variation in the characteristics of host countries, or of affiliate industries, or the interaction of country and industry characteristics. Because early empirical studies on this question found greater affiliate sales in markets with higher GDP, GDP per capita, and high tariffs, they concluded that horizontal customer-seeking FDI was the dominant form of cross-border investment.

Hanson and others (2001) take this approach with their data on the activities of the affiliates of U.S. MNCs available from the U.S. Commerce Department's Bureau of Economic Analysis (BEA). Their findings show the same overall patterns, but they go further by examining the affiliates' ratio of export sales to local sales. Affiliates in larger markets have more local sales, but the share of sales from exports is increasing with GDP per capita, and decreasing with taxes, tariffs, and trade costs, while distance plays no role. They interpret these findings as consistent with an export-platform MNC strategy. Ekholm and others (2007) model this strategy and also find support in the BEA data. Many MNCs have located final assembly in China to serve the local market, export back to the home country, and serve other markets around the world, thus combining horizontal, vertical, and export-platform motives in a single decision. Further, MNCs' expansion strategies may combine vertical and horizontal motives sequentially. For example, Hallward-Driemeier (1997) shows that firms first establish distribution affiliates in a country before starting to produce there.

Hanson and others (2001) also study affiliates' input sourcing. Foreign affiliates import more of their inputs in manufacturing industries where production can be separated into stages. Baldwin and Okubo (2014) examine the importing and exporting behavior of Japanese affiliates and show that many have mixed motives, playing interdependent roles in regional production and sales networks. Alfaro and Charlton (2009) look at the industry classification of MNC affiliates throughout the world. They use different data and document that affiliates are often in activities that are close but not identical to their parent's activities. This fact is consistent with the affiliates supplying related inputs to other entities within the firm, a form of vertical FDI. This distinction would have been obscured by data that classified affiliate activity at a more aggregated level.

Whether an MNC seeks customers or inputs in a host market, the relative appeal of internalizing production in an affiliate versus transacting at arm's length has been related to the institutional characteristics of the host country. Horstmann and Markusen (1987) explore market-seeking motives in a two-country model where a firm's reputation may suffer when transacting in arm's-length relationship. FDI allows firms to access customers without risking their reputation. This work gives rise to predictions about the relative prevalence of MNCs by industry, where the production function varies across industries because of the size of firm-level fixed costs or the extent to which proprietary assets are used as inputs. For example, we may expect more internalization of production in MNCs in R&D-intensive industries.

Viewing MNCs as a means to utilize parent firms' proprietary assets across country borders without risking diminishing their value suggests that host country factors related to the quality of local institutions affect the appeal of locating in a given country. Because local institutional quality is likely correlated with other country level factors, poor quality institutions may be associated with less MNC activity overall. However, conditional on their wanting to access either customers or factors in a given market, MNCs are predicted to be more prevalent in settings where local institutions hamper the efficiency of arm's-length transactions. These relationships are complicated in supply chain settings where production stages vary in factor intensity and products vary in the elasticity of final demand. Bolatto and others (2020) describe when better protection of intellectual property—an intangible asset—leads to more or less integration along a global value chain.[4]

The documented complexity of MNC location strategies has led researchers to conclude that it is important to distinguish between specific types of MNC operations when trying to understand the impact of country or industry characteristics on FDI. Different strategies give rise to similar cross-country, or cross-industry, variation in the extent of affiliate activity (Carr and others (2001)). Furthermore, a large literature examines how variation in corporate taxes and in exchange rates affects the relative appeal of different host countries at different times. Blonigen (2005) presents a review of these issues.

While less common, some empirical work relates host country characteristics to the share of MNC entry and expansion that takes place via acquisition of existing assets versus greenfield investment. Nocke and Yeaple (2007) show that the share of FDI via cross-border acquisition is larger when a host country is more developed. Since it is also known that most FDI flows between developed economies, they suggest that a better understanding of choice of entry mode will be informative about MNC motives overall. They observe that the main difference between an acquisition and greenfield entry is that the parent firm combines existing assets with their own in the former but not in the latter. Their inference is that the assets located in more developed economies are more complementary to multinational production.[5]

Recent Evidence from Eastern Europe

Eastern Europe presents an interesting case study of how host country characteristics relate to MNCs' entry decisions. Since 2004, ten Eastern European countries have acceded to the European Union, and multinational affiliates make up important, but varying, shares of these host country economies. Using various datasets, it is possible to construct the stock of MNC affiliates in each country, by industry, and by parent-firm country, as well as the parent-firm-level investments made between 2008 and 2017. The appendix describes the available data in detail.

There is substantial variation in the stocks and inflows of FDI across the ten host countries. The 25,101 foreign-owned firms in the region account for just under 9 percent of firms with more than ten employees in 2017. Although geographically adjacent, and in a single market, population varies across countries, and population is negatively correlated with country-level GDP per capita and the corporate tax rate in the region.[6] Inward investment flows between 2008 and 2017 were distributed among host countries in similar proportions to the stocks of FDI in 2008, but the investment since 2008 is even more focused on the three countries with the largest populations. The Czech Republic, Poland, and Romania together accounted for more than 64 percent of the foreign-owned firms by 2007 but received 70 percent of the subsequent investments and almost 74 percent of the greenfield investments in the latter period.

Manufacturing firms make up 35 percent of the foreign-owned firms in the region while accounting for only 24 percent of all firms with more than ten employees. Manufacturing investments are relatively frequent in the countries with the largest numbers of foreign investments: the Czech Republic, Poland, and Romania. Services and wholesale and retail firms are also more likely to be foreign-owned than the firms in the social, transport, utilities, and construction sectors, and foreign-owned firms in service sectors are relatively more common in host countries with lower overall MNC affiliate numbers, such as Bulgaria and Latvia. These patterns are more pronounced in the new investments made between 2008 and 2017. The share of each country's affiliates that are in each sector is very stable across sectors. Across all countries, new investments in manufacturing are more likely to be via acquisition than are service-sector investments.

Table 3-1 presents pairwise correlations at the country level between some of the variables mentioned so far. The first column shows that the number of MNC affiliates, total affiliate sales, employment, and total assets in a country, as well as average affiliate sales, employment, and total assets, are all positively correlated with population. Columns 2 and 3 show that the same variables are all negatively correlated with GDP per capita and the corporate tax rate. Column 5 shows that affiliates in countries with a larger share of all firms under foreign control tend to be smaller in sales, employment, and revenues. The final two rows of table 3-1 show that affiliate revenue per employee and total assets per employee are lower in large countries and higher in high-GDP-per-capita countries. They are negatively associated with the number of affiliates in a country and the share of firms under foreign control.

Taken together, these comparisons suggest that the bulk of FDI activity in the region is vertical because it is relatively prevalent in labor-intensive, low-wage countries. Foreign ownership is also more prevalent in manufac-

TABLE 3-1. Pairwise Correlations between Host Country Characteristics

	Population (1)	GDP per capita (2)	Corporate tax rate 2017 (3)	Number of affiliates (4)	Share of firms under foreign control (5)
Population	1				
GDP per capita	−0.39	1			
Corporate tax rate 2017	−0.18	0.76	1		
Number of affiliates	0.72	−0.40	−0.06	1	
Share of firms under foreign control	0.11	0.15	0.37	0.35	1
Total affiliate revenues	0.85	−0.31	−0.28	0.84	0.10
Total affiliate employment	0.85	−0.47	−0.26	0.95	0.20
Total affilate total assets	0.74	−0.30	−0.41	0.72	0.00
Mean affiliate revenues	0.22	−0.07	−0.61	0.02	−0.30
Mean affiliate employees	0.33	−0.31	−0.74	0.18	−0.23
Mean affiliate total assets	0.06	−0.02	−0.55	−0.13	−0.28
Mean affiliate revenue per employee	−0.03	0.58	0.07	−0.30	−0.43
Mean affiliate total assets per employee	−0.31	0.49	0.21	−0.50	−0.12

turing, where vertical motives are expected to be more important because production can be fragmented across locations more easily. The evidence is far from conclusive, however, because MNCs have also entered the largest countries to access consumers and service sectors, which are less amenable to production fragmentation.

BILATERAL SOURCE AND HOST COUNTRY FACTORS

The parent firm's country of origin also affects the appeal of any given host market. Research on the trade of goods and services across borders has long recognized that the sizes of the sending and receiving countries are positively related to flows while distance between countries impedes cross-border trade. Collectively, the research in this area is referred to as the "gravity" literature. Research has established that these empirical regularities also govern various measures of MNC activity abroad. Antràs and Yeaple (2014) show that U.S. affiliate sales decline in distance from the United States, but at a lower rate than aggregate exports. Head and Ries (2008) document that FDI stocks fall with distance from the source country among bilateral country pairs of thirty Organization for Economic Cooperation and Development (OECD) countries and thirty-two OECD investment-partner countries.

The positive role of GDP in both the home and host countries on FDI is relatively straightforward. The greater the size of the host country market, the more desirable it is as a destination for market-serving horizontal FDI. For vertical investments seeking production sites abroad, large host countries provide a greater potential set of targets for acquisitions as well as a richer set of capabilities. Turning to the source country, research on firm heterogeneity shows a strong positive relationship between firm size and performance and the probability that a firm will invest abroad (Helpman and others (2004)). And larger countries are likely to have more large firms. Hence, theory predicts a disproportionately large share of multinationals are based in large source countries.

The theoretical role of distance on FDI flows is less clear-cut. Greater distance means higher costs of communication and coordination between headquarters and affiliates, reducing the probability of investment (Head and Ries (2008)). Alternatively, since local production and exports are substitutes in serving a given market, shorter distances and lower transport costs make it relatively more appealing to serve nearby markets directly through exports and serve more distant markets through affiliates. The empirical evidence, however, is less ambiguous; distance reduces foreign investment in terms of both the number and size of investments.

Last, several studies have documented agglomeration, or herding, in MNC entry decisions for parent firms coming from the same source country. These studies observe that proximity to other firms plays a role in location choice. Head and others (1995) find that Japanese firms tend to locate affiliates in U.S. states that already host many other Japanese-owned firms. Barry and others (2003) argue that such agglomeration could be due to the benefits of co-location or to demonstration effects, whereby previous investors' location decisions are interpreted by other same source–country MNCs as a positive signal about the attractiveness of the host market. If either of these factors are present, bilateral source-host FDI flows are likely to be positively correlated with the levels of preexisting bilateral FDI stocks.

Eastern European Evidence

This section examines the role of gravity on investment flows into Eastern Europe between 2008 and 2017. The analysis uses the gravity dataset from Head and others (2010) that contains the GDP of the origin and destination countries and a measure of distance between them. Bilateral distance between two countries is based on the distance between the biggest cities of those two countries, those intercity distances being weighted by the share of the city in the overall country's population (Head and Mayer (2002)).

Variation in bilateral country-pair FDI flows to the ten Eastern European countries is related to distance in table 3-2. The various measures of FDI include the total count of investments made by each parent firm, as well as the volume of revenues of these new affiliates, local affiliate employment, and local affiliate total assets. These variables permit finding the mean revenues, number of employees, and total assets of each subsidiary in the year of the foreign investment. The variables are then summed or averaged over all investments made during the ten-year period, separately for acquisition and greenfield investments for each country pair. All specifications in table 3-2 contain both source and host country fixed effects to control for differences in GDP, GDP per capita, and other country-specific characteristics. The first independent variable of interest is the natural logarithm of the distance between the two countries.[7] All columns include a variable that specifies whether the investments correspond to acquisition flows or greenfield flows.

TABLE 3-2. Gravity-Type Regression, Extensive and Intensive Margins

	Ln (counts of investments) All pairs (1)	Ln (total revenues year of investment) All pairs (2)	Ln (total employees year of investment) All pairs (3)	Ln (total assets year of investment) All pairs (4)	Ln (mean revenues year of investment) All pairs (5)	Ln (mean employees year of investment) All pairs (6)	Ln (mean total assets year of investment) All pairs (7)
Distance (ln, weighted)	−1.5228***	−2.1449***	−1.9480***	−2.2108***	−0.5758***	−0.3949***	−0.7079***
	(0.116)	(0.212)	(0.207)	(0.214)	(0.162)	(0.142)	(0.172)
Distance (ln, weighted)* Greenfield	0.0260	−0.0229	0.1437	0.0479	−0.1111	0.0580	−0.0095
	(0.047)	(0.135)	(0.099)	(0.118)	(0.121)	(0.078)	(0.105)
Greenfield	−0.9347**	−2.4895**	−3.2674***	−2.9249***	−1.0030	−1.7831***	−1.6794**
	(0.364)	(1.013)	(0.763)	(0.969)	(0.907)	(0.597)	(0.805)
Constant	13.3089***	34.9057***	18.9962***	22.9158***	20.4844***	8.9732***	13.2693***
	(1.119)	(2.027)	(1.400)	(1.425)	(1.558)	(0.981)	(1.155)
Source country FE	Y	Y	Y	Y	Y	Y	Y
Host country FE	Y	Y	Y	Y	Y	Y	Y
Observations	894	820	808	813	820	808	813
R-squared	0.723	0.635	0.668	0.686	0.471	0.475	0.546

Note: Robust standard errors in parentheses, clustered by country pair.

*** $p<0.01$, ** $p<0.05$, * $p<0.1$

Column 1 establishes that the number of FDI investments to countries in the region is decreasing with the distance between the source and host country. Because the ten host countries in this analysis are close together, most of the variation is coming from variation in distance to source countries. This finding reflects that as many as 65 percent of the parent firms are located in a Western EU country, and more than one-quarter of these are in Germany. Columns 2 through 4 find the same effect for the intensive margin of the total activity of new affiliates in the region. The revenues, employment, and total assets of new affiliates are greater for the affiliates of parents whose home country is closer. Columns 5 through 7 show that the mean size of the investment also declines with distance, consistent with vertical motives being the prevalent reason for location choice.

The second row of coefficients in table 3-2 shows no significant difference in the relationship between distance and investment flows for acquisitions or greenfield investments. That is, distance from the source country does not appear to affect the relative appeal of acquiring an existing firm or building an affiliate from scratch.[8] This finding can be related to the analysis in Head and Ries (2008), which explains gravity in FDI stocks as the consequence of information frictions that increase in distance between parent and affiliate. Parents located far away are willing to pay less to acquire a given target, since they will incur larger monitoring costs that decrease the value of the investment. The findings in table 3-2 show that this holds also for greenfield investments.

Another independent variable of interest is the existing stock of FDI from each parent country in each host country. There are several reasons why the presence of MNCs from the same source country could be associated with subsequent investment, and a positive association implies increasing agglomeration of investment activity by source country. Table 3-3 includes measures of prior bilateral investment in the basic gravity regression. This variable is found by aggregating the affiliate-level data by parent-firm country for all foreign firms that are not the result of recent FDI flows. The dependent variables in each of these specifications mirror those in table 3-2. Columns 1 through 4 show that the number of affiliates at the end of 2007 is positively associated with the number of investments made over the following decade and with the total volume of new affiliate activity. For a given source country, subsequent investments are more likely to be in the same host country as past investments. This finding is less pronounced for greenfield investments.

Columns 5 through 7 show that the average revenues, employment, and

TABLE 3-3. Gravity-Type Regression, Extensive and Intensive Margins, Including Bilateral FDI Stock

	Ln (counts of investments) All pairs (1)	Ln (total revenues year of investment) All pairs (2)	Ln (total employees year of investment) All pairs (3)	Ln (total assets year of investment) All pairs (4)	Ln (mean revenues year of investment) All pairs (5)	Ln (mean employees year of investment) All pairs (6)	Ln (mean total assets year of investment) All pairs (7)
Distance (ln, weighted)	−0.4681***	−1.1614***	−0.8449***	−1.2241***	−0.5427**	−0.2826*	−0.6680***
	(0.106)	(0.270)	(0.214)	(0.266)	(0.225)	(0.160)	(0.227)
Distance (ln, weighted)* Greenfield	−0.0723	−0.2329	−0.0513	−0.1456	−0.1584	0.0149	−0.0494
	(0.051)	(0.185)	(0.111)	(0.134)	(0.169)	(0.091)	(0.120)
Log of country-pair old FDI stock	0.6803***	0.6279***	0.7090***	0.6350***	0.0070	0.0695	0.0014
	(0.040)	(0.097)	(0.071)	(0.086)	(0.081)	(0.052)	(0.070)
Log of country-pair old FDI stock * Greenfield	−0.1457***	−0.1931	−0.1496**	−0.1082	−0.0063	0.0237	0.0787
	(0.032)	(0.125)	(0.069)	(0.086)	(0.113)	(0.056)	(0.078)
Greenfield	0.0044	−0.6060	−1.5939*	−1.3954	−0.6519	−1.5339**	−1.6046
	(0.424)	(1.620)	(0.944)	(1.128)	(1.474)	(0.771)	(1.006)
Constant	4.3302***	21.1799***	8.0170***	19.3452***	18.7612***	5.9775***	17.0197***
	(1.098)	(1.760)	(1.348)	(1.865)	(1.463)	(0.991)	(1.556)
Source country FE	Y	Y	Y	Y	Y	Y	Y
Host country FE	Y	Y	Y	Y	Y	Y	Y
Observations	737	682	675	678	682	675	678
R-squared	0.831	0.675	0.735	0.735	0.488	0.510	0.571

Note: Robust standard errors in parentheses, clustered by country pair.

*** $p<0.01$, ** $p<0.05$, * $p<0.1$

total assets of new affiliates are unrelated to the number of preexisting foreign affiliates in a country that are owned by parents from the same source country. That is, the number of entries—but not the size of the entry—is related to the presence of same-parent-country affiliates. While the presence of FDI from the same source country has a significantly lower effect on the number of greenfield entries in a host country than on the number of acquisitions, there are no differential effects on the average size of investments in terms of revenues, employees, or total assets. A comparison of tables 3-2 and 3-3 shows that including the stock of FDI from the same source country and its interaction with a greenfield indicator reduces the magnitude of the negative coefficient on bilateral distance.

ENTRY AND OPERATING FRICTIONS

Prior work has observed that agglomeration in FDI flows from a given source country could be due to inherent advantages of the location or to source country–specific spillovers from co-locating. One version of source country–specific spillovers relates to imperfect information. DeCoster and Strange (2003) and Barry and others (2003) make the point that parent firms may choose to follow the location choices of their compatriots, because in the face of uncertainty about potential host countries, the compatriots' choices might be positive signals about location quality. These so-called demonstration effects differ from any agglomeration benefits in production. To date, most of the empirical research about location herding has focused on FDI from a single source country to multiple hosts, and it has proved difficult to distinguish parent firms' motives.

Eastern European Evidence

The Eastern European data present a way to investigate whether observed agglomeration reflects information frictions based on the idea that an MNC's direct experience increases the information they have about a market. Efficiency-driven motives for FDI agglomeration could be thought of as independent of the extent of any one MNC's local experience. However, the value of the information in a signal from other MNCs from the same source country is less valuable if a parent firm has its own firsthand experience in the region.

An affiliate's parent firm may have multiple affiliates in a host country or in the region. The data contain information about how affiliates' ownership histories have evolved since 2007. Of the 25,101 subsidiaries under foreign control in 2017, 11,459 had been the targets of foreign acquisition between 2008 and 2017, and 4,497 were greenfield investments made by foreign firms over the same period.[9] There are 15,933 parent firms in the data that own at least one affiliate in the region. Of these, 6,288 only have affiliates that existed prior to 2008. An additional 8,256 did not have any prior presence in the region and made at least one investment between 2008 and 2017. The remaining 1,389 parent firms had at least one affiliate in the region in 2007 and made further investments there between 2008 and 2017.

The estimation proceeds as follows: the total number of new investments that a parent firm makes in each year from 2008 to 2017 is taken as given, as is its choice about whether to make an entry via acquisition or greenfield. Conditioning on the number of entries and mode of entry, the probability a parent makes an entry in a given host country is related to the number of affiliates of parents from the same source country that are already present in that host in 2008.[10]

The first two columns in table 3-4 consider all parent firms making new entries in any year between 2008 and 2017. Parent firms are more likely to choose locations where there already are a large number of affiliates of parents from the same source country. The association is larger for entry via acquisition, but remains positive and only slightly reduced for entry via greenfield. The next columns segment the parent firms being considered. Columns 3 and 4 look only at the 1,389 parent firms that had at least one investment in the region by the start of 2008. There is a positive association between the presence of same source–country affiliates and the likelihood of choosing a given host market for a subsequent entry, but it is much smaller in magnitude than for the sample of all parents making entries. Columns 5 and 6 control for whether the parent firm itself had made a prior investment in the same host country. The impact of same source–country affiliates on entry remains unchanged from columns 3 and 4. When distinguishing between the effect on the probability of acquisition and greenfield entry, the role of same source–country affiliates becomes insignificant for both.

Columns 7 through 10 are, however, of particular interest. These are the results for the entry decisions made by the 8,256 parent firms that did not have any affiliates in the region prior to 2008. These results show that these firms choose to enter countries in the region where more same source–country affiliates already exist. A comparison of columns 7 and 9 shows that this

TABLE 3-4. Probability Parent Enters a Host Market as a Function of Source Country Presence in that Market

Conditional logit (conditioning on the number of new investments a parent makes in any one year).

			All Firms That Make at Least One New Investment Post 2007							
	Entries made by all firms		Entries made by firms with prior investment in the region		Entries made by firms with prior investment in the region		Entries made by firms with no prior investment in the region		First entries made by firms with no prior investment in the region	
Variables	(1) entry	(2) entry	(3) entry	(4) entry	(5) entry	(6) entry	(7) entry	(8) entry	(9) entry	(10) entry
Number of MNC affiliates in host from same source country at end 2007	0.0321*** (0.001)	0.0335*** (0.002)	0.0008** (0.000)	0.0006 (0.000)	0.0008** (0.000)	0.0006 (0.000)	0.0696*** (0.004)	0.0704*** (0.005)	0.1211*** (0.010)	0.1128*** (0.010)
Number of same source affiliates in host at end 2007 * Greenfield		−0.0048** (0.002)		0.0006 (0.001)		0.0006 (0.001)		−0.0032 (0.009)		0.0479 (0.032)
MNC itself had an affiliate in host at end 2007					−0.0239 (0.084)	0.0253 (0.103)				
Number of MNC affiliates in host at end 2007 * Greenfield						−0.1470 (0.166)				
Grouped by parent-year	Y	Y	Y	Y	Y	Y	Y	Y	Y	Y
Host country fixed effects	Y	Y	Y	Y	Y	Y	Y	Y	Y	Y
Observations	113,610	113,610	8,268	8,268	8,268	8,268	89,090	89,090	82,550	82,550

Note: Robust standard errors in parentheses, clustered at the parent-firm level.

*** p<0.01, ** p<0.05, * p<0.1

relationship is particularly strong when firms are making their first entry to the region. Columns 8 and 10 show that the effect is not significantly different for entry via acquisition and entry via greenfield.

Table 3-5 narrows the sample even further to those MNCs that made at least two investments between 2008 and 2017. It presents further conditional logistic regressions, focusing only on entries made after the first recent entry to the region. For all parents who have made at least one investment already since 2007 and go on to make at least one more, the presence of same source–country affiliates in a country has only a very small impact on whether the parent firm enters that country next. That is, once a parent has a newly established affiliate in the region, its subsequent entry decisions are unrelated to the presence of affiliates with parents from the same source country. This holds true for acquisition and for greenfield investments. Table 3-5 also shows that a firm is likely to enter elsewhere in the region rather than make subsequent entries in the same market as its first entry. It appears that once MNCs have an affiliate in the region, their decisions to expand to other countries are unrelated to the presence of other firms' affiliates.

DISCUSSION AND CONCLUSION

This chapter describes how empirical researchers use data on MNC entries and affiliate activities to ascertain these firms' motives for operating in multiple markets. One useful summary is that whether the firm is seeking customers or input factors determines whether specific host country characteristics either encourage or deter new FDI. These characteristics include the income level of the population, its size, its proximity to other markets, and trade barriers such as tariffs. Other host country characteristics are seen as potentially conducive to FDI motivated by either market or factor access, such as low corporate taxes and favorable exchange rate movements, although the empirical evidence about these effects is more mixed. On the other hand, local institutional quality is thought to have a direct effect that encourages investment, but also indirect effects on the relative merits of internalization within firm boundaries versus arm's-length transacting.

While the strong association with gravity forces suggests that the distance between source and host is important in shaping FDI flows, a full understanding of the reasons for this remains elusive. Distance has a larger negative effect on vertically fragmented production processes within global value chains spanning country borders, which seek to access low-cost input

TABLE 3-5. Probability Parent Enters a Host Market as a Function of Source Country Presence and Own Recent Entry to that Market

Conditional logit (conditioning on the number of new investments a parent makes in any one year)

	Second or later new investment			
	Entries made by firms with prior investment in the region		Entries made by firms with no prior investment in the region	
Variables	(1) entry	(2) entry	(3) entry	(4) entry
Number of MNC affiliates in host from same source country at end 2007	0.0009* (0.001)	0.0005 (0.001)	−0.0009 (0.001)	−0.0004 (0.001)
Number of same source affiliates in host at end 2007 * Greenfield		0.0012 (0.001)		−0.0023 (0.002)
MNC itself had an affiliate in host at end 2007	−0.5205*** (0.084)	−0.5940*** (0.098)	−3.2051*** (0.219)	−3.3153*** (0.235)
MNC had affiliate in host at end 2007 * Greenfield		0.2215 (0.153)		0.3755 (0.402)
Grouped by parent-year	Y	Y	Y	Y
Host country fixed effects	Y	Y	Y	Y
Observations	4,714	4,714	1,384	1,384

Note: Robust standard errors in parentheses, clustered at the parent-firm level.

*** $p<0.01$, ** $p<0.05$, * $p<0.1$

factors. Distance is perhaps positively correlated with horizontal FDI that acts as a substitute to trade flows. Head and Ries (2008) offer one explanation based on MNC parents having lower value for distant affiliates due to the fact that imperfect monitoring within firm boundaries is more costly for more distant locations. Although empirical work to shed light on the role of entry-mode choice is limited, the Eastern European data suggest that their mechanism holds for greenfield as well as for the global acquisitions they study in their paper.

The analysis discussed here makes some progress on the reasons for parent-country agglomeration using firm-level entry decisions. The findings suggest that the observed agglomeration in the data cannot be due solely to positive operating spillovers among investing firms from the same source country. The observed increase in agglomeration between 2008 and 2017 in Eastern Europe can be attributed to the decisions of MNCs entering the region for the first time. For firms that already had a presence in the region, their subsequent entry was unrelated to the volume of FDI stocks originating from the same parent country. These relationships are consistent with frictions having to do with entry itself. One possibility is that MNCs have more information available to them about markets that are heavily populated by same source–country parents, and this information is valuable only when the MNC has no direct affiliate experience in the market or region.

DATA APPENDIX: EASTERN EUROPEAN ANALYSIS

Context

This chapter examines a new dataset on FDI stocks and recent flows into Eastern Europe. In the thirty years since the end of communist rule in Central and Eastern Europe, the national economies in the region have undergone dramatic transitions. After decades of state-directed economic control, they have been subject to substantial institutional reform and the development of market mechanisms. GDP per capita has increased and foreign investors have directed large flows of capital into the region.

While the focus here is on investment in the recent past, earlier research has considered the levels and types of MNC activity in the immediate aftermath of the opening of these economies. Hanson and others (2001) document that between 1989 and 1998, U.S. affiliates had rapid annual employment growth of 39.7 percent in Central and Eastern Europe. Because the growth rate was high in this region of relatively low GDP per capita, it was interpreted as consistent with an increase in the global prominence of vertical FDI. However, the growing size of the regional market meant that such investment was also consistent with horizontal FDI motives to access the new consumer base. Shatz and Venables (2000) show that MNCs from other regions were also increasing activity in Eastern Europe in the 1990s. From 1993 to 1997, Hungary and Poland were among the top ten global developing economy recipients of FDI. Hanson and others (2001) also show some evidence consistent with a decrease in export-platform strategy in the region in the same period. The ratio of affiliate exports to local sales in non-OECD Europe was at 60 percent in 1982 and had fallen to 20 percent by 1998, although it rose in manufacturing.

Data

Bureau van Dijk databases describe firm ownership by parent companies and enable changes in ownership to be inferred. This chapter uses the latest available information from Orbis for all firms with more than ten employees in ten Eastern European countries.[11] The ten countries are the Eastern European countries that acceded to the EU in 2004—the Czech Republic (CZ), Estonia (EE), Hungary (HU), Lithuania (LT), Latvia (LV), Poland (PL), Slovenia (SI), and Slovakia (SK)—and in 2007—Bulgaria (BG) and Romania (RO). The data include highlights from firms' financial statements, the number of employees, and primary industry according to the nomenclature of economic activities (NACE), Revision 2. Of key importance, the data also reveal each firm's global ultimate owner. These data are combined with historical Orbis, which contains the firms' dates of incorporation and financial information from 2007 to 2018.[12]

The Orbis data record whether a firm is owned by a foreign entity in each year, giving a snapshot of the stock of FDI at each point in time and allowing the measurement of FDI flows in a given year. In this chapter, foreign-owned firms are classified as greenfield investment if they satisfy two criteria: (1) they appear for the first time in the historical Orbis database with a foreign owner, and (2) the firm was incorporated in the year in which it first appeared in the data or in the previous year. Investments are classified as acquisitions if they appear in the historical data in years before they appear for the first time with a foreign owner and if the year of incorporation was at least two years before the new owner was recorded in the data. Some firms were first a greenfield investment and then had a change in ownership to a new foreign owner. These firms are shown as both a greenfield investment and an acquisition. Since the data start in 2007, they show the entry of parents who made new investments from 2008 onward. Thus, the dataset contains two types of foreign-owned companies: those that comprise the stock of old investments made prior to 2008, and those that were new investments made from this year onward. The latter group of subsidiaries are classified as either greenfield or acquisition, or both.[13]

The primary NACE code data are helpful, since the appeal of any one host market for an MNC depends on the industry and set of activities that the affiliate performs there. Also, industries vary in the extent to which they are amenable to the production fragmentation necessary for vertical FDI. The NACE codes allow the grouping of companies according to their business activities. Industries are grouped into five broad sectors: (1) manufacturing, (2) wholesale and retail, (3) services, (4) social services, and (5) transportation, utilities, and construction.

"Manufacturing" includes two-digit NACE codes 0–35, so rather than referring to manufacturing in a narrow sense, it also includes all natural resource–based activities. For instance, farming, fishing, and mining are all in this category. "Transportation, utilities, and construction" includes NACE codes 36–44 and 49–53. "Wholesale and retail" includes NACE codes 45–48. "Services" includes NACE codes 55–84, covering sectors such as food and accommodation, financial and insurance activities, and real estate. "Social services" includes NACE codes 85–90. Health care, education (for example, private schools), and art and entertainment are all in this category.

Focus on Poland

Poland is the largest country in the region, with a population of 38 million. It is the only one of the sample countries broken out in Antràs and Yeaple (2001), table 2.1, of affiliate activity relative to all local firm activity. Their data come from the OECD in 2007, but is reassuringly similar to the aggregate numbers for Poland that emerge from the Orbis data. They document that 16 percent of Poland's enterprises were foreign-owned, and affiliates accounted for 28.1 percent of employment and 45.2 percent of sales. In the data studied here, from 2017, affiliates are 14 percent of the enterprises with available operations data in Poland, and account for 32 percent of employment and 40 percent of sales.

Antràs and Yeaple (2001) also show that, among manufacturing industries, MNC affiliates account for 21 percent of Poland's R&D expenditure in firms and 69 percent of exports. These two numbers are interesting because the relative R&D intensity of Polish affiliates (percentage of total R&D expenditure accounted for by affiliates divided by the percentage of total revenues) is less than for affiliates in Finland, France, Ireland, Holland, and Sweden. It is consistent with affiliates in Poland performing different stages of production to those performed by affiliates in higher-income countries, and suggests that their role in the MNC network is more likely to be vertical. Consistent with this interpretation, Polish affiliates also account for a larger fraction of total host exports relative to total host sales than do the affiliates in the other five countries studied.

Country Comparison

Appendix table A3-1 shows the importance of MNC affiliates in the region overall and in each of the ten countries in 2017. The first column gives the total count of affiliates identified in the Orbis data. Of these 25,101 affiliates, Orbis reports revenues, employee numbers, and total assets for 19,630 firms, which make up 9.7 percent of all the firms in the region with available data on these variables. The average affiliate had revenues of US$41 million, 195 employees, and total assets of US$34 million (see columns 5, 7, and 9). Comparing these mean values to those for the whole available firm population, MNC affiliates' revenues are 4.47 times as large as those of the average local firm, with 2.86 times as many employees, and total assets that are 4.05 times as large. The ratios of these numbers show that MNC affiliates have higher levels of labor productivity and total assets per employee than local firms. These data confirm the finding from other settings and data that multinational affiliates are the largest and most productive firms in any local economy. They are also the most capital-intensive. The next ten rows of table A3-1 give analogous statistics for each of the ten countries in the region separately. MNC affiliates account for between 35 percent and 53 percent of revenues, between 16 percent and 39 percent of employment, and between 21 percent and 53 percent of total assets.

A comparison of Hungary and Latvia is useful. The two countries have

TABLE A3-1. MNC Majority-Owned Foreign Affiliates in the Eastern European EU Countries in 2017

	Number of affiliates 1	% of total firms 2	Number of affiliates with available data 3	Share of total with available data 4	Average affiliate revenues, US$m 5	Average revenues relative to all firms 6	Average employment 7	Average employment relative to all firms 8	Average total assets, US$m 9	Average total assets relative to all firms 10	Affiliate labor productivity 11	Labor productivity relative to all firms 12	Affiliate total assets per employee 13	Total assets per employee relative to all firms 14
Total	25,101	8.7%	19,630	9.7%	41.11	4.47	194.92	2.86	34.44	4.05	0.21	1.56	0.18	1.42
BG	2,150	4.8%	2,007	4.9%	24.36	7.18	176.21	3.35	22.17	6.18	0.14	2.14	0.13	1.84
CZ	4,984	9.9%	2,842	15.8%	57.35	3.37	221.04	2.46	42.22	2.99	0.26	1.37	0.19	1.21
EE	946	13.9%	887	14.2%	17.02	2.52	97.63	2.15	38.78	3.74	0.17	1.17	0.40	1.73
HU	1,383	3.6%	1,282	4.0%	106.08	10.73	359.02	5.87	120.90	11.48	0.30	1.83	0.34	1.96
LT	1,057	5.7%	650	5.9%	46.92	5.88	188.62	2.83	29.85	3.63	0.25	2.08	0.16	1.28
LV	1,467	14.6%	1,356	14.2%	14.68	2.39	78.33	1.55	10.91	2.07	0.19	1.54	0.14	1.33
PL	4,911	10.9%	3,203	13.6%	65.88	2.96	289.84	2.34	46.52	2.59	0.23	1.27	0.16	1.11
RO	7,124	12.6%	6,739	12.4%	22.56	4.06	151.45	2.63	16.77	3.53	0.15	1.54	0.11	1.34
SI	746	10.9%	660	10.4%	45.30	3.36	179.58	2.42	36.67	2.62	0.25	1.39	0.20	1.08
SK	333	3.3%	4	19.0%	78.50	2.29	314.25	0.88	83.25	2.23	0.25	2.61	0.26	2.55

very similar levels of GDP per capita, and while Hungary's tax rate is lower (9 percent versus 15 percent), it was 19 percent up to 2017 (KPMG web page, "tax-rates-online"). One difference between the two countries is in terms of population: Hungary is much larger, at 9.7 million versus 1.9 million for Latvia. Hungary's foreign affiliates, although relatively few, are large in revenues, employment, and total assets, and are very large relative to other Hungarian firms. In fact, Hungarian affiliates have revenues that are seven times as large in revenues, four and a half times as large in terms of employees, and eleven times as large in terms of total assets. Hungarian affiliates have the highest revenues per employee and second-highest total assets per employee. In Latvia, although the share of foreign-owned firms is high, each is only around twice as large as other Latvian firms. Latvian affiliate revenues per employee and total assets per employee fall in the low end of the sample.

Variation across Affiliate Industries and Parent-Firm Region

Appendix table A3-2 documents the main characteristics of foreign direct investments across broad sectors for the stock of foreign-owned firms in 2017. Manufacturing is the largest sector as measured by the number of foreign affiliates, at 35 percent of the total. Services account for 29 percent, and wholesale and retail for 23 percent. The transport, utilities, and construction sectors, and especially the social sectors, are substantially smaller. The FDI inflows between 2008 and 2017 are distributed across sectors remarkably similarly to the FDI stocks in 2007. Manufacturing affiliates are the largest in terms of revenues and total assets, and particularly in terms of employment. Somewhat surprisingly, revenues and total assets per employee are lower in manufacturing than in services and in wholesale and retail.

The global ultimate owners of Eastern European subsidiaries are grouped into six different source regions. Eastern Europe as a host region began as relatively low income and has grown substantially in the past three decades (see appendix figure A3-1). This means that the incentives to undertake FDI in the region for the purpose of wage arbitrage is now lower than in recent history. One factor worth noting is that FDI source countries fall into two categories, those inside and those outside the single market and customs union of the EU. Parent firms within the EU, in Western or Eastern Europe, face very low barriers to trade with any affiliates hosted in the ten countries studied here.

The six groups of source countries are (1) Western Europe—consisting of Austria, Belgium, Denmark, Finland, France, Germany, Greece, Italy, Ireland, the Netherlands, Norway, Portugal, the United Kingdom, Spain, Sweden, and Switzerland; (2) Eastern Europe—the ten Eastern European countries that joined the EU in 2004 and 2007; (3) Asia including China, Hong Kong, Korea, India, Japan, Singapore, and Taiwan; (4) North America comprising the United States and Canada; and (5) tax havens—Bermuda, Cyprus, Cayman Island, the U.S. Virgin Islands, and British Virgin Islands. All other source countries are grouped together as (6) "Other."

Appendix table A3-3 presents the distribution of FDI by source region and host country for existing stocks in 2017 as well as new flows from 2008 to 2017. The large majority of foreign-owned firms have parents in Western Europe: 16,363 or 65 percent. Of these, 26 percent are German parents, and Italy, France, the United Kingdom, the Netherlands, and Austria each source an additional 7 percent to 10 percent. Eastern Europe and North America each have 8 percent, and Asia has 4 percent. Western European firms own more than 70 percent of the foreign-owned firms in Poland, Estonia, and Hungary, whereas Eastern Europe is overrepresented in Latvia, Lithuania, and Slovakia. Panel 3 shows that North American parents are overrepresented in the Czech Republic, Hungary, and Poland, and Asian parents are also found disproportionately in Hungary.

Panel B of appendix table A3-2 describes the relative performance of affiliates owned by parents from different source regions. The subsidiaries of Asian MNCs have the largest revenues, most employees, and most assets, followed by the subsidiaries of North American MNCs. Eastern European–owned affiliates tend to be the smallest. Asian affiliates also have the highest revenues and assets per employee, and Eastern European affiliates have the lowest on both counts. Together with appendix table A3-3, these comparisons reveal that part of the performance premium in Hungarian affiliates relative to those in Latvia, for example, can be attributed to the fact that MNCs from Asia, North America, and Western Europe are more likely to be found in Hungary, and Eastern European parents are more likely to be found in Latvia.

Unreported data show that Western European affiliates are disproportionately in manufacturing activities, and relatively less active in services and wholesale and retail. Asian parents are also more prevalent in manufacturing, and less so in services, although Asian parents also own more

TABLE A3-2. MNC Majority-Owned Foreign Affiliates in the Eastern European EU Countries in 2017

PANEL A. Affiliates by sector group

	Number of affiliates	% of total firms in sector	Number of affiliates with available data	Share of total in sector with available data	Average affiliate revenues, US$m	Average revenues relative to all firms	Average employment	Average employment relative to all firms	Average total assets, US$m	Average total assets relative to all firms	Affiliate labor productivity	Labor productivity relative to all firms	Affiliate total assets per employee	Total assets per employee relative to all firms
	1	2	3	4	5	6	7	8	9	10	11	12	13	14
Total	25,101	9%	19,630	10%	41.10	4.46	195	2.86	34.42	4.06	0.21	1.56	0.18	1.42
Manufacturing	8,739	12%	7,078	13%	54.11	4.25	261	2.89	40.83	3.90	0.21	1.47	0.16	1.35
Services	7,245	10%	5,290	10%	16.24	3.65	168	2.76	39.89	4.54	0.10	1.32	0.24	1.64
Social	344	1%	253	2%	8.50	4.74	141	2.09	7.71	2.08	0.06	2.27	0.05	0.99
Transport, utilities, and construction	3,015	6%	2,372	6%	36.17	4.46	133	2.10	30.65	3.04	0.27	2.13	0.23	1.45
Wholesale and retail	5,758	10%	4,637	10%	53.91	4.06	159	2.99	21.78	3.85	0.34	1.36	0.14	1.29

PANEL B. Affiliates by source region, 2017

	Number of affiliates 1	Number of affiliates with available data 2	Average affiliate revenues, US$m 3	Average employment 4	Average total assets, US$m 5	Affiliate labor productivity 6	Affiliate total assets per employee 7
Total	25,101	19,630	41.10	195	34.42	0.21	0.18
Asia	963	721	100.69	333	61.58	0.30	0.19
Eastern Europe	2,132	1,446	23.86	117	14.94	0.20	0.13
Havens	1,335	1,115	23.41	136	19.10	0.17	0.14
North America	2,090	1,626	54.31	275	47.91	0.20	0.17
Western Europe	16,363	13,003	42.45	204	36.84	0.21	0.18
Other	2,218	1,719	19.66	95	18.73	0.21	0.20

TABLE A3-3. Eastern European MNC Affiliates in Orbis with Ten or More Employees

All firms by country

	BG	CZ	EE	HU	LT	LV	PL	RO	SI	SK	Total
Total	49,242	50,103	6,975	39,615	19,653	11,327	47,258	56,465	7,809	10,239	298,686

All foreign-owned affiliates by parent-firm region and country, as of 2017, share from each source region in each country.

	BG	CZ	EE	HU	LT	LV	PL	RO	SI	SK	Total
Asia	2%	5%	2%	8%	2%	2%	4%	3%	5%	5%	4%
Eastern Europe	6%	11%	10%	3%	15%	21%	3%	7%	9%	49%	8%
Havens	10%	4%	2%	1%	4%	6%	4%	7%	3%	2%	5%
North America	8%	10%	7%	13%	6%	5%	10%	6%	7%	6%	8%
Western Europe	60%	63%	72%	72%	66%	43%	76%	64%	69%	36%	65%
Other	15%	7%	7%	3%	6%	23%	3%	12%	7%	3%	9%
Total	2,150	4,984	946	1,383	1,057	1,467	4,911	7,124	746	333	25,101

All foreign-owned affiliates by parent-firm region and country, as of 2017, share by country from each source region.

	BG	CZ	EE	HU	LT	LV	PL	RO	SI	SK	Total
Parent Region											
Asia	5%	26%	2%	12%	2%	4%	20%	24%	4%	2%	963
Eastern Europe	6%	26%	4%	2%	8%	15%	7%	23%	3%	8%	2,132
Havens	16%	15%	2%	1%	4%	7%	16%	38%	2%	0%	1,335
North America	8%	24%	3%	9%	3%	3%	24%	21%	3%	1%	2,090
Western Europe	8%	19%	4%	6%	4%	4%	23%	28%	3%	1%	16,363
Other	14%	15%	3%	2%	3%	15%	6%	39%	2%	0%	2,218
Total	9%	20%	4%	6%	4%	6%	20%	28%	3%	1%	25,101

All acquisition investments post-2007 by parent-firm region and country, share of total investments by source region and host country

	BG	CZ	EE	HU	LT	LV	PL	RO	SI	SK	Total
Parent Region											
Asia	0.1%	0.7%	0.1%	0.3%	0.1%	0.1%	0.6%	0.6%	0.1%	0.0%	2.7%
Eastern Europe	0.2%	1.3%	0.3%	0.1%	0.3%	0.7%	0.4%	1.0%	0.2%	0.4%	4.8%
Havens	0.9%	0.8%	0.1%	0.1%	0.1%	0.3%	0.8%	1.9%	0.1%	0.0%	5.1%
North America	0.5%	1.6%	0.2%	0.4%	0.2%	0.2%	1.8%	1.2%	0.1%	0.1%	6.4%
Western Europe	3.5%	9.8%	2.2%	3.1%	2.1%	1.9%	12.4%	11.4%	1.5%	0.2%	48.1%
Other	0.6%	0.9%	0.2%	0.1%	0.2%	0.9%	0.5%	1.9%	0.2%	0.0%	5.5%
Total	5.9%	15.2%	3.1%	4.2%	3.0%	4.0%	16.7%	17.9%	2.2%	0.6%	72.7%

All greenfield investments post-2007 by parent-firm region and country, share of total investments by source region and host country

	BG	CZ	EE	HU	LT	LV	PL	RO	SI	SK	Total
Parent Region											
Asia	0.0%	0.3%	0.0%	0.1%	0.0%	0.1%	0.2%	0.4%	0.0%	0.0%	1.3%
Eastern Europe	0.1%	1.1%	0.1%	0.0%	0.1%	0.5%	0.1%	0.8%	0.0%	0.2%	3.1%
Havens	0.1%	0.2%	0.0%	0.0%	0.0%	0.2%	0.1%	0.8%	0.0%	0.0%	1.5%
North America	0.1%	0.5%	0.1%	0.1%	0.1%	0.1%	0.4%	0.8%	0.0%	0.0%	2.3%
Western Europe	0.8%	2.6%	0.6%	0.5%	0.4%	0.9%	2.7%	7.1%	0.3%	0.1%	16.1%
Other	0.2%	0.4%	0.1%	0.0%	0.0%	0.6%	0.1%	1.6%	0.1%	0.0%	3.1%
Total	1.4%	5.3%	0.9%	0.7%	0.6%	2.4%	3.7%	11.5%	0.5%	0.3%	27.3%

FIGURE A3-1. GDP Per Capita, Current US$

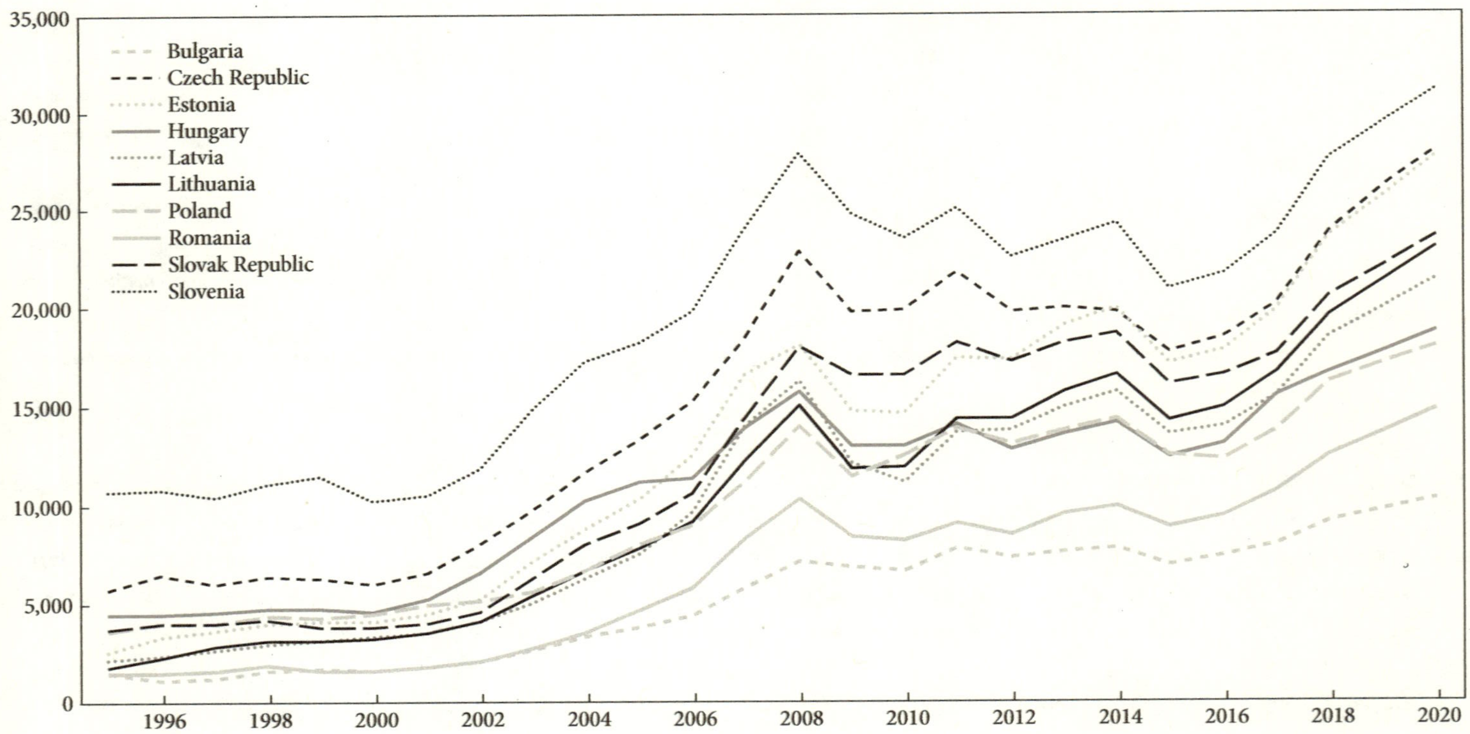

Source: www.imf.org/external/pubs/ft/weo/2018/01/weodata/index.aspx

wholesale and retail affiliates compared to their overall share of affiliates. Eastern European affiliates are overrepresented in services, transport, utilities and construction, and wholesale and retail. North American affiliates specialize in services. Hence, while some of the affiliate performance difference between Hungary and Latvia may be due to the sector composition, it can also be partially attributed to the source country of the parent firms.

Entry Mode

Of the 25,101 foreign-owned firms in 2017, 10,443 had the same foreign owner in 2007 while almost 60 percent were new foreign investment in Eastern Europe, either greenfield or by acquisition. Citing UNCTAD (United Nations Conference on Trade and Development) data, Antràs and Yeaple (2014) comment that mergers and acquisitions accounted for 50 percent of FDI flows globally in 2007, and 68 percent for the flows between developed countries. For the 14,658 affiliates in Eastern Europe in 2017 that had received foreign investment between 2008 and 2017, 73 percent of investments came in the form of acquisition and 27 percent were greenfield entries. The final two panels of appendix table A3-3 show the entries via acquisition and entries via greenfield in the data; the figures are the percentages of all 14,658 investments, by host country and sector. Romania, Latvia, and Slovakia have much higher rates of greenfield relative to acquisitions. In contrast, Hungary, Lithuania, and Slovenia are destinations with much higher shares of acquisitions. The share of new entries via acquisition is much higher in manufacturing than in services. Western European parent firms enter via acquisition three times more often than via greenfield, whereas parent firms from Eastern Europe are only one and a half times as likely to enter via acquisition.

Summation

In sum, when looking at the composition of foreign ownership or recent inflows separately by parent-firm region, by destination industry, or by entry mode, there is little that emerges to clearly differentiate individual host countries. Considering the distribution of parent region and host industry jointly, Western European and Asian parents own proportionally more manufacturing, at 40 percent and 42 percent respectively, relative to the average level of 35 percent. In contrast, North American and Eastern European parent firms own proportionally more service-sector subsidiaries, at

33 percent and 43 percent, relative to the average level of 29 percent. These patterns suggest that being inside the single market and customs union of the EU is not disproportionately important for affiliate activities in manufacturing or services. On balance, manufacturing affiliates in large Eastern European countries are more likely to be owned by Western European parents. Asian and North American parent firms are particularly likely to be the owners of Hungarian affiliates. Finally, Eastern European parents are more likely to invest in the smaller host countries.

NOTES

We thank Chad Bown and the editors for helpful comments during the drafting of this chapter. We also thank Siqin Ding and Camin McCluskey for excellent research assistance, and Paul Horsler and Tommaso Sonno for advice about data availability.

1. A related literature motivates FDI in the form of cross-border mergers and acquisitions as a means to increase the market power of firms that trade internationally. See Neary (2007).

2. The appendix details the data construction and presents summary statistics.

3. The idea that there may be frictions at firm boundaries relates to earlier work motivating the existence of multinationals (Hymer (1976)) and the OLI framework by Dunning (1980).

4. Nunn and Trefler (2009) also appeal to a property-rights logic in developing the prediction that when contracts are incomplete, there are more arm's-length relationships in poor-quality institutional environments when supplier's investments are important, because arm's-length contracting creates incentives that mitigate supplier underinvestment.

5. To the best of our knowledge, little existing empirical work relates entry-mode choice to other host country characteristics, such as trade barriers and institutional quality, or to whether the investment is horizontal or vertical.

6. Data on population come from the World Bank, available at https://data.worldbank.org/indicator/SP.POP.TOTL; data on GDP per capita are from the IMF, available at www.imf.org/external/pubs/ft/weo/2018/01/weodata/index.aspx. Data on corporate tax rates come from KPMG, https://home.kpmg/xx/en/home/services/tax/tax-tools-and-resources/tax-rates-online/corporate-tax-rates-table.html.

7. Taking logs of the dependent variable excludes any information from the absence of any flows, hence the results are limited to variation in the volume of flows between those pairs of countries with positive flows.

8. There is a negative coefficient on the greenfield indicator variable in the third row of each column, reflecting that the majority of investments over the decade are via acquisition.

9. The sum of the number of acquisitions and greenfield investments exceeds the total number of new affiliates between 2008 and 2017, which is 14,658, because some affiliates were first greenfield investments and then acquired by another foreign parent firm.

10. Specifically, the conditional logistic regression asks whether characteristics of the host country, such as the stock of FDI from the same source country, are associated with the investment locations that the parent chooses, given that the parent firm makes a given number of new investments in a particular year.

11. Data on smaller companies with fewer than ten employees can vary across countries due to data-collection techniques. Companies with private individuals as ultimate owners are also excluded.

12. Historical Orbis does not track the change of primary activity. Therefore, there is information about the latest industry activities of the companies only.

13. The data do not contain any information about firms that are no longer active in 2017, or firms that were under foreign ownership prior to 2017 but became domestically owned by 2017. Hence, the findings relate only to the entry mode decisions leading to the current cross-section of MNC activity in the region.

REFERENCES

Alessandrini, Sergio (ed.). *The EU Foreign Direct Investments in Central and Eastern Europe*. A. Giuffré, (2000) Milano.

Alfaro, Laura, and Andrew Charlton. "Intra-Industry Foreign Direct Investment," *American Economic Review*, 99/5 (2009): 2096–19.

Alfaro-Urena, Alonso, Isabela Manelici, and Jose P. Vasquez. "The Effects of Joining Multinational Supply Chains: New Evidence from Firm-to-Firm Linkages." Available at SSRN 3376129 (2019).

Antràs, Pol. "Firms, Contracts, and Trade Structure," *Quarterly Journal of Economics*, 118/4 (2003): 1375–1418.

Antràs, Pol, and Stephen R. Yeaple. "Multinational Firms and the Structure of International Trade," *Handbook of International Economics*, 4, 55–130. Elsevier, 2014.

Arnold, Jens Matthias, and Beata S. Javorcik. "Gifted Kids or Pushy Parents? Foreign Direct Investment and Plant Productivity in Indonesia," *Journal of International Economics*, 79/1 (2009): 42–53.

Barry, Frank, Holger Görg, and Eric Strobl. "Foreign Direct Investment, Agglomerations, and Demonstration Effects: An Empirical Investigation," *Review of World Economics*, 139/4 (2003): 583–600.

Baldwin, Richard, and Takuro Okubo. "Networked FDI: Sales and Sourcing Patterns of Japanese Foreign Affiliates," *World Economy*, 37/8 (2014): 1051–80.

Bernard, Andrew B., J. Bradford Jensen, and Peter K. Schott. *Importers, Exporters, and Multinationals: A Portrait of Firms in the U.S. that Trade Goods*. No. w11404. National Bureau of Economic Research, 2005.

Bevan, Alan A., and Saul Estrin. "The Determinants of Foreign Direct Investment into European Transition Economies," *Journal of Comparative Economics*, 32/4 (2004): 775–87.

Bloom, Nicholas, Raffaella Sadun, and John Van Reenen. "Americans Do IT Better: U.S. Multinationals and the Productivity Miracle," *American Economic Review*, 102/1 (2012): 167–201.

Blonigen, Bruce A. "A Review of the Empirical Literature on FDI Determinants," *Atlantic Economic Journal*, 33/4 (2005): 383–403.

Bolatto, Stefano, Alireza Naghavi, Gianmarco I. P. Ottaviano, and Katja Zajc. "Intangible Assets and the Organization of Global Supply Chains." (2020). CEP Discussion Paper CEPDP1673.

Brainard, S. Lael. *An Empirical Assessment of the Proximity-Concentration Tradeoff between Multinational Sales and Trade.* No. w4580. National Bureau of Economic Research, 1993.

Brouthers, Keith D., and Lance Eliot Brouthers. "Why Service and Manufacturing Entry Mode Choices Differ: The Influence of Transaction Cost Factors, Risk and Trust," *Journal of Management Studies*, 40/5 (2003): 1179–1204.

Carr, David L., James R. Markusen, and Keith E. Maskus. "Estimating the Knowledge-Capital Model of the Multinational Enterprise," *American Economic Review*, 91/3 (2001): 693–708.

Carstensen, Kai, and Farid Toubal. "Foreign Direct Investment in Central and Eastern European Countries: A Dynamic Panel Analysis," *Journal of Comparative Economics*, 32/1 (2004): 3–22.

Caves, Richard E. *Multinational Enterprise and Economic Analysis.* Third edition. Cambridge University Press, 2007.

DeCoster, Gregory P., and William C. Strange. "Spurious Agglomeration," *Journal of Urban Economics*, 33/3 (1993): 273–304.

Devereux, Michael P., and Rachel Griffith. "Taxes and the Location of Production: Evidence from a Panel of U.S. Multinationals," *Journal of Public Economics*, 68/3 (1998): 335–67.

Dunning, John H. "Toward an Eclectic Theory of International Production: Some Empirical Tests," *Journal of International Business Studies*, 11/1 (1980): 9–31.

Egger, Peter, and Michael Pfaffermayr. "Foreign Direct Investment and European Integration in the 1990s," *World Economy*, 27/1 (2004): 99–110.

Ekholm, Karolina. "Proximity Advantages, Scale Economies, and the Location of Production." In *The Geography of Multinational Firms*, 59–76. Springer, 1998.

Ekholm, Karolina, Rikard Forslid, and James R. Markusen. "Export-Platform Foreign Direct Investment," *Journal of the European Economic Association*, 5/4 (2007): 776–95.

Fort, Teresa C. "Technology and Production Fragmentation: Domestic Versus Foreign Sourcing," *Review of Economic Studies*, 84/2 (2017): 650–87.

Gorynia, Marian, Jan Nowak, and Radoslaw Wolniak. "Poland and Its Investment Development Path," *Eastern European Economics*, 45/2 (2007): 52–74.

Grossman, Gene M., and Esteban Rossi-Hansberg. "Trading Tasks: A Simple Theory of Offshoring," *American Economic Review*, 98/5 (2008): 1978–97.

Guadalupe, Maria, Olga Kuzmina, and Catherine Thomas. "Innovation and Foreign Ownership," *American Economic Review*, 102/7 (2012): 3594–3627.

Hallward-Driemeier, Mary Clare. "Foreign Direct Investment by Firms and Local Capital Markets in Hong Kong." PhD diss., Massachusetts Institute of Technology, 1997.

Hanson, Gordon H., Raymond J. Mataloni Jr., and Matthew J. Slaughter. *Expansion Strategies of U.S. Multinational Firms.* No. w8433. National Bureau of Economic Research, 2001.

Head, Keith, and Thierry Mayer. *Illusory Border Effects: Distance Mismeasurement Inflates Estimates of Home Bias in Trade*. Vol. 1. Paris: CEPII, 2002.

Head, Keith, and Thierry Mayer. "Market Potential and the Location of Japanese Investment in the European Union," *Review of Economics and Statistics*, 86/4 (2004): 959–72.

Head, Keith, and Thierry Mayer. "Brands in Motion: How Frictions Shape Multinational Production," *American Economic Review*, 109/9 (2019): 3073–3124.

Head, Keith, Thierry Mayer, and John Ries. "The Erosion of Colonial Trade Linkages after Independence," *Journal of International Economics*, 81/1 (2010): 1–14.

Head, Keith, and John Ries. "FDI as an Outcome of the Market for Corporate Control: Theory and Evidence," *Journal of International Economics*, 74/1 (2008): 2–20.

Head, Keith, John Ries, and Deborah Swenson. "Agglomeration Benefits and Location Choice: Evidence from Japanese Manufacturing Investments in the United States," *Journal of International Economics*, 38/3–4 (1995): 223–47.

Helpman, Elhanan. "A Simple Theory of International Trade with Multinational Corporations," *Journal of Political Economy*, 92/3 (1984): 451–71.

Helpman, E., Melitz, M. J., and Yeaple, S. R. "Export versus FDI with Heterogeneous Firms," *American Economic Review*, 94/1 (2004): 300–16.

Horstmann, Ignatius, and James R. Markusen. "Licensing versus Direct Investment: A Model of Internalization by the Multinational Enterprise," *Canadian Journal of Economics* (1987): 464–81.

Hunya, Gábor. "FDI in Southeastern Europe in the Early 2000s." *Vienna Institute for International Economic Studies* (2002).

Hymer, Stephen Herbert. *The International Operations of National Firms: A Study of Direct Foreign Investment*. MIT Press, 1976.

Javorcik, Beata Smarzynska, and Mariana Spatareanu. "To Share or Not to Share: Does Local Participation Matter for Spillovers from Foreign Direct Investment?" *Journal of Development Economics*, 85/1–2 (2008): 194–217.

Klimek, Artur. "Greenfield Foreign Direct Investment versus Cross-Border Mergers and Acquisitions: The Evidence of Multinational Firms from Emerging Countries," *Eastern European Economics*, 49/6 (2011): 60–73.

Markusen, James R. "Multinationals, Multi-Plant Economies, and the Gains from Trade," *Journal of International Economics*, 16/3–4 (1984): 205–26.

Neary, J. Peter. "Cross-Border Mergers as Instruments of Comparative Advantage," *Review of Economic Studies*, 74/4 (2007): 1229–57.

Navaretti, Giorgio Barba, Anthony J. Venables, and Frank Barry. *Multinational Firms in the World Economy*. Princeton University Press, 2006.

Nocke, Volker, and Stephen Yeaple. "Cross-Border Mergers and Acquisitions versus Greenfield Foreign Direct Investment: The Role of Firm Heterogeneity," *Journal of International Economics*, 72/2 (2007): 336–65.

Nunn, Nathan, and Daniel Trefler. "The Boundaries of the Multinational Firm: An Empirical Analysis." In *The Organization of Firms in a Global Economy*, edited by Elhanan Helpman, Dalia Marin, and Thierry Verdier. Harvard University Press, 2009, 55–83.

Ramondo, Natalia, and Andrés Rodríguez-Clare. "Trade, Multinational Production, and the Gains from Openness," *Journal of Political Economy*, 121/2 (2013): 273–322.

Shatz, Howard. "Gravity, Education, and Economic Development in a Multinational Affiliate Location," *Journal of International Trade and Economic Development*, 12/2 (2003): 117–50.

Shatz, Howard J., and Anthony Venables. *The Geography of International Investment*. Vol. 2338. World Bank Publications, 2000.

Trefler, Daniel. "The Case of the Missing Trade and Other Mysteries," *American Economic Review* (1995): 1029–46.

Wheeler, David, and Ashoka Mody. "International Investment Location Decisions: The Case of U.S. Firms," *Journal of International Economics*, 33/1–2 (1992): 57–76.

Yeaple, Stephen Ross. "The Complex Integration Strategies of Multinationals and Cross Country Dependencies in the Structure of Foreign Direct Investment," *Journal of International Economics*, 60/2 (2003): 293–314.

4

The International Market for Corporate Control

ANUSHA CHARI

Global cross-border merger and acquisition (M&A) volumes have grown at unprecedented rates over the past three decades. Since the 1990s, cross-border mergers and acquisitions account for a very significant fraction of foreign direct investment (FDI) flows around the world. The value of cross-border transactions grew from US$291.4 billion in 2001 to US$728.5 billion in 2017. The growth in the number of deals is also striking: cross-border M&A transactions worldwide rose from 4,163 in 2001 to 14,196 in 2017. The volume of worldwide cross-border M&A activity was 48 percent of total FDI in 2017.

While cross-border M&A share numerous features with domestic M&A, such as technological synergies and financing considerations, cross-border transactions generate many additional complexities. For example, regulatory institutions and market frameworks can vary significantly across countries. In the context of outsourcing production, "make versus buy" considerations for extending firm boundaries across borders also affect cross-border M&A activity.

Explanations for acquiring control across borders, therefore, lie at the intersection of organizational economics and trade. Costly financial contracting and the difficulty of monitoring technologies across borders, especially in countries with weak investor protections, argue for expanding the boundaries of a firm internationally (make) rather than contracting to suppliers outside the firm (buy). Similar to greenfield FDI projects, in which firms build subsidiaries from the ground up rather than acquire them, cross-border M&A are driven by horizontal motivations (to expand market access) or by vertical motivations (to integrate upstream and downstream components of supply chains across borders).

This chapter describes the market for international corporate control in three steps. It documents in some detail a set of facts about the ownership of firms across borders in recent decades. It also examines the incentives that drive firms to extend their boundaries across borders. Finally, it surveys the evidence about post-acquisition outcomes and concludes with some policy considerations.

The chapter begins by documenting the magnitude of cross-border M&A activity and how it varies across industries and locations. It then compares cross-border M&A to levels of greenfield FDI over time. The stylized facts provide an overview of cross-border M&A across time; whether cross-border M&A occur in waves as in the case of domestic M&A; and the regional distribution of cross-border M&A for acquirers and targets by the volume and value of transactions. The facts focus on key features of cross-border M&A, such as (1) whether transactions are horizontal (to obtain market access) or vertical (to integrate supply chains); (2) the mode of financing; (3) transactions that diversify a firm versus those in the same industry; (4) patterns of control acquisition; and (5) strategic versus financially motivated transactions. It also examines whether cross-border M&A activity differs across developed and emerging markets.

Briefly, M&A flows constitute a large part of overall FDI flows, and the number of M&A transactions has tripled over the past two decades. Cross-border M&A activity is concentrated in relatively few countries, mainly the United States and European countries. Cross-border M&A deals occur in waves, and megadeals are on the rise. Most cross-border M&A deals involve private firms, and private-equity transactions have increased significantly. Finally, tax-haven countries account for a substantial share of cross-border M&A activity.

Next, I consider the incentives for firms to buy firms in other countries and to sell divisions to foreign buyers. Existing studies offer several motives, ranging from market-seeking to efficiency (cost reduction) to maintaining control over proprietary technologies in countries with weak contracting institutions. I examine rationales for establishing control through mergers and acquisitions, be it majority or full control, when firms could easily outsource at an arm's length. It is important to note that I discuss how these incentives differ from those that drive M&A activity within countries.

Also, financial considerations such as liquidity provision are often a determining factor in M&A transactions. Here, cheap financial capital based on acquirer-country valuations can drive international buying sprees. Alternatively, undervalued assets in target countries provide an important incentive for cross-border M&A activity. These factors can gain further importance during crises when financial constraints bind.

The evidence suggests that cross-border M&A deals tend to create surplus value through various means—by increasing productivity, improving governance, and boosting stock prices. Cross-border M&A deals also take advantage of undervalued companies in target countries as well as cheap financing in acquiring countries. These factors also relate to other, commonly cited reasons why MNCs establish operations abroad, including those discussed in several other chapters of this volume, such as developing global supply chains through vertical M&A, expanding markets through horizontal M&A, and profit shifting for tax purposes.

Finally, I survey the evidence on post-acquisition outcomes. When a firm based in one country buys a firm based in another, what happens to employment, investment, production, and other measurable aspects of firm activity in the two locations? These considerations are often politically sensitive. When foreign firms acquire control of a country's physical assets, public opposition can run high.

The chapter proceeds as follows. First, it describes M&A characteristics using Moody's Bureau van Dijk's Zephyr database. The advantage of this source over other aggregated sources of FDI data is that the data give detailed transaction characteristics of individual M&A transactions. I provide stylized facts about the frequency, timing, and composition of worldwide cross-border M&A trends over the past two decades. Next, the chapter examines the alternative motivations and explanations for these trends. Then it analyzes post-acquisition outcomes for several real variables, such as employment, investment, and profitability. The last section before the conclusion outlines key policy issues that confront governments with respect to cross-border M&A transactions.

FACTS ABOUT CROSS-BORDER MERGERS AND ACQUISITIONS AROUND THE WORLD

The chapter bases its overview of the structure and evolution of cross-border M&A on Bureau van Dijk's Zephyr database, an extensive worldwide database of M&A transactions. The database includes information on mergers and acquisitions, initial public offerings, private equity, venture-capital deals, and rumors. The data covers European transactions from as early as 1997, North American transactions from 2000, and other global regions from 2003 onward. Zephyr aspires to be comprehensive in that no minimum deal value is applied. As of October 2018, there was information for more than 1.73 million rumored deals and actual transactions in the database.

A typical M&A search query combines variables for geography, timing, deal type, and deal value. This chapter focuses on transactions that involve a cross-border target and are completed—not rumored, pending, postponed, or simply announced. The focus is on transactions with confirmation of completion and not assumed to be complete ("assumed completed" is a data category). From a master sample of 1.21 million announced and completed deals, the cross-border sample consists of 223,405 completed acquisition transactions. Of these transactions, 195,741 are mergers, acquisitions, and minority stake investments. Initial public offerings, institutional buyouts, capital increases, joint ventures, management buy-ins and buy-outs, demergers, and share buybacks are excluded. The final sample consists of 166,311 transactions.

The firms in the final sample are both public and private acquirers and targets from an extensive set of developed and emerging countries. An important advantage of the data is good coverage of private-firm acquisitions that are generally not available in other cross-border M&A data sources. The sample includes majority and minority acquisitions, and mergers as well as exits via private equity transactions, but the sample excludes joint ventures, buyouts, privatizations, reverse mergers, and restructurings. One limitation of the Zephyr database is that it records deal values only beginning in 2001, and it reports deal values for about 61 percent of the transactions. For approximately 45 percent of the sample, the data contain information about the mode of payment, such as cash, equity, or debt.

Table 4-1 provides a broad overview of the data. The total value of deals in the sample is US$9.02 trillion, with a mean transaction value of US$97.9

million. The value of the largest deal—the Vodafone AirTouch takeover of the German telecommunications and engineering group Mannesmann AG—is US$195.6 billion, based on a stock swap between the two firms. About a third of the firms are publicly listed—29.3 percent of acquirers and 26.3 percent of targets. Finally, there are 181 acquirer or source countries and 187 target or destination countries in the sample.

Fact 1: Cross-border mergers and acquisitions comprised nearly 50 percent of FDI flows following the global financial crisis. To highlight the importance of cross-border mergers and acquisitions as a mode of entry into foreign markets, figure 4-1 provides a snapshot of the composition of foreign direct investment into greenfield investments and M&A activity for 2017, the last year in our sample. Data from the *Financial Times* FDI market reports database provides information about the number and value of announced greenfield projects. The number and the aggregate value of cross-border M&A transactions can be calculated using individual transaction information from the Zephyr database.

In 2017, 54.4 percent of FDI transactions were in the form of announced greenfield investments, comprising 50.2 percent of the value of worldwide FDI. The number of cross-border M&A transactions comprised 45.6 percent of the number and 49.8 percent of the value of aggregate FDI. The numbers imply that cross-border M&A activity accounts for nearly half of all FDI transactions. Of the M&A transactions, nearly all (99.9 percent) were in the form of acquisitions, while the relatively uncommon mergers comprised the remainder.[1] Further, acquirers gained majority control in 5.8 percent

TABLE 4-1. Overview of Cross-Border Merger and Acquisitions (CBMA)

No. of completed cross-border transactions (1997–2018)	166,312
Total value of deals (USD billion)	9,016
Mean of total value of deals (USD million)	98
Value of largest deal (USD billion)	196
Share of publicly listed acquirers	29.3%
Share of publicly listed targets	26.3%
No. of acquirer countries	181
No. of target countries*	187

*Excludes island states with total deal value of less than US$1 billion

of transactions and full of their cross-border targets in 27.1 percent of the transactions. Sixty-seven percent of transactions in 2017 involved acquisition stakes of 10 percent to 49 percent, minority stakes classified as FDI—that is, a 10 percent or greater stake.

Figures 4-2 and 4-3 plot the trends of announced greenfield projects and completed M&A transactions, in terms of both numbers and value, between 2003 and 2017. The data suggest that the value of announced greenfield projects peaked in 2007 and has not recovered to its precrisis peak. Mergers and acquisitions, in contrast, have risen steadily since the crisis, and the value of these transactions roughly equaled announced greenfield projects by the end of the data sample period.

Fact 2: The number of cross-border M&A transactions has tripled over the past two decades. Figure 4-2 shows that from 2000 to 2008, before the global financial crisis, the total number of cross-border M&A transactions increased from about 4,500 to 8,500. M&A transactions fell by approximately 30 percent in 2009, mirroring the collapse in global trade in the aftermath of the crisis. The pace of M&A activity recovered and surpassed precrisis levels in 2017, when there were about 14,000 cross-border M&A transactions—more than triple the number at the beginning of the sample.

Fact 3: A rising share of transactions are by Asian and Latin American acquirers, but U.S. and European companies still dominate the market for

FIGURE 4-1. FDI Flow Chart for 2017
(% of number)

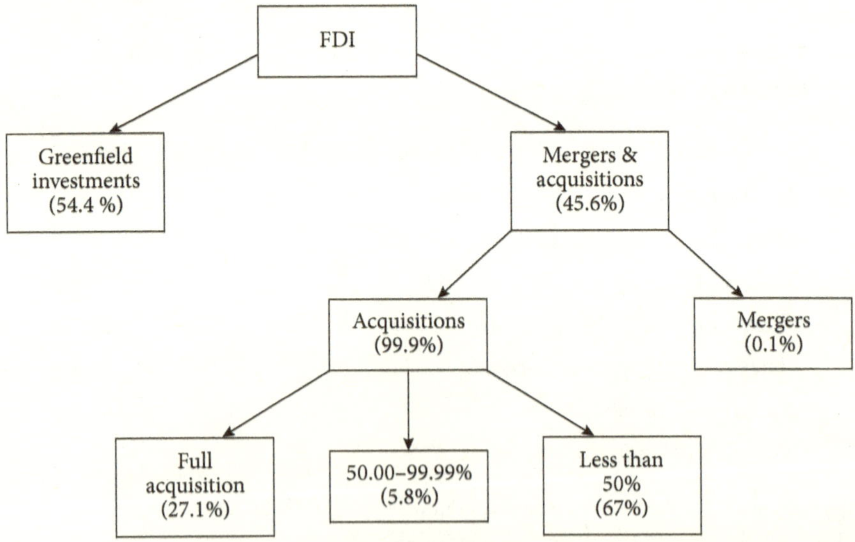

FIGURE 4-2. The Composition of Foreign Direct Investment
(Numbers of transactions)

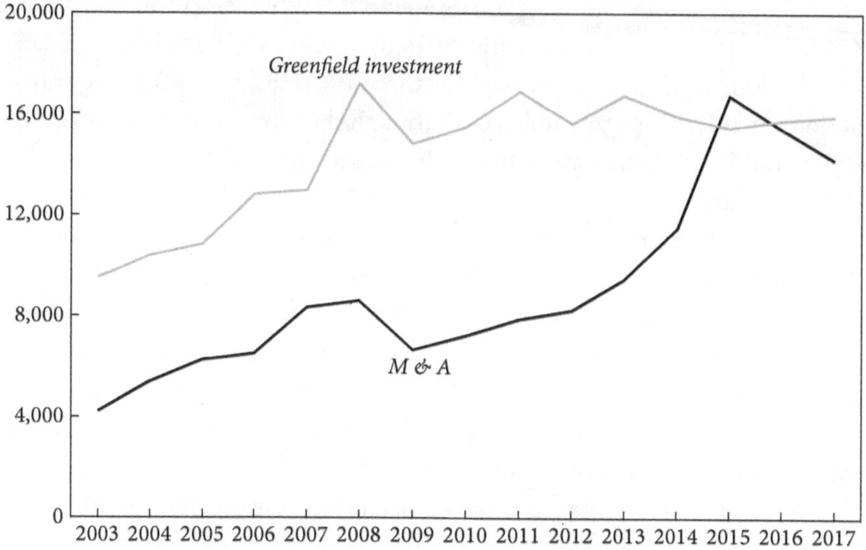

FIGURE 4-3. The Composition of Foreign Direct Investment
(Value of transactions, US$ billion)

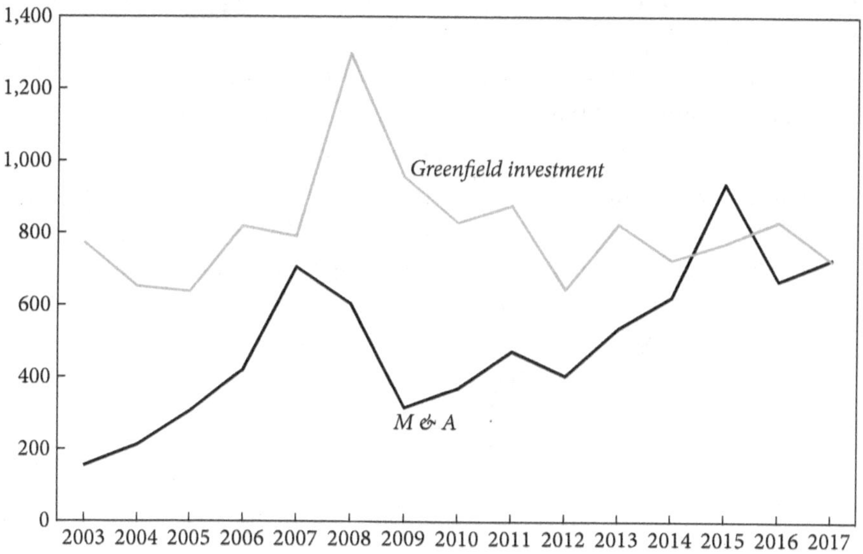

international corporate control. Figure 4-4A shows that in 2000, acquirers from Europe and the United States accounted for 91.2 percent (or 4,095 transactions) of all cross-border M&A activity. While emerging Asian and Latin American acquirers are increasingly important, European and U.S. transactions continued to account for three-fifths (61 percent) of the transactions in 2017. This trend holds even though the number of transactions by Asian and Latin American acquirers increased eight-fold over the past two decades, rising from 383 in 2000 to 2,106 in 2017.

In 2000, Asian transactions accounted for about 6.7 percent of the total. This proportion nearly quadrupled to 23 percent in 2017. Similarly, Latin American transactions rose from 1.97 percent to 10.5 percent of total transactions between 2000 and 2017. In addition, 2.3 percent of the transactions involved African countries in 2017. These numbers suggest that about 35 percent of the M&A transactions in 2017 involved a developing-country target—up from less than 10 percent in 2000.

The United States and Europe also accounted for the bulk of the target firms in cross-border M&A transactions. Figure 4-6 shows that the United States, the United Kingdom, and Germany comprised 28.5 percent of target firms in cross-border M&A transactions. Including target firms from the Netherlands, France, Italy, Spain, Switzerland, Sweden, and Canada, the fraction rises to an impressive 79.2 percent of total cross-border M&A targets. India, China, and Russia account for 10.1 percent of target firms. Including targets from Hong Kong and Australia, the share of target firms from these fifteen nations alone account for nearly 90 percent of all cross-border targets.

North American and European acquirers and targets also dominate the regional distribution of the total value of cross-border M&A activity. Figure 4-5A shows that North American and European acquirers account for 71 percent of the overall value of cross-border transactions. Acquiring firms from Asia and Latin America account for approximately a quarter (26 percent) of the total cross-border transactions by value. Similarly, figure 4-5B shows that North American and European target firms are about 70 percent of total transactions by value, while Asian and Latin American targets account for 24 percent of the total value of transactions. The pattern of concentration in value is similar to the pattern observed in the number of transactions. North America and Europe appear to be the most active regions in cross-border M&A activity.

FIGURE 4-4A. Number of Cross-Border Merger and Acquisitions

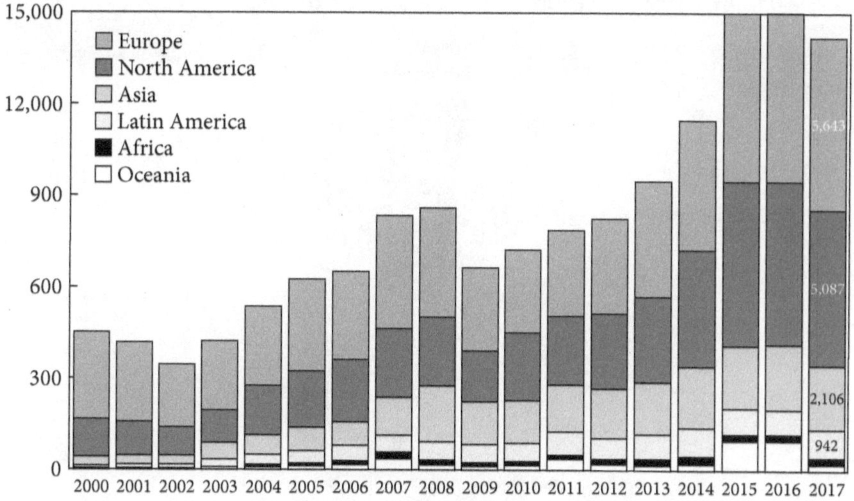

FIGURE 4-4B. Value of Cross-Border Merger and Acquisitions *(US$ billion)*

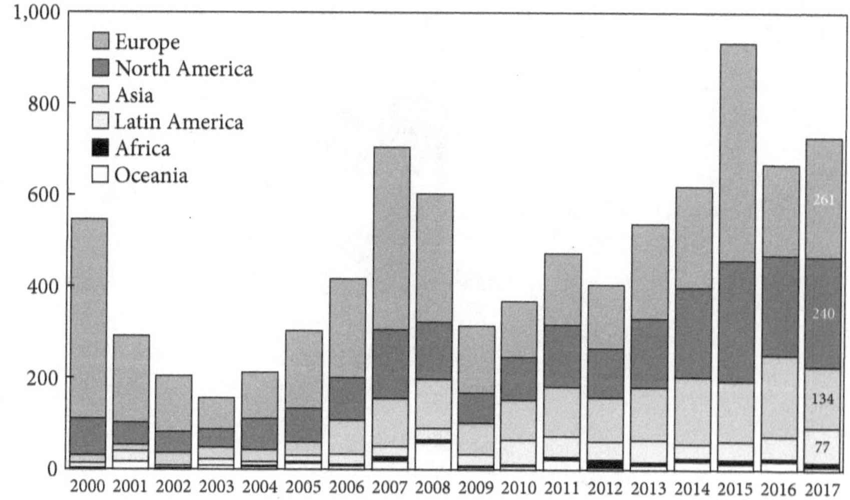

FIGURE 4-5A. Regional Distribution of Acquirer
(Percent of total value of cross-border deals)

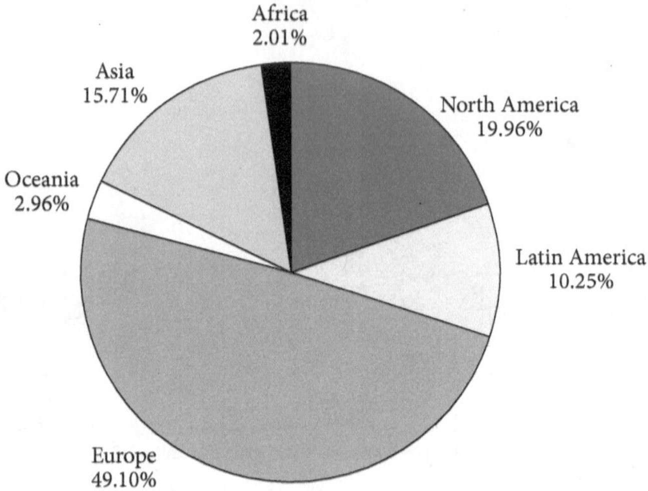

FIGURE 4-5B. Regional Distribution of Target
(Percent of total value of cross-border deals)

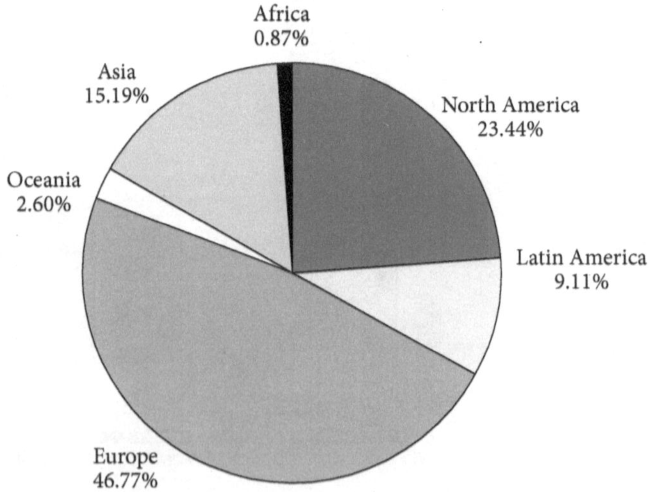

Fact 4: Cross-border M&A activity is highly concentrated among a small set of countries. Fact 3 and fact 4 collectively suggest that cross-border activity is highly concentrated among a small set of countries. A predominantly large fraction of cross-border M&A activity in terms of both acquirers and targets is in North America (the United States and Canada) and Europe, including the United Kingdom. The pattern in cross-border FDI flows in the form of M&A activity appears to mirror patterns in international trade between the two regions.

Fifteen acquirer countries together account for 71 percent of the total number of cross-border transactions. Figure 4-6A shows that acquisitions from the United States and the United Kingdom alone account for 36 percent of overall cross-border M&A activity. Acquiring firms in six countries—the United States, the United Kingdom, Germany, France, the Netherlands, and Canada—account for 52.6 percent of worldwide cross-border M&A transactions. About 11 percent of the acquisitions originate from the tax havens of the British Virgin Islands, the Cayman Islands, Switzerland, Cyprus, Hong Kong, and Singapore. Sweden, Japan, and Australia also rank in the list of top fifteen acquirer nations.

Further, the top fifteen nations comprised 73 percent of the total value of cross-border deals as acquirers and 70 percent as targets. Of these, the United States and the United Kingdom account for 32 percent of the total value as acquirers and 26 percent as targets. Other countries in the top fifteen acquirers, by the total value of deals, are from Europe (Germany, France, Spain, and the Netherlands), Asia (China, India, and Japan), tax-haven countries (Luxembourg, Switzerland, Hong Kong, Singapore, and Bermuda), Canada, and Australia.

Ten of the same countries also are included among the fifteen most popular destination countries by value in terms of target location (figure 4-6B). The exceptions are Italy, India, Russia, Brazil, and Sweden. They are on the list of top destinations in place of Bermuda, Canada, Japan, Hong Kong, and Singapore on the acquirer list. Once again, the concentration of cross-border M&A activity by value comprised a relatively small set of countries, albeit most of the biggest economies in the world. It is worth noting that the sample includes more than 180 acquirer and destination countries.

Figure 4-7 plots the value of transactions by acquiring and target firms from different countries. The picture shows a very high correlation between the total value of transactions by each country as acquirer and target. For example, firms from the United States and the United Kingdom account for a very high value of transactions as both acquirers and targets. In fact, for a sample of 179 countries, the correlation coefficient between the value of transactions by acquirer and target status for each country is 0.959. The finding is robust to sample sizes. For 100, 50, or 40 countries, the correlation coefficient remains greater than 0.95. The figure suggests that countries where firms are active as acquirers are also very active destinations for acquisition targets. Conversely, countries with less activity as acquirers also tend to have less activity as the targets of acquisitions. It is not all that surprising that this pattern seems closely linked to country gross domestic product and consistent with the pattern of concentration documented above.

Fact 5: The industrial composition of acquirers shows the rising global dominance of the services sector. Figures 4-8 and 4-9 show the overall industrial composition of acquirers and targets in cross-border M&A transactions. From the documentation in Zephyr, services include "finance, insurance, real estate, and nonfinancial services." Nonfinancial services include travel accommodations (hotels), recreational and vacation camps, industrial launderers, barber shops, tax preparatory services, and so on. Nearly all industry SIC codes in the 6000–7000 range are classified as services.

Consolidated data from figure 4-8 shows that the services sector accounts for 47 percent of the overall target values, while manufacturing accounts for 38 percent and agriculture for 14 percent. Similarly, figure 4-9 shows that the share of total acquirer value from services sector accounts for a predominant share (65 percent), while manufacturing accounts for 26 percent and agriculture for 8 percent.

Over time, the data show a definite rise in the dominance of the services sector in cross-border transactions. From the acquirer side, services accounted for 52 percent of the total value at the beginning of the sample, rising to 76 percent at the end of the sample in 2017. On average, between 2000 and 2017, manufacturing acquirers had a 27 percent share, and service-sector acquirers 62 percent. The remaining acquirers are from agriculture and construction, utilities, and retail and wholesale trade. On the target side, the industrial composition of total transaction values is more evenly split between manufacturing (38 percent) and services (46 percent), on average.

For developed countries, targets are from both manufacturing (40 percent) and services (46 percent), but acquirers are predominantly from services (63 percent), and about a third (27 percent) from manufacturing. In

FIGURE 4-6A. Total Number of Cross-Border Merger and Acquisitions by Acquirer Country
(Bubble size represents number of transactions of each acquirer country)

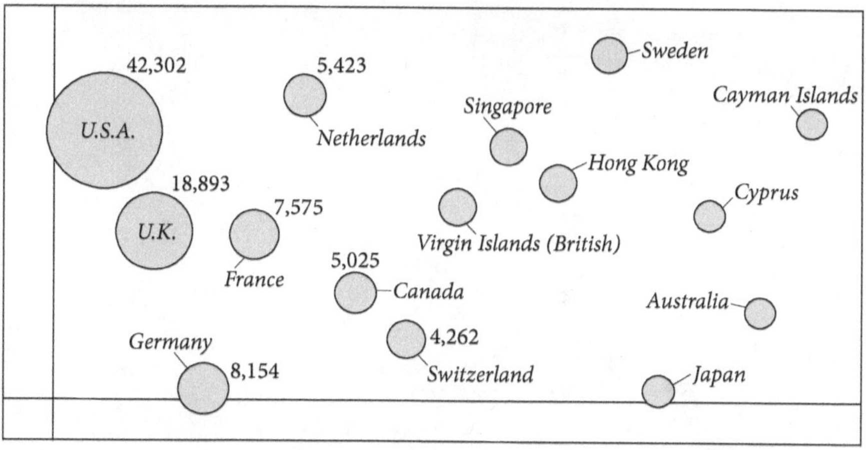

Note: Y-axis values were randomly chosen to create gaps between bubbles for visual purposes and has no economic significance.

FIGURE 4-6B. Total Number of Cross-Border Merger and Acquisitions by Target Country
(Bubble size represents number of transactions of each target country)

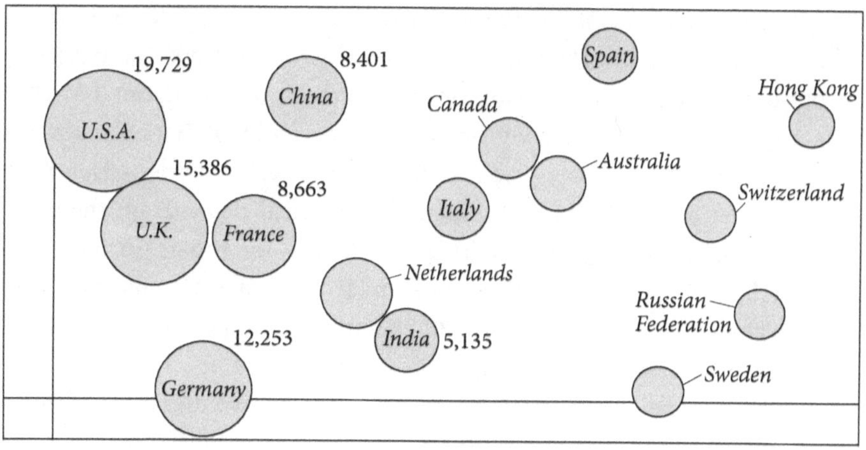

Note: Y-axis values were randomly chosen to create gaps between bubbles for visual purposes and has no economic significance.

FIGURE 4-7. Correlation between Acquirer and Target Values by Country

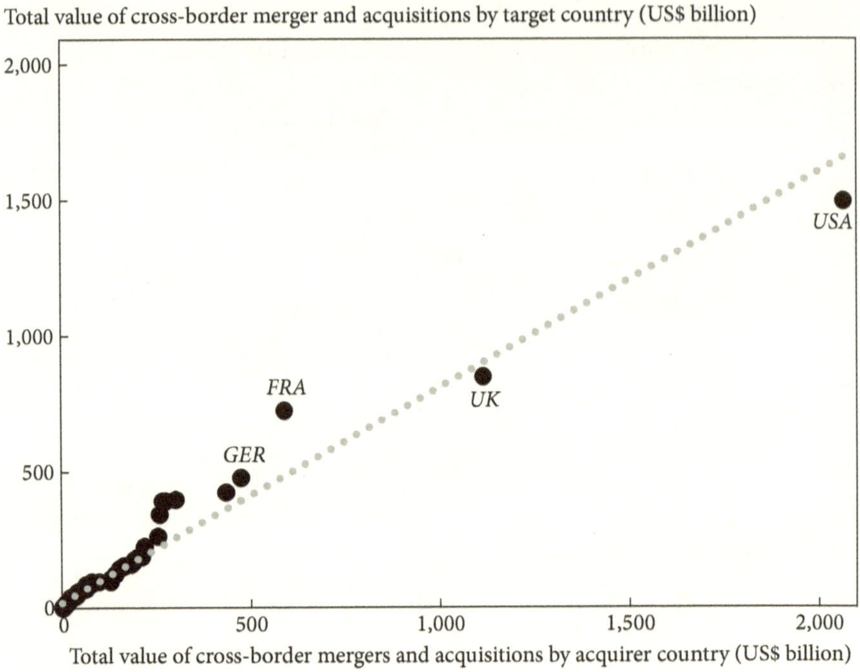

developing and emerging countries, both targets and acquirers fall into shares of 30 percent for manufacturing, 43 percent for services, and 21 percent for agriculture.

Fact 6: A significant fraction of cross-border M&A involve industry diversification integrating global value chains across borders. Rationales for cross-border acquisitions rely on two main categories—horizontal M&A in the acquiring firm's industry primarily for international market access and vertical M&A to integrate global supply chains across borders. Determining whether a transaction is horizontal or vertical depends on the extent to which acquisitions diversify lines of business for the acquiring multinational. However, the crudeness of standard industry classifications presents a challenge for this analysis. For example, it is not clear how to classify large firms that operate in multiple lines of business.

To address this issue, table 4-2 presents alternative measures of industrial diversification based on six-digit, five-digit, four-digit, three-digit, and two-digit North American Industry Classification System (NAICS) codes of acquirers and targets, to get a more nuanced sense of the extent to which acquisitions might diversify. The first column focuses on the nonfinancial

FIGURE 4-8. Value of Cross-Border Merger and Acquisitions by Acquirer Sector *(US$ million)*

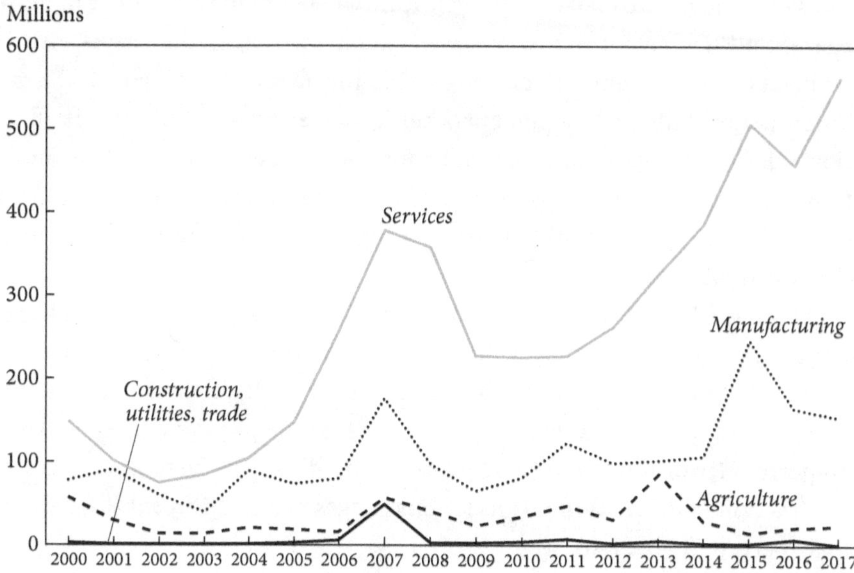

FIGURE 4-9. Value of Cross-Border Merger and Acquisitions by Target Sector *(US$ million)*

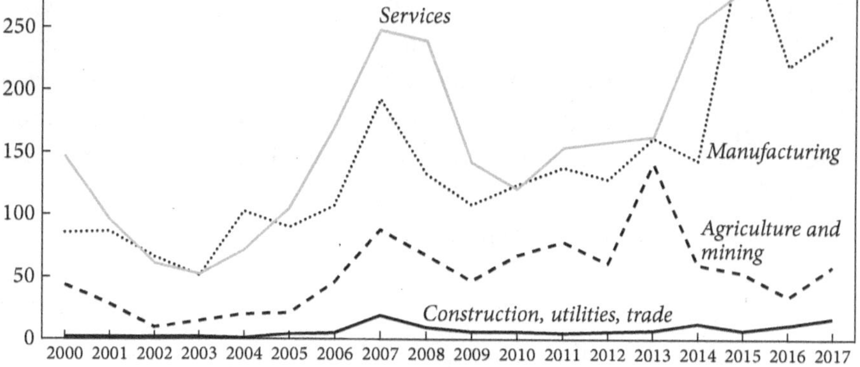

sector—that is, transactions where the acquiring firm is from a manufacturing or primary industry. It is interesting to note that the fraction of transactions classified as diversifying falls steadily when moving from finer to more aggregated degrees of industry classification. At the six-digit level, nearly 50 percent of the transactions are outside the acquirer's primary industry. This fraction falls to 17.8 percent when considering a two-digit classification. The pattern is even more stark for the financial sector, where more than 60 percent of the cross-border M&A transactions constitute industry diversification at the six-digit level, and the fraction is a mere 6.5 percent at the two-digit level.

Standard Industrial Classification (SIC) codes reveal a similar pattern. For a finer four-digit industry classification, 65 percent of the transactions in the nonfinancial real sector are diversifying (outside the acquirer's primary industry). The fraction drops steadily from 60 percent (three-digit), to 46 percent (two-digit), and to 32 percent (one-digit). In the financial sector, the fraction of diversifying transactions ranges from 72 percent (four-digit) to 57 percent (two-digit).

The pattern is consistent with the evidence in Alfaro and Charlton (2009), where data from Dun & Bradstreet (D&B) also presented a more comprehensive and nuanced picture of global multinational activity. The dataset included location, ownership, and detailed sector-level information (at the four-digit level) for each of more than 650,000 multinational subsidiaries in four hundred industries and ninety countries. Given that I did not observe trade within multinational firms, the study used a combination of four-digit sector-level information and input-output tables to distinguish horizontal and vertical FDI.

Similar to the evidence in table 4-2, Alfaro and Charlton (2009) also found that, at the two-digit industry level, a considerably higher fraction of relationships were classified as horizontal (subsidiaries in the same industry as their parents) rather than vertical (subsidiaries that supply their parents with inputs). However, disaggregating to the four-digit level reveals that many of the foreign subsidiaries in the same two-digit industry as their parents were in sectors that produce highly specialized inputs for their parents' production.

Chapter 2 in this volume (Davies and Markusen) classifies multinational enterprise organizational structures according to whether the firm replicates significant amounts of activity across different countries (horizontal FDI) or whether the production process is integrated in stages across borders

TABLE 4-2. Alternative Measures of Industrial Diversification

	Non-financial real sector	Financial sector
2-digit	17.8%	6.5%
3-digit	26.2%	55.4%
4-digit	35.8%	52.2%
5-digit	43.3%	39.8%
6-digit	49.3%	62.9%

(vertical FDI). Alfaro and Charlton (2009) defined vertical FDI as establishments owned by a foreign parent that produce intermediate inputs to the parent's production and export those inputs to the parent country, whereas Alfaro and others (2018) used input-output matrices to characterize the upstream or downstream relationship of activities within multinational firms. The M&A data in Zephyr also provided an unexplored avenue to view the vertical, horizontal, and diversifying motivations of firms to make acquisitions across borders. Table 4-3 shows a snapshot of the data to illustrate the different types of transactions that take place.

For example, Zao's acquisition of Glencore International AG represents vertical integration where a Russian alumina refining and primary aluminum production firm purchased a Swiss metal ore mining firm. Mitsubishi's increasing interest in Chilean Anglo-American Sur Sa is an acquisition of a mining company by a metals wholesaler. On the other hand, in Deutsche Telekom AG's acquisition of the United Kingdom's One-2-One is a diversifying transaction where a wired telecommunication carrier purchases a stake in a wireless telecommunications provider. The German Boehringer Ingelheim–French Merial Sas transaction in the pharmaceutical manufacturing sector appears to be a horizontal acquisition. Similarly, Walgreen's acquisition of Alliance Boots is also a horizontal transaction in retail drugstores. In contrast, Roche's 100 percent acquisition of Bermuda incorporated Corange Ltd., the parent company of Boehringer Mannheim and DePuy, was designed to position Roche as a global leader in diagnostics and strengthen its pharmaceutical division, the foundation of Roche's operations. The transaction, therefore, appears to have both horizontal and vertical features.

Detailed information, on a transaction-by-transaction basis, of the pre-

TABLE 4-3. Overview of Top 10 Deals

Year	Acquiring firm	Target firm	Acquiring country	Target country	Deal value (US$ bn)	Target industry	Acquirer industry
2000	Vodafone Airtouch Plc	Mannesmann Ag	U.K.	Germany	195.64	Information	Information
2015	Altice Nv	Altice Sa	Netherlands	Luxembourg	67.88	Finance and insurance	Finance and insurance
2015	Medtronic Holdings Ltd	Medtronic Inc.	Ireland	U.S.A.	60.75	Manufacturing	Manufacturing
2008	Commonwealth Bank of Australia Ltd	Pt Bank Arta Niaga Kencana Tbk	Australia	Indonesia	52.33	Finance and insurance	Finance and insurance
2007	Acciona Sa	Endesa Sa	Spain	Spain	45.59	Utilities	Transportation and warehouse
2016	Teva Pharmaceutical Industries Ltd	Allergan Plc's Actavis Global Generic Pharmaceuticals	Israel	Ireland	40.5	Manufacturing	Manufacturing
2014	CITIC Pacific Ltd	CITIC Ltd	Hong Kong	China	36.98	Finance and insurance	Mining/Management of companies and enterprise
2018	Linde Plc	Linde Ag	Ireland	Germany	33.19	Manufacturing	Transportation and warehouse
1999	Zeneca Group PLC	Astra Ab	U.K.	Sweden	30	Manufacturing	Manufacturing
2000	BP Amoco PLC	Atlantic Richfield Company	U.K.	U.S.A.	27.73	Mining	Mining

cise nature of the acquisitions along with detailed input-output data would allow a more definitive characterization of the vertical, horizontal, and diversifying motivations for the cross-border transactions. Simply viewing the transactions via the lens of NAICS codes suggests that vertical transactions differ in their four-digit NAICS codes. Horizontal transactions tend to differ in the fifth or sixth digit of their NAICS code. However, some of these horizontal transactions are also diversifying transactions within narrow industry codes, such as wireless (NAICS code: 517312) and wired communications (NAICS code: 517311) or wineries (NAICS code: 312130) and distilleries (NAICS code: 312140). Therefore, the data highlight that distinguishing which transactions are strictly horizontal (to geographically diversify across markets) may not be straightforward, because many of these transactions also had important industrial diversification features.

Returning to table 4-2, nearly two-thirds (64.2 percent) of acquirer and target firms in the nonfinancial real sector share the same industry code at the four-digit NAICS level. However, disaggregating to the five-digit level, the fraction drops to 56.7 percent and, at the six-digit level, to 50.7 percent. Thus, 7.5 percent of transactions that had the same industry code at the four-digit level have different industry codes at the five-digit level and 13.5 percent have different codes at the six-digit level. These differences at the five- and six-digit levels could correspond to diversifying acquisitions across either industries or geographies.

Fact 7: Cross-border M&A transactions occur in waves. Previous studies found two waves of cross-border M&A in the 1980s and 1990s—similar to the pattern for domestic M&A activity. The first occurs between 1987 and 1990, and the second during a period of rapid globalization between 1996 and 2000 (Evenett (2004)). Transaction-level data from the past two decades confirm the wave nature of cross-border M&A. Cross-border M&A declined between 2000 and 2002 following the second wave. The third wave began in 2002 and peaked in 2008—cross-border M&A increased by 105 percent over the period but collapsed by 23 percent in 2009 (figure 4-2). The fourth wave followed the financial crisis, and the number of cross-border M&A in 2017 had increased by 113 percent compared with 2009. Successive waves of M&A had significantly higher numbers of transactions consistent with the evolution of global economic integration.

Evenett (2004) showed that the first wave of cross-border M&A, which took place from 1987 to 1990, reached a peak of US$135 billion in 1990—less than one-fourth the value of the second wave. Figure 4-3 shows the third and fourth waves of cross-border M&A in value (fact 1). Globally, in nominal terms, the value of cross-border M&A declined to US$155 billion in 2003 from a peak value of US$547 billion in 2000. As figure 4-3 makes clear, the third wave peaked in 2007 at a precrisis value of US$705 billion. In nominal terms, cross-border M&A fell by 55 percent in 2009, similar to the collapse in global trade. The fourth wave occurred as cross-border M&A gradually recovered in the aftermath of the crisis to a peak value of US$935 billion in 2015. The value of cross-border M&A declined by approximately 30 percent in 2016 and 2017, coinciding with a period of uncertainty about global trade.

Theories generally attempt to explain the wave phenomenon as stemming from the reactions of firms to shocks in their operating environments. These shocks include deregulation; the emergence of new technologies, distribution channels, or substitute products; and a sustained rise in commodity prices (DePamphilis (2009)).[2] For example, Evenett (2004) suggested that the cross-border M&A wave of the 1990s was dominated by service-sector transactions. In particular, three sectors (transportation and communication; finance; and business services) accounted for about half of the value of all M&A from 1997 to 2000. He suggested that this cross-border M&A can be attributed to deregulation and technological advances in the telecommunications and business services sectors. In banking, consolidation in the form of strategic alliances increased in the 1990s.

Extrapolated to the cross-border context, alternative explanations suggest that overvaluation (either price-to-earnings or market-to-book ratios) of firms in acquirer countries can drive M&A to cluster in waves. Exchange rate appreciation in acquirer countries can also increase the attractiveness of asset valuations in target countries. Alternatively, cross-border M&A waves that follow crises in emerging countries, such as in the aftermath of the Asian financial crisis of the late 1990s, can make target country assets cheap for acquirers from countries not affected by the crisis. It is interesting to note that the Asian financial crisis was followed by massive liberalization in the market for corporate control, which resulted in a wave of cross-border acquisitions in crisis-ridden countries.

Fact 8: Megadeals in cross-border M&A are rising and also occur in waves. Transactions whose value exceeded US$1 billion (megadeals) have increased significantly. The number of megadeals nearly doubled from 2000 to 2007, reaching a precrisis peak of 123. After the crisis, the number of megadeals recovered to a record high of 138 in 2015 (see figure 4-10) and declined in

FIGURE 4-10. Number of Megadeals

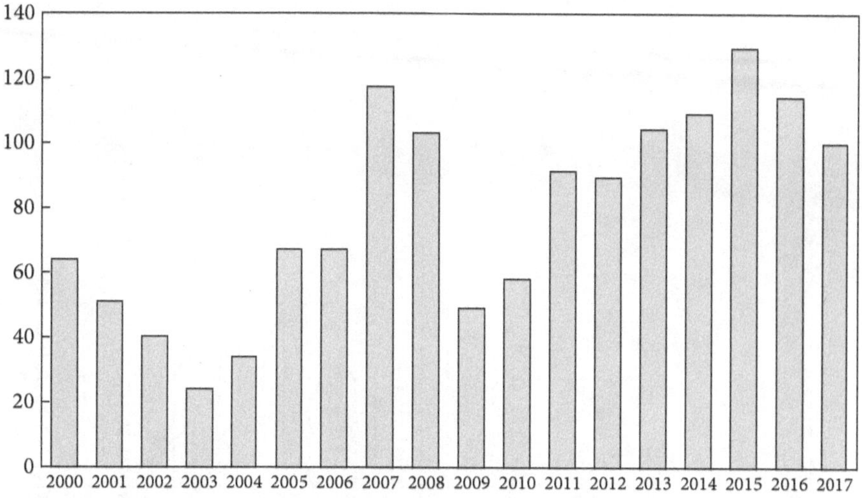

Note: Megadeals defined as those transactions greater than US$ 1 billion

2016 and 2017, consistent with the decline in overall cross-border M&A during these two years. In nominal value terms, megadeals accounted for a striking 60 percent of total cross-border M&A at their peak in 2007 and 53.4 percent at their peak in 2015 (see figure 4-11). The most significant cross-border M&A transaction to date—Vodafone's acquisition in 2000 of Mannesmann AG, valued at US$195 billion—accounted for 35 percent of the total value of cross-border M&A for the year and skewed the share of megadeals to 72 percent of the total.

Table 4-3 lists the top-ten cross-border transactions completed over the sample period. All ten involve developed-market acquirers, and eight of ten targets are also in developed markets. The exceptions are the Commonwealth Bank of Australia's acquisition of Indonesia's Pt. Bank Arta Niaga Kencana, valued at US$50.7 billion, and Hong Kong's CITIC Pacific's acquisition of CITIC Ltd. in China, valued at US$38.1 billion. Target industries predominantly were information technology, financial services, and manufacturing, while acquirer industries also include transport and warehousing companies consistent with the rise of integrated global supply chains. During the internet boom of the late 1990s, Evenett (2004) found that the majority of megadeals involved the service sector, notably the financial and telecommunications industries. In contrast, the industry mix of acquirers

FIGURE 4-11. Value of Megadeals
(US$ billion)

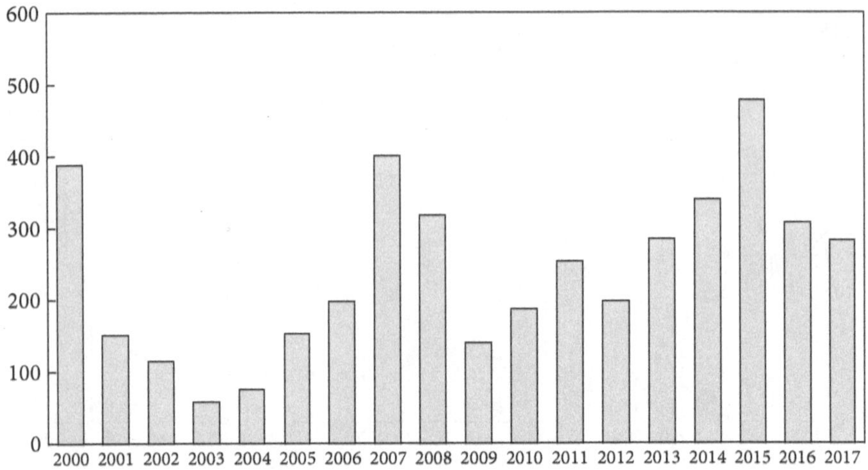

Note: Megadeals defined as those transactions greater than US$ 1 billion

and targets in megadeals since 2000 includes firms from both services and manufacturing.

The average deal size in all cross-border transactions also more than doubled in nominal dollars from US$35.4 million in 2003 to a peak of nearly US$80 million in 2007. After the crisis, average annual transaction values ranged from US$45 million to US$61 million from 2009 to 2017.

Cross-border M&A have been used for corporate inversions for tax purposes; following the M&A deal, the acquiring firm incorporates in the foreign country (that is, inverts) to avoid paying corporate taxes in the home country and to access cash accumulated abroad without paying repatriation taxes. For example, tax-inversion deals accounted for 40 percent of the value of M&A deals by U.S. companies in 2015. In some cases, the newly acquired foreign subsidiary then acquires the original parent in the home country using its tax-advantaged cash, and the transaction is recorded as inward FDI.

Note that the Medtronic transaction in the table represents a tax inversion to Ireland based on Medtronic's acquisition of Covidien plc for US$42.9 billion in cash and stock. The tax inversion allowed Medtronic to relocate its legal headquarters to Ireland, while maintaining its operational and executive headquarters in the United States, thus allowing it to take advantage of the low corporate taxes in Ireland and avoid taxes on more than US$14 billion in profits held overseas.

CITIC Limited (formerly, CITIC Pacific) is a conglomerate headquartered in Hong Kong, whose shares trade on the Main Board of the Hong Kong Stock Exchange. It is majority-owned (58 percent of issued shares) by the Chinese state-owned CITIC Group. Its main lines of business are in financial services, resources and energy, manufacturing, engineering contracting, and real estate. In 2014, CITIC Pacific bought most of the assets from the parent company and issued new shares to the parent, making most of the assets of CITIC Group publicly listed. According to its 2014 annual report, CITIC Limited was one of the largest companies on the Hang Seng Index. "Formerly known as CITIC Pacific, our name changed to CITIC Limited when we acquired the businesses of CITIC Group in August 2014."[3] The deal, therefore, facilitated CITIC's listing in Hong Kong as part of the group's long-term strategy to go public. A reason for choosing the Hong Kong Stock Exchange is that the central government (the controlling shareholder) encourages state-owned enterprises to list on overseas markets, especially the Hong Kong exchange.

Fact 9: Cross-border acquirers tend to be large. The median acquirer firm is five times larger than the median target firm. Median acquirer firm assets are US$330 million, while median target firm assets are US$58 million. The median developed market acquirer has an asset size of US$359 million, while the median developed market target asset size is US$62 million. For emerging markets, the median acquirer firm size is US$196 million and the median target firm size is US$45 million.

A target firm's enterprise value at the time of the acquisition can be computed using information about acquired stakes. The median target enterprise value for this sample is US$50 million. The median enterprise value for developed market targets is US$60 million, and for emerging market targets, US$33 million.

Fact 10: For the most part, firms involved in cross-border M&A deals are privately held. The vast majority of firms in cross-border transactions are private (figure 4-12). Overall, 73.6 percent of the deals involve a private target, 69.9 percent involve a private acquirer, and 94.2 percent have either a private target or a private acquirer. In developed markets, 71.4 percent of the deals involve a private target, 70.0 percent involve a private acquirer, and 94.1 percent have either a private target or a private acquirer. In emerg-

FIGURE 4-12. Public-Private Status of Firms in Cross-Border Mergers and Acquisitions

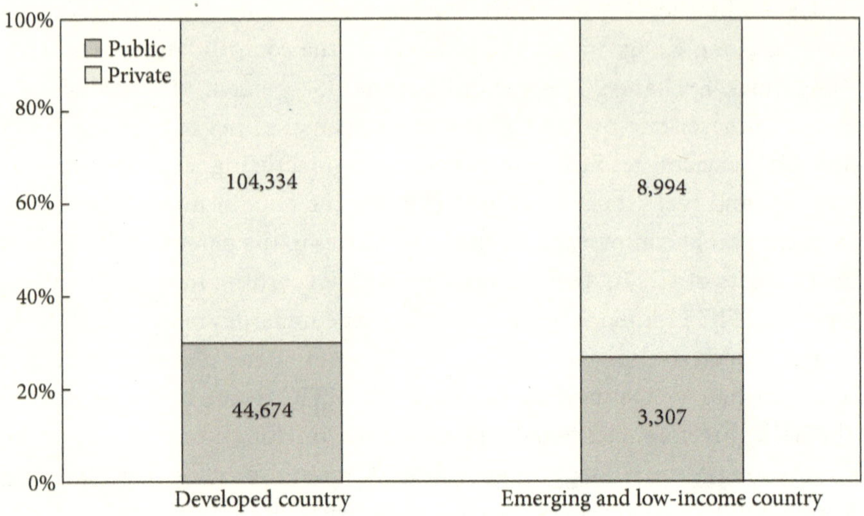

ing markets, 81.4 percent of the deals involve a private target, 73.1 percent involve a private acquirer, and 97.5 percent have either a private target or a private acquirer.

Fact 11: Cash is king. Cash is the predominant payment method in cross-border M&A transactions (figure 4-13). Ninety-four percent of developed market acquirers and 95 percent of emerging market acquirers pay for target firms with cash. A very small fraction of transactions involve payment in stock (5 percent for developed markets and 3 percent for emerging markets) and even fewer in debt instruments (1 percent for developed markets and 2 percent for emerging markets). In contrast, Andrade, Mitchell, and Stafford (2001) reported that 70 percent of M&A transactions within the United States in the 1990s involved stock financing, with 58 percent entirely stock-financed. The proportion of all-cash transactions in the United States was only 17 percent in 1999.

However, more recent evidence shows that the number of merger and acquisition (M&A) transactions paid for entirely in stock in the U.S. market declined sharply after 2001 (de Bodt, Cousin, and Roll (2017)), following regulatory changes in Financial Accounting Standards Board rules, which abolished pooling and goodwill amortization. The authors show that in the past twenty-five years, U.S. merger and acquisition (M&A) transactions

FIGURE 4-13. Method of Financing

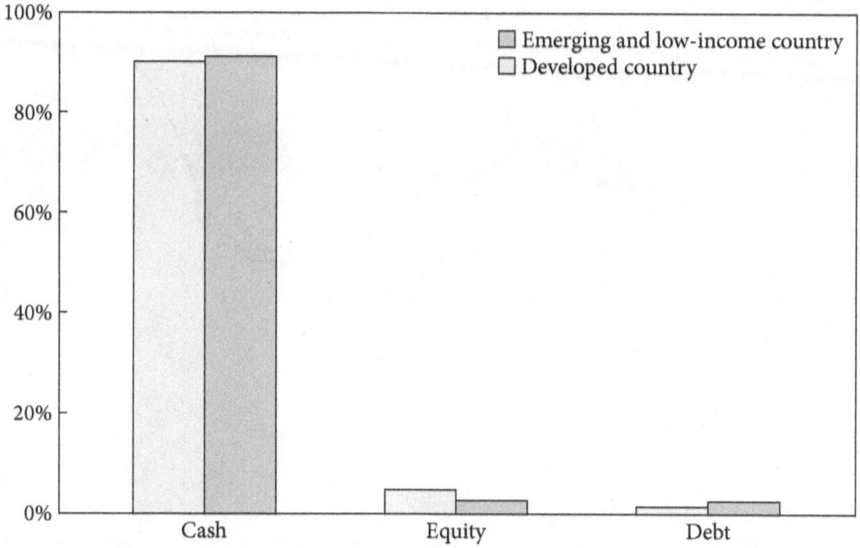

fully paid in stock have displayed a striking pattern: about half of all transactions in value-based percentages featured this payment approach during the 1990s, but fully stock-paid transactions fell to around 10 percent in 2014. According to Thomson Reuters, 33 percent of all deals in the second half of 2016 included some stock in the transaction.

Fact 12: Private equity transactions have increased over time. Cross-border M&A transactions can be motivated by strategic or financial considerations. Strategic motivations usually include market access across geographic regions, synergies between target and acquirer firms that involve cost-cutting or revenue enhancement, vertical or horizontal integration of production processes, and so on. Financial transactions, in contrast, include groups of investors such as private equity (PE) firms. In contrast to strategic acquirers, who look for organizational synergies to enhance profitability, private equity–led investors usually acquire stakes in pursuit of a positive return on their investment and eventually look to exit at a significant profit. Before exit, PE acquirers can help target firms realize operational efficiencies and synergies, and PE acquirers can provide capital to help target firms grow.

Private equity transactions have increased significantly in both number and value in the cross-border market (figures 4-14 and 4-15). The number of

FIGURE 4-14. Number of Private Equity Transactions

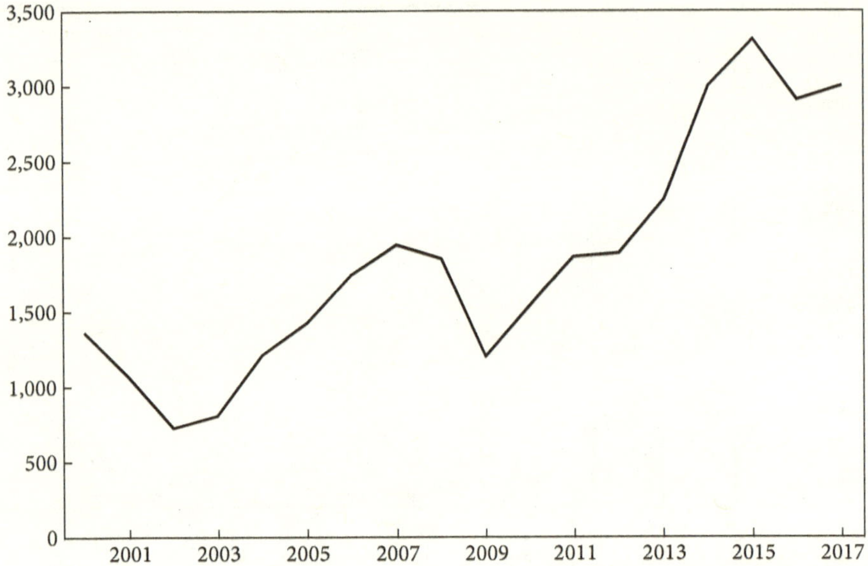

FIGURE 4-15. Value of Cross-Border Private Equity Transactions
(Share of total cross-border M&A)

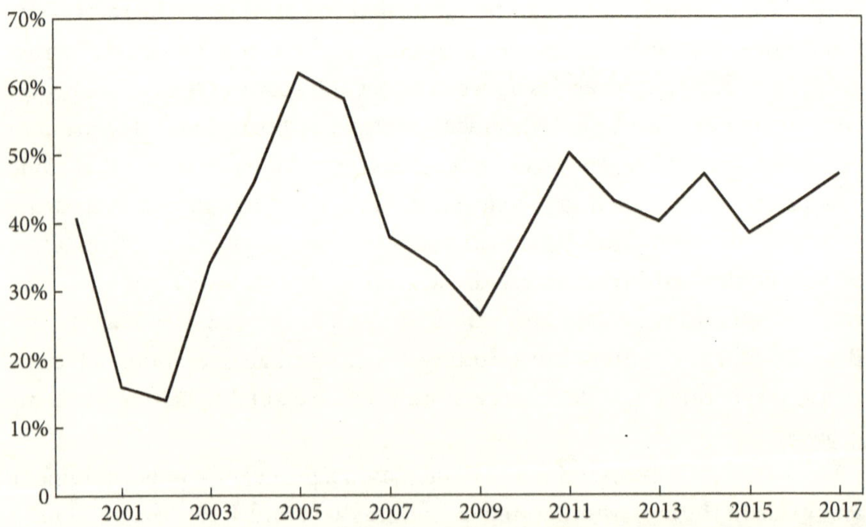

transactions doubled from approximately 1,000 in 2001 to nearly 2,000 in 2007, the pre–financial crisis peak in cross-border PE activity. The number increased after the crisis to more than 3,300 transactions in 2015. The total value of PE transactions rose from US$82 billion in 2000 to approximately US$250 billion in 2007. The value plummeted to US$76 billion in 2009 before rising steadily to more than US$330 billion in 2015. Figure 4-15 presents private equity transactions as a percentage of all transactions. Mirroring the patterns in overall cross-border M&A activity since 2016, both the number and value of PE transactions have declined. The pattern of control acquisition suggests that, on average, PE investors tend to acquire minority stakes. The primary method of payment is cash—98 percent of a sample of 26,881 transactions with available data.

Fact 10 states that firms in cross-border M&A are largely privately held, and fact 12 says private-equity transactions are increasing. Table 4-4 presents confusion matrices to examine whether deal types and the public or private status of firms are systematically related. Panels A and B present the proportions by the frequency and deal values based on the acquirer's public or private status. Panel A shows that about 19 percent of the deals are private equity deals. Of these, approximately 75 percent involve a private acquirer. Panel B shows that, by deal value, nearly 40 percent of the deals are private equity deals and 65 percent of them involve a private acquirer.

Panels C and D examine the same patterns based on the target's public or private status. By the number of transactions, private equity deals are once again about 19 percent of the transactions, and by deal value nearly 35 percent of the deal value for the full sample. Panel C shows that 78 percent of these private equity deals (by frequency) involve a private target, while panel D shows that approximately 68 percent of private equity deals (by value) have a private target. However, these patterns of public and private ownership status are very similar for all other deals as well. Thus, there does not necessarily appear to be a strong relationship between private equity deal status and the public or private status of either acquirers or targets. What remains striking is the proportion of private firms in the number of deals as well as overall deal values (table 4-4, column 3).

Overall, the median deal value in transactions that involve a private target is US$6 million, US$10 million in deals that involve a private acquirer, and US$10 million in deals that have either a private target or a private acquirer. In developed markets, the median value of deals that involve a private target is US$8 million, US$13.5 million in deals that involve a private

TABLE 4-4. Confusion Matrices of Private Equity Deal and Public-Private Firm Status

PANEL A. (Frequency of transactions)

	Private equity deal	All other deals	Total
Public Acquirer	4.60%	24.20%	28.90%
Private Acquirer	14.40%	56.80%	71.10%
Total	19.00%	81.00%	100.00%

PANEL B. (Deal value)

	Private equity deal	All other deals	Total
Public Acquirer	13.80%	37.20%	51.00%
Private Acquirer	26.10%	22.90%	49.00%
Total	39.90%	60.10%	100.00%

PANEL C. (Frequency of transactions)

	Private equity deal	All other deals	Total
Public Target	4.10%	20.70%	24.80%
Private Target	14.80%	60.40%	75.20%
Total	18.90%	81.10%	100.00%

PANEL D. (Deal value)

	Private equity deal	All other deals	Total
Public Target	10.90%	22.40%	33.30%
Private Target	23.40%	43.30%	66.70%
Total	34.30%	65.70%	100.00%

acquirer, and US$12 million in deals that have either a private target or a private acquirer. In emerging markets, the median deal value is much smaller: US$1 million in transactions that involve a private target, US$3 million in deals that involve a private acquirer, and US$1.5 million in deals that have either a private target or a private acquirer.

Do big deals involve publicly held companies and the small ones privately held companies? The data suggest no systematic relationship between the size of the deal and public or private status of the firms. The data show both big and small firms in both big and small deals. Table 4-5, panels A and B show the relationship between deal size and the public or private status of acquirers. Panel A shows the proportions of deals above and below median deal values and the public and private status of firms. For big deals (deal value greater than the median deal value), public and private acquirers appear to be evenly split (panel A, column 1).

Small deals are tilted toward private firms with a 60-40 split (panel A, column 2). When big deals are classified as being in the third quartile of all deals (75th percentile and above) the split between public and private ac-

TABLE 4-5. Confusion Matrices of Deal Size and Public or Private Firm Status

PANEL A. (Frequency of transactions)

	Big deal > median deal value	Small deal <= median deal value	Total
Public	19.90%	23.40%	43.30%
Private	22.20%	34.50%	56.70%
Total	42.10%	57.90%	100.00%

PANEL B. (Frequency of transactions)

	Big deal in 3rd quartile (75th percentile and above)	Small deal in 1st quartile (25th percentile and below)	Total
Public	9.80%	34.40%	44.20%
Private	11.10%	44.70%	55.80%
Total	20.90%	79.10%	100.00%

quirers is once again 50-50 (panel B, column 1). For deals in the first quartile of all deals (25th percentile and below), private deals account for 56 percent of the number of small deals (panel B, column 2). Note that Zephyr records many transactions as zero (that is, below a US$10 million threshold), and these tiny deals get recorded in the below-median cell and below the 25th percentile.

Fact 13: Tax-haven countries play a significant role in cross-border M&A transactions. Evidence suggests that tax-haven countries host a significant fraction of FDI. Multinational firms use tax havens for tax planning purposes (Dharmapala (2008))—and to facilitate tax avoidance by shifting taxable income out of high-tax jurisdictions and by reducing the burden of foreign taxable income (Desai, Foley, and Hines (2006)). Further, tax havens tend to be countries with better corporate governance practices (Dharmapala and Hines (2009)). Evidence also suggests that firms that use tax havens are larger and more international, and have extensive intra-firm trade and high research and development intensities (Desai, Foley, and Hines (2006)).

Relatedly, Dharmapala (2018) pointed to a wide body of evidence that suggests that residence-based taxation of foreign income significantly affects the ownership patterns and value of cross-border M&A. For example, Huizinga and Voget (2009) showed that the prospect of international double taxation affects the parent-subsidiary structure of multinational firms created by cross-border mergers and acquisitions. Further, countries with a high international double taxation of foreign-source income attract fewer parent firms and reduce the likelihood, following a cross-border M&A transaction, that the country is chosen as a headquarters location. Moreover, higher repatriation taxes significantly increase the propensity of multinational firms to relocate their headquarters. Conversely, in 2009, when Japan abolished repatriation taxes, transactions with a Japanese acquirer increased significantly (Voget (2011); Feld and others (2013)).

There is, however, relatively little information about the use of tax havens in cross-border M&A transactions. The data in figure 4-16 show that the role of tax havens rose significantly between 2000 and 2017. At the beginning of the sample, in 2000, transactions that had either a target or an acquirer firm from a tax-haven country accounted for 7 percent of the total number of cross-border transactions and 6 percent of the value. On average, in the pre–financial crisis period, tax havens accounted for approximately 17 percent of the value and 10 percent of the number of cross-border M&A transactions. The data suggest that these fractions rose in the 2009–17 post-crisis

FIGURE 4-16. Role of Tax Havens in Cross-Border Merger and Acquisitions

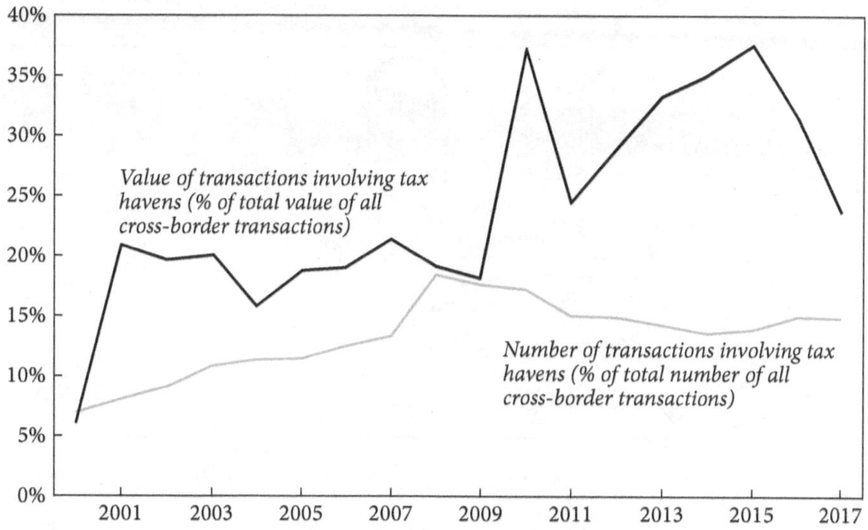

period—to 15 percent of the number and 30 percent of the value of total cross-border M&A transactions.

Figure 4-17 shows a bubble chart of the value of transactions that took place across different tax-haven countries. The bubble size representing the significance of cross-border transactions based in tax havens increases over time. In tax-haven transactions, the mean acquirer-firm size, according to available data for pre-deal total asset values, was US$11.29 billion, and the median US$330 million; the mean target-firm size was US$4.19 billion, and the median US$195 million. This pattern is consistent with evidence that large firms tend to use tax havens. The industry composition suggests that 75 percent of the acquirers based in tax havens are from the financial sector, while 55 percent of targets domiciled in tax havens are from the nonfinancial real sector.

Fact 14: The pattern of control acquisition in cross-border transactions varies across developed- and emerging-market acquirers. Similar to domestic M&A, cross-border acquisitions can take the form of a minority stake, a majority stake, or full takeover of the target firm (figure 4-18). Cross-border transactions by developed-market acquirers involve acquisitions of minority stakes in approximately 55 percent of transactions when the target is in a

FIGURE 4-17. Value of Transactions Across Different Tax Havens
(Bubble size represents value of transactions across acquirers and targets)

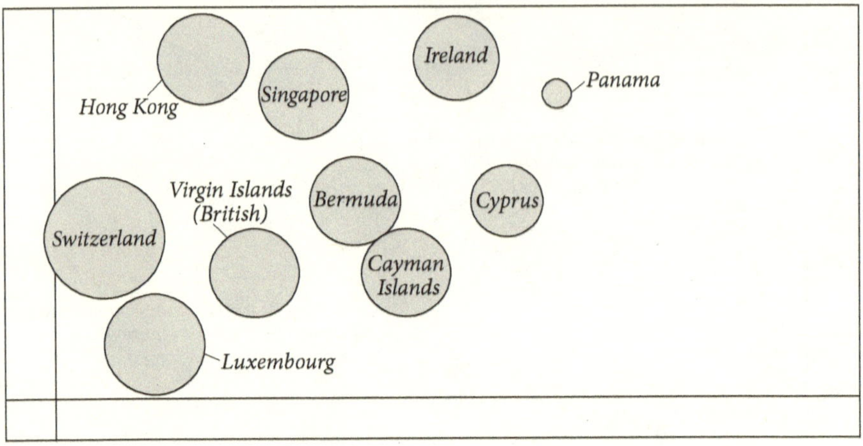

FIGURE 4-18. The Pattern of Control Acquisition in Emerging and Developed Economies

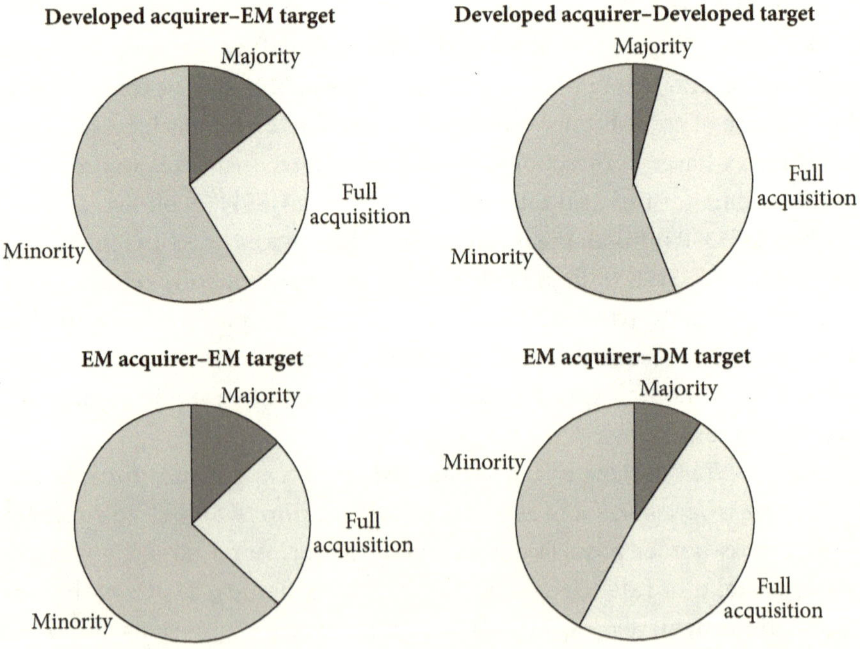

developed market and 57 percent when the target is in an emerging market. When a developed-market firm acquires a developed-market target, about 40 percent of transactions involve the full purchase of the target. But when a developed-market firm acquires a target in an emerging market, only 26 percent of transactions involve the full purchase. Developed-market firms acquire majority control in 17 percent of transactions in emerging markets, but only 5 percent when the target is in a developed market. Thus, the data suggest that developed-market acquirers either acquire full control or minority stakes in developed-market targets while, in acquisitions in emerging markets, approximately 60 percent involve acquiring a minority stake and 40 percent either a majority stake or full acquisition.

The pattern is different when the acquiring firm is from an emerging market. Emerging market acquirers tend to acquire minority stakes in about 60 percent of the transactions when the target firm is also from an emerging market. A striking difference is that emerging-market acquirers gain majority or full control in 60 percent of the transactions when the target is in a developed market. Emerging market firms acquire full control of developed-market targets in 49 percent of transactions.

The data show that on average, foreign firms acquire a 9 percent initial minority stake in target firms—the fraction ranges from 6 percent for developed-market targets to 18.5 percent for emerging-market targets. After an initial stake is acquired, approximately 40 percent of transactions involve further acquisitions in the same target firm. Sixty percent of further acquisitions lead to additional minority stakes and 40 percent to majority stakes. In transactions involving majority control, on average, 15 percent lead to additional stakes that fall shy of full control and 22 percent of the transactions result in a complete transfer of ownership to the foreign acquirer.

Arguments for cross-border acquisitions often rely on the degree of investor protection provided by institutions across the globe as well as the very different levels of capital-market development in target-firms' countries. For example, Antras, Desai, and Foley (2009) showed that, in countries where monitoring is non-verifiable, multinational firms were more likely to establish subsidiaries rather than license proprietary technologies to unrelated third parties. Arm's-length transactions to unrelated third parties were more likely to occur in countries with stronger investor protections. Further, multinational parents decreased their ownership stakes, financing, and scale of operations in host economies with weaker institutional environments. The evidence from cross-border M&A transactions corroborates

BOX 4-1. Brexit: Implications for European M&A

Given potential disruptions from uncertainty about Britain's exit from the European Union, it is worth examining European M&A activity in more detail. Panels A and B of table 4-6 describe both numbers and values of transactions. The table treats the European Union (without the United Kingdom) as one large country to explicitly consider the importance of the United Kingdom in intra-European cross-border M&A activity.

Panel A examines the frequency of transactions between 2000 and 2017. The columns (targets) and rows (acquirers) classify countries and regions as the EU bloc (excluding the United Kingdom), the United Kingdom, Non-EU European countries, and the rest of the world. The diagonal elements of the table, therefore, represent domestic M&A activity for each of these classifications. The top left quadrant represents M&A activity between and within the European Union and the United Kingdom. The patterns are striking. Intra-EU (domestic) M&A activity (about 28,000 transactions) accounts for more than 60 percent of the approximately 44,000 total domestic and cross-border M&A transactions, and in about 35 percent of the 44,000 transactions, one-party is from the European Union and the other from the United Kingdom. Of the 15,432 EU-U.K. cross-border transactions, 70 percent involve U.K. acquirers and EU targets, while EU firm acquisitions of U.K. targets account for 30 percent.

The data show that a disproportionate fraction of European M&A activity is intra-European. But in M&A flows between the European Union and the United Kingdom, a significantly higher proportion of the acquirers are based in the United Kingdom. The overwhelming representation of U.K. acquirers is also evident if we include Non-EU European countries in the mix. In cross-border transactions across Europe, nearly 40 percent of the acquirers and 15 percent of the targets were based in the United Kingdom. It is not clear how Brexit will affect cross-border M&A flows in Europe. It is worth noting that U.K. acquirers accounted for 36 percent of the cross-border M&A flows from Europe to the rest of the world. Notably, 8,511 transactions involved pairs of firms from the United States and the United Kingdom. There were 2,898 transactions between U.K. acquirers, and U.S. targets—40 percent of outbound M&A from the United Kingdom to the rest of the world and 5,613 transactions involve U.S. acquirers and U.K. targets—55 percent of inbound M&A into the United Kingdom from the rest of the world. Britain's partnerships with countries outside the EU bloc will doubtless remain significant.

Panel B shows the breakdown of M&A activity based on the value of the transactions. A similar picture of U.K. dominance on the acquirer-side emerges. Valued at US$487 billion, U.K.-based acquirers account for 75 percent of cross-border M&A activity between the United Kingdom and the EU bloc. Including non-EU countries, U.K. acquirers account for 40 percent of the total value of cross-border transactions within Europe and 10 percent of the total value of cross-border transactions globally.

The United Kingdom clearly has been an active destination for inbound M&A flows from around the world and also an important acquirer in cross-border M&A. Less clear is what sorts of foreign direct investment policies will emerge in a post-Brexit world. There is uncertainty about what type of regulatory equivalence will operate for the U.K. acquirers and targets in the European Union and how free trade agreements will change between the European Union and United Kingdom. Brexit could affect takeover laws, intellectual property right protections, and employment and tax laws.

Foreign firms that used the United Kingdom as a gateway to European markets may have to rethink their cross-border M&A strategies. Acquiring operations in an EU country may help international firms retain European market access but divert activity away from the United Kingdom. Conversely, the rapid depreciation of the British pound and post-referendum share prices may present opportunistic buying opportunities in the United Kingdom.

Ultimately, cross-border M&A activity involving the United Kingdom and the European Union will depend on the exact form Brexit takes and the precise nature of the United Kingdom's arrangements with the European Union. For example, if the United Kingdom follows the "Norwegian model"—that is, leaves the European Union but joins the European Economic Area and the European Free Trade Association and allows for the free movement of capital, labor, and trade—it will retain access to the single market. This model also means that the EU Takeover Directive and EU Merger Regulations will continue to apply to U.K.-based firms.

Conversely, the "Swiss model," which would require the United Kingdom to negotiate bilateral agreements with EU countries individually, would give the United Kingdom greater flexibility to change its laws but also require changing the regulatory framework governing foreign firms considering the United Kingdom as an M&A investment destination. Complete exit from the European Union and the single market would leave the United Kingdom the choice of relying on World Trade Organization rules to engage with the European Union or negotiating an entirely new free trade agreement. And, complete exit would pose the most significant uncertainty regarding the regulatory framework governing M&A activity involving the United Kingdom.[a]

---

a. For an excellent summary of legal issues, see Sam Pearse, "What Could Brexit Mean for M&A?" July 15, 2016, www.pillsburylaw.com/images/content/1/0/v2/104451/AcquisitionsDaily-Pearse-July152016.pdf.

TABLE 4-6. European M&A Activity

PANEL A. Number of M&A transactions

	Target region				
Acquirer Region	European Union (Excl. U.K.)	United Kingdom	Non-EU	Rest of the world	Total
European Union (Excl. U.K.)	27,658	4,662	5,892	13,121	51,333
United Kingdom	10,770	1,130	889	7,410	20,199
Non-EU	4,883	785	1,460	2,451	9,579
Rest of the world	20,602	10,188	3,457	69,219	103,466
Total	63,913	15,386	9,424	77,589	166,312

PANEL B. Total value of M&A transactions (US$ billion)

	Target region				
Acquirer Region	European Union (Excl. U.K.)	United Kingdom	Non-EU	Rest of the world	Total
European Union (Excl. U.K.)	1,337	164	329	930	2,760
United Kingdom	487	34	49	405	976
Non-EU	162	34	92	219	507
Rest of the world	1,069	510	270	3165	5,014
Total	3,055	742	540	4679	9,016

some of these patterns. The section "Determinants of Cross-Border M&A" explores the motivations for acquiring control in greater detail.

DETERMINANTS OF CROSS-BORDER M&A

When looking at the organization of firms across borders, a natural first-order question is why multinational enterprises exist at all or why firms choose to become multinational enterprises. In theory, in a world of complete contracting (one in which the parties to agreements could specify their rights and duties for every possible state of the world), global firms could outsource production at various stages of the value chain to third parties via arm's-length contracts. Outsourcing is evident across numerous industries where segments of the production process are fragmented across suppliers and countries. Therefore, the rationale for keeping stages of production within the boundaries of the firm across borders must depend on what drives firms to maintain control over their international operations. Fact 14 suggests that the pattern of control acquisition in cross-border transactions varies across developed- and emerging-market acquirers.

Theories of firm organization often put forward contracting frictions as a primary rationale for extending firm boundaries. In the context of multinational firms, these contracting frictions can span vastly different institutional settings around the world—with varying investor and legal protections that lie at the heart of enforcing property rights. These institutional differences can be particularly important in industries that are research-and-development intensive or specialize in intangible asset production where the protection of intellectual property is paramount. Multinational parents may, therefore, be more likely to share proprietary technologies and intangible assets when they acquire majority control of the target, especially in settings with non-verifiable monitoring and weak investor protection.

Like domestic M&A, in theory, the potential for synergies or the creation of surplus value is an important rationale for firms acquiring targets across borders. If foreign owners run domestic firms more efficiently, the transfer of ownership from domestic to foreign hands can lead to efficiency gains and be welfare-improving (Krugman (1998)). Therefore, the question arises of whether the transfer of ownership through cross-border mergers and acquisitions generates surplus value. Alternatively, how profitable are these transactions? Several studies examine this question.

Borrowing from a vast literature on mergers and acquisitions in corporate finance, Chari (2007) turned to the stock market for an answer. Since stock prices represent the present discounted value of expected future cash flows, changes in stock prices provide estimates of surplus value creation at the time of foreign acquisition announcements. In particular, on the date of a foreign M&A transaction announcement, changes in acquirer- and target-firm stock prices reveal information about the potential wealth creation from the transaction. Changes in market-weighted joint returns for acquirers and targets can, therefore, serve as summary statistics for M&A value creation (Andrade, Mitchell, and Stafford (2001))—in other words, can help assess the profitability of M&A.

Using announcement returns offers an advantage because the effects of M&A on productivity or other measures of economic output may occur over many years. The stock market, in contrast, assesses the discounted value of future cash flows and provides an immediate indicator of whether investments are expected to generate value for the acquirer firm's shareholders.

Buiter (2006) argued that FDI flows are extraordinarily productive and profitable because they come bundled with investors' technical and managerial skills and knowledge. Therefore, the cumulated historical value of these cross-border M&A flows likely represents but a small fraction of the fair or fundamental value today of the equity claims on the assets abroad. Surplus value creation (or profitability) through the transfer of control is likely to be high if the investing country is very different from the recipient country; for example, investments from developed markets to risky emerging markets. However, putting a firm figure on the value of these flows is daunting (Buiter (2006)). Abnormal announcement returns associated with M&A transactions can be used to estimate the market-capitalized returns generated by developed-market M&A flows to emerging markets.

In Chari (2007), I focused on developed to emerging market, cross-border M&A flows and used a transaction-level dataset (the Securities Data Corporation (SDC) Thompson's International Mergers and Acquisitions database) to identify transactions from 1988 to 2003. Similar to the Zephyr database, the SDC data provide information about the transacting parties, the dates the acquisitions were announced and completed, the stakes sought by the acquiring firms, and a variety of other transaction characteristics, such as deal size and method of payment. The stock-price information comes from Datastream, Bloomberg, and national stock exchanges.

The data confirm that foreign acquisitions in emerging markets create surplus value. On average, following a foreign acquisition announcement, market capitalization–weighted joint returns for targets and acquirers increase a statistically significant 5.8 percent when majority control is acquired. The joint-return increases are robust to the inclusion of controls for country, time, industrial diversification, method-of-payment effects, as well as acquirer- and target-firm characteristics such as size and liquidity. The findings are consistent with studies that conclude that FDI results in improved productivity (Aitkin and Harrison (1999)) and that productivity gains that resulted from FDI are concentrated in plants where multinational firms acquire majority or full ownership (Perez-Gonzalez (2004)).

The findings also suggest that acquiring majority control may be a necessary prerequisite to improving productivity, especially in countries where it is difficult to write or enforce complete contracts. Since ineffective monitoring and incomplete contracting are especially relevant in emerging markets, by acquiring majority control, developed-market acquirers in effect extend the boundaries of the firm across borders to encompass the emerging-market targets.

Similarly, in Chari, Ouimet, and Tesar (2010), we examined shareholder value gains from cross-border mergers and acquisitions involving developed-country acquirers and emerging-market targets. For a sample of 390 transactions, we found that market-adjusted returns total US$111.5 billion for acquiring-firm shareholders. On average, acquirers realize a positive return of 4.43 percent when they announce the acquisition of control of a publicly held target from an emerging market. The median net return ratio (acquirer's dollar value gain/transaction value) is 1.37 when control of an emerging-market target transfers to a developed-market acquirer. The study found that improved governance (via control rights) and the transfer of intangibles (such as research and development or brand value) from acquirers to targets explained the revaluation in acquirer stock prices and the resulting dollar-value gains in emerging-market transactions.

Another set of explanations for cross-border M&A focuses on imperfect capital market integration across countries. Multinational firms with deep pockets can make purchases around the world, especially when foreign assets are available cheaply. These explanations rely on financial frictions in international capital markets as determinants of cross-border M&A. For example, Erel, Liao, and Weisbach (2015) examined differences in valuations between acquirer and target firms, which can vary substantially over time or any pair of countries as exchange rates and stock markets fluctuate. The authors find that countries with appreciated currencies are more likely to have acquiring firms, while firms in countries where currencies have depreciated are more likely to be targets. Valuation differences may also explain the wave nature of M&A activity (fact 7).

Baker, Wurgler, and Foley (2009) suggested a role for cross-border arbitrage by multinational firms. Their study found that FDI flows increased sharply as source-country stock market valuations rose and suggested a "cheap financial capital" channel in which FDI flows in part reflect the use of relatively low-cost capital available to parent firms overvalued in their own countries. Similarly, Erel and others (2015) found that firms in countries with high-performing stock markets were more likely to be buyers, while firms in countries with relatively poor-performing stock markets tended to be targets.

Blonigen, Fontagne, Sly, and Toubal (2012) also found a valuation effect that drives cross-border M&A: productivity losses among target firms provide an opportunity for multinational acquirers to obtain desired assets relatively cheaply. Finally, Erel and others (2014) provided evidence that, in a large sample of European acquisitions, both foreign and domestic acquisitions ease financial frictions in target firms. They found that the investment levels of target firms increased significantly following an acquisition.

Studies of cross-border M&A that examine financial frictions also focus on a "cheap assets" channel labeled "fire-sale FDI." Countries with financial crises provide ample opportunity to purchase liquidity-constrained and otherwise stressed assets at bargain prices. To explain the surge in foreign acquisitions of Asian firms during the 1997–98 financial crisis at a time when portfolio investors were fleeing from Asia, Krugman (1998) first put forward the idea of fire-sale FDI. Krugman provided anecdotal evidence from the financial press that sharp nominal exchange rate depreciations combined with a rapid deterioration in domestic macroeconomic conditions severely constrained domestic firms' liquidity. As a result, foreign investors purchased distressed domestic firms at discounted, or fire-sale, prices. Motivated by this idea, Aguiar and Gopinath (2005) found evidence of fire-sale FDI in East Asia during the Asian financial crisis. Specifically, countries that experienced dramatic reversals in portfolio equity and debt flows simultaneously experienced an increase in foreign acquisitions, particularly of liquidity-constrained firms.

Acharya and Shin (2009) developed a theoretical model that explains an inflow of FDI and outflow of foreign portfolio investment during financial crises. They show that the transfer of control in the form of direct ownership of failed firms' assets can circumvent agency problems—namely, a divergence between shareholder and manager objectives, but during crises, efficient owners (such as other domestic firms) also face financing constraints. The result is a transfer of ownership to foreign firms at fire-sale prices. Their model predicts that this fire-sale FDI should be associated with flipping acquired firms back to domestic owners once the crisis abates.

However, the evidence regarding fire-sale FDI is mixed. In Chari (2007), I used stock returns to examine whether foreign acquirers took advantage of cash-strapped targets during crises. By exploiting the cross-time variation in acquiring firm returns, I investigated whether the gains to acquiring firms increased significantly during crises compared with relatively calm periods. The results showed that crises do not coincide with substantially higher acquirer returns, suggesting that it is not clear that the developed-market acquisitions represent fire sales by firms in emerging markets. The crises (especially in Asia) coincide with the deregulation of the market for corporate control. Several countries liberalized their M&A laws, making it easier for foreign companies to acquire domestic firms under the policy direction of the International Monetary Fund. Therefore, it is important to recognize that crisis period returns also reflect these liberalization measures.

Similarly, Alquist, Mukherjee, and Tesar (2016) developed a model to compare cross-border acquisitions during financial crises with acquisitions during non-crisis periods. The study cited two motivations for foreign acquisitions: first, a liquidity motive where foreign-firm acquisitions relax credit constraints on the targets and, second, a synergistic motive where acquisitions exploit operational synergies between the target and the acquirer. The authors suggested that during crises, credit conditions tighten in the target economy and the liquidity motive dominates. Their model predicts that during crises, relative to non-crisis periods, (1) foreign acquisitions are more likely; (2) the proportion of foreign acquisitions that involve industry diversification are higher; (3) average ownership stakes are lower; and (4) acquisition duration is lower (that is, acquisition stakes are more likely to be flipped). Their empirical analysis found support for the first prediction but not for the remaining three. These results, therefore, suggest that foreign acquisitions in emerging markets do not differ between crises and normal periods in these important ways.[4]

A final set of explanations about the determinants of cross-border M&A activity focuses explicitly on institutions and corporate governance. Legal and institutional features can significantly affect the property rights setting and the incomplete contracting problem. In Chari and others (2009), we examined whether the ability of developed-market acquirers to bring better institutional practices to emerging-market targets may drive up expected future cash flows (Coffee (1999)). We used the legal and institutional measures proposed by La Porta and others (1998) as proxies for institutional differences between countries in our sample.

The study found that acquirers from countries with better investor protections experienced significant gains after the announcement of majority control of a target in a country with weak investor protections. However, these gains only occurred when the acquirer attained control of the target. The results are consistent with our hypothesis that, with control, acquirers can bond target firms to the institutions in their home countries, increasing shareholder value.

Other international M&A studies focus on the gains to target firms when they are acquired by firms operating in an environment with better investor protection. For example, Rossi and Volpin (2004) showed that firms in countries with inadequate investor protections are more likely to be targets in cross-border acquisitions. Bris and Cabolis (2008) found—using a sample of developed- and emerging-market transactions for wholly acquired targets—that targets' abnormal returns increase with better shareholder protection and accounting standards in the acquirer's country of origin.

While numerous reasons motivate firms to make cross-border acquisitions, a few major themes broadly summarize these transactions. First, factors that drive cross-border control acquisition, referred to in fact 14, are key and fall under the rationales of protecting intellectual property or improving corporate governance structures, especially in countries with weak institutions. Second, valuation differences between acquirer- and target-firm countries, referred to in fact 7, are either due to stock market valuations or exchange rates in source countries (booms or appreciations) or destination countries (most frequently, crises and depreciations). Finally, the rules of the game (deregulation or protectionism) or changes in regulatory frameworks lead to significant changes in the ownership patterns of firms across borders and the organization of global supply chains.

POST-ACQUISITION OUTCOMES

In the context of foreign acquisition of domestic targets, it is important to examine whether foreign ownership leads to improvements in firm-profitability or plant-productivity.[5] Studies about the effects of FDI focus on plant-level productivity measures, such as total factor productivity (TFP) or labor productivity (output per worker). Antras, Desai, and Foley (2009) documented the productivity-improving role of U.S. multinational firms.

Fukao and others (2006) showed that Japanese target firms that received foreign investment experienced rapid improvement in productivity and profitability compared with Japanese firms acquired by domestic firms. Akben-Selçuk (2008) found the same result using data on Turkish firms. Doms and Jensen (1998) also found that foreign-owned companies in their sample were more productive than domestically owned ones. Studies of industrial-country firm acquisitions of developing-country targets indicate that both parties' valuations improve following the transactions (Chari, Ouimet, and Tesar (2009)). In the developed-market context, Girma and coauthors, in a series of papers concentrating on acquisition targets in the United Kingdom, documented improved firm performance following foreign acquisitions.

The return on assets (ROA) of targets following their acquisition is the most direct test of the performance of developed-market acquisitions. In Chari and others (2009), we investigated a change in ROA in the second year following cross-border acquisition for a sample of developed- and emerging-market targets and found a correlation between the transfer of majority control of emerging-market targets and higher post-acquisition ROA.[6] We also found that (1) stock-financed acquisitions are associated with lower accounting returns; (2) transactions where the acquirer comes from an industry with high patent-intensity correlate with higher accounting returns; and (3) the acquisition of emerging-market targets is associated with higher accounting returns than the acquisition of developed-market targets.

After a spate of emerging-market acquisitions of U.S. firms, in Chari, Chen, and Dominguez (2012), we analyzed the performance of firms acquired by firms in emerging markets. We examined stock prices, accounting measures, and employment outcomes. In the study, abnormal announcement returns provided a forward-looking estimate of expected shareholder value creation. We also examined post-acquisition changes in other aspects of target-firm operations, such as property, plant, and equipment (PP&E), employment, and sales. We evaluated post-acquisition changes in accounting measures of performance, such as profitability, investment, and sales, as well as employment outcomes in U.S. targets that were acquired by emerging-market firms.

Our results suggested that emerging-market firms tended to acquire public targets with relatively high levels of sales, employment, and total assets. We also found that the stock price response of target firms was positive and significant around the time of the acquisition announcement. On average, target stock price returns on a cumulated basis over a three-day window around the acquisition announcement date increased by 8 percent. This abnormal return remains significant and positive for extended windows of ten and twenty-one business days. Consistent with the positive announcement returns, we found that, after the acquisition, the profitability of acquired targets improved. The target firm's ROA increased by 7 percent in the five years following the acquisition.

We also found strong evidence that acquiring firms significantly restructured target firms. Measures of employment, sales, and PP&E in the target firms all declined in the post-acquisition years. This pattern of increasing profits (income as a percent of assets) but declining sales is consistent with post-acquisition firm-efficiency improvements. For instance, if acquiring firms shut down or sell unprofitable divisions, declining sales by the target firm will be accompanied by rising profits. The decline in employment and net PP&E we observed also suggests downsizing to improve overall profitability as a percent of assets.

Employment downsizing is consistent with a comparative-input-cost hypothesis, given that emerging-market acquirers may take advantage of low wages in their home countries by cutting labor-intensive activities in the United States following an acquisition. Whereas industrial-country acquirers often seek emerging markets for their lower labor costs, emerging-market acquirers can relocate (or in-source) manufacturing activity while keeping existing distribution networks in the host country of the acquired business.

Chen (2011) explored whether the acquirer's country of origin matters for post-acquisition target performance. Compared with domestic acquisitions, Chen found that target firms acquired by foreign firms experienced higher returns on assets. However, the channels of performance improvement varied across foreign acquirer types. Emerging market acquisitions led to reductions in sales and employment, whereas acquisitions by industrial-country firms increased sales and employment in targets. This study showed that targets experience similar patterns in performance improvements and restructuring processes after being acquired by emerging-market firms, as found by the Chari and others (2012) study.

A wide body of literature documents the economy-wide effects of FDI on economic growth. (See Alfaro and Johnson (2012) for a nice survey.) The evidence suggests that FDI can affect target sectors through competition, technology diffusion, and so on, and the beneficial effects generally depend on the strength of local institutions. It is possible that cross-border M&A activity also generates these types of positive effects.

In general, a wide body of evidence suggests that cross-border mergers and acquisitions are key drivers of productivity improvements in target firms, with spillovers to other firms in the destination countries. This evidence is generally consistent with the broader evidence related to the productivity-enhancing role of foreign direct investment. The productivity-improvement patterns also contrast with purely domestic M&A activity, where the evidence about value creation is more mixed. However, both cross-border and domestic M&A result in reorganizations that fundamentally change, in terms of employment and capital investment, the structure of the merged firms and the industries to which they belong.

POLICY CONSIDERATIONS

A rapid increase in foreign acquisitions often generates a heated debate in host countries. Popular sentiment sees little value to the host nation in foreign acquisitions that merely transfer existing assets from domestic to foreign hands.[7] For instance, in the aftermath of the Asian crisis, following a spate of foreign acquisitions, Prime Minister Mahathir of Malaysia proclaimed, "If we are not careful, we will be recolonized."[8] Furthermore, foreign acquisitions coinciding with crises in the host nations have the added controversy of domestic firms being forced to liquidate assets at fire-sale prices (Krugman (1998)).

In the United States, a spate of acquisitions by foreign firms also produces consternation in policy circles. For example, considerable resistance met, and ultimately thwarted, the proposed acquisition of commercial operations at six U.S. ports by Dubai Ports World in 2006, and the 2005 bid by CNOOC—the Chinese state-owned oil company—to acquire Unocal. Unocal ultimately favored Chevron's lower offer of US$17.4 billion over CNOOC's. Another high-profile emerging-market acquisition was the Indian Tata Motors 2008 purchase of Ford's Jaguar and Land Rover divisions. More recently, in 2013, China's biggest pork producer, Shuanghui International, acquired Smithfield Foods, the nearly hundred-year-old Virginia-based meat giant, for US$4.7 billion in cash.

Policy implications stemming from cross-border M&A activity, therefore, arise from two separate concerns. When foreign firms try to acquire domestic natural resources or critical technology, it is legitimate to ask whether national security may be compromised. On the other hand, if national security is not at risk, nationalist sentiments such as those expressed by Prime Minister Mahathir often play a role in whether cross-border acquisitions are completed or derailed.

An interesting study by Dinc and Erel (2013) examined the impact of economic nationalism on cross-border mergers and acquisitions. Using data from the European Union for more than ten years, the study documented government reactions to significant corporate M&A attempts. The paper presented compelling evidence for widespread economic nationalism where governments prefer that firms remain domestically owned. Moreover, these preferences were stronger in countries with active far-right parties and weak governments. The study showed that nationalist government reactions not only affect the outcome of M&A transactions but also deter future foreign investment in these countries.

The United States remains the largest recipient of FDI flows in the world. It is also the largest provider of direct investment abroad. In 2017, total FDI in the United States was US$4.03 trillion and U.S. direct investment abroad was US$6.01 trillion (Bureau of Economic Analysis, U.S. Department of Commerce). Historically, the United States has therefore taken an open and rules-based approach to foreign investment flows and more or less allowed the market to determine the extent and nature of these flows. However, increasingly, foreign acquisitions considered threats to either the security of critical technologies or natural resources are under review by the interagency Committee on Foreign Investment in the United States (CFIUS).

Consideration of economic threats under the umbrella of national security has also increased. Congressional scrutiny of the review process at CFIUS has increased with the emergence of state-owned enterprises as acquirers and the attempted foreign acquisitions of sensitive and critical technologies. CFIUS reviews these transactions to determine whether they threaten to impair national security, or whether the foreign entity is government-controlled and the transaction would result in control of any "critical infrastructure that could impair the national security."[9] CFIUS regulations apply directly to cross-border M&A. Between 2008 and 2015, CFIUS received 925 notices from foreign investors of plans to acquire, take over, or merge with a U.S. firm.

In 2018, the CFIUS statute was amended through the Foreign Investment Risk Review Modernization Act (FIRRMA), which expanded the scope of transactions subject to CFIUS review to include, for example, foreign purchases of distressed assets or bankrupt firms to acquire critical technologies. It is worth noting that, to date, spanning three administrations, only six foreign M&A transactions (five involving Chinese acquirers) were blocked by presidential action based on CFIUS recommendations.

Fundamental policy issues, therefore, arise in weighing the benefits of foreign investment against national security interests. Foreign investment can create jobs, spur local investment, and contribute to tax revenues at the state, local, and federal levels. Strategically, how can the United States, the biggest beneficiary of inward foreign direct investment, protect its national security interests while promoting a liberalized international economic order that facilitates U.S. investment abroad and encourages the free movement of capital across other countries' borders?

At the same time, how should policymakers determine whether foreign investment in an industry (critical or not) is too high or too concentrated? Do these concerns outweigh the functioning of a free and efficient market for international corporate control? Additionally, how should national security be defined in a rapidly evolving global economic and technological landscape? These are some of the open policy questions that will directly affect cross-border M&A, for which easy answers will be hard to come by and in all likelihood continue to be handled on a case-by-case basis rather than by policy decree.

While CFIUS scrutiny has gained importance in the United States, EU antitrust issues have also heated up. The European Commission must be notified of planned mergers and acquisitions of firms that do significant business in the European Union if the combined businesses exceed certain revenue thresholds.[10] If the commission concludes that a merger would distort competition, it may block it unless the companies propose remedies. More than 7,500 cases have been referred to the commission since 1990, and 30 cases were blocked on anti-competitive grounds.

In 2019, for example, EU regulators blocked the proposed merger between rail manufacturers Siemens and Alstom, leading to calls from Germany and France for an overhaul of EU competition policy to better meet global challenges such as competition from China. Other examples include the prohibition of a joint venture between Tata Steel and ThyssenKrupp, and the rejection of a bid by the German copper company Wieland-Werke AG to buy a business unit from Aurubis, Europe's biggest copper smelter, on the grounds that the deals were anti-competitive and would lead to increased prices for different types of steel and copper.

The European Union's merger review process has been controversial, given instances of mergers that were approved by non-European regulatory authorities but rejected by the European Commission. For example, the U.S. Department of Justice cleared the US$42 billion acquisition of Honeywell by General Electric in 2001, but the European Commission blocked it.[11] Critics argue that the European merger policy advances protectionist industrial policy rather than competition (Bradford and others (2018)).[12] U.S. officials have charged that the commission deviates from the norm that "the antitrust laws protect competition, not competitors" and accused the commission of "using its merger-review process as a tool to protect and promote European industry at the expense of U.S. competitors." U.S. tech giants such as Apple, Google, Facebook, chipmaker Broadcomm, and Amazon have faced high-profile investigations and been fined by the commission for antitrust violations. Looking ahead, antitrust considerations loom large in the context of cross-border M&A in the European Union.

More generally, a broad range of public policy issues around cross-border M&A arise as governments weigh the balance of the potential benefits of M&A activity (for example, increased productivity growth, inward flows of capital financing, technological diffusion) against the potential costs (loss of markets to foreign firms, a loss of corporate control, national security concerns, and greater market concentration). Here, as in many instances, some countries might welcome greenfield investment, but not foreign firms taking over their domestic companies.

CONCLUDING REMARKS

This chapter documents salient features of recent trends in cross-border M&A activity around the world. Transactions-level data show that over the past two decades, cross-border mergers and acquisitions comprised nearly 50 percent of FDI flows. The number of cross-border M&A transactions has tripled over the past two decades. It is interesting to note that cross-border M&A activity is highly concentrated among a small set of countries. In particular, both in numbers and value of transactions, the United States and Europe dominate the market for international corporate control.

The industrial composition of acquirers shows the rising global dominance of the service sector. Further, a significant fraction of cross-border M&A involve industry diversification integrating global value chains across borders. Similar to domestic M&A, cross-border M&A transactions occur in waves—over the past two decades, there were two waves: one that peaked in 2007 before the global financial crisis and a second that peaked in 2015. Successive waves are bigger; both the numbers of transactions and the value of transactions increase dramatically. The past decade also saw the rise of mega-deals, or deals greater than US$10 billion, in cross-border M&A.

Acquirers in cross-border M&A tend to be considerably larger than target firms. The median acquirer is five times larger than the median target firm. For the most part, firms involved in cross-border M&A deals are privately held, and cash is the predominant form of payment in these transactions. The importance of private-equity transactions in cross-border M&A has increased over time and around the globe. Further, a group of tax-haven countries play a significant role in cross-border M&A transactions.

The data show that the pattern of control acquisition in cross-border transactions varies across developed and emerging-market acquirers. Alternative motivations and incentives for acquiring control across borders range from extending the boundaries of the firm to encompass foreign targets in settings of unverifiable and costly monitoring, to providing liquidity to financially constrained target firms. The evidence suggests that by and large target profitability improves following acquisitions, and the acquisitions seem to create significant surplus value. However, it is also the case that employment and investment can be affected if foreign acquirers significantly restructure target firms. The chapter concludes with a discussion of policy implications as policymakers weigh national security concerns against a desire to increase foreign investment in their economies.

NOTES

I thank Sharjil Haque for stellar research assistance and Steve Kamin for a thoughtful discussion of an earlier draft.

1. Zephyr's glossary defines "merger" as follows: "A true merger is, in reality, actually quite rare, and many acquisitions are incorrectly described as 'mergers' in the press. In a true merger, there is a one-for-one share swap for shares in the new company, and the deal involves a 'merging of equals.' If the swap is not on equal terms, the deal would be coded as an acquisition. However, in a true merger, the original companies are entered into the deal record as the acquirer and the target (in no particular order). In the case of a three-way (or more) merger, multiple companies can be entered in both acquirer and target fields. Where a Newco has been used, the Newco is added as the acquirer and the newly merged company as the target. The newly merged company name would be added to the comments. Mergers do often occur as 'partnerships,' and are most typically carried out by organizations such as law firms and accountancy firms."

2. Donald M. DePamphilis, "Why Merger and Acquisition Waves Occur," understandingmanda (website), October 10, 2009, https://understandingmanda.wordpress.com/article/why-merger-and-acquisition-waves-occur-2y7l67l8la2ns-19/.

3. CITIC Limited, *2014 Annual Report*, www1.hkexnews.hk/listedco/listconews/sehk/2015/0417/ltn20150417394.pdf.

4. Using data on M&A transactions from 27 EU countries from 1999 to 2012, Wietzel, Kling, and Gerritson (2014) find little evidence for "fire-sale FDI," suggesting an integrated European market without significant financial frictions. Similarly, Stoddard and Noy (2015) find that financial crises have a significant adverse impact on FDI flows and M&A activity. They also do not find empirical evidence of fire-sale FDI.

5. See, for example, Caves (1996); Aitken and Harrison (1999); Perez-Gonzales (2004); Arnold and Javorcik (2005); and Petkova (2008). Aitken and Harrison (1999) concluded from a sample of Venezuelan firms that foreign ownership is correlated with productivity improvements. Arnold and Javorcik (2005) used Indonesian plant-level data and found that foreign ownership led to significant improvements in productivity in the year of acquisition as well as in subsequent years. Petkova (2008) conducted a study using Indian plant-level data and concluded that foreign-owned plants experienced improvements in productivity three years following foreign investment. In the literature concerned with spillovers from FDI, Aitken and Harrison (1999) found adverse effects on domestic firm productivity from FDI. Javorcik (2004) identified positive FDI spillover effects on domestic firms through backward linkages.

6. Standard accounting rules stipulate that firms must include the profits or losses of any majority-owned subsidiaries in their consolidated accounting statements. Thus, in cases of control acquisition, the acquirer's accounting performance includes the target's performance.

7. "When Japanese-owned Bridgestone takes control over the U.S. firm Firestone . . . in such an acquisition, there is no investment expenditure; merely an international transfer in the title of corporate assets." See K. A. Froot, "Japanese Foreign Direct Investment," NBER Working Paper No. 3737, June 1991, and *U.S.-Japan Economic*

Forum, vol. 1, edited by M. Feldstein and Y. Kosai, National Bureau of Economic Research and Japan Center for Economic Research, 1991.

8. Televised speech, January 29, 1998.

9. James K. Jackson, "The Committee on Foreign Investment in the United States (CFIUS)," Congressional Research Service, updated February 14, 2020, https://fas.org/sgp/crs/natsec/RL33388.pdf, 22.

10. The commission enforces merger control in the European Union, on the basis of the merger regulation (ec.europa.eu/competition/mergers/legislation/regulations.html#merger_reg).

11. See MacLaren (2001).

12. Anu Bradford, Robert Jackson, and Jonathan Zytnick, "Does the European Union Use Its Antitrust Power for Protectionism?" ProMarket, April 3, 2018, https://promarket.org/european-union-use-antitrust-power-protectionism/.

REFERENCES

Acharya, Viral V., Hyun-Song Shin, and Tanju Yorulmazer. 2011b. "Fire-Sale FDI," *Korean Economic Review*, 27 (2): 163–202.

Aguiar, Mark and Gita Gopinath. 2005. "Fire-Sale FDI and Liquidity Crises," *Review of Economics and Statistics*, 87 (3): 439–52.

Aitken, Brian J. and Ann E. Harrison. 1999. "Do Domestic Firms Benefit from Direct Foreign Investment? Evidence from Venezuela," *American Economic Review*, 89: 605–18.

Alfaro, Laura and Andrew Charlton. 2009. "Intra-Industry Foreign Direct Investment," *American Economic Review*, 99 (5): 2096–2119.

Alfaro, Laura and Matthew Johnson. 2012. "Foreign Direct Investment and Growth," in *The Evidence and Impact of Financial Globalization*, edited by Gerard Caprio (Elsevier, Netherlands), 299–307.

Alquist, Ron, Rahul Mukherjee, and Linda Tesar. 2016. "Fire Sale FDI or Business as Usual?" *Journal of International Economics*, 98: 93–113.

Akben-Selcuk, Elif. 2008. "The Impact of Cross-Border M&A Target Company Performance: Evidence from Turkey," *Economics Bulletin*, 13 (5): 1–9.

Andrade, Gregor, Mark Mitchell, and Erik Stafford. 2001. "New Evidence and Perspectives on Mergers," *Journal of Economic Perspectives*, 15 (2): 103–20.

Antras, Pol, Mihir Desai, and Fritz Foley. 2009. "Multinational Firms, FDI Flows and Imperfect Capital Markets," *Quarterly Journal of Economics*, 124 (3): 1171–1219.

Arnold, Jens M. and Beata S. Javorcik. 2005. "Gifted Kids or Pushy Parents? Foreign Acquisitions and Plant Performance in Indonesia," Development Studies Working Paper No. 197. Centro Studi Luca D'Agliano, March.

Baker, Malcolm, C. Fritz Foley, Jeffrey Wurgler. 2009. "Multinationals as Arbitrageurs: The Effect of Stock Market Valuations on Foreign Direct Investment," *Review of Financial Studies*, 22 (1): 337–69.

Blonigen, Bruce, Lionel Fontagne, and Nicholas Sly, and Farid Toubal. 2014. "Cherries for Sale: Incidence and Timing of Cross-Border M&A," *Journal of International Economics*, 94: 341–57.

Bris, Arturo and Christos Cabolis. 2008. "The Value of Investor Protection: Evidence from Cross-Border Mergers," *Review of Financial Studies*, 21 (2): 605–48.

Buiter, Willem. 2006. "Dark Matter or Cold Fusion?" Goldman Sachs Global Economics Paper No. 136. January. www.nber.org/~wbuiter/dark.pdf.

Caves, Richard. 1996. *Multinational Enterprise and Economic Analysis* (Cambridge University Press).

Chari, Anusha. 2007. The Net Present Value of Foreign Direct Investment. Mimeo.

Chari, Anusha, Paige Ouimet, and Linda Tesar. 2010. "The Value of Control in Emerging Markets," *Review of Financial Studies*, 23 (4): 1741–70.

Chari, Anusha, Wenjie Chen, and Kathryn M. E. Dominguez. 2012. "Foreign Ownership and Firm Performance: Emerging Market Acquisitions in the United States," *IMF Economic Review*, 60: 1–42.

Chen, Wenjie. 2011. "Does the Country of Origin of the Acquiring Firm Impact Performance?" *Journal of International Economics*, 83 (2): 219–28.

de Bodt, Eric, Jean-Gabriel Cousin, and Richard Roll. 2018. "Full-Stock-Payment Marginalization in Merger and Acquisition Transactions," *Management Science*, 64 (2): 760–83.

Desai, Mihir A., C. Fritz Foley, and James R. Hines Jr. 2006. "The Demand for Tax Haven Operations," *Journal of Public Economics*, 90 (3): 513–31.

Dharmapala, Dhammika. 2008. "What Problems and Opportunities Are Created by Tax Havens?" *Oxford Review of Economic Policy*, 24 (4): 661–79.

Dharmapala, Dhammika. 2018. "The Consequences of the Tax Cut and Jobs Act's International Provisions: Lessons from Existing Research," *National Tax Journal*, 71 (4): 707–28.

Doms, Mark E. and J. Bradford Jensen. 1998. "Comparing Wages, Skills, and Productivity Between Domestically and Foreign-Owned Manufacturing Establishments in the United States," in *Geography and Ownership as Bases for Economic Accounting*, edited by R. E. Baldwin, R. E. Lipsey, and J. D. Richardson (University of Chicago Press): 235–58. NBER Book Series Studies in Income and Wealth, vol. 59.

Dinc, I. Serdar and Isil Erel. 2013. "Economic Nationalism in Mergers and Acquisitions," *Journal of Finance*, 68: 2471-2514.

Erel, Isil, Rose C. Liao, and Michael S. Weisbach. 2012. "Determinants of Cross-Border Mergers and Acquisitions," *Journal of Finance*, 67 (3): 1045–83.

Erel, Isil, Yeejin Jang, and Michael S. Weisbach. 2015. "Do Acquisitions Relieve Target Firms' Financial Constraints?" *Journal of Finance*, 70: 289–328.

Evenett, Simon. 2004. "The Cross-Border Mergers and Acquisitions Wave of the Late 1990s," in R. Baldwin and A. Winters, *Challenges to Globalization: Analyzing the Economics* (Boston: National Bureau of Economic Research).

Feld, Lars P., Martin Ruf, Uwe Scheuering, Ulrich Schreiber, and Johannes Voget. 2013. "Effects of Territorial and Worldwide Corporation Tax Systems on Outbound M&As." ZEW-Centre for European Economic Research Discussion Paper 13-088. ZEW-Centre for European Economic Research, Mannheim, Germany.

Fukao, Kyoji, Ito Keiko, Ug Kwon Hyeog, and Takizawa Miho. 2006. "Cross-Border Acquisitions and Target Firms' Performance: Evidence from Japanese Firm-Level Data," NBER Working Paper No. 12422.

Huizinga, Harry P. and Johannes Voget. 2009. "International Taxation and the Direction and Volume of Cross-Border M&As." *Journal of Finance* 64 (3): 1217–49.

Girma, Sourafel. 2005. "Technology Transfer from Acquisition FDI and the Absorptive Capacity of Domestic Firms: An Empirical Investigation," *Open Economics Review*, 16: 175–87.

Girma, Sourafel and Holger Goerg. 2007. "Evaluating Foreign Ownership Wage Premium Using a Difference-in-Differences Matching Approach," *Journal of International Economics*, 72 (1): 97–112.

Girma, Sourafel, Richard Kneller, and Mauro Pisu. 2007. "Do Exporters Have Anything to Learn from Foreign Multinationals?" *European Economics Review*, 51: 981–98.

Javorcik, Beata S. 2004. "Does Foreign Direct Investment Increase the Productivity of Domestic Firms? In Search of Spillovers through Backward Linkages," *American Economic Review*, 94: 605–27.

Krugman, Paul. 2000. *Fire-Sale FDI* (University of Chicago Press).

La Porta, Rafael, Florencio López-de-Silanes, Andrei Shleifer, and Robert Vishny. 1998. "Law and Finance," *Journal of Political Economy*, 106 (6): 1113–55.

MacLaren, Malcolm. 2001. "The GE/Honeywell Merger Case Reaching the Limits of International Competition Policymaking," *German Law Journal*, vol. 2 (12).

Perez-Gonzales, Francisco. 2004. "The Impact of Acquiring Control on Productivity: Evidence from Mexican Manufacturing Plants." Mimeo.

Petkova, Neviana. 2008. "Does Foreign Ownership Lead to Higher Firm Productivity?" Mimeo.

Rossi, Stefano and Paolo Volpin. 2004. "Cross-Country Determinants of Cross-Border Mergers and Acquisitions," *Journal of Financial Economics*, 74: 277–304.

Stoddard, Olga and Ilan Noy. 2015. "Fire-Sale FDI? The Impact of Financial Crises on Foreign Direct Investment," *Review of Development Economics*, 19 (2): 387–99.

Voget, Johannes. 2011. "Relocation of Headquarters and International Taxation," *Journal of Public Economics*, 95 (9): 1067–81.

Weitzel, Utz, Gerhard Kling, and Dirk Gerritsen. 2014. "Testing the Fire-Sale FDI Hypothesis for the European Financial Crisis," *Journal of International Money and Finance*, 49 (PB): 211–34.

5

The Corporate Finance of Multinational Firms

ISIL EREL
YEEJIN JANG
MICHAEL S. WEISBACH

As the world economy has become more integrated, the number of multinational firms has increased. As of 2017, about half of the publicly traded firms in the United States were multinationals.[1] For the average multinational firm, foreign income and sales represented about 40 percent of aggregate income and sales. The extent of multinational firms' international operations was similar for international firms in MSCI World Index of developed countries.[2] As the global economy became more integrated, the fraction of firms with foreign sales also rose rapidly in emerging markets. Given that multinational firms are such significant players in the world economy, understanding their financial policies is important.

Operating in more than one country can affect a firm's financial decisions in several ways. Most important, multinational firms appear to enjoy both a lower cost of finance and a greater access to capital during poor economic times, in large part because they have more flexibility than domestic firms in their potential sources of financing.

In principle, any firm could borrow from any bank in the world or issue public equity or debt in any country. However, it is usually much more cost-effective for firms to raise capital in locations where they have operations (see Jang (2017)). Financing international activities from local capital provides a natural hedge against currency risks. Furthermore, by operating in more than one location, multinational firms have additional choices of where to raise capital, allowing them to obtain lower loan rates and also to diversify their sources of financing, which can be valuable when financing becomes scarce in one part of the world.

In addition, being multinational diversifies a firm's cash flows across countries and minimizes the effect of country-specific shocks. Therefore, multinational firms have lower cash-flow volatility than otherwise similar domestic firms. This lower cash-flow volatility likely reduces a firm's credit risk and cost of financing and increases its overall debt capacity. We document empirically that multinational firms, consistent with their wider choice of borrowing locations, pay lower spreads on their bank loans, holding other factors constant. However, some studies find that being multinational lowers the cost of equity, while others find that it raises the cost of equity.

While multinational firms benefit through diversification of capital sources and from tax arbitrage across countries, they also incur costs. Firms operating in multiple countries are likely to face larger political risks than domestic companies. A multinational company is a "foreign" company in at least one country, and regulatory authorities often discriminate against foreign companies. Dinc and Erel (2013) provide empirical evidence that economic nationalism, defined as a preference for the native firm over the foreign one, has both direct and indirect economic effects on acquisitions and impedes international capital flows. The authors show that governments implement national policies against foreign acquisitions through several methods, including delaying regulatory approvals, using golden shares in previously privatized companies, publicly opposing the deals, and providing financing to the rival bidders from their national banks. Even when a multinational firm is treated well by a host government, it always faces the risk of a policy shift, potentially occurring when the government changes. Domestic firms do not face this political risk.

Multinational firms also face exchange rate risk. They receive revenues in a mix of currencies while their expenses, such as for production costs and interest payments, likely are in a different mix of currencies. Therefore, movements in exchange rates create a mismatch between the income the company receives and its expenses, creating a demand for hedging foreign exchange risk.

This chapter surveys the academic literature on the corporate financing costs and benefits of multinational firms relative to domestic ones. The section following the introduction characterizes multinational firms and presents detailed characteristics of multinationals in the United States and overseas. In the next section, we provide detailed summary statistics on the capital structure of multinational firms and compare their capital structure with the capital structure of domestic firms. The section following discusses the ways firms diversify their sources of financing and the impact of this diversification on multinational firms' financing costs. The next-to-last section discusses the additional risks faced by multinational firms in comparison to the domestic counterparts. The last section provides a short summary.

CHARACTERISTICS OF MULTINATIONAL FIRMS

A multinational firm can be defined in several ways. Since no definition is perfect, we utilize two different approaches. First, we use foreign pretax income to characterize multinational firms. Following Jang (2017), we define a firm as multinational when it reports any foreign income in the previous three years.[3] However, this approach could mischaracterize firms that do not report foreign income when their percentage of foreign income is relatively low compared with their overall income or when it is negative. Therefore, as a second measure, following Denis, Denis, and Yost (2002), we define internationally diversified firms by using information on foreign sales from the Compustat Geographic Segment database in the United States, or Worldscope for foreign firms.[4] Specifically, a firm is defined as multinational if at least 5 percent of its sales are from outside of its home country. According to this definition, however, a firm that exports goods to other countries would be defined as a multinational firm even if it does not have any assets outside its home country.[5]

Panel A of table 5-1 presents statistics on the number of multinational and domestic public firms in the United States between 1986 and 2017, using both definitions. The percentage of multinational firms defined using foreign income (sales) increased from 20 percent (18 percent) to 48 percent (40 percent) over the thirty-two-year period. It is interesting to note that panel A, table 5-1 documents the increase in the ratio of multinational firms despite the significant decline in the number of U.S. public firms (see Doidge, Karolyi and Stulz (2017)). The number of public firms in the United States decreased almost by half over the thirty-two years, with surviving firms being more than twice as likely to be multinational.

Several reasons explain the sharp decline in the number of public firms

TABLE 5-1. Descriptive Statistics: Distribution of Multinational Firms

PANEL A. Number of multinational firms in the United States

Definition of MNC:		(1) Non-missing foreign income in past 3 years		(2) Foreign sales ≥ 5% total sales	
Year	# Firms	% MNC	Average % foreign income of MNC	% MNC	Average % foreign sales of MNC
1986	5,149	20%	29%	18%	27%
1987	5,376	20%	31%	19%	29%
1988	5,189	20%	31%	19%	30%
1989	5,024	20%	31%	20%	31%
1990	4,979	20%	33%	20%	32%
1991	5,090	21%	30%	21%	32%
1992	5,273	22%	30%	22%	32%
1993	6,364	22%	28%	20%	30%
1994	6,707	20%	29%	21%	30%
1995	6,834	20%	30%	22%	32%
1996	7,233	21%	30%	23%	32%
1997	7,208	21%	29%	24%	33%
1998	6,824	22%	31%	26%	33%
1999	6,625	22%	31%	29%	35%
2000	6,323	21%	31%	31%	35%
2001	5,683	23%	30%	33%	35%
2002	5,284	26%	31%	34%	37%
2003	4,998	27%	34%	35%	38%
2004	4,936	30%	34%	36%	39%
2005	4,844	32%	34%	36%	40%
2006	4,726	33%	35%	36%	40%
2007	4,554	35%	36%	36%	42%
2008	4,271	36%	35%	37%	43%
2009	4,065	38%	35%	38%	42%
2010	3,923	39%	37%	38%	43%
2011	3,822	41%	37%	39%	44%
2012	3,771	42%	35%	39%	42%
2013	3,824	43%	35%	39%	42%
2014	3,929	44%	34%	39%	41%
2015	3,878	43%	34%	38%	39%
2016	3,752	44%	33%	39%	39%
2017	2,647	48%	38%	40%	40%

Note: Tables show the descriptive statistics of multinational firms around the world. In panel A, the sample covers 1986 to 2017 for U.S. publicly traded firms with positive total assets and sales in Compustat (U.S. firms). In panel B, the sample covers 2000 to 2017 for publicly traded firms in forty-one countries with positive total assets and sales in Worldscope (international firms). We report statistics for twenty-two developed countries included in the MSCI World index (except the United States) as well as for nineteen emerging-market countries in the MSCI Emerging Markets index (except Argentina, Egypt, Pakistan, Peru, Qatar, Saudi Arabia, and the United Arab Emirates). We use two ways to identify multinational firms (MNC). In the first definition (1), a firm is defined as *multinational* if it reports non-zero foreign income (Compustat item: PIFO; Worldscope item: WC07126) at any point in the past three years, and as *domestic* otherwise. In the second definition (2), a firm is flagged as a *multinational* if it has foreign sales (geographic segment data in Compustat; Worldscope item: WC07101) larger than or equal to 5 percent of its total sales. In panels A and B, the table shows the total number of firms, the percentage of multinational firms based on two definitions, the average ratio of foreign sales to total sales, and the average ratio of foreign income to total income across multinational firms by fiscal year. The ratio of foreign income is calculated as the absolute value of foreign income, divided by the sum of absolute values of domestic and foreign income. In panel C, we list the percentage of multinationals across forty-one countries, including the United States, based on two definitions. In the last four columns, the averages of debt-to-asset and cash-to-asset ratios are reported separately for multinationals and domestic firms. Statistics are averaged over the 2000–2017 time period.

PANEL B. Number of multinational firms around the world

Sample:	MSCI world (developed) Countries					MSCI emerging-market countries				
Definition of MNC:		(1) Foreign income		(2) Foreign sales			(1) Foreign income		(2) Foreign sales	
Year	# Firms	% MNC	Average % foreign income of MNC	% MNC	Average % foreign sales of MNC	# Firms	% MNC	Average % foreign income of MNC	% MNC	Average % foreign sales of MNC
2000	8,767	17%	35%	39%	47%	3,601	8%	28%	10%	39%
2001	9,221	19%	33%	40%	48%	3,979	9%	28%	13%	39%
2002	9,330	20%	32%	40%	48%	5,259	10%	23%	14%	39%
2003	9,691	20%	32%	40%	49%	6,054	9%	23%	14%	40%
2004	10,248	20%	33%	39%	49%	6,615	7%	27%	13%	42%
2005	10,814	21%	31%	37%	49%	8,061	7%	31%	13%	42%
2006	11,094	21%	31%	36%	51%	8,494	7%	30%	13%	44%
2007	11,116	20%	33%	36%	51%	8,962	6%	30%	13%	43%
2008	10,928	20%	35%	36%	52%	9,562	7%	32%	13%	45%
2009	10,742	20%	33%	37%	54%	10,069	7%	32%	14%	43%
2010	10,718	19%	26%	37%	56%	10,557	7%	23%	15%	47%
2011	10,709	18%	27%	37%	57%	11,415	6%	13%	18%	48%
2012	10,999	13%	35%	41%	56%	11,844	5%	19%	28%	44%
2013	11,020	12%	28%	41%	55%	12,283	4%	23%	36%	45%
2014	10,981	11%	29%	40%	57%	12,711	4%	22%	35%	45%
2015	10,890	8%	31%	36%	57%	12,769	3%	24%	32%	44%
2016	10,717	7%	33%	35%	57%	12,732	3%	25%	32%	44%
2017	10,473	5%	38%	34%	58%	12,583	3%	26%	33%	44%

PANEL C. Number of multinational firms across countries

Definition of MNC:		(1) Foreign income		(2) Foreign sales					
Country	# Firm-year	% MNC	Average % foreign income of MNC	% MNC	Average % foreign sales of MNC	Debt/assets MNC vs. domestic		Cash/assets MNC vs. domestic	
Australia	23,851	16.2%	27.2%	18.3%	53.0%	0.164	0.143	0.225	0.282
Austria	1,141	18.8%	38.4%	70.9%	64.0%	0.249	0.240	0.118	0.131
Belgium	1,682	13.2%	40.4%	54.8%	60.1%	0.248	0.245	0.098	0.157
Brazil	4,182	2.6%	25.6%	14.5%	36.9%	0.346	0.322	0.147	0.121
Canada	21,795	10.4%	35.6%	25.1%	64.6%	0.205	0.197	0.142	0.199
Chile	2,404	3.2%	40.4%	14.2%	50.1%	0.326	0.237	0.069	0.069
China	38,197	0.4%	24.5%	22.3%	33.7%	0.255	0.198	0.203	0.208
Colombia	448	0.7%	8.4%	15.2%	40.4%	0.410	0.173	0.033	0.084
Czech Republic	257	7.1%	16.1%	20.4%	29.9%	0.124	0.157	0.210	0.103
Denmark	2,010	9.2%	36.3%	46.5%	68.4%	0.234	0.246	0.113	0.167
Finland	2,162	10.1%	37.7%	66.7%	61.6%	0.243	0.251	0.116	0.143
France	10,824	19.2%	35.5%	55.4%	49.2%	0.222	0.219	0.147	0.172
Germany	10,650	11.6%	35.3%	52.8%	51.5%	0.180	0.198	0.169	0.173
Greece	3,180	7.7%	29.5%	22.9%	44.7%	0.389	0.343	0.088	0.085
Hong Kong	2,293	24.1%	30.6%	56.7%	66.4%	0.170	0.189	0.199	0.207
Hungary	331	6.5%	38.0%	45.3%	50.2%	0.269	0.162	0.057	0.090
India	32,059	2.0%	37.0%	14.9%	47.1%	0.266	0.307	0.124	0.083
Indonesia	5,500	3.3%	17.1%	14.3%	43.8%	0.286	0.311	0.131	0.109
Ireland	965	31.1%	43.3%	65.5%	67.2%	0.228	0.190	0.179	0.185

Israel	4,109	4.7%	31.7%	27.0%	70.2%	0.291	0.252	0.200	0.250
Italy	4,061	7.0%	35.2%	48.9%	55.3%	0.263	0.277	0.096	0.118
Japan	51,288	15.1%	23.8%	28.2%	35.2%	0.200	0.212	0.167	0.191
Malaysia	14,095	11.2%	21.7%	27.1%	41.4%	0.246	0.210	0.128	0.147
Mexico	1,513	14.9%	24.5%	36.9%	40.0%	0.237	0.229	0.098	0.092
Netherlands	2,193	20.7%	41.5%	72.0%	63.1%	0.230	0.237	0.134	0.132
New Zealand	1,864	19.5%	24.2%	28.1%	49.8%	0.281	0.232	0.085	0.119
Norway	2,816	10.3%	37.0%	45.9%	63.7%	0.277	0.274	0.152	0.193
Philippines	2,706	3.0%	23.6%	10.1%	35.8%	0.275	0.229	0.157	0.146
Poland	5,488	2.7%	28.2%	21.9%	38.2%	0.204	0.181	0.079	0.114
Portugal	805	12.2%	38.8%	48.6%	47.5%	0.379	0.392	0.078	0.069
Russia	2,882	1.4%	17.0%	15.1%	42.4%	0.382	0.264	0.056	0.099
Singapore	8,467	12.3%	35.6%	56.1%	58.0%	0.180	0.206	0.196	0.205
South Africa	4,063	17.9%	24.1%	30.3%	36.8%	0.204	0.176	0.126	0.139
South Korea	14,891	9.1%	17.1%	28.0%	40.9%	0.279	0.252	0.138	0.165
Spain	2,148	15.1%	37.1%	61.8%	49.2%	0.352	0.298	0.096	0.101
Sweden	7,158	8.8%	35.2%	38.0%	62.9%	0.188	0.169	0.123	0.200
Switzerland	3,213	15.3%	35.7%	73.4%	65.1%	0.189	0.204	0.165	0.184
Taiwan	24,145	13.0%	28.7%	33.6%	58.7%	0.211	0.196	0.197	0.223
Thailand	7,492	5.7%	23.1%	15.7%	46.0%	0.264	0.261	0.125	0.116
Turkey	3,717	3.2%	26.4%	10.5%	37.7%	0.318	0.225	0.115	0.095
United Kingdom	22,963	31.1%	35.8%	48.4%	55.8%	0.181	0.180	0.167	0.199
U.S.A.	79,230	34.4%	34.4%	36.4%	39.9%	0.211	0.235	0.200	0.167

in the early 2000s, but a particularly important one is the increasing role of private capital markets. Many public firms had leveraged buyouts and went private, initial public offerings (IPOs) were rare despite the strong economy, and private capital markets allowed startups to remain private for a very long time. For example, Uber, one of the most successful startups during this period, was founded in 2009 and remained private until 2019, raising US$24.7 billion privately over that period.[6] Moreover, as shown by Doidge, Karolyi, and Stulz (2017), the delisting rate increased significantly in the past twenty years, largely due to an increased pace of acquisitions of public firms by other public firms. These acquisitions have also increased the average size of remaining public firms.

Currently, U.S. public firms are fairly evenly split between domestic and multinational, with 1,257 firms classified as multinational and 1,390 as domestic, using the definition based on the existence of foreign income in the previous three years. The split is similar when we concentrate on foreign sales as a measure of being multinational (with 1,061 multinational and 1,586 domestic firms). For a typical U.S. multinational firm, 40 percent of sales are attributed to foreign sales in 2017, and we get a similar ratio (38 percent) when we use foreign income relative to total income.

Panel B of table 5-1 presents frequencies for an international sample of firms. We report results using both the definition based on foreign income and the one based on foreign sales. We first report statistics for the twenty-two developed countries (excluding the United States) included in the MSCI World Index and then for nineteen emerging-market countries included in the MSCI Emerging Markets Index (except Argentina, Egypt, Pakistan, Peru, Qatar, Saudi Arabia, and the United Arab Emirates).[7] This panel indicates that the ratio of multinational firms has been stable between 30 percent and 40 percent over the eighteen years of our sample when we use foreign sales to identify multinational firms. As of 2017, 34 percent of firms from MSCI developed countries and 33 percent of firms from MSCI emerging-market countries are multinational firms. In 2017, the average multinational firm in developed countries attributed 58 percent of sales to foreign sales and the average multinational firm in emerging-market countries attributed 44 percent of sales to foreign sales; both figures were slightly higher than the 40 percent average for U.S. multinational firms. These differences likely reflect variations in the nature of firms in diverse countries and also the likelihood that firms in respective countries go public.

Using foreign income to identify multinational firms in countries other than the United States could be problematic due to variations in reporting requirements across countries. In addition, as we noted, it is possible for firms not to report foreign income when the percentage of foreign income is relatively low compared with overall income or when it is negative. According to this definition, the percentage of firms that were multinationals was 17 percent (8 percent) in 2000 and 5 percent (3 percent) in 2017 in MSCI developed (emerging) markets. However, we know that, among firms that report foreign income in the past three years, on average, 38 percent (26 percent) of their income was foreign in 2017.

Panel C presents the same numbers across individual countries averaged over 2000–2017. While the United States, Ireland, the United Kingdom, Hong Kong, and the Netherlands have the highest ratio of multinational firms (classified using the foreign income definition), China, Columbia, Russia, India, and Brazil have the lowest ratios. Panel C also reports debt-to-assets and cash-to-assets ratios of multinational and domestic firms in these countries. In figure 5-1, we visualize the differences in these ratios between multinational firms and domestic firms. The reference line identifies the zero difference in leverage or cash ratios for multinational and domestic firms. Consistent with the idea that multinational activity increases a firm's debt capacity, many countries are located above the reference line, showing that the leverage ratio of multinational firms tends to be higher than the leverage ratio of domestic firms, especially in emerging markets. We also find that, with a few exceptions of emerging-market countries such as the Czech Republic, India, and Brazil, multinational firms have much lower cash holdings than domestic firms. One exceptional case is the United States, where multinational firms hold more cash than domestic firms on average, consistent with the evidence documented by Pinkowitz, Stulz, and Williamson (2016).

Next, we characterize the industry distribution of multinational firms. Table 5-2 presents the percentage of multinational firms across industries in the United States (panel A), and in MSCI developed and emerging-market countries (panels B and C)[8] across twelve Fama-French industries.[9] As also shown in figure 5-2, some industries show a high fraction of multinational firms in the United States: chemical and allied products (61 percent), manufacturing (49 percent), business equipment (48 percent), and consumer durables (48 percent). The other U.S. industries have much lower percentages of multinational firms—33 percent or much less. Differences across industries are less evident in both other developed countries

FIGURE 5-1. Leverage and Cash Holding: Multinational versus Domestic Firms

PANEL A. Total debt/assets: MNC vs. domestic

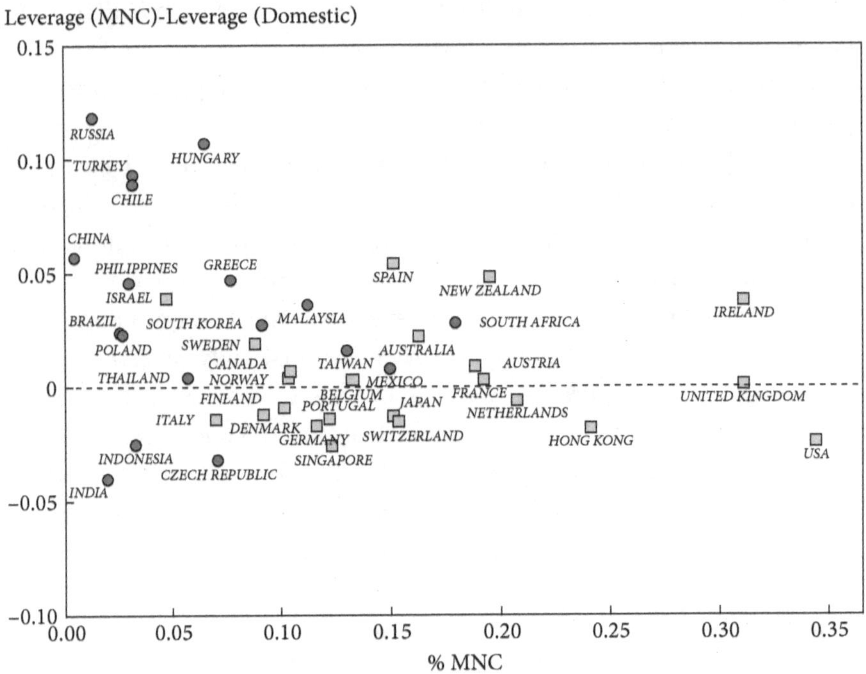

PANEL B. Cash/assets: MNC vs. domestic

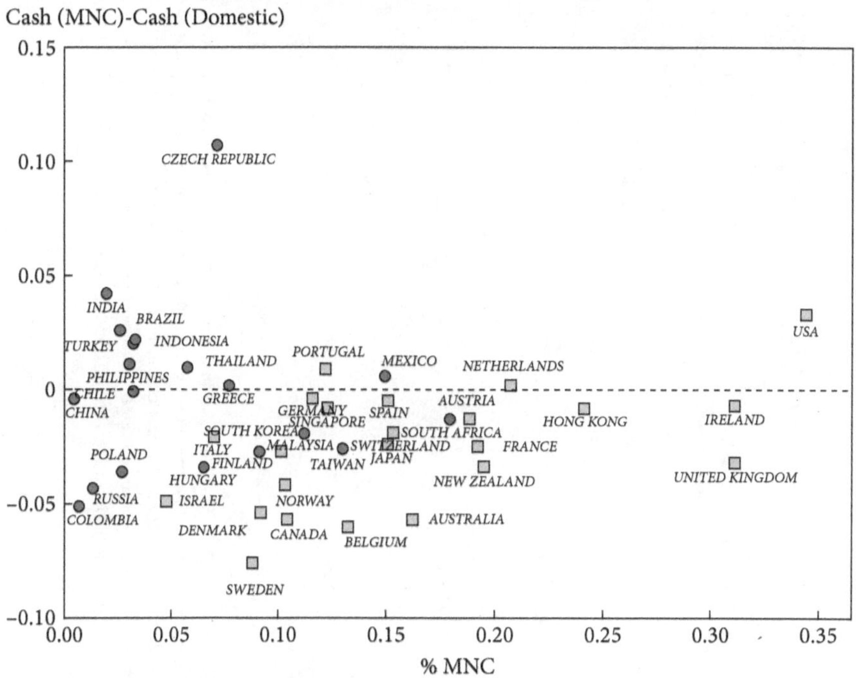

Note: These scatter plots show the percentage of multinational firms and the differences in debt-to-asset ratio and cash-to-asset ratio of multinational firms and domestic firms by country. In a given year, a firm is defined as a multinational firm (MNC) if it reports non-zero foreign income at any point in the past three years, and as a domestic firm otherwise. Each point represents a country. The X-axis represents the average percentage of multinational firms of each country based on the foreign income–based definition. The Y-axis represents the differences in debt-to-asset ratios (panel A) and cash-to-asset ratios (panel B), which are calculated as the average of debt-to-asset ratios (cash-to-asset ratios) of multinational firms minus the ratios of domestic firms from 2000 to 2017. Squares represent developed countries, and circles emerging markets. The dotted line is the reference point where the ratios of multinational and domestic firms are equal.

TABLE 5-2. Industry Distribution of Multinational Firms around the World

	Panel A. United States			Panel B. MSCI world (developed) countries			Panel C. MSCI emerging countries		
Industry	**# Firm-year**	**% MNC**	**Average % foreign income**	**# Firm-year**	**% MNC**	**Average % foreign income**	**# Firm-year**	**% MNC**	**Average % foreign income**
Consumer nondurables	8,718	33.2%	30.8%	14,173	17.4%	33.5%	22,657	4.8%	23.1%
Consumer durables	3,905	47.5%	32.4%	5,600	27.9%	32.9%	9,715	5.2%	27.7%
Manufacturing	16,687	49.4%	33.8%	25,115	18.7%	29.9%	38,567	5.4%	24.9%
Oil, gas, and coal extraction	6,238	27.0%	43.8%	6,086	25.1%	39.2%	3,331	4.7%	18.3%
Chemical and allied products	3,510	61.1%	40.8%	5,473	24.6%	31.3%	10,863	4.6%	22.3%
Business equipment	28,499	48.1%	33.3%	28,062	17.9%	30.1%	27,202	9.5%	28.9%
Telephone and television transmission	3,960	15.0%	21.5%	3,541	13.5%	24.0%	3,357	4.8%	20.3%
Utilities	4,693	1.3%	17.5%	2,277	12.6%	27.8%	4,163	2.4%	28.5%
Wholesale and retail	16,799	19.5%	24.8%	20,641	13.8%	28.3%	11,927	5.3%	20.2%
Healthcare and medical equipment	15,661	23.7%	32.9%	10,574	15.1%	30.0%	8,993	2.5%	23.6%
Finance	34,768	5.5%	28.8%	1,127	12.2%	28.6%	815	6.8%	19.7%
Other	19,667	24.6%	31.6%	43,714	13.5%	32.2%	25,843	4.7%	24.9%

Note: Percentage of multinationals across industries in the United States (panel A), in MSCI developed countries (panel B), and in MSCI emerging-market countries (panel C). A firm is defined as *multinational* if it reports non-zero foreign income (Compustat item: PIFO; Worldscope item: WC07126) at any point in the past three years, and as *domestic* otherwise. Industry is based on the Fama-French twelve-industry classification. The first column lists the total number of firm-years, the second column lists the percentage of multinational firms, and the third column lists the industry-level average ratio of foreign income for multinational firms. The ratio of foreign income is calculated as the absolute value of foreign income, divided by the sum of absolute values of domestic and foreign income. Statistics are for 1986 to 2017 for the U.S. sample (panel A) and for 2000 to 2017 for the international sample (panels B and C).

FIGURE 5-2. Number of Multinational Firms by Industry

PANEL A. U.S. multinational firms by industry 1986–2017

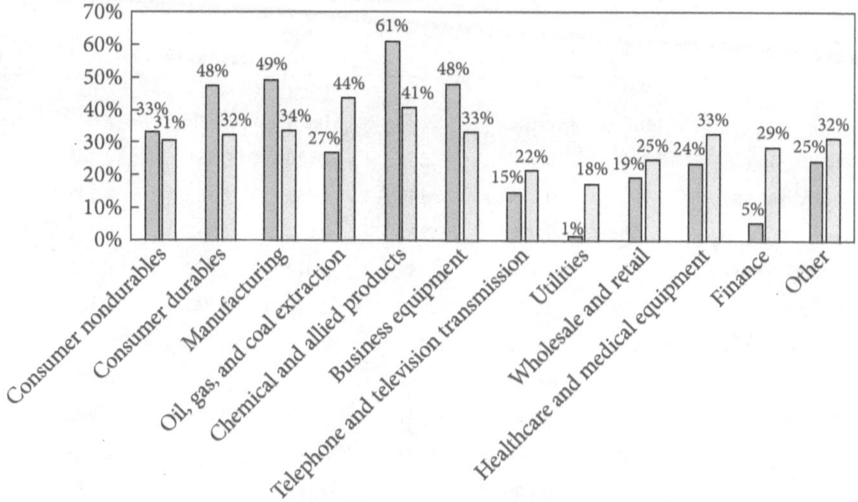

PANEL B. International multinational firms by industry 2000–2017

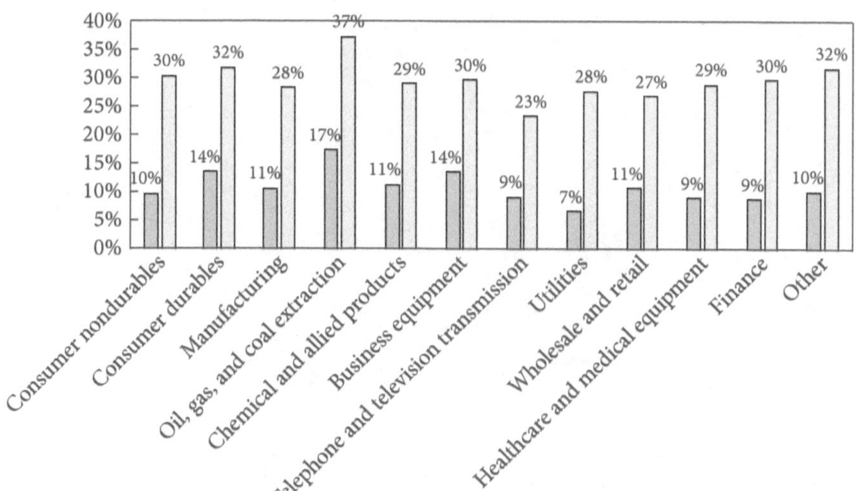

Note: This figure shows the percentage of multinationals (MNC) and the average percentage of foreign income of multinationals across industries in the United States (panel A) and non-U.S. MSCI developed and emerging-market countries (panel B). In a given year, a firm is defined as a multinational firm (MNC) if it reports pretax foreign income at any point in the past three years, and as a domestic firm otherwise. Industries are based on the Fama-French twelve-industry classification.

TABLE 5-3. Characteristics of Multinationals

PANEL A. U.S. firms

	Multinational			Domestic			Diff. in mean
	Mean	Median	Std	Mean	Median	Std	MNC—domestic
Total assets	6.266	0.437	43.246	3.880	0.181	44.046	2.386***
Market capitalization	4.902	0.479	22.140	1.332	0.106	8.223	3.570***
Sales growth	0.108	0.075	0.267	0.132	0.082	0.321	-0.024***
Cash flow/total assets	0.115	0.124	0.147	0.074	0.078	0.168	0.041***
Std of cash flow	0.070	0.046	0.078	0.076	0.042	0.103	-0.006***
Rated	0.315	0.000	0.465	0.180	0.000	0.384	0.135***
Investment grade	0.152	0.000	0.359	0.080	0.000	0.272	0.071***
Speculative grade	0.135	0.000	0.341	0.082	0.000	0.274	0.053***
Cash/total assets	0.189	0.114	0.197	0.158	0.061	0.215	0.031***
Total debt/total assets	0.212	0.176	0.203	0.244	0.189	0.233	-0.033***
Zero debt	0.147	0.000	0.354	0.128	0.000	0.334	0.019***
# Firm-year obs.	47,337			115,768			
# Unique firm	5,367			14,736			

and emerging-market countries. While finance and utilities have the lowest fraction of multinational firms in the United States (with 1 percent and 5 percent, respectively), firms in those industries are much more globalized in other developed countries (with about 12 percent and 13 percent, respectively). In addition, compared with multinational firms in emerging-market countries, the ones in developed countries rely more on foreign income—in particular, in oil, gas, and coal extraction industries and in chemical and allied products industries (40–44 percent in the United States and 31–40 percent in other developed countries). While the fraction of multinational

PANEL B. International firms

	MSCI world (developed) countries			MSCI emerging countries		
	Multi-national	Domestic	Diff. in mean MNC— domestic	Multi-national	Domestic	Diff. in mean MNC— domestic
Total assets	4.806	1.640	3.166***	2.575	0.887	1.688***
Market capitalization	2.944	1.038	1.906***	1.638	0.771	0.867***
Sales growth	0.070	0.070	-0.000	0.097	0.115	-0.018***
Cash flow/total assets	0.077	0.043	0.034***	0.112	0.102	0.010***
Std of cash flow	0.110	0.147	-0.038***	0.062	0.078	-0.016***
Cash/total assets	0.167	0.198	-0.031***	0.150	0.151	-0.000
Total debt/total assets	0.197	0.202	-0.005***	0.245	0.239	0.006**
Zero debt	0.140	0.192	-0.052***	0.052	0.114	-0.062***
# Firm-year obs.	30,077	157,433		9,298	157,840	
# Unique firm	4,126	17,273		1,389	14,969	

Note: This table reports firm-level statistics for fundamental firm-level characteristics. In panel A, the sample includes all publicly traded U.S. firms available in Compustat with positive total assets and sales. The sample period covers 1986 to 2017. We report mean, median, and standard deviation. In panel B, we report only the means (to save space) for international firms available in Worldscope with positive total assets and sales. The sample covers 2000 to 2017 for developed and emerging-market MSCI countries. A firm is defined as *multinational* if it reports non-zero foreign income (Compustat item: PIFO; Worldscope item: WC07126) at any point in the past three years, and as *domestic* otherwise. *Total assets* and *market capitalization* are in U.S. billions of dollars. *Cash flow* and *cash* are scaled by total assets. *Std of cash flow* is calculated as the standard deviation of *cash flow/total assets* over previous five years with the minimum three-year observations. *Rated* is an indicator variable for a firm that has an S&P issuer rating. *Investment grade* is an indicator of a firm that has an S&P investment grade issuer rating (AAA, AA+, AA, or AA-) and *speculative grade* is an indicator of a firm that has an S&P speculative grade issuer rating (A+, A, A-, BBB+, BBB, or BBB-). *Zero debt* is an indicator for a firm-year with zero or missing long-term debt. Ratio variables are winsorized at 1 percent and 99 percent. The difference reported is based on t-test of the mean. The symbols ***, **, and * denote statistical significance at the 1 percent, 5 percent, and 10 percent levels.

firms in the United States is relatively low, multinational firms in utilities and finance generate 17–29 percent of income overseas.

Multinational firms are likely to differ from domestic firms in several ways. In table 5-3, we present firm-level characteristics of multinational and domestic firms. Panel A contains statistics for the U.S. sample, covering 1986–2017. This panel indicates that multinational firms tend to be larger and more stable than domestic firms. Average total assets are almost twice as high for multinationals as for domestic firms, and multinationals' average market capitalization is almost four times as high. Cash flows are also much higher, and, it is important to note, the standard deviation of cash flows is statistically significantly lower for multinationals, possibly because multinationals' cash flows are diversified across countries. In addition, multinational firms are more likely to have public bond rating. Finally, compared with domestic firms, multinational firms hold more cash, carry less leverage as a ratio of their asset size, and are more likely to have zero debt.

In panel B, we present the average statistics for MSCI World (developed) versus MSCI emerging-market countries for 2000–2017. Multinationals from developed countries, with mean total assets of US$4.8 billion, are on average smaller than U.S. multinationals, with US$6.3 billion in average total assets. Multinationals from emerging-market countries are, on average, much smaller, with US$2.6 billion in total assets. The average market capitalization follows the same rankings, with multinationals from the United States at US$4.9 billion, developed countries at US$2.9 billion, and emerging-market countries having US$1.6 billion of average market capitalization.

When we compare multinational firms with domestic firms, we see that multinationals are larger than domestic firms in terms of both total assets and market capitalization. Like U.S. multinational firms, foreign multinationals have higher cash flows and lower cash-flow volatility. Consistent with the pattern observed in figure 5-1, foreign multinationals in developed countries other than the United States keep less cash in reserve than domestic firms. While multinational firms in developed countries have a lower debt ratio, MNCs in emerging markets tend to have a slightly higher debt ratio and are less likely to carry zero debt than domestic firms. This pattern potentially reflects the higher debt capacity of multinationals, especially in emerging-market countries with weak external financial markets.

THE CAPITAL STRUCTURE OF MULTINATIONAL FIRMS

Capital Structure of U.S. Multinationals

In table 5-4, we provide detailed summary statistics for capital structures of U.S. multinational firms, first for the entire universe of public firms and then for firms of differing credit quality. We start by reporting detailed characteristics for all firms, where the majority of firms are unrated. To compare similarly rated firms, we analyze investment-grade firms (panel B) and speculative-grade firms (panel C) separately.

Table 5-4 indicates that U.S. multinational firms are more likely to hold cash, as a percentage of their assets, and less likely to borrow in the debt market. The average cash-to-assets ratio is 16.7 percent for multinationals while it is only 13.5 percent for domestic firms in the United States. However, the mean total debt-to-asset ratio is 23.7 percent for multinationals and 26.5 percent for domestic firms (although median ratios are both 21 percent). Larger cash holdings likely reflect tax incentives for multinationals to hold cash earned overseas rather than pay repatriation taxes for cash returned to domestic shareholders. The differences in debt ratios would occur if these firms followed the "pecking order" theory of capital (Myers and Majluf (1984)).[10] Since multinationals are likely to have been successful in generating cash flows and diversifying internationally, they would not have fallen down the pecking order as often as similar domestic firms. Thus, compared with domestic firms, multinational firms would carry less debt on their balance sheets.

When we examine the details of the debt structure (such as senior bonds, subordinated bonds, commercial paper, or bank debt), we see that the lower total debt ratio for multinational firms occurs because multinationals' bank loans are lower as a ratio of total debt. Term bank loans, on average, form 20 percent of total debt for domestic firms but only 14 percent for multinational firms, with the difference being statistically significant at the 1 percent level. Compared with domestic firms, an average multinational firm relies more on senior bonds or notes (30 percent of total debt versus 19.3 percent of total debt). They are also more likely to issue convertible debt and commercial paper. On the other hand, domestic firms, since they tend to be less creditworthy, are 11 percent more likely to borrow with collateral (38 percent versus 27 percent).

Next, we compare capital structures of U.S. multinational and domestic firms grouped by credit ratings. We first compare investment grade–rated firms (panel B of table 5-4) and then speculative grade–rated ones (panel C of table 5-4). Rated multinational firms, investment grade or speculative grade, hold more cash but have less total debt, especially long-term debt, compared with domestic firms. As expected, investment-grade firms rely more on senior bonds or notes and less on bank debt. The ratio of senior bonds or notes, as a fraction of debt, increases to 58.4 percent for investment grade–rated multinational firms from 30 percent overall. The ratio of bank term loans, as a fraction of debt, drops to 3 percent for investment grade–rated multinational firms from 14 percent overall. For speculative-grade

TABLE 5-4. Capital Structure Characteristics (U.S. Sample)

PANEL A. All firms

	Multinational			Domestic			Diff. in mean
	Mean	Median	Std	Mean	Median	Std	MNC—domestic
Cash/total assets	0.167	0.105	0.172	0.135	0.052	0.193	0.032***
Total debt/total assets	0.237	0.211	0.200	0.265	0.208	0.235	-0.028***
Long-term debt/total debt	0.708	0.889	0.358	0.698	0.863	0.350	0.010***
Debt structure (% total debt)							
By type							
Sr. bonds and notes	0.300	0.000	0.386	0.193	0.000	0.337	0.107***
Sub. bonds and notes	0.047	0.000	0.175	0.031	0.000	0.135	0.016***
Commercial paper	0.009	0.000	0.056	0.003	0.000	0.029	0.006***
Convertible debt	0.072	0.000	0.222	0.041	0.000	0.168	0.031***
Bank debt	0.261	0.004	0.369	0.296	0.002	0.383	-0.034***
Revolving credit	0.127	0.000	0.266	0.103	0.000	0.240	0.024***
Term loans	0.140	0.000	0.279	0.196	0.000	0.329	-0.056***
Cap. leases	0.046	0.000	0.183	0.037	0.000	0.163	0.009***
By interest type							
Fixed rate debt	0.365	0.116	0.406	0.321	0.000	0.396	0.044***
Variable rate debt	0.225	0.000	0.345	0.193	0.000	0.321	0.032***
Zero coupon debt	0.004	0.000	0.053	0.002	0.000	0.032	0.003***
By priority							
Senior debt	0.620	0.987	0.462	0.560	0.848	0.466	0.060***
Sub. debt	0.048	0.000	0.177	0.033	0.000	0.138	0.016***
Secured debt	0.273	0.001	0.391	0.379	0.099	0.426	-0.106***
Unsecured debt	0.404	0.133	0.440	0.247	0.000	0.364	0.157***
# Firm-year obs.	25,031			52,660			
# Unique firm	3,197			7,510			

PANEL B. Investment grade

	Multinational			Domestic			Diff. in mean
	Mean	Median	Std	Mean	Median	Std	MNC—domestic
Cash/total assets	0.105	0.068	0.109	0.056	0.027	0.086	0.049***
Total debt/total assets	0.257	0.242	0.143	0.289	0.292	0.179	-0.031***
Long-term debt/total debt	0.809	0.893	0.231	0.794	0.884	0.249	0.015**
Debt structure (% total debt)							
By type							
Sr. bonds and notes	0.584	0.744	0.388	0.459	0.536	0.400	0.125***
Sub. bonds and notes	0.012	0.000	0.074	0.025	0.000	0.079	-0.013***
Commercial paper	0.044	0.000	0.112	0.025	0.000	0.075	0.019***
Convertible debt	0.032	0.000	0.130	0.016	0.000	0.084	0.016***
Bank debt	0.064	0.000	0.149	0.112	0.000	0.204	-0.048***
Revolving credit	0.034	0.000	0.109	0.047	0.000	0.117	-0.013***
Term loans	0.030	0.000	0.097	0.065	0.000	0.159	-0.035***
Cap. leases	0.008	0.000	0.037	0.006	0.000	0.034	0.002*
By interest type							
Fixed rate debt	0.576	0.750	0.400	0.492	0.590	0.400	0.085***
Variable rate debt	0.069	0.000	0.148	0.085	0.000	0.162	-0.016***
Zero coupon debt	0.005	0.000	0.048	0.002	0.000	0.023	0.003***
By priority							
Senior debt	0.705	0.993	0.437	0.611	0.878	0.444	0.094***
Sub. debt	0.012	0.000	0.074	0.025	0.000	0.079	-0.013***
Secured debt	0.045	0.000	0.139	0.190	0.010	0.279	-0.145***
Unsecured debt	0.694	0.971	0.426	0.498	0.568	0.408	0.196***
# Firm-year obs.	4,527			5,074			
# Unique firm	505			629			

PANEL C. Speculative grade

	Multinational			Domestic			Diff. in mean
	Mean	Median	Std	Mean	Median	Std	MNC—domestic
Cash/total assets	0.108	0.069	0.118	0.087	0.042	0.123	0.021***
Total debt/total assets	0.394	0.369	0.200	0.478	0.459	0.225	−0.084***
Long-term debt/total debt	0.897	0.971	0.195	0.923	0.988	0.174	−0.025***
Debt structure (% total debt)							
By type							
Sr. bonds and notes	0.386	0.355	0.370	0.371	0.264	0.382	0.015*
Sub. bonds and notes	0.119	0.000	0.251	0.109	0.000	0.241	0.009
Commercial paper	0.000	0.000	0.005	0.000	0.000	0.006	0.000
Convertible debt	0.109	0.000	0.247	0.072	0.000	0.198	0.037***
Bank debt	0.287	0.180	0.318	0.240	0.102	0.297	0.047***
Revolving credit	0.079	0.000	0.167	0.083	0.000	0.162	−0.004
Term loans	0.211	0.016	0.297	0.158	0.000	0.271	0.052***
Cap. leases	0.018	0.000	0.086	0.014	0.000	0.060	0.005**
By interest type							
Fixed rate debt	0.513	0.562	0.373	0.483	0.539	0.384	0.030***
Variable rate debt	0.256	0.108	0.313	0.221	0.062	0.290	0.035***
Zero coupon debt	0.004	0.000	0.053	0.001	0.000	0.020	0.003***
By priority							
Senior debt	0.675	0.933	0.400	0.595	0.783	0.430	0.081***
Sub. debt	0.120	0.000	0.252	0.110	0.000	0.242	0.010
Secured debt	0.351	0.253	0.358	0.316	0.175	0.351	0.035***
Unsecured debt	0.474	0.495	0.386	0.432	0.414	0.390	0.042***
# Firm-year obs.	4,596			5,868			
# Unique firm	837			1,171			

Note: This table reports details of capital structure for U.S. multinational firms versus domestic firms. Panel A includes all firms. Panel B is for investment-grade firms, while panel C is for speculative grade firms. The sample covers publicly traded Compustat firms between 1997 and 2017 due to data availability in Capital IQ. A firm is defined as *multinational* if it reports non-zero pretax foreign income (Compustat item: PIFO) at any point in the past three years, and as *domestic* otherwise. All debt structure variables are scaled by the total debt. Variables are winsorized at 1 percent and 99 percent. The difference reported is based on t-test of the mean. The symbols ***, **, and * denote statistical significance at the 1 percent, 5 percent, and 10 percent levels.

firms, we see different patterns in the details of debt structure for multinationals compared with domestic firms: the average multinational firm has more term loans, as a fraction of its total debt, than the average domestic firm (21 percent versus 16 percent) while the ratio of senior bonds and notes is weakly different from each other for speculative-grade firms.

Holding credit ratings constant is one way to limit the sample to comparable multinational and domestic firms. Another way is to focus on firms with similar asset sizes. Next, in table 5-5, we analyze multinationals' capital structures relative to those of domestic firms within different size buckets. We first compare large multinational firms with similarly sized domestic firms (panel A). These large domestic firms have total assets larger than or equal to the median total assets of multinational firms, with the median estimated for each year. The match creates relatively similar firms in terms of total assets, with mean total assets of US$19.64 billion for multinational firms and mean total assets of US$15.53 billion for large domestic firms. Grouping by asset size, the difference in market capitalization is still substantial, about US$14 billion for multinational firms compared with US$4.7 billion for domestic firms of similar asset size. Although large multinational firms carry lower leverage than large domestic firms, they are more likely to issue long-term debt, which is dominated by senior bonds and notes (44 percent versus 28 percent). The cash ratio for these large multinational firms is, on average, 12.5 percent, which is almost double the ratio for large domestic firms (6.7 percent). Large multinationals tend to have a higher leverage than a typical multinational firm (28 percent versus 24 percent) and, again, lower than the leverage of similar domestic firms.

In panel B, we compare smaller-than-median domestic firms with multinational firms whose assets are smaller than or equal to the median assets of the domestic firms, with the median estimated for each year. Average total assets for this subsample of multinational firms is US$252 million and average market capitalization is US$401 million. Again, cash ratios are larger, and leverage is lower, for multinational firms than for domestic firms. However, for these smaller multinational firms, bank loans are relatively more important than senior bonds or notes (35 percent bank debt versus 12 percent senior bonds and notes, as a percentage of total debt).

In summary, these tables show clear differences in cash holdings, debt ratios, or capital structure details between U.S. multinational and domestic firms. These differences exist within size and credit rating categories.

TABLE 5-5. Capital Structure Characteristics—Subsamples Based on Firm Size (U.S. Sample)

PANEL A.

	Large multinational			Large domestic			Diff. in mean
	Mean	Median	Std	Mean	Median	Std	MNC—domestic
Cash/total assets	0.125	0.079	0.131	0.067	0.033	0.101	0.058***
Total debt/total assets	0.280	0.260	0.184	0.312	0.278	0.228	−0.032***
Long-term debt/total debt	0.815	0.934	0.270	0.786	0.925	0.285	0.029***
Debt structure (% total debt)							
By type							
Sr. bonds and notes	0.441	0.461	0.396	0.283	0.000	0.372	0.159***
Sub. bonds and notes	0.054	0.000	0.180	0.039	0.000	0.139	0.015***
Commercial paper	0.017	0.000	0.073	0.008	0.000	0.043	0.009***
Convertible debt	0.073	0.000	0.212	0.034	0.000	0.140	0.039***
Bank debt	0.201	0.017	0.300	0.278	0.097	0.338	−0.078***
Revolving credit	0.084	0.000	0.197	0.079	0.000	0.181	0.005*
Term loans	0.119	0.000	0.239	0.201	0.000	0.308	−0.082***
Cap. leases	0.022	0.000	0.111	0.011	0.000	0.073	0.010***
By interest type							
Fixed rate debt	0.494	0.556	0.398	0.443	0.444	0.397	0.051***
Variable rate debt	0.185	0.000	0.289	0.168	0.026	0.262	0.017***
Zero coupon debt	0.005	0.000	0.055	0.001	0.000	0.023	0.004***
By priority							
Senior debt	0.680	0.988	0.432	0.628	0.879	0.431	0.052***
Sub. debt	0.055	0.000	0.181	0.040	0.000	0.141	0.015***
Secured debt	0.188	0.001	0.311	0.365	0.199	0.389	−0.177***
Unsecured debt	0.568	0.723	0.429	0.358	0.187	0.384	0.210***
# Firm-year obs.	13,415			21,904			
# Unique firm	1,532			2,832			

PANEL B.

	Small multinational			Small domestic			Diff. in mean
	Mean	Median	Std	Mean	Median	Std	MNC—domestic
Cash/total assets	0.233	0.177	0.206	0.205	0.102	0.236	0.028***
Total debt/total assets	0.171	0.103	0.205	0.221	0.144	0.235	-0.050***
Long-term debt/total debt	0.537	0.652	0.409	0.595	0.729	0.387	-0.057***
Debt structure (% total debt)							
By type							
Sr. bonds and notes	0.120	0.000	0.283	0.131	0.000	0.295	-0.011**
Sub. bonds and notes	0.027	0.000	0.138	0.022	0.000	0.118	0.005**
Commercial paper	0.001	0.000	0.028	0.000	0.000	0.005	0.001**
Convertible debt	0.062	0.000	0.217	0.047	0.000	0.186	0.015***
Bank debt	0.349	0.000	0.434	0.312	0.000	0.419	0.036***
Revolving credit	0.179	0.000	0.325	0.126	0.000	0.282	0.053***
Term loans	0.177	0.000	0.329	0.189	0.000	0.343	-0.012**
Cap. leases	0.089	0.000	0.260	0.063	0.000	0.217	0.025***
By interest type							
Fixed rate debt	0.198	0.000	0.351	0.219	0.000	0.365	-0.021***
Variable rate debt	0.283	0.000	0.405	0.219	0.000	0.366	0.064***
Zero coupon debt	0.005	0.000	0.057	0.002	0.000	0.041	0.002**
By priority							
Senior debt	0.571	0.994	0.483	0.523	0.814	0.485	0.048***
Sub. debt	0.030	0.000	0.144	0.024	0.000	0.124	0.005**
Secured debt	0.407	0.023	0.457	0.404	0.002	0.457	0.003
Unsecured debt	0.194	0.000	0.355	0.155	0.000	0.317	0.039***
# Firm-year obs.	8,679			23,888			
# Unique firm	1,792			4,739			

Note: This table reports details of capital structure for large/small multinational firms versus domestic firms. Large domestic firms, in panel A, are identified as with total assets larger than or equal to the median total assets of multinational firms, with the median estimated each year. In panel B, smaller-than-median domestic firms are compared with multinational firms with assets smaller than or equal to the median asset of the domestic firms, with the median estimated each year. All debt structure variables are scaled by the total debt. The difference reported is based on t-test of the mean. The symbols ***, **, and * denote statistical significance at the 1 percent, 5 percent, and 10 percent levels.

Capital Structures of Non-U.S. Multinational Firms

In table 5-6, we tabulate details of capital structures for multinationals in comparison to their domestic counterparts, first for MSCI developed countries (panel A) and then for MSCI emerging-market countries (panel B). An important difference with the U.S. sample is that foreign multinational firms in developed countries, compared with domestic firms in their respective regions, hold less cash as a fraction of their total assets (14.6 percent versus 16.6 percent). Also, even though their leverage ratio is similar to U.S. counterparts, non-U.S. multinational firms rely less on the senior bond market for financing, but more on the bank debt market. For example, as discussed above, bank debt is, on average, 26 percent of total debt for U.S. multinational firms (and 20 percent of total debt for large U.S. multinationals, which are similar in size to the multinationals from other developed countries). However, for multinationals from MSCI developed or emerging-market countries, this ratio is more than 50 percent.

CAPITAL RAISING BY MULTINATIONAL FIRMS

Where Do Multinationals Get Financing?

An important consideration when a firm raises capital is the location of the capital provider. Being geographically closer to the capital provider reduces information asymmetry between the lenders and the borrowers (see, for example, Sufi (2007)). Given that multinationals have assets in multiple countries, they can more easily raise capital from multiple countries. Where to raise capital represents an important corporate financial decision faced by multinational firms.

Debt Financing

The two most important forms of debt finance are publicly traded bonds and bank debt. Henderson, Jegadeesh, and Weisbach (2006) document that between 1990 and 2001, about 20 percent of all capital raised through bond issues came from outside the issuing firm's home country. The most common places of issue of international bonds were the United States and Europe, and many issuers were multinationals from countries with less liquid capital markets.[11]

Most large bank loans are syndicated across multiple banks, and the participating banks often come from different countries. Table 5-7 summarizes these patterns for syndicated loans made to U.S. firms between 1990 and 2018. For multinationals, 33 percent of loans had at least one participating bank from Canada and 32 percent had at least one from the United Kingdom. Foreign banks also participate in syndicated loans to domestic firms, but to a lesser degree: 22 percent of syndicated loans to domestic firms had at least one lender from Canada and 16 percent had at least one lender from the United Kingdom.

Next, we examine the difference in bank loan sources between multinational firms and domestic firms in a regression setting. The sample includes syndicated loans issued to U.S. public firms between 1990 and 2018, obtained from Dealscan, aggregated at the loan-package level. We estimate ordinary least squares (OLS) regressions, where the dependent variable is the indicator for including at least one foreign lender in its syndicate in columns 1 and 2, and the percentage of foreign lenders as the total number of syndicate members in columns 3 and 4. The main independent variables are the multinational indicator based on non-zero foreign income in the past three years and the percentage of foreign income. The regressions include controls of loan features and borrower characteristics and year, industry, borrower rating, and deal-purpose fixed effects.

Table 5-8 examines the differences in the sources of loans between multinational and domestic firms, with controls for a number of variables that could potentially affect the structure of the loan. This table illustrates that multinationals are 5 percent more likely to have at least one foreign lender in the syndicate. In addition, they have a 3.5 percent higher fraction of foreign lenders in the syndicate, which is equivalent to a 16 percent increase at the mean (0.22). The fraction of a firm's foreign income positively and significantly affects both variables. The effects are economically large: they imply that a one-standard-deviation of foreign income (0.245) would increase the fraction of foreign lenders in the syndicate by 2.2 percentage points, which is equivalent to a 10 percent increase.

Equity Financing

Firms can also issue equity outside their own country. Henderson, Jegadeesh, and Weisbach (2006) document that about 12 percent of capital raised by equity issues comes from outside a firm's home country. While international equity issues are less common than debt issues, they still represent an important consideration in multinational firms' financial decisions.

TABLE 5-6. Capital Structure Characteristics (International Sample)

PANEL A. MSCI World (developed) countries

	Multinational	Domestic	Diff. in mean
	Mean	Mean	MNC-domestic
Cash/total assets	0.146	0.166	−0.019***
Total debt/total assets	0.217	0.234	−0.017***
Long-term debt/total debt	0.519	0.495	0.024***
Debt structure (% total debt)			
By type			
Sr. bonds and notes	0.142	0.099	0.043***
Sub. bonds and notes	0.006	0.006	0.000
Commercial paper	0.008	0.003	0.005***
Convertible debt	0.043	0.036	0.008***
Bank debt	0.520	0.520	−0.001
Revolving credit	0.115	0.103	0.013***
Term loans	0.406	0.419	−0.013***
Cap. leases	0.056	0.063	−0.008***
By interest type			
Fixed rate debt	0.287	0.229	0.058***
Variable rate debt	0.183	0.162	0.021***
Zero coupon debt	0.008	0.010	−0.002***
By priority			
Senior debt	0.759	0.697	0.062***
Sub. debt	0.008	0.009	−0.001
Secured debt	0.236	0.267	−0.031***
Unsecured debt	0.534	0.454	0.080***
# Firm-year obs.	26,799	133,281	
# Unique firm	3,862	15,867	

PANEL B. MSCI emerging countries

	Multinational	Domestic	Diff. in mean
	Mean	Mean	MNC-domestic
Cash/total assets	0.144	0.136	0.009***
Total debt/total assets	0.251	0.258	−0.006**
Long-term debt/total debt	0.397	0.366	0.030***
Debt structure (% total debt)			
By type			
Sr. bonds and notes	0.132	0.072	0.060***
Sub. bonds and notes	0.001	0.001	0.001**
Commercial paper	0.011	0.005	0.006***
Convertible debt	0.035	0.019	0.015***
Bank debt	0.564	0.579	−0.015***
Revolving credit	0.159	0.155	0.003
Term loans	0.409	0.434	−0.025***
Cap. leases	0.028	0.030	−0.002
By interest type			
Fixed rate debt	0.191	0.175	0.017***
Variable rate debt	0.276	0.184	0.092***
Zero coupon debt	0.019	0.015	0.004***
By priority			
Senior debt	0.744	0.720	0.024***
Sub. debt	0.002	0.001	0.001
Secured debt	0.326	0.381	−0.055***
Unsecured debt	0.447	0.357	0.090***
# Firm-year obs.	8,921	142,704	
# Unique firm	1,364	14,576	

Note: This table reports details of capital structure for multinational firms versus domestic firms in MSCI developed countries in panel A and in MSCI emerging countries in panel B. The sample covers publicly traded firms covered in Worldscope and Capital IQ between 2000 and 2017. A firm is defined as *multinational* if it reports non-zero foreign income at any point in the last three years, and as *domestic* otherwise. All debt structure variables are scaled by the total debt. We report only the means and the difference in mean between multinational firms and domestic firms. Variables are winsorized at 1 and 99 percent. The difference reported is based on t-test of the mean. The symbols ***, **, and * denote statistical significance at the 1 percent, 5 percent, and 10 percent levels.

TABLE 5-7. Sources of Bank Loans

Lender country	Loans to multinational	Loans to domestic
Canada	32.56%	22.46%
United Kingdom	31.79%	15.76%
Japan	28.76%	16.37%
France	24.50%	16.31%
Germany	22.40%	13.39%
Netherlands	16.30%	7.86%
Switzerland	14.22%	9.27%
Italy	7.34%	1.51%
Australia	4.55%	1.60%
Belgium	3.83%	2.07%
Spain	3.61%	0.90%
China	3.26%	0.92%
Norway	2.97%	0.94%
Taiwan	2.06%	1.90%
Ireland	1.64%	0.96%
Sweden	1.55%	0.25%
Hong Kong	1.50%	0.64%
Israel	1.43%	1.30%
Denmark	1.35%	0.38%
Singapore	1.27%	0.42%
Observations	15,051	24,641

Note: This table presents the percentage of the number of loans that include at least one lender from each country in loan syndicates. The sample includes syndicated bank loans issued to U.S. public firms in Compustat during the period from 1990 to 2018 from Dealscan. *Multinational* is the indicator denoting a multinational borrower that reports non-zero foreign income (PIFO) at any point in the last three years, and *% foreign income* is the absolute value of foreign income (PIFO), divided by the sum of absolute values of domestic (PIDOM) and foreign income (PIFO). Each column shows the percentage of number of loans to multinational firms and domestic firms, respectively, that include at least one lender from each country in a loan syndicate. The list of lender countries is in descending order of loans to multinational firms.

The most common way to issue equity in other countries is to cross-list the stock on a local exchange.[12] International equity issues through cross-listings are more common for multinational firms than for domestic ones (see Doidge and others (2009)). In addition, foreign institutional ownership increases with foreign sales (Ferreira and Matos (2008)).

Table 5-9 compares foreign ownership and the incidence of equity offers from other countries across multinationals and domestic U.S. firms. It is evident from this table that multinational firms have more foreign ownership (4.3 percent for multinationals versus 1.8 percent for domestic firms). Foreign institutional ownership has constantly increased since 2000 and, as of 2017, 8.4 percent of equity of multinational firms and 4.0 percent of domestic firms was held by institutional investors outside the United States. Despite the increase in capital flow overseas, the difference in foreign ownership between multinational and domestic firms still remains significant. Multinational firms are more likely to raise equity overseas, just as they are more likely to borrow overseas.

Why Multinational Firms Have a Financing Advantage

Jang (2017) addresses one financing advantage of multinational firms over domestic firms. She considers whether the presence of an operation can facilitate capital-raising in the country where the operation is located. Presumably, the foreign operations can lower a capital provider's information asymmetry and monitoring costs. Jang (2017) documents that firms are more likely to receive bank loans from foreign lenders in countries where foreign subsidiaries are located. In addition, this better access to foreign capital markets can help multinationals raise capital if there are financial market disruptions in one part of the world.

For example, during the financial crisis of 2008, capital raising in the United States and Europe became extremely difficult. Firms with Asian operations, where capital markets continued to function more or less normally, consequently had an advantage in raising capital and so were better able to weather the crisis. This funding advantage makes multinational firms' income more stable than domestic firms' income. Consistent with this idea, figure 5-3 documents that U.S. multinationals' foreign income as a percentage of sales has been growing irrespective of business cycles, while their domestic income declines during down cycles.

Multinational firms also can take advantage of interest rate differences

TABLE 5-8. Regressions: Access to Foreign Bank Loans

	(1)	(2)	(3)	(4)
Dep. Var. =	Borrow from foreign lender = 1		% foreign lender in syndicate	
Multinational	0.050***		0.035***	
	(7.35)		(7.19)	
% foreign income		0.108***		0.092***
		(9.07)		(10.26)
Loan size	0.015***	0.015***	0.008***	0.008***
	(4.59)	(4.64)	(3.09)	(3.12)
Maturity	−0.018***	−0.018***	−0.010***	−0.010***
	(-4.57)	(−4.55)	(−3.56)	(−3.63)
Secured	0.012**	0.013**	0.010***	0.011***
	(2.00)	(2.05)	(2.67)	(2.80)
Revolver	−0.013**	−0.014**	−0.025***	−0.025***
	(−2.10)	(−2.19)	(−5.53)	(−5.50)
Term loan	0.025***	0.024***	0.026***	0.026***
	(4.18)	(4.01)	(6.95)	(6.83)
# Lenders	0.252***	0.252***	0.060***	0.059***
	(71.30)	(71.11)	(21.54)	(21.43)
Firm size	0.029***	0.029***	0.034***	0.033***
	(9.69)	(9.71)	(14.63)	(14.53)
Firm profitability	0.007	0.008	−0.067***	−0.068***
	(0.28)	(0.30)	(−3.70)	(−3.76)
Firm tangibility	0.006	0.004	−0.002	−0.001
	(0.34)	(0.25)	(−0.15)	(−0.11)
Year FE	Y	Y	Y	Y
Industry FE	Y	Y	Y	Y
Borrower rating FE	Y	Y	Y	Y
Deal purpose FE	Y	Y	Y	Y
Observations	34,135	33,717	34,135	33,717
Adj-R^2	0.499	0.499	0.291	0.294

Note: This table presents estimates of the relation between having multinational operations and access to foreign lenders in bank loans. The estimation is from the OLS regression, where the dependent variable is the indicator that a syndicate includes at least one foreign lender in columns (1) to (2) and the percentage of the foreign lenders in the syndicate in columns (3) to (4). The sample includes syndicated bank loans issued to U.S. public firms in Compustat from 1990 to 2018 from Dealscan. All firm-level controls are obtained from Compustat, and they are estimated in one year prior to the loan issuance year. *Multinational* is the indicator denoting a multinational borrower that reports non-zero foreign income (PIFO) at any point in the last three years, and *% foreign income* is the absolute value of foreign income (PIFO), divided by the sum of absolute values of domestic (PIDOM) and foreign income (PIFO). We define *loan size* as log of loan amount in US$ millions, *maturity* as log of maturity in months, *secured* as an indicator variable equal to one if the loan package is secured and equal to zero otherwise, *revolver* as an indicator variable equal to one if the loan package includes a revolver, *term loan* as an indicator variable equal to one if the loan package includes a term loan, *# lenders* as log of the number of lenders in the syndicate, *firm size* as log of total assets (AT), *firm profitability* as operating income before depreciation (OIBDP) scaled by total assets, and *firm tangibility* as property, plant, and equipment (PPENT) scaled by total assets. S&P rating is based on long-term public bond rating (SPLTICRM) coded into eight categories as AAA, AA, A, BBB, BB, B, CCC+ and below, and unrated. All regressions include loan issuance year fixed effects, industry (measured in SIC two-digit code) fixed effects, S&P rating fixed effects, and deal purpose fixed effects. Standard errors are corrected for clustering of observations at the firm level and associated t-statistics are in parentheses. The symbols ***, **, and * denote statistical significance at the 1 percent, 5 percent, and 10 percent levels.

TABLE 5-9. Equity Ownership

	Multinational (A)	Domestic (B)	Diff. (A) – (B)
Foreign ownership	4.27%	1.77%	2.50***
Ownership by country			
United Kingdom	1.41%	0.62%	0.79***
Canada	0.86%	0.44%	0.42***
Germany	0.41%	0.26%	0.15***
Norway	0.35%	0.13%	0.22***
China	0.24%	0.13%	0.12***
Japan	0.20%	0.07%	0.13***
Netherlands	0.18%	0.07%	0.12***
France	0.16%	0.07%	0.10***
Sweden	0.12%	0.06%	0.06***
# Firm-year obs.	25,852	49,241	

Note: This table presents the percentage of foreign institutional ownership of equity of U.S. public firms. The sample includes firm-year panel of publicly traded U.S. firms in Compustat from 2000 to 2017 with positive total assets and sales reported. A firm is defined as *multinational* if it reports non-zero foreign income at any point in the past three years, and as *domestic* otherwise. The institutional holding information is obtained from Factset, and we aggregate mutual fund holdings and institutional holdings reported in 13F filings at the firm level to estimate the percentage of number of shares held by foreign institutional investors. When a firm-year observation is not matched to the Factset institutional holding data, we treat missing information as zero. The columns show the average of foreign ownership and the ownership by institutional investors from each country as the percentage of total number of shares outstanding of multinational firms (A) and domestic firms (B). The difference reported is based on t-test of the mean. The symbols ***, **, and * denote statistical significance at the 1 percent, 5 percent, and 10 percent levels.

across countries. If rates differ in countries and firms do not perceive that the differences are offset by changes in expected currency movements, then firms can benefit by issuing debt in countries with lower rates. In principle, domestic firms could raise debt in any country. However, in practice, multinational firms are much more likely to raise capital outside their own country, and as Jang (2017) documents, they are especially likely to raise debt in countries where their foreign operations are located. Consistent with this idea, Henderson, Jegadeesh, and Weisbach (2006) and McBrady, Mortal, and Schill (2010) find that firms are more likely to issue bonds in countries with lower rates, and Keloharju and Niskanen (2001) find that a sample of Finnish companies were more likely to issue foreign bank debt when interest rates in Finland were relatively high. Allen (2019) links these decisions directly to monetary policy; he finds that when one country's central bank lowers rates, multinational firms in other countries become more likely to raise debt in that country's currency.

Multinational firms, even if they focus on one industry, are like a multidivisional firm in that each country's operation usually operates separately from the others and thus has different exposures to country-specific shocks. Consequently, much of the internal capital markets literature is relevant to multinational firms as well. Diversifying operations and using internal capital markets could, in principle, lead to cross-subsidization that lowers financial constraints (see, for example, Stein (1997, 2003)). Since a firm's cash flows in different countries are exposed to different shocks, international diversification could reduce the overall volatility of cash flows and lower default risk through cross-subsidization across countries. The diversification of cash flows across countries provides multinationals with a financing advantage over domestic firms even if their marginal source of finance is from domestic sources.

To examine the importance of the cross-country internal capital markets generated by multinational firms, Desai, Foley, and Forbes (2008) compare the way in which large currency depreciations affect multinational and domestic firms. Consistent with the notion that multinationals have more diverse sources of capital, these authors find that U.S. multinational corporations increased sales, assets, and investment significantly more than domestic firms during and after these currency depreciations. They also provide direct evidence suggesting that the cross-country internal capital markets created by multinationals' operations in multiple countries give them a competitive advantage during large currency depreciations.

FIGURE 5-3. Domestic Income versus Foreign Income for U.S. Multinational Firms over NBER Business Cycles

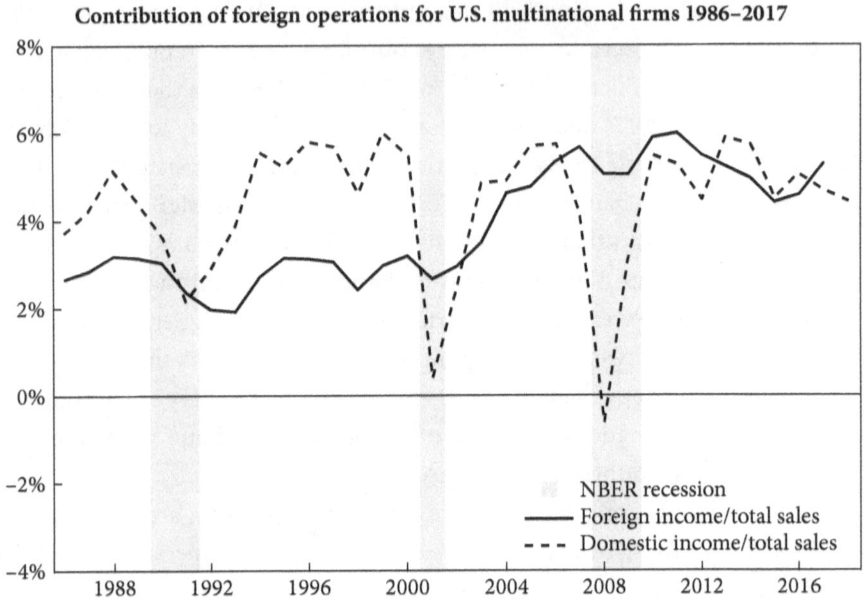

Note: This figure documents the domestic income and foreign income for U.S. multinational firms from 1986 to 2017. The sample includes the U.S. multinational firms that report pretax foreign income at any point in the past three years. The solid line depicts the average of the ratio of foreign income to sales, and the dotted line depicts the average of the ratio of domestic income to sales. The gray areas denote the NBER recession years.

Estimates of the Multinationals' Cost of Finance

The Cost of Debt

Multinationals have several financing-cost advantages over domestic firms. Shocks that affect one country but not others have limited impact on multinationals, lowering the volatility of their cash flows and decreasing their likelihood of a default. In addition, if there is a credit crunch in one part of the world, a multinational can take advantage of short-term borrowing opportunities in areas not affected by the crunch. However, multinationals also face additional costs not borne by domestic firms—from political risk and exchange rate risk. So, it is not obvious whether, on net, multinationals' cost of capital should be higher or lower than domestic firms.

Reeb, Mansi, and Allee (2001) estimate the cost of debt for multinationals, focusing on corporate bond markets. These authors compare the rates paid on newly issued bonds by multinationals and domestic firms. They find that firms with international operations tend to have better credit ratings and therefore higher debt capacities. This finding suggests that, consistent with the diversification arguments, all else being equal, multinational firms have lower costs of debt than otherwise identical domestic firms. In addition, Reeb, Mansi, and Allee (2011) suggest that the lower cost of debt goes beyond what debt ratings convey; the market evidently incorporates the international aspects of firms' operations even more than debt-rating analysts.

Houston, Itzkowitz, and Naranjo (2007) analyze the time series of syndicated loans in ten countries. They find that loans to European firms carry significantly lower spreads than loans to North American firms. They find that multinationals enjoy this cheaper bank funding only by using lead arrangers in Europe. They also find that larger firms, on average, pay lower spreads on their loans when they borrow from a foreign lender. This evidence suggests that global competition has helped reduce borrowing costs for multinational firms with greater access to lending markets around the world.

We present our own analysis of whether multinationals have a lower cost of debt than domestic firms in table 5-10. This analysis uses the Dealscan database, and presents estimates of equations predicting loan spreads as a function of whether the firm is multinational, as well as a host of other firm-level and loan-level factors that potentially affect spreads. In column 1, the coefficient on the multinational dummy is −4.4 and is statistically significantly different from zero. This estimate implies that multinational firms pay about 4.4 basis points less on their debt than an otherwise identical domestic firm. In column 2, we replace the multinational dummy with the fraction of foreign income; the coefficient is also negative (−8.2) and statistically significantly different from zero. Overall, these equations suggest that when firms are more geographically diverse, they pay lower lending rates.

An important consideration in interpreting these results is the extent to which they are causal. The literature finds that multinational firms pay lower borrowing rates than domestic firms, holding other things constant. However, it is possible that other factors could potentially cause a spurious correlation between multinationality and lower rates. For example, if more profitable firms with more stable cash flows are more likely to diversify internationally, then these firms would likely borrow at lower rates regardless of the marginal effect of their multinational status. While the correlation between being multinational and lending rates appears robust, we cannot definitively say that the causal interpretation is appropriate. Identifying this relationship more precisely would be an excellent topic for future research.

The Cost of Equity

Measuring the cost of equity is typically more difficult than measuring the cost of debt, since equity does not have an observable promised yield that equals the amount of interest the firm will pay if it does not default. Perhaps for this reason, the literature's conclusion on the effect of multinationality on the cost of equity is not as clear as it is for the cost of debt, with the results varying depending on the method used.

Baker, Foley, and Wurgler (2009) study the effect of domestic stock market valuations on firms' foreign direct investment (FDI) decisions. When valuations are unusually high, firms face a particularly low cost of equity, so they have an incentive to invest. The authors find that when multinationals appear to be overvalued in their home country, they take advantage of their valuation and act as cross-border arbitragers through FDI. At least some of the time, Baker, Foley, and Wurgler's results suggest that multinationals have a relatively low cost of equity.

A more direct way to estimate the effect of multinationality on the cost of issuing equity is by considering the returns that are earned by investing in multinationals relative to the returns earned by investing in otherwise identical domestic firms. Both Fillat and Garetto (2015) and Jang, Wang, and Zhang (2018) use this approach. Both papers document that multinationals pay return premiums relative to domestic firms of about twenty-three basis points per month after controlling for local and global pricing factors. These papers attribute multinationals' higher cost of equity to foreign operational risks that cannot be easily reversed when a global downturn hits. Consistent with this idea, Fillat, Garetto, and Oldenski (2015) and Jang, Wang, and Zhang (2018) find evidence that risk premiums are higher for firms operating in countries with higher entry and operational costs from factors such as tax rates and the levels of financial market development and property rights. Other papers focus on the information costs investors must pay to obtain and process information as an explanation for multinational firms' higher cost of equity. For example, Huang (2015) documents a delay in the incorporation of global news into multinational firms' stock prices.

This financing discussion does not include tax considerations. Ample evidence suggests that taxes affect financing in multinationals—perhaps more so than domestic firms, because of the possibility of tax arbitrage across countries.

RISK PROFILES

As companies operate more globally, they face additional risks beyond those faced by domestic firms. In this section, we discuss two such sources of risk: *country risk* (including *political risk*) and *foreign exchange risk.*

Country Risk

The term *country risk* refers to any factor that varies by country (see Damodaran (2018). Country-level risk could occur because of uncertainty about economic conditions that vary across countries—about the country's economic growth, the development and stability of a country's political and legal institutions, and the extent to which the political system favors local firms over foreign ones. Damodaran (2018) concludes that a firm's exposure to country risk is not determined by where the firm is incorporated or traded; it is determined by where a firm operates. Multinational firms can face substantial country risk because they operate across many different countries.

Desai, Foley, and Hines (2008) study the effects of country-specific political risk on U.S. multinational firms' capital structure. Investment returns for subsidiaries from the same parent have different levels of risk in different countries. These returns are more volatile in countries with greater political risk, and these volatile returns are reflected in aggregate foreign returns of the multinational corporations. Desai, Foley, and Hines document that parent companies respond to political risk by increasing leverage in subsidiaries in politically risky countries. Therefore, to limit their aggregate leverage, they also end up reducing their domestic leverage. In other words, multinationals mitigate country-level risks by passing these risks to foreign capital providers for whom it is relatively less costly. They adjust their opera-

TABLE 5-10. Cost of Debt

	(1)	(2)
Dep. Var. =	Loan spread	
Multinational	−4.432** (−2.56)	
% foreign income		−8.235*** (−2.73)
Loan size	−11.137*** (−11.29)	−11.157*** (−11.32)
Maturity	−14.499*** (−11.46)	−14.483*** (−11.39)
Secured	57.915*** (35.20)	57.770*** (34.95)
Revolver	9.255*** (4.35)	9.443*** (4.42)
Term loan	54.887*** (30.84)	54.722*** (30.74)
# Lenders	−7.857*** (−8.41)	−7.885*** (−8.45)
Firm size	−6.626*** (−7.31)	−6.769*** (−7.47)
Firm profitability	−230.751*** (−26.90)	−231.976*** (−26.86)
Firm tangibility	−0.580 (−0.13)	−0.629 (−0.14)
Year FE	Y	Y
Industry FE	Y	Y
Borrower rating FE	Y	Y
Deal purpose FE	Y	Y
Observations	29,016	28,660
Adj-R^2	0.549	0.550

Note: This table presents estimates of the relation between having multinational operations and cost of debt. The estimation is from the OLS regression, where the dependent variable is the all-in-drawn spread in basis points. The sample includes syndicated bank loans issued to U.S. public firms in Compustat during the period from 1990 to 2018 from Dealscan. All firm-level controls are obtained from Compustat and they are estimated in one year prior to the loan issuance year. *Multinational* is the indicator denoting a multinational borrower that reports non-zero foreign income (PIFO) at any point in the past three years, and *% foreign income* is the absolute value of foreign income (PIFO), divided by the sum of absolute values of domestic (PIDOM) and foreign income (PIFO). We define *loan size* as log of loan amount in U.S. million dollars, *maturity* as log of maturity in months, *secured* as an indicator variable equal to one if the loan package is secured and equal to zero otherwise, *revolver* as an indicator variable equal to one if the loan package includes a revolver, *term loan* as an indicator variable equal to one if the loan package includes a term loan, *# lenders* as log of the number of lenders in the syndicate, *firm size* as log of total assets (AT), *firm profitability* as operating income before depreciation (OIBDP) scaled by total assets (AT), and *firm tangibility* as property, plant and equipment (PPENT) scaled by total assets. S&P rating is based on long-term public bond rating (SPLTICRM) coded into eight categories as AAA, AA, A, BBB, BB, B, CCC+ and below, and unrated. All regressions include loan issuance year fixed effects, industry (measured in SIC two-digit code) fixed effects, S&P rating fixed effects, and deal purpose fixed effects. Standard errors are corrected for clustering of observations at the firm level, and associated t-statistics are in parentheses. The symbols ***, **, and * denote statistical significance at the 1 percent, 5 percent, and 10 percent levels.

tions accordingly, as well. For example, U.S. MNCs serving customers in politically risky countries are more likely to serve these customers through exports from the United States rather than local production.

Multinational firms often enter foreign markets through acquisitions. Political and cultural differences can affect cross-border acquisitions, since political pressure in host countries often favors local companies over foreign acquirers, representing an important risk facing multinational firms.

Dinc and Erel (2013) evaluate this risk by studying governments' reactions to merger and acquisition (M&A) bids by foreign and domestic firms. They provide strong evidence of economic nationalism in the M&A markets; many local governments prefer that target companies remain domestically owned rather than foreign-owned. The authors show that governments implement national policies against foreign acquisition through several methods, including delaying regulatory approvals, using golden shares in previously privatized companies, publicly opposing the deals, and providing financing to the rival bidders from their national banks. These nationalistic reactions directly and indirectly affect the functioning of M&A markets. They not only lead active cross-border acquisition bids to fail but also deter foreign companies from bidding for other companies in that country. Consequently, this type of political risk can impede international capital flows.[13]

Foreign Exchange Risk

Currency fluctuations can affect the value of multinational firms' foreign earnings.[14] Adler and Dumas (1984) and Dumas and Solnik (1995) show that all firms, either domestic or multinational, are exposed to currency risk to some extent. However, this risk tends to be larger for multinational firms, because a substantial fraction of their cash flows and costs are in foreign currencies. Jorion (1990) documents that exposure of U.S. multinationals to foreign exchange risk increases with the fraction of their foreign operations.

Dewenter, Schrand, and Wang (2016) study U.S. multinationals' net exposure to currency risk by analyzing twenty-three countries that shifted from fixed to floating exchange rate regimes. Fifteen of these currencies initially were tied to the U.S. dollar, and eight were tied to other currencies. The authors observe whether multinationals exposed to these currency regime shifts hedged their foreign exchange exposure, either operationally or financially. Using a difference-in-differences design, which exploits changes for currencies tied to the U.S. dollar versus other currencies for hedgers and non-hedgers, the authors conclude that the net exposure to currency risk is significant for U.S. multinational firms. While hedging offsets the exposure, the net currency risk positions are value-relevant. However, strategic considerations appear to outweigh currency-risk considerations in the multinationals' cross-border investment decisions.

SUMMARY

Multinational firms are becoming the predominate type of public corporation. They amount to about half of publicly traded firms in the United States and a substantial fraction worldwide as well. Value-weighted, the numbers are even higher, with multinationals accounting for 57 percent of the U.S. public equity market. Thus, understanding how multinational factors affect corporate financial decisions is important.

Multinational firms can better access capital markets outside their home countries. They can take advantage of interest rate differentials in different parts of the world when raising debt and equity externally. However, multinational firms also face costs not borne by domestic firms; they face both country risk and foreign exchange risk.

As global markets become more integrated and firms become even more multinational, the financial issues facing these firms are likely to become increasingly important. The ability of financial managers to choose between alternative capital markets will increase, and capital markets will become more competitive internationally. Unfortunately, the rise of nationalism is likely to adversely affect multinational firms as well. Consequently, the issues raised in this chapter likely will be increasingly important over time, so they should demand attention both from practitioners managing their balance sheets and from academics studying financial management practices.

NOTES

We thank Fritz Foley, Jim Hines, David Wessel, and participants in a presentation at Brookings for very helpful suggestions. Greg Allen, Hyeik Kim, and Rick Ogden provided excellent research assistance.

1. Forty-eight percent of publicly traded firms in the U.S. were multinationals, defined as corporations with any foreign income reported in the previous three years, a definition slightly different from the one used in chapter 1 of this volume.

2. Index of stocks of twenty-three developed countries compiled by MSCI Inc. of New York, N.Y.

3. We use pretax foreign income (PIFO) in Compustat and international operating income (WC07126) in Worldscope. Although Jang (2017) complements this definition using information on the location of subsidiaries from the firms' 10K filings with the U.S. Securities and Exchange Commission, we concentrate on this definition based on non-zero foreign income due to data constraints.

4. We use international sales (WC07101) in Worldscope.

5. The definitions for multinational firms in both approaches might not be comparable across countries, as reporting requirements for foreign income or foreign sales might vary by country. In the case of the United States, all publicly traded firms are required to disclose foreign income or foreign sales separately for material foreign operations or sales. For example, SEC regulation §210.4-08(h) requires any U.S. public firm to separately disclose pretax income and income tax expenses for domestic and foreign operations, if any of these measures for non-U.S. operations exceed 5 percent of the consolidated total. Under SFAS No. 131, any U.S. public firm must separately report information about an operating segment if its reported revenue is 10 percent or more of the combined revenue of all reported operating segments.

6. See Crunchbase for details of Uber's financing history.

7. We drop seven countries—Argentina, Egypt, Pakistan, Peru, Qatar, Saudi Arabia, and the United Arab Emirates—because of poor coverage of foreign sales or foreign income variables in Worldscope.

8. We rely on the foreign income–based definition of multinational firms here and throughout the rest of the chapter. Similar tables created based on the foreign sales–based definition are available upon request from the authors.

9. Each company listed on the NYSE, AMEX, and NASDAQ is assigned in the Fama-French database to an industry portfolio, based on its four-digit SIC code.

10. The "pecking order" theory holds that a firm should prefer to finance itself through retained earnings first. If those are not available, it should turn to debt issuance and then equity issuance.

11. See Henderson, Jegadeesh, and Weisbach (2006), appendix C, for details on the amount of different types of capital that firms from several countries receive from each other's country.

12. Issuing capital through a cross-listing rather than a private placement or a sale on the local exchange allows investors to receive communications in their home language and binds the issuing firm to comply with local securities laws. For a detailed

discussion of the way cross-listings work, and the regulations that affect them, see Karolyi (1998).

13. See also Ahern, Daminelli, and Fracassi (2015), which documents that the volume of cross-border mergers is lower when countries of merging firms are culturally more distant.

14. Shapiro (1975) presents a formal model of exposure to exchange rate changes for multinational firms.

REFERENCES

Adler, M., and B. Dumas (1984). "Exposure to Currency Risk: Definition and Measurement," *Financial Management, 13* (2), 41.

Ahern, K. R., D. Daminelli, and C. Fracassi (2015). "Lost in Translation? The Effect of Cultural Values on Mergers Around the World," *Journal of Financial Economics, 117 (1)*, 165–89.

Allen, G. D. (2019) "Foreign Monetary Policy and the Currency Composition of Corporate Debt." working paper, Ohio State University.

Baker, M., C. F. Foley, and J. Wurgler (2009). "Multinationals as Arbitrageurs: The Effect of Stock Market Valuations on Foreign Direct Investment," *Review of Financial Studies, 22* (1), 337–69.

Damodaran, A. (2017). "Country Risk: Determinants, Measures, and Implications—The 2017 Edition" (July 9). Available at SSRN: http://dx.doi.org/10.2139/ssrn.3000499.

Denis, D. J., D. K. Denis, and K. Yost (2002). "Global Diversification, Industrial Diversification, and Firm Value," *Journal of Finance, 57* (5), 1951–79.

Desai, M. A., C. F. Foley, and K. J. Forbes (2008). "Financial Constraints and Growth: Multinational and Local Firm Responses to Currency Depreciations," *Review of Financial Studies, 21* (6), 2857–88.

Desai, M. A., C. F. Foley, and J. R. Hines Jr. (2008). "Capital Structure with Risky Foreign Investment," *Journal of Financial Economics*, 88, 534–53.

Dewenter, K. L., C. M. Schrand, and C. Wang (2016). "The Impact of Currency Risk on U.S. MNCs: Evidence from Currency Crises," *Critical Finance Review*, 7 (1), 1–53.

Dinc, S. and I. Erel (2013). "Economic Nationalism in Mergers and Acquisitions," *Journal of Finance*, 68, 2471–2514.

Doidge, C., A. Karolyi, and R. Stulz (2009). "Has New York Become Less Competitive than London in Global Markets? Evaluating Foreign Listing Choices over Time," *Journal of Financial Economics*, 91, 253–87.

Doidge, C., A. Karolyi, and R. Stulz (2017). "The U.S. Listing Gap," *Journal of Financial Economics*, 123, 464–87.

Dumas, B. and B. Solnik (1995). "The World Price of Foreign Exchange Risk," *Journal of Finance, 50* (2), 445–79.

Ferreira, M. and P. Matos (2008). "The Colors of Investors' Money: The Role of Institutional Investors around the World," *Journal of Financial Economics*, 88, 499–533.

Fillat, J. L. and S. Garetto (2015). "Risk, Returns, and Multinational Production," *Quarterly Journal of Economics, 130* (4), 2027–73.

Fillat, J. L., S. Garetto, and L. Oldenski (2015). "Diversification, Cost Structure, and the Risk Premium of Multinational Corporations," *Journal of International Economics, 96* (1), 37–54.

Henderson, B., N. Jegadeesh, and M. S. Weisbach (2006). "World Markets for Raising New Capital," *Journal of Financial Economics*, 82, 63–101.

Houston, J. F., J. Itzkowitz, and A. Naranjo (2007). "Borrowing Beyond Borders: The Geography and Pricing of Syndicated Bank Loans." *SSRN* (March).

Huang, X. (2015). "Thinking outside the Borders: Investors' Underreaction to Foreign Operations Information," *Review of Financial Studies*, 28 (11), 3109–52.

Jang, Y. (2017). "International Corporate Diversification and Financial Flexibility," *Review of Financial Studies, 30* (12), 4133–78.

Jang, Y., X. Wang, and X. Zhang (2018). "The Multinational Return Premium: Investor's Perspective," working paper, University of New South Wales.

Jorion, P. (1990). "The Exchange-Rate Exposure of U.S. Multinationals," *Journal of Business, 63* (3), 331–45.

Karolyi, A. (1998). "Why Do Companies List Their Shares Abroad? A Survey of the Evidence and Its Managerial Implications," *Salomon Brothers Monograph Series* 7 (1).

Keloharju, M. and M. Niskanen (2001). "Why Do Firms Raise Foreign Currency Denominated Debt? Evidence from Finland," *European Financial Management*, 7, 481–96.

McBrady, M. R., S. Mortal, and M. J. Schill (2010). "Do Firms Believe in Interest Rate Parity?" *Review of Finance*, 14, 695–726.

Myers, S. and N. Majluf (1984). "Corporate Financing and Investment Decisions: When Firms Have Information Investors Do Not Have," *Journal of Financial Economics*, 13, 187–221.

Pinkowitz, L., R. M. Stulz, and R. Williamson (2016). "Do U.S. Firms Hold More Cash than Foreign Firms Do?" *Review of Financial Studies*, 29 (2), 309–48.

Reeb, D., S. A. Mansi, and J. M. Allee (2001). "Firm Internationalization and the Cost of Debt Financing: Evidence from Non-Provisional Publicly Traded Debt," *Journal of Financial and Quantitative Analysis, 36* (3), 395–414.

Shapiro, A. C. (1975). "Exchange Rate Changes, Inflation, and the Value of the Multinational Corporation," *Journal of Finance, 30* (2), 485–502.

Stein, J. (1997). "Internal Capital Markets and the Competition for Corporate Resources," *Journal of Finance*, 52, 111–33.

Stein, J. (2003). "Agency, Information, and Corporate Investment," in *Handbook of the Economics of Finance*, edited by G. M. Constantinides, M. Harris, and R. M. Stulz.

Sufi, A. (2007). "Information Asymmetry and Financing Arrangements: Evidence from Syndicated Loans," *Journal of Finance*, 62, 629–68.

6

Do Multinational Firms Export Jobs?

LINDSAY OLDENSKI

By definition, multinational firms do some of their work outside of their headquarters country. As a result, it may seem inevitable that they "export jobs" by hiring employees in other countries. This process, known as offshoring, often has very negative connotations, conjuring up images of firms that fire workers at home and replace them with cheaper labor in another country. And this type of offshoring certainly does occur, which results in real harm to the displaced workers. Yet multinational firms are large and complex. They expand abroad in many different ways and for many different reasons, which may have different consequences for workers in their home country, some positive and some negative. For example, a U.S. firm may set up a plant abroad not to replace U.S. production, but to gain access to a market that would have been otherwise difficult to serve. This market access may allow the firm to grow and expand in ways that benefit its employees at home as well as abroad.

This chapter will examine the evidence on offshoring by multinational firms and draw conclusions about the aggregate effects on U.S. workers, as well as identify which types of workers are more likely to gain or lose from offshoring and how big those gains and losses are likely to be. It will also evaluate programs designed to help workers displaced by offshoring.

Because the United States has much higher wages and worker benefits than other countries, firms have an incentive to cut costs through offshoring and labor-substituting technologies. However, the data show that while some U.S. workers are displaced, new high-paying jobs are created in the United States by firms that offshore production. In general, more highly skilled workers are likely to gain, and lower-skilled workers are more likely to lose, jobs. Programs that help retrain displaced workers have been shown to mitigate the losses, though these programs would need to be greatly expanded if all workers who have been negatively affected by offshoring are to be assisted.

In this chapter, the word "offshoring" will be used to describe any production done by a multinational enterprise (MNE) outside of its headquarters country. Offshoring can take the form of a U.S. company shutting down a factory in the United States and moving those jobs to another country. In this case, some U.S. workers are clearly hurt. They are left unemployed and competing with other unemployed workers for potentially scarce jobs. But this is not the only effect of offshoring on U.S. workers. While some U.S. workers are clearly hurt by offshoring, others gain as their firms become more competitive, allowing the firms to expand and hire more employees in the United States. Sorting out the different effects of offshoring is challenging. One problem is that the jobs that are lost due to offshoring and the jobs that are gained are often in different cities or different occupations. Not only does this complicate our understanding of how offshoring works, it also does not reassure an auto assembly worker in Detroit to say that new sales jobs are available in California. In many cases, it is extremely difficult for workers to find jobs that are similar to the ones that were offshored, which results in very real costs.

Ford Motor company provides one example of the complexity of multinational production. Ford announced plans in 2016 to shift all of its small-car production from the United States to Mexico. But around the same time, it also announced plans to invest US$4.5 billion over the subsequent four years in new battery-powered models and reiterated its commitment to developing an autonomous vehicle, work that would primarily be done in the United States (Gardner (2016)). By itself, the decision to shift small-car production to Mexico could be seen as a huge loss for U.S. workers and the U.S. manufacturing sector more broadly. Yet that step freed resources for the development of the next generation of battery-powered and driverless cars. As jobs were destroyed in the old production lines, new ones were created in the forward-looking models. The problem is that workers who used to assemble small cars may not have the skills needed to work on more technologically advanced battery-powered or driverless cars. This leads to unemployment and increased income inequality at the same time that it creates new high-paying jobs.

It is also extremely difficult to separate the effects of offshoring from other factors affecting employment, such as technology change, consumer demand, and the overall health of the economy. U.S. manufacturing employment, as a share of total U.S. employment, has been declining steadily since the 1950s, long before offshoring became a trend. Much of that decline has been due to technology and a shift in consumption away from goods and toward services. At the same time, technological advances have made it easier to offshore services as well as goods, leading to greater concerns among white-collar workers. Measuring the offshoring of services presents its own problems. They are less tangible than goods, and thus harder to measure.

The following sections will review what we know about the various effects of different types of offshoring on different types of workers, and try to paint a more complete picture of how those effects fit together to affect the overall economy. They will look at who is hurt by offshoring, and how big those costs are, as well as who benefits and how large those gains are. Conclusions will be drawn about the net effects on the U.S. economy as well as distributional consequences and concerns for individual workers.

WHAT, WHERE, WHY, AND HOW DO FIRMS OFFSHORE?

To understand the effects of offshoring on U.S. workers, it is important to first understand where and how firms operate abroad.

Figure 6-1 shows the top ten locations for offshoring by U.S. MNEs. Offshoring is measured using the value added by U.S.-owned firms in each host country. This value-added measure is preferable to measures of financial flows, because it captures the actual economic activity performed by U.S. firms in each country. Only two of the top ten destinations, Mexico and China, are developing countries, and they only account for 14 percent of the total value added in the top ten offshoring locations. When U.S. firms produce abroad, they are much more likely to do so in high-income countries than in low-income countries. This suggests that taking advantage of low wages is not the primary motivation for firms to produce abroad. Instead, firms consider a variety of factors, including worker skills, local institutions, tax policy, proximity to global value chains, and the size of the local market.

In almost all cases, U.S. MNEs sell at least some of what they produce

FIGURE 6-1. Top Ten U.S. Foreign Direct Investment Destinations in 2016 *(US$ billion of value added)*

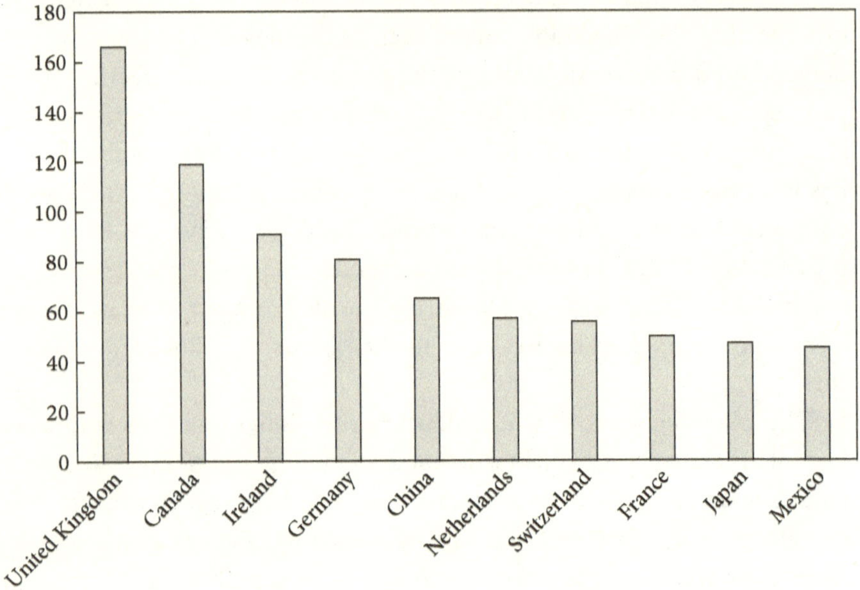

Source: Author's calculations based on data published by the U.S. Bureau of Economic Analysis

abroad to customers in the host country. From 1987 to 2011, about 95 percent of foreign affiliates of U.S. MNEs in the manufacturing sector sold some goods to the local market, and about 37 percent sold exclusively to their host market (Garetto, Oldenski, and Ramondo (2019)). In many cases, market-seeking is the primary reason for expanding internationally in the first place. In 2009, affiliates of U.S. MNEs abroad accounted for 75 percent of U.S. sales to foreign customers. It is likely that at least some of these sales would not have been made if U.S. firms had not located close to their customers. Proximity to customers is necessary for the sale of many goods and services and motivates a large share of foreign direct investment (FDI) by U.S. firms (Oldenski (2012)). In this case, FDI may allow U.S. firms to expand and gain market share relative to their foreign competitors, benefiting their U.S. workers rather than substituting for them.

Most MNEs do some combination of different types of FDI, including assembling goods to be consumed at home, sourcing intermediate inputs, and selling to local markets. However, when people discuss offshoring, it is often global sourcing and assembly that they have in mind. When firms expand to find customers, they may be more likely to do so to higher-income countries where customers can afford to buy their goods and services. But offshoring that is done to cut production costs may be more likely to take place in countries where workers earn much lower wages than workers in the United States. To focus on this second motive, it is useful to consider only U.S. MNEs that produce something abroad that is then shipped back to the United States. Figure 6-2 shows the volumes of U.S. imports from majority-owned affiliates of U.S. firms in 2016 (the latest year for which data are available) for the top ten source countries. These represent goods that were produced abroad by U.S. MNEs and then shipped to the United States. Unfortunately, the data do not distinguish between imports that are sold to consumers in the United States and imports of intermediates, which may have been used in the production of goods that could either be consumed in the United States or eventually exported. However, this category does remove pure market-seeking FDI, and focuses on sales to the United States (either to U.S. consumers or U.S. firms). Even within this group, most of these within-firm imports are from other developed countries. Only three of the top ten are developing countries—Mexico, China, and Hong Kong—

FIGURE 6-2. U.S. Imports from Majority-Owned Foreign Affiliates of U.S. MNEs in 2016
(US$ billion)

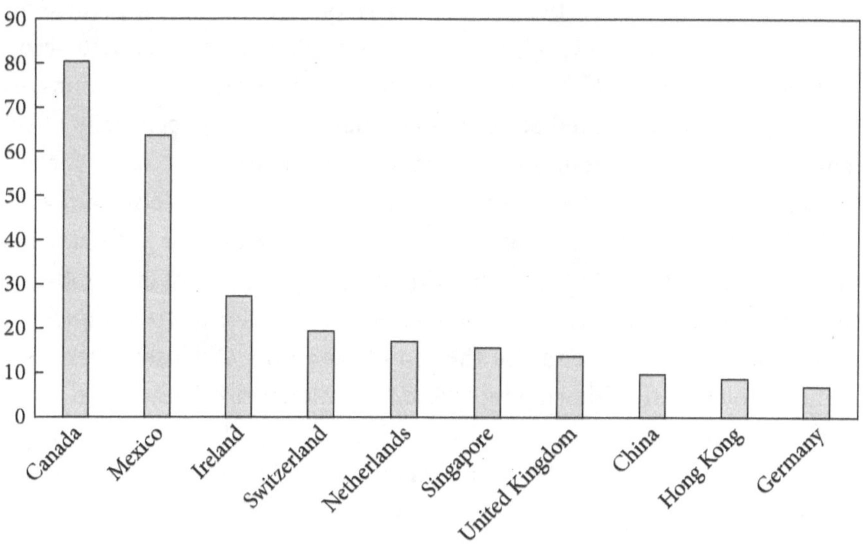

Source: Author's calculations based on data published by the U.S. Bureau of Economic Analysis

making up 31 percent of within-firm imports from the top ten countries. Again, this suggests that low wages are not the primary motivation for offshoring by U.S. MNEs.

Even the most global firms do not offshore all of their production, because, as studies show, to do so would be infeasible. Blinder and Krueger (2013) asked U.S. workers detailed questions about the nature of their jobs, then used that information to create an index of how feasible it would be to offshore each job. The authors used several approaches, including asking workers directly about the possibility of offshoring their job, hiring professional coders to create offshorability measures using characteristics of the job requirements, and creating an index themselves. All of these approaches concluded that about 25 percent of U.S. jobs were offshorable, much more than estimates from other studies. For example, by looking at data on sector in which at least some offshoring has already taken place, Bardhan and Kroll (2003) conclude that about 11 percent of all U.S. jobs are potentially offshorable. Similarly, a McKinsey Global Institute study (2005) concluded that about 11 percent of service-sector employment was technically capable of being offshored. Note that these estimates are all upper bounds, as they capture the share of jobs that *could* be offshored, not the share of jobs that *will* be offshored. These studies suggest that even when U.S. firms take advantage of offshoring opportunities, they still need to perform much of their work in the United States for practical reasons related to technology, the need for customer interaction, or legal restrictions. Moreover, as pointed out by Jensen and Kletzer (2008), referring to jobs that can be relocated across borders as "offshorable" misses the fact that many of these occupations are areas in which the United States has comparative advantage. Many of the characteristics that are used to classify "offshorability" actually capture "tradability." Trade includes exports as well as imports, so some of the so-called offshorable products may actually be exported by the United States instead of offshored. Rather than a threat, the tradability of these jobs can present an opportunity for U.S. workers, who can perform services and, to a lesser extent, produce goods for the rest of the world. Oldenski (2012) used data on the actual offshoring by U.S. multinationals to characterize which types of goods and services U.S. firms are more likely to produce in the United States and which are more likely to be produced abroad. The results suggest that U.S. MNEs move the most routine tasks to other countries, keeping jobs that require more complex skills, decisionmaking, and communication in the United States. This is, in part, because routine tasks are easier to separate from the firm's headquarters. But the United States also has a comparative advantage in nonroutine tasks such as problem solving, creative thinking, and making decisions. These results are consistent with the findings of other studies, including Firpo, Fortin, and Lemieux (2011) and Ebenstein, Harrison, McMillan, and Phillips (2014), which use data for the United States, as well as Baumgarten, Geishecker, and Görg (2013) and Becker, Ekholm, and Muendler (2013), which use data on Germany.

CHANGES IN OFFSHORING OVER TIME

Some of the concerns over MNE offshoring stem from the perception that it has been increasing. Figure 6-3 shows that, indeed, the share of total employment by U.S. MNEs that is located outside of the U.S. has been increasing in recent decades, going from about 25 percent in 1997 to about 35 percent in 2016. The foreign employment share seems to have leveled off, or even decreased, between 2013 and 2016. This could mean that U.S. MNEs began to do more work in the United States, relative to other countries, in 2013–2016. But it is important to note that figure 6-3 shows employment only *within* multinational companies. If firms are purchasing goods and services from contractors in other countries rather than making them in the majority-owned affiliates, this could also show up as a decline in the share of MNE employment at foreign affiliates.

THE ROLE OF CONTRACTING AND ARM'S-LENGTH OFFSHORING

Thus far, this chapter has focused on production within multinational firms. But firms may also contract out the provision of goods or services to unrelated companies. Unfortunately, it is extremely difficult to observe this arm's-length offshoring in the data, as U.S. firms are only required by law to report what they produce themselves. Information published by the U.S. Census Bureau, however, is instructive.

Census Bureau data break out the share of total imports that are shipped between related versus unrelated parties. This information, however, has some limitations. Although it includes unrelated-party imports from offshore outsourcing purchases, a large portion of these trade flows are traditional imports that do not involve a multinational firm at all. In addition, the import data are only available for goods, and do not capture any off-

FIGURE 6-3. Share of U.S. MNE Employment Located Outside the United States

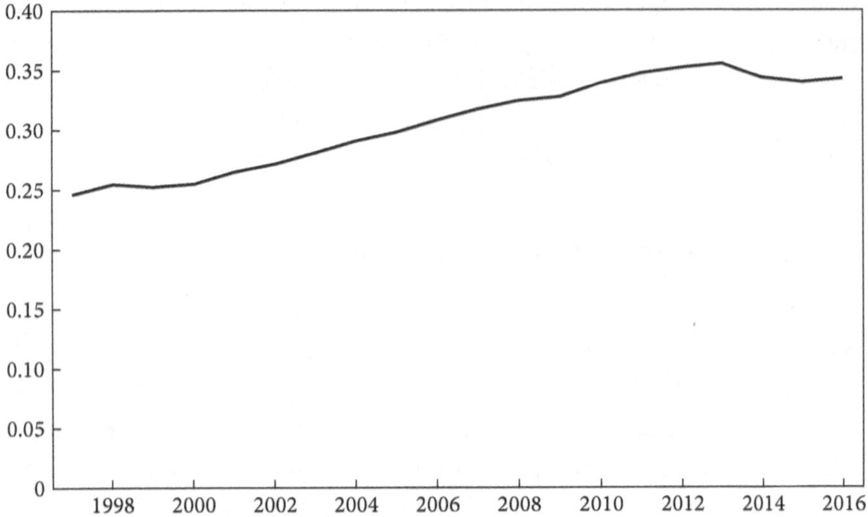

Source: Author's calculations based on data published by the U.S. Bureau of Economic Analysis

shoring of services. With these caveats, figure 6-4[1] shows that related-party imports (those that happen within multinational firms) have consistently made up about 50 percent of all U.S. imports over the past decade. This pattern suggests that even given recent reports of firms using external contractors, production within MNEs is still extremely important. However, if it is becoming increasingly common for MNEs to contract out services—as opposed to goods—that had previously been performed within the firm, then the statistics presented in figure 6-4 may understate the extent to which foreign sourcing by MNEs is growing.

Figure 6-4 suggests that offshoring within multinational firms has not declined as a share of total U.S. imports, even with the option of external contracting. However, because it is difficult to measure the exact extent of outside contracting, it is possible that this type of offshoring is more widespread than the data suggest. From the perspective of workers, the important question is whether U.S. workers will be affected differently by arm's-length offshoring than by MNEs producing at affiliates abroad. Research suggests that workers would not be affected differently, as long as a U.S. MNE is doing the offshoring. Evidence suggests that U.S. workers at non-multinational firms are more negatively affected by imports than workers at multinational firms

FIGURE 6-4. Share of U.S. Imports That Occur within Firms

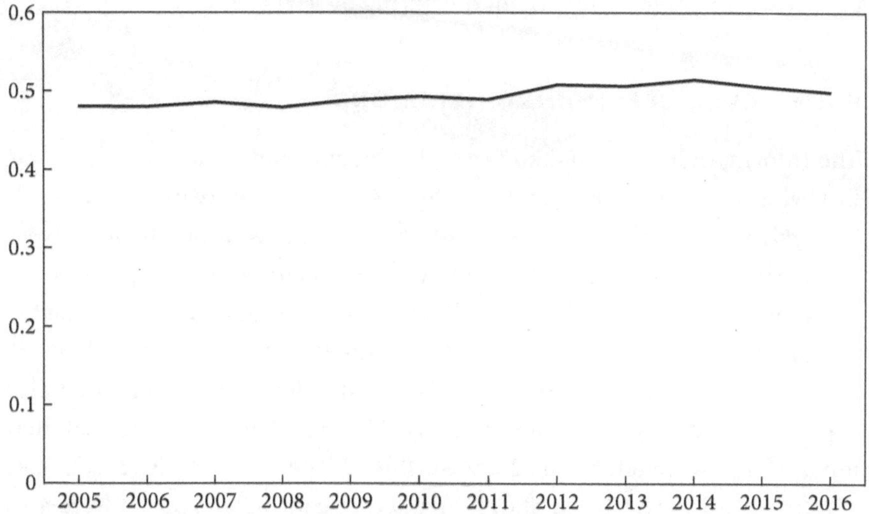

Source: Author's calculations using data from the U.S. Census Bureau Related-Party Trade Database

(Kovak, Oldenski, and Sly (2019); Autor, Dorn, and Hanson (2013)). This is because multinationals experience productivity gains from offshoring that allow them to expand domestically as well as internationally. Imports that consumers purchase from purely foreign firms do not have these benefits. When U.S. workers perform tasks that are complementary to imported goods, most likely (but not necessarily) because the U.S. firm doing the importing employs these workers, then imports can be beneficial. Consider a U.S. electronics firm that hires engineers, project managers, and marketing employees in the United States to design and sell their products, and may also produce some components in the United States. If the firm is able to import some of its inputs or assemble its products abroad, then cost savings may allow it to lower prices and sell more, leading to greater demand for workers in the United States. What matters for the productivity gains in this scenario is that the firm has a presence in the United States, where Americans can be hired when gains from offshoring lead to expansion. These positive effects are likely to exist regardless of whether offshoring happens at arm's length or within the firm. The more negative effects materialize when there is no U.S. presence to gain from the efficiency effects. Of course, in the case of imports, consumers gain from lower prices, and firms that use the imports as inputs into their production are better off, but the employment effects are different in the case of offshoring by MNEs.

FIRM-LEVEL OFFSHORING DECISIONS

The information presented so far looks at aggregate trends in offshoring. But what about within individual firms? The U.S. Bureau of Economic Analysis surveys all U.S.-based multinational firms annually, and every five years conducts a more detailed benchmark survey. Column 1 of table 6-1 shows the number of U.S. MNEs that have expanded and contracted in the United States and abroad between the two most recent benchmark survey years, 2009 and 2014.[2] Most U.S. firms that expanded abroad also expanded in the United States. Of the 1,345 U.S. MNEs that increased their foreign employment between 2009 and 2014, 72 percent also increased their employment in the United States. Firms that contracted abroad were also more likely to add workers in the United States, but they did not expand in the United States at the same rate as the firms that grew both at home and abroad. Of the 908 U.S. MNEs that decreased their foreign employment between 2009 and 2014, 58 percent increased their employment in the United States. This means that the firms that were most likely to hire more workers in the United States were also the firms that hired more workers in other countries.

Of all 2,253 U.S. multinational firms, the largest group expanded both at home and abroad, followed by firms that contracted abroad and expanded at home. In fact, more U.S. firms have grown domestically while reducing their employment abroad than have added workers abroad while scaling back at home. Thus, the raw data show no systematic replacement of U.S. jobs with foreign jobs.

Table 6-1 reports the number of firms with net employment gains and losses. Growth at the median firm was slightly higher in the United States than abroad, and the rate of job loss was lower in the United States than at foreign affiliates. Between 2009 and 2014, the median firm that expanded in the United States had job growth of about 24 percent, and the median foreign employment growth of firms that expanded abroad was 23 percent.[3] For firms with net job losses, those numbers were a 14 percent reduction in the United States and a 23 percent reduction abroad. However, the average employment changes were much larger than the medians, as some large firms had much greater gains and losses. The average employment growth of

TABLE 6-1. Number of Firms That Increased and Decreased Their U.S. and Foreign Employment

	1 2009–2014	2 2010–2015	3 2004–2014	4 2009–2014 Manufacturing	5 2009–2014 Services
Firms that expanded abroad					
. . . and expanded in the U.S.	974 (72%)	959 (73%)	704 (67%)	499 (71%)	475 (74%)
. . . and contracted in the U.S.	371 (28%)	360 (27%)	354 (33%)	200 (29%)	171 (26%)
Firms that contracted abroad					
. . . and expanded in the U.S.	524 (58%)	512 (58%)	293 (47%)	298 (60%)	226 (55%)
. . . and contracted in the U.S.	384 (42%)	372 (42%)	336 (53%)	200 (40%)	184 (45%)

Note: This table was constructed using firm-level data on U.S. multinational companies at the Bureau of Economic Analysis (U.S. Department of Commerce) under arrangements that meet legal confidentiality requirements. The views expressed are those of the author and do not reflect official positions of the U.S. Department of Commerce.

firms that expanded in the United States was 31 percent, while the average growth abroad was 52 percent. Average losses in the United States were 23 percent, and average losses abroad were 32 percent.

The patterns described focus on changes from 2009 to 2014, because they are the two most recent benchmark survey years. But using 2009 as a comparison year may be problematic because of the Great Recession. For that reason, column 2 of table 6-1 reports the same figures for 2010–15. The pattern is very similar. Column 3 of table 6-1 considers changes from 2004 to 2014. Even when the recession years are included in the middle of the sample, the largest category of firms is still those that increase both in the United States and abroad. The main difference between the 2004–14 period and the post-recession years is that firms that contracted abroad between 2004 and 2014 were more likely to also contract in the United States.

Columns 4 and 5 of table 6-1 break down the results by manufacturing and non-manufacturing (service) firms. The patterns are very similar across these two sectors, with service firms exhibiting a slightly higher correlation of hiring patterns in the United States and abroad.

EFFECTS OF OFFSHORING ON DOMESTIC WORKERS

Sorting out the effects of offshoring on domestic workers is extremely difficult, given that many forces other than offshoring may cause job losses. This section reviews the data sources and methodologies that have been used to identify the winners and losers from offshoring, and describes what is known about the magnitude of the effects of offshoring on various types of workers. While some individual workers may be badly hurt by offshoring, the likelihood of any given worker being hurt is relatively low, and the gains to workers who benefit from offshoring are high. Worker training programs have been shown to mitigate the negative effects, but have not been widely implemented in the United States.

Using Trade Adjustment Assistance Data to Identify and Assist Displaced Workers

As mentioned in the introduction, it is much easier to observe the workers who are hurt by offshoring than to observe those who gain. However, even that has its challenges. When a plant closes, it can be difficult to distinguish the role played by offshoring relative to other factors, such as technology, demand, or the overall health of the firm. One approach is to focus on firms and workers that qualify for Trade Adjustment Assistance (TAA). TAA is a U.S. government program that offers assistance to workers hurt by trade and offshoring. Before assistance is provided, a group of three or more workers, a company official, or a union representative must submit a petition to the U.S. Department of Labor (DOL), which then verifies the role of trade in the job dislocation. While some unions, such as the United Steelworkers, publicize and coordinate the process for their members, as of 2011, two-thirds of TAA participants were not union members (Solis and Kirk (2011)).[4] For a petition to be approved, the workers must be harmed either by increased imports or because their firm has shifted production or services to a foreign country. If a petition is approved, individual workers covered by it may apply for benefits. In 2009, 42 percent of certified petitions were due to a shift in production abroad rather than import competition (DOL (2009)). Benefits include subsidized training, career counseling, job search and reallocation allowances, income support for participants in training, and wage insurance for workers older than fifty. From 2007 to 2012, an average of 2,464 TAA petitions were filed annually, covering an average of 158,280 workers per year. Of these, about two-thirds were certified as eligible for TAA by the Department of Labor. However, less than 40 percent of certified workers end up participating in the TAA programs. Thus, a total of about 375,493 U.S. workers received TAA benefits from 2007 to 2012. (Cimino-Isaacs and Hufbauer (2015)). This is an extremely small number, especially compared with the total U.S. jobs that are destroyed and created on a regular basis for reasons other than trade. For example, from September 2018 to December 2018, the United States lost 6.9 million jobs from closing and contracting private-sector establishments. Over the same period, gross job gains from opening and expanding private-sector establishments were 7.7 million, which resulted in a net employment gain of 814,000 jobs in the private sector during the fourth quarter of 2018 (U.S. Bureau of Labor Statistics (2019)). TAA-certified individuals make up a very small share of total laid-off workers.

Table 6-2 shows the distribution of TAA petitions filed and approved by state in fiscal year 2017. These petitions were distributed more or less evenly with state population, showing surprisingly little geographic concentration. Petitions were not filed in only three states (Alaska, Delaware, and Wyoming) in 2017.

TAA-certified individuals are not likely to be representative of all workers affected by trade for several reasons. First, only workers who lose their jobs as a result of trade or offshoring have an incentive to apply, so the statistics do not capture workers who were positively affected by offshoring. Second, laid-off workers who are quickly reemployed have no incentive to apply. Finally, the TAA numbers likely miss many workers who are hurt by trade or offshoring but do not apply for benefits because they lack information about the program or because their employers lack an incentive to apply. Despite these caveats, studying workers who qualify for TAA still can be useful, as it provides information on a specific group that can be easily identified as being negatively affected by offshoring.

Monarch, Park, and Sivadasan (2017) look at about a thousand firms that were certified as offshorers through the TAA program between 1999 and 2006. The authors were not able to follow the outcomes for individual workers, but instead looked at what happened to the firms. Firms whose workers received TAA benefits due to offshoring experienced overall declines in U.S.

TABLE 6-2. Trade Adjustment Assistance Petitions Filed and Approved by State, FY 2017

State	Petitions filed	Petitions certified	Est. # of workers	State	Petitions filed	Petitions certified	Est. # of workers
Alabama	1	4	1,627	Nebraska	11	9	578
Alaska	0	1	13	Nevada	2	1	8
Arizona	12	9	2,294	New Hampshire	5	2	40
Arkansas	13	10	502	New Jersey	35	29	1,567
California	114	91	12,338	New Mexico	3	3	1,842
Colorado	19	18	2,073	New York	85	59	3,065
Connecticut	20	17	949	North Carolina	23	20	3,472
Delaware	0	0	0	North Dakota	1	0	0
DC	1	0	0	Ohio	35	21	3,934
Florida	17	15	1,333	Oklahoma	15	21	2,312
Georgia	11	7	1,334	Oregon	73	58	3,949
Hawaii	1	1	13	Pennsylvania	94	72	4,219
Idaho	7	4	788	Puerto Rico	3	3	299
Illinois	44	35	2,830	Rhode Island	3	1	263
Indiana	14	12	1,416	South Carolina	21	17	2,291
Iowa	4	8	1,196	South Dakota	2	3	321
Kansas	21	17	936	Tennessee	17	16	3,653
Kentucky	11	15	1,143	Texas	80	63	5,501
Louisiana	1	3	397	Utah	7	6	535
Maine	5	7	351	Vermont	5	4	90
Maryland	8	4	411	Virginia	10	8	1,170
Massachusetts	36	31	2,870	Washington	30	23	7,416
Michigan	43	26	7,135	West Virginia	3	7	593
Minnesota	27	22	1,444	Wisconsin	22	18	1,050
Mississippi	2	2	387	Wyoming	0	0	0
Missouri	15	13	1,552				
Montana	5	8	517	**Total**	**1,037**	**844**	**94,017**

Source: U.S. Department of Labor

employment, and their employment remained lower than that of similar non-offshoring firms up to six years after the initial offshoring occurred. After six years, the TAA firms used capital and skilled labor more intensively than their peers, though average wages paid to both their production or nonproduction workers did not change. Firms that were certified as offshorers through TAA were also more likely to shut down over the following three to five years. This suggests that offshoring can have lasting negative consequences for some workers and firms.

These results are in stark contrast to the results for all multinational firms presented in table 6-1, which show that 72 percent of firms that increase their offshore employment also increase their domestic employment. They also differ from other empirical studies, such as Sethupathy (2013), which examines offshoring by U.S. firms in Mexico and finds an increase in U.S. wages and no U.S. job losses at the offshoring firms. This contradiction is most likely because firms that qualify for TAA assistance are the firms whose employees are most negatively affected by offshoring. Employees of firms that offshore but also create more jobs in the United States have less need to apply for government assistance. However, the existence of the TAA firms and the job losses experienced by their employees suggests that offshoring affects different workers differently. Workers fortunate enough to be employed by a growing firm, even one that does a considerable amount of offshoring, may be sheltered from the negative effects of offshoring. But workers employed by a less dynamic or shrinking firm, such as those whose workers are eligible for TAA benefits, are worse off as a result of their firm's offshoring. Even though the results in table 6-1 show an overall positive correlation between expansion at home and expansion abroad, they also suggest that about 28 percent of firms that expand abroad reduce their employment in the United States.

It is also useful to look at what happens to TAA workers after they lose their jobs to offshoring. The Department of Labor publishes annual reports of the uptake and outcomes of TAA programs. According to Department of Labor data, from October 1, 2016, to September 30, 2017, an estimated 94,017 workers became eligible for TAA benefits and 43,615 received these benefits. More than 63 percent of individuals who participated in TAA programs received job training, and more than 89 percent of those who completed training received a credential. Performance among TAA recipients was high, with 75 percent of TAA participants obtaining new employment within six months of completing the program. More than 71 percent of participants who completed the program were reemployed in non-manufacturing industries (DOL (2017)). Table 6-3 provides more detail on the employment outcomes of workers who participated in TAA training programs between 2013 and 2017. In each of these years, more than 70 percent of the workers were employed within three months of completing TAA training. Of these, more than 90 percent were still employed six months later.

Taken together, these data suggest that some workers suffer large negative consequences as a result of offshoring, but that trade adjustment assistance can be a potentially effective way of helping them find employment. Unfortunately, the Department of Labor only publishes data on employment rates and average incomes after the training programs, but not on the wages of participants before they lost their jobs to offshoring. It is possible that displaced workers are earning less than they were before the offshoring and retraining occurred. In a study of Connecticut workers affected by mass layoffs for reasons not directly related to offshoring, Couch and Placzek (2010) estimate that some laid off workers experienced wage reductions that were initially more than 30 percent, and as much as 15 percent after

TABLE 6-3. Trade Adjustment Assistance Worker Training Outcomes

Fiscal Year	Employed in the first quarter after training[1]	Still employed after 6 months[2]	Average earnings in the first 6 months[3]
2013	71.6%	91.7%	US$18,104
2014	72.4%	91.4%	US$17,857
2015	74.1%	92.4%	US$17,910
2016	74.3%	92.2%	US$18,750
2017	72.9%	90.9%	US$19,129

Note: "Trade Adjustment Assistance for Workers Program," Employment and Training Administration, United States Department of Labor, 2017, www.doleta.gov/tradeact/docs/AnnualReport17.pdf.

1. Percentage of TAA participants who were employed in the first quarter after exit as reported in the third quarter after exit.

2. Percentage of TAA participants employed in the first quarter after exit who are still employed in the third quarter after exit. This six-month retention rate is based on data collected five quarters after exit to allow for time to collect and report data.

3. Average (mean) earnings for TAA participants in the second and third quarters after exit. These earnings are based on data collected five quarters after exit to allow for time to collect and report data.

six years. That study considers workers who were laid off for reasons other than offshoring, but it is possible that there could be similar wage effects for workers who lost their jobs because their firms shifted production to another country.

Recent research by Ben Hyman (2018) combines worker-level data from the Census Bureau with data on all TAA petitions filed with the Department of Labor. To measure the effects of the TAA program on displaced workers, the author uses the data to track approximately 300,000 displaced workers as they move in and out of unemployment and across employers in diverse industries and regions, both before and after their initial job separation. To avoid the problem of selection into TAA programs, this study uses the fact that some TAA case investigators are more or less likely to approve petitions. If assigned to more lenient investigators, displaced workers have a higher likelihood of receiving TAA benefits, for reasons not related to their own work experience. The results suggest that workers who undergo TAA training give up about US$10,000 in income while training, yet ten years later have approximately US$50,000 higher cumulative earnings relative to similar workers who do not retrain. About 33 percent of these returns are driven by higher wages, which suggests that the benefits to TAA-trained workers do not only come through greater labor force participation or receiving higher priority in hiring. Rather, TAA workers also appear to be paid a premium for their newly acquired skills and knowledge. Again, these workers make up only a small share of those potentially affected by offshoring, but the results do suggest that TAA training can be a valuable tool for helping this group of workers.

Are Foreign Workers Substitutes for U.S. Workers?

Whether foreign workers can easily substitute for U.S. workers is another important question when trying to understand how vulnerable U.S. workers are to offshoring. If a foreign worker can perform a job as well as a worker in the United States, why would firms not locate production where wages are lower? But it is also possible that U.S. workers have unique skills and experience that make them difficult to replace with foreign workers. Assessing how similar workers are across countries can be challenging. Many of the important differences among workers cannot be summed up by simple statistics like years of schooling or work experience. To address this, some researchers use multinational firm cost functions to estimate the elasticity of substitution between domestic and foreign workers. To isolate substitution effects, this approach explicitly holds firm output fixed. Thus, it cannot capture the overall effect of offshoring. But it is useful for estimating the extent to which domestic and foreign workers can be used to produce the same level of output. This approach generally looks at how responsive firms' offshoring decisions are when foreign wages fall. The results are mixed. Slaughter (2000) finds that offshoring by U.S. firms to low-wage countries has no detectable effect on their U.S. employment. Harrison and McMillan (2011) find that offshoring to low-wage countries substitutes for domestic employment, but for firms that perform very different tasks at home than abroad, foreign and domestic employment are complements. Other studies have looked at offshoring by European firms to low-wage countries and found little or no substitution (Braconier and Ekholm (2000); Konings and Murphy (2006); and Marin (2004)). Some firm-level studies have found that wages or per capita incomes are not significant predictors of where MNEs decide to locate their production in the first place (Devereux and Griffith (1998); Buch, Kleinert, Lipponer, and Toubal (2005)). Other studies, however, have found low wages to be a significant predictor of offshoring location choice (Disdier and Mayer (2004); Becker, Ekholm, Jackle, and Muendler (2005)). Muendler and Becker (2010) point out that there may be bias in studies that only look at changes within existing offshorers, without controlling for location selection, or that only consider one potential offshoring destination at a time. They use data on German multinationals and find that foreign and domestic labor are substitutes at both the extensive margin (when firms open new affiliates) and the intensive margin (when firms expand their existing operations in other countries). However, they find evidence of intensive margin substitution only for other European countries, but not for developed or developing countries outside of Europe. And even the effects within Europe are small. A 1 percent wage reduction in Central and Eastern Europe, for instance, is associated with a 0.03 percent drop in home employment at German MNE parents. As mentioned, all of these papers are looking at the technical substitutability of workers across countries. To accomplish this, they must hold output fixed. This means that they do not allow for any increases in the size of the firm that are enabled by the cost savings that result from offshoring. In other words, what they capture is not the overall effect of offshoring—including the positive productivity effects as well as the negative substitution effects—but instead they ask a more technical question about the extent to which domestic and foreign workers can be substituted for each other in production. Even with that caveat, the available evidence suggests that there is not a high degree of substitutability between domestic and foreign workers.

Of course, some jobs are easier to perform abroad than others. As a result, offshoring does not affect all workers in the same way, with effects varying based on several different dimensions. In general, high-skilled workers are most likely to gain from offshoring, and low-skilled workers are most likely to be made worse off. This has been shown for both employment (Crino (2010)) and wages (Baumgarten, Geishecker, and Görg (2013); Hummels, Jorgensen, Munch, and Xiang (2014)). The effects also depend on the country in which the offshoring takes place. Negative effects on U.S. workers are more likely when offshoring takes place in low-income countries. But these negative effects are small, as developing countries are more likely to compete with each other for offshoring jobs than they are to compete with U.S. workers (Brainard and Riker (1997)). For firms that perform significantly different tasks at home and abroad, foreign and domestic employment are complements (Harrison and McMillan (2011)). This is due in part to the fact that the United States has a comparative advantage in higher-skilled jobs and occupational tasks. Another reason is that some jobs are simply more difficult to perform abroad, because they require communication with U.S. customers or management or because they are simply too complex for a firm to trust to workers in another country (Oldenski (2012)).

Quantifying the Negative Effects of Offshoring

How large are the effects of offshoring on vulnerable workers? The negative effects of offshoring are generally small, even for groups of workers who are most likely to be negatively affected. For low-wage workers, a 10 percent increase in offshoring leads to an average wage decrease of 0.22 percent (Hummels, Jorgensen, Munch, and Xiang (2014)) to 0.40 percent (Ebenstein, Harrison, McMillan, and Phillips (2014)). Liu and Trefler (2011) find that the probability of switching to a lower-wage occupation increases by about 0.039 percent. Offshoring has been found to increase the unemployment risk of low-skilled workers, but the quantitative effect is modest. Munch (2010) estimated the employment effects of offshoring using Danish data and found, for example, that a thirty-to-thirty-nine-year-old male with only a high school education experienced a 1 percentage point increase in the risk of unemployment—from 26.1 percent in 1991 to 27.1 percent in 2002, a period when outsourcing by Danish firms increased by 2.7 percentage points. These results suggest that while the potential effects on an individual worker may be large (for example, the loss of a job), the odds of any given low-skilled worker being negatively affected are low enough to make the aggregate effects quite small. There is ample evidence that low-skilled workers, and manufacturing workers in particular, have experienced widespread job loss and wage declines in the United States (see, for example, Fort, Pierce, and Schott (2018)). But little evidence relates these losses to offshoring, suggesting that other factors, such as technology, changes in demand, and import competition, may be much larger factors.

Quantifying the Positive Effects of Offshoring

Much less is known about workers who gain from offshoring. This is in part because job gains are generally not as concentrated as losses. It is also much more difficult to establish a causal relationship between offshoring and job creation. One reason is that the gains are often in different industries, different geographic locations, or even different firms relative to where the initial offshoring took place. Consider Apple. It offshores the production and assembly of most of the components for its smartphones and tablets. Yet doing so allows the firm to sell more products, which creates jobs in the United States—from engineers in Silicon Valley to Apple Store clerks in the Midwest. On its website, Apple claims to be responsible for creating 2 million jobs in the United States. This includes 80,000 Apple employees, 450,000 jobs through their U.S.-based suppliers, and 1.53 million U.S. jobs "attributable to the App Store ecosystem."[5] These jobs are spread over all fifty states. Apple employment outside of California was twenty-eight times higher in 2019 than it was in 2000. The problem is that it is difficult to know the counterfactual—in other words, how many Apple-related workers would be employed in the United States if Apple could not offshore production. It is possible that Apple might employ even more workers in the United States if it no longer produced its components abroad. It is also possible that without the ability to offshore, Apple would not be the highly successful company that it is today, and that could cost jobs in the United States. Clearly, however, Apple is responsible for a large number of U.S. jobs—80,000 of them direct employees of the firm—even with a substantial amount of its production located abroad.

Despite the difficulties of establishing causality, several studies have managed to address this problem by studying exogenous decreases in the cost of offshoring—that is, factors that affect the firms' decisions to offshore but are not a result of decisions made by the firms themselves. These studies have generally found positive effects of offshoring on some U.S. workers. Offshoring does not mean simply shifting production abroad. Instead, when firms offshore, they also increase their production in the United States, and we observe greater output (Wright (2014)) and greater employment (Desai, Foley, and Hines (2009); Criscuolo and Garicano (2010); Kovak, Oldenski, and Sly (2019)) as a result. These effects do not change the fact that some workers lose their jobs, but they do suggest that offshoring brings strong positive effects to the U.S. economy and some U.S. workers, and is not a purely negative shock.

As shown in table 6-1, firms that expand abroad tend to expand in the United States at the same time. This is generally good news for workers. But it does not tell us much about the causal effects of offshoring on U.S. employment. It could just be that productive, growing firms hire more workers in all of their locations, and that the offshoring has no direct effect on hiring abroad. It is also possible that the sign of the relationship is reversed, and that even though we see firms expanding simultaneously in the United States and abroad, they would have actually hired more workers in the United States if offshoring had not been an option. It is extremely difficult to sort out the causal relationship between offshoring and domestic employment, because firms make decisions about both of these things simultaneously, based on their own productivity and other characteristics. Kovak, Oldenski, and Sly (2019) address this problem by looking at an exogenous shock to the cost of offshoring, in the form of bilateral tax treaties. These treaties between the United States and other countries lower the cost of offshoring by U.S. multinational firms, yet they are not correlated with the firms' productivity or other characteristics. Thus, it is possible to see what happens to the U.S. employment of firms that already have an affiliate in a treaty country after the treaty reduces their cost of offshoring. The results suggest that a reduction in the cost of offshoring helps employees of multinational firms in the United States. A 10 percent increase in affiliate employment drives a 1.8 percent increase in employment at the U.S. parent firm. However, these gains are mostly offset by losses to workers at other, non-MNE firms in the United States. At the industry level, a 10 percent increase in affiliate employment induced by bilateral tax treaties only leads to a 0.14 percent increase in U.S. domestic employment.

Who Wins and Loses?

So what determines who wins and who loses as a result of offshoring? Workers at MNEs are more likely to gain than workers at non-MNEs. As mentioned, workers who are likely to be hurt the most are those with less education (Hummels, Jorgensen, Munch, and Xiang (2014)), who perform routine tasks (Ebenstein, Harrison, McMillan, and Phillips (2014); Hummels, Jorgensen, Munch, and Xiang (2014); Ottaviano, Peri, and Wright (2013); and Oldenski (2012)), and who work in industries that offshore more to low-income countries (Ebenstein, Harrison, McMillan, and Phillips (2014)). Yet these losses are often offset by gains to workers with more education or who perform nonroutine tasks. Hummels, Jorgensen, Munch, and Xiang (2014) use data on offshoring by Danish firms and find that offshoring lowers the wages of low-skilled workers and raises the wages of high-skilled workers, while exporting increases the wages of both high- and low-skilled workers. They find that if a firm doubles its offshoring, the average low-skilled worker at that firm loses 4.2 percent of their pre-offshoring earnings over the next five years. This loss includes any wage changes in their current job, wage changes in new jobs, and losses due to time spent in unemployment. In contrast, the average high-skilled worker gains 4.9 percent of their pre-offshoring earnings. Because higher earners gain and lower earners lose, offshoring can have an effect on income inequality. Oldenski (2014) uses firm-level data on offshoring paired with occupation-level data on employment and wages to estimate the effect that offshoring has had on U.S. workers from 2002 to 2008. The results suggest that offshoring by U.S. firms has contributed to relative gains for the most highly skilled workers and relative losses for middle-skilled workers. An increase in offshoring in an industry is associated with an increase in the wage gap between workers at the 75th percentile and workers with median earnings in that industry, and with a decrease in the gap between workers earning the median wages and those at the 25th percentile. This pattern can be explained by the tasks performed by workers. Offshoring is associated with a decrease in wages for occupations that rely heavily on routine tasks and an increase in wages if the occupation is nonroutine and communication intensive. Workers who perform routine tasks tend to be in the middle or bottom of the wage distribution, while workers who perform nonroutine and communication-intensive tasks are more likely to be in high-paying jobs.

In the aggregate, employees of U.S. MNEs that offshore gain, albeit with much churning and distributional consequences. Given the presence of both gains and losses, the most relevant policy question is whether it is possible to mitigate the losses from offshoring, without forgoing the benefits. The available evidence suggests that worker training programs may be effective at achieving this goal.

Much of the research on the labor market effects of offshoring focus on U.S. multinationals. However, research using data on firms from other countries suggests that the effects are likely similar, at least across other developed countries. The labor market effects of offshoring by firms from less developed countries has not been studied in much detail, in large part due to lack of sufficiently detailed data on firms from these countries, and thus remains an open question.

EFFECTS OF FOREIGN MNEs ON DOMESTIC WORKERS

U.S. workers are not only affected by the actions of U.S.-owned MNEs. They are also affected by foreign-owned multinationals in the United States. Thus, the global expansion of multinational production implies not only that U.S. firms will expand abroad, but also that foreign firms will increasingly perform more work, and create more jobs, in the United States.

In 2016, affiliates of foreign-owned multinational firms in the United States employed more than 7.6 million U.S. workers. As shown in figure 6-5, these foreign investors in the United States pay, on average, higher wages than U.S. employers. They even pay higher wages than U.S. multinationals, which are among the highest-paying of all U.S. firms. This should not be surprising. First, multinational firms are the largest and most productive of all firms, and are known to pay higher wages than purely domestic firms, which results in a multinational wage premium. Second, foreign firms are not locating in the United States to take advantage of low wages. Instead, they are drawn by the highly skilled workforce, culture of innovation, and large consumer market. That implies a selection effect, in which foreign firms create jobs that require higher skills than the average U.S. firm. Setzler and Tintelnot (2019) are able to separate the relative contributions of the MNE premium and worker composition by studying workers who move between foreign and domestic firms. They find that the typical worker earns 7 percent more at the average foreign firm than at the average domestic firm. In their aggregate data, foreign firms pay 25 percent higher average wages than domestic firms, after controlling for industry and location. Together, these results suggest that most of the foreign firm wage differential can be attributed to the types of workers they hire, but there is also a substantial foreign firm premium for a given worker. The wage premium paid by foreign multinationals is quite large in the aggregate—US$34 billion annually.

In addition to creating high-paying jobs, foreign firms may also have indirect effects on domestic firms. When foreign firms enter a market, they bring new production technologies and management practices that can spill over to the local market. These FDI spillovers can take the form of horizontal technology transfers from foreign to domestic firms in the same industry. For example, workers may leave the foreign-owned firm and take the techniques that they have learned to their next job in a domestic firm. Domestic firms may also learn by observing their competitors. Spillovers may also be vertical. For example, if foreign-owned firms wish to source inputs locally, they may demand higher quality or even share production technology with their suppliers, which would result in greater productivity of local firms in upstream industries. Research on multinational spillovers initially focused on developed-country firms in less developed markets.[6] In this situation, the gap between the technology level of the firm's headquarters location and the host country is the greatest, and thus the potential for

FIGURE 6-5. Average Annual Compensation of U.S. Workers in 2015

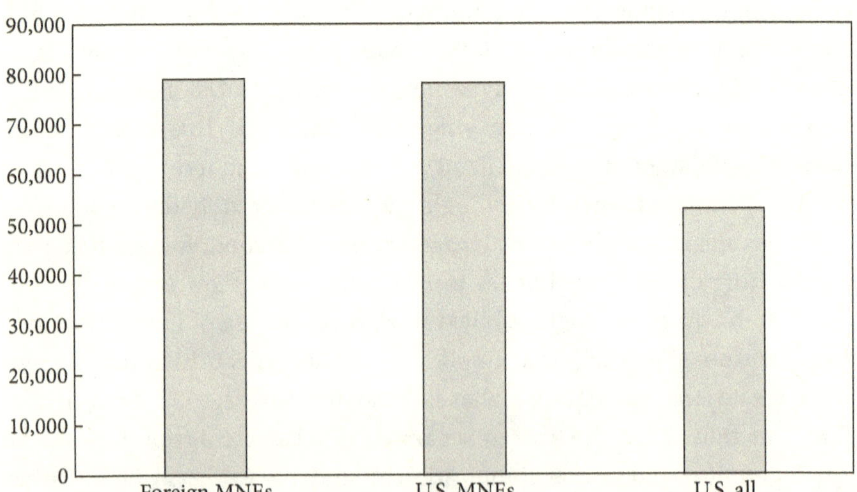

Note: Average annual compensation of workers is the cost to the firm of employing workers, including wages and benefits.

Source: Author's calculations based on data published by the U.S. Bureau of Economic Analysis

gains may be the highest. However, several studies have also found evidence of positive spillovers from FDI in developed countries.[7] For example, Moran and Oldenski (2013) found that a 1 percentage point increase in the share of total employees in an industry who work at foreign-owned firms in the United States increases the productivity of all firms in the industry by an average of 0.81 percent after one year and by 2.75 percent in the second year, or a total of more than 3.5 percent. These numbers imply that productivity spillovers from FDI alone are responsible for U.S. total factor productivity (TFP) growth of about 3 percent from 1987 to 2007.[8] This 3 percent is more than one-tenth of the 25 percent U.S. TFP growth over that period. In other words, about 12 percent of the total productivity growth in the United States from 1987 to 2007 can be attributed to spillovers from inward FDI. Setzler and Tintelnot (2019) find that an increase in employment at foreign-owned firms significantly raises value added, employment, and total wages at domestically owned firms in the same commuting zone. Their estimates imply that, for every job created by a foreign multinational, approximately 0.42 jobs and US$91,000 in value added are generated by domestic firms in the same local labor market. Their combined estimates of the direct and indirect effects imply that one additional job created by a foreign multinational generates, on average, annual aggregate wage gains for local workers of approximately US$16,000, two-thirds of which is due to the indirect effects. This has important implications for workers as the expansion of both foreign and domestic firms can lead to job creation in the United States.

SUMMARY: WHAT PROPOSITIONS ON OFFSHORING ARE SUPPORTED BY RESEARCH?

To summarize the results described in this chapter, some conventional wisdom on offshoring is supported by careful research, but some is not. The proposition that foreign workers can be easily substituted for domestic workers only has limited support, suggesting that U.S. and foreign workers are, at most, imperfect substitutes, and that substitution is more likely between similar countries. There is also no evidence of widespread replacement of U.S. jobs with foreign jobs. However, research has shown that the effects of offshoring are heterogenous—that is, offshoring has very different effects on different workers. Employees of multinational firms and more highly skilled workers are more likely to benefit from offshoring, while less skilled workers and those at purely domestic firms are more likely to be worse off. Trade adjustment assistance in the United States has been relatively limited, but research on TAA suggests that it can be effective in helping displaced workers, especially through job training programs.

CONCLUSIONS

The answer to the question "Do multinational firms export jobs?" is a definite "Yes." However, they also import jobs, and in many cases, offshoring enables that job creation at home. Overall, the net effect of MNE offshoring on domestic jobs and wages is close to zero or possibly a small positive. But that net effect masks the fact that some workers are hurt by offshoring while others gain. In general, less educated workers and those who perform routine tasks are more likely to experience job losses and reduced wages as a result of offshoring, while more highly educated workers gain. Evidence suggests that TAA, particularly in the form of worker training, can help mitigate some of the negative effects of offshoring without sacrificing the benefits.

NOTES

1. These numbers differ from those presented in chapter 1, figure 1-13, in this volume. Figure 6-4 presents data on related-party trade from the U.S. Census Bureau, which is constructed using U.S. Customs data that classifies all imports entering the United States according to whether or not they occur between related parties. Figure 1-13 of chapter 1 presents data from the U.S. Bureau of Economic Analysis, which collects data on intrafirm trade directly from multinational companies in their annual surveys of U.S. multinational enterprises and U.S. affiliates of foreign parents. Due to differences in the coverage of these datasets and their definitions of intra-firm trade, the total volumes of intra-firm trade that they report are not identical.

2. The findings presented in table 6-1 are based on the statistical analysis of firm-level data on U.S. multinational companies at the Bureau of Economic Analysis, U.S. Department of Commerce, under arrangements that maintain legal confidentiality requirements. The views expressed are those of the authors and do not reflect official positions of the U.S. Department of Commerce.

3. To avoid disclosing values for individual firms, reported medians average the values of the nine firms around the median.

4. United Steelworkers, "Trade Adjustment Assistance Services," www.usw.org/members/laid-off-members/trade-adjustment-assistance-services.

5. "Two Million U.S. Jobs. And Counting," www.apple.com/job-creation/.

6. For example, evidence of positive spillover effects from FDI have been found for Mexico (Blomström (1986), Kokko (1994)); Mauritius (Rhee, Katterback, and Whie (1990)); Malaysia (Rasiah (1995), Canpanelli (1997)); Indonesia (Blomström and Sjo-

holm (1999), Blalock and Gertler (2005, 2008)); Lithuania (Javorcik (2004)); Ghana (Gorg and Strobl (2005)); and Thailand (Kohpaiboon (2007, 2009)).

7. Branstetter (2006); Haskel, Pereira and Slaughter (2007); Keller and Yeaple (2009); Moran and Oldenski (2013).

8. From 1987 to 2007, employment at foreign-owned firms as a share of total U.S. employment grew from about 3.8 to 4.6 percent (a 0.8 percentage point increase). That implies that productivity spillovers from FDI are responsible for U.S. TFP growth of about 3 percent (0.008*(0.81+2.75)).

REFERENCES

Autor, David, David Dorn, and Gordon Hanson. 2013. "The China Syndrome: Local Labor Market Effects of Import Competition in the United States," *American Economic Review*, 103 (6): 2121–68.

Bardhan, Ashok D. and Cynthia Kroll. 2003. "The New Wave of Outsourcing. Fisher Center for Real Estate & Urban Economics." Working Paper No. 1103, University of California, Berkeley, Fall 2003.

Baumgarten, Daniel, Ingo Geishecker, and Holger Görg. 2013. "Offshoring, Tasks, and the Skill-Wage Pattern," *European Economic Review*, 61: 132–52.

Becker, Sascha O., Karolina Ekholm, Robert Jackle, and Marc-Andreas Muendler. 2005. "Location Choice and Employment Decisions: A Comparison of German and Swedish Multinationals," *Review of World Economics/Weltwirtschaftliches Archiv*, 141/4 (December 2005): 693–731.

Becker, Sascha, Karolina Ekholm, and Marc-Andreas Muendler. 2013. "Offshoring and the Onshore Composition of Tasks and Skills," *Journal of International Economics*, 90 (1): 91–106.

Blinder, Alan S. and Alan B. Krueger. 2013. "Alternative Measures of Offshorability: A Survey Approach," *Journal of Labor Economics*, 31(2): S97–S128.

Braconier, Henrik and Karolina Ekholm. 2000. "Swedish Multinationals and Competition from High- and Low-Wage Locations," *Review of International Economics*, 8/3 (August 2000): 448–61.

Brainard, S. Lael and David A. Riker. 1997. "Are U.S. Multinationals Exporting U.S. Jobs?" Technical Report, National Bureau of Economic Research.

Buch, Claudia M., Jorn Kleinert, Alexander Lipponer, and Farid Toubal. 2005. "Determinants and Effects of Foreign Direct Investment: Evidence from German Firm-Level Data," *Economic Policy*, 41 (January 2005): 51–98.

Bureau of Labor Statistics. Business Employment Dynamics—Fourth Quarter 2018.

Cimino-Isaacs, Cathleen and Gary Clyde Hufbauer. 2015. "The Fate of Trade Adjustment Assistance: The Basics." Peterson Institute for International Economics Trade and Investment Policy Watch. June 11, 2015.

Couch, Kenneth A. and Dana W. Placzek. 2010. "Earnings Losses of Displaced Workers Revisited," *American Economic Review*, 100 (1): 572–89.

Crinò, Rosario. 2010. "Service Offshoring and White-Collar Employment," *Review of Economic Studies*, 77 (2): 595–632.

Criscuolo, Chiara and Luis Garicano. 2010. "Offshoring and Wage Inequality: Using Occupational Licensing as a Shifter of Offshoring Costs," *American Economic Review*, 100 (2): 439–43.

Department of Labor. "Trade Adjustment Assistance for Workers Program: Fiscal Year 2017."

Department of Labor. "Trade Adjustment Assistance for Workers Program: Fiscal Year 2009."

Desai, Mihir A., C. Fritz Foley, and James R. Hines Jr. 2009. "Domestic Effects of the Foreign Activities of U.S. Multinationals," *American Economic Journal: Economic Policy*, 1 (1): 181–203.

Devereux, Michael P. and Rachel Griffith. 1998. "Taxes and the Location of Production: Evidence from a Panel of U.S. Multinationals, Journal of Public Economics," 68/3 (June 1998): 335–67.

Disdier, Anne Celia and Thierry Mayer. 2004. "How Different Is Eastern Europe? Structure and Determinants of Location Choices by French Firms in Eastern and Western Europe," *Journal of Comparative Economics*, 32/2 (June 2004): 280–96.

Ebenstein, Avraham, Ann Harrison, Margaret McMillan, and Shannon Phillips. 2014. "Estimating the Impact of Trade and Offshoring on American Workers Using the Current Population Surveys," *Review of Economics and Statistics*, 96 (4): 581–95.

Firpo, Sergio, Nicole M. Fortin, and Thomas Lemieux. 2011. "Occupational Tasks and Changes in the Wage Structure." IZA Discussion Paper No. 5542.

Fort, Teresa, Justin Pierce, and Peter Schott. 2018. "New Perspectives on the Decline of U.S. Manufacturing Employment," *Journal of Economic Perspectives*, 32 (2): 47–72.

Gardner, Greg and Brent Snavely. 2016. "Ford Shifting All U.S. Small-Car Production to Mexico," *Detroit Free Press*, September 14, 2016.

Garetto, Stefania, Lindsay Oldenski, and Natalia Ramondo. 2019. "Multinational Expansion in Time and Space." NBER Working Paper No. 25804.

Harrison, Ann and Margaret McMillan. 2011. "Offshoring Jobs? Multinationals and U.S. Manufacturing Employment," *Review of Economics and Statistics*, 93 (3): 857–75.

Hummels, David, Rasmus Jorgensen, Jakob Munch, and Chong Xiang. 2014. "The Wage Effects of Offshoring: Evidence from Danish Matched Worker-Firm Data," *American Economic Review*, 104 (6): 1597–1629.

Hyman, Ben. 2018. "Can Displaced Labor Be Retrained? Evidence from Quasi-Random Assignment to Trade Adjustment Assistance," working paper.

Jensen, J. Bradford and Lori G. Kletzer. 2008. "Fear and Offshoring: The Scope and Potential Impact of Imports and Exports of Services." Peterson Institute for International Economics Policy Brief PB08-1.

Konings, Jozef and Alan Patrick Murphy. 2006. "Do Multinational Enterprises Relocate Employment to Low-Wage Regions? Evidence from European Multinationals," *Review of World Economics/Weltwirtschaftliches Archiv*, 142/2 (July 2006): 267–86.

Kovak, Brian, Lindsay Oldenski, and Nicholas Sly. 2020 (forthcoming). "The Labor Market Effects of Offshoring by U.S. Multinational Firms," *Review of Economics and Statistics*.

Liu, Runjuan and Daniel Trefler. 2011. "A Sorted Tale of Globalization: White Collar Jobs and the Rise of Service Offshoring." NBER Working Paper No. 17559.

Marin, Dalia. 2004. "A Nation of Poets and Thinkers—Less So with Eastern Enlargement? Austria and Germany." CEPR Discussion Paper 4358.

McKinsey Global Institute. 2005. "The Emerging Global Labor Market" (June 2005).

Monarch, Ryan, Jooyoun Park, and Jagadeesh Sivadasan. 2017. "Domestic Gains from Offshoring? Evidence from TAA-Linked U.S. Microdata," *Journal of International Economics*, 105 (March 2017).

Moran, Theodore H. and Lindsay Oldenski. 2013. "Foreign Direct Investment in the United States: Benefits, Suspicions, and Risks." Peterson Institute for International Economics (September 2013).

Muendler, Marc-Andreas and Sascha O. Becker. 2010. "Margins of Multinational Labor Substitution," *American Economic Review*, 100 (5): 1999–2030.

Munch, Jakob R. 2010. "Whose Job Goes Abroad? International Outsourcing and Individual Job Separations," *Scandinavian Journal of Economics*, 112 (2): 339–60.

Oldenski, Lindsay. 2012. "Export Versus FDI and the Communication of Complex Information," *Journal of International Economics*, 87/2 (July 2012).

Oldenski, Lindsay. 2012. "The Task Composition of Offshoring by U.S. Multinationals," *International Economics*, 131.

Oldenski, Lindsay. 2014. "Offshoring and the Polarization of the U.S. Labor Market," *Industrial and Labor Relations Review*, 67 (May 2014).

Ottaviano, Gianmarco, Giovanni Peri, and Greg Wright. 2013. "Immigration, Offshoring, and American Jobs," *American Economic Review*, 103/5 (August 2013).

Sethupathy, Guru. 2013. "Offshoring, Wages, and Employment: Theory and Evidence," *European Economic Review*, 62 (C): 73–97.

Setzler, Bradley and Felix Tintelnot. 2019. "The Effects of Foreign Multinationals on Workers and Firms in the United States." NBER Working Paper No. w26149.

Slaughter, Matthew J. 2000. "Production Transfer within Multinational Enterprises and American Wages," *Journal of International Economics*, 50 (2).

Solis, Hilda L. and Ron Kirk. 2011. "The Truth about Trade Adjustment Assistance," *The Hill* (June 28).

Wright, Greg. 2014. "Revisiting the Employment Impact of Offshoring," *European Economic Review*, 66 (February 2014).

7

Do Multinational Corporations Exploit Foreign Workers?

EMMA AISBETT
ANN E. HARRISON
DAVID I. LEVINE
JASON SCORSE
JED SILVER

> To exploit someone is to take unfair advantage of them. It is to use another person's vulnerability for one's own benefit. Of course, benefiting from another's vulnerability is not always morally wrong—we do not condemn a chess player for exploiting a weakness in his opponent's defense, for instance. But some forms of advantage-taking do seem to be clearly wrong, and it is this normative sense of exploitation that is of primary interest . . .
>
> —*Stanford Encyclopedia of Philosophy*[1]

Do multinational corporations (MNCs) exploit foreign workers? If we assume the world is perfectly competitive and define exploitation as paying below-market wages, then MNCs generally do not exploit workers in poor nations. Yet answers differ if we consider richer models of labor markets and more demanding definitions of exploitation. The definition of exploitation from the *Encyclopedia of Philosophy* leads us to ask what it would mean to take "unfair advantage [of] another person's vulnerability." To answer this question, we identify three sets of theories of exploitation: theories based on market outcomes, theories based on sharing an unfair portion of the surplus, and theories based on assumptions about fundamental human rights.

A *market-based* or *consequentialist* definition of exploitation considers whether workers would be better off had they not been employed by an MNC. *Unfair-share* exploitation occurs when profitable firms do not sufficiently share their profits with their employees. Utilitarian ethics is one of several approaches that argue that above-market wages are sometimes ethically desirable. These fairness approaches also raise concerns about a system of production in which MNCs depress labor's share of income, either in source or in destination labor markets.

The third approach to exploitation defines exploitation as a *violation of human rights*. We focus on human rights that almost all nations have agreed to, such as limits on child labor, forced overtime, unsafe conditions, and discrimination and violence against women. Any violations of human rights at MNCs matter, regardless of whether MNCs pay higher wages than domestic employers. Under the *unfair-share* or *human rights* approaches, a multinational can be said to exploit workers even when the job is better than most jobs at domestic employers. In that case, exploitation would occur either if the multinational firm is keeping almost all the surplus generated by the worker's efforts or if labor conditions violate some aspect of basic human rights—such as forced overtime, child labor, or discrimination.

We focus much of our analysis on the effects of multinationals in poor nations. However, we also analyze the effect of MNCs moving operations to lower-income countries on wages and employment of home-country workers. The widespread public perception is that MNCs exploit workers in poor regions. We find almost no evidence of exploitation defined as compensation below the market wage. Multinational firms tend to offer workers slightly better wages and conditions than domestic firms. They generally also increase the demand for workers in high-paying industries and occupations. At the very least, there is little evidence that their effects on wages and working conditions are negative relative to domestic firms.

There also is little direct evidence that multinationals share an unfairly low portion of their surplus. One study[2] shows that the wage premium offered by MNCs in Europe corresponds to rent-sharing rather than compensating employees for other attributes of their jobs. Yet the relatively low wage premiums reported by many studies shows that most multinationals do not share very much surplus. Shifting to the market level, there is suggestive evidence that the expansion of MNCs decreases labor's share of income.

There is more conclusive evidence that offshoring by MNCs to low-income countries leads to lower wages and fewer jobs for low-skilled home-country workers performing routine tasks. However, import competition and technical change may have displaced many of these jobs even without offshoring.

Finally, we find evidence that MNCs violate basic human rights in poor nations. Examples include discrimination against women and migrant workers, suppression of the right to organize, and poor health and safety conditions. These conditions are also prevalent, and may be worse, at local firms in developing countries. However, under the human rights definition of exploitation, doing as well or better than domestic employers does not exonerate MNCs.

Both the multinational company's country of origin and host country influence compensation and other labor practices. It is reasonable to assume that a multinational based in Germany or Sweden, where labor rights are relatively strong, typically treats workers in poor countries more favorably than an MNC whose home base is a low-income country, where labor rights are often weak. Knowing that a multinational produced a product tells consumers little about the living standards or human rights of the workers who made it. Sometimes the host nation is an important signal. For example, Saudi Arabia and Kazakhstan agreed to respect core International Labor Organization (ILO) agreements, but few workplaces in Saudi Arabia avoid gender discrimination, and few in Kazakhstan permit free unions.[3]

In short, most low-skilled workers in poor nations receive low wages and have poor working conditions, regardless of the employer's ownership. Indeed, MNCs typically offer slight improvements relative to domestic firms. The perception of MNCs as particularly exploitative seems to arise from the assumption that these companies have a greater surplus that they could share with their workers, not from evidence that MNCs treat workers worse than domestic firms.

Policy and activism to improve working conditions and wages can be effective in ensuring that companies become better at sharing the surplus with their workers. As Harrison and Scorse (2010) demonstrate, MNCs that were under pressure by anti-sweatshop activists in Indonesia in the 1990s raised wages in the textile, apparel, and footwear sectors. Wage increases were a win-win in the sense that employment and benefits remained strong. MNCs, especially those that sell highly visible branded products, may be more sensitive to pressure from nongovernmental organizations (NGOs) and consumers because their markups are higher and they want to avoid negative publicity.[4] Nonetheless, focusing on policies that aim to broadly increase labor productivity and improve the enforcement of labor standards in developing countries may have larger effects on the well-being of workers in poor nations than focusing solely on multinationals.

This survey proceeds as follows. We begin by discussing several definitions of exploitation. In particular, we review the literature on how MNCs affect wages, focusing on whether MNCs provide a wage premium relative to domestic firms, while also considering the effects of MNCs on the structure of the economy. We then analyze the slim evidence regarding whether MNCs share an unfairly small portion of their surplus with workers. One interesting question is the effect of MNCs offshoring on workers who remain in the home country, which we then analyze. We also discuss whether MNCs exploit workers by violating their human rights, and finish by presenting our conclusions.

DEFINITIONS OF EXPLOITATION

We focus on three approaches to define exploitation. The first approach is the market-based or consequentialist one. Market-based or consequentialist arguments define exploitation as actions that make workers worse off than they would have been otherwise. Second, both utilitarian arguments and regularities in behavioral economics suggest it is sometimes fair for profitable employers to share surplus with employees. These fairness arguments depend on the employer and its ability to pay. Third, deontological or human rights arguments define exploitation as actions that violate principles of human rights, dignity, and fairness, which hold regardless of what would have occurred otherwise. These deontological or human rights approaches focus on objective standards rather than the employer's ability to pay.

Market-based or Consequentialist Arguments

In the language of philosophy, the neoclassical approach—which focuses on the outcomes of actions and transactions—uses consequentialist arguments to make a normative judgment. For example, an action is considered "good" if its consequence is an improvement in global welfare. Applying the consequentialist approach to questions of exploitation, neoclassical economists will typically judge a transaction between a worker and firm as "good" (hence, non-exploitative) if it is a Pareto improvement—that is, both the worker and firm are better off. A benchmark for exploitation is, therefore, whether employees of MNCs fare better than they would have at their next best option.

The assumption of perfect competition embedded in most of these models means that workers make perfectly rational decisions with perfect information, with no costs of mobility, no social or familial constraints on their decisions, and full agency. These assumptions imply that if a worker accepted a job at a multinational, then that job was the best option available. By this definition of exploitation, this transaction is not exploitative. An alternative definition of exploitation, by John Bates Clark (1899), asks whether workers are paid less than the incremental revenue they create (what economists call the worker's marginal revenue product). Again, assuming perfect competition rules out Clark's definition of exploitation.

When we relax the critical assumption of perfect competition, and envision more realistic labor market conditions, then information asymmetry, market power, and the costs of switching jobs make exploitation of workers possible. When firms are monopsonists, such as in a "factory town," or when labor market frictions are important, wages can be lower than workers' marginal revenue products. Workers may not be informed about conditions at their workplace, ranging from risks of immediate injury to long-term exposure to carcinogens, and from sexual harassment to mandatory overtime. With labor market frictions, workers have less ability to threaten to change jobs in response to poor treatment or violations of the terms of their employment.

In theory, either MNCs or purely domestic firms could exploit workers more. Multinationals might exploit workers less, because MNCs are formal-sector firms that are subject to more domestic and international labor standards that guarantee basic conditions for workers. Market failures, such as market power in product markets, can raise MNCs' ability to share rents with workers, reducing managers' incentives to treat workers poorly. At the same time, MNCs tend to be larger than average. Thus, they may wield more labor market power than domestic firms. In addition, MNCs' importance to local economies may lead to preferential treatment and weaker enforcement of labor and other standards. Workers may also be less familiar with some hazards (such as the long-term risks posed by carcinogens) that may be more common at multinationals than at domestic employers.

Where social norms may penalize the first firm that implements an effective anti-sexual harassment policy, a requirement from an MNC that all its suppliers implement policies against sexual harassment can benefit workers. To the extent that employers must pay workers a compensating difference for the risk of sexual harassment (or face higher turnover costs due to harassment), owners can also benefit (Hersch (2011)) from adopting effective anti-sexual harassment policies. Finally, both firms and owners may dislike standards, such as limits on voluntary overtime and requirements for uncomfortable safety equipment. However, if workers have imperfect information or present bias related to safety and health hazards, such standards may benefit them. In addition, workers may gain collectively by limiting child labor or long hours, even if an individual family prefers more work at the going wage (Basu and Van (1998)).

Fair Share of the Surplus

Many observers consider that paying "better than the alternative" may still fall short of a fair wage. We define "unfair-share" economic exploitation as occurring when the worker is made better off by the MNC, but there remains something reasonably construed as "unfair" about the transaction. The definition of exploitation from the *Encyclopedia of Philosophy* suggests that exploitation of workers in poor nations occurs if multinationals "take unfair advantage of" the workers' low market wages. That language leads us to ask what makes a wage or working condition "fair." We discuss several overlapping theories.

A utilitarian theory of fairness asks if raising the poor workers' wage would improve average well-being in the world. If most owners and customers of branded MNCs have lower marginal utility of income than poor workers, then a utilitarian will classify the higher wage as fair. At the same time, if a multinational paying high wages lost a lot of market share or laid off many workers, the resulting job loss and inefficiency would offset distributional gains to workers who received the higher wages.

Behavioral economics provides a complementary approach to defining the fair share of surplus. A large body of research suggests that most people consider it fair to share some of the surplus that arises from a profitable relationship. In particular, evidence from behavioral economics suggests that humans value fairness in transactions. The ultimatum game (Thaler and Camerer (2005)) is a widely reproduced experiment in behavioral economics that shows this behavior. In a typical ultimatum game, the experimenter gives the players US$100. The Proposer must make a single take-it-or-leave-it offer to the Responder of an amount Q between 0 and US$100. If the Responder accepts the offer, the Responder receives Q and the Proposer keeps US$100 – Q. If the Responder declines the offer, they both get zero. Economic theory has a simple prediction: the Proposer offers one cent, which the Responder accepts. In a vast array of settings, Proposers typically offer 20 percent to 50 percent of the pot. These offers are rational, as Responders frequently decline "unfair" offers that do not provide them with what they consider a sufficient share of the surplus. In experiments in poor nations, Responders sometimes decline offers equal to several days' wages (Steffen and others (2011)).[5] The evidence from these experiments suggests the vast majority of people around the world consider it morally wrong for one party (the Proposer) to exploit their advantage built into the game's structure and capture the lion's share of the surplus.

If these (and many other) laboratory experiments generalize, many people perceive it is morally wrong for MNCs with high ability to pay not to share some of their surplus with workers. In other words, MNCs paying at or slightly above-market wage is insufficient to conclude that they are not exploiting their workers in the sense of unfair sharing. On the one hand, we did not find any research on questions such as how profits from a product development center in California (Apple) affects perceptions of the fair wage for assembly workers (FoxConn) at a supplier in China or Vietnam. On the other hand, the anti-sweatshop campaigns against Nike and Adidas in the 1990s and the new concerns about market power and excess profits (Philippon (2019)) suggest that some activists perceive a link between profits and fair wages.[6]

The above discussion takes individual firms as the unit of analysis. At the same time, multinationals may change the structure of the economy or politics in ways that help or harm workers—the latter being what some have called "structural exploitation." For example, multinationals may either increase local labor demand through vertical linkages or decrease it by competing with labor-intensive local firms. Other examples of potential structural exploitation include reducing labor's bargaining power, lowering governments' ability to tax capital, and using political influence to support antidemocratic institutions. However, MNCs may also increase productivity, reduce cartel power, and promote more efficient government policies.

Deontological or Human Rights Approaches

Kant and other philosophers posit that humans have basic human rights (Kant, *Groundwork of the Metaphysic of Morals* (1785)). Deontological, or human rights, arguments suggest it is unethical to benefit from the poverty of (or discrimination faced by) poor workers in poor nations. Instead, every worker is entitled to be treated with dignity. One common condition for dignity is that employers should pay workers enough to afford decent accommodation, food for their families, and education for their children, regardless of the wage employees are willing to work for.

The human rights approach also considers it unfair to pay a woman less than a similarly qualified man, regardless of differences in market wages. There is substantial evidence of large discrimination by gender and often ethnicity in many nations. More generally, the ILO assumes there are human rights in workplaces regardless of whether the market transaction is voluntary. Child labor, forced labor, discrimination, and suppression of unions constitute violations of these rights. Almost all nations have signed treaties endorsing these rights. Many NGOs lobbying for worker rights use this human rights approach to define exploitation.

In contrast to a consequentialist approach, a deontological approach will condemn a multinational that adequately compensates workers yet has high rates of sexual harassment, or has many easily preventable injuries, even if domestically owned employers treat employees worse. Thus, this approach suggests measuring the *absolute* performance of MNCs (such as adhering to ILO agreements or to universal ethical standards), not just MNCs' performance relative to workers' alternatives.

MNC EFFECTS ON WAGES

We now turn to the evidence regarding the market-based theories of exploitation. We start by examining wages. Wage rates are one of the most important, and easiest to measure, factors in assessing employees' well-being. In most studies of how multinationals affect wages, the wage is the dependent variable and the authors interpret a positive partial correlation with foreign ownership as evidence of a wage premium at multinationals.

These studies may overestimate the effects of MNCs by not controlling for unobservable worker characteristics, such as human capital, that influence hiring by MNCs (see Almeida (2007)). These studies may underestimate the wages paid by MNCs by controlling for employer characteristics such as size and industry. For example, large firms may pay above-market wages due to efficiency wage effects or rent sharing while certain sectors may also be associated with wage premiums. If the MNC wage premium is driven at least partially by locating in large and profitable sectors, thereby creating more opportunities for better paying jobs, it may make sense to credit MNCs for this benefit, even if a similarly positioned domestic firm would pay equivalent wages.

A few studies have examined how wages change in firms as ownership shifts from domestic to foreign (or vice versa) or follow workers as they move between domestic and foreign-owned firms. Such longitudinal designs provide more convincing evidence of a causal link between foreign ownership and higher wages. Given the fairly large number of studies, we focus primarily on studies that control for worker characteristics.

MNC Wages in Developing Countries

Public and academic discourse on the effect of MNCs on foreign workers typically refers to MNCs based in countries belonging to the Organization for Economic Cooperation and Development (OECD) and operating in lower- and middle-income countries. Some of the first work on the MNC wage premium was done by Aitken, Harrison, and Lipsey (1996), who examine whether manufacturing foreign direct investment (FDI) in Mexico, Venezuela, and the United States is associated with higher wages. In their cross-sectional analysis, they find that a 10 percent increase in manufacturing FDI in Mexico and Venezuela corresponds to a 2.2 percent increase in production worker wages, and a 2.9 percent increase in non-production wages. In a time-series analysis that controls for firm-level size, capital intensity, and industrial composition, the foreign ownership wage premium persists, but is only about a third as large. The authors interpret these results as suggesting that FDI is associated with higher productivity in MNCs, some of which is passed on to workers in the form of higher wages. Lipsey and Sjoholm (2004) use cross-sectional data to control for worker education along with firm size, location, industry, and input mix to isolate the effect of MNC ownership on wages in Indonesia. In the regression with the most controls, they find wage premiums of 12 percent for production workers and 22 percent for non-production workers, although this does not rule out the possibility of upward bias caused by unobservable characteristics. Their

2006 study uses Indonesian panel data from 1975–1995 to examine how changes in firm ownership, from domestic to MNC and vice versa, affect wages. While their panel findings are similar to their 2004 cross-section results, they find that plants that underwent a foreign takeover during the sample period paid 17 percent and 28 percent higher wages for production and non-production workers, respectively, than plants that remained domestic. These effects are significantly larger than the effects of a domestic takeover. However, the authors note that these results are still subject to selectivity bias from time-varying unobservables that influence multinational takeovers.

Arnold and Javorcik (2009) attempt to overcome these endogeneity issues by comparing trends in Indonesian firms that become acquired by a multinational to trends in firms that have similar observable characteristics prior to the acquisition but are *not* acquired. (Economists call these methods propensity score matching with a difference-in-difference approach.) Using data from 1983–2011, they find that foreign takeovers result in 41 percent higher wages after two years relative to the counterfactual they construct, and that foreign privatizations led to 27 percent higher wages after two years. They also find significant increases in employment and investment, and that foreign plants actually become less skill-intensive—inconsistent with the idea that takeovers displace low-skilled workers within the firm.

Martins and Esteves (2006) and Poole (2008) use matched-worker and firm-panel data for 1995–1999 to analyze the effect of foreign ownership on wages in Brazil. Like Earle and Telegdy (2007), Martins and Esteves (2006) use changes in firm ownership as a way to control for unobserved firm-specific effects that could be correlated with wage premiums.[7] They also follow workers who move to or leave foreign enterprises, to control for unobserved worker-specific effects. They find that workers moving from foreign to domestic firms typically take wage cuts when they move, while movers from domestic to foreign firms increase their pay. However, compared with the unconditional wage gaps of 50 percent, the wage premium associated with working for a foreign firm falls to between 3 percent and 7 percent once they control for worker and firm characteristics. Both Martins and Esteves (2006) and Poole (2008) conclude that their results support a small positive effect of foreign firms in the Brazilian labor market.

To summarize, there is varyingly robust evidence that the higher wages paid by multinationals in developing countries do, in fact, represent a premium. However, only one of the above studies provides a causal estimate, and only two studies follow the same enterprises over time using matched worker-employer data. The evidence is consistent with positive wage premiums, which drop to single digits once worker and firm characteristics can be controlled for.

MNC Wages in Developed Countries

The literature on MNC wages in developed countries faces similar identification challenges as in developing countries. Breau and Brown (2011) examine MNC ownership in Canadian manufacturing in 1999 and 2001. They find that when controlling for worker and firm characteristics, foreign ownership results in a wage premium of 7 percent. Bircan (2011) examines the MNC wage premium in Turkish manufacturing from 1993–2001 and uses a continuous instead of binary measurement of foreign ownership. She finds that for every 10 percent increase in foreign ownership at the firm level, there is a corresponding 4 percent increase in non-production wages, but finds no premium for production workers.

Martins (2004) examines the MNC wage premium using matched employee-employer data from 1991–1999 in Portugal. Using ordinary least squares (OLS) regressions at the firm level, he finds an average wage premium of 32 percent for MNC-owned plants. These statistically significant effects generally disappear when applying propensity score matching, and the study finds negative wage effects of foreign acquisitions from a combined propensity score difference-in-difference approach similar to that used by Arnold and Javorcik (2009). However, Martins does not present balance tests to ensure the appropriateness of the matching procedure (Girma and Gorg (2007)).

Girma and Gorg (2007) use a similar difference-in-difference approach coupled with propensity scores, and examine the effect of foreign acquisition on the wages of workers in the U.K. food and electronics sectors from 1980–1994. They find that acquisitions by U.S. MNCs led to wage increases of 13 percent for production workers and 8 percent for non-production workers, while acquisitions by EU MNCs did not lead to any wage premiums. However, the authors point out that since they were unable to control for worker characteristics, these wage premiums may be the result of "poaching" the best workers from domestic firms. Heyman and others (2007) also combine propensity score matching and difference in differences using data from 1996–2000 in Sweden. While they find that foreign ownership is associated with a 20 percent wage premium when using firm-level variables, they actually find a negative wage effect when using individual worker fixed effects.

The latest study, by Setzler and Tintelnot (2019), uses matched employee-employer data for the United States to examine the effect of multinational employment on wages. They find that when firm-specific factors are not accounted for, the wage premium is 25 percent. Moving from a non-multinational to a multinational firm, after accounting for other factors, reduces the wage premium to 7 percent. Setzler and Tintelnot (2019) also use an instrumental variable approach inspired by Bartik to get at the possible endogeneity of foreign firm location.

Overall, industry and worker attributes appear to mostly explain the large gap between multinational and domestic. The most rigorous studies find that a small premium from MNCs does persist in developing countries (to the extent that selectivity bias is successfully controlled for by propensity score matching), and recent studies get estimates ranging from 0 percent to 7 percent for developed countries.

MNCs AND FAIR SHARING OF SURPLUS

We now turn to arguments that judge exploitation by MNCs absolutely, rather than relative to domestic firms. We start with theories about fairly sharing surplus. As noted, utilitarian theories and behavioral economic experiments suggest it is fair for employers with high ability to pay to share their profits with their employees. Inequality-averse utilitarians also worry if MNC activity increases market-level inequality.

Sharing Surplus with MNC Employees and Their Suppliers

As discussed, MNCs typically pay slightly higher wages than similar domestic firms when controlling for worker characteristics. Evidence suggests that the premium is quite small—almost certainly less than 10 percent and likely in the range of 3 to 7 percent. Also, as discussed, it is unclear how much of this premium is due to rent sharing; MNCs could pay higher wages to reward unmeasured skills. The wage gap could overstate employee benefits if it compensates workers for unmeasured poor working conditions (Lipsey and Sjoholm (2006)), or understate employee rents if MNCs have above-average working conditions (for example, due to customers enforcing their codes of conduct). With those cautions in mind, it appears that many MNCs share some small amount of their rents with employees.

Budd, Konings, and Slaughter (2005) find evidence of rent sharing using panel data across Europe; a doubling of parent profits raises affiliate wages by 1 percent to 5 percent. However, we are not aware of any such studies in a developing country. At the same time, the small size of the wage premium suggests any rent sharing through wages is small. In addition, the scattered evidence on employee turnover rates for factories in poor nations (often more than 100 percent per year) suggests that sharing surplus via better working conditions is not large.

MNCs' Effects on Labor Markets in Poor Nations

While the studies discussed only focus on multinational affiliates, multinational entry may also affect wages and employment at the industry and local labor market levels. In theory, this entry could either benefit or harm workers in host countries. If the MNC competes with local firms, then local firms may contract. In extreme cases, there may even be a net loss of jobs. However, the MNC may also increase labor demand for other firms in the labor market as well. For example, MNCs may increase labor demand for intermediate inputs produced by local firms, or they spread knowledge on technology or on good management.

Not many studies address these factors. In Ethiopia, Abebe, McMillan, and Serafinelli (2018) find some evidence of increased employment at domestic manufacturing firms in locations that experienced an FDI entry but no discernible effect on wages. In contrast, Atkin, Faber, and Gonzalez-Navarro (2018) find that despite overall welfare gains, foreign retail entry in Mexico was associated with a 3.9 percent reduction in the number of domestic retail establishments. This job loss occurred along with a 4.4 percent to 5.1 percent reduction in profits for traditional retailers and a 5.9 percent decline in monthly income for traditional retail workers.[8] In the former context, the authors find strong linkages and knowledge transfer between foreign and domestic firms, while in the latter, foreign and domestic firms compete against each other directly. These two papers are not an exhaustive treatment of labor market effects of MNCs; rather, they illustrate the potential for positive or negative effects of MNC entry on employees of local firms.

More generally, a utilitarian is concerned with how a system of production dominated by MNCs affects inequality as well as productivity. Labor shares have been declining globally over the past few decades (Dao and others (2017)), while corporate profits as a share of national economies have been increasing (Harrison (2004)). This pattern raises questions about the extent to which MNCs drive these trends. Harrison (2004) develops a bargaining game between labor and capital owners in a framework where imperfect competition leads to excess profits, which must be shared. In her model, capital owners are more likely to achieve a stronger bargaining position when it is easier for them to relocate than it is for workers. She then tests the implications of the model for changes in global labor shares. Determinants of such shares include restrictions on labor and capital mobility. The evidence suggests that higher foreign investment flows (consistent with fewer restrictions on capital) are associated with lower labor shares globally.

The underlying theory motivating this research is that capital account openness increases the relative bargaining power of capital with respect to labor and weakens labor's relative position. Jayadev (2007) correlates measures of capital account openness with national labor shares. Consistent with Harrison's work, Jayadev (2007) finds a negative correlation in developed countries between openness and labor shares, possibly a negative correlation in middle-income countries, and no correlation for the poorest nations. Jaumotte and Tytell (2007) examine labor shares in the advanced economies and find that measures of globalization, such as share of imported intermediate inputs and levels of immigration, are negatively correlated with labor share. They also find that technological change in the information and communication sector has a larger negative correlation with the labor share.

Research on the relationship between MNCs and labor shares generally relies on macro rather than firm-level data. Moreover, it is difficult to separate the effects of MNCs on the labor share from the effects of market concentration, technological change, and trade. More evidence is needed on the linkages between differential mobility and labor shares at the micro as well as the aggregate level.

THE EFFECT OF MNC OFFSHORING ON DOMESTIC WAGES

We now turn to the effects of offshoring by MNCs on home-country workers. Media and politicians (on both sides of the aisle) have criticized companies that offshore routine manufacturing jobs to low-income countries.

Critics often assume offshoring supplants American workers one-for-one with cheaper workers abroad. In this view, offshoring puts downward pressure on wages at home by threatening to replace workers with cheaper labor abroad. The fairness theories reviewed above suggest it is not always fair for companies to profit while workers in their home nations lose.

However, economic theory suggests that the motive for offshoring, type of work, and destination of the offshored jobs will determine effects of offshoring on workers. While offshoring could substitute for home-country workers, it could also allow firms to expand, or simply stay in business, increasing wages and employment at home.

Given the mixed predictions of theory, we turn to the data. The literature we discuss is largely at an aggregate level—most papers deal with industry, labor market, and supply chain effects, while only a few limit their analysis to within-firm effects. However, empirical research on offshoring's effects is challenging from an identification standpoint, because employers with expanding product demand are likely to increase employment both at home and abroad. While some studies use instrumental variables or assume some prices are exogenous, it is hard to justify all the assumptions needed to interpret the estimates as causal.

Despite the concerns about causality, the bulk of the literature is consistent with theory. The average effect of offshoring on employment and earnings in industrialized nations is not typically large, and may be positive. However, this average effect hides predictable heterogeneity. Specifically, most studies find that offshoring to low-wage nations lowers demand for routine labor in source nations. Similarly, offshoring to high-wage nations lowers demand for non-routine labor in source nations. The same studies also find outsourcing to low-wage countries *increases* demand for non-routine labor, and that outsourcing to high-wage countries increases demand for routine labor in the source nations.

Distributional effects say more about the possibility for exploitation as defined earlier in the chapter. There are both winners and losers from offshoring, and it is important to identify and compensate the losers (Bernanke (2006)). As discussed, participants in experiments view an outcome as "unfair" when one party chooses an option that benefits themselves while knowingly significantly harming another. However, it is difficult to conclude that offshoring itself harms workers if the same job losses would have occurred anyway. We therefore measure consequentialist exploitation against the counterfactual of how workers would have fared in the absence of offshoring.

How Prevalent Is Offshoring?

Before delving into the effects of offshoring, we highlight a few facts presented in the literature that show its importance to the U.S. economy. Between 1993 and 2011, U.S. manufacturing employment fell by more than one-third, with American multinationals accounting for a disproportionate share (41 percent) of this decline (Boehm, Flaaen, and Pandalai-Nayar (2019)). According to Slaughter (2009), U.S. multinational parents accounted for about 19 percent of total U.S. employment, while, more recently, Boehm, Flaaen, and Pandalai-Nayar (2019) find that multinationals accounted for 29 percent of U.S. manufacturing employment as of 2011. Much offshoring consists of production of intermediate inputs. The same authors calculate that in 2011, 49 percent of U.S. multinationals sourced intermediate inputs from affiliates in low-income countries, and 73 percent sourced from unaffiliated suppliers in low-income countries, compared with 25 percent and 44 percent in 1993, respectively. This constitutes a major share of U.S. trade; as reported in Kovak, Oldenski, and Sly (2018), more than 40 percent of U.S. imports were through related-party transactions and more than 60 percent of manufacturing imports in 2007 were intermediate goods (Boehm, Flaaen, and Pandalai-Nayar (2019)). Thus, much of the effects of foreign import competition in general include offshoring—both through related-party imports and offshoring through unrelated parties. However, to keep our task manageable, we focus on papers explicitly covering foreign-affiliate employment and related-party trade.

The modern literature on the effects of offshoring on domestic wages arguably begins with Feenstra and Hanson (1999). They first identify the effect of offshoring and technical change on industry prices and productivity, which they use to decompose each channel's effect on wages. They find that offshoring led to no discernible change in the wages of production workers and a small increase in wages of non-production workers. Some other studies also find offshoring improves labor outcomes. For example, Desai, Foley, and Hines (2009) use data matching domestic firms to foreign affiliates to show that a 10 percent increase in a multinational's overseas investment is associated with a 2.6 percent increase in domestic investment, and a 10 percent increase in overseas employee compensation is associated with a 3.7 increase in domestic employment compensation. However, their analysis is limited to what occurs within a firm, not at the industry or occupational level. They also do not distinguish between the types of labor and the destination of offshoring. Moreover, they use foreign growth rates to instrument for investment in foreign affiliates. This estimation strategy assumes that U.S. wage bills and investment are uncorrelated with foreign growth rates. However, it is plausible that firms respond to foreign growth by increasing production at home. This would lead to an overestimate of the effect of offshoring on domestic employment.

A second approach is to construct measures of exposure to offshoring at the industry and occupational level. This permits a broader analysis than that of Desai, Foley, and Hines (2009), since offshoring by one firm may affect workers differentially across geography and worker-skill levels. Oldenski (2014) finds results suggesting offshoring complements non-routine U.S. labor and substitutes for routine U.S. labor, but glosses over the distinction between high- and low-income destinations. Offshoring—measured through firm-level foreign affiliate sales rather than employment—increases overall wages and employment for the average occupation within an industry. Oldenski also finds that the overall wage increase is accompanied by wage polarization, with increases at the top and bottom of the wage distribution and a decline in the middle. Occupations with non-routine and communication-intensive tasks obtain higher wages, while occupations that involve computer use see wage declines. On the other hand, Hummels and others (2014) find positive effects of offshoring for high-skilled workers in Denmark, and negative effects for low-skilled workers; they also find that routine jobs, as well as jobs using natural science and engineering knowledge, undergo larger wage losses due to offshoring.

Hummels and others (2014) and Oldenski (2014) show that offshoring is associated with wage losses for less skilled workers and wage gains for more skilled employees. Ebenstein and others (2014) and Ebenstein, Harrison, and McMillan (2017) study the effects of exposure to offshoring to high- and low-income countries as well as the effects of exposure to import penetration at the industry and occupation level, broken down by the degree of routineness. At the industry level, they find that offshoring to high-income countries has a small positive effect on wages (a 10 percent increase in industry foreign affiliate employment leads to a 0.14 percent increase in wages), but find no effect of offshoring to low-income nations. However, at the occupational level, Ebenstein and others (2014) find that offshoring to high-income countries significantly increases U.S. wages (a 10 percent increase in occupational foreign affiliate employment leads to a 0.34 percent rise in wages), but offshoring to low-income countries has a larger negative effect

(0.40 percent) on wages. However, their estimates can only be interpreted as causal under the assumptions that offshoring is not a response to changes in domestic wages, and that technical change is uncorrelated with offshoring.

The fall in wages reported by Ebenstein and others (2014) are entirely driven by workers performing the most routine tasks. Using more recent data, Ebenstein, Harrison, and McMillan (2017) show that these effects are partially offset by small but significant increases in wages in low-income regions and decreases in wages in high-income countries for non-routine workers. This reflects the fact that routine tasks are performed in low-income countries, while non-routine tasks are performed in high-income countries, and is consistent with evidence that workers are more easily able to switch industry than occupation (Kambourov and Manovskii (2009)). Such interpretations are consistent with standard trade theory applied within multinational firms—gains accrue to the factor in which the United States has a comparative advantage and losses to the factor in which the United States has a comparative disadvantage. These effects have been increasing over time, reflecting the growth of offshoring and globalization in general (Ebenstein and others (2014); Ebenstein, Harrison, and McMillan (2017)).

Mechanisms

In this section, we explore how offshoring affects labor demand and individual worker wages in the home country. Offshoring to low-income countries affects wages of U.S. workers at the individual level, as well as at the local labor market level and within firms exposed to offshoring through upstream and downstream linkages. One mechanism is worker displacement—when jobs are offshored, workers are forced to seek a new job or leave the labor force. Other mechanisms include induced changes in labor intensity and supply chain consequences that indirectly affect labor demand and wages. The results discussed indicate that the negatives outweigh the positives primarily for U.S. workers performing routine, highly substitutable tasks.

Worker Displacement

When jobs are offshored, workers are forced to transition to other occupations or sectors, become unemployed, or drop out of the labor force. Ebenstein and others (2014) and Ebenstein, Harrison, and McMillan (2017) match a sample of individual workers observed in the Current Population

Survey (CPS) in consecutive years. Ebenstein, Harrison, and McMillan (2017) find no significant effect of switching industries within manufacturing, but switching industries and leaving manufacturing leads to 2.7 percent lower wages, and leaving manufacturing and switching occupation leads to 4 percent lower wages. Hummels and others (2014) tracked cohorts that left a firm after an offshoring event in Denmark, finding that the present discounted value of lost earnings exceeded 50 percent of pre-displacement earnings for both high- and low-skilled workers. This implies that changing occupation and industry is costly for workers. Kambourov and Manovskii (2009) find that occupational rather than industry tenure represents a stock of human capital—five years is associated with a 12 percent wage premium—that is depleted when an individual switches occupation. Ebenstein, Harrison, and McMillan (2017) find that occupational exposure to offshoring in China is associated with a small but statistically significant negative effect on labor force participation. Nevertheless, they also find that technology, proxied for by computer use, explains much more of the decline in labor force participation.

Changes in Factor Intensity

Offshoring also changes optimal factor allocations within domestic operations, which can compound job losses. Given that the United States typically has a comparative advantage in capital and high-skilled labor, standard trade theory suggests that increasing inter- or intra-firm trade would lead domestic plants to use these factors more intensively. Pierce and Schott (2016) find that exposure to Chinese import competition (including related-party imports, which, they find, constitutes nearly 60 percent of the increase in U.S. firms importing from China) after the establishment of permanent normal trade relations in 2001 led plants to become significantly more capital- and skill-intensive, with production workers experiencing 1.5 times the decrease in employment of non-production workers. Similarly, offshoring routine tasks may decrease routine manufacturing activities domestically, but having a larger and more dispersed supply chain may increase the number of executive, managerial, and administrative jobs performed at headquarters (Kovak, Oldenski, and Sly (2018)). This indicates effects beyond direct substitution of domestic for foreign labor and suggests that technology replaces labor directly and indirectly through offshoring and import competition.

Labor Market and Supply Chain Effects

In an analysis that does not separate high- and low-income offshoring, Kovak, Oldenski, and Sly (2018) find that a 10 percent increase in foreign affiliate employment is associated with a 0.67 percent increase in local labor market employment in addition to a 1.8 percent increase in domestic employment. Boehm, Flaaen, and Pandalai-Nayar (2019) develop a model of multinational firm sourcing that allows them to estimate an upper bound of a single parameter—the elasticity of firm size with respect to production efficiency—that determines the effect of foreign sourcing by multinationals on domestic employment at affiliated and non-affiliated plants. They estimate this upper bound (in most specifications) to be well below one—implying negative effects of multinational sourcing. In a simple counterfactual analysis, they find that offshoring accounted for about 810,000 manufacturing job losses between 1997 and 2007, roughly one-fifth of the total decline in manufacturing employment in that period. Slightly more than half of these job losses occur at unaffiliated domestic suppliers rather than within multinationals, alongside a smaller effect of greater foreign sourcing by non-multinationals. In a similar model, Antràs, Fort, and Tintelnot (2017) estimate this elasticity to be greater than one but find that the recent growth in sourcing from China reduces domestic sourcing by 0.53 percent on net leads. However, this masks considerable heterogeneity: firms not linked to China contract or exit, while those linked with China increase their domestic sourcing. While they do not map changes in sourcing to employment outcomes, they predict substantial churn in the labor market, compounding these net effects. These recent models underscore the importance of the effects of offshoring outside the parent firm.

Is Offshoring Exploitation?

We find that *some* types of offshoring have negative effects on *some* workers. However, our consequentialist definition of exploitation requires that workers would not have been exposed to these negative effects had offshoring not taken place. How many of the American workers whose jobs were replaced by cheaper overseas labor would still be employed if their employer had not engaged in offshoring? Would their firms have automated their jobs instead of offshoring them? Would they be able to keep pace with increasingly competitive foreign firms if they did not produce their optimal product mix at the cheapest cost?

To the best of our knowledge, no empirical work addresses this counterfactual. However, technological change and increasing import competition would likely have reduced U.S. manufacturing employment even in the absence of offshoring. First, domestic firms have been contracting and dying at similar rates to U.S. multinationals' domestic operations. Summary statistics reported by Boehm, Flaaen, and Pandalai-Nayar (2019) show that the number of domestic manufacturing firms decreased by nearly 3 percent per annum on average from 2001 to 2011, while the number of U.S. multinationals only decreased by 1.3 percent and the count of foreign multinationals increased by 2.3 percent per annum, on average. Likewise, employment at domestic firms contracted by 5.04 percent per annum, compared with 4.17 percent for U.S. multinationals and 0.35 percent for foreign multinationals. Obviously, some of this could be due to the supply-chain effects of multinational offshoring, but they alone cannot plausibly explain these downward trends. While employees of domestic firms are different (in ways both observed and unobserved) from employees of multinationals, this nevertheless suggests that employees would have been no better insulated from layoffs and plant closures had they worked for a domestic firm rather than a multinational.

Moreover, the effects of offshoring—particularly through related-party intermediate input imports—are a small part of the effects due to foreign import competition in general. Ebenstein and others (2014) find that a 10 percent increase in occupational exposure to import competition is associated with about four times the decline in wages as the same increase in exposure to offshoring. Similarly, Ebenstein, Harrison, and McMillan (2017) find that the effect of import competition from China was three times that of related-party offshoring. In this vein, the forces that encourage multinationals to establish and expand operations in China and other low-wage countries—rural-urban migration, liberalization, industrialization, technological advances—are the same forces that threaten to compete with them should they continue to produce in the United States.

While technical change and automation are interlinked with offshoring, their direct labor–substituting effects are likely greater than the effects of offshoring. Proxying for technical change with computer use, Feenstra and Hanson (1999) find that technical change explains roughly three times as much of the decline in employment as offshoring. Similarly, Ebenstein, Harrison, and McMillan (2017) show that both computer use and prices of investment goods are much more important determinants of employment than exposure to Chinese offshoring. Autor and others (2003), who develop the routineness measure used by Ebenstein and others (2014), Oldenski (2014), and Ebenstein, Harrison, and McMillan (2017), initially use this framework to show that computers substitute for routine labor and increase the skill bias within manufacturing plants. Moreover, by the logic of applying this framework, the jobs vulnerable to offshoring are the same as the jobs vulnerable to replacement through technical change.

However, technical change runs far beyond computer use, with rapidly increasing automation in both the manufacturing and service sectors. Economists are still grappling with a theoretical framework for automation, and few empirical analyses exist. Like offshoring, automation of certain tasks could be associated with substitution or crowding-in effects on employment. Acemoglu and Restrepo (2017) find that the substitution effects of robots dominate, with each robot per thousand workers leading to a 0.18 to 0.37 percentage point decline in manufacturing employment but find that exposure to robot use is only weakly correlated with measures of offshoring. On the other hand, Autor and Salomons (2018) provide some evidence that adoption of robots has not displaced employment but has reduced labor's share in value added, especially in recent years. With the number of robots expected to triple or quadruple over the next few years (Acemoglu and Restrepo (2017)), the magnitude of these effects will likely outpace the effects of offshoring.

The literature discussed shows the nuanced and disaggregated effects that offshoring by multinationals has had on American workers. Despite disagreement over whether positive or negative channels dominate, offshoring clearly generates winners and losers. Even when effects balance out in the aggregate, distributional consequences do not. The evidence suggests that blue-collar manufacturing workers performing routine tasks that can easily be replicated in low-wage countries stand to lose the most. It will be important for policy to ensure that workers most vulnerable to globalization can be insulated from, or compensated for, the inevitable changes the U.S. labor market will continue to face.

These changes appear to be part of broader trends affecting U.S. manufacturing, as well as manufacturing in Europe and even China (where manufacturing employment shares have also begun to decline). While offshoring is an important factor, it does not appear plausible that offshoring is the only factor driving these trends, given the larger roles import competition and technical change play. Many of the jobs lost due to offshoring could have been lost through these other channels, although a rigorous analysis of this question would require substantial extensions of existing models of multinational sourcing.

DO MNCs EXPLOIT WORKERS BY DENYING THEM BASIC RIGHTS?

A wide array of domestic and international laws and standards provide clear, although not exhaustive, descriptions of conditions that lead to exploitation. This section addresses the extent to which MNCs deny workers what many consider to be basic rights.[9] Many claims of MNC exploitation are not based on relative wages, as discussed in the previous section. Rather, the claims refer to evidence of "unacceptably" or "immorally" bad standards of treatment, including child labor, physical and verbal abuse, excessive working hours, and inadequate health and safety measures. As discussed, exploitation may arise from violations of moral rights, irrespective of the distributional outcome (Zwolinski and Wertheimer (2017)). Nevertheless, we do compare outcomes between MNCs and other firms in some instances, which may shed light on the extent to which MNCs may either improve conditions to international standards or reduce them by subverting domestic standards.

A rights-based approach is central to the International Labor Organization (International Labor Organization (2016)). The 1998 ILO Declaration on Fundamental Principles and Rights at Work commits all member states to respecting rights in four categories:

- the elimination of all forms of forced or compulsory labor
- freedom of association and the right to collective bargaining
- the abolition of child labor
- the elimination of discrimination with respect to employment and occupation

We structure the available evidence according to these categories. In addition, we summarize available evidence related to health and safety of workers. These working conditions arise repeatedly in the literature and public debate on MNCs' treatment of foreign workers. They are also a component of key ILO conventions.

Presumably because these rights are enshrined in ILO conventions, they are also found in the code of conduct adopted by many MNCs. For example, the Fair Labor Association (FLA) has based its standards on the ILO conventions. Twenty-eight U.S. companies and suppliers have signed on to these standards and the FLA's monitoring and compliance programs. FLA members include major brands such as Nike, New Balance, Fruit of the Loom, and Patagonia.[10]

An important element of the concept of exploitation is the use of another person's vulnerability. To that end, we pay specific attention to the working conditions of more vulnerable workers, such as women and migrants. As noted in a 2016 ILO Statement to the UN General Assembly in New York, the "situation is often bleaker for groups working in vulnerable circumstances, including migrants, refugees, women, and domestic workers" (International Labor Organization (2016)). Similarly, the International Organization for Migration's 2003 World Migration Report notes the "particular vulnerability to exploitation and abuse of women migrant workers" (International Organization for Migration (2003), 105–06). This is not to say that employing a vulnerable person is exploitation; however, given that vulnerable workers have fewer recourses, simply requiring that MNCs improve on their next-best option may still condone unethical behavior.

This section presents evidence on labor rights at MNCs. The rights-based approach to exploitation uses absolute standards rather than relative ones. Nonetheless, comparing labor rights at MNCs relative to domestic employers provides additional insights.

Relatively few studies directly compare how well MNCs meet non-wage labor standards to similar domestic firms. For this reason, we include studies that compare conditions inside and outside export processing zones (EPZs) in the same city. This evidence is relevant because nations create EPZs largely to encourage FDI and increase participation in MNC supply chains. The proportion of establishments with substantial foreign ownership was between 70 percent and 96 percent in the EPZs we discuss. These inside-outside EPZ comparisons do, however, mix MNC versus local with cross-sectoral comparisons—comparing, for example, formal manufacturing jobs with informal service-sector jobs. As such, they answer a different question than that examined in within-sector analyses of wage differentials.

Because the academic literature on non-wage working conditions is limited, we also bring in evidence from international organizations such as the OECD, the World Bank, and ILO, research institutes such as the Centre for Research on Multinational Corporations (SOMO), and high-profile NGOs such as Human Rights Watch and Oxfam. We acknowledge that one reason there is relatively little academic literature on this topic, compared with wages, is that there is relatively little data of high quality. This topic seems to be too important to simply exclude, however, so we have used the best-quality sources we could find.

Finally, we note that much of the available evidence does not distinguish the home country of the MNC. The studies that do distinguish tend to show variation in compliance with the home country. A recent high-quality study for Ontario, Canada, found that U.S.-based firms had lower compliance than Canadian or continental European firms, but higher than Mexican or Chinese (Pohler and Riddell (2019)).

Forced Labor and Working Hours

We found no evidence of MNCs involved in slavery in the sense of workers being forced to work for no pay. At the same time, there is extensive evidence of employers requiring workers to work overtime in excess of two hours per day, often without compensation (Milberg and Amengual (2008)).[11] Workers can be compelled to work more overtime than they want to by threats of dismissal, violence, or (in some cases) deportation.

The 2018 compliance report from Better Factories Cambodia (BFC) provides high-quality evidence from a garment industry with one of the best reputations for maintaining labor standards (International Finance Corporation (2018). Almost all (96 percent) of the factories assessed were foreign-owned, predominantly by Chinese multinationals. More than 70 percent of assessed factories did not comply with the requirement that overtime never exceed two hours per day. However, in only 5 percent to 10 percent of factories was there involuntary overtime or failure to pay the penalty rates for overtime (with the exception of meal allowances, where the non-compliance rate was more than 30 percent).

Compulsory overwork in export processing zones is documented by Hein (1988) and ILO (2016) for the Mauritius apparel EPZ, and Yonghong (1989) for Shenzhen EPZ in China. Similarly, in 2016, FLA assessors in twenty-seven countries, including Myanmar, Vietnam, Bangladesh, China,

Indonesia, India, and Sri Lanka, found "more than three-quarters of all facilities [to be] in need of improvement regarding excessive hours of work" (Fair Labor Association (2017)).

Little evidence compares working hours in MNCs with hours at domestic firms. One exception is Hijzen and Swaim (2008). Using linked employer-employee data, they find no statistically significant effect of moving to an MNC on logged weekly hours in Germany, Portugal, or the United Kingdom. For Brazil, they find a decrease in working hours of around 0.2 percent.[12]

Turning to evidence from EPZs, Cirera and Lakshman's summary of eight studies was: "While long working hours appear to be a common element in many EPZs, the comparison with working hours outside the zone is mixed" (Cirera and Lakshman (2017)). Kabeer and Mahmud (2004) compare workers and working conditions inside and outside export processing zones (EPZs) in Dhaka, Bangladesh.[13] They find workers inside the EPZs were substantially more likely to receive a contract letter, paid leave, and payment for overtime worked, and less likely to work more than ten hours per day.

Freedom of Association and Right to Organize

The Preamble to the Constitution of the International Labor Organization declares "recognition of the principle of freedom of association" to be a means of improving conditions of labor and of establishing peace. One of the first declarations of the ILO was the Freedom of Association and Protection of the Right to Organize Convention in 1948. In addition, the presence of unions is a strong predictor of compliance with local employment laws (Pohler and Riddell (2019).

Evidence on whether MNCs discourage labor organizations more than domestic firms is limited and mixed. Using linked employer-employee data, Hijzen and Swaim (2008) find workers in Germany and the United Kingdom are less likely to be in a union when they are working for a multinational firm.[14] Using time-series data to compare segmented production (MNC supply chain) to the traditional integrated production sector in El Salvador and Honduras, Anner (2011) finds segmentation strongly associated with a decrease in unionization. Also in Honduras, a survey found that EPZ workers are relatively less likely to be employed in workplaces with unions (compared with workers applying to work in the EPZ). At the same time, in their survey of the literature, Cirera and Lakshman (2017) conclude that in a majority of cases, unionization in EPZs is slightly higher than, or similar to, in firms outside the zones. Arnal and Hijzen (2008) also find that simple comparisons between MNC affiliates and (not necessarily similar) domestic firms show higher unionization rates in MNC affiliates. These mixed results suggest that on the question of unionization, it is important to carefully disentangle selection effects from causal effects of MNC ownership and multinational production processes. National norms and government policy also play an important role (Distelhorst and others (2015).

EPZs in some countries explicitly forbid unions and labor organization (Cirera and Lakshman (2017)). Even where legal, unions are de facto prohibited in many places, because workers are threatened with dismissal or blacklisting, or occasionally even violence if they attempt to organize (Milberg and Amengual (2008); also Manjoo (2012) provides one example). BFC's review of 464 Cambodian garment factories found 243 incidents of noncompliance with the right to organize among 155 different factories (International Finance Corporation (2018)).

Despite potential reputational costs, wholly owned factories of major international brands sometimes actively prohibit rights to organize. An investigation by Cividep India (2017) found workers in one of Samsung India's factories claimed they were asked during job interviews if they knew what a union was, and not hired if they responded affirmatively. The report also claimed that leaders of attempts to unionize the plant workforce were subsequently dismissed. Finally, contract letters revealed restrictions on rights to join any social organization without the permission of the management (Cividep India (2017)).

In some places, union participation in MNC supply chains is violently suppressed. The Bangladeshi garment sector is one example. Union organizers have been attacked with machetes or found dead, with their bodies showing signs of torture (Human Rights Watch (2015)).[15]

Child Labor

Few actions are as universally condemned in the West as child labor. For this reason, over the past decade, Western-based MNCs have almost universally announced zero-tolerance policies on employment of children in their affiliates and supply chains. Enforcement of these policies can vary, however, and cases of child labor are still routinely uncovered even in best-practice monitoring settings like the FLA and the Cambodian garment sector (Halegua (2006)). Child labor may be harder to detect and prevent at suppliers of multinationals. While studies and audits have shown improving compliance of suppliers with child labor laws (Egels-Zandén (2007) and (2014); Donaghey and others (2014)), enforcement is imperfect. Moreover, audits at factories may mask labor done by children of employees who bring their work home, as documented by Husselbee (2000) and Khan, Munir, and Willmott (2007) among soccer ball producers in Pakistan.

More recently, campaigns have started to focus on the ways in which MNCs may indirectly contribute to child labor by paying workers low wages. A 2017 report on the children of Bangladeshi garment workers (Theuws, Sandjojo, and Vogt (2017)) found some families took their children out of school not only to reduce expenses but also to complete childcare and housework tasks that their mothers could not perform due to long working hours. Some children also supplemented family income by working in sectors that do not have a zero-tolerance policy for child labor.

Health and Safety

Some MNCs and (more often) their suppliers provide very dangerous workplaces. For example, more than a thousand workers died when the 2013 Rana Plaza building collapsed in Bangladesh. Workers in that building produced clothes for many major brands. That tragedy highlighted concerns that multinationals exploit workers' ignorance of safety conditions such as the structural integrity of a building.

It is possible that the MNC wage premium observed in some studies may reflect that these jobs are more dangerous than others. This premium could be inefficiently (and unfairly) low when health and safety risks are hard for workers to evaluate. This problem is especially true in industries and jobs of which workers have little prior knowledge, when workers cannot observe hazards (such as poor building construction), or when workers are unfamiliar with the hazard (such as many chemicals that lead to long-term harm).

Manjoo (2012) interviewed MNC employees in Honduras, who had reportedly "witnessed coworkers succumb to chronic fatigue, depression, and musculoskeletal disorders as a result of the hazardous working conditions." Similarly, field research on foreign firms in the Malaysian electronics industry by SOMO (2013) found workers were required to stand for their work during the entire shift. Furthermore, the workers reported exposure to toxic fumes and chemicals during the process of lead welding. Employers do not provide protective equipment, such as masks. Many workers said they suffered from allergic reactions and often developed coughs. Bangladeshi garment workers interviewed by Human Rights Watch claimed the water the factory supplied was so dirty it was undrinkable (Human Rights Watch (2015)). Of course, interviews with workers identify only the hazards workers know about.

Systematic data collection supports the anecdotal evidence above. A survey from Better Factories Cambodia (International Finance Corporation (2018)) shows that even in one of the most high-profile, best-practice industries in a low-wage nation, health and safety problems are common (table 7-1).

Studies of EPZs are also generally grim. In their review, Cirera and Lakshman (2017) found "significant health and safety issues in EPZs documented in the literature, ranging from anecdotal evidence to more robust studies." Similarly, Milberg and Amengual (2008) conclude: "Many workplaces in EPZs throughout the world still fail to provide safe environments." These studies, however, suggest employers in EPZs have fewer violations

TABLE 7-1. Safety Hazards Reported in Cambodian Factories with the Highest Rate of Noncompliance

Nature of noncompliance	Extent of noncompliance (% of factories assessed)
Inadequate lighting	93% of 433
Inadequately equipped/staffed infirmary	85% of 394
Improper labeling of chemicals	56% of 464
Failure to meet ergonomic standards	58% of 464
Failure to adhere to occupational safety and health workplace policy	62% of 464
Failure to assess workplace occupational safety and health issues	64% of 464
No mechanism(s) for managing employee occupational safety and health matters	64% of 464
Unacceptable temperature and/or ventilation	65% of 464
No requirement for pre-employment medical assessment	63% of 464

than employers not in an EPZ. Cirera and Lakshman (2017) find no studies showing worse health and safety conditions inside EPZs, and some showing better conditions. Milberg and Amengual (2008) conclude that MNCs' efforts to improve health and safety are making progress.

Discrimination and Treatment of Women

In many countries, women face substantial discrimination in the home and workplace, including lack of access to education. Female workers in poor countries are a particularly vulnerable group, and hence prone to exploitation.

Female workers at suppliers for MNCs in many nations report recurrent violations of their rights. Examples include verbal and physical abuse by supervisors, sexual harassment, preemployment pregnancy tests, unfair dismissal and discrimination on the grounds of pregnancy, and denial of maternity leave and other legally required benefits (Raworth (2004)).[16] Manjoo (2012) found women working in EPZs in Honduras earn between 28 percent and 51 percent less than the minimum wage, with employers justifying lower wages for women with the stereotype that women's work is less demanding.

Some discrimination is overt. To find examples, we downloaded employment ads from leading websites in Korea, India, Indonesia, and Thailand. Except for Korea, all websites were in English. We first searched for terms such as "female" and "male." We then read candidate ads to be sure they referred to looking for only male or only female applicants.[17] Many globally recognizable MNCs posted ads seeking only males or females for different types of positions, in violation of ILO standards. However, domestically owned firms placed the vast majority of ads both with and without overt discrimination.

There is little evidence on whether MNCs are more or less likely than domestic employers to adhere to the ILO right for equal pay for equal work. There have, however, been some recent studies on the gender pay gap in foreign affiliates compared with domestic firms.[18] Vahter and Masso (2019) find that in Estonia foreign ownership is associated with a substantial increase in the gender pay gap (controlling for worker and firm characteristics). They posit that their result may be driven by lower tolerance for flexible work hours among foreign-owned firms. Their results are consistent with the results of Bøler, Smarzynska Javorcik, and Ulltveit-Moe (2018), which show that the gender wage gap is higher among exporting firms in Norway.

In contrast, Kodama, Javorcik, and Abe (2018) find that foreign affiliates in Japan employ more women and are more likely to provide telecommuting, childcare subsidies, and flexible working arrangements.

Tang and Zhang (2017) suggest that whether MNC affiliates exhibit more or less gender discrimination may depend on the cultures of the home and host countries. They find that, among manufacturing firms in China, foreign affiliates from countries with a more gender-equal culture tend to employ proportionally more women and promote female managers. Notably, the UNDP Gender Inequality Index, which the authors use to measure home-country culture, ranks European countries as more equal and the United States as less equal than China.[19]

Discrimination and Treatment of Migrant Workers

Migrant workers are more vulnerable than local workers (International Labor Organization (2016)). Among other things, migrant workers lack social and political networks, they may not proficiently speak or read the local language, and their employer may have the ability to have them deported (legally or otherwise). Because of their migration status, especially if they are undocumented, they may not be able to seek legal recourse without fear of deportation, or may not be aware of their rights.

If MNCs are not exploiting their workers, they should treat migrant workers as well as local workers—to avoid benefitting at the expense of migrants' higher vulnerability. There are well-documented cases of MNCs providing worse conditions to migrant workers, but we do not know the extent of the mistreatment and how MNCs' discrimination compares with treatment by domestic firms.

The Center for Research on Multinational Corporations (a Dutch NGO) investigated the relative treatment of migrant and foreign workers at three Malaysian electronics factories owned by multinationals (SOMO (2013)).[20] Migrants are a substantial part of the workforce in the industry, facilitated by government policy and a set of intermediary firms who bring the migrants in. Often migrants are employed formally by one of the intermediary firms, not the factory.

Migrant workers were treated substantially worse than local workers. Local workers reported working "eight to ten hours a day, five days a week, and mainly work in the morning shift, while outsourcing agency workers work twelve hours a day, six days a week, and all shifts" (SOMO (2013)).

Migrant workers also reported that their pay was docked if they were late or sick, supervisors threatened them with deportation if they made complaints, that the outsourcing agency held their passports, and that the pay was as little as half what they were promised. Many had never seen their formal employment contract, and even fewer had seen their contract in a language they could read.

Enforcement of Standards and Intention to Exploit?

Most large MNCs have codes of conduct for their subsidiaries and their suppliers. While these codes vary widely, almost all encompass the labor standards we discuss. This raises an interesting question. Do the human rights violations described persist because the MNCs benefit from them? Or do they persist because, despite best effort, MNCs are not able to eliminate violations from their supply chains?

The answer to this question matters to our question of exploitation. As Rabin's work shows, intentions matter in many people's determination of whether an action is fair or not. Furthermore, the rights-based approach emphasizes the correctness of the choices made by an agent, not their outcomes. So long as MNCs allow human rights violations, they are exploiting workers.

In the 1990s, many MNCs introduced codes of conduct for their suppliers. In some cases, the MNCs announced workplace inspections ahead of time, had managers choose workers to interview, and had managers present during interviews. These standards did not look at second tier suppliers. In the last generation, many large companies have implemented more serious efforts to ensure their suppliers adhere to the agreed-on standards. Most obviously, more codes have consequences, where suppliers are dismissed if they do not improve (Boudreau (2019)). At the same time, the literature on supplier adherence paints a complex picture of how often codes lead to improvement in supplier behavior. For example, one study found that, on average, adherence improved over time (Hugill, Short, and Toffel (2016b)). Improvement was faster if auditors have more training and if audit visits also help train suppliers (Hugill, Short, and Toffel (2016); Short, Toffel, and Hugill (2016); and Thorlakson and others (2018)). Hugill, Short, and Toffel (2016), Short, Toffel, and Hugill (2016), and Stroehle (2017) find adherence is higher if domestic institutions promote compliance (for example, there is a free press).[21]

In short, codes of conduct do not automatically ensure high compliance. With sufficient effort and resources, it is possible for MNCs to validate their supplier standards to show the standards are achieving their stated goals (and to improve their compliance process if adherence remains low). Only then can MNCs be confident that they are not responsible for the exploitation of foreign workers.

CONCLUSION

We have introduced three different approaches to define exploitation of workers by MNCs. The market-based or consequentialist approach asks if MNCs create worse outcomes for workers than they would have had otherwise. We find that MNCs typically pay slightly higher wages than local firms in developing countries. While much of this can be attributed to worker and industry characteristics, there is still suggestive evidence of a wage premium from MNCs. It is unclear whether this represents rent sharing, unmeasured skills, or a compensating differential for uncertainty over job tenure or other differences between MNCs and local firms. In either case, there is no evidence that MNCs systematically pay lower wages than their domestic counterparts.

Likewise, our analysis of offshoring by MNCs finds no effects on wages or employment at the aggregate or industry levels. However, at the occupational level, there is strong evidence that offshoring by MNCs to low-income affiliates hurts workers performing routine tasks, but that offshoring to high-income locations benefits them. Nevertheless, given the costliness of job transitions, such churn is likely to have deleterious effects on many workers. These workers are also more exposed to the labor-substitution effects of foreign import competition and technical change. Although we cannot observe a counterfactual in which offshoring never took place, it appears likely that these channels, whose effects are much larger than the effects of offshoring, would have driven much of these job losses. Therefore, it is difficult to conclude that offshoring constitutes our first definition of exploitation by making workers worse off than they otherwise might have been.

Our second set of definitions of exploitation founded in utilitarian ethics and behavioral economics asserts that it is fair for rich employers to share some of their surplus with employees. Budd and Slaughter (2004) and Budd, Konings, and Slaughter (2005) find evidence of MNC rent sharing in Canada and Europe, respectively, but we are not aware of any such study in a developing country. The small wage gaps and relatively high turnover we find suggest that any sharing of surplus is modest.

At the market level, an inequality-averse utilitarian worries that MNCs may harm workers. Labor shares are declining in many nations as multinationals have risen in importance. We review a handful of papers associating MNCs with this trend, but robust causal evidence linking multinational activity with the robust decline in labor shares is limited.

Our third definition of exploitation occurs if MNCs violate workers' rights. These rights include, but are not limited to, rights defined by local laws and international standards, such as rights set forth by the ILO. This definition of exploitation does not depend on whether domestic firms also commit these violations. We find well-documented evidence that multinationals do violate workers' rights, including discrimination by gender and preventing workers from exercising their right to unionize. We do not have consistent evidence whether MNCs exacerbate, ameliorate, or simply participate in the poor treatment of workers in poor parts of global supply chains.

Some Limitations

The key question to understanding the effects of multinationals involves the relevant counterfactual. As we noted, this counterfactual is difficult for studies of wages and working conditions. Moreover, those studies focused more on MNCs, not on the multinational supply chains that are often of interest to activists and policymakers. At a deeper level, our view of MNCs might differ if we think the counterfactual of working for a multinational is (a) working for a multinational's supplier, (b) working for a domestic employer who exports because the multinational never entered, or (c) remaining a peasant farmer.

Our literature review has focused on the wages and working conditions of multinationals and their suppliers. However, many of the harshest critics examine how MNCs change the structure of the economy and of politics to "rig the rules of the game." Multinationals' willingness to relocate can reduce the bargaining power of all workers. That same mobility makes MNCs harder to tax, requiring nations to shift to more regressive taxes or to lower spending that might help the poor. Multinationals' size can give them disproportionate influence in politics, reducing democratic accountability. At the same time, multinationals can increase living standards globally by increasing efficiency and facilitating knowledge transfer to developing countries (Abebe, McMillan, and Serafinelli (2018)). MNCs also sometimes fight for efficient policies and reduce the monopoly power of domestic cartels. We leave a review of these important arguments for others.

We also did not have sufficient data to separate out when MNCs enter a poor nation to create an export platform versus when they are producing for the poor nation's market. Entering a poor nation to produce for the domestic market is more likely to displace local workers, and also to improve product variety for consumers.[22] In addition, there is increasing anecdotal evidence that MNCs originating in rich countries are likely to have very different behaviors and effects than MNCs originating in emerging markets. Since multinationals often import their home-country approaches to their host country, MNCs originating in countries with robust labor standards and generous compensation schemes are likely to behave quite differently from others.

Implications

Overall, asking whether MNCs exploit their workers may be the wrong question when it comes to preventing exploitation and improving workers' outcomes. Meaningful improvements in living standards will require enforcing existing minimum-wage laws and ILO standards and implementing policies to raise worker productivity. To improve economic outcomes, researchers and policymakers should shift their attention away from MNC status and instead focus on the firm characteristics that more strongly influence wage rates—firm size and industrial sector—as well as the related issues of market concentration and monopsony power that are correlated with declining labor shares across the world.

Given that MNCs employ only a modest share of the workforce, addressing violations of workers' rights at MNCs only puts a dent in widespread poor conditions. Nevertheless, addressing MNCs' violations of workers' rights may be efficacious to the extent that MNCs and their suppliers are more visible to governments, watchdogs, and conscious consumers, potentially making violations easier to sanction and providing a profit incentive for MNCs to treat employees more fairly (and to require the same of suppliers). While the marginal returns to activism may thus be higher for MNCs, solely focusing on them will not end all violations of human rights.

Thus, improving the welfare of vulnerable workers will require much more than pressure on MNCs. It is beyond our scope to recommend policies toward achieving these goals. However, common sense suggests focusing on improving human capital, creating healthy work spaces, encouraging the functioning of labor markets, helping workers defend their rights through collective action, training workers and managers on employees' rights, and increasing enforcement of labor laws already on the books.

NOTES

The authors thank Maria Lopez Godoy for outstanding research assistance and Jeseo Park for collecting data on multinationals with gender-specific job ads.

1. "Exploitation," *Stanford Encyclopedia of Philosophy*. Available at https://plato.stanford.edu/entries/exploitation/.

2. Budd, J. W., Konings, J. and Slaughter, M. J. 2005. "Wages and International Rent Sharing in Multinational Firms," *Review of Economics and Statistics*, 87(1), 73–84.

3. ITUC has an index of poor labor rights, from a trade union perspective. Available at www.ituc-csi.org/ituc-global-rights-index-2018.

4. These sectors in Harrison and Scorse (2010) were linked to high-profile retail brands, such as Nike, Adidas, and Reebok. At the same time, these wage gains did not carry over to other industries.

5. Andersen, Steffen, Seda Ertaç, Uri Gneezy, Moshe Hoffman, and John A. List. "Stakes matter in ultimatum games," *American Economic Review*, 101/7 (2011): 3427–39.

6. Theories of procedural justice also posit that outcomes can be "unfair" or "unjust" on the basis of how they arose. For example, many people consider it fairer to react to an exogenous shock than to take the initiative and cause harm (Rabin 1993)). The seminal quasi-experiment of Kahneman, Knetsch, and Thaler (1986) found that people are more likely to judge layoffs and pay cuts by an employer as unfair if they were undertaken to increase the employer's profits: in particular, to hire cheaper alternative workers. These original Canadian findings have since been reproduced in several countries, including the United States (Charness and Levine (2000) and (2002)) and Germany (Gerlach, Levine, Stephan, and Struck (2008)).

7. Of course, we want to control for unobserved differences in skill and working conditions, but not for unobserved differences in firm-specific rents that could be shared with workers. Firm-specific fixed effects are too crude a tool to untangle these three sources of firm-specific differences.

8. These effects are offset by large but regressive gains in consumer surplus. The authors also note that these results are likely specific to retail FDI.

9. For additional research on the extent to which market concentration has increased in the United States, see Abdela and Steinbaum (2018) and Krueger and Posner (2018).

10. Fair Labor Association, "Improving Workers' Lives Worldwide." Available at www.fairlabor.org.

11. For example, Manjoo (2012): "Women EPZ workers were allowed two timed bathroom breaks per shift and were not paid for their overtime if their production requirements were not met."

12. It should be noted that this decrease was also correlated with an increased likelihood of working a low-paid job. In combination, these findings are consistent with arguments that MNCs' distributed supply chains reduce the number of middle-income jobs compared with traditional integrated production facilities. For more on this argument, see, for example, Anner (2011).

13. Seventy-two percent of firms in Bangladesh's EPZs have some foreign ownership (58 percent are wholly foreign owned), and 100 percent of firms are part of multinational supply chains. Available at www.bepza.gov.bd/pages/details/about.

14. The difference is only statistically significant for the United Kingdom. No data was available for unionization in Portugal and Brazil.

15. As one of the Human Rights Watch (2015) interviewees explains:

> I was beaten with metal curtain rods in February, when I was pregnant. I was called to the chairman's room, and taken to the third floor management room that is used by the management and directors—and there I was beaten by the local goons. . . . There were other women who were called at other times, and they were beaten the same way as well. They were threatening me, saying, "You need to stop doing the union activities in the factory, why did you try and form the union."

16. See Manjoo (2012) for evidence from Honduras, Ngai (2007) for evidence from China, and Human Rights Watch (2015) for evidence from Bangladesh.

17. For example, in Korea, Domino's Pizza (subsidiary of a U.S. firm) wanted a male cook/server, and the German firm Adidas wanted a male salesperson. In Thailand, a subsidiary of the Japanese multinational Canon advertised for a male waste management professional. Not all ads from multinationals favored men: in Korea, the French clothing firm Le Coq Sportif wanted a female salesperson; in Thailand, the Austrian fashion company Swarovski advertised for a female sales executive; and in Indonesia, the U.S.-based Marriott wanted a female food and beverage manager. Jeseo Park collected these data. The downloads were a single snapshot for each website: February 10, 2019, for the Korean-language sites in Korea (www.alba.co.kr, www.albamon.com, www.saramin.com); February 12, 2019, for the Korean site in English (https://incruit.com); February 15, 2019, for the Thai sites (https://th.jobsdb.com, https://jobtopgun.com); and February 18, 2019, for the Indian (www.shine.com, www.wisdomjobs.com, www.naukri.com) and Indonesian sites (https://id.jobsdb.com, www.glassdoor.co.uk). We did not code all employers for multinational status; instead, we skimmed the list to identify a handful of recognizable brands. Thus, the true number of multinationals is almost surely larger than the few we note here. This study updates Levine (1989): https://doi.org/10.1111/0019-8676.00078.

18. Studies of gender pay gap do not necessarily get at exactly the issue of equal pay for equal work, as it is often not clear whether workers being compared are performing the same tasks.

19. Gender Inequality Index (GII), United Nations Development Programme. Available at http://hdr.undp.org/en/composite/GII.

20. Migrant workers come predominantly from Indonesia, Nepal, India, Thailand, China, the Philippines, Burma, Cambodia, Bangladesh, Pakistan, and Vietnam.

21. Some of the challenges to monitoring is that (as noted) it is difficult to monitor labor standards that workers do not see as a benefit. One of the authors (Levine) had a graduate student with family connections to several garment factories in Pakistan. These factories largely supplied multinationals. She first toured each factory wearing a white lab coat and holding a clipboard. As expected, workers assumed she was auditing working conditions in the factory. She observed all workers wearing their safety equipment. During interviews, the workers reported working within the legal overtime limits. She then removed the lab coat and explained that she was just a friend of the factory owner pretending to audit. The workers admitted that they rarely wore the safety equipment and that they worked longer hours than on the official timesheet. A second student carried out a similar small study near a very large furniture factory in Vietnam, also supplying an MNC. When she presented herself as a possible inspector, workers reported zero work at home. When she explained she was a visiting student, many students discussed how they and their children wove rattan at home in the evening. As noted, employee resistance to endorsing a standard does not mean that the standard is ineffective in improving workers' collective well-being, especially if workers lack information about exposure to harm or are present-biased. At the same time, such challenges in measurement show how difficult it can be to enforce rules that workers do not endorse.

22. Of course, if the added product varieties create positive or negative externalities, the effects are even more complex. Think of new drugs versus harmful infant formula, or high or low pollution.

REFERENCES

Abebe, G., M. S. McMillan, and M. Serafinelli. (2018). "Foreign direct investment and knowledge diffusion in poor locations: Evidence from Ethiopia." NBER Working Paper No. w2446.

Abdela, A. and M. Steinbaum (2018). "The United States Has a Market Concentration Problem: Reviewing Concentration Estimates in Antitrust Markets, 2000–Present." Roosevelt Institute Issue Brief.

Acemoglu, D. and P. Restrepo (2017). "Robots and Jobs: Evidence from U.S. Labor Markets." NBER Working Paper No. 23285.

Acemoglu, D. and others (2016). "Import Competition and the Great U.S. Employment Sag of the 2000s," *Journal of Labor Economics*, 34 (S1), S141–S198.

Aitken, B., A. Harrison, and R. E. Lipsey (1996). "Wages and Foreign Ownership: A Comparative Study of Mexico, Venezuela, and the United States," *Journal of International Economics*, 40, 345–71.

Almeida, R. (2007). "The Labor Market Effects of Foreign Owned Firms," *Journal of International Economics*, 72 (1), 75–96.

Anner, M. (2011). "The Impact of International Outsourcing on Unionization and Wages: Evidence from the Apparel Export Sector in Central America," *ILR Review*, 64 (2), 305–22.

Antràs, P., T. C. Fort, and Tintelnot, F. (2017). "The Margins of Global Sourcing: Theory and Evidence from U.S. Firms," *American Economic Review*, 107 (9), 2514–64.

Arnal, E. and A. Hijzen. 2008. "The Impact of Foreign Direct Investment on Wages and Working Conditions," OECD Social, Employment and Migration Working Paper No. 68.

Atkinson, A. B. (2015). *Inequality* (Harvard University Press).

Autor, D. H., D. Dorn, L. F. Katz, C. Patterson, and J. Van Reenen (2017). "The Fall of the Labor Share and the Rise of Superstar Firms." CEPR Discussion Paper No. DP12041. Available at SSRN: https://ssrn.com/abstract=2968382.

Autor, D. and A. Salamons (2018). "Is Automation Labor-Replacing? Productivity Growth, Employment, and the Labor Share." Brookings Papers on Economic Activity.

Autor, D. H., D. Dorn, and G. H. Hanson (2013). "The China Syndrome: Local Labor Market Effects of Import Competition in the United States," *American Economic Review*, 103 (6), 2121–68.

Autor, D. H., F. Levy, and R. J. Murnane (2003). "The Skill Content of Recent Technological Change: An Empirical Exploration," *Quarterly Journal of Economics*, 118 (4), 1279–1333.

Basu, K., and V. H. Pham (1998). "The Economics of Child Labor," *American Economic Review*, 88 (3): 412–27.

Bernanke, B. S. (2006). "Global Economic Integration: What's New and What's Not." Jackson Hole, Wyoming, Federal Reserve Bank of Kansas City 30th Annual Economic Symposium.

Bircan, Ç. (2011). "Foreign Direct Investment and Wages: Does the Level of Ownership Matter?" Research Seminar in International Economics Working Paper No. 618, University of Michigan.

Boehm, C., A. Flaaen, and N. Pandalai-Nayar (2019). "Multinationals, Offshoring and the Decline of U.S. Manufacturing." NBER Working Paper No. 25824.

Bøler, E. A., B. Smarzynska Javorcik, and K. H. Ulltveit-Moe (2015). "Globalization: A Woman's Best Friend? Exporters and the Gender Wage Gap." CESifo Working Paper.

Boudreau, L. (2019). "Multinational Enforcement of Labor Law: Experimental Evidence from Bangladesh's Apparel Sector." Working paper.

Breau, S. and W. M. Brown (2011). "Exporting, Foreign Direct Investment, and Wages: Evidence from the Canadian Manufacturing Sector." *Growth and Change*, 42, 261–86.

Budd, J. W. and M. J. Slaughter (2004). "Are Profits Shared across Borders? Evidence on International Rent Sharing," *Journal of Labor Economics*, 22 (3), 525–52.

Budd, J. W., J. Konings, and M. J. Slaughter (2005). "Wages and International Rent Sharing in Multinational Firms," *Review of Economics and Statistics*, 87 (1), 73–84.

Camerer, C. F. and R. H. Thaler (1995). "Anomalies: Ultimatums, Dictators, and Manners," *Journal of Economic Perspectives*, 9 (2), 209–19.

Cirera, X. and R. W. Lakshman (2017). "The Impact of Export Processing Zones on Employment, Wages and Labour Conditions in Developing Countries: Systematic Review." *Journal of Development Effectiveness*, 9 (3), 344–60.

Cividep India (2017). "Samsung's Sub-standard Labour Practices in India: A Profile of Samsung Electronics in Tamil Nadu." Good Electronics, March.

Conyon, M. J. and others (2002). "The Productivity and Wage Effects of Foreign Acquisition in the United Kingdom," *Journal of Industrial Economics*, 50 (1), 85–102.

Desai, M. A., C. F. Foley, and J. R. Hines Jr. (2009). "Domestic Effects of the Foreign

Activities of U.S. Multinationals," *American Economic Journal: Economic Policy*, 1 (1), 181–203.

Distelhorst, G., R. M. Locke, T. Pal, and H. Samel (2015). "Production Goes Global, Compliance Stays Local: Private Regulation in the Global Electronics Industry." *Regulation & Governance*, 9 (3), 224–42.

Donaghey, J., J. Reinecke, C. Niforou, and B. Lawson (2014). "From Employment Relations to Consumption Relations: Balancing Labor Governance in Global Supply Chains." *Human Resource Management*, 53 (2), 229–52.

Ebenstein, A., A. Harrison, and M. Margaret (2017). "Why Are American Workers Getting Poorer? China, Trade, and Offshoring," In *The Factory-Free Economy: Outsourcing, Servitization and the Future of Industry*, edited by L. Fontange and A. Harrison (Oxford University Press), 222–56.

Ebenstein, A., A. Harrison, M. McMillan, and S. Philips (2014). "Estimating the Impact of Trade and Offshoring on American Workers Using the Current Population Surveys," *Review of Economics and Statistics*, 96 (4), 581–95.

Egels-Zandén, N. (2007). "Suppliers' Compliance with MNCs' Codes of Conduct: Behind the Scenes at Chinese Toy Suppliers," *Journal of Business Ethics*, 75 (1), 45–62.

Egels-Zandén, N. (2014). "Revisiting Supplier Compliance with MNC Codes of Conduct: Recoupling Policy and Practice at Chinese Toy Suppliers," *Journal of Business Ethics*, 119 (1), 59–75.

Feenstra, R. C. and G. H. Hanson (1999). "The Impact of Outsourcing and High-Technology Capital on Wages: Estimates for the United States, 1979–90," *Quarterly Journal of Economics*, 114 (3), 907–40.

Gutiérrez, G. and T. Philippon (2019). "Fading Stars." NBER Working Paper No. 25529. Available at NBER: www.nber.org/papers/w25529.

Halegua, A. (2007). "The Debate Over Raising Chinese Labor Standards Goes International," *Harvard Law Policy Review*, 5 (April).

Harrison, A. and M. McMillan (2011). "Offshoring Jobs? Multinationals and U.S. Manufacturing Employment," *Review of Economics and Statistics*, 93 (3), 857–75.

Harrison, A. and J. Scorse (2010). "Multinationals and Anti-Sweatshop Activism," *American Economic Review*, 100 (1), 247–73.

Hersch, J. (2011). "Compensating Differentials for Sexual Harassment," *American Economic Review*, 101 (3), 630–34.

Heyman, F., F. Sjöholm, and P. Tingvall (2007). "Is There Really a Foreign Ownership Wage Premium? Evidence from Matched Employer-Employee Data," *Journal of International Economics*, 73 (2), 355–76.

Hein, C. (1998). "Multinational Enterprises and Employment in the Mauritian Export Processing Zone." International Labour Office, Multinational Enterprises Programme Working Paper No. 52, Geneva.

Hijzen, A. and P. Swaim (2008). "Do Multinationals Promote Better Pay and Working Conditions?" *OECD Observer* (269), 15.

Hugill, A., J. L. Short, and M. W. Toffel (2016). "Beyond Symbolic Responses to Private Politics: Examining Labor Standards Improvement in Global Supply Chains," *SSRN Electronic Journal*. Available at 10.2139/ssrn.2806966.

Human Rights Watch (2015). "'Whoever Raises Their Head Suffers the Most': Workers' Rights in Bangladesh's Garment Factories," April 24.

Hummels, D., R. Jørgensen, J. Munch, and C. Xiang (2014). "The Wage Effects of Offshoring: Evidence from Danish Matched Worker-Firm Data," *American Economic Review*, 104 (6), 1597–1692.

Husselbee, D. (2000). "NGOs as Development Partners to the Corporates: Child Football Stitchers in Pakistan," *Development in Practice*, 10 (3), 377–89.

International Finance Corporation (2018). "Better Factories Cambodia: An Industry and Compliance Review," International Labor Office, Geneva.

International Labor Organization (2016). "ILO Statement to the Third Committee of the 71st General Assembly," www.ilo.org/newyork/speeches-and-statements/WCMS_532963/lang--en/index.htm.

International Organization for Migration (2003). *World Migration Report*, The United Nations.

Jaumotte, F. and I. Tytell (2007). "How Has the Globalization of Labor Affected the Labor Share in Advanced Countries?" IMF Working Paper, Research Department.

Jayadev, A. (2007). "Capital Account Openness and the Labour Share of Income," *Cambridge Journal of Economics*, 31 (3), 423–43.

Kambourov, G. and I. Manovskii (2009). "Occupational Mobility and Wage Inequality," *Review of Economic Studies*, 76 (1), 731–59.

Kant, I. (1785). *Groundwork of the Metaphysic of Morals*, edited by A. Wood (Yale University Press).

Khan, F., K. Munir, and H. Willmott (2007). "A Dark Side of Institutional Entrepreneurship: Soccer Balls, Child Labor, and Postcolonial Impoverishment," *Organization Studies*, 28, 1055–77.

Kodama, N., B. S. Javorcik, and Y. Abe (2018). "Transplanting Corporate Culture across International Borders: Foreign Direct Investment and Female Employment in Japan," *World Economy*, 41, 1148–65. Available at https://doi-org.virtual.anu.edu.au/10.1111/twec.12612.

Kovak, B., L. Oldenski, and N. Sly (2018). "The Labor Market Effects of Offshoring by U.S. Multinational Firms." NBER Working Paper No. 23947.

Krueger, A. B. and E. A. Posner (2018). "A Proposal for Protecting Low-Income Workers from Monopsony and Collusion," The Hamilton Project, Brookings.

Lipsey, R. E. and F. Sjöholm (2004). "Foreign Direct Investment, Education and Wages in Indonesian Manufacturing," *Journal of Development Economics*, 73 (1), 415–22. Available at https://doi.org/10.1016/j.jdeveco.2002.12.004.

Lipsey, R. E. and F. Sjöholm (2006). "Foreign Firms and Indonesian Manufacturing Wages: An Analysis with Panel Data." Economic Development and Cultural Change.

Mai Chi, D., D. Mitali, K. Zsoka, and L. Weicheng (2017). "Why Is Labor Receiving a Smaller Share of Global Income? Theory and Empirical Evidence." IMF Working Papers 17/169, International Monetary Fund.

Manjoo, R. (2012). "Report of the Special Rapporteur on Violence Against Women, Its Causes and Consequences," United Nations.

Manning, A. (2003). *Monopsony in Motion: Imperfect Competition in Labor Markets* (Princeton University Press).

Martins, P. S. (2004). "Do Foreign Firms Really Pay Higher Wages? Evidence from Different Estimators." IZA Discussion Papers 1388, Institute for the Study of Labor (IZA).

Matthias, A. J. and B. S. Javorcik (2009). "Gifted Kids or Pushy Parents? Foreign Direct Investment and Plant Productivity in Indonesia," *Journal of International Economics*, 79 (1), 42–53.

Milberg, W. and M. Amengual (2008). "Economic Development and Working Conditions in Export Processing Zones: A Survey of Trends," ILO, Geneva.

Muendler, M.-A. and S. O. Becker (2010). "Margins of Multinational Offshoring," *American Economic Review*, 100 (1), 1999–2030.

Oldenski, L. (2014). "Offshoring and the Polarization of the U.S. Labor Market," *ILR Review*, 67 (3), 734–61.

Philippon, T. (2019). *The Great Reversal: How America Gave Up on Free Markets* (Harvard University Press).

Pierce, J. R. and P. K. Schott (2016). "The Surprisingly Swift Decline of U.S. Manufacturing Employment," *American Economic Review*, 106 (7), 1632–62.

Pohler, D. and C. Riddell (2019). "Multinationals' Compliance with Employment Law: An Empirical Assessment Using Administrative Data from Ontario, 2004 to 2015," *ILR Review*, 72 (3), 606–35.

Rabin, M. (1993). "Incorporating Fairness into Game Theory and Economics," *American Economic Review*, 83 (5), 1281–1302.

Raworth, K. (2004). "Trading Away Our Rights: Women Working in Global Supply Chains," *Oxfam Policy and Practice: Private Sector*, 1 (1), 1–52.

Short, J. L., M. W. Toffel, and A. R. Hugill (2016). "Monitoring Global Supply Chains," *Strategic Management Journal*, 37, 1878–97.

Slaughter, M. (2009). *How U.S. Multinational Companies Strengthen the U.S. Economy*, Technical Report, Business Roundtable and the United States Council Foundation.

Stroehle, J. C. (2017). "The Enforcement of Diverse Labor Standards through Private Governance: An Assessment," *Transfer: European Review of Labor and Research*, 23 (4), 475–93.

Tang, H. and Y. Zhang (2017). "Do Multinationals Transfer Culture? Evidence on Female Employment in China." CESifo Working Paper Series No. 6295. Available at SSRN: https://ssrn.com/abstract=2917193.

Thaler, R. H. (1988). "Anomalies: Ultimatum Games," *Journal of Economic Perspectives*, 2 (4), 195–206.

Theuws, M., V. Sandjojo, and E. Vogt (2017). "Branded Childhood: How Garment Brands Contribute to Low Wages, Long Working Hours, School Dropout and Child Labour in Bangladesh," SOMO (Centre for Research on Multinational Corporations) and Stop Child Labour, Amsterdam, January.

Thorlakson, T., J. Hainmueller, and E. F. Lambin (2018). "Improving Environmental Practices in Agricultural Supply Chains: The Role of Company-Led Standards," *Global Environmental Change*, 48, 32–42.

Vahter, P. and J. Masso (2019). "The Contribution of Multinationals to Wage Inequality: Foreign Ownership and the Gender Pay Gap," *Review of World Economics*, 155 (1), 105–48.

Yonghong, S. (1989). "Export Processing Zones in China Buji: A Case Study," *Economic and Political Weekly*, 24 (7), 355–65.

Zwolinski, M. and A. Wertheimer (2017). "Exploitation," *The Stanford Encyclopedia of Philosophy* (Summer), edited by Edward N. Zalta.

8

The New Global Invention Machine

A Look Inside the R&D Networks of U.S. Multinationals

LEE BRANSTETTER
BRITTA GLENNON
J. BRADFORD JENSEN

THE RISE OF OVERSEAS R&D

For decades, U.S. multinational companies (MNCs) performed nearly all of their research and development (R&D) within the United States, even as they expanded overseas production and sales of goods and services. The relatively small amount of R&D they conducted outside the United States tended to be concentrated in a small number of advanced industrial economies. Over the past two decades, however, the amount of R&D conducted overseas by U.S. MNCs has grown nearly four-fold, and its geographic distribution has substantially expanded and now includes parts of the developing world. U.S. MNCs have developed an innovation system that spans the globe.

Like many aspects of globalization, the globalization of R&D offers opportunities and may pose risks. Some observers fear that the increasing globalization of R&D might lead to a loss of U.S. technological leadership. However, we observe that U.S. innovators remain involved in important ways in U.S. MNCs' global R&D for decades—suggesting fears of hollowing out may be overstated. Furthermore, we note that the large and growing pool of highly educated scientists and engineers in the developing world offers the possibility of increasing the rate of global productivity growth. Our research suggests that the best way to productively utilize this resource is by combining emerging market talent with MNC innovation experience through the globalization of MNC R&D.

However, several challenges could limit these benefits. The global rise of economic nationalism potentially risks progress in this area, particularly if the United States retreats from international trade policy leadership. The U.S. government's aggressive use of tariffs is already signaling to companies that it no longer supports the internationalization of commercial activities. It may take years to measure the impact on global R&D with any precision, but it is not difficult to imagine that current policy moves and public statements by government officials will reduce overseas R&D by U.S. MNCs or, potentially worse, decrease integration and collaboration between U.S. MNCs' domestic R&D labs and their foreign affiliates.

In addition, some important developing countries are resisting effective protection of intellectual property rights and openness to foreign direct investment (FDI), preventing MNCs from taking full advantage of these nations' potential as R&D sites. As the locus of R&D shifts from manufacturing to services, and digitally traded services become a greater component of global consumption, liberalization of global trade in services would increase progress in innovation. The global effort to restrict (or tax) international data flows is another potential impediment. Because movement of skilled workers is a vital element of this system, rising opposition to immigration is another risk. Finally, growing U.S.-China tensions pose a special challenge because of the important role these two economies play in the global economic system. Public policies should strengthen intellectual property rights, encourage labor mobility, and liberalize trade in services so that innovation can flourish and thereby improve living standards and fuel economic progress.

This chapter begins by examining R&D globalization as a possible (partial) response to one of the global economy's most pressing challenges—the significant and persistent slowdown in productivity growth in the advanced economies. As we argue in the next section, the mobilization of human talent enabled by R&D globalization may be essential to revive and sustain innovation and productivity growth. This makes R&D globalization not just an interesting phenomenon but something potentially foundational for future growth.

We move on from that initial discussion to describe the data we use to create a statistical portrait of the R&D globalization phenomenon, at least with regard to U.S. multinationals. These data point to some important shifts in the distribution of multinational inventive activity across geography and across technological fields. We also note that the nature of R&D appears to be changing. Within multinationals, there appears to be a sharp increase in R&D cooperation across borders, evidenced by a rise in the number of patents that contain inventor teams with both U.S. and non-U.S. addresses. We argue that movements of R&D across geography and technological fields are closely related to one another. The sharp increase in the role of information technology (IT) hardware and software in invention helps explain the significant shift in the geography of U.S. foreign affiliate R&D. The most important new hubs of foreign R&D all have extensive and growing human resource assets in IT hardware and software. The inherent modularity of IT hardware and software facilitates the distribution of inventive activity across geographies, and software-mediated design tools and modern communications technologies facilitate the intensive information exchange that still must take place.

Having described the forces driving increased R&D globalization, the chapter concludes by noting the policy trends around the world that are limiting its expansion. These policy challenges exist in both developing and developed countries, and appear to be intensifying in the current environment of rising trade friction and antiglobalization sentiment. As always, the benefits of globalization are contingent on pursuing policies that will enable them to be fully realized.

R&D GLOBALIZATION AS A RESPONSE TO THE GLOBAL PRODUCTIVITY SLOWDOWN

Promoting the effective globalization of R&D may be especially important in light of the challenge posed by the global productivity slowdown (Byrne, Fernald, and Reinsdorf (2016); Syverson (2017)). Despite hopeful talk by industry leaders and consultants of an imminent fourth industrial revolution, the available data suggest that the most important hallmark of past industrial revolutions—a significant and persistent acceleration in the growth rate of labor productivity—is still missing. Gordon (2016) argues that the productivity slowdown evident since just before the global financial crisis is only the beginning of a persistent deceleration in the productivity growth rate—a consequence, he argues, of the grim reality that no current or future inventions will have the same impact on human welfare as the "great inventions" of the nineteenth and twentieth centuries.

Many knowledgeable commentators have dismissed Gordon's techno-pessimism, but leading economic theories of endogenous innovation suggest that Gordon's basic tenet has a core of truth—innovation is getting harder.[1] According to the widely cited model of Jones (2009), it is harder to innovate now because of the "burden of knowledge." Human technological knowledge has expanded dramatically, but every generation must first master the knowledge accumulated by previous generations before it can build upon that knowledge. As the amount of prior knowledge grows, it becomes more difficult to master. Increasingly, would-be innovators are forced to specialize in narrow domains of expertise, and innovation requires ever-larger and more difficult-to-manage teams to bring this expertise together. Jones (2009) presents persuasive evidence of these increasing costs, and Bloom and others (2020) provide even starker evidence of apparent diminishing returns to innovative effort in advanced countries.

However, there is a silver lining in these pessimistic models of innovation. They all imply that the scale of investment in innovation matters, and the globalization of knowledge creation could be a powerful force for boosting productivity growth. A small number of mostly British engineers, tinkerers, and entrepreneurs produced the breakthroughs of the first Industrial Revolution. The second Industrial Revolution went further, and it achieved more, because it could draw upon a larger pool of potential inventors that extended beyond Great Britain. This broader mobilization of Western inventive talent had its limits: the research technology of the era required collaborators to be in the same place at the same time. Innovation labor markets were, at best, national in scope, which limited the array of research teams that could be created. Industrial advances still rested on a narrow foundation, with most of the human race effectively excluded from participation.

The changing situation today has important implications for future productivity growth. Higher education is spreading rapidly in emerging markets such as China and India (Freeman and Huang (2015)). In just the past dozen years, China expanded the number of bachelor's degrees it grants in science and engineering by about 300,000 per year, to more than 1.3 million (National Science Board (2016)). China now graduates more newly minted scientists and engineers than all the technological superpowers of the West put together. By contrast, the United States awards only about 250,000 bachelor's degrees in science and engineering per year. Various sources in the literature suggest, though, that despite the rapid expansion of the scale of engineering education in India and China, its average quality may still lag behind Western countries, and the ability of either China or India to innovate at the global technology frontier through the efforts of its indigenous firms may still be limited (Freeman and Huang (2015)). Nevertheless, ample evidence points to India and China's top engineering students' extremely high level of skill. Multinationals have responded to this growing talent pool by ramping up the amount of R&D they undertake in emerging-market countries. With computer-assisted design software, internet videoconferencing, and the ability to quickly access terabytes of test data, it is now increasingly possible for Chinese and Indian engineers to collaborate closely, in almost real time, with seasoned technology experts in the United States, Western Europe, and Japan.

This combination of developed-economy technological experience and emerging-market talent appears to produce impressive results.[2] In a comprehensive study of U.S. patents granted to teams that included at least one Indian or Chinese inventor, Branstetter, Li, and Veloso (2015) find that Chinese engineers working for foreign-based multinationals produced inventions in China that appear to be at least as good as the inventions produced by the same multinationals in their home countries. IBM or Intel engineers in China can be as productive as IBM or Intel engineers in Silicon Valley—and the number of good engineers in China is rapidly growing. China is not the only emerging market where U.S. multinationals are finding high returns to their R&D investments. Figure 8-1 presents results from a comparison of patent output across R&D sites.[3]

This graph raises the possibility that the foreign engineers, whom U.S. MNCs can access through their global R&D systems, could power an acceleration in the rate of productivity growth around the world.[4] Fernald and Jones (2014) estimate that about 1.3 percentage points of the average 2 percent annual increase in U.S. labor productivity from 1950 to 2007 stemmed from higher research intensity (that is, the rising fraction of the population engaged in invention) in the advanced countries. Research intensity outside the traditional developed economies is already increasing rapidly and will likely continue for decades. As investment in higher education spreads

FIGURE 8-1. Patents Generated per R&D Dollar (Controlling for Industry and Firm) by Country

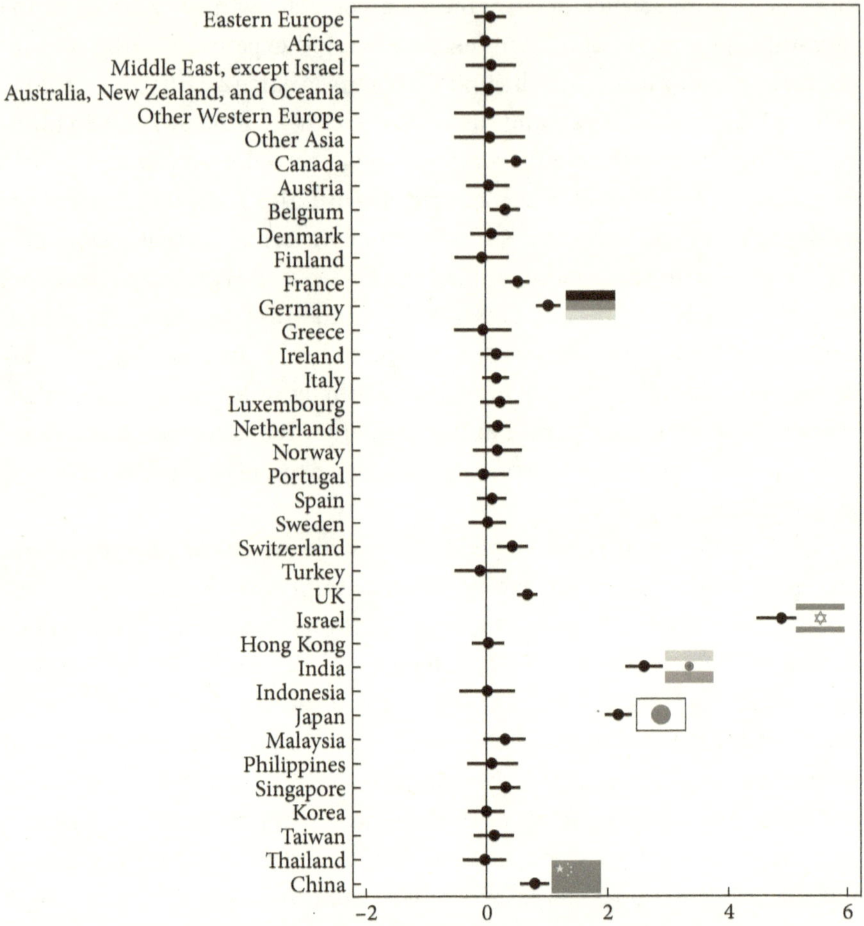

Note: This figure originally appeared as figure 9 in Branstetter, Glennon, and Jensen (2019b).

Source: Confidential data from the U.S. Bureau of Economic Analysis and authors' calculations.

through the developing world, it is possible global research intensity could double or more than double in coming decades. R&D globalization could help ensure that this growing global talent pool is utilized in the most efficient and effective possible way, maintaining the expansion of the global technology frontier even in the face of powerful economic forces. As Nobel laureate Paul Krugman (1992) once noted, productivity is not everything, but in the long run, it is *almost* everything. R&D globalization could be a key contributor to maintaining or increasing global productivity growth.

DATA FOR MEASURING THE GLOBALIZATION OF R&D

We use a combination of two data sources to generate a unique panel dataset for analysis of U.S. multinational innovative activity abroad. The first is the Bureau of Economic Analysis (BEA) annual survey on U.S. Direct Investment Abroad.[5] The database contains financial and operating characteristics of both the U.S. parent companies and their foreign affiliates, including R&D expenditures, which is the primary variable of interest for this chapter.

The second source of data is U.S. Patent and Trademark Office (USPTO) patent data, obtained using the PatentsView database, and includes all utility granted patent applications through August 2017.[6] Patents are an imperfect measure of innovation; there is heterogeneity across countries, firms, and industries in the propensity to patent.[7] However, patenting does reflect an important piece of a country's innovative output, and it is highly correlated with other measures of innovation.

Our final dataset is at the firm-country-year level and varies across firms, countries, and time. A more complete description of the data can be found in the appendix to this chapter.

DATA SHOW A SIGNIFICANT RISE IN OVERSEAS R&D CONDUCTED BY U.S. MNCs

Total U.S. R&D spending as a share of gross domestic product (GDP) increased slightly from 2.5 percent in 1999 to 2.7 percent in 2016.[8] Multinationals are an important driver of that R&D spending[9]—their share of the total was 57 percent in 2015[10]—and the innovation that R&D generates. At the same time, U.S. MNCs have dramatically increased their overseas R&D expenditures; U.S. MNCs' foreign R&D expenditures increased from approximately US$14 billion in 1997 to more than US$55 billion in 2015. In some industries, the growth of overseas R&D has been especially striking. R&D expenditures by overseas affiliates in professional, scientific, and technical services increased by more than a factor of eighteen between 1999 and 2014, and the ratio of overseas R&D to domestic R&D for multinationals in this industry has gone from less than 10 percent in 1999 to more than 40 percent in 2015. However, this industry is at the extreme end of the distribution. While U.S. MNCs' foreign R&D expenditures have increased dramatically, they still conducted about 83 percent of their R&D in the United States in 2015 (down from 92 percent in 1989).

THE CHANGING FOOTPRINT OF U.S. MNCs' OVERSEAS R&D

U.S. MNCs' foreign R&D is growing not only on the intensive margin (more spending in existing locations) but also on the extensive margin (conducting R&D in more locations), with an average firm conducting R&D in more places than before.

In 1989, U.S. MNCs conducted 74 percent of all foreign R&D in just five countries—the United Kingdom, Germany, Japan, France, and Canada. They were prominent R&D locations because of their historical importance as global centers of scientific research (and as lucrative consumer markets for U.S. MNC products). By 2014, however, only 43 percent of all foreign R&D was conducted in these five countries. Figure 8-2 shows the growing importance of new locations and the corresponding decline in the relative importance of the traditional R&D hubs.

Many of these new hubs have only recently graduated from the ranks of developing countries, and two of the most important new destinations for U.S. MNC R&D, China and India, still have relatively low per capita incomes. Most economists would expect that only the most advanced industrial countries possess a comparative advantage in innovation, so the shift in R&D investment away from traditional hubs appears to challenge traditional views of comparative advantage and economic development. The apparent paradox fades, however, as we examine the inner workings of the global R&D system. In the same way that multinationals have created global value chains that provide low-wage developing countries with the sophisticated inputs they need to manufacture and export technology-intensive products, U.S. multinationals have created a kind of intellectual value chain that combines the impressive engineering talent available in developing countries with sophisticated, specialized knowledge needed to produce frontier innovations for the global market. To see this intellectual value chain in action, we turn to our second principal source of data on

FIGURE 8-2. The Rise of New R&D Hubs

R&D expenditures of U.S. MNC foreign affiliates, in millions USD

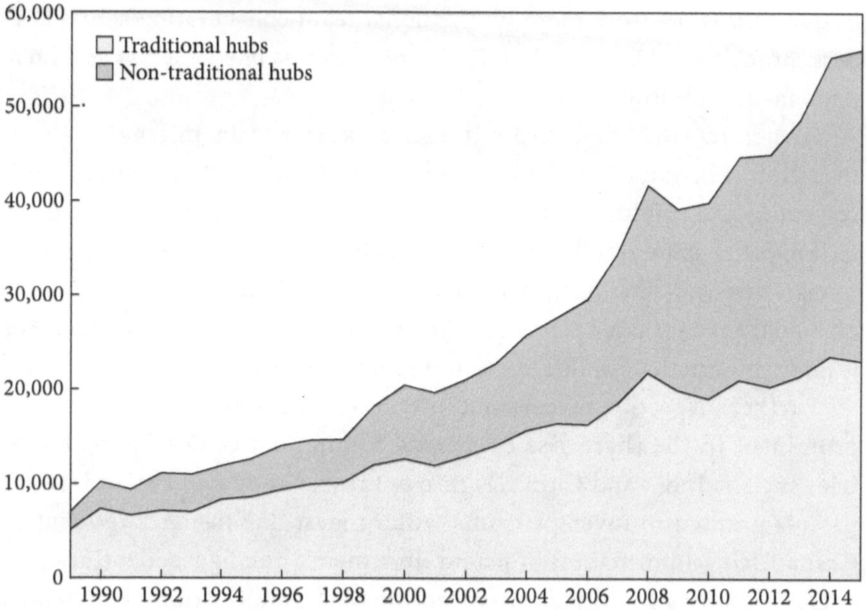

Note: This figure previously appeared in Branstetter, Glennon, and Jensen (2019b).

Source: Confidential data from the U.S. Bureau of Economic Analysis and authors' calculations.

U.S. MNCs' global innovation system—patents—and use them to analyze the striking rise in cross-border research collaboration evidenced by patent documents from the USPTO.[11]

U.S. PATENTS REVEAL RAPID GROWTH IN CROSS-BORDER R&D COLLABORATION

U.S. patent law requires that applicants include a list of inventors and their addresses in the patent application. This requirement implies that patents generated with substantive input from scientists and engineers employed by the foreign affiliates of U.S. MNCs will list the foreign addresses of those R&D personnel. Because we know the locations of R&D-performing affiliates around the world, we can match R&D investments made by U.S. MNCs abroad with the patents those investments generate. This matching, however, revealed that many patents listing the addresses of foreign inventors also list the addresses of U.S.-based inventors, suggesting that the patent in question is the work of an international team collaborating across borders. Branstetter, Li, and Veloso (2015) refer to this phenomenon as "international co-invention."

Earlier research has already noted a rapid rise in international co-invention (Kerr and Kerr (2018); Branstetter, Li, and Veloso (2015)). With respect to U.S. multinational firms in particular, this trend is even more striking; the share of all U.S. MNC patents, including patents granted to foreign inventors that have inventors from more than one country, has increased from less than 2 percent in 1980 to more than 10 percent in 2014. For leading multinationals, this fraction is likely even higher.

Further inspection reveals that international co-invention is especially prominent in the sharp rise of patents coming out of developing countries such as India and China. Figure 8-3 tracks the rapid rise in USPTO patents granted to inventor teams with at least one member resident in China. Using information in patent documents, the figure identifies patents owned by all multinationals (not just U.S. multinationals) in which all the inventors have Chinese addresses and patents in which the inventor team contains both Chinese and non-Chinese addresses.[12] Figure 8-4 presents a similar breakdown of USPTO patents granted to inventor teams with at least one member resident in India.

These figures show that the dramatic rise of USPTO patent grants to Chinese and Indian inventors was driven disproportionately by multinationals, with a conspicuously large role for patents generated through international co-invention. Branstetter, Li, and Veloso (2015) show that the patents owned by multinationals are of systematically higher quality than patents owned and generated by indigenous Chinese or Indian firms.[13] These authors introduce the idea that the intellectual inputs provided by the rest of the MNCs' global R&D system help make up for the lack of a sufficiently developed indigenous knowledge base in developing countries. In the same way that a developing country can export a complex product because it imports some of the most advanced components, an R&D center based in a developing country can contribute to innovation for the global market because local staff can "import" the R&D expertise of their colleagues who are often based in advanced industrial economies. The high-bandwidth communications technologies enabled by the internet and, in some industries, the diffusion

FIGURE 8-3. USPTO Patents Granted to Chinese Inventors

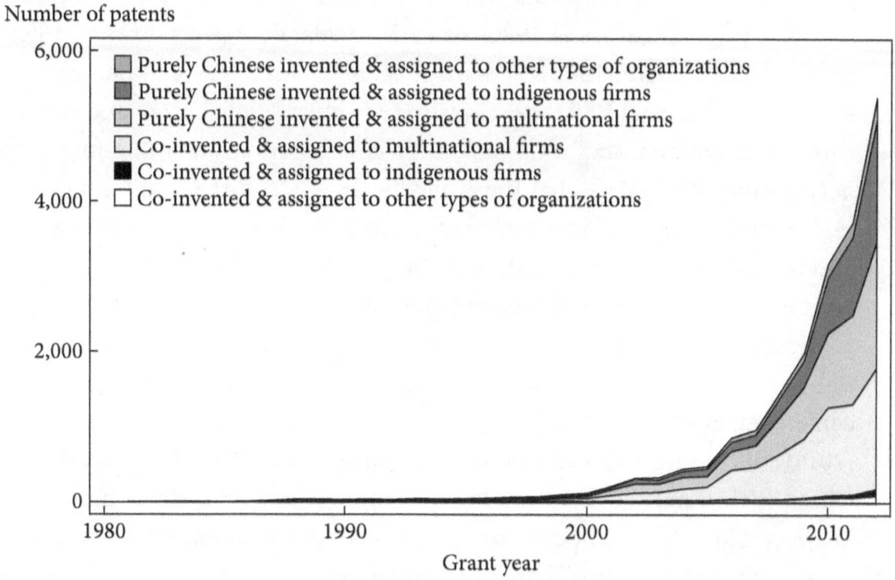

Source: Branstetter, Li, and Veloso (2015)

FIGURE 8-4. USPTO Patents Granted to Indian Inventors

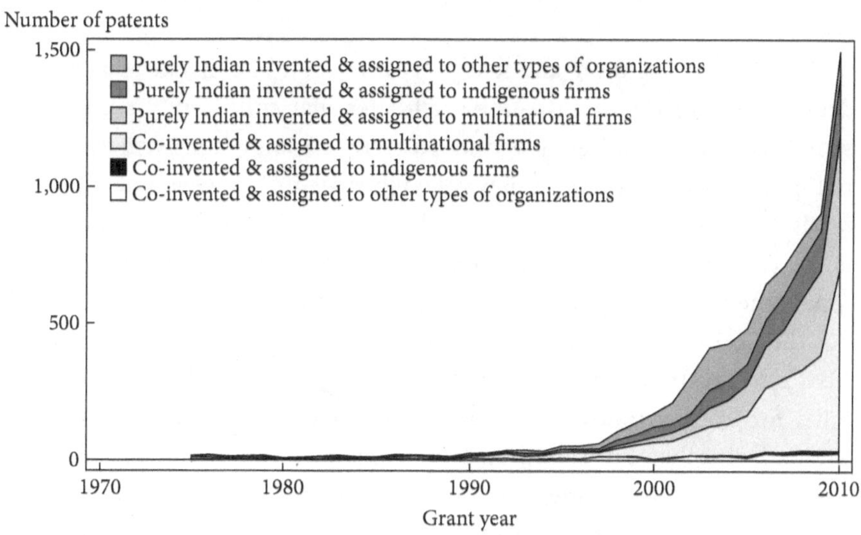

Source: Branstetter, Li, and Veloso (2015)

of design software explicitly engineered to facilitate collaboration by geographically distributed teams, allows for a degree of remote collaboration that was impossible in the 1980s or early 1990s. Further, a series of interviews we conducted with R&D managers in U.S. MNCs reveal that many of the firms with global R&D consciously try to create global innovation teams through intentional staff rotation, online collaboration, and other intrafirm networking. We believe that these efforts allow U.S. MNCs to tap into the raw talent available in emerging markets in ways that they could not before, and this is a key factor in understanding the geographic shift in R&D that has taken place since the rise of the internet.

Interestingly, international co-invention not only makes up for the initial absence of frontier innovative capabilities in emerging-market R&D centers but also can help build those capabilities. Branstetter, Li, and Veloso (2016) follow clusters of patents generated by foreign MNCs operating in China within particular technological domains and show that these firms are very likely to rely heavily on foreign-based inventors at first, but over time, the patents become more likely to be invented by teams of indigenous researchers. They suggest that foreign MNCs use international R&D collaboration as a way of sharing advanced expertise with local Chinese teams. This expertise gets transferred to the local team, and Chinese teams become more intellectually independent, as evidenced by a decline in the number of foreign inventors appearing in the patent documents generated by a given research stream.

Branstetter, Glennon, and Jensen (2018) expand on this idea, using data drawn from all U.S. multinational affiliates that consistently report R&D spending and patenting. We find patterns strongly consistent with the notion that the inception of new research streams in developing countries tends to be more reliant on intellectual input from U.S.-based inventors than is the case in developed countries, though the degree of reliance on U.S. input tends to converge over long periods of time. This work further builds out the notion of international co-invention as a mechanism for enabling MNCs to do frontier research in countries with limited indigenous capability for frontier innovation. Our interviews with R&D managers at U.S. MNCs strengthen our interpretation of the declining significance of U.S.-based inventors in the research streams of foreign affiliates. R&D managers and engineers describe the organizational structures and practices designed to promote knowledge sharing within the firm. International collaboration is deliberately enhanced through short-term personnel exchanges between more and less established R&D subsidiaries, and regular videoconferences help maintain these ties once the exchanges end. Internal systems track expertise networks around the world, enabling research teams in one location to find necessary expertise elsewhere within the system. All interviewees pointed to the growing capabilities of research teams in emerging markets.

Figure 8-5, reproduced below from Branstetter, Glennon, and Jensen (2018), illustrates the core finding of that paper. The solid lines trace out the propensity for a patent produced in a given year after the inception of a new research stream to include at least one U.S.-based inventor, and it does so separately for research streams begun in "lower knowledge stock" countries and "higher knowledge stock" countries. As is evident from the figure, this propensity starts high—and it begins at a substantially higher point for patents generated in lower knowledge stock countries—but it falls quickly, and propensities tend to converge across low- and high-knowledge-stock countries within a decade of the research stream's inception.

FIGURE 8-5. Propensity for a Patent Generated by a Foreign Affiliate to Have a U.S.-Based Inventor

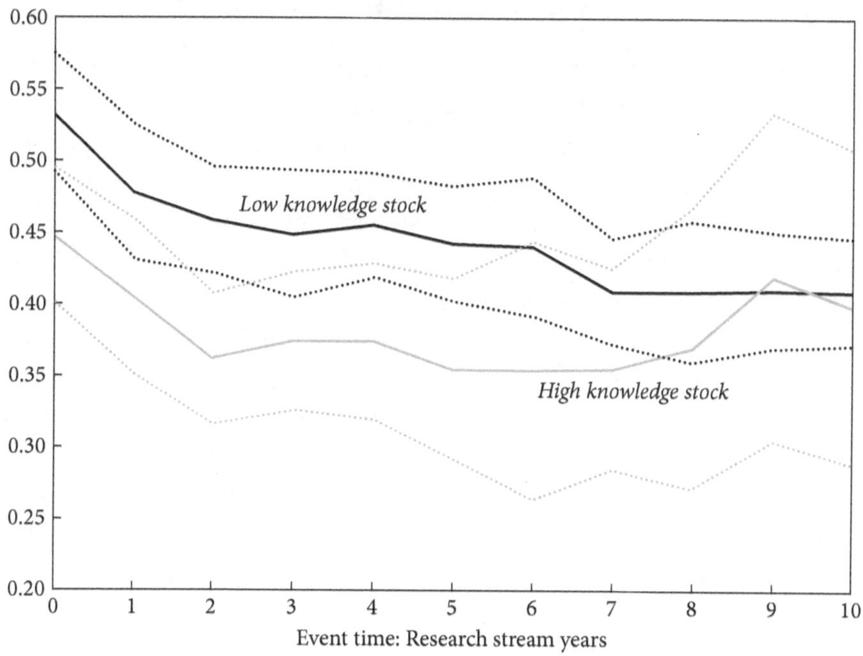

Source: Branstetter, Glennon, and Jensen (2018)

The figure conveys another important message: the apparently enduring reliance of foreign affiliates everywhere on intellectual inputs from U.S.-based research personnel. Examination of the patents generated by even mature, long-running research streams suggests an enduring centrality of U.S.-based R&D facilities within U.S. multinationals' global R&D systems. Patents generated by foreign research streams seem to show that the United States remains an important source of new ideas for all foreign hubs, even in the very long run and even in the most mature research streams. The measure of reliance on U.S. intellectual inputs traced in figure 8-5 generally does not fall below 30 percent, suggesting that those who worry that the globalization of R&D will eliminate demand for U.S.-based engineers might be overly pessimistic. Our results are consistent with the results of Macher and Mowery (2008) and Hufbauer, Moran, and Oldenski (2013). Arora and Gambardella (2005b) hold a similar view for the India case, arguing that the type of software work offshored to India is software production rather than software design, which continues to be located in the United States.

THE GROWING SOFTWARE AND IT INTENSITY OF U.S. MNC INVENTION

Software and IT patents have been growing in importance since the 1990s; the share of software patents in all USPTO patents grew from 6 percent in 1990 to nearly 40 percent by 2014.[14] More important than the simple fact that software and IT intensity in innovation is increasing is evidence that firms that do not invest sufficiently in software and IT can fall behind their competitors. Arora, Branstetter, and Drev (2013) show that in the IT industry, differences in software intensity can explain at least part of the success of American IT firms relative to Japanese firms since the 1990s. Japanese IT firms that were less software-intensive were characterized by lower rates of R&D productivity relative to their American counterparts. Branstetter, Drev, and Kwon (2018) document that the importance of software is not limited to the IT hardware sector alone. They show that innovation in four traditional manufacturing industries (autos and auto parts, aerospace and defense, medical devices, and pharmaceuticals) has also become more software-intensive. Furthermore, firms that took a more software-intensive approach to innovation tended to outperform their less software-intensive peers.

The increasing use of software and IT hardware is an important global development (Branstetter, Drev, and Kwon (2018)).[15] Increasingly, engineers can now enhance product functionality through software engineering rather than mechanical, chemical, or electrical engineering. Decades of rapid advance in the computational power of microprocessors had, by the 1990s, created a suite of cheaper tiny computers that could be easily programmed to direct the behavior of very different devices in increasingly sophisticated ways.[16] Advances in microprocessors were complemented by advances in sensors and digital control systems that made it easier for microprocessors to alter the way these devices worked, often through rapid response to even fairly subtle changes in the devices' environment. As these trends advanced, software engineers built a steadily expanding menu of routines and subroutines in standardized languages that could be used and reused to direct the actions of different devices.

The economic literature on general-purpose technologies (Bresnahan and Trajtenberg (1995); Helpman and Trajtenberg (1998)) explains these developments as a new wave of technological change. The basic hardware components that had arrived as early as the 1980s—microprocessors, sensors, memory, and digital control systems—were extremely broadly applicable. But every effective application required product- and industry-specific knowledge, embodied in the software that made these standardized components work in fundamentally different contexts. So, firms across a broad range of industries increasingly needed to invest in IT and software engineering capabilities.

The widespread use of software and IT has enabled and reinforced the globalization of R&D in two important ways. First, the inherently modular nature of IT hardware and software facilitates the division of innovative effort across multiple locations within an MNC. Because different components of a larger system fit together through standardized interfaces, product development of the components can take place simultaneously and, to some extent, independently. This capability allows multinational firms to decompose innovation in these domains into pieces that can be distributed to the location that can perform the R&D most efficiently. The internet has enabled a richer, faster, cheaper exchange of data than was possible in earlier eras, and in some fields, software-enabled collaboration tools have been specifically developed to enable teams of engineers separated by distance to work on the same project. To put it differently, advances in IT and software have created technologies of collaboration that make cross-border R&D far more feasible. Then, a lead R&D center, possibly in the United States, can reassemble the constituent pieces to produce the full innovation.

All of this suggests that technology has partly driven the globalization of R&D. As IT hardware and software have become much more important parts of the R&D portfolios of U.S. firms, research in these domains is inherently easier to distribute across countries, and modern telecommunications and computer-aided design technologies facilitated the dense exchange of information necessary to support cross-border collaboration in R&D.

The second way in which software and IT contributed to the globalization of R&D is in human resources. As demand for IT and software engineers expanded in the 1990s, the United States began importing foreign engineers on a large scale. Bound and others (2015) document the increase in high-skilled foreign-born IT workers in parallel to the rising importance of IT in the United States. According to the National Survey of College Graduates,[17] the U.S. IT workforce, made up of programmers, computer scientists, and electrical engineers, grew by 112 percent between 1993 and 2010, while the overall U.S. workforce grew by only 70 percent. The share of foreign IT workers in total IT workers grew from 16 percent in 1993 to 32 percent by 2010. The H-1B visa program for skilled workers helped bring foreign engineers into the U.S. labor market. This entire visa program became dominated by workers in computer-related occupations. The annual quotas (that is, the maximum number of new H-1B visas issued every year to private-sector firms) were raised substantially during the internet boom of the 1990s. Arora, Branstetter, and Drev (2013) argue that the ability of American firms to access foreign-born software engineers enabled them to respond to technological opportunities much more effectively than their Japan-based rivals, reinforcing the speed and extent of the IT revolution in the United States.

However, while American firms were largely unconstrained in their ability to import foreign talent as needed to meet growing demand for IT and software workers in the 1990s, the H-1B annual quota was cut to a quarter of its previous size in 2004. That began a new era in which firms were increasingly constrained in their ability to hire foreign skilled workers. Access to talented engineers and programmers is critical for firms to stay at the technological frontier, and Glennon (2019) documents that many U.S. multinational firms found a creative response: when unable to hire the foreign labor they needed in the United States, they simply hired at their foreign affiliates instead, as shown in figure 8-6. The figure, supported by extensive regression analysis, shows how multinational firms highly dependent on the H-1B visa system changed their foreign employment when the H-1B quota was lowered by roughly 75 percent. The relative change is clearly visible in the raw data, and the impact also clearly emerges in a series of careful difference-in-differences regressions.

Glennon also finds evidence that, in addition to hiring more skilled labor abroad in response to skilled immigration restrictions, U.S. multinational firms also opened more R&D-performing foreign affiliates and produced more patents abroad, suggesting that restrictions on importing foreign skilled labor were—and continue to be—an important driver of the globalization of R&D. In particular, the shift abroad was concentrated in three main countries: China and India (or the places where companies had been recruiting engineers and IT workers) and Canada, whose skilled-immigration regime made it possible for U.S. multinational firms to easily hire the immigrant workers they needed at their Canadian foreign affiliates. In short, the demand for skilled labor has been a major driver of the globalization of R&D, and a combination of tightened policies on the immigration of skilled workers and an abundant supply of human capital abroad have been important drivers of the foreign R&D location choice.

FIGURE 8-6. Changes in the Foreign Employment of U.S. MNCs in Response to 2004 H-1B Quota Tightening

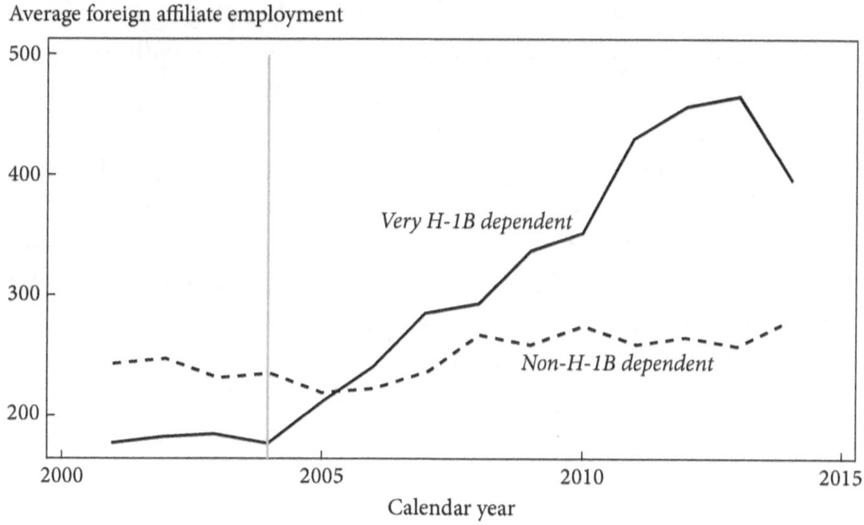

Source: Glennon (2019)

These changes suggest an extremely large increase in demand for IT and software engineering talent that was partially met by importing talent from abroad in the 1990s, through mechanisms like the H-1B program, then met by moving high-skilled tasks abroad as immigration policy was tightened in the 2000s. A closer examination of the countries supplying this talent suggests that technically skilled workers are abundant in many of the same countries—notably India and China—where we see a parallel increase in U.S. MNC foreign R&D. Applications from employers for Indian workers made up 62 percent of new H-1B visa applications in 2016,[18] and Indian and Chinese students combined made up 18 percent of doctorates in science and engineering from U.S. universities in 2016,[19] and this share is even larger for some key disciplines. If the large number of Indian and Chinese students pursuing graduate education at American research universities represents only a slice of the countries' science and engineering talent, most of which remains at home, then this suggests a massive amount of software- and IT-trained human capital is available in China and India. Arora and Gambardella (2005a) and Arora and Gambardella (2005b) likewise document the abundant supply of engineering and technology graduates in emerging economies.

The evidence also suggests that the talent in key emerging markets has been available for hire at wages well below U.S. wages. Within many U.S. multinationals, the rise in demand for IT and software engineers was especially acute, and the supply of foreign engineers in these disciplines was especially abundant. This leads to another important finding of our research: software-intensive and IT-intensive U.S. multinationals rapidly expanded their R&D in emerging markets where high-quality workers were relatively abundant.

Figure 8-7 shows the positive correlation between U.S. MNC R&D activity in a country—based on published Bureau of Economic Analysis (BEA) statistics on the worldwide activities of U.S. multinational enterprises—and a country's software and IT hardware intensity, conditioning on country fixed effects.[20] Figure 8-8 illustrates the strong positive correlation between U.S. firms' IT and software intensity and their innovative activity in emerging markets.[21] These two graphs together suggest that foreign R&D is most pronounced in IT- and software-intensive countries and that it is most intensively done by IT- and software-intensive firms.

FIGURE 8-7. Affiliate R&D Expenditure and Host Country Software Intensity

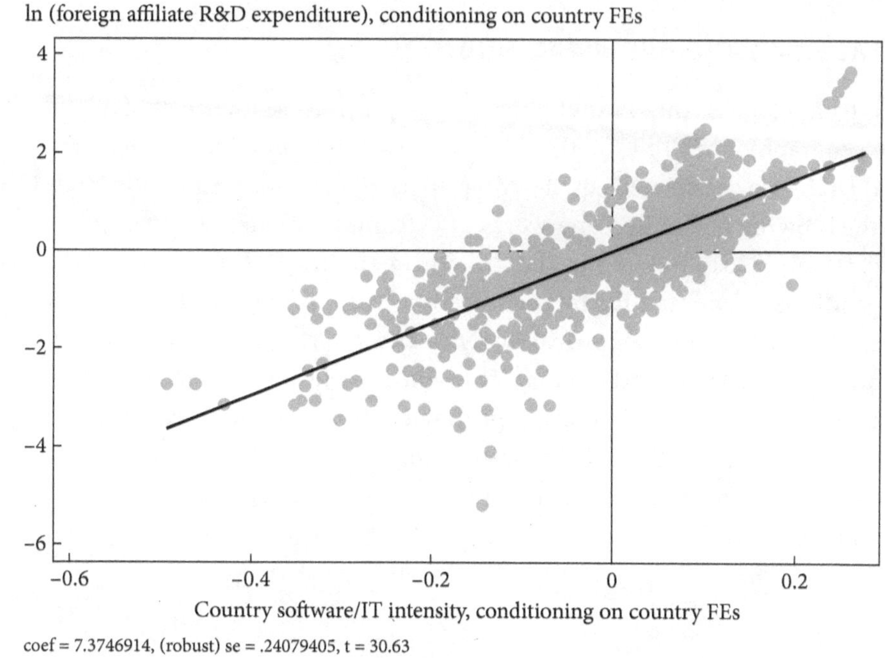

Source: Branstetter, Glennon, and Jensen (2019a).

FIGURE 8-8. Firm Reliance on Developing Country Inventors and Firm-Level Software and IT Intensity

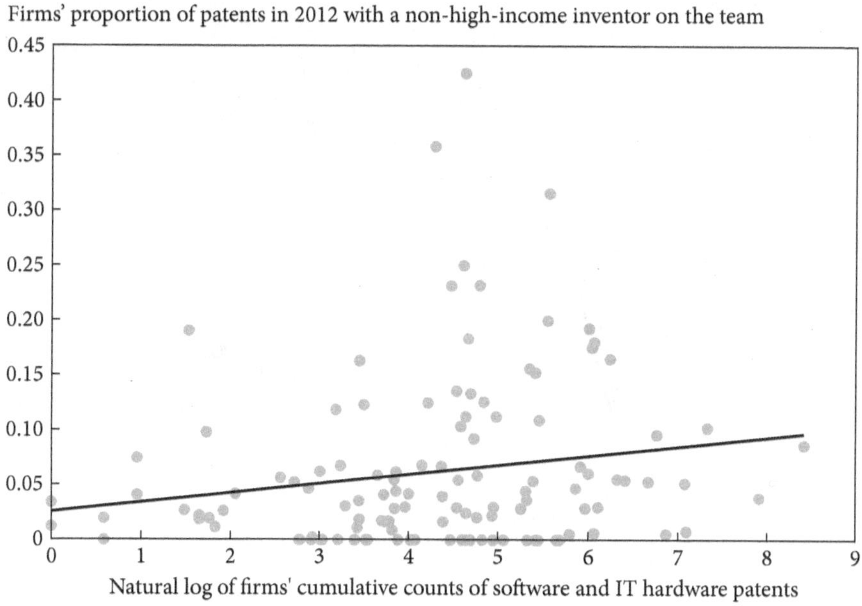

Source: Branstetter, Glennon, and Jensen (2019a)

A TALE OF THREE NEW R&D HUBS

The technological shifts highlighted in the previous section help explain the geographic shift in U.S. MNC R&D outside the United States. All new R&D hubs are not created equal—three, in particular, loom especially large in the growing global R&D networks of U.S. multinationals: China, India, and Israel. Figure 8-9 shows the growth in the fraction of global R&D expenditure accounted for by each of these three countries. This section draws upon both our empirical analysis and a series of interviews with country-based MNC R&D managers to illustrate how and why these particular nations have become disproportionate drivers of the market shift in the distribution of U.S. MNC R&D spending across countries. In all three places, local human resources in the IT and software domain were an important attractor.[22]

FIGURE 8-9. The Rise of China, India, and Israel

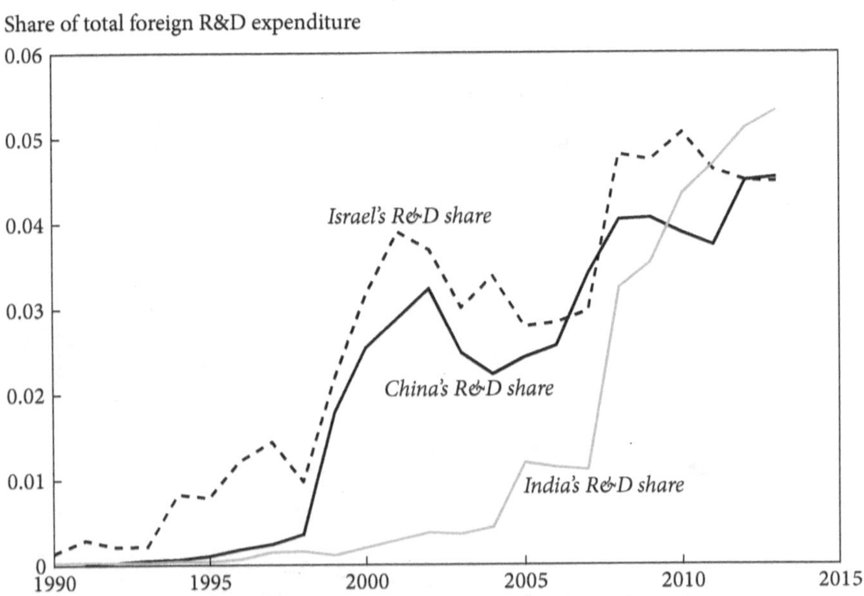

Source: Branstetter, Glennon, and Jensen (2019a)

A Passage to India

Software invention looms large in the patents generated by U.S. MNC R&D affiliates in India, and the abundance in India of relatively low-cost software engineers[23] was repeatedly emphasized in interviews as a reason for U.S. multinationals to expand their R&D in that country. India's success in exporting software- and business process–outsourcing services demonstrated the relative quality of Indian software engineers, and U.S. firms in these service sectors have proactively shifted some of their research and development to India. Largely because of India's prominent role, professional services is the U.S. industry with the most globalized R&D. In recent years, the ratio of R&D performed by foreign affiliates in professional services relative to R&D undertaken by the U.S. parent companies is more than 40 percent, and India makes up an important component of that foreign-affiliate R&D. Because software has increasingly become a critical input to innovation across many products, manufacturers have joined services firms in hiring Indian software engineers.

The Indian case also casts a particularly strong light on the difference between the "knowledge-seeking" motivation described in the earlier management literature and the search for talent we highlight here. U.S. multinationals were not investing in India to tap new technologies developed autonomously by indigenous Indian corporations or to learn about new scientific discoveries developed by pioneering Indian academic institutions. For the most part, the innovative capabilities of indigenous Indian firms are still viewed as relatively limited compared with the capabilities of the multinationals resident in India. Therefore, one can draw a distinction between the knowledge-seeking FDI explored in the empirical literature of the 1990s and early 2000s and what seems to be happening in India. Multinationals are not seeking to tap into an indigenous body of knowledge, in the same way that they might have sought to tap into Japanese expertise in cutting-edge consumer electronics in earlier decades. Instead, many multinationals were tapping raw Indian talent and integrating that talent into multinational R&D systems in which a significant amount of the intellectual leadership and direction still came from outside India (Branstetter, Glennon, and Jensen (2018)). In the more mature and developed R&D centers, Indian staff are beginning to exert more intellectual leadership in some areas, but there is still a gap between indigenous and multinational innovation. Our interviewees consistently emphasized the importance of a common language and the role of the Indian diaspora in the United States in successfully integrating Indian talent into U.S. MNC R&D systems.

Israel, the (R&D) Promised Land

Software and IT loom large in the patents generated by the Israeli foreign affiliates of U.S. MNCs, although not as large as in the Indian case. The attraction of human capital was also a major theme of our interviews in Israel. However, the nature and genesis of that human capital differed in significant ways from the case of India. In Israel, universal conscription of the Jewish population places much of the nation's brainpower under the authority of the nation's national defense establishment, and tests administered to new recruits sort the most intellectually gifted among them into elite groups like Unit 8200, a signals intelligence unit often compared to America's National Security Agency. At an early stage in their lives, young Israelis assigned to these units receive intensive exposure to high-level computer science concepts and skills, and they are assigned challenging software engineering tasks central to Israeli national security. This experience often exerts a lasting influence on the education and career choices of conscripts recruited into these units after their return to civilian life. Imagine the impact on the U.S. software-engineering workforce if the top 0.1 percent of U.S. high school graduates could be locked in the basement of the National Security Agency for several years, given a crash course in digital intelligence, cyberwar, and cybersecurity, and required to produce mission-critical software.

Israel has thus created a unique set of institutions that steer a disproportionate fraction of their most gifted citizens into computer-science careers, and the stock of veterans of these elite units was growing to significant levels just as the global trajectory of innovation made software more central to nearly every domain of technological innovation. Israeli wages are not cheap. Nevertheless, MNCs are investing in Israeli talent, because the quality of Israeli human capital is distinctively high. Not surprisingly, areas of Israeli strength like machine vision or cybersecurity often have a connection to the national security functions that are the focus of investment by Unit 8200. Some Israeli firms in these domains have become leaders in their fields, and previous success with initial public stock offerings (IPOs) helped induce an impressive flow of energetic and creative Israeli start-ups. However, acquisition by a U.S. multinational is now a more likely outcome for these start-ups than an IPO in the United States or elsewhere. Upon acquisition, the most successful start-ups often become Israel-based R&D hubs for the acquiring U.S. firms.

These acquisitions and the successful integration of the firms into the R&D operations of U.S. multinationals are abetted, as with the case of India, by an extensive Israeli diaspora in the United States. The interaction between Israeli and American academics, managers, engineers, and financiers is substantial, especially when scaled to the size of the Israeli economy. Many Israeli managers of U.S. MNC R&D operations in Israel have personal connections to the United States, received part of their education at an American university, and spent years in Silicon Valley before returning to Israel. Many prominent American managers, venture capitalists, and scientists also have strong personal and family ties to Israel and have spent substantial time there. American multinationals are investing in Israel to take advantage of distinctive Israeli competencies, but these competencies have been jointly developed by Israel's unique human capital institutions, American firms, and the Israeli corporate entities they have established or acquired, rather than wholly developed by a cluster of indigenous firms.

China: Enter the Dragon

Multinational investment in China is more complex. Interviewees maintained that the cost, scale, and quality of Chinese engineering talent was a significant draw, and that Chinese engineers participated in international teams creating inventions for the global market. However, multinationals conducting R&D in China were often seeking to redesign Western technology for a Chinese market that is large and rapidly growing, but substantively different from high-income Western markets. In this new hub, there are clearly some older motives (market adaptation) for MNC R&D investment, as well as newer ones. Chinese R&D is also more hardware-focused than Israeli or Indian R&D, reflecting China's emergence as the leading exporter of IT hardware and components. The Chinese diaspora in the United States played an important role in helping U.S. multinationals recruit talent and navigate the complex business environment of contemporary China.

The presence of strong diasporas for all three of our new hubs is significant when we consider findings from Kerr and Kerr (2015) and Foley and Kerr (2013), which show that the ethnic composition of a firm's inventors is associated with increases in the share of that firm's affiliate activity in countries related to that ethnicity.

R&D GLOBALIZATION, COMPARATIVE ADVANTAGE, AND THE ROLE OF NON-U.S. MNCs

The growth in R&D in new hubs has been a significant driver of the overall increase in overseas R&D spending, but traditional hubs still remain an important component of the global R&D system created by U.S. MNCs. Nevertheless, R&D performed by U.S. MNC affiliates in the new hubs of China, India, and Israel is concentrated in different industries than in the traditional R&D hubs. R&D by affiliates in Germany, Japan, Canada, the United Kingdom, and France is concentrated in traditional manufacturing sectors such as chemicals, goods, and machinery, while much of the R&D by affiliates in China, India, and Israel is in professional, scientific, and technical services (a category dominated by software engineering). Figure 8-10 presents the breakdown of recorded expenditure across broad industry categories. It is a crude reflection of specialization in different kinds of R&D in different host nations, but it is hard to reconcile these numbers with the notion that R&D-performing affiliates are doing the same thing in these different countries.

No particular hub completely specializes in one domain, and, as noted, U.S.-based co-inventors play an important role in the innovative activities of all hubs. Nevertheless, the data reveal a clear pattern of specialization, with U.S. MNCs clearly focusing their R&D investment in ways that reflect the distinctive relative strengths of the host countries. The ability to access this broad range of strengths through a global R&D system helps maintain the innovative dynamism of U.S. MNCs.

How does the pattern of R&D growth in the new hubs relate to the problem of the global innovation slowdown? Regardless of whether Robert Gordon (2016) is correct that the inventions of our present and near future will fail to pack the productivity-enhancing punch of past inventions, or whether Brynjolfsson and McAfee (2017) are correct that we are on the verge of a new series of dramatic technological revolutions, in the long run, the compelling endogenous growth models of Jones (2009) and supportive evidence put forward by Bloom and others (2020) suggest that innovative progress will require that an ever-increasing fraction of the human race be recruited to support innovative efforts. If these efforts relied solely on brainpower already resident in the advanced industrial countries, the potential limits to these human resources would seem to be relatively proximate. Educated workers talented enough to participate in the advance of the techno-

FIGURE 8-10. Specialization According to Comparative Advantage?

R&D performed in "old hubs" in 2014, by industry of affiliate

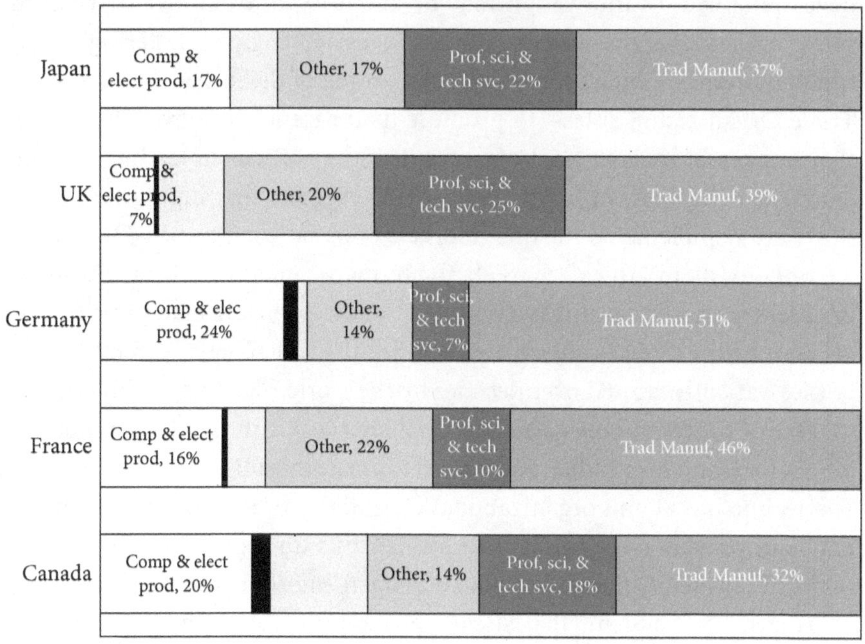

R&D performed in "new hubs" in 2014, by industry of affiliate

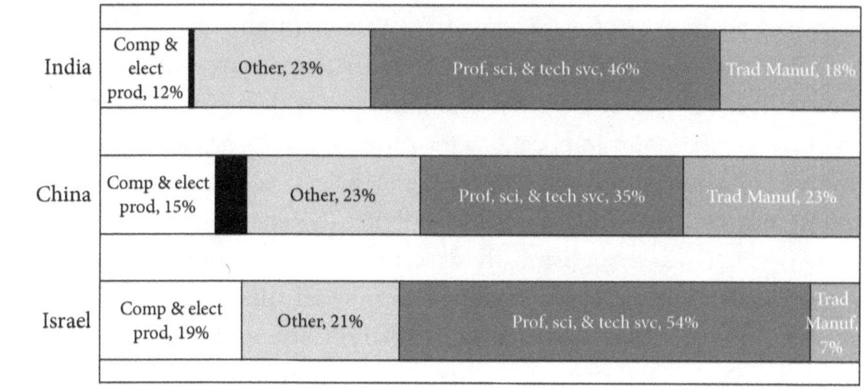

logical frontier have many alternative, equally remunerative potential uses of their human capital and ability, and an ever-increasing fraction of talented workers could only be procured at an ever-increasing cost.

The recent massive expansion of higher education outside the advanced industrial countries—particularly in China—raises the possibility that the developing world's innovation may be about to shift into overdrive at the same moment that the Western world's invention engine is faltering. Unfortunately, despite China's intense efforts—some of them illegal under World Trade Organization rules—to promote its indigenous innovation abilities, they appear, at least so far, to fall short of the abilities in leading Western countries. The work of Jones (2014, 2015) suggests that highly specialized skills are complements for one another, but that the incentive to specialize only exists in "thick" markets for human capital (markets with many job seekers and many employers), and it could plausibly take years or even decades before China's enterprises acquire the full array of inventive capabilities patiently crafted over decades by the world's leading multinationals.

One of the central messages of this chapter is that the world does not have to wait for Chinese or Indian enterprises to create this full range of capabilities. The technological and organizational capabilities of the leading U.S. multinationals provide mechanisms and frameworks through which the growing ranks of talented Chinese, Indian, and Israeli engineers can be plugged into globalized R&D systems that already possess this full range of capabilities. While our exposition and figures have emphasized the interaction of U.S.-based inventors with foreign teams in a particular country, U.S. MNCs can also pair an Indian software engineer with a German mechanical engineer or a Japanese electrical engineer, as circumstances warrant. The matching possibilities and achievable team configurations within these MNC networks could have first-order implications for future research productivity, because the sobering model of Jones (2009) suggests that it is not only the scale of R&D teams, but also their diversity that contributes to R&D outcomes.

An extensive, though mostly descriptive literature on national innovation systems has already made the point that different nations tend to evolve different R&D systems with different strengths and weaknesses: (Nelson 1992); (Okimoto and Rohlen 1988); (Mansfield 1988a and 1988b); and (Branstetter and Kwon 2018). Because the components of these systems co-evolve over long periods and tend to cohere in mutually reinforcing ways, it often proves quite difficult to transplant a conspicuously successful element from one national system into another. Germany, the nation that invented research universities and dominated the earliest science-intensive industries, has struggled in the post–World War II era to incubate a start-up infrastructure like Silicon Valley's. A particularly painful setback came in the early 2000s with the collapse of Germany's Neuer Markt. Around the same time, the nation's efforts to lure immigrant engineers from source nations like India generated a significant backlash and yielded few results. Conversely, the United States has struggled to transplant German institutions like the vocational training systems and the Fraunhofer Institutes, specializing in applied research, that have contributed significantly to the export strength of Germany's *mittelstand* (small- and medium-size firms). The rise of globalized R&D networks within MNCs means that no single nation—not even the most advanced—needs to contain within its borders the full range of capabilities for enterprises to utilize them. These international systems broaden the array and diversity of invention teams that can be created, raising the productivity of R&D investment.

This chapter has emphasized the role of U.S. MNCs in the creation of global R&D networks, but existing research clearly shows that other countries' firms also have created global R&D networks. Related studies suggest that Japanese firms (Branstetter (2006)) and British firms (Griffith, Harrison, and Van Reenen (2006)) have created global networks of R&D-performing affiliates that route useful knowledge back to the parent firm. Unfortunately, a full exploration of recent developments within non-U.S. multinationals is limited by the lack of data. Few nations maintain a database on multinational activity as extensive and comprehensive as the BEA data for the United States, so a quantitatively precise assessment of the relative role of U.S. multinationals within the broader phenomenon of R&D globalization is well beyond the scope of this chapter and may be all but impossible, given current data constraints. However, it seems likely that U.S. firms play an especially important role, for many reasons, of which we will highlight two. First, many places in this chapter note the apparent importance of an ethnic diaspora in helping connect U.S. firms to foreign sources of talent. As resident firms within an immigrant nation that hosts many multinationals, U.S. MNCs may have a decided advantage over firms based elsewhere, an idea that gets some evidentiary support in Arora, Branstetter, and Drev (2013), Branstetter, Drev, and Kwon (2018), and Foley and Kerr (2016). Second, this chapter has stressed the particular salience of IT and software in R&D globalization, and these are sectors in which U.S. firms have traditionally led, especially in software.

POLICY CHALLENGES TO THE GLOBAL INNOVATION SYSTEM

Over the past twenty years, the growing importance of software and IT has driven U.S. MNCs to significantly increase the scale and scope of their R&D outside the United States. New R&D hubs like China and India are not only yielding high returns for U.S. MNCs but also, as hosts of these R&D activities, benefiting directly from the innovation supported by U.S. MNCs and indirectly from spillovers through technology transfers to local firms. The globalization of R&D, and the global innovation system it supports, has the potential to increase global productivity growth—a mutually beneficial opportunity for the entire world.

Yet, in spite of the promise this opportunity brings, a number of policy challenges threaten the continued health of the global innovation system. As already noted, the trade policies of the Trump administration increasingly posed a risk to the global innovation system. It may take years before data are available to measure the impact of these policies on global R&D, but the risk that they will decrease cross-border collaboration is real.

We have also emphasized how critical skilled immigration is for the global R&D system. Immigrant engineers have long served as a human bridge between their American employers and the research communities in their former countries (Foley and Kerr (2013)). While the Trump administration undertook policy shifts to reduce immigration, these follow a substantial decline in annual H-1B visa quotas implemented more than a decade ago, which have had measurable effects on the global allocation of high-skilled tasks within U.S. multinationals, as shown by Glennon (2019).[24] The EU nations and Japan have long maintained relatively more restrictive immigration policies, which hold back their own economic growth. A greater global commitment to (skilled) immigration and temporary movement would facilitate the development of a more global R&D system.

Another ongoing concern is the protection of intellectual property. Prior research documents that stronger intellectual property rights in reforming countries attract more investment and more technologically intensive MNC activity (Branstetter, Fisman, and Foley (2006); Branstetter and Saggi (2011); Bilir (2014)). The shortcomings of enforcement systems in China and India are particularly salient, because both countries have so much to contribute to human innovation through greater participation in a global R&D

system. R&D managers we interviewed suggest that global MNCs would invest more in R&D-intensive activity in China if intellectual property were better protected there and technology transfers were not forced. Likewise, the unwillingness of the Indian government to enact pharmaceutical patent reform truly consistent with the Agreement on Trade-Related Aspects of Intellectual Property Rights (TRIPS) has gravely discouraged MNCs from investing in R&D in the Indian pharmaceutical industry. This is a major lost opportunity, given this sector's rising potential (Arora, Branstetter, and Chatterjee (2008)). Strengthening intellectual property rights in places where they are currently weakly protected would foster a more robust global innovation system.

This chapter has repeatedly emphasized the rising importance of software and IT in the broader innovation activities of U.S. multinationals, and it has offered evidence in support of the idea that the growing intensity in software and IT innovation has powerfully reinforced the globalization of R&D. In this broader context, it is clear that a global innovation system will depend on the free flow of data between the R&D facilities of MNCs. Efforts that restrict these data flows (for example, forced data localization) could significantly impede the operation of a global innovation system. A greater global commitment to the free international flow of data, with appropriate safeguards to ensure privacy and other important social goals, could help ensure the healthy development of a global R&D system. Of course, these considerations make clear that national efforts to close the internet of particular nations to the broader global system constitute a serious impediment to international trade in ideas. China's distinctive digital protectionism will become a more important challenge to the global trading system as the importance of international data flows continues to rise.

The last challenge is the emerging Western response to an increasingly authoritarian and ambitious China. China is an important destination for U.S. MNC R&D and an important supplier of scientists and engineers to the U.S. education system and U.S. firms. The Trump administration sought to limit technology transfers and exchange of researchers (for example, by limiting visas to Chinese engineers) in a series of policies that look increasingly like an attempt to decouple the U.S. and Chinese economies. This chapter does not assess the relative merits of a U.S. policy of economic engagement with China versus a U.S. policy seeking to isolate it economically. But a major bipartisan discussion is underway over how best to engage (or not) with

China in the hope of incentivizing changes in its political and economic behavior. It is difficult to foresee how the economic relationship between China and the United States will evolve, but the current direction will likely harm the global R&D system. The potential costs and benefits of having China inside the global innovation system should be carefully weighed in any reassessment of these policies. Branstetter (2018) outlines a series of policies that could provide a useful response to the challenges China presents, while maintaining a significant degree of economic integration.

APPENDIX: DATA FOR MEASURING THE GLOBALIZATION OF R&D

We use a combination of two sources to generate a unique panel dataset for analysis of U.S. multinational innovative activity abroad. The first is the Bureau of Economic Analysis (BEA) annual survey on U.S. Direct Investment Abroad. BEA is under a congressional mandate[25] to track investment into and out of the United States, and as such, its data comprise the most comprehensive available data for U.S. multinational activity abroad. The database contains financial and operating characteristics of both the U.S. parent companies and their foreign affiliates, including R&D expenditures, which is the primary variable of interest for this chapter. We constructed a panel dataset of this activity from 1989 through 2014.[26] Each firm may report on a consolidated basis for multiple affiliates in the same country under certain conditions.[27] Therefore, rather than conduct analysis at the affiliate level, we aggregate all foreign affiliate activity up to the country level for a given firm for a given year.

The second source of data is U.S. Patent and Trademark Office (USPTO) patent data, obtained using the PatentsView database, and it includes all utility granted patent applications through August 2017.[28] We restrict our analysis to USPTO patents rather than the Japan Patent Office (JPO) or European Patent Office (EPO) patents, for three primary reasons: (1) our sample is U.S. multinationals, (2) the use of USPTO patents ensures a common standard that is close to or at the global technological frontier, and (3) the use of USPTO patents allows a comparable measure across countries. Patents are an imperfect measure of innovation; there is heterogeneity across countries, firms, and industries in the propensity to patent.[29] However, patenting does reflect an important piece of a country's innovative output, and it is highly correlated with other measures of innovation. Because obtaining a patent from the USPTO is costly and requires a degree of novelty as judged by professional patent examiners, the use of USPTO patents helps to ensure that the counted inventions are close to the technological frontier. It also ensures the application of a common standard. While this measure of innovation is not ideal, we believe it is the best available measure of innovation that is consistent for both cross-country comparison and across-time comparison. Furman, Porter, and Stern (2002) provide further support for our use of patenting as a comparison measure of a country's innovation. They provide an extensive overview of other measures of a country's national innovative capacity and come to the conclusion that patents are "the most concrete and comparable measure of innovative output over countries and time."

No numerical identifiers exist in both the BEA data and the USPTO patent data, so we matched the two databases using firm names. We conducted several rounds of probabilistic record linkage between BEA multinationals and patent assignees,[30] followed by manual verification to ensure the generated matches were correct. If a firm appeared in the BEA data but not in the patent data in a given year, we assumed that it did not apply for any patents in that year. Following the prior literature, we consider the patent inventors' country of residence as the country where an innovation takes place, and we consider a patent as having originated (at least in part) from a foreign country if any of its inventors list their address as from that country. Using these data, we are able not only to see whether a firm is patenting in a country, but we are also able to see the firm's R&D expenditures there, using the BEA data. This means that we are uniquely able to eliminate instances where patents appear to originate in a country with no R&D-performing affiliate. Our final dataset is at the firm-country-year level and varies across firms, countries, and time.

NOTES

This chapter draws upon earlier work by the authors, including Branstetter, Glennon, and Jensen (2018), Branstetter, Glennon, and Jensen (2019a), and, especially, Branstetter, Glennon, and Jensen (2019b), a Peterson Institute Policy Brief upon which much of the exposition in this chapter is closely based. The statistical analysis of firm-level data on U.S. multinational companies was conducted at the Bureau of Economic Analysis (BEA), U.S. Department of Commerce, under arrangements that maintain legal confidentiality requirements. We thank Bill Zeile, Jim Fetzer, and Ray Mataloni for helpful discussions on the BEA data. We gratefully acknowledge financial support from the Portuguese National Science Foundation (FCT) through its support of the Carnegie Mellon University Portugal program and financial support from the National Science

Foundation through two grants: SciSIP 1360165 and SciSIP 1360170. All errors and omissions remain our own responsibility. The views expressed are those of the authors and do not reflect official positions of the U.S. Department of Commerce.

1. For a more optimistic take on America's productivity growth prospects, see Branstetter and Sichel (2017).

2. For example, Hufbauer, Moran, and Oldenski (2013) report that U.S. MNCs that do not perform R&D outside the United States also do not perform R&D within the United States, suggesting that foreign R&D and domestic R&D are complements, not substitutes, for U.S. MNCs.

3. These results were obtained by regressing patents on foreign R&D expenditure by U.S. MNCs, controlling for firm-country and year effects. The residuals from this regression were then regressed indicator variables, one for each country. The figure then plots the coefficients of the country indicator variables.

4. This paragraph draws from Branstetter and Sichel (2017).

5. BEA is under a congressional mandate to track investment into and out of the United States, and as such, its data comprise the most comprehensive available information regarding the U.S. multinational activity abroad.

6. "Where Innovation Happens: Patents Granted (since 2013)," PatentsView. Available at www.patentsview.org/web/.

7. For instance, the propensity to patent tends to be much higher in industries like IT and biotechnology than in less technologically dynamic domains, and it tends to be higher in manufacturing than in services. Simple comparisons of patent counts could, therefore, obscure changes in the true level of innovation across firms and technological fields. In regression analysis, however, the incorporation of firm and/or industry fixed effects can partially control for time-invariant differences across firms in their propensity to patent that stem from the fact that different firms are inventing in different technological domains characterized by different propensities to patent. Given our rich BEA data, we can also examine changes in the mix of R&D expenditure across affiliates, industries, countries, and time, which provide us with another window into the changing mix of inventive activities that offers a useful check on the potential biases present in patent data.

8. World Bank, research and development expenditure data, https://data.worldbank.org/indicator/GB.XPD.RSDV.GD.ZS?locations=U.S.

9. U.S. Bureau of Economic Analysis (BEA) data, www.bea.gov/iTable/index_MNC.cfm. The BEA is our first principal source of data on U.S. MNCs' global innovation system.

10. National Science Board, Science and Engineering Indicators 2018, chapter 4, "Research and Development: U.S. Trends and International Comparisons," https://nsf.gov/statistics/2018/nsb20181/assets/1038/research-and-development-u-s-trends-and-international-comparisons.pdf; U.S. Bureau of Economic Analysis, Activities of U.S. Multinational Enterprises in 2015, https://apps.bea.gov/scb/pdf/2017/12-December/1217-activities-of-us-multinational-enterprises.pdf.

11. We restrict our analysis to USPTO patents for three primary reasons: (1) our sample is U.S. multinationals, and the use of USPTO patents (2) ensures a common

standard that is close to or at the global technological frontier and (3) allows for comparison across countries.

12. Figures 8-3 and 8-4 track patents assigned to all multinationals, not just MNCs based in the United States. As it turns out, Taiwan-based multinationals generate even more U.S. patent grants through their China-based R&D operations than U.S.-based multinationals do. What is clear, however, is that much of China's recent rapid rise in U.S. patent grants has been driven by the actions of foreign firms, not indigenous ones.

13. Branstetter, Li, and Veloso (2015) show that U.S. MNCs play an even more important role in generating U.S. patents granted to teams with at least one Indian inventor than they do in the case of China.

14. The ideas in this paragraph were first introduced in Branstetter, Glennon, and Jensen (2019a), and the language here closely follows that earlier paper.

15. The discussion in this paragraph and the paragraph that follows draws upon Branstetter, Drev, and Kwon (2018), and the language here closely follows that earlier paper.

16. Byrne, Oliner, and Sichel (2018) review the literature on rapid declines in the prices of semiconductor devices and show that these price declines continued through the 2010s.

17. National Science Foundation, National Survey of College Graduates, https://nsf.gov/statistics/srvygrads/.

18. According to USCIS Fiscal Year 2016 Annual Report to Congress: "Characteristics of H-1B Specialty Occupation Workers."

19. National Science Foundation, National Center for Science and Engineering Statistics, Survey of Earned Doctorates.

20. We define a country's software or IT hardware intensity as the share of its cumulative USPTO citation-weighted patent stocks classified as software or IT hardware. We determine the location of a patent using inventor addresses; if an inventor lists their address on a patent in country J, we define that patent as originating in country J. Software is defined using the Arora, Branstetter, and Drev (2013) methodology, and IT hardware is defined using the Hall, Jaffe, and Trajtenberg (2001) NBER technology classification. We define IT hardware as encompassing the following NBER technology classifications: 21 (communications), 22 (computer hardware and software), 23 (computer peripherals), 24 (information storage), 41 (electrical devices), and 46 (semiconductor devices).

21. U.S. firm IT and software intensity are measured as the firm's USPTO software or IT hardware patent stock, with software and IT hardware patents classified in the same way as described for country IT or software intensity. We define a firm's innovative activity in emerging markets as the proportion of its USPTO patents with an inventor from a non-high-income country, as classified by the World Bank.

22. The ideas in this section on the newly emerging hubs of India, China, and Israel were first introduced in Branstetter, Glennon, and Jensen (2019a), and some of the language in this section closely follows that in the earlier paper.

23. Arora and Gambardella (2006) have described the sequence of developments that enabled India to produce such a large number of software engineers.

24. For example, President Trump signed a "Buy American and Hire American" executive order, directing government officials to "rigorously enforce" immigration laws. As a result, more H-1B and L-1 visa applications have been rejected, with rejection rates for H-1B visas tripling. Starting in April 2018, the Trump administration suspended premium processing of H-1B petitions subject to the visa cap. In November 2018, the administration introduced a new Labor Condition Application form, requiring more information from companies applying for H-1B visas, which some believe might reduce interest in H-1B visas. The Trump administration is also proposing changes to the H-1B visa application process. These changes, at a minimum, increase uncertainty around the visa process.

25. The mandate comes from the International Investment and Trade in Services Survey Act. The data are collected for the purpose of producing publicly available aggregate statistics on the activities of multinational enterprises.

26. The most extensive data are collected in benchmark years: 1989, 1994, 1999, 2004, 2009, and 2014. The reporting requirement threshold varies by year, size of the affiliate, and the parent's ownership stake. BEA estimates values of some variables of some affiliates in non-benchmark years in order to estimate a consistent universe across years. We only use the reported data in this chapter.

27. These conditions are that the affiliates operate in the same country and same industry classification or are integral parts of the same business operation.

28. http://www.patentsview.org/web/.

29. For instance, the propensity to patent tends to be much higher in industries like IT and biotechnology than in less technologically dynamic domains, and it tends to be higher in manufacturing than in services. Simple comparisons of patent counts could therefore obscure changes in the true level of innovation across firms and technological fields. In regression analysis, however, the incorporation of firm and/or industry fixed effects can partially control for time-invariant differences across firms in their propensity to patent that stem from the fact that different firms are inventing in different technological domains characterized by different propensities to patent. Given our rich BEA data, we can also examine changes in the mix of R&D expenditure across affiliates, industries, countries, and time, which provide us with another window into the changing mix of inventive activities that provides a useful check on the potential biases present in patent data.

30. A technique typically used for merging two datasets with no common record linkage.

REFERENCES

Arora, Ashish, Lee Branstetter, and Chirantan Chatterjee. 2008. Strong Medicine: Patent Reform and the Emergence of a Research-Driven Pharmaceutical Industry in India. Paper prepared for NBER Conference on Location of Biopharmaceutical Activity, March 6–8.

Arora, Ashish, Lee G. Branstetter, and Matej Drev. 2013. "Going Soft: How the Rise of Software-Based Innovation Led to the Decline of Japan's IT Industry and the Resurgence of Silicon Valley," *Review of Economics and Statistics*, 95 (3): 757–75.

Arora, Ashish and Alfonso Gambardella, eds. 2005a. *From Underdogs to Tigers: The Rise and Growth of the Software Industry in Brazil, China, India, Ireland, and Israel* (Oxford University Press).

Arora, Ashish and Alfonso Gambardella. 2005b. "The Globalization of the Software Industry: Perspectives and Opportunities for Developed and Developing Countries," *Innovation Policy and the Economy*, 5: 1–32.

Bilir, Kamran. 2014. "Patent Laws, Product Life-Cycle Lengths, and Multinational Activity," *American Economic Review*, 104 (7): 1979–2013.

Bloom, Nicholas, Charles Jones, John Van Reenen, and Michael Webb. 2020. "Are Ideas Getting Harder to Find?" *American Economic Review*, 110 (4): 1104–44.

Bound, John, Breno Braga, Joseph M. Golden, and Gaurav Khanna. 2015. "Recruitment of Foreigners in the Market for Computer Scientists in the United States," *Journal of Labor Economics*, 33 (S1): S187–223.

Branstetter, Lee. 2018. China's Forced Technology Transfer Problem—and What to Do about It. PIIE Policy Brief 18-13. Washington: Peterson Institute for International Economics.

Branstetter, Lee and Kamal Saggi. 2011. "Intellectual Property Rights, Foreign Direct Investment, and Industrial Development," *Economic Journal*, 121/555 (September): 1161–91.

Branstetter, Lee and Daniel Sichel. 2017. *The Case for an American Productivity Revival.* PIIE Policy Brief 17-26. Washington: Peterson Institute for International Economics.

Branstetter, Lee G., Raymond Fisman, and C. Fritz Foley. 2006. "Do Stronger Intellectual Property Rights Increase International Technology Transfer? Empirical Evidence from U.S. Firm-Level Panel Data," *Quarterly Journal of Economics*, 121/1 (February): 321–49.

Branstetter, Lee, Matej Drev, and Namho Kwon. 2018. "Get with the Program: Software-Driven Innovation in Traditional Manufacturing," *Management Science*, 65 (2): 541–58.

Branstetter, Lee, Britta Glennon, and J. Bradford Jensen. 2018. "Knowledge Transfer Abroad: The Role of U.S. Inventors within Global R&D Networks," NBER Working Paper No. 24453.

Branstetter, Lee G., Britta Glennon, and J. Bradford Jensen. 2019a. "The IT Revolution and the Globalization of R&D," *Innovation Policy and the Economy*, 19: 1–37.

Branstetter, Lee G., Britta Glennon, and J. Bradford Jensen. 2019b. "The Rise of Global Innovation by U.S. Multinationals Poses Risks and Opportunities," Policy Brief 19-9, Peterson Institute for International Economics, June.

Branstetter, Lee, Guangwei Li, and Francisco Veloso. 2015. "The Rise of International Co-Invention." In *The Changing Frontier: Rethinking Science and Innovation Policy*, edited by Adam B. Jaffe and Benjamin F. Jones (University of Chicago Press): 135–68.

Branstetter, Lee, Guangwei Li, and Francisco Veloso. 2016. "Bridge to Excellence: The Impacts of International Co-invention on Multinational R&D in China," unpublished working paper.

Bresnahan, Timothy F. and M. Trajtenberg. 1995. "General Purpose Technologies 'Engines of Growth'?" *Journal of Econometrics*, 65 (1): 83–108.

Brynjolfsson, Erik and Andrew McAfee. 2014. *The Second Machine Age: Work, Progress, and Prosperity in an Age of Brilliant Technologies* (Cambridge, Mass.: W. W. Norton) .

Byrne, David M., John G. Fernald, and Marshall Reinsdorf. 2016. "Does the United States Have a Productivity Slowdown or a Measurement Problem?" *Brookings Papers on Economic Activity* (Spring): 109–82.

Byrne, David M., Stephen D. Oliner, and Daniel E. Sichel. 2018. "How Fast Are Semiconductor Prices Falling?" *Review of Income and Wealth*, 64 (3): 679–702.

Fernald, John G. and Charles Jones. 2014. "The Future of U.S. Economic Growth," *American Economic Review: Papers & Proceedings*, 104 (5): 44–49.

Foley, C. Fritz and William R. Kerr. 2013. "Ethnic Innovation and U.S. Multinational Firm Activity," *Management Science*, 59 (7): 1529–44.

Freeman, Richard B. and Wei Huang. 2015. "China's 'Great Leap Forward' in Science and Engineering." In *Global Mobility of Research Scientists: The Economics of Who Goes Where and Why*, edited by Aldo Guena (Cambridge, Mass.: Academic Press): 155–75.

Furman, Jeffrey L., Michael E. Porter, and Scott Stern. 2002. "The Determinants of National Innovative Capacity," *Research Policy*, 31: 899–933.

Glennon, Britta. 2019. "How Do Restrictions on High-Skilled Immigration Affect Offshoring? Evidence from the H-1B Program," unpublished working paper.

Gordon, Robert J. 2016. *The Rise and Fall of American Growth: The U.S. Standard of Living since the Civil War* (Princeton University Press).

Griffith, Rachel, Rupert Harrison, and John Van Reenen. 2006. "How Special Is the Special Relationship: Using the Impact of U.S. R&D Spillovers on U.K. Firms as a Test of Technology Sourcing," *American Economic Review*, 96 (5): 1859–75.

Hall, Bronwyn H., Adam B. Jaffe, and Manuel Trajtenberg. 2001. "The NBER Patent Citations Data File: Lessons, Insights and Methodological Tools," NBER Working Paper No. 8498.

Helpman, Elhanan and Manuel Trajtenberg. 1998. A Time to Sow and a Time to Reap: Growth Based on General Purpose Technologies. In *General Purpose Technologies and Economic Growth*, edited by Elhanan Helpman (MIT Press): 55–83.

Hufbauer, Gary Clyde, Theodore H. Moran, and Lindsay Oldenski, assisted by Martin Vieiro. 2013. *Outward Foreign Direct Investment and U.S. Exports, Jobs, and R&D: Implications for U.S. Policy*. Policy Analyses in International Economics 101. Washington: Peterson Institute for International Economics.

Jones, Benjamin F. 2009. "The Burden of Knowledge and the 'Death of the Renaissance Man': Is Innovation Getting Harder?" *Review of Economic Studies*, 76: 283–317.

Jones, Benjamin F. 2014. "The Human Capital Stock: A Generalized Approach," *American Economic Review*, 104/11 (November).

Jones, Benjamin. 2014. "The Knowledge Trap: Human Capital and Development Reconsidered," NBER Working Paper No. 14138.

Kerr, Sari Pekkala and William R Kerr. 2018. "Global Collaborative Patents," *Economic Journal*, 128 (612): 1–38.

Krugman, Paul. 1992. *The Age of Diminished Expectations: U.S. Economic Policy in the 1990s* (MIT Press).

Macher, Jeffrey T., and David C. Mowery, eds. 2008. *Innovation in Global Industries: U.S. Firms Competing in a New World (Collected Studies)*. (Washington: National Academies Press).

National Science Board. 2016. *Science and Engineering Indicators 2016* (NSB-2016-1). Arlington, Va.: National Science Foundation.

Syverson, Chad. 2017. "Challenges to Mismeasurement Explanations for the U.S. Productivity Slowdown," *Journal of Economic Perspectives*, 31 (2): 165–86.

9

Multinationals in the Digital Economy

BENJAMIN EDELMAN

Modern digital services largely come from multinational corporations (MNCs) whose size and scope are unprecedented. It has not always been this way. Just a few decades ago, users typically turned to local firms for most kinds of information technology (IT). And, historically, software was known for its low barriers to entry and the quick rise of startups and small firms. This chapter examines the forces contributing to the rise of digital MNCs, as well as the challenges they face.

THE DIGITAL REVOLUTION AND MULTINATIONALS

The digital revolution has affected nearly every business. For some, improved technology calls for adjusting supply chains and reworking operations to increase efficiency. For others, new technologies bring new competitors. In certain sectors, new technology effectively reworks an entire business, which must now operate digitally.

As digital technologies permeate MNCs, the impacts in many respects match digital technologies at domestic firms. For most, the fundamental benefits are better collection and processing of more information, and greater ability to find patterns and insights in that information. But these capabilities distinctively benefit large firms. For example, large firms typically must allocate inventory across multiple and distant facilities, and so must collect information that cannot be observed from any single location.

Digital tools are massively faster and more accurate than the paper-based processes firms used decades ago and yield better analyses and more prudent business decisions. Large firms also must track customer purchases to predict demand and ensure adequate supply. Here, too, digital solutions offer major advances—tracking more data, more quickly, at lower cost, and with greater opportunity for analysis and insight. Meanwhile, large firms manage workforces spread across numerous sites, and digital methods bring efficiency to both the assignment of employees (how many staff will be needed at a given site on a given day and time) and other operational tasks (for instance, ensuring that staff are properly paid for time worked). Large firms also need data and analysis to rigorously assess myriad marketing efforts over numerous regions, while mom-and-pop marketers often have an intuitive sense of what advertising strategies work best. Ultimately, the size and scope of a large firm are a clear match for the breadth, accountability, and control provided by effective digital tools. MNCs, being especially large, tend to particularly enjoy all these benefits.

Indeed, large firms have made, and continue to make, striking investments in digital technologies. For example, in 2018, Walmart spent an estimated US$11.7 billion on IT, including handheld devices and advanced cash registers for store staff, as well as increased robotics for both warehouses and stores.[1] This amount totaled approximately 2 percent of company revenue, about four times what the company spent on new stores, expansions, relocations, and remodels.[2] Clearly, Walmart views digital investments as important. While Walmart is distinctive in its overall size, other firms usually spent more on IT as a proportion of revenue. A survey of IT spending found that, across a range of industries, even the firms in the 25th percentile spent more than 1 percent of firm revenue on IT, while top-spending financial services firms spent more than 11 percent of revenue on IT, and top-spending health care firms spent more than 5 percent of revenue on IT. Table 9-1 summarizes the survey results.

It is easy to shrug off multinationals' digital functions as routine and unremarkable. But the firms have gained significant advantages from faster or better implementation of digital technologies. Airlines' early use of IT offers many notable examples. Consider American Airlines' 1970s efforts to provide SABRE computer terminals to interested travel agencies. Participating travel agents could browse and confirm American flights nearly instantly, whereas booking another airline's flights required making a phone call and often waiting several hours for confirmation that the desired seats

TABLE 9-1. IT Spending as a Percentage of Revenue by Industry

Industry	IT spending range (25th to 75th percentiles)
Discrete manufacturing	1.4% to 3.2%
Financial services	4.4% to 11.4%
High tech	2.6% to 4.7%
Retail	1.2% to 3.0%
Health care	3.0% to 5.9%

Source: Frank Scavo and others, "IT Spending as a Percentage of Revenue by Industry, Company Size, and Region," Computer Economics—Metrics for IT management, 2019, www.computereconomics.com/article.cfm?id=2626.

Note: Based on survey of 232 IT organizations in the United States and Canada, stratified between small, mid-sized, and large organizations. Firms with less than US$1 million of IT spending were excluded.

were available. American reported that its first two hundred travel agent installations yielded a 500 percent return on investment.[3] American benefited from its early efforts at yield management, employing digital technology to adjust prices so that each seat was sold for as much as possible. As of 1992, American estimated that yield management added more than US$500 million per year to its profits.[4] In comparison, American's operating profit for the three-year period from 1991 to 1993 averaged US$168 million per year—so without yield management, the company would have posted substantial losses in those years. For both travel agent connections and yield management, American enjoyed particularly large benefits because, at the outset, competitors lacked similar methods.

More recently, digital technologies have been often most striking when they run amok. Continuing with the airlines as an example, consider the chaos when a reservation system fails. A power outage in 2017 disabled British Airways computers and stranded 75,000 passengers.[5] When Delta Air Lines' operations computers failed for five hours in 2016, two thousand flights were canceled at a cost to the company of approximately US$150 million.[6] Perhaps the most harmful digital failures are those that linger for months or years without significant attention. While Walmart touts its efficient supply chain that predicts inventory needs and avoids stock outages,[7] analysts criticized struggling retailers Kmart and Sears for, among other things, inventory mismatch that kept unpopular items on shelves and left shelves bare of items customers were more likely to buy.[8] Clearly, Kmart and Sears faced a range of operational and strategic challenges. But better IT—and better use of IT—would have offered the beginning of a path forward.

Airlines and retailers ordinarily are not thought of as core digital firms. But as these examples show, digital strengths can offer distinctive advantages, while digital failures can undermine a firm's value. The balance of this chapter will look at firms we might call "core digital MNCs," distinctive in that they build digital offerings as their primary product or service.

CORE DIGITAL MULTINATIONALS

The obvious digital multinationals are the tech titans that have become established household names: Amazon, Apple, Facebook, Google, and Microsoft. These firms provide a range of partially overlapping software and services that have transformed information technology, communication, and marketing. Box 9-1 lists key offerings from these firms. Box 9-2 presents selected milestones in digital technologies—reminding us how far we have

BOX 9-1. Selected Offerings from Digital Titans

Amazon: Retail, marketplace, cloud computing, advertising services, streaming

Apple: Phone hardware and software, computer hardware and operating systems

Facebook: Social networking, advertising services, communication tools

Google: Search engine, advertising services, phone software, communication tools

Microsoft: Computer operating systems, productivity tools, developer tools, cloud computing

Note: Each firm has numerous additional offerings not listed.

Source: Author.

come and how quickly. The figures reveal a pronounced shift from business services (such as early computing for business and government operations) to leisure (such as media and entertainment).

The largest digital firms have enjoyed a striking rise in size, prowess, and overall power. Table 9-2 lists the top worldwide firms by market capitalization, with core digital multinationals now occupying seven of the top ten spots. Figure 9-1 plots the market capitalization of selected firms fairly classified as core digital multinationals, showing their rapid growth. These high valuations imply that capital markets think these digital MNCs are likely to remain profitable and are here to stay. These high valuations are also striking because core digital multinationals tend not to employ large numbers of workers. Table 9-3 ranks the top global employers, with only two digital firms present among the top ten. The only U.S. digital MNC with both high valuation and high employment is Amazon. Amazon's presence on both lists results from its business model: it not only runs a website where customers make purchases, but also stores goods in its own warehouses and increasingly delivers goods via its own trucks—providing significant employment. In contrast, other digital MNCs tend to forgo warehousing and delivery; for example, Google and Facebook hold no inventory and deliver no goods, instead leaving those tasks to their advertisers.

FACTORS CAUSING THE RISE AND PERSISTENCE OF DIGITAL MULTINATIONALS

Multinational corporations dominate many parts of economy, with distinctive dominance in software, because they can ship their final products reliably, instantly, and cost-free. Furthermore, the costs of creating software are mostly fixed, with little to no cost for each additional customer. As a result, any local firm's effort to make its own version would be, in a certain sense, both duplicative and inefficient. These factors provide reason to expect that the digital economy will remain, and increasingly be dominated by, multinational firms—with correspondingly fewer digital services confined by national boundaries.

Meanwhile, standardization across countries, providing the ability to communicate with and interoperate with others, offers significant benefits. Standardization begins with hardware: two decades ago, world travelers struggled with a dozen-plus different telephone sockets used around the world, but Ethernet connectors (for wired internet) and WiFi are global stan-

BOX 9-2. Selected Milestones in Digital Technologies

1969 ARPANET, a predecessor to the internet, begins operation with funding from the U.S. government

1979 The VisiCalc electronic spreadsheet launches, demonstrating the benefit of personal computers in the workplace

1981 IBM releases its Personal Computer, with 16KB of user memory

1983 Cellular telephone service is introduced

1989 British computer scientist Tim Berners-Lee proposes a distributed information system that became what we now call the World Wide Web

1994 Netscape releases version 1.0 of its Navigator web browser

1995 Microsoft releases Windows 95, with multitasking to run multiple programs simultaneously

1998 E-commerce takes off in the United States, and as many as 50 million U.S. households purchase products over the internet

1998 Google begins public usage of its search engine

2000 Concerns about the new century and millennium spark upgrades to IT infrastructure, but few significant disruptions occur

dards that work equally everywhere. File formats have similarly been standardized: the Unicode character set lets a modern digital document present text in substantially any language used anywhere in the world.[9] At the dawn of the personal computer era, U.S. firms focused their efforts on domestic customers and largely supported only English, leaving firms outside the United States to devise software for other languages. For example, in 1978, Toshiba released the JW-10 word processor for Japanese users, including an innovative solution for phonetic entry of the 40,000-plus kanji characters in Japanese writing.[10] Two decades later, Microsoft Office accommodates substantially all languages while serving as a de facto global standard. Users in

2001	Struggling to sell programs that users install on their computers, software developer Concur reinvents itself as "software as a service"—running programs on internet servers
2007	Apple releases the first iPhone, with a touch screen and support for viewing most web pages
2007	Netflix mails its billionth DVD and announces its planned shift to streaming video delivery
2008	HTC releases the first smartphone running Google Android
2009	Airbnb begins its peer-to-peer booking service for overnight accommodations
2010	Google's YouTube reaches 1 billion video views per day and twenty-four hours of video uploaded per minute
2010	Apple releases iPad tablet, with a larger screen and extended battery life
2013	Uber and Lyft launch electronic ride hailing with casual drivers driving their own cars
2017	Netflix achieves as many U.S. subscriptions as all U.S. cable TV networks combined

Source: Author.

Japan no longer need a special "Japanese-compatible" computer or software, because standard global computers can do the job.

Online services similarly demonstrate the benefits of efficient global firms. In principle, each community could devise its own classified ad marketplace, but the Craigslist goliath offers standardized categories and functionality in seven hundred cities across seventy countries. As social networks began, some countries favored locally developed versions of the "friend," messaging, and photo features now routine at Facebook, but Facebook ultimately subsumed those competitors almost everywhere. Multinational standard-bearers benefited from the cost-effectiveness of building their features once

TABLE 9-2. Largest Global Firms by Market Capitalization

Rank	Company name	Location	Sector	Market cap (US$B)
1	Microsoft	U.S.	Technology	US$905
2	Apple	U.S.	Technology	US$896
3	Amazon	U.S.	Technology	US$875
4	Alphabet	U.S.	Technology	US$817
5	Berkshire Hathaway	U.S.	Financials	US$494
6	Facebook	U.S.	Technology	US$476
7	Alibaba	China	Technology	US$472
8	Tencent	China	Technology	US$438
9	Johnson & Johnson	U.S.	Health care	US$372
10	Exxon Mobil	U.S.	Oil and gas	US$342
11	JP Morgan Chase & Co.	U.S.	Financials	US$331
12	Visa	U.S.	Financials	US$314
13	Nestle	Switzerland	Consumer goods	US$292
14	ICBC	China	Financials	US$287
15	Walmart	U.S.	Consumer goods	US$280
16	Bank of America	U.S.	Financials	US$266
17	Procter & Gamble	U.S.	Consumer goods	US$266
18	Royal Dutch Shell	UK	Oil and gas	US$256
19	Novartis	Switzerland	Health care	US$245
20	Verizon Communications	U.S.	Technology	US$244

Note: Market capitalization as of March 31, 2019. Technology companies shown in bold.

Source: Author, adapted from Bloomberg with PwC Analysis, "Global Top 100 Companies 2019," at section "Top 100 global companies 1–20," July 2019, www.pwc.com/gx/en/audit-services/publications/assets/global-top-100-companies-2019.pdf.

FIGURE 9-1. Growth in Market Capitalization of Core Digital Multinationals

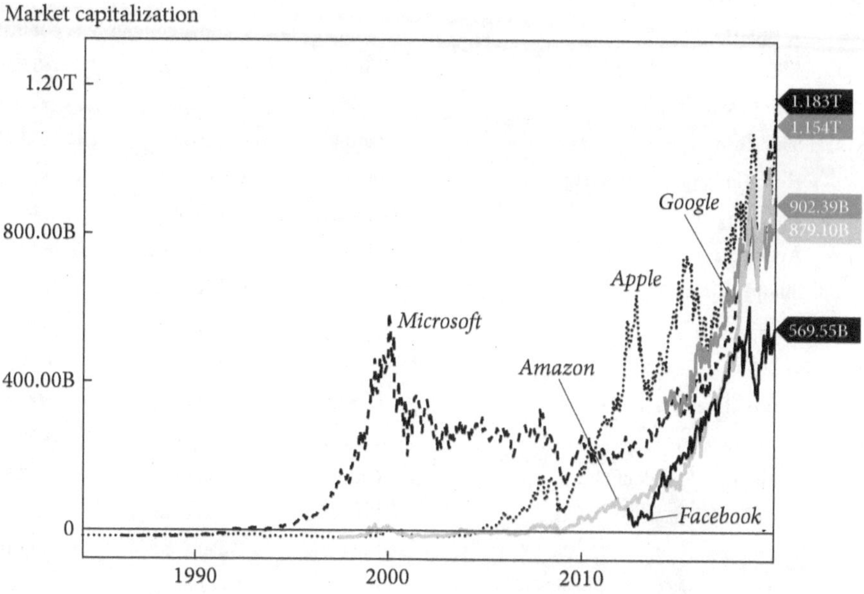

Note: Chart shows each firm's market capitalization, beginning with its IPO. The labels in the right margin give market capitalizations of the respective firms as of November 25, 2019.

Source: Adapted from Ycharts.com

to deploy globally: a classified ad site that served a small city would struggle to justify building a complex category structure, cross-linking, or neighborhood filters. But Craigslist can build these features once and offer them globally, so even small markets get them automatically and with near-zero cost. Furthermore, fundamental requirements for general-purpose tools have been similar across countries. The same features that make Craigslist useful in Chicago make it useful in Cairo. Local or national digital service providers struggle to match these capabilities, which, in turn, encourages users to switch to the feature-rich offerings from multinational firms.

FACTORS LIMITING DIGITAL MULTINATIONALS

While the provision of digital services clearly gravitates toward multinationals, some offsetting factors encourage local production. Local firms sometimes have materially greater unit revenues or lower costs, either of which can give local firms an advantage over multinationals.

TABLE 9-3. Largest Global Employers

Rank	Company name	Location	Sector	Employees
1	Walmart	U.S.	Consumer goods	2,200,000
2	China National Petroleum	China	Oil and gas	1,382,401
3	China Post Group	China	Postal	935,191
4	State Grid	China	Energy	917,717
5	Hon Hai Precision Industry	Taiwan	Technology	667,680
6	Volkswagen	Germany	Automotive	664,496
7	Amazon	U.S.	Technology	647,500
8	Sinopec Group	China	Oil and gas	619,151
9	Compass Group	U.S.	Food	595,841
10	U.S. Postal Service	U.S.	Postal	565,802
11	Huaxia Life Insurance	China	Financials	500,000
12	Deutsche Post	Germany	Postal	499,018
13	Agricultural Bank of China	China	Financials	477,526
14	Jardine Matheson	China	Financials	469,000
15	Gazprom	Russia	Oil and gas	466,100
16	China Mobile Communications	China	Technology	462,046
17	Accenture	U.S.	Professional services	459,000
18	Kroger	U.S.	Food	453,000
19	Industrial and Commercial Bank of China	China	Financials	449,296
20	Aviation Industry Corp. of China	China	Aerospace	446,613

Note: Data as of fiscal year 2018. Technology companies shown in bold.

Source: Author, adapted from Statista, "The World's 50 Largest Companies Based on Number of Employees in 2018."

A local firm's revenue advantage typically comes from a better understanding of customer requirements, letting the firm generate greater revenue from the same users. We have seen some evidence of the importance of local services distinctively tuned to local tastes or local requirements. For example, Japanese users seem to prefer "full" screens (with more text, including numerous advertisements), compared to U.S. users often enjoying sparse screens. By all indications, this difference historically helped Japan's e-commerce platforms hold off global competitors. A multinational competing in Japan would miss the greater revenue from intensive advertising, putting itself at a perpetual disadvantage.

Local firms' cost advantage can come from a superior ability to understand and comply with local regulatory requirements. Regulation was a particularly prominent factor in China, where the government banned various sensitive terms and subjects and required removing certain material. In many circumstances, China even required online services to link users' online activities to their offline identifies; for example, by asking users to upload photos of themselves holding government-issued ID cards.[11] These requirements were distinctively difficult for global firms. First, these requirements differed from standard practices elsewhere, so complying would require building all manner of features for use solely in China. Despite the obvious appeal of China's huge market, global firms often viewed these features as a lower priority, since they would not be used elsewhere. Second, employees at global firms tended to find China's requirements distasteful—in tension with Western norms of free expression and unfettered communication. Collectively, these factors helped preserve and strengthen China's national services and prevent consolidation onto global platforms. The limits on MNCs' ability to operate in China's market, the large size of the market, and the country's ample technical talent positioned local firms to build their own versions of internet standard-bearers. For example, Chinese users tend to turn to Baidu rather than Google, WeChat rather than Facebook, Taobao rather than eBay, and similarly to national replacements for most of the well-known services otherwise used worldwide. But Chinese services need not stop at mimicking the functions of MNC services. In numerous areas, Chinese firms developed faster, better, or simply differently. For example, WeChat went well beyond features familiar to Facebook users; WeChat includes modules for paying bills, ordering food, and online shopping.

Local firms can also enjoy a cost advantage from local servers, which provide faster service than remote servers. Historically, this difference was most important for services with large files (especially video) or latency-sensitive functions (where speed of transmission from user to server and back was particularly important, such as when editing a document on a server). But global firms have found ways to address these needs. For one, improved software design reduces pressure on these technical requirements. Rather than send each keystroke to a remote server before it is shown on-screen (as was standard in early remote-computing services such as Telnet), edits can be made locally and synchronized to and from a server periodically (as Dropbox, Google Drive, and Microsoft OneDrive do). Furthermore, MNCs can arrange local servers when improved performance is important. (Google says it has fourteen data centers on four continents.[12] Microsoft offers Azure cloud hosting in fifty data centers on all six inhabited continents.[13]) Finally, "content distribution networks," such as Akamai and CloudFlare, help even small sites get the benefits of local servers without the cost of placing servers in myriad locations around the world.[14]

One might also question the need for goliath MNCs, because software has low barriers to entry. Proponents of this view emphasize that software tends not to be capital-intensive, leveling the playing field for startups and already established firms. There is some evidence in support of this perspective, including some large offerings that originated with small teams and little capital. (Mark Zuckerberg, Facebook cofounder and chief executive, personally coded much of the company's initial site from his dorm room—using his own know-how instead of raising capital to pay professional developers. A decade later, communication service WhatsApp needed a staff of just nineteen to provide communication service to 465 million users.[15]) Nonetheless, experience reveals that successful firms quickly evolve into MNCs providing global service from a centralized location. Simple as Facebook might have been at its outset, the company now employs approximately forty thousand people,[16] from engineers to product managers to sales staff, along with some fifteen thousand "moderator" contractors (who evaluate sensitive or disputed content).[17] This scale could hardly be more different from a dorm room hobby. Doing the job right—amply understanding users' and advertisers' requirements in order to build services they value; evaluating processes and partners to protect privacy; examining and removing improper material—has proven difficult at every turn. If it can be done at all, it appears to require the scale that only an MNC can bring. (To be sure, there is no consensus that Facebook does it well.)

The bottom line is that the digital economy is more centralized than intuition might have predicted.

LABOR AND TRADE

MNCs' entry into tech services notably implies increased remote production. Of course, remote production is nothing new; factories have long produced cars, electronics, and even prefabricated homes for export. But remotely produced software portends remote production of an ever-growing share of value in the economy. Previously, local advertising supported local news media. (Think of a Cleveland car dealership advertising in a Cleveland newspaper or on a Cleveland radio station.) These days, remotely produced advertising services targeted to local users can yield funding for remote production of other online services. (Consider that same car dealership advertising on Google or Facebook.) Changes in advertising and media bring the loss of reliable middle-class jobs—reporters, radio announcers—along with weighty questions about the future of journalism. But changes need not stop at the media. If a small business stores its financial records in online accounting software, it may prefer remote accountants rather than local accountants working on site. Digital transformation similarly destabilizes the local loop that previously kept most advertising expenditures within a local economy: for instance, a local car dealership paid a newspaper that employed a reporter who bought a car at that dealership. But when a dealership advertises on Google or Facebook, funds flow to software engineers in Silicon Valley, who are unlikely to shop at that car dealership.

Historically, customer service jobs appeared safe from transfer overseas, as face-to-face service was widely seen as fundamental. But this, too, is beginning to change, thanks to superior software and telecommunications. For some years, a call to a bank, credit card issuer, or airline could be answered by a representative half a world away. These days, the intercom at a fast-food restaurant's drive-through window may connect to a clerk in another state, or, for that matter, another country.[18] With cheap communications and an easy mechanism for that clerk to enter the order into reliable IT, the clerk need no longer be on site. Here, too, the digital economy further expands what jobs can be outsourced, to where, and with what ease.

A potential offsetting factor is that digital tools can facilitate local innovation and employment. Consider tech tools productively customized or modified in-country to make custom software. Historically, Microsoft embodied this model through its tools division, offering such systems as Visual Basic, which let nontechnical staff build software for their companies' idiosyncratic requirements. Historically, Microsoft's tools began with the basics—providing pre-built user interface components and standardized methods for file storage, so developers could focus on business logic. Google subsequently added higher-level services, such as mapping functions, to facilitate the presentation and analysis of geographic data. Under this approach, firms seek to distinguish themselves through software and business processes embodied in software. For example, a mom-and-pop appliance repair shop could deliver superior service not just through friendly and skilled technicians but through custom software that helps the firm recognize repeat customers and recurring problems. More recently, Amazon, Google, and Microsoft all have been providing software libraries to help software developers harness the power of artificial intelligence—giving a developer many of the advanced capabilities used by large firms without the need to understand the statistics and data science that support these methods.

Nonetheless, custom software seems to be an imperfect fit for most customers. By all indications, companies largely want pre-built software. A goliath like UPS may want to schedule and dispatch its own trucks, and may perceive that it can gain competitive advantage from a better algorithm or from software uniquely tailored to its requirements. But a typical mom-and-pop appliance repair shop just wants a program to tell its half-dozen technicians which customers to visit each day. Rare is the small firm inclined to design and build this software itself. More often, a small firm prefers to license an off-the-shelf solution such as a standard suite for scheduling and dispatching field staff. The software—and the value-add it brings—thus end up being remotely produced.

REGULATION

Initially, some companies and analysts thought that multinational tech companies might not be subject to local laws. If a company had no servers or staff within a country, it often saw little need to comply with that country's laws. In an influential early essay, political activist John Perry Barlow declared that not only were governments "not welcome" in cyberspace, but they would have no ability to enforce their rules there.[19]

An early dispute between Yahoo and French activists demonstrates the broad contours of such disputes. In 2000, complainant LICRA (the International League against Racism and Anti-Semitism) challenged Yahoo Auctions' sales of Nazi memorabilia. LICRA charged that these sales violated Article R645-1 of the French Criminal Code and were, in LICRA's view, an attack on the cohesiveness of French society. But Yahoo saw itself as a U.S. company, noting that its servers were located entirely in the United States, its services were primarily aimed at U.S. residents, and that U.S. courts would not enforce any judgment arising out of these facts. The French court ruled for LICRA, noting that French law was clear, that the auctions at issue were open to bidders from any country, including France, and, most of all, that Yahoo was clearly aware that French residents used its auction site. In particular, the court noted that Yahoo showed French-language advertisements on its pages when they were accessed from computers in France. With Yahoo able to recognize French users for the purpose of showing targeted advertising, the court thought Yahoo should similarly restrict French users from accessing, not to mention bidding in, the offending auctions. Rather than continue to fight in France, Yahoo brought its own lawsuit in the United States, seeking an order that the French ruling was inapplicable and unenforceable in the United States. The district court was receptive, finding the underlying French law to be inconsistent with the First Amendment to the U.S. Constitution, but the U.S. Court of Appeals for the Ninth Circuit pointed out that U.S. courts lacked personal jurisdiction over LICRA, a French nongovernmental organization with no ties to the United States.[20] Meanwhile, Yahoo chose to disallow the sale of Nazi memorabilia from its service worldwide, and in 2007 Yahoo shut most of its auctions site worldwide. These developments effectively mooted the dispute, yet the proceedings were instructive in revealing the nuances of cross-border disputes involving multinational tech firms.

More recently, MNC tech firms have come to recognize the power of national sovereignty. First, MNCs typically find they need significant resources in most countries to deliver the best possible service. Often, MNCs want servers in-country to provide rapid and cost-effective data transmission. This is particularly important for services with high sensitivity to delay (such as online applications) and high data volume (like video).

Second, MNC tech firms increasingly employ staff within most countries. For example, as of 2019, Google reported seventy offices in fifty countries.[21] As online services have become more widely used, sales efforts are correspondingly broader—which calls for a larger sales staff, including sales staff in most countries where advertisers are located. When selling advertising to car dealerships, dermatologists, lawn care services, and countless others, a large in-country sales force is far more productive, because of its local knowledge and cultural and language connections. Effectively, that requires MNC tech titans to employ at least its sales staff worldwide. Google's U.K. team is instructive: of 3,658 Google employees in the U.K. in 2018, 1,451 were in marketing and sales[22]—despite the company's substantial research and development and engineering offices. In countries where MNC tech firms lack research and development and engineering offices, sales staff represent an even larger proportion of in-country employees (often, substantially all).

National sovereignty considerations have further grown in power, because many countries have found ways to block access to MNC sites and services they dislike. At least thirty-nine countries have blocked material they find unlawful or unwanted.[23] (Table 9-4 presents a list.) Some of these countries have mixed records on freedom of expression. (Fifteen of these thirty-nine countries appear in the bottom 20 percent of the Reporters without Borders 2019 World Press Freedom Index.) Other countries are widely perceived to support freedom of expression but nonetheless block certain material. A third set of countries increasingly challenge the historic U.S. norm of tech platforms hosting and distributing all manner of content, and seek restrictions on information disfavored under national law.[24] Blocking technology remains imperfect—often suffering false positives, such as blocking entire websites to disable individual pages.[25] Furthermore, a country typically incurs an up-front cost to begin blocking—compelling all internet service providers in the country to receive and process block requests,

TABLE 9-4. Countries that Have Blocked Material on the Internet

Armenia	Moldova
Azerbaijan	Morocco
Bahrain	Oman
Belarus	Pakistan
Burma (Myanmar)	Qatar
China	Russia
Colombia	Saudi Arabia
Ethiopia	Singapore
Gaza and the West Bank	South Korea
Georgia	Sudan
India	Syria
Indonesia	Tajikistan
Iran	Thailand
Italy	Turkey
Jordan	Turkmenistan
Kazakhstan	United Arab Emirates
Kuwait	Uzbekistan
Kyrgyzstan	Vietnam
Libya	Yemen
Mauritania	

Source: Adapted from OpenNet Initiative, Internet Filtering Data, https://opennet.net/research/data

or redesigning the country's internet infrastructure to send data through checkpoints where government equipment can block disfavored communications. But as more countries implement these changes, the path for others becomes increasingly clear. Today's MNCs cannot assume that their online presence is unblockable.

Indeed, governments have developed increasingly flexible and multifaceted strategies to impose their requirements on MNCs. As discussed, governments can block access to disfavored sites. Countries can increase their likelihood of imposing restrictions globally by seeking to seize the domain name that makes a website available worldwide. Best-known in this vein is the United States' 2012 seizure of Megaupload, a filesharing site accused of copyright infringement.[26] The United States is particularly well positioned to block domain names, because many are registered in the United States. (Indeed, the registries for the largest top-level domains, including .com, .net, and .org, reside in the United States, and U.S. courts have held that domains can be seized at the location of their registry.[27])

Governments also can pressure MNCs via legislative hearings and, potentially, new laws. Dissatisfied with MNCs using material from Spanish publishers, the Spanish government in 2014 effectively required search engines to make certain payments to news sites.[28] Such new laws do not always work perfectly. Indeed, Spain's 2014 approach let search engines avoid the payments by closing their news businesses in Spain, as Google did in response to the law. Nonetheless, when a MNC's tactics raise urgent concerns that draw legislators' attention, the legislative power gives governments more power than skeptics initially thought.

Finally, governments can invoke traditional law enforcement mechanisms. Box 9-3 lists selected fines against digital MNCs. In important respects, these mechanisms work especially well against the largest companies. On one hand, MNCs have ample resources to fight the fines, including vigorous opposition on the merits as well as procedural wrangling designed to cause delay. But when legal avenues are exhausted, MNCs have little choice but to comply. In that regard, MNCs are significantly different from tiny firms that are more likely to change names and shift tactics. For example, when litigation led to the demise of Napster,[29] copycats created Grokster and dozens more, and piracy continued unabated.[30] In contrast, large companies have much less ability to defy the law.

Nonetheless, many MNCs can avoid laws they do not like, and in a

BOX 9-3. Selected Fines against Digital MNCs

March 2004—European Commission fined Microsoft €497 million for withholding information as to Windows interoperability and for including Media Player in Windows.

February 2008—European Commission fined Microsoft €899 million for charging unreasonable royalty rates for information pertaining to Windows interoperability.

May 2009—European Commission fined Intel €1.06 billion for pricing CPUs to discourage computer manufacturers and retailers from using and selling competing chips.

August 2012—FTC fined Google US$22.5 million for circumventing Apple privacy protections to collect more information about users.

March 2013—European Commission fined Microsoft €561 million for malfunctions in the screen that let users choose a preferred web browser.

June 2017—European Commission fined Google €2.4 billion for favoring Google Shopping in Google's search results.

July 2018—European Commission fined Google €4.3 billion for blocking competing mobile operating systems, including requiring mobile device manufacturers to install certain Google apps if they wanted other Google services, banning manufacturers from selling devices based on modified versions of open-source Android software, and giving financial incentives for exclusivity.

March 2019—European Commission fined Google €1.49 billion for requiring exclusivity from certain online publishers that showed Google ads.

July 2019—FTC fined Facebook US$5 billion for failing to protect users' data from third parties, serving ads using phone numbers that users had provided only for security, and falsely telling users that its face recognition software was turned off by default.

Note: Each item describes the violation as alleged by the corresponding enforcement agency. The companies disputed the allegations. This figure lists only a fraction of enforcement actions. The listed digital MNCs, and others, also faced numerous enforcement actions in a variety of countries on multiple other subjects.

Source: Author.

range of situations can largely do what they want, despite laws and regulations. Uber is an informative example, though in some respects an outlier. Uber was repeatedly found to violate national or local law as it dispatched vehicles without the licenses and formalities some jurisdictions sought to require. A city or country seeking to rein in Uber could order it to cease operations, but often Uber continued anyway,[31] correctly perceiving that governments would be ill equipped to stop it. With most Uber engineers and systems in its California headquarters or otherwise out of reach, local regulators could not attach Uber assets or directly enforce their rules as they might against an ordinary local firm. An aggressive jurisdiction could pursue criminal sanctions against local Uber managers, and indeed France briefly jailed two Uber regional managers in 2015.[32] But most jurisdictions seemed to consider that approach excessive and disproportional—reinforcing Uber's sense that it could proceed without significant risks. Uber often pushed for the revision of laws it deemed unwelcome or ill advised—and, more often than not, it prevailed.[33] YouTube's experience is broadly similar: despite controversial videos prompting partial or complete bans in at least twenty-six countries,[34] YouTube retained its overall business model, including receiving and distributing videos without advance human review. Courts may criticize aspects of YouTube's operation as improper, harmful, or unlawful, but so far, they have found no practical way to significantly change its approach.

TAX

The tax questions posed by multinational technology companies are broadly similar to other tax questions for large firms. Often, the most fundamental question is where value is created, and thus where it should be properly taxed. But large technology companies have a particularly clear opportunity to use transfer pricing (for instance, when a parent company sells goods or services to a subsidiary) to assign value to low-tax jurisdictions. Notably, for most technology companies, value results in large part from the underlying intellectual property, which, as an intangible, can be placed almost anywhere. Compare classic manufacturing, where the location of a factory is usually importantly constrained by factors such as transportation costs, location of inputs, and location of customers.

Scott Dyreng (Duke University), Michelle Hanlon (Massachusetts Institute of Technology), and Dhammika Dharmapala (University of Chicago) further explore questions of multinational tax in chapters 10 and 11 in this volume.

INNOVATION AND VALUE

Analysts sometimes remark on both the high value of tech startups and the ease of starting them. Indeed, in 1938, Bill Hewlett and David Packard began developing their first product in a garage in Palo Alto, California. More recently, Amazon and Google continued the tradition of reducing overhead by beginning in suburban garages. As mentioned, Facebook's Zuckerberg personally wrote much of Facebook's code alone in his dorm room. Facebook was an instant hit across the Harvard campus before the company paid a dollar of rent. Capital requirements have declined further because modern startups rent servers in the cloud, paying by the hour for computer capacity as needed rather than buying servers up-front.

Despite historically low barriers to entry, analysts subsequently observed that the greatest tech innovations now come from tech giants. One might cite self-driving cars, but also balloons providing internet access to remote areas, voice assistants, facial recognition, and cloud computing. Furthermore, critics suggest that established tech firms tend to favor their own products; Google hesitating to link to other companies' review sites or travel tools;[35] Facebook trying to prolong users' sessions in its tool rather than send users to publishers' sites.[36] In this view, the prototypical startup in a garage increasingly fades into the past. Indeed, by some metrics, a declining share of tech-firm value flows to startups, and a growing share to giants.[37] Investors increasingly counsel startups to design their products to stay out of the way of tech giants.[38]

The growing power of MNC tech giants shifts the tone of discussion about their regulation. By all indications, countries increasingly perceive themselves as subject to the whims of tech giants rather than vice versa. Tech incumbents previously trumpeted low barriers to entry and new startups as reasons why governments need not fear incumbent firms' size and power, but that argument increasingly rings hollow. For MNCs, these developments are a mixed bag. On one hand, large business opportunities truly benefit from MNCs' scale. At the same time, governments' increased concerns compel greater accountability to ensure that MNCs truly advance shared values. Ultimately, these developments set virtuous incentives—for MNCs to both set lofty goals and then deliver on them.

LOOKING AHEAD

MNC tech giants have brought undeniable advances. Not long ago, it would have been inconceivable to search the world's information with the scale and insight Google routinely provides. Self-publishing videos on YouTube, or almost anything on Facebook, gives unprecedented opportunities to an army of enthusiasts—a new band seeking an audience, a handyman teaching do-it-yourselfers, or a teacher explaining elementary mathematics. And Amazon delivers an unmatched assortment of products at speed and cost that were, until recently, unthinkable. Consumers relish these offerings, and clamor for more.

Yet the tech backlash is equally undeniable. Millions of users install special web browsers or plug-ins designed to impede advertising and tracking they see as inappropriate. A growing meme celebrates deleting Facebook accounts. Regulators the world over identified a range of tech-giant practices they seek to change, and every tech giant seems to carry a giant regulatory bullseye.

While regulators raise diverse concerns, questions of international boundaries loom large. European regulators wonder why so few European companies are leaders in tech—and what it means if European consumers and firms must rely on, and are obliged to pay for, American technologies. Meanwhile, American tech firms criticize European requirements for privacy, competition, and more. In parallel, China built its own tech titans, making it independent of global standards but hindering some kinds of cross-border communication and commerce. The international openness that allowed the rise of global tech titans—and the internet itself—seems increasingly tenuous.

Separately, the growth of tech giants raises questions about where MNC dominance will lead. Whatever their preferences, many critics seem to have made peace with computer software that establishes global standards and disproportionately emanates from the United States. But the tech giants continually seek to expand. Witness Google's moves toward driverless cars (via its parent company, Alphabet), Amazon's moves toward both movie production and logistics, and Facebook's moves toward internet access—

each among countless others. For these firms, these are logical extensions of their supply and distribution chains, and opportunities to continue to grow to meet investor expectations. Yet these expansions also bring new kinds of opposition and increasingly diverse firms. In the next two decades, MNC tech firms may look quite different from those we have seen in the last two.

NOTES

1. Kim Nash, "Amazon, Alphabet, and Walmart Were Top IT Spenders in 2018," *Wall Street Journal*, January 17, 2019.

2. Walmart Inc. 10-K for the fiscal year ending January 31, 2019, section "strategic capital allocation."

3. U.S. District Court, Central District of California, "Memorandum from T. G. Plaskett to A. V. Casey," American Airlines documents AA080713–AA080714, January 17, 1977.

4. Barry Smith, John Leimkuhler, and Ross Darrow, "Yield Management at American Airlines," *Interfaces* 22/1 (January–February 1992): 8–31.

5. "British Airways: Thousands Disrupted as Flights Axed amid IT Crash," BBC News, May 27, 2017.

6. Chris Isidore, "Delta: 5-Hour Computer Outage Cost U.S. $150 Million," CNN Business, September 7, 2016.

7. Christy Brooks, "Why Smarter Inventory Means Better Customer Service," Walmart, August 16, 2017, https://corporate.walmart.com/newsroom/business/20170816/why-smarter-inventory-means-better-customer-service; Charisse Jones, "What's Killing Sears and Kmart?" *USA Today*, March 22, 2017.

8. Jessica Tyler, "We Went to a Kmart Store and Saw Why the Company Is in Danger of Shutting Down," *Business Insider*, April 8, 2018.

9. Unicode Consortium, https://home.unicode.org/.

10. "Historical Computers in Japan—Japanese Word Processors—Toshiba JW-10," IPSJ Computer Museum, http://museum.ipsj.or.jp/en/computer/word/0049.html.

11. "China," OpenNet Initiative, https://opennet.net/research/profiles/china-including-hong-kong.

12. "Google Datacenters," www.google.com/about/datacenters/.

13. "Azure Regions," Microsoft Azure, https://azure.microsoft.com/en-us/global-infrastructure/regions/.

14. "CloudFlare Plans," www.cloudflare.com/plans/.

15. Reed Albergotti, Douglas MacMillan, and Evelyn Rusli, "Facebook to Pay $19 Billion for WhatsApp," *Wall Street Journal*, February 19, 2014; J. Clement, "Number of Monthly Active WhatsApp Users Worldwide from April 2013 to December 2017," Statista, www.statista.com/statistics/260819/number-of-monthly-active-whatsapp-users/.

16. "Facebook Newsroom," https://newsroom.fb.com/company-info/.

17. Joshua Brustein, "Facebook Grappling with Employee Anger over Moderator Conditions," *Bloomberg*, February 25, 2019.

18. Matt Richtel, "The Long-Distance Journey of a Fast-Food Order," *New York Times*, April 11, 2006.

19. John Perry Barlow, "A Declaration of the Independence of Cyberspace," *Wired*, June 1, 1996.

20. *Yahoo! Inc. v. LICRA and UEJF*, 433 F.3d 1199 (9th Cir. 2006).

21. Our Offices, Google, https://about.google/intl/en_us/locations/.

22. Mark Sweney, "Google's U.K. Staff Paid Package of £226,000 on Average in 2018," *Guardian*, April 3, 2019.

23. Author's calculations from OpenNet Initiative, Internet Filtering Data, https://opennet.net/research/data.

24. See generally OpenNet Initiative reports and articles, https://opennet.net/reports.

25. Benjamin Edelman, 2003, "Web Sites Sharing IP Addresses: Prevalence and Significance," https://cyber.harvard.edu/people/edelman/ip-sharing/.

26. *United States v. Kim Dotcom, Megaupload Limited, et al.* (E.D.Va. 2002).

27. *Mattel v. Barbie-Club.com*, 310 F.3d 293 (2nd Cir. 2002).

28. Spain, Law 21/2014, Revising the Intellectual Property Act.

29. *A&M Records, Inc. v. Napster*, 239 F.3d 1004 (9th Cir. 2001).

30. See, for example, Brendan Koerner, "Why Is Napster Shut Down but Grokster's Still Running?" *Slate*, March 8, 2002.

31. Mike Isaac, *Super Pumped* (New York: W. W. Norton & Company, 2019).

32. Romain Dillet, "Uber France Leaders Arrested for Running Illegal Taxi Company," *TechCrunch*, June 29, 2015.

33. See, for example, Olivia Solon, "How Uber Conquers a City in Seven Steps," *Guardian*, April 12, 2017.

34. Representative examples: A Turkish court ordered the blocking of YouTube in 2007 due to videos insulting Mustafa Kemal Atatürk, incident to a barrage of online insults among users from Armenia, Greece, and Turkey. Jeffrey Rosen, "Google's Gatekeepers," *New York Times*, November 28, 2008. The UAE's Telecom Regulatory Authority briefly blocked YouTube from August to October 2006 due to concerns regarding adult content. Ronald Deibert and others, *Access Controlled: The Shaping of Power, Rights, and Rule in Cyberspace* (MIT Press, 2010).

35. Conor Dougherty, "Inside Yelp's Six-Year Grudge against Google," *New York Times*, July 1, 2017; Foo Yun Chee, "Expedia Files Google Complaint to EU Regulators," Reuters, March 30, 2012. The author historically wrote and spoke about a range of similar concerns.

36. Alexis Madrigal, "When the Facebook Traffic Goes Away," *Atlantic*, October 24, 2017.

37. See, for example, Pamela Parker, "Google, Facebook Ad Gains Continue to Shrink What's Left for Everyone Else, Says Analyst Firm," *Marketing Land*, March 28, 2019 (finding a 7.2 percent year-over-year decline in ad spend available to all other online media).

38. "American Tech Giants Are Making Life Tough for Startups," *Economist*, June 2, 2018.

10

Tax Avoidance and Multinational Firm Behavior

SCOTT DYRENG
MICHELLE HANLON

This chapter reviews, and at times extends, research that examines tax avoidance by multinational corporations (MNCs) and how taxes and tax avoidance behavior influence MNCs' investing, financing, accounting, and other practices. The chapter also reviews existing tax avoidance literature as it relates to purely domestic firms to the extent that comparisons of domestic and multinational firms are informative, or in circumstances where evidence has not been compiled separately for both types of firms.

By operating in multiple jurisdictions with distinct tax policies, MNCs have unique opportunities to reduce their tax obligations by structuring activities strategically across international borders. In addition, countries often compete via tax policy to attract multinational firms. Governments worry that tax avoidance activities, coupled with tax competition among countries, are eroding their existing tax bases, and they have lamented their inability to impose taxes on multinational firms in the modern business environment. These concerns have become much more acute in recent years with growing coverage of corporate tax avoidance issues in the popular press, which, in turn, has heightened political awareness of multinational tax avoidance issues. The Base Erosion and Profit Shifting (BEPS) initiatives of the Group of 20 (G-20) and the Organization for Economic Cooperation and Development (OECD), the U.S. Senate investigations into tax avoidance, and European Union reactions to alleged illegal state aid are recent examples. In addition, worldwide and government actions to combat tax avoidance seem to be increasing, given the breadth of the recent proposed Global Anti-Base Erosion Proposal (GloBE) by the OECD.[1]

For the purposes of this chapter, corporate income tax avoidance (hereafter, "tax avoidance," for simplicity) is defined as anything that reduces cash income taxes paid relative to pretax financial accounting income. This is the definition adopted in numerous studies that require a firm-specific measure, including Dyreng, Hanlon, Maydew (2008) and Hanlon and Heitzman (2010). Admittedly, not all research uses this definition, but having such a working definition makes an evaluation and summary of tax avoidance research as it applies to multinational firms more tractable. This definition of tax avoidance involves a broad set of both (1) actions taken by the firm to lower taxes and (2) outcomes of tax laws established by governments. In other words, tax avoidance under this definition captures both aggressive tax avoidance and also statutorily intended avoidance such as accelerated depreciation deductions, research tax credits, or other laws and agreements instituted by governments. However, it is important to recognize that this measure does not capture all tax planning, because it does not capture tax planning that reduces both taxes and reported accounting income (known as conforming tax avoidance).

This chapter begins by examining data on how much U.S. MNCs pay in taxes. Despite many articles in the press that highlight specific situations where MNCs paid very little or even no taxes, the fact is that MNCs pay billions of dollars in income taxes. For example, between 2009 and 2018, publicly traded U.S. multinational corporations paid, in aggregate, more than US$2.7 trillion in income taxes to governments around the world.[2] These same firms reported an aggregate of about US$10.7 trillion in pretax earnings during the same period, suggesting that, in aggregate, about 25 percent of pretax earnings were paid in income taxes around the world during that ten-year period. MNCs also pay (or remit) other taxes, and these are discussed near the end of the chapter. These so-called indirect taxes are also substantial.

While some firms significantly reduce their income tax liabilities, the totality of the evidence suggests that multinational firms face significant operational and reputational constraints on tax avoidance, a narrative that is often missing in media portrayals of tax avoidance, which focus on a few specific examples. In light of this, the chapter discusses questions and related research about (1) the extent to which firms can avoid taxes, (2) the variation in tax avoidance, (3) characteristics associated with tax avoidance, (4) the pervasiveness of tax avoidance, (5) the costs that deter tax avoidance, and (6) the consequences of tax avoidance.

This chapter reviews and extends the literature that measures and quantifies tax avoidance at the firm level. Similar to prior research, it provides evidence consistent with considerable cross-sectional variation in tax avoidance, with some firms appearing to pay taxes at rates significantly lower than the statutory tax rate, while other firms appear to pay taxes at rates that are higher than the statutory tax rate. Even when effective tax rates are measured over long periods to reduce the influence of unusual years or one-time shocks, the variation in tax avoidance remains high. For example, when measured over a ten-year period, about 17 percent of observations have cash effective tax rates below 20 percent, while 15 percent have a cash effective tax rate higher than 50 percent (during years when the U.S. statutory tax rate was between 34 percent and 35 percent). Consistent with prior research, when firm-specific cash effective tax rates are measured over longer horizons, the distribution tightens.[3]

This chapter then reviews and extends the literature that examines how tax avoidance has changed. Consistent with Dyreng, Hanlon, Maydew, and Thornock (2017), the data presented in this chapter suggests that tax avoidance (as we define it) has increased over the past thirty years. Contrary to the conventional wisdom that multinational firms have more tax avoidance opportunities than purely domestic firms, and thus benefit from tax-based cost advantages, the evidence suggests that tax avoidance has increased (that is, cash effective tax rates have decreased) at purely domestic firms as much as at multinational firms over the past thirty years. In addition, looking at the level of rates, purely domestic firms have lower cash effective tax rates than multinational firms over the entire thirty-year period. Moreover, following the recent U.S. tax reform, known as the Tax Cuts and Jobs Act (TCJA) of 2017, purely domestic firms experience a much sharper decline in cash effective tax rates than multinational corporations. This is consistent with expectations, because all of a purely domestic firm's income is subject to the U.S. tax rate (which the TCJA dropped from 35 percent to 21 percent) and because some international provisions in the TCJA may increase the taxes multinationals pay.

Researchers have devoted substantial resources to understanding the determinants of tax avoidance. This chapter reviews the findings from these studies and concludes that, despite some progress, the field still cannot explain a large portion of the variation in tax avoidance. The unexplained variation arises, in part, because (1) idiosyncratic business models and idiosyncratic business managers engender idiosyncratic tax avoidance opportunities and varying proclivities to take those opportunities that are unlikely to be explained by traditional regression techniques, and (2) because tests that include all known tax avoidance factors simultaneously are difficult to design. A few of the factors associated with tax avoidance beyond traditional firm characteristics (industry and size) have been recently studied, including financial accounting incentives, reputation, and the identity of executive-level managers.

Part of the chapter discusses the techniques multinational firms use to avoid taxes, including income shifting. This is difficult, because many techniques are highly technical and context-specific. Additionally, the specific structures employed by firms are generally proprietary or not widely known. Where possible, the chapter highlights information that has been revealed publicly in court cases, congressional testimonies, academic literature, and investigative reports in the press. Nevertheless, for much of the discussion, the technical details and intricate nuances of these strategies are omitted in favor of describing more generalizable patterns. One of the most common techniques multinational firms use is to shift income from one jurisdiction to another. Because income shifting is impossible to directly observe, researchers use a variety of econometric techniques to generate estimates of the phenomenon. This chapter reviews this literature, and notes, as other studies have, that the economic magnitudes of income shifting estimated in these studies are wide-ranging and at times seem implausibly large when compared with other data.

Finally, the chapter turns to the literature that examines how taxes and tax avoidance affect other decisions, such as investment location, corporate capital structure, and employment. For example, the evidence suggests that jurisdictions with low tax rates attract investment, all else constant. Further, firms may choose to shift income to a low-tax jurisdiction, which might only be possible if some real production activities are performed in the low-tax jurisdiction (or at least performed outside of the United States). Prior to the TCJA, the income recognized in the low-tax jurisdiction could have become "trapped" abroad, as the company could not repatriate the earnings to the United States without paying incremental U.S. taxes. Research suggests that companies with trapped foreign earnings engaged in relatively more investment in foreign jurisdictions and relatively more domestic borrowing, creating a situation where tax avoidance, including income shifting, seemed to affect foreign investment, which opened the door for more tax avoidance.

Most of the chapter focuses on U.S. MNCs and primarily discusses research that was conducted between the Tax Reform Act of 1986 and before the TCJA was effective in 2018. At the end of the chapter, some very recent research about the effects of the TCJA is discussed.

DO MULTINATIONAL FIRMS PAY TAXES?

Many U.S. multinational firms pay substantial income taxes, despite many anecdotes in the press to the contrary. In addition, some companies disclose and discuss the amount of taxes they pay. For example, in 2004, Lee Scott, president and CEO of Walmart, wrote in his annual letter to shareholders:

> I also will report that Walmart paid US$4 billion in U.S. federal income taxes in fiscal year 2004. To borrow a page from my friend Warren Buffett's annual report letter to the shareholders of Berkshire Hathaway, this means that if 446 other taxpayers paid the same amount as Walmart, no other business or individual in the United States would have had to pay federal taxes last year (based on 2003 U.S. federal tax receipts of US$1.782 trillion).

To estimate, in a large sample, how much firms pay, much of this chapter uses information from financial statements. Thus, it is important to understand what financial statements disclose about taxes. The most crucial distinction to make and understand is the difference between income tax expense on the income statement and cash taxes paid.

The income tax expense on a firm's income statement is computed using the accrual method of accounting (like everything else on the income statement). Thus, income tax expense is not equal to cash taxes paid. At a high level, the total income tax expense in a reporting period reflects taxes that have been and will be paid on the accounting earnings reported on that income statement for the same period. In simple terms, the income tax expense is matched with the current-year pretax earnings. Or, alternatively stated, tax expense captures future tax costs and benefits incurred in the current period. The accounting income tax expense amount consists of two parts—current tax expense and deferred tax expense.[4] Each of these expense amounts is disclosed by broad jurisdiction—United States, international, and state (generally). The current tax expense is the portion of the expense that most closely mirrors cash taxes paid. However, it is not equal to cash taxes paid, because the current tax expense will include some accruals as well (for example, tax expense recorded for changes in contingent tax liabilities arising to account for possible future taxes from assessments by tax authorities). In the sample of public multinational firms, the correlation between cash taxes paid and total current tax expense is 92 percent.

In contrast to tax expense, cash taxes paid is the amount of cash firms remitted to all governments around the world for income tax payments, net of any refunds received. Cash taxes paid is not disclosed by jurisdiction. Cash taxes paid could be related to this year's income or could include such things as payments made as a result of a tax audit or settlement for a prior tax year. In other words, cash taxes paid is literally just that: the amount of cash paid during the year for income taxes.[5] Because cash taxes paid is not disclosed by jurisdiction, current tax expense is used as a proxy for cash taxes paid when by-jurisdiction amounts are needed.

In figure 10-1, panel A reports the aggregate amount of income taxes paid to all governments by publicly traded U.S. multinational companies each year over the past thirty years in the line labeled "Cash Taxes Paid." The figure reports that these companies paid a total of US$64 billion in income taxes to governments around the world in 1988. The amount rises to as much as US$332 billion in 2014, and is US$259 billion in 2018, the year immediately after the passage of the TCJA.[6] Figure 10-1, panel A, also reports the federal current tax expense each year for the past thirty years in the line labeled "Federal Current Tax Expense." In 1988, publicly traded U.S. multinational firms reported US$34 billion in federal current tax expense, and in 2018 reported US$167 billion in federal current tax expense.[7]

Though the amount of taxes paid is large, it is difficult to interpret without context. In 2014, the most recent data available, the Internal Revenue Service collected just over US$336 billion in corporate income taxes, which accounted for about 11 percent of U.S. revenue. In 2014, publicly traded U.S. multinational firms reported US$187 billion in current federal tax expense, or about 56 percent of all U.S. federal corporate income taxes (assuming that current tax expense is a reasonable proxy for cash taxes paid in aggregate for such purposes).

In addition to comparing the amount of taxes paid by publicly traded multinational firms with the total amount of corporate tax collected in the United States, it is also informative to examine the amount of taxes paid relative to measures that capture the scale of the economy. In figure 10-1, panel B plots cash taxes paid divided by U.S. gross domestic product (GDP)

FIGURE 10-1. Taxes Paid by Multinational Firms

PANEL A. Sum of taxes paid each year between 1988 and 2018

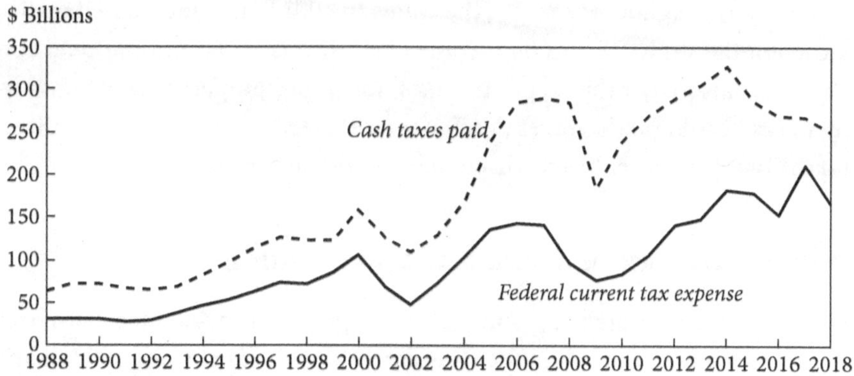

PANEL B. Sum of taxes paid scaled by U.S. GDP each year between 1988 and 2018

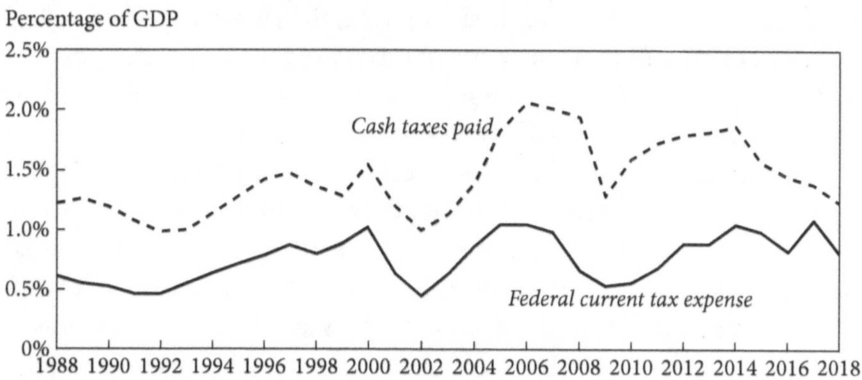

Note: The sample comprises all U.S.-incorporated multinational firm-year observations in Compustat with beginning total assets (AT) of at least US$10 million. Firm-years are defined as multinational if they report non-missing values of pretax foreign earnings (PIFO) or foreign tax expense (TXFO, TXDFO). In panel B, GDP data was gathered from www.bea.gov.

and federal current tax expense divided by U.S. GDP. As the figure shows, worldwide cash taxes paid hovers between 1 percent and 2 percent of GDP. As might be expected, federal current tax expense captures a smaller fraction of GDP, and hovers between about 0.5 percent and 1 percent of GDP.

In sum, the results, juxtaposed against the common narrative that large public multinational corporations pay very little income tax, suggest that the reality of the corporate income tax is nuanced and difficult to convey in a single statistic or simple conclusion. Indeed, many multinational corporations clearly pay substantial income tax, while other companies undeniably pay relatively little income tax. The wide variation in income tax burdens are discussed throughout the rest of the study. In addition, as mentioned earlier, although the study focuses on income taxes throughout, multinational corporations also pay other types of taxes, including property taxes, employment taxes, value added taxes (VATs), excise taxes, tariffs, and other indirect taxes. These taxes are briefly discussed before the conclusion.

CORPORATE TAX PLANNING AND AVOIDANCE

Research on corporate tax planning and corporate tax avoidance dates back many decades. In the economics literature, foundational work by Hall and Jorgensen (1967) established that tax policies could affect investment and other corporate decisions. Similarly, Modigliani and Miller (1963) argued that corporate taxes could affect corporate financing policies. Over the ensuing years, researchers have devoted substantial efforts to understanding how tax policies affect investment and financing policies. In effect, the fact that corporate taxes influence so many corporate actions is evidence of tax planning. If firms simply blindly complied with tax laws without any tax planning at all, taxes would have no effect on corporate behavior.

Myron Scholes and Mark Wolfson provided significant structure to the literature on corporate tax planning in the 1980s and published what has become a seminal textbook in 1992. In the wake of the Scholes and Wolfson textbook, research on tax planning and tax avoidance began to grow in the 1990s. Moreover, the rise of corporate tax shelters became more widely documented in the late 1990s, due, in part, to a white paper by the U.S. Treasury (1999) and substantial media coverage (for example, Novack and Saunders (1998); Frank (2003)). In an influential review of the tax literature, Shackelford and Shevlin (2001) called for research on the determinants of tax aggressiveness, while Weisbach (2002) identified the "undersheltering puzzle," where he asked why tax avoidance ("sheltering," in his paper) is not more pervasive. Additionally, Slemrod (2004), Chen and Chu (2005), and Crocker and Slemrod (2005) developed the theoretical foundation of corporate tax avoidance within an agency framework. The combination of these factors, and undoubtedly others, has led to a recent explosion of corporate tax research.

What Is Corporate Tax Planning?

For the purposes of this chapter, the term "tax planning" refers to any alteration of corporate activity relative to a zero-tax world. The chapter assumes the objective of a representative firm is to maximize after-tax returns. For example, tax planning might consist of altering investments, finances, operations, employment, mergers and acquisitions, or any other of myriad corporate activities to maximize the after-tax return on those activities, even though the choices might be suboptimal in a zero-tax world. Thus, the definition of tax planning is consistent with Scholes and Wolfson (1992), who argue that "effective tax planning involves considering the role of taxes when implementing the decision rule of maximizing after-tax returns."

As a practical matter, tax planning is impossible to observe directly, because the world absent taxes cannot be observed. Corporate tax planning encompasses every type of tax that might affect a corporation either directly or indirectly. Thus, firms maximize profits after taking into consideration both explicit taxes, which are taxes paid to the government, and implicit taxes, which are taxes that are not paid to a government but are borne economically, because the returns on tax-favored projects might be lower than the returns on non-tax-favored projects. Firms maximize income after taking into consideration not only corporate income taxes, but also property taxes, value-added taxes, sales taxes, and so forth (to the extent they are not simply collected and remitted by the entity). Furthermore, and at least in theory, firms maximize returns by taking into consideration shareholder investment taxes (although the empirical evidence on this is not strong). In other words, effective corporate tax planning requires that firms take into account all parties, all taxes, and all costs (Scholes and Wolfson (1992)).

What Is Corporate Income Tax Avoidance?

For the purposes of this chapter, corporate income tax avoidance (again, referred to herein as "tax avoidance," for simplicity) is defined as anything that reduces cash income taxes paid relative to pretax financial accounting income.[8] This definition of tax avoidance is broad enough to capture activities as egregious as tax evasion, where earnings are simply not reported to the taxing authorities, or aggressive forms of avoidance that might be technically legal but push the boundaries of the law. The definition also encompasses benign activities that reduce taxes, such as investments in municipal bonds that generate tax-exempt interest income, and the effects of statutory provisions such as accelerated depreciation, research and development tax credits, or other laws and agreements established by governments. It is important to note that the definition of tax avoidance used in this chapter encompasses most common tax planning strategies used by multinational firms, including shifting income to low-tax foreign jurisdictions using strategically set transfer prices, or intercompany debt, as well as decisions that generate tax savings such as establishing manufacturing, research and development, or sales operations in low-tax foreign jurisdictions.

Although this definition of tax avoidance encompasses a wide range of activities, it misses some forms of tax planning. Because avoidance is defined as taxes paid relative to pretax accounting earnings, any actions a firm takes that reduces both taxes and pretax accounting earnings will not fall within the scope of tax avoidance as measured here. For example, interest payments on most forms of third-party debt reduce both cash taxes paid and pretax financial accounting earnings.[9] Tax planning that reduces pretax financial accounting earnings and cash taxes paid is sometimes referred to as "conforming tax avoidance," while this chapter's definition of tax avoidance might be more precisely referred to as "non-conforming tax avoidance."[10]

Estimating Corporate Tax Avoidance

Following Dyreng, Hanlon, and Maydew (2008), this chapter empirically measures corporate tax avoidance, using the cash effective tax rate, by summing cash income taxes paid over some period (usually one, five, or ten years), and dividing by pretax earnings summed over the same period, as follows:

$$CASH\ ETR = \frac{\sum_t CASH\ TAX\ PAID_t}{\sum_t PRETAX\ INCOME_t}. \tag{1}$$

Although data necessary to calculate CASH ETR (cash effective tax rate) is available annually for publicly traded U.S. multinational firms, relatively long-run versions of the measure are preferable, because they minimize the effect of several problems. First, CASH ETR is difficult to interpret when pretax income (defined as pretax financial accounting income) is negative. Increasing the length of the period over which the measure is calculated reduces the fraction of observations with negative pretax income, because fewer firms have cumulative losses over a longer period. Second, because both cash tax paid and pretax income can be volatile for many reasons, summing over a long period allows random fluctuations to wash out, thereby creating a more stable measure. Third, because the numerator is cash-based, but the denominator is accrual-based, summing over a long period allows for many of the accruals in pretax earnings to reverse, creating a better (though still not perfect) match between numerator and denominator.[11] Fourth, using a cash-based number in the numerator removes the effect of tax accruals, which can sometimes significantly alter the tax expense relative to cash taxes paid.

Figure 10-2 uses data from Compustat between 1988 and 2017 to plot the distribution of CASH ETR calculated over various horizons for all publicly traded non-financial, non-utility MNCs and domestic-only corporations (DOCs) with total assets greater than US$10 million and pretax income greater than zero.[12] Following Dyreng, Hanlon, and Maydew (2008), if CASH ETR is greater than one, it is reset to one, and if it is less than zero, it is reset to zero.[13]

Panel A of figure 10-2 provides histograms of one-year CASH ETR (that is, where the numerator and denominator are annual measures). Also, the number of observations, the moments of the distribution, and values of various quantiles of the distribution are presented in the first row of table 10-1, panel A for MNCs and table 10-1, panel B for DOCs. The mean of the distribution for MNCs is 0.293, about 5 or 6 percentage points below the statutory tax rate during the sample period of 34 percent or 35 percent. The mean of the distribution for DOCs is 0.261, about 8 or 9 percentage points below the statutory tax rate. As can be seen by looking at panel A of figure 10-2, more firm-years appear in the lower ranges of CASH ETR than in the higher ranges. For example, for both MNC and DOC firm-years, 70 percent have CASH ETR below the statutory tax rate (that is, 35 percent), but only 30 percent have CASH ETR above the statutory tax rate. Moreover, 37 percent of MNC firm-years and 45 percent of DOC firm-years report CASH ETR below 20 percent. With both groups, a relatively large number of observations have CASH ETR very near 0 percent, and this is particularly obvious in the sample of DOC firm-years, suggesting many of these observations have zero or negative cash taxes paid, despite earning profits during the year. These observations can often be attributed to unusual or extreme earnings or tax realizations, including losses in prior years that result in large tax loss carryforwards. For example, if a firm records a pretax financial accounting loss in year *t*-1 (and let's assume, just for the purposes of this discussion,

FIGURE 10-2. Distribution of CASH ETR for Firms over Various Horizons

PANEL A. One-year CASH ETR

Multinationals

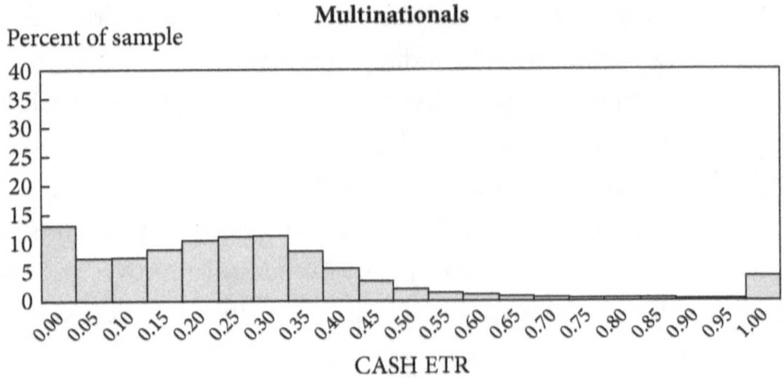

Domestics

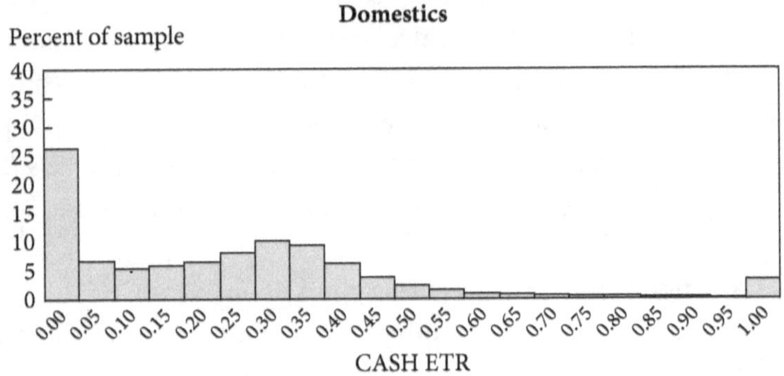

PANEL B. Five-year CASH ETR

Multinationals

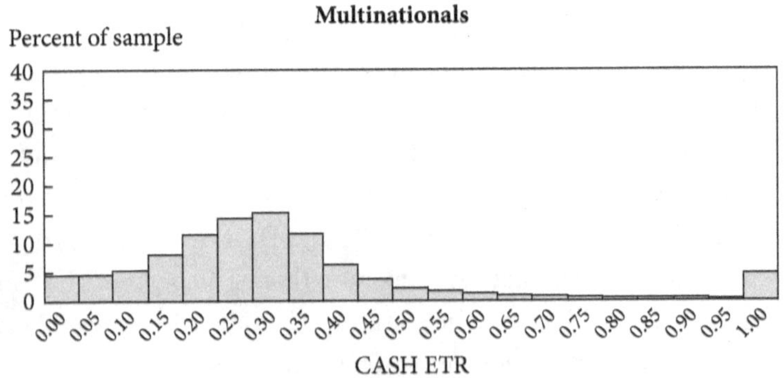

Domestics

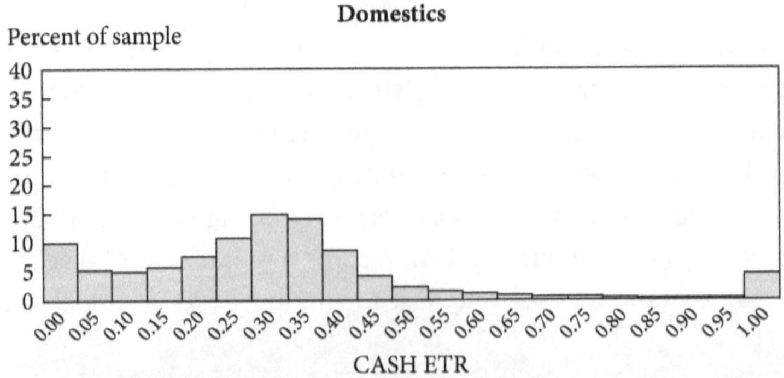

PANEL C. Ten-year CASH ETR

Multinationals

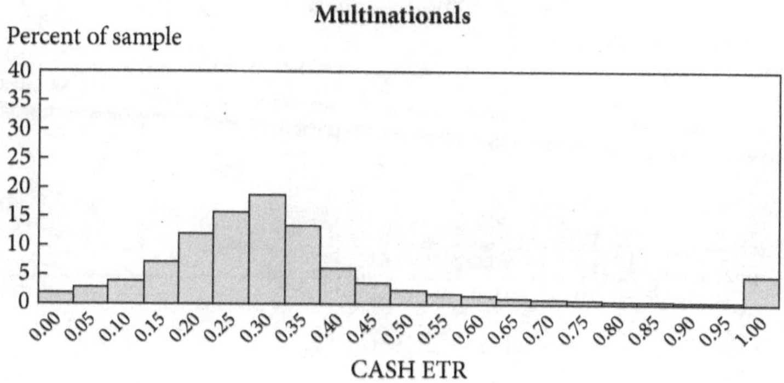

Domestics

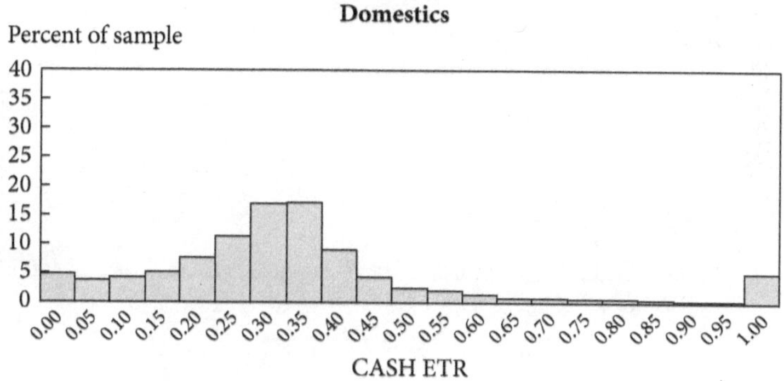

PANEL D. Thirty-year CASH ETR

Multinationals

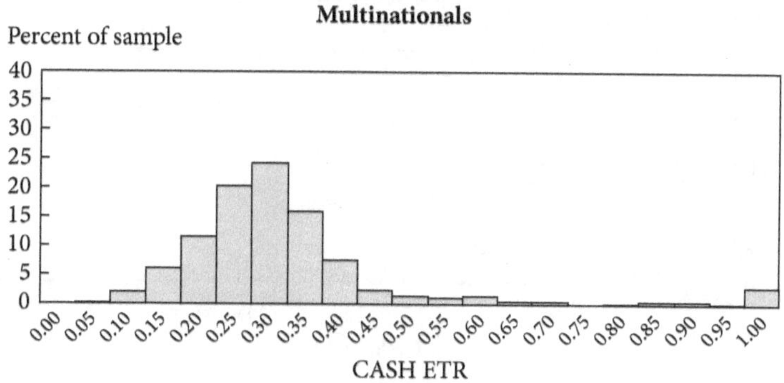

Domestics

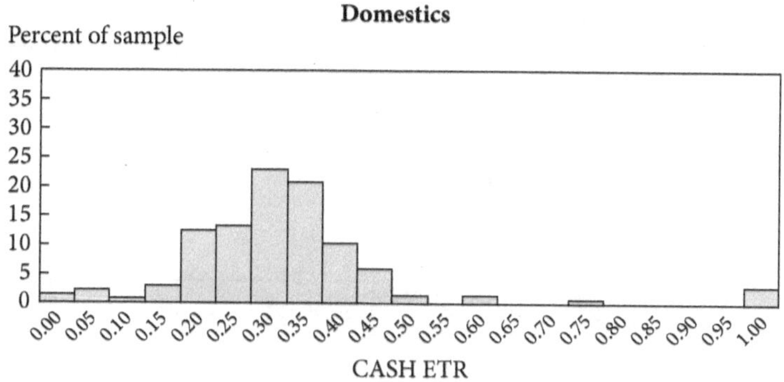

PANEL E. One-year CASH ETR for firms with non-missing thirty-year CASH ETR

Multinationals

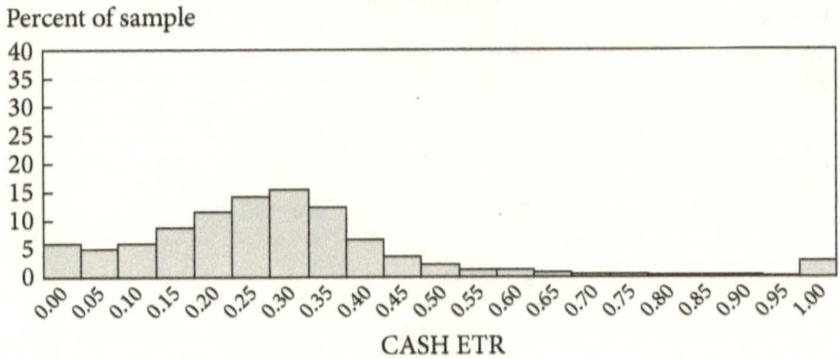

Domestics

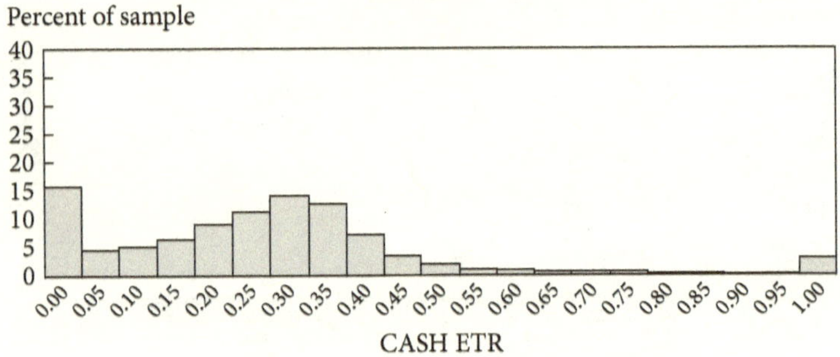

PANEL F. One-year CASH ETR for 2018

Multinationals

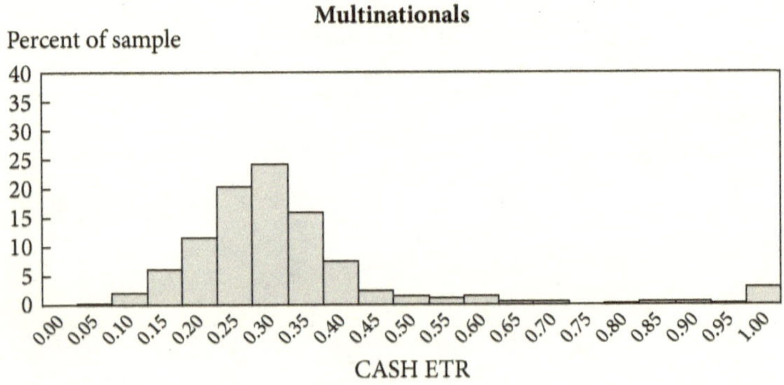

Domestics

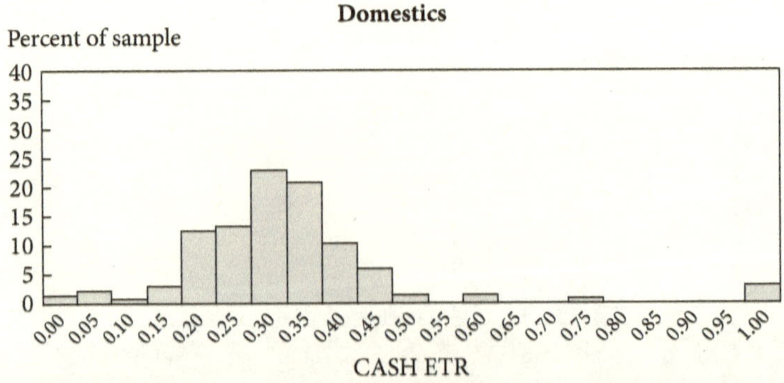

Note: The sample comprises all non-financial, non-utility U.S.-incorporated multinational and domestic firm-year observations in Compustat (Compustat data pneumonics in parentheses with all caps) between 1988 and 2017 (panel F includes the year 2018 only) with necessary data to calculate CASH ETR, defined as Σ_t *CASH TAX PAID*$_t$ / Σ_t *PRETAX INCOME*$_t$, where *CASH TAX PAID*$_t$ is cash taxes paid as reported by the firm in the financial statement footnotes (TXPD) and *PRETAX INCOME*$_t$ is pretax accounting income as reported by the firm in the income statement (PI). Observations where Σ_t *PRETAX INCOME*$_t$ is negative are deleted. Observations with CASH ETR > 1 are reset to 1, and observations with CASH ETR < 0 are reset to 0. In panel A, we show the distribution of one-year CASH ETR (that is, $t = 0$). In panel B, we show the distribution of five-year CASH ETR (that is, $t = -4$ to $t = 0$). Panel C presents the distribution of ten-year CASH ETR (that is, $t = -9$ to $t = 0$), and in panel D we show thirty-year CASH ETR (that is, $t = -29$ to $t = 0$). Panel E is the distribution of one-year CASH ETR for firms that have non-missing thirty-year CASH ETR. We define firm-years as multinational if they report non-missing values of pretax foreign earnings (PIFO) or foreign tax expense (TXFO, TXDFO) in any of the years necessary to compute the corresponding CASH ETR, domestic otherwise.

that the firm records a tax loss as well), that observation would be excluded from the sample in year *t*-1 because CASH ETR is difficult to interpret when pretax earnings are negative. If the same firm records a profit for financial accounting in year *t*, CASH ETR might be very low or even zero, because the firm might be able to use the tax loss carryover from year *t*-1 to reduce or eliminate taxes in year *t*, thus reducing the numerator of CASH ETR to zero, over a positive denominator of pretax income (because financial accounting losses are not carried over).

Panel B of figure 10-2 presents a histogram of five-year CASH ETR (that is, where the numerator and denominator are separately summed from

TABLE 10-1. Descriptive Statistics of CASH ETR over Various Horizons

PANEL A. Multinationals

Variable	N	Mean	StdDev	P5	p25	p50	p75	P95
1-year CASH ETR	37,020	0.293	0.233	2.052	0.131	0.262	0.378	0.892
5-year CASH ETR	29,095	0.339	0.219	0.055	0.211	0.304	0.395	0.954
10-year CASH ETR	19,752	0.356	0.209	2.806	0.239	0.317	0.395	0.971
20-year CASH ETR	424	0.351	0.165	6.710	0.264	0.320	0.375	0.700
1-year CASH ETR*	11,557	0.313	0.197	3.244	0.197	0.295	0.381	0.708
1-year CASH ETR* for 2018	1,106	0.239	0.227	3.777	0.097	0.190	0.282	0.799

PANEL B. Domestics

Variable	N	Mean	StdDev	P5	p25	p50	p75	P95
1-year CASH ETR	39,777	0.261	0.240	0.000	0.043	0.244	0.380	0.765
5-year CASH ETR	23,577	0.331	0.227	0.014	0.019	0.319	0.405	0.934
10-year CASH ETR	11,941	0.363	0.219	0.051	0.246	0.338	0.415	1.000
20-year CASH ETR	135	0.350	0.158	0.167	0.276	0.336	0.396	0.602
1-year CASH ETR*	3,502	0.290	0.214	0.000	0.144	0.287	0.382	0.719
1-year CASH ETR* for 2018	476	0.158	0.196	0.000	0.005	0.119	0.222	0.530

*Only for firms with non-missing 30-year CASH ETR

Notes: The sample comprises all non-financial, non-utility U.S.-incorporated firm-year observations in Compustat (Compustat data pneumonics in parentheses with all caps) between 1988 and 2018 with necessary data to calculate CASH ETR, defined as Σ_t *CASH TAX PAID*$_t$ / Σ_t *PRETAX INCOME*$_t$, where *CASH TAX PAID*$_t$ is cash taxes paid as reported by the firm in the financial statement footnotes (TXPD) and *PRETAX INCOME*$_t$ is pretax accounting income as reported by the firm in the income statement (PI). Observations where Σ_t *PRETAX INCOME*$_t$ is negative are deleted. Observations with CASH ETR > 1 are reset to 1, and observations with CASH ETR < 0 are reset to 0. The different rows in the table show the descriptive statistics for CASH ETR computed over various horizons, as labeled in the first column.

t-4 to *t*, then divided), and the associated characteristics of the distribution are reported in the second row each of the two panels of table 10-1. As can be seen in table 10-1, the mean of the distribution rises several percentage points relative to the one-year CASH ETR, for both MNCs and DOCs achieving a value of 0.339 for MNC firm-years and 0.331 for DOC firm-years. Both of these values are lower than the statutory tax rate, but higher than the mean of one-year CASH ETR. The distribution of five-year CASH ETR remains asymmetric, with more mass in the left side of the distribution, but less asymmetric than one-year CASH ETR. In addition, there are fewer extreme observations so that the masses at the ends of the distribution are smaller, a fact that is particularly visible for DOC observations.

Panel C of figure 10-2 presents histograms of ten-year CASH ETR (that is, where the numerator and denominator are separately summed from *t*-9 to *t*, then divided), and the associated characteristics of the distributions are reported in the third row of the two panels of table 10-1. Once again, the mean of the distribution rises a few percentage points relative to one-year CASH ETR and five-year CASH ETR, with a value of 0.356 for MNC firm-year observations and 0.363 for DOC observations. The distribution also becomes more symmetric, and even fewer extreme observations are reset to zero from below or to one from above, so the abnormal masses at the ends of the distribution are smaller. Even though the distribution becomes more symmetric, 16 percent of MNC and 18 percent of DOC observations have cash effective tax rates below 20 percent.

Panel D of figure 10-2 contains histograms of thirty-year CASH ETR (that is, where the numerator and denominator are separately summed from $t = -29$ to *t*, then divided), which covers the entire sample period from 1988 to 2017. The associated characteristics of the distributions are reported in the fourth row of each panel of table 10-1. This panel reports data from 559 firms (424 MNCs and 135 DOCs), each with only one observation, because the sample comprises thirty years of data. The mean thirty-year CASH ETR is 0.351 for multinational (domestic) firms and 0.350 for domestic firms, relatively close to the statutory tax rate of either 34 or 35 percent during the sample period. The standard deviation of this distribution is relatively tight, and the extreme tails continue to shrink. When calculated over a thirty-year period, one MNC and five DOCs had a CASH ETR less than 10 percent, and thirty-six MNCs and ten DOCs had a CASH ETR less than 20 percent.

Obviously, because data are required for thirty consecutive years when calculating thirty-year CASH ETR, only firms with long histories as publicly traded companies appear in the figure. To determine if the shape of the distribution is driven by the calculation of thirty-year CASH ETR, or whether it is driven by special characteristics of firms that survive for thirty years, the chapter reexamines one-year CASH ETR, but only for firm-years that correspond to the 559 firms with a non-missing thirty-year CASH ETR. The resulting histograms are in figure 10-2, panel E, and the fifth row of table 10-1, panel A and panel B. Even though all of the observations in this figure are derived from firms that survive the full thirty years, the distributions are asymmetric and have significant extreme values, similar to the distributions plotted in panel A for all available firm-years. This confirms that in any given year, CASH ETR might be unusually low or high because of random fluctuations in earnings or taxes, unusual corporate events (for example, mergers), changes in tax policies, tax enforcement actions, or other short-lived factors.

Finally, panel F of figure 10-2 presents one-year CASH ETR for 2018. Although the distributions appear similar to the distributions presented in panel A, which covers firm-years between 1988 and 2017, the mean of each of the distributions in panel F is lower than the corresponding distributions in panel A. This can be easily seen by comparing the values in the sixth row of panels A and B of table 10-1 with the values in the first rows of panels A and B of table 10-1. The mean of one-year CASH ETR is 0.239 for MNCs and 0.158 for DOCs in 2018 compared to 0.293 for MNCs and 0.261 for DOCs from 1998 to 2017. In addition, more firms bunch in the bar close to zero for DOCs—nearly 40 percent of the sample of DOCs are in the bar nearest zero for 2018 versus a roughly 27 percent in from 1988 to 2017. These effects are likely due to the TCJA, which lowered the statutory tax rate from 35 percent to 21 percent and allowed for immediate expensing of qualified assets.

Overall, there are five key observations related to figure 10-2. First, the distribution of CASH ETR tightens as the time horizon lengthens. Second, even when calculated using a thirty-year horizon, there is still variation in the distribution of CASH ETR (though the mean rises to 35 percent). Third, the distribution is asymmetric—fewer firms have CASH ETR higher than the statutory tax rate than below the statutory tax rate. Fourth, there are a substantial number of firms that achieve CASH ETR lower than 20 percent even over longer-run periods (but again, the percentage of firms that can do this does decline as the horizon lengthens).[14] Fifth, the mean value of CASH ETR appears to have dropped significantly in 2018 after the TCJA, especially for domestic-only firms, consistent with the corporate statutory tax rate being lowered from 35 percent to 21 percent.

Overall, the data presented in this section using CASH ETR provides evidence that some firms pay taxes at rates lower than the U.S. statutory tax rate, over the period 1988–2017, and this is the case for both multinational entities and purely domestic firms. Later, the chapter describes some of the common mechanisms firms use to achieve these relatively low tax rates, with a special focus on strategies employed by multinational firms.

Trends in Tax Avoidance

Over the past thirty-one years, firms have become increasingly multinational, and this trend is readily apparent in the data using any number of measures. One of the simplest measures of multinationality used in the literature is whether a firm reports any foreign earnings or foreign taxes in its annual report (as used above). In figure 10-3, panel A replicates and extends figure 10-1 from Dyreng, Hanlon, Maydew, and Thornock (2017); the data reveal that about 34 percent of firm-years in Compustat reported evidence of foreign earnings or foreign taxes in their annual reports in 1988, and that this fraction has steadily grown to about 70 percent in 2018.

Dyreng, Hanlon, Maydew, and Thornock (2017) study profitable firm-years on Compustat, and require other conditioning variables. One possible concern with the trend observed in figure 10-3, panel A, is that the trend toward multinationality might be biased because perhaps older, surviving firms are more likely to become multinational. To investigate this possibility, in figure 10-3, panel B examines whether rates of multinationality are systematically different for relatively young versus relatively old firms.[15] In 1988, about 14 percent of firms between one and ten years old have multinational operations, while the fraction is about 32 percent of firms between twenty-one and thirty years old. This suggests that older firms are more likely to have multinational operations, and this is true in each of the other years examined: 1998, 2008, and 2018. The results reveal that a larger fraction of older firms have multinational operations than younger firms in every decade of the sample studied. However, the figure also shows that firm-years in both age groups, young and old, are more multinational in each successive decade, consistent with globalization trends.

Not only has the fraction of U.S. public corporations that report foreign earnings or foreign taxes grown, but the number of unique countries in which U.S. multinationals report significant operations has also increased. The SEC requires publicly traded U.S. firms to disclose a list of their signifi-

FIGURE 10-3. Multinationality over Time

PANEL A. Fraction of profitable firm-years with evidence of multinational operations in earnings and tax disclosures

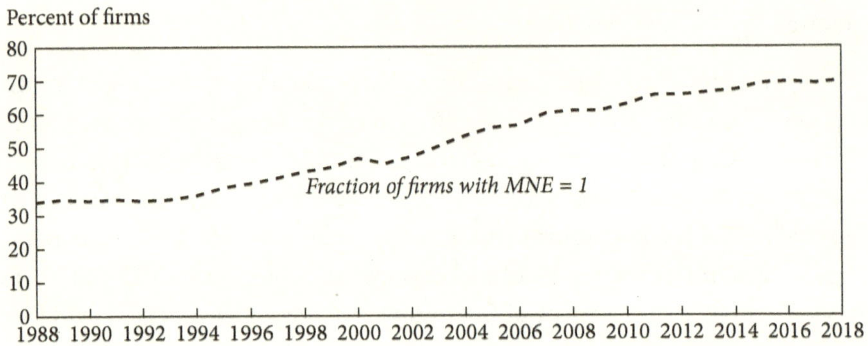

PANEL B. Fraction of young and old firm-years with evidence of multinational operations in earnings and tax disclosures

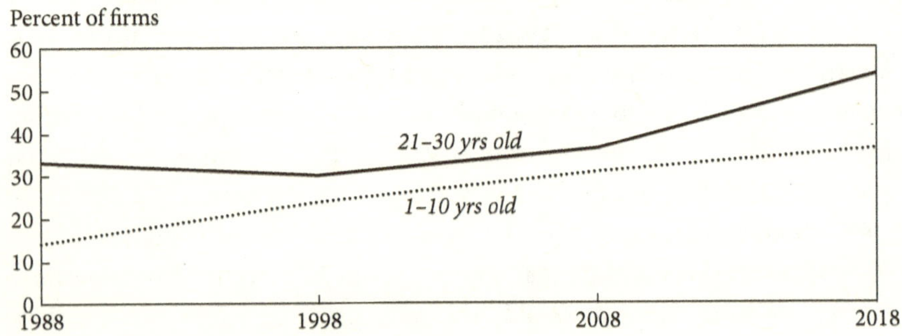

PANEL C. Number of distinct countries hosting significant subsidiaries for the mean U.S. multinational firm

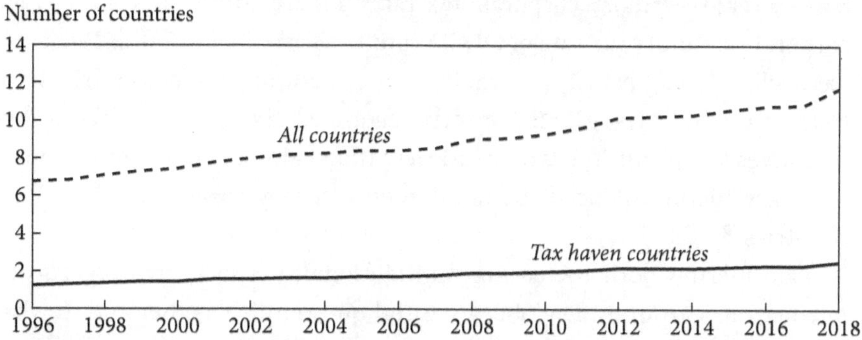

Note: MNE is equal to one if the firm has non-missing values of pretax foreign income (PIFO), current foreign-tax expense (TXFO), or deferred current-tax expense (TXDFO), zero otherwise. In panel A, the sample selection follows Dyreng, Hanlon, Maydew, and Thornock (2017) and requires firms to be incorporated in the United States in non-financial, non-utilities industries, have positive pretax income (PI) and sales (SALE), and non-missing values of cash taxes paid (TXPD) and total assets (AT) at the beginning and end of the period. Panel B relaxes the sample requirements by retaining all industries, and not requiring cash taxes paid (TXPD) or positive values of pretax income (PI). Panel C uses all firms with Exhibit 21 from Form 10-K filed with the SEC (see Dyreng and Lindsey (2009) and Dyreng, Hoopes, Langetieg, and Wilde (2019) for additional details).

cant subsidiaries each year.[16] As can be seen in figure 10-3, panel C, among firms that disclose at least one significant foreign subsidiary, the number of distinct countries in which the mean firm has a material foreign subsidiary has grown from 6.78 in 1996 to 11.79 in 2018. Moreover, among this same set of firms, the mean firm had a significant subsidiary in 1.27 tax-haven countries in 1996 compared with 2.52 tax-haven countries in 2018.

Over this same period, foreign countries (and the United States in 2018) have lowered statutory corporate tax rates. Figure 10-4 shows the average corporate statutory tax rate of OECD countries was 44 percent in 1988, and has declined steadily to 24 percent in 2018. In addition, many countries have enacted tax holidays, granted special negotiated tax rates, or provided tax incentives for specific types of investment (for example, patent box regimes), that have further reduced the tax burden faced by corporations in many countries.[17]

Considering both increasing multinationality and decreasing corporate tax rates around the globe, a natural question is whether and to what extent tax avoidance (defined as cash taxes paid divided by pretax accounting income) has increased among multinational firms. Dyreng, Hanlon, Maydew, and Thornock (2017) provide evidence on this question by examining the trends in corporate tax avoidance for U.S. multinational firms com-

FIGURE 10-4. Statutory Tax Rate of OECD Countries over Time

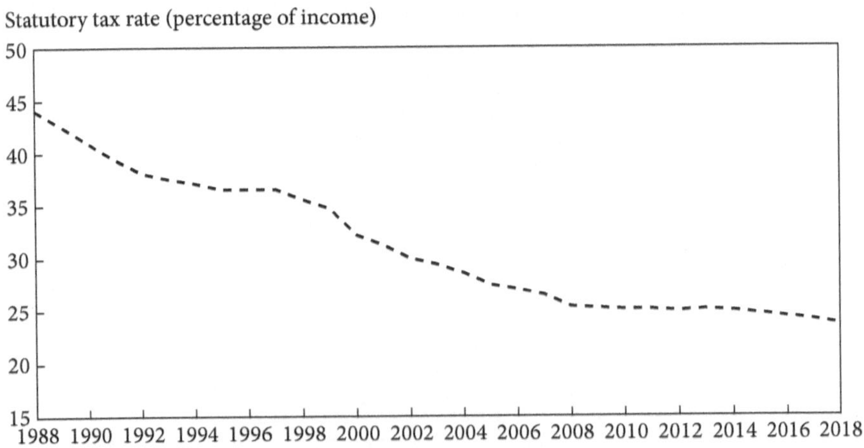

Note: This figure plots the average combined national and subnational statutory tax rate of OECD countries.

Source: OECD.stat (https://stats.oecd.org)

pared with purely domestic firms. Consistent with expectations, the authors find that the cash effective tax rates of U.S. multinational firms declined substantially in the twenty-five years between 1988 and 2012. Surprisingly, however, the authors also find that purely domestic U.S. firms report similar declines in their effective tax rates. Figure 10-5, panel A, reproduces and extends figure 3 from Dyreng, Hanlon, Maydew, and Thornock (2017). The figure provides evidence consistent with (1) the cash effective tax rates of U.S. multinational firms declining, and (2) the cash effective tax rates of purely domestic firms declining at a similar pace, which is somewhat surprising because the U.S. statutory tax rate was effectively constant between 1988 and 2017, rising only once from 34 percent to 35 percent in 1994. The trends of both types of U.S. companies merit further discussion.

First, the evidence in Dyreng, Hanlon, Maydew, and Thornock (2017) suggests that the declining effective tax rates of U.S. multinationals appear to be partially driven by (1) U.S. multinationals becoming more global, more intangibles-based, and reporting more foreign earnings (either via fundamental business purposes or via income shifting) and (2) foreign statutory tax rates declining. Prior to the TCJA, the United States had a worldwide tax system that allowed deferral of U.S. taxes on foreign subsidiary operating earnings until repatriation. Thus, any earnings (1) recognized in a foreign subsidiary in a country with a relatively low tax rate, and (2) held abroad and not subject to immediate U.S. taxation, lowered the firm's cash effective tax rate. As more operating earnings were reported in foreign jurisdictions (and not repatriated), cash effective tax rates declined.[18]

Second, the fact that domestic firms have declining cash effective tax rates is puzzling, and calls into question the conventional wisdom that multinational firms have a tax-based competitive advantage. Many believe that because purely domestic firms do not have opportunities to earn income in low-tax jurisdictions, and cannot engage in strategic behaviors to recognize earnings in tax havens, their tax avoidance opportunities are limited. Nevertheless, the data reveal that their cash effective tax rates are lower and have been declining at the same pace as multinational firms.

Several researchers have proposed explanations for these two puzzles. Dyreng, Hanlon, Maydew, and Thornock (2017) speculate that one partial explanation resides in temporary statutory tax changes (and possibly other domestic tax changes) designed to stimulate the economy and encourage investment such as bonus depreciation from 2001 to 2004 and starting again in 2008 (now scheduled through 2026 in the TCJA), and special deductions

FIGURE 10-5. Mean CASH ETR over Time for U.S. Multinational and U.S. Domestic Firms

PANEL A. Multinationals and domestics

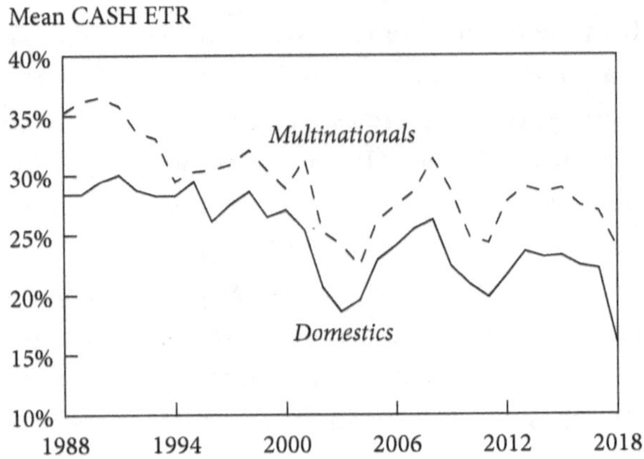

PANEL B. CASH ETR over time comparing high tech and other industries

High tech industries

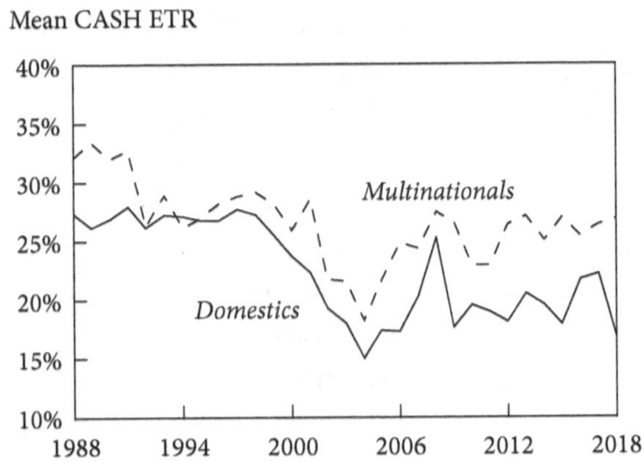

Other industries

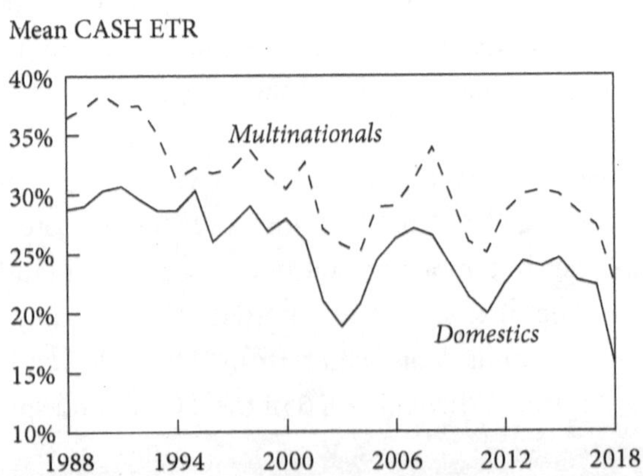

PANEL C. CASH ETR over time comparing high market cap to low market cap firms

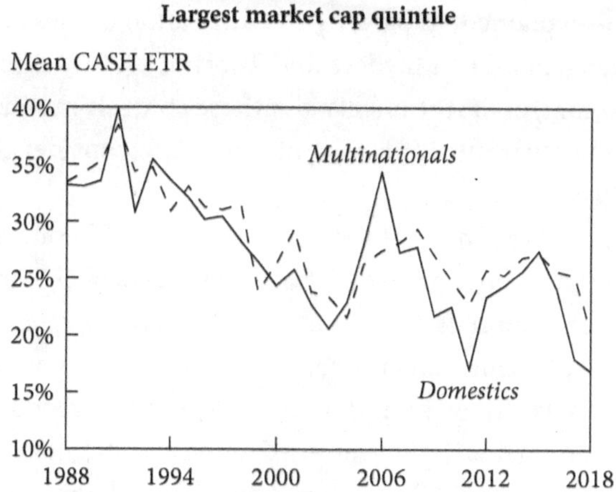

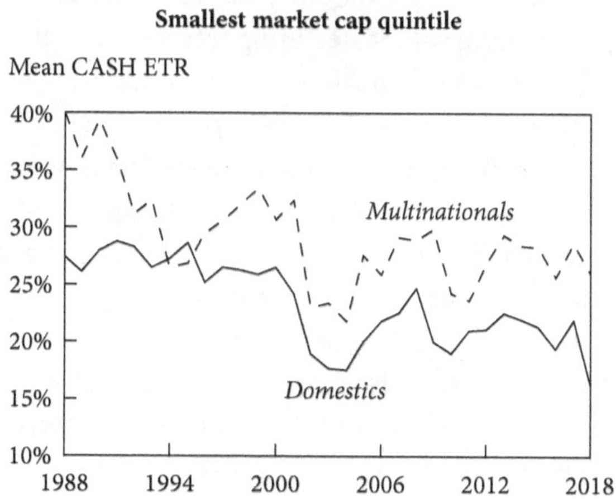

Note: The sample comprises all non-financial, non-utility U.S.-incorporated multinational firm-year observations in Compustat (Compustat data pneumonics in parentheses with all caps) between 1988 and 2018 with total assets greater than US$10 million and necessary data to calculate one-year CASH ETR (TXPD/PI). We define firm-years as multinational if they report non-missing values of pretax foreign earnings (PIFO) or foreign tax expense (TXFO, TXDFO). In panel B, high tech industries are defined as firms with three-digit SIC codes equal to 283, 357, 366, 367, 382, 384, 481, 482, 489, 737, or 873, following Kile and Phillips (2009). In panel C, we assign firms to quintiles based on the quintiles of market value of equity of multinationals in each year. Domestics are then assigned to quintiles using the quintiles from the market value of equity of multinationals.

like the domestic production activities deduction (now expired). Drake, Hamilton, and Lusch (2019) argue that purely domestic firms, on average, have larger tax loss carryforwards than other firms, and their low effective tax rates can be explained, in part, by the utilization of these tax loss carryforwards. Dyreng, Hanlon, Maydew, and Thornock (2017) discuss tax losses and attempt to control for the effects, but these controls may have been limited due to data constraints. It is also important to consider that tax losses are not entirely exogenous.

Thomsen and Watrin (2018) extend Dyreng, Hanlon, Maydew, and Thornock (2017) by comparing the effective tax rates of U.S. multinationals to European multinationals. They find that effective tax rates have declined for both groups of firms, but more for European multinationals than for U.S. multinationals. They find that the downward trends of European multinationals are primarily driven by declines in statutory corporate tax rates around Europe. Dyreng, Hanlon, Maydew, and Thornock (2017) also find that the decline in foreign statutory tax rates (for example, European tax rates) is a partial driver of the declining trend for U.S. multinationals.

To provide further insight, possible effects of industry and size are examined in this chapter. Figure 10-5, panel B, presents the data by industry—high-tech firms versus firms in other industries.[19] The general trends shown in panel A generally also apply to firms in both high-tech industries and in other industries; namely, that tax rates are declining and that domestics generally have lower tax rates than multinationals.[20]

Figure 10-5, panel C, presents the data by size of firm—large and small firms. Cutoff points were created for each quintile of market value of equity of multinational firms in each year, and these cutoff points were used to assign all firms (multinationals and domestics) to five groups. By construction, the multinational firm-years are evenly spread across the five groups. The domestics are skewed to the smaller quintiles. Nevertheless, there are sufficient domestic and multinational observations in each quintile to facilitate analysis. In the subset of the largest firms, domestics and multinationals are fairly similar, with both groups exhibiting declining tax rates. And, for this subset of observations, neither domestic nor multinational firms have consistently lower cash effective tax rates. In contrast, in the smallest quintile, domestics have generally lower effective tax rates than multinationals. This finding appears consistent with Drake, Hamilton, and Lusch (2019), suggesting that small domestic firms possibly have greater loss carryforwards, resulting in their cash effective tax rates being relatively lower in profitable years. However, the data also suggest that large domestics do not achieve those types of benefits— large domestics and large multinationals are more similar to each other than are small domestics and small multinationals.[21] Thus, while the subset of large firms does not reveal that domestic firms have lower cash tax rates than multinationals, the totality of our analysis does not support the conventional narrative that multinationals have vastly lower tax rates or a steeper downward trend in tax avoidance than domestics.

After presenting data on tax avoidance in the cross-section and over time, the chapter now turns to literature on the factors associated with tax avoidance, methods of tax avoidance, and consequences of tax avoidance.

CHARACTERISTICS AND FACTORS ASSOCIATED WITH TAX AVOIDANCE

As noted earlier, the distribution of tax avoidance varies widely.[22] Over the past decade, researchers have published numerous studies attempting to explain this variation, with some progress. Nevertheless, researchers typically report adjusted R-squared statistics between 5 percent and 20 percent, suggesting that the bulk of the variation remains unexplained. For example, even with a full set of firm- and manager-fixed effects, Dyreng, Hanlon, and Maydew (2010) report an adjusted R-squared of at most 24 percent when examining one-year CASH ETR, while Chen, Chen, Cheng, and Shevlin (2010) report in their study of family firms an adjusted R-squared between 12 percent and 20 percent.

Despite difficulty explaining the variation in CASH ETR (and GAAP ETRs) overall, researchers have identified numerous factors that are correlated with ETRs (however defined).[23] First, several studies illustrate the effect of executive compensation packages on tax avoidance. Rego and Wilson (2012) report evidence consistent with a positive association between stronger equity risk incentives for the manager (designed to encourage the manager to take on risky projects) and tax avoidance (using various measures, one of which is CASH ETR), consistent with tax avoidance activities being risky investments. Phillips (2003) finds that compensating business unit managers on an after-tax basis is correlated with lower effective tax rates, and Armstrong, Blouin, and Larcker (2012) report that the tax director's incentive compensation is correlated with Generally Accepted Accounting Principles (GAAP) effective tax rates (rather than cash taxes paid), suggesting the importance of reported earnings numbers.

Not only do explicit managerial incentives affect tax avoidance, so do the managers themselves. In other words, compensation packages motivate behavior, but the managers themselves matter, separate from the firms, firm characteristics, and incentives. Dyreng, Hanlon, and Maydew (2010) find evidence that individual managers affect tax avoidance (that is, a manager fixed effect for tax avoidance), but the authors cannot isolate any particular factor that explains why (for example, age, education, power, and so forth). Subsequent research reports evidence consistent with some attributes of the executives mattering, such as prior military service (Law and Mills (2017)), personal tax aggressiveness (Chyz (2013)), religious social norms (Dyreng, Mayew, and Williams (2012); Boone, Khurana, and Raman (2013)), civic-mindedness (Hasan, Hoi, Wu, and Zhang (2017)), social connections (Brown and Drake (2014)), and political preferences (Francis, Hasan, Sun, and Wu (2016)).

Managers are also concerned with financial accounting earnings, and often appear to favor reporting high accounting earnings, even if this means paying more cash tax. For example, Erickson, Hanlon, and Maydew (2004) study firms that were accused by the SEC of overstating financial accounting earnings and were subsequently required to restate their financial results to remove the overstatement. By comparing restated financial results to the original overstated amounts, the authors find that the average firm in their sample paid eleven cents in cash taxes for an additional one dollar of overstated financial accounting earnings.[24] Graham, Hanlon, and Shevlin (2011) survey tax directors and report evidence that (1) top management at public firms often place more weight on GAAP effective tax rates than on cash taxes paid, and (2) the impact of repatriating foreign earnings on financial accounting income is an important determinant in the repatriation decision. Blouin, Krull, and Robinson (2012) use archival data and report evidence consistent with Graham, Hanlon, and Shevlin (2011).

The relationship of additional firm characteristics and tax avoidance has also been examined. For example, Badertcher, Katz, and Rego (2013) report evidence consistent with managers of closely held firms being more risk-averse, and consequently avoiding less tax. This finding is consistent with Chen, Chen, Cheng, and Shevlin (2010), who interpret their evidence as suggesting that family firms avoid less tax. In addition, McGuire, Wang, and Wilson (2014) study firms with dual-class ownership structures and find that as the wedge between voting rights and cash flow rights increases, tax avoidance declines. However, the results need to be interpreted with care.

The measures of tax avoidance employed in many of these studies were not designed to be employed across public and private firms, nor perhaps across firms with otherwise different ownership structures. The measures are usually some type of effective tax rate—cash taxes paid or income tax expense divided by pretax accounting earnings. As discussed, cash effective tax rates only capture non-conforming avoidance, meaning tax avoidance that lowers taxes paid but does not lower pretax accounting income. It is plausible that private firms and firms with otherwise lower capital-market pressures would be willing to engage in conforming tax avoidance (that is, the type that also lowers pretax accounting earnings). Thus, comparing effective tax rates across firms with different ownership structures, and different capital-market pressures, cannot be interpreted in the same manner as comparing effective tax rates across a sample of publicly traded firms. Effective tax rates are likely not as good a measure of tax avoidance in private firms (Hanlon and Heitzman (2010)).

Rego (2003) examines economies of scale and multinationality as determinants of GAAP effective tax rates.[25] Using data from 1990 to 1997, Rego (2003) finds that larger firms have higher GAAP effective tax rates, consistent with the political costs argument from Zimmerman (1983). Holding firm size constant, Rego (2003) also reports that firms with higher incomes have lower GAAP effective tax rates, consistent with the marginal benefit of tax avoidance increasing with profitability. Finally, Rego's results are consistent with multinational firms having lower GAAP effective tax rates than purely domestic firms, holding size and income level constant. In addition, Rego's evidence also suggests that multinational firms with more extensive foreign operations have lower GAAP effective tax rates than multinational firms with less extensive foreign operations, consistent with economies of scale for tax planning.[26]

Markle and Shackelford (2012 and 2013) study multinational companies from around the world, not just the United States. The authors document that Japanese and U.S. multinational corporations have the highest GAAP effective tax rates, while multinationals based in tax havens have the lowest. However, they find little difference between the effective tax rates of domestic and multinational firms. They also find that entering a tax haven is associated with subsequent declines in effective tax rates, consistent with Dyreng and Lindsey (2009).

Overall, the studies find that firms with more financial leverage, higher research and development expenses, and more property plant and equipment generally have relatively lower cash effective tax rates. Executives seem to matter, though it is not clear what the executive does to lower rates. In terms of multinationality, specifically, firms with more foreign earnings (especially in tax havens) are able to achieve relatively low tax rates, and this effect is stronger when the firm is also more intangible in nature (for example, more R&D spending). Nevertheless, the overall effect of multinationality on tax avoidance remains somewhat mixed, as some studies find that, when compared to domestic firms, multinational firms have lower rates (Rego (2003)), similar rates (Markle and Shackelford (2012)), or higher rates (Dyreng, Hanlon, Maydew, and Thornock (2017)).[27]

Although researchers have documented that tax avoidance is correlated with a multitude of factors, significant issues remain unresolved. First, it is difficult, if not impossible, to simultaneously study all the factors that have been shown to be correlated with tax avoidance. Thus, researchers have difficulty understanding just how much total variation in the tax avoidance distribution can be explained. Additionally, researchers struggle to determine with confidence which factors are the primary drivers of the variation in tax avoidance, because it is difficult to control for all known determinants of tax avoidance in a single model. Second, researchers commonly face problems of endogeneity, including both simultaneity and omitted correlated variables, and have had difficulty finding satisfying identification strategies. For example, R&D is correlated with tax avoidance, but it is unclear if the tax benefits of engaging in R&D per se causes lower CASH ETR, or if firms that engage in R&D also have a greater ability and propensity to shift income to low-tax jurisdictions, resulting in lower CASH ETR. The reality is that both effects are probably occurring, but it is difficult to identify which matters the most. To date, researchers have not identified a "silver bullet" that explains the cross-sectional variation in tax avoidance. To the extent that tax avoidance arises through actions beyond idiosyncratic personality traits or business models, researchers likely will use advanced econometric techniques and identify clever natural experiments to improve the understanding of the cross-sectional variation in tax avoidance.

HOW DO FIRMS AVOID TAXES?

Though many studies identify characteristics of firms and managers that are correlated with corporate tax avoidance, researchers generally stop short of identifying the exact nature of the actions taken that caused fewer taxes to be paid. This is partly because of the myriad options available to those considering how to avoid income taxes, as well as the lack of required public disclosures about firms' tax situations. Indeed, as discussed, managers' tax planning can range from using incentives clearly granted by statutory authority (for example, accelerated depreciation deductions, interest deductions, tax exempt municipal bond interest) to illegal tax evasion (for example, not reporting known taxable income), with many possibilities in between. This section identifies some of the known methods managers use to avoid taxes.[28]

Tax Avoidance via Provisions in the Tax Code

The tax code explicitly provides some methods of tax avoidance. For example, firms can take accelerated depreciation deductions on many types of capital assets and claim deductions for most types of interest paid. They can receive tax credits for certain research or experimentation, for investments in solar or wind energy (or the provision of equity by financial institutions to solar and wind developers), and for investments in low-income housing, among many other tax breaks. Each year, the U.S. Department of Treasury identifies the cost associated with these tax breaks in a report on tax expenditures. In 2015, the government identified 169 different types of corporate tax breaks, with deferral of tax on foreign earnings, research and experimentation credits, domestic production activities deductions, and low-income housing investment credits among the largest.

One of the largest statutory tax deductions is for interest.[29] Firms that use debt financing instead of equity financing can reduce their tax payments. Researchers have long debated just how significantly this tax break affects corporate capital structure and other corporate behaviors. Early researchers hypothesized that firms with non-debt tax shields (for example, depreciation deductions) would employ less leverage, but they often found the opposite because firms with high non-debt tax shields often had high financing needs (large physical capital assets drive both large amounts of depreciation and large needs for capital financing).

In the 1990s, researchers made progress in estimating firm-specific marginal tax rates (Shevlin (1990); Graham (1996)), which led to significant progress in documenting a relation between debt and taxes (Graham (1996 and 2000)).[30] However, some questions remain because estimating marginal tax rates is notoriously complicated and fraught with measurement error (for example, Shevlin (1990); Graham (1996); Blouin, Core, and Guay

(2010)), and because separating the effect of the marginal tax rate from other correlated factors can be difficult. For example, firms with low marginal tax rates are also more likely to experience existing or future losses, and are thus more likely to face higher bankruptcy costs and other frictions that make borrowing difficult. In addition, measuring leverage can be complicated. For example, financial reports do not capture some economic liabilities, and other liabilities can be "off-balance sheet" for financial accounting but deductible for tax purposes (see Mills and Newberry (2005)).[31] However, overall, the evidence suggests an association between debt and taxes; but how important taxes are in corporate capital structure (that is, what order effect) is still an open question.

Some companies have also significantly reduced their cash effective tax rates by using stock-based compensation. Until 2004, companies were not required to record a financial accounting expense for stock option compensation, but received tax deductions for the intrinsic value (market price less the strike price) of the compensation at exercise.[32] This created situations where tax liabilities were reduced significantly, but financial accounting income was not affected, resulting in very low CASH ETRs for some firms.[33] Since 2004, firms have been required to record financial accounting expense for share-based compensation in the amount of the "fair value" of the compensation on the grant date, with the financial accounting expense typically being recorded over the vesting period. Even with this expensing, during some years with high stock market appreciation, the deduction for stock compensation can be significantly larger than the financial accounting expenses recorded, such that some firms still report a very low CASH ETR. In addition, while the prior accounting standards did not require the book-tax difference for options to be accounted for in income tax expense (instead, the excess tax benefits were recorded in equity), current rules require the recording of a temporary difference related to the amount expensed for financial accounting and a permanent difference for any amount in excess of the compensation expense for financial accounting. As a result, income tax expense is now also lowered by any excess (for tax relative to book) deductions for stock options. Such an excess deduction for stock-based compensation was likely the major factor that reduced Amazon's federal current tax expense to zero in 2018.[34]

Just because the aforementioned tax breaks are explicitly listed in the tax code, does not mean that they are without controversy. For example, significant gray areas arise when determining what qualifies as an interest payment (and therefore deductible) versus a dividend payment (and therefore not deductible)—for example, in hybrid debt-equity investments. Likewise, there is substantial room for disagreement over what qualifies as a research or experimentation expenditure that might qualify for a tax credit instead of a less valuable deduction. With almost every codified tax deduction, there is some scope for companies to reduce taxes by interpreting the law to their benefit. Moreover, some countries (and states) negotiate directly with companies and grant special tax rates or tax holidays. Chow, Hoopes, and Maydew (2018) report that about 9.7 percent of U.S. public multinational firms reported participating in at least one tax holiday. Some special tax deals have recently been scrutinized; for example, the illegal state aid case brought by the European Union against Ireland and Apple.[35]

Tax Avoidance via "Tax Shelters"

In addition to favorable tax legislation, and the discretion allowed within those rules, companies also cleverly interpret the tax law to reduce tax payments. In the 1990s, some companies engaged in what became known as "corporate tax shelters" with colorful names and acronyms such as COLI (Corporate Owned Life Insurance), LILO (Lease-In, Lease-Out), BOSS (Bond and Option Sales Strategy), and so forth. These strategies were technically legal but widely viewed as being contrary to the intent of the law. Often they were sold to clients by law firms, accounting firms, or investment banks. Many researchers and others have described and examined these shelters. Prior research includes Bankman (2004), Graham and Tucker (2006), Hanlon and Slemrod (2009), Wilson (2009), and Brown (2011). The U.S. Treasury analyzed the shelters in 1999, investigative reporters have written about them (Byrnes and Lavelle (2003), Novack and Saunders (1998)), and there have been books—for example, *Perfectly Legal* (Johnson (2003)). While the nuances of these shelters are beyond the scope of this chapter, most of these transactions have been curtailed in recent years through increased penalties for taxpayers and advisors, and through more thorough reporting to the IRS and to the public in required financial reports.

Tax Avoidance via Income Shifting

Income shifting is high on the menu of tax avoidance options available to multinational firms.[36] This method of tax avoidance for MNCs has attracted the most attention, thus this chapter devotes more attention to the method, including a discussion of the various magnitude estimates.

Firms shift income by strategically using intercompany transactions to recognize earnings in low-tax jurisdictions. These intercompany transactions generally involve payments for goods and services, known as transfer prices, or intercompany interest payments on internal debt. Transfer prices and intercompany interest rates are required when doing business as a multinational whenever transactions happen between related entities, but they are also subject to strategic manipulation by companies because the same decisionmakers control both sides of the transaction.

Current rules require that intercompany transactions take place at an arm's-length price—a price that would have been used if the parties to the transaction were unrelated. In practice, however, the arm's-length price is difficult to enforce because open-market prices are difficult to observe or simply do not exist for many goods, services, and financing transactions. For example, when an internet user in France clicks on an advertisement delivered by Google, it seems reasonable for Google's French subsidiary to pay a royalty for use of the Google search algorithm and other intellectual property; after all, the algorithm was likely developed by engineers located outside France. But an open market does not exist for search algorithms, and hence an arm's-length royalty rate is unobservable and essentially nonexistent. Without an observable market price, Google necessarily makes assumptions about what the price should be, but those assumptions are influenced by Google's incentives, including the tax incentives. Thus, the theory of requiring an arm's-length price is sound, but perhaps in practice it is a difficult method of mitigating income shifting.

Recognizing the limitations of arm's-length pricing in controlling tax-motivated income shifting in some cases, countries have erected a wide variety of additional barriers, known as anti-base erosion provisions. These barriers include limitations on interest deductibility, withholding taxes on dividends, royalties, and interest payments, taxes on passive income, and many others (including the base erosion and anti-abuse tax (BEAT) in the United States in the TCJA). These anti-base erosion provisions increase the cost of income shifting, thereby reducing its prevalence.

Because tax rules are generally created at the individual-country level, and different countries seek different objectives with their tax systems, the existing international tax landscape is disjointed and extremely complicated.[37] Some countries tax the earnings of resident companies regardless of where they are earned. Other countries tax only the earnings generated within the home country. Some countries define residence as the location of management while others define it as the location of incorporation. Some countries have wide bilateral treaty networks that enable tax-efficient movement of capital, earnings, and goods and services between the two countries; others do not have large treaty networks.[38] The ultimate outcome of the uncoordinated nature of the international tax landscape is that some companies have opportunities to create complex structures and clever intercompany transactions that cause these tax systems to interact in the company's favor.

Anecdotal evidence of income shifting is pervasive, and a few of those anecdotes are cited below to illustrate several strategies used by some U.S. multinational companies.[39] First, some U.S. multinational companies with valuable intangible assets such as patents, copyrights, or trademarks arrange their global organizations so that the intangible asset is owned by a subsidiary in a low-tax country.[40] The transfer of ownership (or some ownership rights) usually requires a taxable payment by the low-tax subsidiary to the high-tax entity at a "fair market" arm's-length price. Thus, firms have an incentive to transfer ownership of intangible assets early in their life when their market value is low, or when market values are difficult to determine. For example, Uber transferred the rights to many of its intangible assets to foreign subsidiaries in the Netherlands in early 2013, shortly before a new round of venture capital financing increased the value of the company from US$330 million to about US$3.5 billion.[41] Once the low-tax subsidiary owns or controls the asset, it licenses the right to use it to other subsidiaries of the company that are located in other countries. Subsidiaries in these other countries (often with higher tax rates) pay royalties, license fees, or other compensation to the low-tax subsidiary each time they use the intangible asset owned by the low-tax subsidiary. As the value of the intangibles grows and they generate more income, these payments from the operating companies to the entity in the low-tax country grow. The payments to the entity in the low-tax country are generally tax deductible in the high-tax countries, thereby lowering, or even eliminating, the taxes owed to high-tax countries by entities in the high-tax countries. For example, Starbucks was accused of shifting income out of the United Kingdom by compelling its U.K. subsidiary to pay royalties for the Starbucks brand and business processes to its Dutch holding company. The net effect was that Starbucks reported no profits and paid no taxes in the United Kingdom, despite robust U.K. sales and claims by management to shareholders that U.K. operations were profitable. As in most of these cases, there are two sides to the story and the truth is not clear-cut. Sales and financial accounting profitability do not determine tax liabilities; rather, the tax rules of the jurisdictions determine taxation. Starbucks claimed the tax planning was legal and it did not technically owe U.K. tax. Some argued that the case was brought on moral, not legal, grounds. Regardless of whether Starbucks's actions were legal or moral, it falls within this chapter's definition of tax avoidance (a reduction of cash taxes paid relative to financial accounting income). Additionally, the case illustrates that when the apparent economics do not align with taxation, journalists and regulators notice. Indeed, reporters and regulators have raised similar accusations against other well-known companies. These accusations seem to be bringing about real change in the perception of tax avoidance and the regulations around the world.[42]

Second, many U.S. multinationals have been accused of using intercompany lending arrangements to strip earnings out of high-tax countries and report them in low-tax jurisdictions. In these arrangements, a subsidiary located in a low-tax country lends to a subsidiary in a high-tax country. The entity in the high-tax country pays interest on the loan, which is tax deductible in the high-tax country. The interest payments are taxable in the country where they are received, but because the lending subsidiary is generally located in a low-tax country, the overall company's tax bill is reduced. A recent example of a U.S. MNC involved in income shifting using intercompany debt is Hess, Inc. Hess's Norwegian subsidiary borrowed from Hess's Dutch subsidiary at an unusually high interest rate. The high interest rate reduced income in Norway and increased income in the Netherlands, where it was taxed at a lower rate than it would have been taxed in Norway. In 2017, the Norwegian government determined that the interest rate was not arm's length, and disallowed some of the deductions that the Norwegian subsidiary had claimed.

In some situations, complicated corporate structures are necessary for income shifting. Consider structures such as the Double Irish—or the Double Irish with the Dutch Sandwich—that have been implemented by U.S. companies (via Ireland) for the purpose of generating untaxed foreign earnings that are not immediately subjected to U.S. taxation.[43] In general, the structures involve a cost-sharing agreement where the low-tax jurisdiction foreign subsidiary acquires intellectual property (IP) from the U.S. parent company (either through a purchase or a licensing agreement).[44] The foreign subsidiary then shares in the cost to further develop the IP or to develop the market for the sales of the IP in other jurisdictions. As the foreign subsidiary bears risks and costs, it is entitled to the income from the sales of the product, effectively shifting the income (revenue and the shared costs) to the low-tax jurisdiction. This transaction is described in detail in Kleinbard (2011). Often in such strategies, the foreign earnings were ultimately recognized in other haven nations, giving rise to terms like the "Bermuda Black Hole" to describe the final destination of international profits of U.S. multinational firms.

The examples above illustrate how international tax rules can motivate firms to form complicated chains of ownership and intercompany transactions. Many of the structures require various subsidiaries and a series of intercompany contracts and payments. While many income-shifting anecdotes have been identified in the popular press and by academic researchers and policymakers, researchers have struggled to systematically study income shifting on a large scale. As a result, the extent to which income shifting occurs (that is, is it concentrated in a few sensational examples or is it more pervasive across firms?) and the overall magnitude of income shifting are not yet reliably known.

By its nature, income shifting is not directly observable, because the counterfactual—that is, what income would have been absent the income shifting—is not reported (or otherwise observable). As such, researchers must first estimate (using observable data) what earnings would have been had they not been shifted, and then compare this estimated quantity to reported income to infer shifted income. Thus, income shifting research is largely an exercise in estimating what earnings would have been if income were determined by economic factors of production, and testing to see whether the difference between actual earnings and estimated "as-if" earnings varies predictably with tax incentives to shift income.

It is important to note that companies expand and operate overseas for many reasons that have nothing to do with taxes (location of customers, labor costs, natural resources, and so forth). At the same time, the evidence suggests tax rates playing a significant role in location decisions and income reporting. In addition to the academic studies discussed below, government reports provide evidence that is consistent with income shifting. For example, the Government Accountability Office (GAO) reported in 2008 that foreign operations of U.S. multinationals in low-tax countries have income shares significantly larger than their share of other measures, such as physical assets, compensation, and employment. The relation was the opposite for most of the operations in high-tax foreign locations. Furthermore, the U.S. Treasury, in a study of transfer-pricing rules, examined the relation between controlled foreign corporation profitability and the statutory tax rate of the jurisdiction in which the controlled foreign corporation is located. Using tax filing data, the Treasury found an inverse relation between pretax profitability and tax rates. The evidence that some shifting likely occurs is pervasive. However, evidence that firms shift income does not necessarily mean they are doing any illegal tax planning. Many of the estimates, as described above (and below), measure income relative to what would be expected based on the location of the factors of production. However, the tax laws do not compute taxation based on the factors of production (or formulary apportionment).[45]

There is a large academic literature on income shifting, including some early seminal work, that this chapter cannot fully cover: for example, Altshuler and Grubert (2001), Altshuler, Grubert, and Newlon (2001), Grubert (2003), Harris (1993). Grubert and Slemrod (1998) and Grubert (2003) were early papers that recognized the importance of intangible assets for income shifting. For example, Grubert (2003) uses Treasury corporate tax return files for 1996 and finds that income derived from R&D-based intangibles account for about half of the income shifted from high-tax to low-tax countries. Grubert (2003) also reports that R&D-intensive subsidiaries engage in more intercompany transactions and thus have more opportunities to shift income. This chapter primarily focuses on more recent studies that attempt to quantify the shifting and also the studies that examine the determinants and the consequences of income shifting.

Estimating income shifting using macroeconomic data

In one line of studies, researchers use macroeconomic data to estimate income shifting. One early example is Hines and Rice (1994). They aggregate data at the country level and estimate variations on a model that takes the general form of

$$\log \pi_z = \beta_1 + \beta_2 logL_z + \beta_3 logK_z + \beta_4 logA + \beta_5 \tau_z + v_z, \tag{2}$$

where π_z is the sum of profits of all non-bank subsidiaries of U.S. parent firms in country z, L_z is labor input in country z, K_z is capital input in country z, A is a measure of the productivity of economic activity in country z, and τ_z is the country's tax rate. If reported earnings arise through the application of economic factors of production (that is, capital, labor, and country productivity), and taxes are not an economic factor of production, then the tax rate should not affect earnings. However, taxes might explain reported earnings if firms use intercompany transactions to report income in jurisdictions different from where it was economically generated. Hines and Rice (1994) conclude that high tax rates reduce reported profits, and that firms strategically shift earnings to low-tax countries to reduce their tax.

Other researchers have studied income shifting using macroeconomic data, including, most recently, Clausing (2020), Wright and Zucman (2018), and Torslov, Wier, and Zucman (2020). Clausing (2020) uses data from the U.S. Commerce Department's Bureau of Economic Analysis (BEA) on direct investment earnings to infer income shifting. She first provides evidence consistent with direct investment earnings being sensitive to the tax rate on those earnings (higher tax rates are correlated with lower direct investment earnings). She estimates that income shifting by U.S. multinationals reduced tax revenue collections by about US$100 billion in 2017. As mentioned, estimating income shifting is important but very difficult work, and there is no consensus in the literature of the economic magnitude of the problem. In recent work, for example, Blouin and Robinson (2019) argue that estimates of income shifting and revenue losses using macroeconomic data from the BEA are overstated due to double counting of some earnings.

Moreover, based on a simple back-of-the-envelope calculation, the estimate of US$100 billion in Clausing (2020) seems high. Consider that the sum of all foreign profits of publicly traded U.S. multinational firms in 2017 was US$513 billion.[46] Thus, if publicly traded U.S. multinational firms paid no tax at all on their earnings to foreign governments in 2017, then an upper bound of lost tax revenue would be 35 percent of US$513 billion, or about US$180 billion. But it is also the case that those same firms had a foreign current tax expense (which, as discussed above, is a rough proxy for taxes paid) of about US$111 billion during that same year. That means, ignoring any foreign tax credit limitations, that about US$69 billion in tax revenue was lost (US$180 billion minus US$111 billion). While it is possible that the discrepancy could be accounted for by private firms shifting income to low-tax foreign jurisdictions, it seems unlikely that the discrepancy could be so large.

Using a different approach, Torslov, Wier, and Zucman (2020) compare the profit-to-wage ratios of foreign firms to the ratios of local firms. They estimate that 40 percent of the foreign profits of multinational firms were shifted to tax havens in 2015. In a related study, Wright and Zucman (2018) argue that 60 percent of the foreign profits of U.S. multinational firms were in tax haven affiliates in 2015. This estimate also seems very high when compared to data derived from publicly available financial reports. Publicly traded U.S. multinational firms recorded pretax foreign income of US$416 billion in 2015. Applying the Wright and Zucman (2018) estimate that 60 percent of foreign income (or US$250 billion) was recognized in a tax haven (where presumably the tax rate is zero or very low), the remaining 40 percent (or US$166 billion) would have been taxed at a rate of 59 percent to account for the approximately US$98 billion in foreign current taxes recorded by these firms to foreign governments, a far higher rate than the OECD average statutory tax rate of about 25 percent in 2015. While it is plausible that a few companies recognized very large profits in tax havens, it seems unlikely that 60 percent of the foreign earnings of the typical U.S. multinational firm were recognized in a tax haven. In sum, while the evidence based on macroeconomic data suggests there is income shifting, the extent of the issue and magnitude of the income shifted is very much an open question.

Estimating Income Shifting Using Microeconomic Data

Because there are inherent limitations to research on income shifting using macroeconomic data, researchers have also employed firm-level data to estimate the magnitude of income shifting and study the factors associated with it.[47] Early work by Collins, Kemsley, and Lang (1998) examines the foreign profits of U.S. multinational firms relative to the same firms' consolidated worldwide profits. During their sample period, some foreign countries had higher statutory corporate tax rates than the U.S. statutory corporate tax rate. The authors report evidence consistent with abnormally high U.S. profits for firms that have relatively high foreign tax rates. The authors interpret the evidence as being consistent with tax-motivated income shifting into the United States. Their estimates imply that for each percentage point difference between the foreign tax rate and the U.S. tax rate, 1 percent of income is shifted for tax purposes. Using essentially the same methodology, Klassen and Laplante (2012) estimate that from 2005 to 2009, U.S. multinational firms shifted US$10 billion of income more per year *out* of the United States than from 1998 to 2002.

Huizinga and Laeven (2008) extend Hines and Rice (1994) by applying the Hines and Rice (1994) method to firm-level data (usually from public sources concentrated in Europe) instead of country-level data. In addition, the authors develop a new proxy for the tax incentives to shift income that takes into account all of the statutory tax rates of the firm's subsidiaries simultaneously, and varies for each of the firm's subsidiaries each year (but includes only subsidiaries and tax rates of countries of subsidiaries included in their data). Huizinga and Laeven (2008) primarily study the economic magnitude of income shifting and find that a decrease of the statutory tax rate of 1 percentage point increases reported profits in the country by less than 1 percent in many countries, a semi-elasticity that is similar to that reported by Collins, Kemsley, and Lang (1998). Overall, they report an average semi-elasticity of about 1.31, but the estimate varies significantly, depending on the empirical specification.

Dharmapala and Riedel (2013) use a different approach to identify income shifting. They first identify exogenous shocks to the income of parent firms and then trace the shocks through to affiliates of the firm. They find evidence that shocks to income at the parent firm are more likely to manifest in higher reported profits in low-tax affiliates than in high-tax affiliates, suggesting tax-motivated income assignment. Davies, Martin, Parenti, and Toubal (2018) examine French firm-level data on export prices to both related affiliates and to unrelated third parties. The authors find evidence that tax avoidance through transfer pricing is large and the activity is concentrated—most of it is driven by exports of 450 firms to ten tax havens.

Although many recent income-shifting studies use affiliate-level (micro) data, the data have some weaknesses. First, publicly available datasets (for example, data from the Bureau van Dijk Amadeus database (BVD)) generally do not contain detailed affiliate-level data on the financial results of the entire firm. Instead, information about some parts of the firm exist in reasonable levels of detail (for example, European subsidiaries), while information about other parts of the firm is almost nonexistent (for example, Asian subsidiaries, tax havens outside of Europe—the Cayman Islands, Bermuda, and so forth). This compels researchers to make estimates by examining only a fraction of the firm's geographic footprint that is not randomly selected, but possibly is correlated with key variables such as a country's tax status. An example of this problem is highlighted by Torslov, Wier, and Zucman (2020). Torslov, Wier, and Zucman (2020) discuss micro data and its problems to explain their use of macro data. They state that of the more than US$50 billion in consolidated profits reported by Apple in 2016, only about US$2 billion can be identified in Apple's subsidiaries using publicly available data sources commonly used to apply the Huizinga and Laeven (2008) model, which is an affiliate-level model. They argue that this discrepancy suggests that estimates calculated using publicly available micro-level data generate unreliable point estimates, because the data cover such a small fraction of some firms. We note that while the lack of complete coverage by the BVD database is concerning, some researchers have developed clever techniques to minimize the effect of the incomplete data problem (for example, Dharmapala and Riedel (2013)).

Second, and related to the first, because BVD data (commonly used in firm-level and affiliate-level) income-shifting studies only provide a partial view of the entire firm, researchers cannot easily track the flow of funds. In principle, one advantage to micro-level data is that it can be used to observe subsidiaries with abnormally low earnings and corresponding subsidiaries with abnormally high earnings, and thereby determine the flow of funds within the firm. Unfortunately, with such sparse data, such estimates are difficult.

Finally, some researchers have used consolidated public filings for U.S. multinational firms, which contain earnings numbers that are disaggregated to show domestic and foreign components (for example, Dyreng and Markle (2016), Klassen and Laplante (2012)). These data are advantageous because they include all of the firm's earnings, but they come at a major cost. They do not contain detailed information on the specific countries where the earnings were reported. Thus, using these data, researchers are forced to examine only shifting into or out of the United States, but cannot examine shifting from one subsidiary to another within the same family group, nor can they identify which tax haven countries receive the shifted income.

Overall, and with the above data limitations in mind, the estimated magnitude of income shifting using firm-level (or affiliate-level; microeconomic) data is generally smaller than the estimated magnitude using country-level (macroeconomic) data (Dharmapala (2014)). Indeed, Heckemeyer and Overesch (2013) systematically evaluated the elasticities estimated in twenty-seven unique empirical studies, most of which used microeconomic data, and found that the consensus elasticity is about 0.8, which is significantly smaller than the elasticities typically found in studies that use macroeconomic data.[48]

Summary of Income Shifting Literature

The weight of the evidence is consistent with firms shifting income away from high-tax countries into low-tax countries. The evidence is consistent with this outcome across studies that employ public and private data, macro and micro data, and with a variety of techniques. Nevertheless, these same studies report widely varying estimates of the magnitude of the phenomenon. Thus, the extent to which income shifting occurs is still debated and is still an open question. More progress will (hopefully) be made as additional data become available, as econometric techniques advance, and by conducting tests as tax rules change.

Tax Avoidance via Location Decisions Regarding Investment, Incorporation, and Debt

Multinational firms can also go beyond merely shifting reported income to different locations; they can reduce their tax bill by relocating real activities. Indeed, the two actions are not mutually exclusive. Firms make location decisions based on many factors, taxes being one. Once an investment is made in a low-tax jurisdiction, it is likely that opportunities for tax avoidance (for example, income shifting) expand. In addition, if a firm engages in income shifting, sometimes structural changes (for example, local investments) are required to support the income shifting (a type of feedback effect).

The most straightforward action is that firms will locate investment in low-tax jurisdictions. Indeed, the literature finds that a decrease in a country's tax rate leads to an increase in foreign direct investment. DeMooij and Ederween (2003) conducted a meta-analysis and concluded that across the outcomes in the twenty-five studies they analyze, the median value of the tax elasticity is around minus 3.3; a 1 percent reduction in the host country tax raises foreign direct investment in that country by 3.3 percent.[49]

Studies on the recent "innovation- or patent-box" regimes, which provide lower effective tax rates on income derived from intellectual property, report some evidence that firms change the location of patents and also capital expenditures (see Böhm, Karkinsky, Knoll, and Riedel (2015); Bradley, Dauchy, and Robinson (2015); Bradley, Robinson, and Ruf (2018); and others) when innovation-box legislation becomes effective, suggesting that lower tax rates attract investment.

Companies can also change their tax residence to a low-tax jurisdiction, an action sometimes known as a tax inversion. The goal of an inversion is generally to escape U.S. taxation on foreign earnings and to strip income out of the United States via deductible payments from the U.S. entity to the new foreign "parent" (for example, interest). There have been waves of inversions, in the United States and in other countries as well (specifically, the United Kingdom before it became a more tax-favorable jurisdiction). The United States has countered with increasingly strict tax rules that make inversions less beneficial, and the TCJA, based on the evidence so far, seems to have stopped inversions out of the United States.

There was a significant inversion wave from the late 1990s through 2001. Inverting firms during this period would often state that part of the reason to invert was to save taxes. For example, Ingersoll-Rand stated that it expected to save US$40 million a year, and Cooper Industries expected to save US$55 million a year in U.S. taxes (Cloyd, Mills, and Weaver (2003)). Another wave of inversions occurred in the mid-2010s. Pfizer tried to invert in 2015 (via merging with Allergan), but the U.S. government implemented rules to stop the transaction. Seida and Wempe (2004) examined inverting firms' effective tax rates and showed that they do indeed decline after inversions. Several studies looked at the market reaction to inversion announcements during the earlier wave (Cloyd, Mills, Weaver (2003); Desai and Hines (2002)) and found somewhat mixed evidence, with Cloyd, Mills, and Weaver (2003) finding no statistical market reaction to inversion announcements, but Desai and Hines (2002) finding a small positive market reaction to inversion announcements.

Finally, firms can also locate financial debt capital in foreign locations to take advantage of tax treatment and tax rules and use debt location to shift income. Newberry and Dhaliwal (2001) provide evidence that U.S. multinationals allocate debt based on jurisdiction-specific tax loss carryforwards and foreign tax credit considerations. Furthermore, Huizinga, Laeven, and Nicodeme (2008), Egger, Keuschnigg, Merlo, and Wamser (2014), and Buettner and Wamser (2013) provide evidence for European firms of tax-motivated income shifting via debt. Fuest, Hebous, and Riedel (2011) examined income shifting via debt in developing countries and provide evidence that the effects are larger than in developed countries.[50]

Thus, firms can choose to locate their investment, place of incorporation, and debt across the globe in a manner that will save taxes. Setting up such structures often enables income shifting to occur and then sometimes income shifting requires a further commitment for real investment offshore.

CONSEQUENCES OF TAX AVOIDANCE

Beyond simply documenting the existence of tax avoidance (for example, shifting income and changing real behavior to lower taxes), and attempting to estimate the economic magnitude of the phenomenon, researchers have examined many subsequent economic outcomes associated with tax avoidance. The research that has examined some of the significant consequences of tax avoidance by U.S. multinational firms is discussed below.

Consequences: Lost Revenues

The most obvious consequence of tax avoidance is that governments around the world lose revenue. Estimates of just how much are difficult to compute with much reliability, because, of course, the revenue that would be raised in a world where no one avoided paying taxes is unknowable. In addition, tax incentives can potentially raise revenue for governments, and even perhaps provide other valuable economic benefits, such as increased investment and employment. The value of those benefits would need to be estimated and offset against lost revenue. As discussed above, the magnitude of lost revenue from tax avoidance of any type, including income shifting, is unsettled.[51]

Consequences: Pre-TCJA "Trapped Cash" and Its Effect on Corporate Capital Structure, Payout Policy, and Investment

As discussed, many tax avoidance strategies of multinationals included moving operations and investments to low-tax jurisdictions and shifting income to low-tax jurisdictions. As investments were made in low-tax foreign jurisdictions and income was shifted to low-tax foreign jurisdictions, U.S. companies had earnings and cash in those jurisdictions that would be subject to the relatively high U.S. tax rate if repatriated to the United States. As a result (at least in part due to the U.S. tax), U.S. multinationals had large and growing cash balances in foreign entities (Foley, Hartzell, Twitman, and Twite (2007)). In other words, the companies had what came to be known as *trapped* cash.[52]

Effect of "Trapped Cash" on Capital Structure and Payout Policy

Many anecdotes suggest that U.S. firms increased U.S. borrowing because they did not have access to their foreign cash. For example, back in

1993, Apple Computer Inc. (now Apple Inc.) was preparing to issue US$500 million in debt and was being questioned about why it needed to issue debt. The company responded that it was considering issuing debt to pay for new research and development facilities. Analysts at the time noted that the situation was unusual because Apple had more than US$1 billion in cash on hand and no long-term debt obligations. The investor relations spokesperson for Apple at the time, Bill Slakey, responded that Apple was reluctant to draw on its cash reserves because much of the cash was outside the United States and repatriating it would produce a significant tax bill (Weber (1993)). Potentially even more costly than issuing debt, a few years later Apple considered merging or selling itself to Sun-Microsystems because its "financial condition was worsening." Apple noted that its board contemplated the merger as potentially ". . . the best way to save the company, which is facing a cash crunch to pay future restructuring charges and an upcoming debt payment." An analyst from Brown Brothers Harriman said that Apple had US$1.1 billion in cash, but most of it was in foreign subsidiaries. He stated, "If they were to draw it out, it would be subject to taxation. It's liquid, but it's like drawing money from a 401(k) (retirement plan) or something" (Poletti (1996)).[53] Several academic studies support the idea that many U.S. firms borrowed in the United States to fund U.S. operations and payouts.[54] For example, Graham, Hanlon, and Shevlin (2010), in a survey of tax executives, report that nearly 45 percent of firms stated they borrow money in the United States to avoid the repatriation tax. Beyer, Downes, and Rapley (2017) examine internal capital market inefficiencies (for example, the repatriation tax) and how such inefficiencies affect payout policy and corporate leverage. The authors conclude that domestic cash is a typical determinant of payouts, but that increases in foreign cash are also significantly associated with shareholder payout for investment-grade firms that can borrow. In a related paper, De Simone and Lester (2018) find that firms with large foreign cash balances have relatively high domestic debt.

Effect of "Trapped Cash" on Investment

Researchers have also examined the effects of tax avoidance behavior and trapped cash on investment. Faulkender and Petersen (2012) find that financially constrained firms appear to forgo domestic investments because of the frictions repatriation taxes create in internal capital markets. Hanlon, Lester, and Verdi (2015) investigate the merger-and-acquisition activity (and capital expenditures and R&D) of firms with large amounts of trapped cash due to the repatriation tax. The authors examine whether the locked-out cash is associated with more foreign acquisitions (in other words, whether the cash is burning a hole in managers' pockets). They find that locked-out cash is associated with a higher likelihood of foreign acquisitions (as well as foreign capital expenditures and R&D spending), but not domestic acquisitions and capital spending. The authors also document a negative association between locked-out cash and the market reaction to a foreign deal, which they interpret as evidence the market views those acquisitions as less value-enhancing. Similarly, Edwards, Kravert, and Wilson (2016) examine the market reaction to foreign acquisitions and report evidence that firms with high levels of trapped cash make less profitable (measured as lower returns and lower return-on-assets after the transaction) acquisitions of foreign targets.

Bird, Edwards, and Shevlin (2017) examine acquisition behavior of foreign acquirers. The authors' evidence suggests foreign acquirers are tax-favored relative to U.S. acquirers when the target company has substantial trapped cash. The hypothesis is that foreign firms can acquire U.S. targets and avoid the U.S. tax on the locked-out cash, whereas U.S. acquirers cannot avoid the tax. The authors' results are consistent with their hypothesis.

Thus, the evidence suggests that, before the TCJA, investment and investment location were affected by tax avoidance behavior and the resulting trapped cash of U.S. multinational firms.

Consequences: Employment

Some evidence suggests that tax rates affect employment, and some recent evidence suggests that tax avoidance affects both employment and the location of employment. Much of this work is conducted using data at the state level in the United States. For example, Giroud and Rauh (2019) use data from the U.S. Census Bureau to examine whether state-level business taxation affects employment and capital. Their research design tests the responses of different organizational forms to different tax rates. Their data span 1977 to 2011, and they find that increases in the state corporate tax rates are associated with fewer establishments and fewer employees at corporations, but not at businesses not taxed as corporations. Moretti and Wilson (2014) provide evidence that state-level subsidies for biotech employers is associated with significant increases in the number of star biotech scientists in that state. They also estimate that much of the response is due to the relocation of the scientists across state lines.[55]

The effect of tax incentives on labor in an international setting is even more lightly studied, likely due to the paucity of data. One example, however, is Williams (2018), who studies whether tax incentives explain job offshoring. He cites the congressional testimony of attorney Paul Oosterhuis of Skadden, Arps, Slate, Meagher & Flom LLP (2013), who explained that, under the then-current transfer pricing rules, the party that bears the costs and risks in an arm's-length transaction is entitled to the bulk of the return. Hence, moving labor offshore, in some cases, supports the rights to the income in the offshore location (in other words, manufacturing had to follow the income shifting). Oosterhuis, in his testimony, attributed much of the loss of manufacturing (investment and labor) in the United States to these tax incentives. Indeed, the outcome of manufacturing following income shifting was implied by the models presented in prior literature (for example, Hines and Rice (1994), Grubert and Slemrod (1998), and Gordon and Hines (2002)). Williams (2018) uses data reported by the Department of Labor's Trade Adjustment Assistance (TAA) program that covers 80,000 offshored jobs during his sample period, 2003 to 2009. Williams finds a negative association between the number of jobs offshored to a country and the corporate tax rate in that country. He finds significant cross-sectional variation in that firms where the jobs are kept within the worldwide firm are much more likely to be responsive to tax rates as compared to instances when the jobs are outsourced to a third party.

Fuest, Peichl, and Siegloch (2018) examine data on corporate taxes imposed by German municipalities—the German local business tax (LBT)—to estimate how much of the corporate tax falls on workers in the form of lower wages. This setting is useful for several reasons, one of which is that the municipality determines the rate of tax but the base is determined at the federal level. In addition, there is substantial variation in rates and almost 18,000 changes (6,802 are used in their study) in tax rates across thousands of municipalities over their twenty-year sample period. They conclude that wages decrease significantly after tax increases; indeed, they estimate that workers bear about half of the total tax corporate burden. Other results in their study suggest that wages are more sensitive to tax rates in more profitable firms, but at the same time, the wage effects are almost zero for very large firms, foreign-owned firms, and firms that operate in multiple jurisdictions. One possible explanation is that these firms can engage in more profit shifting to avoid the tax increase, and thus there is no response in wages.

More recent evidence on the effects of tax provisions, such as the domestic production activities deduction (DPAD) (Lester (2019); Dobridge, Landefeld, and Mortenson (2019); and Ohrn (2018)), is also informative. The DPAD was enacted as part of the American Jobs Creation Act in 2004. It allowed firms to deduct a portion of income related to domestic production when determining their U.S. income tax liability; effectively equivalent to a 3.15 percentage point rate decrease on domestic manufacturing income. The evidence from the studies suggests that the DPAD increased capital expenditures by firms who claimed the deduction and that the increase in investment was greatest when the benefits of the tax provision were fully phased in.[56] In addition, the evidence suggests employment costs did not increase (and indeed decreased) after the tax cut in the DPAD. Thus, the lower tax rate on certain activities is associated with greater investment related to those activities and what seems like a substitution effect of capital for labor in that setting.

Consequences: Transparency and Shareholder Value

Several studies examine the hypothesis that having subsidiaries in tax-haven countries reduces transparency and drains shareholder value. Bennedsen and Zeume (2018) argue that tax havens enable managers to derive private benefits at the expense of shareholders, because operating in tax havens creates opacity that allows managers to hide information from shareholders.[57] They argue that when tax-haven countries sign tax information exchange agreements (TIEAs), both transparency and shareholder value increase. They find that the value of firms with subsidiaries in tax-haven countries that sign TIEAs increases by 2.5 percent, suggesting that the benefits of transparency accrue to shareholders. These findings are consistent with Balakrishnan, Blouin, and Guay (2018), who provide evidence that aggressive tax planning is correlated with lower corporate transparency; with Hope, Ma, and Thomas (2013), who find that managers that engage in tax planning give less information about the location of their earnings in geographic segment disclosures; and with Durnev, Li, and Magnan (2016), who provide evidence that firms incorporated in tax havens trade at a discount.[58]

WHY NOT? WHAT ARE THE CONSTRAINTS ON TAX AVOIDANCE?

So far, this chapter has presented data showing that, in the aggregate, multinational firms pay a substantial amount of income tax. However, it has also presented evidence suggesting a significant amount of tax avoidance is occurring, especially by firms with certain characteristics and managers, and that tax avoidance is increasing. A question that naturally arises is why firms do not avoid more taxes. In other words, what are the constraints on tax avoidance?[59] An easy answer is tax avoidance stops when the marginal costs exceed the marginal benefits. But what are the costs?

Some limited evidence is available in the literature. For example, in their survey of tax executives in 2007, Graham, Hanlon, Shevlin, and Shroff (2014) asked the question, "Has your company ever considered *but decided not to* implement a tax planning strategy proposed and/or marketed by an accounting, law, investment, or tax consulting firm?" For those that answered yes, the authors asked, "What factors were important in your company's decision not to implement the tax planning strategy that was proposed?" Admittedly, this is narrower than the general question posed in this section, but such an approach is necessary in survey questions and provides helpful insights nonetheless.

The responses are summarized in their figure 1 and reproduced in this chapter's figure 10-6. The data are presented separately in the figure for public firms and private firms. The factor attracting the most (86 percent of the sample) "important and very important" responses (a rating of 3 or 4 on a Likert scale from 0 to 4) was that "the transaction lacked business purpose and/or economic substance." Related, the factor that received the third-most "important or very important" responses (62 percent) was "risk of detection by the IRS." Thus, the validity of the tax planning, whether the company will be caught, and whether the tax planning benefits would be retained are among the most important costs considered by firms.

The factors that received the second- and fourth-most responses concern the company's reputation. The second most important factor in limiting engaging in tax planning was "potential harm to your company reputation" (69.5 percent overall rated it important or very important; 72.2 percent of publicly traded companies did). The fourth most important factor was "risk of adverse media attention (for example, *Wall Street Journal* coverage)" with 57.6 percent of companies (60 percent of public companies) stating that this

FIGURE 10-6. Incentives and Disincentives to Tax Plan

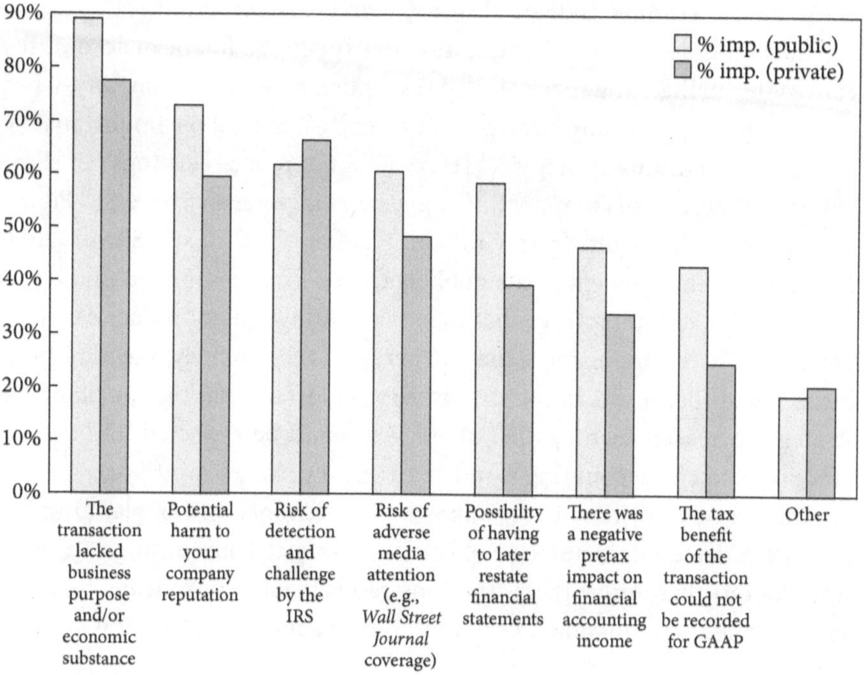

Note: This figure is taken from Graham, Hanlon, Shevlin, and Shroff (2014) where data are analyzed from six hundred tax directors' responses to survey questions about tax planning (and other topics). The figure is figure 1 in the Graham, Hanlon, Shevlin, and Shroff (2014) paper. The figure presents the responses to the survey question "What factors were important in your company's decision not to implement the tax planning strategy that was proposed?" The survey provides a 5-point rating scale ranging from 0 to 4 with a rating of 0 labeled "Not at all important" and a rating of 4 labeled "Very important." This figure presents the percentages of respondents that gave a rating of 3 or 4 for each factor. The results are shown separately for public and private firms.

factor was "important or very important" at their company in limiting tax planning. Thus, reputation effects seem to be a significant deterrent to engaging in tax planning strategies.[60]

Another factor that attracted a high importance rating by at least a large minority of firms was the financial accounting implications of tax planning. Figure 10-6 reveals that more than 50 percent of publicly traded firms considered the possibility of having to restate accounting earnings when deciding on a tax planning strategy. In addition, more than 40 percent of publicly traded firms cited two other factors that were important in their decisions not to engage in tax planning: (1) a negative financial accounting effect (that is, financial accounting earnings that had to be reduced to lower taxable income), and (2) not being able to record the tax benefits for financial accounting (for example, a deferral strategy, or a too-risky strategy).

The authors asked another question to explore the financial accounting constraint further. The survey asked respondents, "At your company, when evaluating a tax planning strategy that saves cash taxes, how important is it that the tax planning strategy . . . (1) . . . does not reduce earnings per share (EPS) and (2) . . . leads to reporting higher earnings per share (EPS)." Figure 10-7 presents the results from Graham, Hanlon, Shevlin, and Shroff (2014; figure 3). Seventy percent of the publicly traded firms responded that it was important or very important that the tax planning did not reduce earnings per share. Furthermore, more than 50 percent of the publicly traded respondents stated that it was important or very important that the tax planning strategy increased earnings per share. As would be expected, the importance of financial accounting is much lower for private firms.[61]

Thus, based on these data, important constraints on tax planning are the risk of detection, reputation effects, and financial accounting concerns. And there are certainly others. The constraints must be significant, because, as mentioned, multinational corporations are paying a substantial amount of taxes.

EARLY EVIDENCE ON BEPS AND TCJA

Earlier, this chapter replicated and extended Dyreng, Hanlon, Maydew, and Thornock (2017) through 2018. One advantage of extending the trends is that it enables an examination of the early effects of the TCJA, which lowered the corporate statutory tax rate in the United States to 21 percent beginning in 2018. As figure 10-5 shows, both purely domestic firms and multinational firms had distinct drops in cash effective tax rates in 2018 (as also shown in figure 10-2, panel F). The decrease is particularly noticeable for purely domestic firms, probably because their entire incomes were subjected to the lower tax rates, while only a fraction of multinational firms' incomes benefit from the reduced rates. The remaining fraction of multinationals' income continued to be subject to the tax rates of the foreign countries in which they operated (and potentially subject to the new tax on global intangible low-taxed income in the United States).

Many researchers are studying the immediate effects of the TCJA. One early study by Hanlon, Hoopes, and Slemrod (2019) examined firm actions and firm disclosures about their actions in response to the TCJA. The au-

FIGURE 10-7. Financial Accounting Incentives for Tax Planning

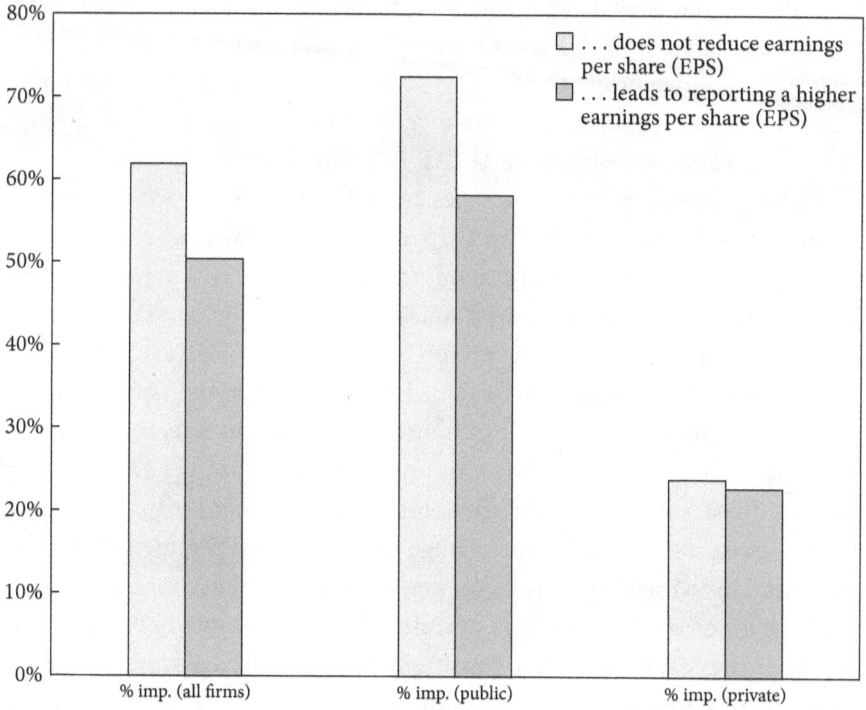

Note: Figure 10-7 is from Graham, Hanlon, Shevlin, and Shroff (2014; figure 3). The figure presents the responses to the survey question "At your company, when evaluating a tax planning strategy that saves cash taxes, how important is it that the tax planning strategy . . . (1) . . . does not reduce earnings per share (EPS) and (2) . . . leads to reporting a higher earnings per share (EPS)." The survey provides a 5-point rating scale ranging from 0 to 4 with a rating of 0 labeled "Not at all important" and a rating of 4 labeled "Very important." This figure presents the percentages of respondents that gave a rating of 3 or 4 for each factor. The results are shown separately for public and private firms.

thors find that, in their sample, 4 percent of firms disclosed worker bonuses or increases in wages, and 22 percent disclosed that they would increase investment. The authors find an increase in share repurchases, but the increase (at that time) was concentrated in a small number of firms. Other studies examined the limitations on interest deductibility and the effect on corporate leverage (Carrizosa, Gaertner, and Lynch (2019)), the investment effects of the TCJA (for example, Beyer, Downes, Mathis, and Rapley (2019)), compensation effects (Luna, Schuchard, and Stanley (2019)), and stock-repurchase behavior (Bennet, Thakor, and Wang (2019)). Many of these studies are not fully vetted yet, and the post-TCJA time series of data is limited.

Many articles also provide anecdotes, commentary, and institutional details about what is occurring and what might be expected after the TCJA. For example, Horst (2020) provides excellent insights into companies repatriating intangible property after the TCJA. In addition, Horst (2019b) provides preliminary estimates of the revenue effects of the TCJA, and Horst (2019a) describes the impact on GAAP ETRs for large companies.

The experience of other countries can offer insight into what to expect, namely the United Kingdom and Japan when they lowered corporate tax rates and moved to territorial systems (though neither country adopted exactly the same rules as the United States). One paper that studied the move to territorial taxation by the United Kingdom is Liu (2019). It reports evidence that the territorial tax reform increased the investment of U.K. multinationals in low-tax countries by almost 16 percent. Liu tests investment in high-tax countries by U.K. firms and investment within the United Kingdom by these same firms and finds no statistically significant changes in either. Thus, she concludes the change to a territorial regime led to more outbound investment by U.K. firms and more investment overall.

Hasegawa and Kiyota (2017) examine the repatriation effects of Japan's changes. They report evidence consistent with increased dividend repatriation, but in a varied way. Firms with large amounts of retained earnings were more responsive and increased repatriations more. It is interesting to note that the authors find withholding tax rates on dividends became more important in the decision to repatriate after the law change.

Whether or not similar results will occur in the United States remains to be seen. Identifying the different effects of the TCJA will be difficult because many of the provisions in the TCJA affected all companies at once and many tax rules were changed at the same time. In addition, many other events were occurring roughly around the same time as the law change, such as tariffs, and also international tax rules from the OECD.

INDIRECT TAXES

This chapter focuses on income taxes, but businesses also pay substantial amounts in other taxes. Some examples include payroll taxes, property taxes, customs and export duties, tariffs, and extractive taxes. In addition, businesses are often responsible for collecting and remitting consumption taxes, such as the state retail sales taxes in the United States and the value-added tax or goods and services tax in many other countries. While consumption taxes in theory are passed on to consumers, evidence suggests businesses bear part of these taxes.[62]

Firms are not required to make substantial detailed disclosures about indirect tax payments, which makes these taxes more difficult to study. A few companies, however, voluntarily disclose information about indirect taxes. The appendix presents a few examples, including disclosures from Verizon and Exxon Mobil. Panel A of the appendix provides Verizon's disclosure on income taxes, employment taxes, and property and other taxes. In 2017, taxes other than income taxes accounted for about 40 percent of the total taxes paid by Verizon. In 2018, indirect taxes constituted nearly 55 percent of total taxes paid, which reflects the decline in the statutory corporate income tax rate from 35 percent to 21 percent. Panel B provides Exxon Mobil's disclosure. Exxon Mobil reports income and "other taxes and duties" (that is, indirect taxes) separately for those incurred in the United States and foreign countries. In 2016, the company reported U.S. income tax expense of about negative US$3 billion but positive U.S. indirect taxes of US$4.4 billion. In 2016, the company reported nearly US$27 billion in indirect taxes in non-U.S. jurisdictions constituting 91 percent of its total tax expense for the year. In 2018, the company paid nearly US$5 billion in indirect taxes to the United States and more than US$30 billion to non-U.S. jurisdictions. Indirect taxes constitute 81 percent of total U.S. tax expenses and 78 percent of the total non-U.S. tax expenses.

As more companies provide corporate social responsibility reports (CSR reports), environmental, sustainability, and governance reports (ESG), and reports under the Extractive Industries Transparency Initiative (EITI), somewhat more disclosures about various taxes will become available. For example, Freeport-McMoRan, a mining company, issues a report titled "Transparency of Government Payments" as part of its disclosures via the EITI. Its table from this report is in panel C of the appendix.

RioTinto, another mining company, issues what is likely the most comprehensive set of disclosures. The company's thirty-three-page report in 2018, "Taxes Paid: Our Economic Contribution," highlights that it paid US$6.6 billion in global taxes and royalties to various governments. It reports a global effective income tax rate of 28.6 percent for 2018 and a global effective tax rate of all taxes and royalties paid of 37.4 percent.[63]

Indirect taxes can also affect foreign affiliate investments and output (Desai, Foley, and Hines (2004)), and cross-border mergers (Herger, Kotsogiannis, and McCorriston (2016)). In addition, researchers have found that indirect tax benefits affect location decisions, and in some cases increase employment (for example, Greenstone and Moretti (2003)).[64]

Researchers have also found evidence that firms attempt to avoid indirect taxes. Opportunities for tax avoidance arise because there are differences in the location of taxation—place of supply (destination) or place of incorporation (origin) for different goods and services, and sometimes differences based on whether the sale is digital. Using value-added taxes as an example, companies can channel sales through affiliates in low-VAT-tax countries and sell into higher-VAT-tax countries when the origin principle is applied. For example, Poniatowski, Bonch-Osmolovskiy, and Belkindas (2016) reported a "VAT gap" (that is, underpayment of VAT) of 159.5 billion euro in 2014. There is also evidence in the United States that online retailers, in contrast to brick-and-mortar retailers, avoid a taxable nexus when consumption taxes increase (Bruce, Fox, and Luna (2015)).[65]

CONCLUSIONS

This chapter reviews, and at times extends, the literature on tax avoidance by multinational firms and its effects. First, multinational corporations pay a substantial amount of taxes, both direct and indirect. Nevertheless, there is (1) evidence of tax avoidance via income shifting, and (2) evidence that real investment, debt, and employment are sensitive to taxation. Naturally, the two effects are not independent of each other. As noted in Hines (2014), if shifting income were possible without accompanying real changes to investments, those real investments would be insensitive to taxation, because the negative consequences of taxes could be eliminated by simply shifting income to a more favorable jurisdiction. Instead, firms face complex investment problems where the optimal solution often results in distorted real activities and accounting choices relative to a world without taxes. In addition, the fact that multinational firms pay substantial taxes suggests that there are constraints on tax avoidance. Also, the data suggest a great deal of variation in tax avoidance, meaning some firms seem to avoid taxes over a long period while others do not. Prior literature has identified some factors associated with this variation, but to date no single factor has been identified as really driving tax avoidance.

Multinational corporations, relative to domestic-only corporations, can avoid taxes by shifting income to low-tax jurisdictions. The literature provides a plethora of evidence that income shifting occurs, but the extent to which it occurs is still an open question. It appears, based on the evidence and many sources of data, that some of the estimates of income shifting seem implausibly large. Improvements may be obtained if (when) future researchers invent new methods of estimating income shifting or when new data become available. Better estimates (and more agreement about the estimates) will be imperative in evaluating the recent tax policies of the United States, the European Union, and the OECD (barring other research design issues).

Finally, most of this chapter's evidence is about U.S. multinational corporations in the pre-TCJA tax regime. During the period over which most of the studies referenced in this chapter were conducted, the data suggests that tax avoidance begets more tax avoidance. Once a company sets up a tax avoidance structure, future behavior generally must fit within or support the structure. In addition, one consequence of tax avoidance in the pre-TCJA period for a multinational firm was trapped cash in foreign subsidiaries that led to more U.S. borrowing, more investment (capital expenditures and M&A) in foreign locations, and at times a higher likelihood of having the subsidiary acquired by a foreign company.

What will occur post-TCJA and after the anti-BEPS initiatives remains to be seen. Presumably, the rules aim to more effectively mitigate tax avoidance. But, in general, it seems likely firms will continue to try to maximize shareholder value by lowering costs, including tax costs. However, there is a movement toward viewing firms via a stakeholder lens rather than a shareholder-only lens. This movement—combined with large government deficits, concerns about income inequality, and pressure from activist organizations and the media about taxes—may lead to less tax avoidance. Separately, identifying all these effects—rule changes, social changes, and political changes, and most recently COVID-19 and related governmental responses—will be both challenging and important work.

APPENDIX: DISCLOSURES OF NON-INCOME TAXES

PANEL A. Verizon Communications

The amounts of cash taxes paid by Verizon are as follows: *(dollars in millions)*

Years ended December 31	2018	2017	2016
Income taxes, net of amounts refunded	**US$ 2,213**	US$ 4,432	US$ 9,577
Employment taxes	**1,066**	1,207	1,196
Property and other taxes	**1,598**	1,737	1,796
Total	**US$ 4,877**	US$ 7,376	US$ 12,569

PANEL B. Exxon Mobil

NOTES TO CONSOLIDATED FINANCIAL STATEMENTS

19. Income and Other Taxes

	2018			2017			2016		
	U.S.	Non-U.S.	Total	U.S.	Non-U.S.	Total	U.S.	Non-U.S.	Total
					(millions of dollars)				
Income tax expense									
Federal and non-U.S.									
Current	459	9,001	9,460	577	6,633	7,210	(214)	4,056	3,842
Deferred—net	518	(614)	(96)	(9,075)	754	(8,321)	(2,801)	(1,422)	(4,223)
U.S. tax on non-U.S. operations	42	-	42	17	-	17	41	-	41
Total federal and non-U.S.	1,019	8,387	9,406	(8,481)	7,387	(1,094)	(2,974)	2,634	(340)
State	126	-	126	(80)	-	(80)	(66)	-	(66)
Total income tax expense	1,145	8,387	9,532	(8,561)	7,387	(1,174)	(3,040)	2,634	(406)
All other taxes and duties									
Other taxes and duties	3,498	29,165	32,663	3,330	26,774	30,104	3,209	25,811	29,020
Included in production and manufacturing expenses	1,245	857	2,102	1,107	747	1,854	1,052	808	1,860
Included in SG&A expenses	153	312	465	147	354	501	133	362	495
Total other taxes and duties	4,896	30,334	35,230	4,584	27,875	32,459	4,394	26,981	31,375
Total	6,041	38,721	44,762	(3,977)	35,262	31,285	1,354	29,615	30,969

PANEL C. Freeport-McMoRan

Cash Payments to Governments[a] ($ Millions)						
For the year ended December 31, 2018	U.S.	Chile	Peru	Indonesia	Other Countries[b]	Total
Corporate Income Taxes, Net of Refunds	$ (3)	$ 16	$ 162	$ 705	$ 22	$ 902
Withholding Taxes on Foreign Dividends	-	2	1	182	-	185
Employee Payroll Taxes[c]	309	11	83	54	23	480
Dividends	-	-	-	148	-	148
Royalties and Net Severance Taxes	24	1	41	214	-	280
Property Taxes	81	-	-	17	2	100
Other Taxes and Fees[d]	52	13	68	207	(26)	314
Total	**$ 463**	**$ 43**	**$ 355**	**$ 1,527**	**$ 21**	**$ 2,409**

a. This schedule reflects a voluntary effort by Freeport-McMoRan to capture its cash payments to governments (net of refunds).

b. Represents cash payments to governments by Freeport-McMoRan's other business groups that are located outside of the countries where Freeport-McMoRan conducts its primary operations.

c. Includes payroll taxes collected on behalf of employees and paid to governments.

d. Includes customs and export duties, as well as withholding tax on foreign services.

NOTES

We thank the editors, Fritz Foley, Jim Hines, and David Wessel, for comments on an earlier draft. We also thank Tom Horst, Rebecca Lester, Kevin Markle, Terry Shevlin, and Nemit Shroff for comments.

1. See www.oecd.org/tax/beps/ for information about the OECD base-erosion and profit-shifting initiative; www.hsgac.senate.gov/subcommittees/investigations/hearings/offshore-profit-shifting-and-the-us-tax-code for information about the U.S. Senate investigations on tax avoidance; and http://europa.eu/rapid/press-release_IP-18-6889_en.htm for an example of the European Union's actions on illegal state aid.

2. The US$2.7 trillion tax total is calculated by summing the value of income taxes paid (Compustat data item TXPD) on Compustat for all U.S.-incorporated firms with non-missing beginning assets (Compustat data item AT), revenues (Compustat data item SALE) greater than zero, and non-missing pretax income (Compustat data item PI) from 2009 to 2018.

3. The effects of changes are discussed in the sample below.

4. Deferred tax expense is the expense related to changes in deferred tax assets and liabilities. A discussion of this is beyond the scope of this paper. For more information about the accounting for income taxes, see any intermediate accounting textbook.

5. Compustat data items for the items discussed are as follows: cash taxes paid (TXPD), total income tax expense (TXT), federal current income tax expense (TXFED), foreign current income tax expense (TXFO), and state current income tax expense. The Compustat year convention is used. For example, a firm with a year starting June 2018 and ending May 2019 will be labeled as having a fiscal year in Compustat of 2018. The convention puts calendar year-end 2018 firms as 2018, as well as firms with fiscal years where the majority of months fall in 2018. This will cause some mismatch in timing as firms with a fiscal year-end of, say, October 2018 will be labeled as a 2018 firm year, but would have to apply a blended rate for tax purposes, and the financial accounting effects would occur in a year labeled 2018 even though the act was passed in 2017. However, for most firms (including calendar year-end firms) the classification lines up. The one exception is that the immediate expensing provisions of the TCJA start in 2017. This is discussed more, to some extent, below.

6. Taxes paid appears to decline after 2014. Why this occurs is unclear. In examining the data, the sample deciles by 192 observations in 2014. This chapter does not investigate this further or examine the changes in observations year-to-year.

7. In figure 10-1, there is a spike in current federal tax expense in 2017, but no corresponding spike in cash taxes paid. This is an example of where the two can differ. In 2017, with the passage of the TCJA, for financial accounting purposes, companies were required to accrue the tax expense for some provisions in the TCJA, for example, the mandatory deemed repatriation tax (the transition tax) on unrepatriated foreign earnings (Section 965(a) inclusion). However, the tax did not need to be paid in 2017, but could be paid over an eight-year period following the TCJA. This creates a large difference in the two measures. Astute readers may wonder if immediate expensing in the TCJA resulted in a similar difference. In the measures used in figure 10-1, the answer is no. The immediate expensing of qualified assets enacted as part of the TCJA

had an effective date of September 27, 2017. Immediate expensing would lower cash taxes paid for companies that took advantage of the provision. The provision would also lower current federal tax expense for financial accounting. Thus, there would not be a difference in the two measures we present due to immediate expensing. However, if we were to examine *total* income tax expense (current plus deferred), there would be a difference between cash effective tax rates and the effective tax rate where total income tax expense is in the numerator. This is because bonus depreciation from immediate expensing on the tax return would increase deferred federal tax expense for financial accounting. Thus, immediate expensing would lower cash taxes paid and current federal tax expense similarly (in general), but would not lower total income tax expense (because financial accounting pretax income and financial accounting depreciation are not affected by the new tax rule).

8. Tax planning and tax avoidance are sometimes used interchangeably in extant literature.

9. See Hanlon and Heitzman (2010) for their discussion of interest expense. To be clear, the use of debt to third parties will generally not affect the (CASH ETR) measure, because the interest expense would often reduce accounting income and provide a deduction for taxable income. Thus, interest expense to third parties often constitutes conforming tax avoidance. However, intercompany debt would likely affect the measure, because intercompany interest expense would be eliminated upon consolidation for financial accounting but have the effect of reducing taxable income in a high-tax jurisdiction and increasing taxable income in a low-tax jurisdiction. Thus, cash taxes paid for the worldwide entity would be lower but accounting income would likely not be lowered.

10. Conforming means accounting and taxable incomes are conformed to be the same with respect to that transaction.

11. Note that the measure could be affected by management in attempts to manipulate earnings to achieve certain benchmarks, such as analysts' earnings forecasts. Imagine a company "manages income upward" but does not pay tax on that income. The measured tax rate will fall. This should be less of a concern over the long run, as some portion of the earnings management will reverse. In addition, this is still considered tax avoidance under this chapter's broad-based definition, because the company avoided paying tax on the managed earnings.

12. The sample attrition from deleting firm-years with negative pretax income varies with the horizon over which the CASH ETR is calculated. For one-year CASH ETR, 34.7 percent of observations are deleted because of negative pretax income; for five-year CASH ETR, about 31.0 percent of observations are deleted because of negative five-year pretax income; for ten-year CASH ETR, about 23.6 percent of observations are deleted because of negative ten-year pretax income; and for thirty-year CASH ETR, about 8.6 percent of observations are deleted because of negative thirty-year pretax income.

13. In panel A of figure 10-2, about 3.7 percent (4.1 percent) of the multinational (domestic) observations were below zero, and thus reset to zero; about 4.3 percent (3.3 percent) of the multinational (domestic) observations were greater than one, and thus reset to one. In panel B, about 1.3 percent (1.7 percent) of the multinational (domestic) observations were below zero, and thus reset to zero; about 4.7 percent (4.6 percent)

of the multinational (domestic) observations were greater than one, and thus reset to one. In panel C, about 0.5 percent (0.7 percent) of the multinational (domestic) observations were below zero, and thus reset to zero; about 4.8 percent (5.1 percent) of the multinational (domestic) observations were greater than one, and thus reset to one. In panel D, none of the observations were below zero; about 3.1 percent (3.0 percent) of the multinational (domestic) observations were greater than one, and thus reset to one. In panel E, about 2.6 percent (4.5 percent) of the multinational (domestic) observations were below zero, and thus reset to zero; about 2.9 percent (2.9 percent) of the multinational (domestic) observations were greater than one, and thus reset to one. In panel F, about 4.1 percent (9.5 percent) of the multinational (domestic) observations were below zero, and thus reset to zero; about 4.2 percent (1.9 percent) of the multinational (domestic) observations were greater than one, and thus reset to one.

14. Rather than classifying firms in the distribution, other approaches include subtracting the firm's rate from a cross-sectional constant/benchmark of some type, for example, the statutory U.S. tax rate or an industry average.

15. The sample for this analysis is all U.S.-incorporated firm-years in Compustat with positive values of total assets and sales.

16. The disclosure is Exhibit 21 of Form 10-K. There is some selective disclosure in Exhibit 21, though Dyreng, Hoopes, Langetieg, and Wilde (2019) find that most disclosures are accurate. Moreover, we gather data using text search algorithms that may miss or misclassify subsidiaries (for example, if the company includes the name of the country in the subsidiary name, the subsidiary might be double-counted). In addition, Exhibit 21 requires disclosure of the country of incorporation, but many tax structures rely on differences in incorporation location and the location of management and control (for example, an Irish incorporated subsidiary managed in Bermuda), and Exhibit 21 does not have information on the location of management or control.

17. Clearly, statutory tax rates do not tell the whole story. Tax rate changes are often accompanied by other changes that affect the tax base or tax enforcement, as discussed in Kawano and Slemrod (2015). Moreover, some countries have imposed new taxes on multinationals to prevent profit shifting (for example the diverted profits tax in Australia and the United Kingdom).

18. Depending on how a firm accounted for unremitted foreign earnings, the effective tax rate for financial reporting (known in the literature as the GAAP—or Generally Accepted Accounting Principles—effective tax rate) may or may not have been affected. If a firm treated the earnings as temporarily reinvested, then the U.S. tax was accrued for financial reporting purposes and the GAAP effective tax rate was not reduced. However, if the earnings were treated as indefinitely reinvested, then the U.S. tax was not accrued, and the GAAP effective tax rate was reduced.

19. High-tech industries are defined as firms with three-digit SIC codes equal to 283, 357, 366, 367, 382, 384, 481, 482, 489, 737, or 873, following Kile and Phillips (2009).

20. The trends are broadly similar in unreported results if firms are split into those that report research and development expense (a variable commonly used to identify high tech firms) and those that do not report research and development expense.

21. Additionally, the largest hundred domestic firms in each year were matched to the multinational firm that was closest in size in the same year. The unreported results again suggest that large domestic firms and large multinational firms have

similar levels and trends in CASH ETR. Again, in unreported results with similar conclusions, this exercise was repeated, but with the matched firm required to come from the same industry (using the Fama French 30 industry classification).

22. As shown earlier, CASH ETR displays significant variation. Other proxies for tax avoidance (for example, GAAP ETR, book-tax differences, permanent book-tax differences) also display significant variation.

23. The numerator of a GAAP ETR is tax expense rather than cash taxes paid.

24. For more on this issue, see Shackelford and Shevlin (2001) and their review of the book-tax tradeoff literature, including accounting method choice decisions, disqualification of incentive stock options, and other firm decisions.

25. GAAP effective tax rates are calculated as income tax expense per the financial statements divided by pretax income per the financial statements, where the financial statements are computed according to Generally Accepted Accounting Principles (GAAP).

26. Interestingly, Rego motivates her study quoting Leblang's (1998) *Tax Notes* article, which states that multinational corporations ". . . may have significantly greater opportunities to escape tax with respect to cross-border investments than with respect to strictly domestic investments" (181) and by quoting Collins and Shackelford's (1999) *Tax Notes* article, which concludes that ". . . empirical findings in the area are insufficient and inconclusive and fail to support or undermine Leblang's assertions" (131). Rego (2003) was an important paper in trying to reconcile these views, but the question still seems open today.

27. We caution that these discrepancies could be driven by different time periods and differences in the research designs of the studies, and in particular driven by the fact that Dyreng, Hanlon, Maydew, and Thornock (2017) examine CASH ETR, while Rego (2003) and Markle and Shackelford (2012) examine GAAP effective tax rates.

28. See Beer and others (2018) for a discussion of international corporate tax avoidance methods and estimated magnitudes.

29. Notably, the government does not include interest expense deductions on the list of corporate tax breaks.

30. Shevlin (1990) and Graham (1996) focus on deriving firm-specific marginal tax rates in contrast to the prior literature at the time. Auerbach (1983) estimated marginal tax rates on the earnings of corporate investments in plant and equipment. In addition, Altshuler and Auerbach (1990) examine and clearly describe the restrictions on the ability of firms to utilize tax losses and credits. Shevlin (1987, 1990) and Graham's work (starting with the 1996 paper) incorporate the insights and details about loss carryovers and credit utilization from Auerbach (1983) and Altshuler and Auerbach (1990) in developing the firm-specific marginal tax rates.

31. See Hanlon and Heitzman (2010) and Graham (2008) for more complete reviews.

32. This same amount is taxable to the employee as compensation in the same reporting period.

33. But the GAAP ETRs were not affected. See Hanlon and Shevlin (2002) for an explanation of the prior accounting for income taxes when options were not expensed for financial accounting.

34. See Richard Rubin, "Does Amazon Really Pay No Taxes? Here's the Com-

plicated Answer," *Wall Street Journal*, June 14, 2019, for further information about Amazon. The deduction lowered tax payments for many companies in the 1990s during the dot-com bubble, but these reductions were not reflected in income tax expense (see Hanlon and Shevlin (2002) and Graham, Lang, and Shackelford (2004)).

35. See https://europa.eu/rapid/press-release_IP-16-2923_en.htm for a press release by the European Commission related to the case, and https://en.wikipedia.org/wiki/EU_illegal_State_aid_case_against_Apple_in_Ireland for a summary of events. See also Apple's 10-K at SEC.gov.

36. Income shifting has, at times, been important for other cross-jurisdictional tax avoidance, for example across states in the United States. This chapter focuses on cross-country income shifting.

37. Efforts around the world are currently underway to improve coordination of tax rules among countries, and thus change how global income is allocated and taxed.

38. Many countries have made substantial changes to their international tax rules during the sample period studied.

39. There are variations on the structures. For example, the foreign subsidiary may not own the intangible asset but rather license it from the parent company in some cases. For ease of discussion, only the relatively simple case for the transactions is presented.

40. In some instances, ownership is not transferred, but licensing rights are granted. In the text that follows, "owned" is used for simplicity, but actual transactions can take many forms.

41. See Brian O'Keefe and Marty Jones, "How Uber Plays the Tax Shell Game," *Fortune*, October 22, 2015, for additional details.

42. For more on both sides of the Starbucks issue, see Kleinbard (2013), Worstall (2014), and Lawson (2012).

43. For discussions of these, see Kleinbard (2011) and Drucker (2010) for the Double Irish and Double Irish Dutch Sandwich. The Double Irish is no longer allowed, but Ireland has replaced it with the Single Malt. See Coyle (2017) for a description of the Single Malt. The Capital Allowances for Intangible Assets (CAIA) (also known as the Green Jersey) is another strategy used in Ireland (for a description of the CAIA, see Ernst & Young (2017)).

44. This initial transfer of ownership or control is a taxable transaction, with tax liability based on the purchase price or royalty payment of the transfer.

45. See also Joint Committee on Taxation (2010).

46. The sum of US$513 billion was calculated by adding all pretax foreign income (Compustat data item PIFO) of U.S.-incorporated firms with positive values of assets at the beginning of the period, positive revenues, and non-missing values of cash taxes paid, pretax income, pretax foreign income, and foreign current tax expense (Compustat data items TXPD, PI, PIFO, and TXFO, respectively).

47. When using macroeconomic data to estimate income shifting, researchers face limits on the conclusions they can draw. For example, macroeconomic data series are often difficult to compare across countries because of variations in calculations driven by cultural or political climates. Moreover, because the data arises at an aggregated level, researchers using macroeconomic data are unable to determine the characteristics of companies that are associated with income shifting, how many

companies shift income, and what organizational or operational consequences might follow the choice to shift income.

48. The Huizinga and Laeven (2008) approach has been widely adopted in recent years to examine specific questions regarding the association of income shifting and other firm outcomes. As examples, Markle (2016) estimates that multinational firms subjected to territorial tax regimes appear to shift more income than multinational firms subjected to worldwide regimes; Dischinger, Knoll, and Riedel (2014) report evidence suggesting firms are biased toward recognizing profits in the country of their headquarters; and De Simone, Klassen, and Seidman (2018) report some evidence that income shifting is negatively related to investment efficiency. In addition, De Simone (2016) provides evidence that the adoption of International Financial Reporting Standards increases estimated income shifting. The evidence suggests that a mechanism behind this result is that the standards created cross-jurisdictionally comparable financial statements, and therefore allow firms to draw from a larger pool of observations when justifying profit margins to demonstrate compliance with arm's-length standards. See also Bilicka (2019). Bilicka (2019) examines U.K. administrative data and compares U.K. subsidiaries of foreign multinationals to domestic-only U.K. companies. Her evidence is consistent with multinational subsidiaries having a lower ratio of taxable profits to assets in the United Kingdom than domestic-only companies in the United Kingdom.

49. DeMooij and Ederween (2003) provide an excellent summary of the literature. Hines (1997 and 1999) reviews the U.S. literature and finds that a 1 percent higher tax rate on companies leads to a reduction in inbound investment of around 0.5 percent and 0.6 percent. See also Hassett and Hubbard (2002), a comprehensive review on taxes and investment. For some other important papers, see Desai and Hines (1999); Barrios, Huizinga, Laeven, and Nicodeme (2012); Hebous, Ruf, and Weichenrieder (2011); Becker and Riedel (2012); Becker, Fuest, and Riedel (2012). Note, however, that the literature has, at times, had a difficult time documenting that aggregate investment responds to taxes, so much so that Hines and Park (2019) state that "The apparently small power of tax incentives to stimulate aggregate investment spending is one of the puzzles of the empirical investment literature."

50. For other studies, see Desai, Foley, and Hines (2004) and Buettner, Overesch, Schreiber, and Wamser (2012).

51. In addition to the academic studies discussed above, we note that as part of the Base Erosion and Profit Shifting Project, the OECD published an estimate of US$240 billion for the global annual revenue loss due to income shifting (https://www.oecd.org/tax/beps/). Likewise, the IMF reported that in 2013 more than US$400 billion of tax was lost for OECD countries and US$200 billion for non-OECD countries (Crivelli, de Mooij, and Keen (2016)).

52. Harford, Wang, and Zhang (2017) provide evidence consistent with shareholders valuing foreign cash less than domestic cash, because the firm will face repatriation taxes on foreign cash and because the agency costs of foreign cash appear to be higher than domestic cash.

53. This example is from Graham, Hanlon, and Shevlin (2010). Apple issued an additional US$17 billion in debt in 2013 and again had to explain to the market why it was borrowing, even though it had so much cash on its balance sheet. The *Wall Street Journal*

(Burne and Cherney (2013)) stated, "Apple has a huge cash stockpile, but much of its money is overseas. Raising cash in the bond market helps Apple avoid the big tax bill that would hit if the company brought its cash back to the U.S., executives said last week."

54. See also Altshuler and Grubert (2003) about repatriation taxes and financial policy at multinationals.

55. However, see Gale, Krupkin, and Rueben (2015) for a counter view that the economic effects of state tax rate changes on labor and capital spending are small, and thus, cuts in state income tax rates will not necessarily generate growth.

56. Ohrn (2018) estimates that a one percentage point reduction in effective tax rates generated by the policy increases investment by 4.7 percent of installed capital, increases payouts by 0.3 percent of sales, and decreases debt by 5.3 percent of total assets.

57. See also Desai, Dyck, and Zingales (2007), who examine the interaction between corporate taxes and corporate governance. The authors predict and find evidence consistent with the sensitivity to corporate tax changes varying with the quality of corporate governance.

58. The literature also examines other effects. For examples, see Desai, Foley, and Hines (2003), who study direct versus indirect ownership and the sensitivity to tax, and Dyreng, Lindsey, Markle, and Shackelford (2015), who study ownership chains.

59. See Weisbach (2002) for a discussion of the costs and benefits of tax shelters in particular.

60. For other studies on reputation and tax avoidance, see Hanlon and Slemrod (2009) and Dyreng, Hoopes, and Wilde (2016).

61. This differential between public and private firms demonstrates the importance of being careful in comparing public and private firms using measures such as an effective tax rate, or cash effective tax rate, or any similar measure that is a tax measure relative to an accounting measure. Private firms place much less weight on financial accounting earnings and thus the metrics are not comparable across the two types of firms.

62. See Baugh, Ben-David, and Park (2018), who study the effects of the implementation of the "Amazon tax."

63. The report is too large to reproduce, but can be found at https://www.riotinto.com/documents/RT_taxes_paid_2018.pdf for interested readers.

64. See also Jacob, Michaely, and Muller (2018) for a study of consumption taxes and investment more generally, using a value added tax change in the Netherlands. The authors find evidence consistent with consumption taxes decreasing investment, especially so for firms facing more elastic demand.

65. There is evidence regarding the elasticities of goods and how this benefited online retailers such as Amazon. When online sales required a sales tax to be charged, households living in the states where the sales tax increased reduced Amazon purchases by more than 9 percent and for large purchases by roughly 30 percent (Baugh, Ben-David, and Park (2018)).

REFERENCES

Altshuler, R. and A. Auerbach. 1990. "The Significance of Tax Law Asymmetries: An Empirical Investigation," *Quarterly Journal of Economics*, 105 (1): 61–86.

Altshuler, R. and H. Grubert. 2001. "Where Will They Go If We Go Territorial? Dividend Exemption and the Locations Decisions of U.S. Multinational Corporations," *National Tax Journal*, 54 (4): 787–809.

Altshuler, R. and H. Grubert. 2003. "Repatriation Taxes, Repatriation Strategies, and Multinational Financial Policy," *Journal of Public Economics*, 87 (1): 73–107.

Altshuler, R., H. Grubert, and S. Newlon. 2001. *Has U.S. Investment Abroad Become More Sensitive to Tax Rates? International Taxation and Multinational Activity*, edited by James R. Hines Jr. (University of Chicago Press), 9–32.

Armstrong, C. S., J. L. Blouin, and D. F. Larcker. 2012. "The Incentives for Tax Planning," *Journal of Accounting and Economics*, 53 (1–3): 391–411.

Auerbach, A. J. 1983. "Corporate Taxation in the United States," *Brookings Papers on Economic Activity*, 2: 451–513.

Badertcher, B. A., S. P. Katz, and S. O. Rego. 2013. "The Separation of Ownership and Control and Corporate Tax Avoidance," *Journal of Accounting and Economics*, 56 (2–3): 228–50.

Balakrishnan, K., J. L. Blouin, and W. R. Guay. 2018. "Tax Aggressiveness and Corporate Transparency," *Accounting Review*, 94 (1): 45–69.

Bankman, J. 2004. "The Tax Shelter Problem." *National Tax Journal*, 57 (4): 925–36.

Barrios, S., H. Huizinga, L. Laeven, and G. Nicodeme. 2012. "International Taxation and Multinational Firm Location Decisions," *Journal of Public Economics*, 96: 946–58.

Baugh, B., I. Ben-David, and H. Park. 2018. "Can Taxes Shape an Industry? Evidence from the Implementation of the 'Amazon Tax,'" *Journal of Finance*, 73 (4): 1819–55.

Becker, J., C. Fuest, and N. Riedel. 2012. "Corporate Tax Effects on the Quality and Quantity of FDI," *European Economic Review*, 56 (8): 1495–1511.

Becker, J. and N. Riedel. 2012. "Cross-Border Tax Effects on Affiliate Investment: Evidence from European Multinationals," *European Economic Review*, 56 (3): 436–50.

Beer, S., R. de Mooij, and L. Liu. 2018. "International Corporate Tax Avoidance: A Review of the Channels, Effect Sizes, and Blind Spots." IMF working paper.

Bennedsen, M. and S. Zeume. 2018. "Corporate Tax Havens and Transparency," *Review of Financial Studies*, 31 (4): 1221–64.

Bennett, B., A. V. Thakor, and Z. Wang. 2019. "Stock Repurchases and the 2017 Tax Cuts and Jobs Act." Working paper.

Beyer, B., J. Downes, and E. T. Rapley. 2017. "Internal Capital Market Inefficiencies, Shareholder Payout, and Abnormal Leverage," *Journal of Corporate Finance*, 43: 39–57.

Beyer, B., J. Downes, M. Mathis, and E. Rapley. 2019. "Early Evidence on the Use of Foreign Cash Following the Tax Cuts and Jobs Act of 2017." Working paper.

Bilicka, K. A. 2019. "Comparing U.K. Tax Returns of Foreign Multinationals to Matched Domestic Firms," *American Economic Review*, 109 (8): 2921–53.

Bird, A., A. Edwards, and T. Shevlin. 2017. "Does U.S. Foreign Earnings Lockout Advantage Foreign Acquirers?" *Journal of Accounting and Economics*, 64 (1): 150–66.

Blouin, J., J. Core, and W. Guay. 2010. "Have the Tax Benefits of Debt Been Overstated?" *Journal of Financial Economics*, 98 (2): 195–213.

Blouin, J., L. K. Krull, and L. A. Robinson. 2012. "Is U.S. Multinational Dividend Repatriation Policy Influenced by Reporting Incentives?" *Accounting Review*, 87 (5): 1463–91.

Blouin, J. and L. Robinson. 2019. "Double Counting Accounting: How Much Profit of Multinational Enterprises Is Really in Tax Havens?" Working paper.

Böhm, T., T. Karkinsky, B. Knoll, and N. Riedel. 2015. "The Impact of Corporate Taxes on R&D and Patent Holdings." Working paper, University of Munster, Oxford University, and University of Bochum.

Boone, J. P., I. K. Khurana, and K. K. Raman. 2013. "Religiosity and Tax Avoidance," *Journal of the American Taxation Association*, 35 (1): 53–84.

Bradley, S., E. Dauchy, and L. Robinson. 2015. "Cross-country Evidence on the Preliminary Effects of Patent Box Regimes on Patent Activity and Ownership," *National Tax Journal*, 68 (4): 1047–71.

Bradley, S., L. Robinson, and M. Ruf. 2018. "The Impact of IP Box Regimes on the M&A Market." Working paper, Drexel University, Dartmouth College, and University of Tuebingen.

Brown, J. 2011. "The Spread of Aggressive Corporate Tax Reporting: A Detailed Examination of the Corporate-Owned Life Insurance Shelter," *Accounting Review*, 86 (1): 23–57.

Brown, J. and K. Drake. 2014. "Network Ties Among Low-Tax Firms," *Accounting Review*, 89 (2): 483–510.

Bruce, D., W. F. Fox, and L. Luna. 2015. "E-Tailer Sales Tax Nexus and State Tax Policies," *National Tax Journal*, 68 (35): 735–65.

Buettner, T., M. Overesch, U. Schreiber, and G. Wamser. 2012. "The Impact of Thin Capitalization Rules on the Capital Structure of Multinational Firms," *Journal of Public Economics*, 96: 930–38.

Buettner, T. and G. Wamser. 2013. "Internal Debt and Multinational Profit Shifting: Empirical Evidence from Firm-level Panel Data," *National Tax Journal*, 66 (1): 63–96.

Burne, K. and M. Cherney. 2013. "Apple's Record Plunge into Debt Pool," *Wall Street Journal*, April 30.

Byrnes, N. and L. Lavelle. 2003. "The Corporate Tax Game," *Bloomberg Businessweek*, March 31.

Carrizosa, R., F. B. Gaertner, and D. Lynch. 2019. "Debt and Taxes? The Effect of TCJA Interest Limitations on Capital Structure." Working paper.

Chen, K. P. and C. Chu. 2005. "Internal Control vs. External Manipulation: A Model of Corporate Income Tax Evasion," *RAND Journal of Economics*, 36: 151–64.

Chen, S., X. Chen, Q. Cheng, and T. Shevlin. 2010. "Are Family Firms More Tax Aggressive Than Non-Family Firms?" *Journal of Financial Economics*, 95 (1): 41–61.

Chow, T., J. Hoopes, and E. Maydew. 2018. "Firms on Foreign (Tax) Holidays." Working paper.

Chyz, J. 2013. "Personally Tax Aggressive Executives and Corporate Tax Sheltering," *Journal of Accounting and Economics*, 56 (2–3): 311–28.

Clausing, K. 2020. "Profit Shifting Before and After the Tax Cuts and Jobs Act." Working paper.

Cloyd, B., L. Mills, and C. Weaver. 2003. "Firm Valuation Effects of the Expatriation of U.S. Corporations to Tax Haven Countries," *Journal of the American Taxation Association*, 25 (Suppl): 87–109.

Collins, J. and D. Shackelford. 1999. Writers Challenge Claim of Favorable Cross-Border Taxation, *Tax Notes*, 82 (January 4): 131–34.

Coyle, D. 2017. "Multinationals Turn from 'Double Irish' to 'Single Malt' to Avoid Tax in Ireland," *Irish Times*, November 14.

Collins, J., D. Kemsley, and M. Lang. 1998. "Cross-Jurisdictional Income Shifting and Earnings Valuation," *Journal of Accounting Research*, 36 (2): 209–29.

Crivelli, E., R. de Mooij, and M. Keen. 2016. "Base Erosion, Profit Shifting, and Developing Countries," *FinanzArchiv*, 72: 268–301.

Crocker, K. and J. Slemrod. 2005. "Corporate Tax Evasion with Agency Costs," *Journal of Public Economics*, 89: 1593–1610.

Davies, R. B., J. Martin, M. Parenti, and F. Toubal. 2018. "Knocking on Tax Haven's Door: Multinational Firms and Transfer Pricing," *Review of Economics and Statistics*, 100 (1): 120–34.

De Mooij, R. A. and S. Ederveen. 2003. "Taxation and Foreign Direct Investment: A Synthesis of Empirical Research," *International Tax and Public Finance*, 10: 673–91.

Desai, M. A., A. Dyck, and L. Zingales. 2007. "Theft and Taxes," *Journal of Financial Economics*, 84: 591–623.

Desai, M. A., C. F. Foley, and J. R. Hines Jr. 2003. "Chains of Ownership, Regional Tax Competition, and Foreign Direct Investment." In *Foreign Direct Investment in the Real and Financial Sector of Industrial Countries* (Berlin, Heidelberg: Springer), 61–98.

Desai, M. A., C. F. Foley, and J. R. Hines Jr. 2004. "Foreign Direct Investment in a World of Multiple Taxes," *Journal of Public Economics*, 88 (12): 2727–44.

Desai, M. A., C. F. Foley, and J. R. Hines Jr. 2004. "A Multinational Perspective on Capital Structure Choice and Internal Capital Markets," *Journal of Finance*, 59 (6): 2451–87.

Desai, M. A. and J. R. Hines Jr. 1999. "'Basket' Cases: Tax Incentives and International Joint Venture Participation by American Multinational Firms," *Journal of Public Economics*, 71 (3): 379–402.

Desai, M. and J. R. Hines Jr. 2002. "Expectations and Expatriations: Tracing the Causes and Consequences of Corporate Inversions," *National Tax Journal*, 55: 409–40.

De Simone, L., 2016. "Does a Common Set of Accounting Standards Affect Tax-Motivated Income Shifting for Multinational Firms?" *Journal of Accounting and Economics*, 61 (1): 145–65.

De Simone, L., K. J. Klassen, and J. K. Seidman. 2018. "The Effect of Income-Shifting Aggressiveness on Corporate Investment." Working paper.

De Simone, L. and R. Lester. 2019. "The Effect of Foreign Cash Holdings on Internal Capital Markets and Firm Financing." Working paper, Stanford.

Dharmapala, D. 2014. "What Do We Know about Base Erosion and Profit Shifting? A Review of the Empirical Literature," *Fiscal Studies*, 35 (4): 421–48.

Dharmapala, D. and N. Riedel. 2013. "Earnings Shocks and Tax-Motivated Income-Shifting: Evidence from European Multinationals," *Journal of Public Economics* 97: 95–107.

Dischinger, M., B. Knoll, and N. Riedel. 2014. "The Role of Headquarters in Multinational Profit Shifting Strategies," *International Tax and Public Finance*, 21 (2): 248–71.

Dobridge, C., P. Landefeld, and J. A. Mortenson. 2019. "Corporate Taxes and the Wage Distribution: Effects of the Domestic Production Activities Deduction." Working paper, Joint Committee on Taxation.

Drake, K., R. Hamilton, and S. Lusch. 2019. "Are Declining Effective Tax Rates Indicative of Tax Avoidance?" Insight from Effective Tax Rate Reconciliations. Working paper.

Drucker, J. 2010. "Google 2.4% Rate Shows How US$60 Billion Is Lost to Tax Loopholes," *Bloomberg*, October 21.

Durnev, A., T. Li., and M. Magnan. 2016. "Are Offshore Firms Worth More?" *Journal of Corporate Finance*, 36: 131–56.

Dyreng, S., M. Hanlon, and E. Maydew. 2008. "Long-Run Corporate Tax Avoidance," *Accounting Review*, 83: 61–82.

Dyreng, S., M. Hanlon, and E. Maydew. 2010. "The Effects of Executives on Corporate Tax Avoidance," *Accounting Review*, 85: 1163–1189.

Dyreng, S., M. Hanlon, E. Maydew, and J. Thornock. 2017. "Changes in Corporate Effective Tax Rates over the Past 25 Years," *Journal of Financial Economics*, 124: 441–63.

Dyreng, S., J. L. Hoopes, P. Langetieg, and J. H. Wilde. 2019. "Strategic Subsidiary Disclosure." Working paper.

Dyreng, S. D., J. L. Hoopes, and J. H. Wilde. 2016. "Public Pressure and Corporate Tax Behavior," *Journal of Accounting Research*, 54 (1): 147–86.

Dyreng, S. and B. Lindsey. 2009. "Using Financial Accounting Data to Examine the Effect of Foreign Operations Located in Tax Havens and Other Countries on U.S. Multinational Firms' Tax Rates," *Journal of Accounting Research*, 47 (5): 1283–16.

Dyreng, S., B. Lindsey, K. Markle, D. Shackelford. 2015. "The Effect of Tax and Nontax Country Characteristics on the Global Equity Supply Chains of U.S. Multinationals," *Journal of Accounting and Economics*, 59 (2): 182–202.

Dyreng, S. and K. Markle. 2016. "The Effect of Financial Constraints on Income Shifting by U.S. Multinationals," *Accounting Review* 91 (6): 1601–27.

Dyreng, S., W. J. Mayew, and C. D. Williams. 2012. "Religious Social Norms and Corporate Financial Reporting," *Journal of Business Finance and Accounting*, 39 (7–9): 845–75.

Edwards, A., T. Kravet, and R. Wilson. 2016. "Trapped Cash and the Profitability of Foreign Acquisitions," *Contemporary Accounting Research*, 33 (1): 44–77.

Egger, P., C. Keuschnigg, V. Merlo, and G. Wamser. 2014. "Corporate Taxes and Internal Borrowing within Multinational Firms," *American Economic Journal: Economic Policy*, 6 (2): 54–93.

Erickson, M., M. Hanlon, and E. Maydew. 2004. "How Much Will Firms Pay for Earnings that Do Not Exist? Evidence of Taxes Paid on Allegedly Fraudulent Earnings," *Accounting Review*, 79: 387–408.

Ernst & Young. 2017. "Ireland Announces Changes to Capital Allowances for Intangible Assets," October 12, https://taxinsights.ey.com/archive/archive-news/ireland-announces-changes-to-capital-allowances-for-intangible-assets.aspx.

Faulkender, M. and M. Petersen. 2012. "Investment and Capital Constraints: Repatriations under the American Jobs Creation Act," *Review of Financial Studies*, 25: 3351–88.

Foley, C. F., J. Hartzell, S. Titman, and G. Twite. 2007. "Why Do Firms Hold So Much Cash? A Tax-Based Explanation," *Journal of Financial Economics*, 86: 579–607.

Francis, B. B., I. Hasan, X. Sun, and Q. Wu. 2016. "CEO Political Preference and Corporate Tax Sheltering," *Journal of Corporate Finance*, 38: 37–53.

Frank, M. 2003. "The Rise of the Wall Street Tax Machine," *Bloomberg Businessweek*, March 31.

Fuest, C., S. Hebous, and N. Riedel. 2011. "International Debt Shifting and Multinational Firms in Developing Countries," *Economics Letters*, 113 (2): 135–38.

Fuest, C., A. Peichl, and S. Siegloch. 2018. "Do Higher Corporate Taxes Reduce Wages? Micro Evidence from Germany," *American Economic Review*, 108 (2): 393–418.

Gale, W. G., A. Krupkin, and K. Rueben. 2015. "The Relationship Between Taxes and Growth at the State Level: New Evidence." Working paper, Urban-Brookings Tax Policy Center.

Giroud, X. and J. Rauh. 2019. "State Taxation and the Reallocation of Business Activity: Evidence from Establishment-Level Data," *Journal of Political Economy*, 127 (3): 1262–1316.

Gordon, R. H. and J. R. Hines Jr. 2002. "International Taxation" in *Handbook of Public Economics*, edited by A. J. Auerbach and M. S. Feldstein (Amsterdam: North Holland), vol. 3.

Government Accounting Office. 2008. "Comparison of the Reported Tax Liabilities of Foreign and U.S.-Controlled Corporations, 1998–2005." GAO-08-957.

Graham, J. 1996. "Debt and the Marginal Tax Rate," *Journal of Financial Economics*, 41: 41–74.

Graham, J. 2000. "How Big Are the Tax Benefits of Debt?" *Journal of Finance*, 55: 1901–41.

Graham, J. 2008. "Taxes and Corporate Finance" in *Handbook of Corporate Finance: Empirical Corporate Finance*, edited by E. Eckbo (Amsterdam: Elsevier Science).

Graham, J., M. Hanlon, and T. Shevlin. 2010. "Barriers to Mobility: The Lockout Effect of U.S. Taxation of Worldwide Corporate Profits," *National Tax Journal*, 63 (December): 1111–44.

Graham, J., M. Hanlon, and T. Shevlin. 2011. "Real Effects of Accounting Rules: Evidence from Multinational Firms' Investment Location and Repatriation Decisions," *Journal of Accounting Research*, 49 (March): 137–88.

Graham, J., M. Hanlon, T. Shevlin, and N. Shroff. 2014. "Incentives for Tax Planning and Avoidance: Evidence from the Field," *Accounting Review*, 89: 991–1024.

Graham, J., M. H. Lang., and D. A. Shackelford. 2004. "Employee Stock Options, Corporate Taxes and Debt Policy," *Journal of Finance*, 59 (4): 1585–1618.

Graham, J. and A. Tucker. 2006. "Tax Shelters and Corporate Debt Policy," *Journal of Financial Economics*, 81: 563–94.

Greenstone, M. and E. Moretti. 2003. "Bidding for Industrial Plants: Does Winning a 'Million Dollar Plant' Increase Welfare?" NBER Working Paper No. w9844.

Grubert, H. 2003. "Intangible Income, Intercompany Transactions, Income Shifting, and the Choice of Location," *National Tax Journal*, 56 (1): 221–42.

Grubert, H. and J. Mutti. 2000. "Do Taxes Influence Where U.S. Corporations Invest?" *National Tax Journal*, 53: 825–83.

Grubert, H. and J. Slemrod. 1998. "The Effect of Taxes on Investment and Income Shifting to Puerto Rico," *Review of Economics and Statistics*, 80 (32): 365–73.

Hall, R. E. and D. Jorgenson. 1967. "Tax Policy and Investment Behavior," *American Economic Review*, 57 (3): 391–414.

Hanlon, M. and S. Heitzman. 2010. "A Review of Tax Research," *Journal of Accounting and Economics*, 50 (December): 127–78.

Hanlon, M. and T. Shevlin. 2002. "The Tax Benefits of Employee Stock Options: The Accounting and Implications," *Accounting Horizons*, 16: 1–16.

Hanlon, M. and J. Slemrod. 2009. "What Does Tax Aggressiveness Signal? Evidence from Stock Price Reactions to News about Tax Shelter Involvement," *Journal of Public Economics*, 93: 126–41.

Hanlon, M., R. Lester, and R. Verdi. 2015. "The Effect of Repatriation Tax Costs on U.S. Multinational Investment," *Journal of Financial Economics*, 116: 179–96.

Hanlon, M., J. Hoopes, and J. Slemrod. 2019. "Tax Reform Made Me Do It!" *NBER Tax Policy and the Economy*, 33: 33–80.

Harford, J., C. Wang, and K. Zhang. 2017. "Foreign Cash: Taxes, Internal Capital Markets, and Agency Problems," *Review of Financial Studies*, 30 (5): 1490–1538.

Harris, D., 1993. "The Impact of U.S. Tax Law Revision on Multinational Corporations' Capital Location and Income-Shifting Decisions," *Journal of Accounting Research*, 31: 111–40.

Hasan, I., C. K. Hoi, Q. Wu, and H. Zhang. 2017. "Does Social Capital Matter in Corporate Decisions? Evidence from Corporate Tax Avoidance," *Journal of Accounting Research*, 55 (3): 629–68.

Hasegawa, M. and K. Kiyota. 2017. "The Effect of Moving to a Territorial Tax System on Profit Repatriation: Evidence from Japan." Working paper.

Hassett, K. and R. G. Hubbard. 2002. "Tax Policy and Business Investment" in *Handbook of Public Economics*, edited by A. Auerbach and M. Feldstein (Amsterdam: Elsevier Science), vol. 3: 1294–1343.

Hebous, S., M. Ruf, and A. J. Weichenrieder. 2011. "The Effects of Taxation on the Location Decision of Multinational Firms: M&A Versus Greenfield Investments," *National Tax Journal*, 64 (3): 817–38.

Heckemeyer, J. H. and M. Overesch. 2013. "Multinationals' Profit Response to Tax Differentials: Effect Size and Shifting Channels." Working paper, ZEW.

Herger, N., C. Kotsogiannis, and S. McCorriston. 2016. "Multiple Taxes and Alternative Forms of FDI: Evidence from Cross-Border Acquisitions," *International Tax and Public Finance*, 23 (1): 82–113.

Hines, J. R. Jr. 1997. "Tax Policy and the Activities of Multinational Corporations" in *Fiscal Policy: Lessons from Economic Research*, edited by A. Auerbach (MIT Press).

Hines, J. R. Jr. 1999. "Lessons from Behavioral Responses to International Taxation," *National Tax Journal*, 52 (3): 385–404.

Hines, J. R. Jr. 2014. "How Serious Is the Problem of Base Erosion and Profit Shifting?" *Canadian Tax Journal*, 62 (2): 443–53.

Hines, J. R. Jr. and J. Park. 2019. "Investment Ramifications of Distortionary Tax Subsidies," *Journal of Public Economics*, 172: 36–51.

Hines, J. R. Jr. and E. Rice. 1994. "Fiscal Paradise: Foreign Tax Havens and American Business," *Quarterly Journal of Economics*, 109 (1): 149–82.

Hope, O. K., M. S. Ma, and W. B. Thomas. 2013. "Tax Avoidance and Geographic Earnings Disclosure," *Journal of Accounting and Economics*, 56 (2–3): 170–89.

Horst, T. 2019a. "The TCJA's Impact on GAAP Effective Tax Rates of Large U.S. Non-financial Corporations," *Tax Notes International*, May 27.

Horst, T. 2019b. "Preliminary Estimates of the Likely Actual Revenue Effects of the JCJA's Provisions," *Tax Notes International*, September 16.

Horst, T. 2020. "The TCJA's Incentives for and Impediments to Repatriating Intangible Property," *Tax Notes International*, February 10.

Huizinga, H., L. Laeven, and G. Nicodeme. 2008. "Capital Structure and International Debt Shifting," *Journal of Financial Economics*, 88: 88–118.

Huizinga, H. and L. Laeven. 2008. "International Profit Shifting within Multinationals: A Multi-Country Perspective," *Journal of Public Economics*, 92 (5): 1164–82.

Jacob, M., R. Michaely, and M. A. Muller. 2018. "Consumption Taxes and Corporate Investment," *Review of Financial Studies*, 32 (8): 3144–82.

Johnson, D. C. 2003. *Perfectly Legal: The Covert Campaign to Rig Our Tax System to Benefit the Super Rich—and Cheat Everybody Else* (London: Penguin Books).

Joint Committee on Taxation. 2010. "Present Law and Background Related to Possible Income Shifting and Transfer Pricing. Scheduled for Public Hearing Before the House Committee on Ways and Means on July 22, 2010." JCX-37-10.

Kawano, L. and J. Slemrod. 2015. "How Do Corporate Tax Bases Change When Corporate Tax Rates Change? With Implications for the Tax Rate Elasticity of Corporate Tax Revenues," *International Tax and Public Finance*, 23 (3): 401–33.

Klassen, K. and S. Laplante. 2012. "Are U.S. Corporations Becoming More Aggressive Income Shifters?" *Journal of Accounting Research*, 50 (5): 1245–85.

Kleinbard, E. 2011. "Stateless Income," *Florida Tax Review* (11): 699.

Kleinbard, E. 2013. "Through a Latte, Darkly: Starbucks' Stateless Income Tax Planning," *Tax Notes* (June 24): 1515–35.

Kile, C. O., and M. E. Phillips. 2009. "Using Industry Classification Codes to Sample High-Technology Firms: Analysis and Recommendations," *Journal of Accounting, Auditing & Finance*, 24 (1): 35–58.

Law, K. F. and L. F. Mills. 2017. "Military Experience and Corporate Tax Avoidance," *Review of Accounting Studies*, 22 (1): 141–84.

Lawson, D. 2012. "In Defense of Starbucks and Amazon," *Independent*, December 4, www.independent.co.uk/hei-fi/views/dominic-lawson-in-defence-of-starbucks--and-amazon-8381303.html.

Leblang, S. 1998. "International Double Non-Taxation," *Tax Notes International*, 134 (10): 181–83.

Lester, R. 2019. "Made in the U.S.A? A Study of Firm Responses to Domestic Production Incentives," *Journal of Accounting Research*, 57 (4): 1059–1115.

Liu, L. 2019. "Where Does Multinational Investment Go with Territorial Taxation? Evidence from the United Kingdom," *American Economic Journal: Economic Policy*, forthcoming.

Luna, L., K. Schuchard, and D. Stanley. 2019. "Changes in CEO Compensation after the Tax Cuts & Jobs Act and the Impact of Corporate Governance: Initial Evidence." Working paper.

Markle, K. 2016. "A Comparison of the Tax-Motivated Income Shifting of Multinationals in Territorial and Worldwide Countries," *Contemporary Accounting Research*, 33 (1): 7–43.

Markle, K. and D. Shackelford. 2012. "Cross-Country Comparisons of Corporate Income Taxes," *National Tax Journal*, 65 (3): 493–528.

Markle, K. and D. Shackelford. 2013. "The Impact of Headquarter and Subsidiary Locations on Multinationals' Effective Tax Rates," *Tax Policy and the Economy*, 28: 33–62.

McGuire, S. T., D. Wang, and R. J. Wilson. 2014. "Dual Class Ownership and Tax Avoidance," *Accounting Review*, 89 (4): 1487–1516.

Mills, L. and K. Newberry. 2005. "Evidence of Off-Balance-Sheet Financing from Book-Tax Differences," *Journal of Accounting Research*, 43: 251–82.

Modigliani, R. and M. Miller. 1963. "Corporate Income Taxes and the Cost of Capital: A Correction," *American Economic Review*, 53: 433–43.

Moretti, E. and D. J. Wilson. 2014. "State Incentives for Innovation, Star Scientists and Jobs: Evidence from Biotech," *Journal of Urban Economics*, 79: 20–38.

Newberry, K. and D. Dhaliwal. 2001. "Cross-Jurisdictional Income Shifting by U.S. Multinationals: Evidence from International Bond Offerings," *Journal of Accounting Research*, 39: 643–62.

Novack, J. and L. Saunders. 1998. "The Hustling of Corporate Tax Shelters," *Forbes* (December 14): 198–208.

Ohrn, E. 2018. "The Effect of Corporate Taxation on Investment and Financial Policy," *American Economic Journal: Economic Policy*, 10 (2): 272–301.

Olbert, M. and A. Werner. 2019. "Consumption Taxes and Corporate Tax Planning—Evidence from European Service Firms." Working paper, University of Mannheim.

Oosterhuis, P. 2013. Testimony before the House Committee on Ways and Means (June 13). Available at: http://waysandmeans.house.gov/UploadedFiles/Oosterhuis_Testimony.pdf.

Phillips, J. 2003. "Corporate Tax-Planning Effectiveness: The Role of Compensation-Based Incentives," *Accounting Review*, 78: 847–74.

Poletti, T. 1996. "Apple Talks Stalled Again over Price," Reuters News Wire, February 7.

Poniatowski, G., M. Bonch-Osmolovskiy, and M. Belkindas. 2016. "Study and Reports on the VAT Gap in the EU-28 Member States: 2016 Final Report." Case Research Paper (483).

Rego, S. 2003. "Tax Avoidance Activities of U.S. Multinational Corporations," *Contemporary Accounting Research*, 20: 805–33.

Rego, S. and R. Wilson. 2012. "Equity Risk Incentives and Corporate Tax Aggressiveness," *Journal of Accounting Research*, 50 (3): 775–809.

Scholes, M. and M. Wolfson. 1992. *Taxes and Business Strategy: A Planning Approach*, 1st ed. (Upper Saddle River, N.J.: Pearson Prentice-Hall).

Shackelford, D. and T. Shevlin. 2001. "Empirical Tax Research in Accounting," *Journal of Accounting and Economics*, 31: 321–87.

Shevlin, T. 1987. "Taxes and Off-Balance Sheet Financing: Research and Development Limited Partnerships," *Accounting Review*, 62 (3): 480–509.

Shevlin, T. 1990. "Estimating Corporate Marginal Tax Rates with Asymmetric Tax Treatment of Gains and Losses," *Journal of American Taxation Association*, 11 (2): 51–67.

Slemrod, J., 2004. "The Economics of Corporate Tax Selfishness," *National Tax Journal*, 57: 877–99.

Seida, J. and W. Wempe. 2004. "Effective Tax Rate Changes and Earnings Stripping Following Corporate Inversions," *National Tax Journal*, 57: 805–27.

Slemrod, J. 2004. "The Economics of Corporate Selfishness," *National Tax Journal*, 57: 877–99.

Thomsen, M. and C. Watrin. 2018. "Tax Avoidance over Time: A Comparison of European and U.S. Firms," *Journal of International Accounting, Auditing and Taxation*, 33: 40–63.

Torslov, T., L. Wier, and G. Zucman. 2020. "The Missing Profits of Nations." Working paper.

Weber, T. 1993. "Apple Edges Toward First Bond Offer with US$500 Mln Shelf," Dow Jones News Service, May 7.

Weisbach, D. 2002. "Ten Truths about Tax Shelters," 55 *Tax L. Rev.* 215.

Williams, B. 2018. "Multinational Tax Incentives and Offshored U.S. Jobs," *Accounting Review*, 93 (5): 293–324.

Wilson, R. 2009. "An Examination of Corporate Tax Shelter Participants," *Accounting Review*, 84: 969–99.

Wright, R. and G. Zucman. 2018. "The Exorbitant Tax Privilege." NBER Working Paper No. 24983.

Worstall, T. 2014. "They're Spouting Nonsense About the Starbucks Tax Situation Again," *Forbes*, December 2.

U.S. Department of Treasury. 1999. "The Problem of Corporate Tax Shelters: Discussion, Analysis and Legislative Proposals." July. Washington, D.C.: Governmental Printing Office.

U.S. Department of Treasury. 2019. "Tax Expenditures FY2021," https://home.treasury.gov/system/files/131/Tax-Expenditures-2021.pdf

Zimmerman, J. 1983. "Taxes and Firm Size," *Journal of Accounting and Economics*, 5: 119–49.

11

Do Multinational Firms Use Tax Havens to the Detriment of Non-Haven Countries?

DHAMMIKA DHARMAPALA

The activities of multinational corporations (MNCs) in countries and territories described as tax havens have attracted growing public and academic attention in recent years. Tax-haven activity appears to be an important component of MNCs' wider global operations. Thus, the topic is important for understanding the global activities of MNCs as well as the role of tax-haven jurisdictions in the global economy. It also illuminates aspects of the wider process of global economic integration that is central to many policy debates and political developments in the current, highly fraught global environment. This chapter describes and explains the academic literature on this topic. It does not aim to be a comprehensive survey of the literature, although it covers a wide range of studies. It builds on prior surveys of the role of tax havens (for example, Dharmapala (2008); Hines (2010)) and of profit shifting by MNCs (for example, Dharmapala (2014a)), but develops a largely distinct set of themes and arguments. It is aimed at a general audience of those interested in international economic issues, rather than at tax specialists.

The chapter uses a pragmatic working definition of tax havens that corresponds to usage in the prior academic literature, without any judgmental intent. In particular, the definition used here is based on the list of tax havens constructed in Dharmapala and Hines (2009), with some minor updates described in the next section.[1] While most of the data and illustrations are drawn from U.S.-based MNCs, the discussion is applicable to MNCs based in all countries. Since profit shifting is important to MNCs' haven use, the chapter discusses the evidence on profit shifting across jurisdictions. However, this chapter's primary focus is not on the analysis of firms' profit shifting (which is more fully addressed in Dharmapala (2014a) and in chapter 10, by Dyreng and Hanlon, in this volume), but rather on the reasons governments adopt policies that facilitate or restrict haven use and profit shifting.

Much of the public debate about havens tends to conflate the use of havens by MNCs with the use of havens by individual residents of non-haven countries and emphasizes the role of tax havens' secrecy. In general, these activities are quite distinct—MNCs' activities in havens are generally thought to be lawful (although MNCs' tax planning may involve adopting more or less aggressive positions in the face of legal uncertainty). In contrast, individuals' use of havens is typically unlawful and relies on secrecy (although the spread of information exchange among governments is arguably in the process of eliminating individual evasion via foreign financial accounts). Thus, this distinction corresponds quite closely to the distinction between tax avoidance or tax planning (the lawful reduction of taxes owed) and tax evasion (the failure to pay legally owed taxes). While tax-haven secrecy and tax evasion have not generally been thought to be very relevant for MNCs' tax-haven activities, some nuances have been introduced by a recent literature that finds evidence that MNCs' haven activity may respond to information exchange, and that secrecy may play some role in firms' haven activities. A section of this chapter seeks to place this new evidence within a broader conceptual framework (derived from Desai and Dharmapala (2006), (2008), (2009a), (2009b), and (2018)) that highlights the relationship between tax avoidance and agency costs (that is, the imperfect alignment of the interests of managers and shareholders).

The chapter begins with a summary of the most salient facts about MNCs' haven activities, drawing on the aggregate country-level data on the foreign operations of U.S. MNCs provided by the Bureau of Economic Analysis (BEA) at the U.S. Department of Commerce. These aggregate data reveal patterns of MNC activity that are highly consistent with the disproportionate use of havens (relative to indicators of "real" activity, such as employment and tangible assets) for the location of holding companies within MNC groups, for the location of intangible assets, and for financing activities. However, an important caveat is that the accounting system used by the BEA for foreign affiliates that serve as holding companies may substantially overstate certain measures of MNCs' haven activity (notably the fraction of income reported in havens). Notwithstanding this, the differences between haven and non-haven affiliates in the BEA data are not as pronounced as might be expected based on the tenor of much of the public discussion.

The tax motivations for MNCs' use of havens are obvious, and there are clearly large potential gains for MNCs from cross-border tax planning. Nonetheless, there is also considerable evidence of significant frictions that limit MNCs' use of havens. The factors limiting MNCs' haven usage can be classified as follows: nontax frictions (such as the legal and business environment in different jurisdictions, a consideration that has largely been neglected in discussions of MNCs and havens), tax law provisions limiting profit shifting (which are discussed in detail in this chapter), and the costs of tax planning. The available evidence suggests the relevance of each of these elements. For instance, while MNCs locate holding companies disproportionately in havens, holding companies are also often found in non-havens (suggesting the importance of nontax considerations in their location). Extensive evidence also suggests that MNCs' profit shifting responds to anti-tax avoidance rules in various countries. Most strikingly, many MNCs (indeed, a majority in certain widely used datasets) do not have any haven affiliates at all, suggesting that tax planning is far from frictionless. The evidence for these different types of frictions casts some doubt on the widespread notion that MNCs are readily able to avoid taxes via the use of havens, and raises important questions about how to conceptualize the tax and nontax motivations for MNCs' haven activity.

In conventional accounts, MNCs' use of tax havens erodes the tax base of non-havens by facilitating profit shifting. These accounts imply that MNCs' haven activities are detrimental to non-haven countries' welfare, and depict non-haven countries—even large and powerful ones such as the United States—as hapless victims of havens. However, as discussed in the middle of this chapter, tax-law mechanisms that enable non-haven countries to neutralize the effect of MNCs' use of havens have long existed. These include controlled foreign corporation (CFC) rules and thin capitalization rules (TCRs). Under CFC rules, countries where MNCs are headquartered tax certain types of income earned by the haven affiliates of their resident MNCs. TCRs limit the deductibility of interest in certain circumstances. The use of these provisions has grown markedly in recent decades. Of course, they could potentially be implemented even more extensively. However, the failure to do so is a (presumably deliberate) policy choice of non-haven countries' governments rather than an unwelcome imposition by havens. MNCs' use of tax havens thus appears to rely crucially on its facilitation by the laws of non-haven countries.

There are potential alternative accounts in which non-haven countries are less complicit. For instance, MNCs' use of havens may exploit unintended interactions between the tax laws of different countries, as argued by the Organization for Economic Cooperation and Development (OECD (2013)). However, this chapter suggests that this is unlikely to be the primary explanation of MNCs' tax-haven use. It is also possible that non-havens' failure to fully neutralize MNCs' use of havens may represent a policymaking error or oversight, or may be the result of political dysfunction. This explanation would require, however, that non-haven countries' errors are systematic rather than random, and that policymakers are failing to respond to the highly salient public concern about MNCs' profit shifting.

After explaining the tax provisions noted above, the middle section of this chapter seeks to reframe the fundamental intellectual and policy issues raised by havens. In particular, it argues that the most relevant question is not how non-haven countries should combat havens, but rather why non-havens facilitate MNCs' use of havens.[2] Framing the question in this way suggests (at least) two possible answers. One is that non-haven countries use their tax-law tools suboptimally due to a collective action problem (such as a situation in which eliminating MNCs' haven use is collectively optimal for non-havens, but where no individual non-haven has an incentive to strengthen its anti-avoidance rules). This is theoretically possible, but there are reasons to doubt that it is a complete explanation. The main alternative possibility is that MNCs' haven activity serves the interests of non-haven countries, at least as those interests are construed by their political systems. A strand of the public finance literature suggests that under certain political and informational constraints (that prevent countries from directly taxing mobile and immobile capital differentially), MNCs' tax-haven use can increase the welfare of non-havens. To paraphrase what Voltaire wrote in an entirely different context, in this view, "If tax havens did not exist, it would be necessary for non-havens to invent them." The middle section of the chapter evaluates these possibilities and other potential explanations. It concludes that, regardless of the mechanism, it seems clear that MNCs' haven activity serves the interests of non-haven countries (either individually or collectively, or both). Of course, this does not in itself settle the question of whether MNCs' haven activity promotes non-haven countries' "true" welfare, or merely their interests as refracted through the prism of various political distortions.

This chapter also reviews empirical estimates of the magnitude of profit shifting by MNCs to havens. This section of the chapter highlights the discrepancy between micro-econometric estimates using affiliate-level data (which tend to find smaller magnitudes) and macro studies using aggregate data (which tend to find larger magnitudes). It links these differences to the distinction commonly drawn in public finance theory between tax avoidance and behavioral responses to taxation, suggesting that micro-econometric estimates may better capture tax avoidance. This distinction rests on the significance of nontax frictions. Tax avoidance involves minimal nontax frictions, although it entails tax-planning costs, whereas behavioral responses distort firms' nontax activities. As noted, some evidence indicates that nontax frictions (such as the legal and business expertise available in different jurisdictions) constrain MNCs' tax-haven use. This evidence suggests that some of what has traditionally been viewed as profit shifting (that is, as cross-border tax avoidance) might arguably be reconceptualized as a type of behavioral response to tax differences across countries that is limited by nontax legal and business considerations. In any event, the concept of behavioral responses to taxation appears sorely in need of updating for a contemporary world in which physical infrastructure is often less important than the legal and business environment.

MNCs' TAX-HAVEN ACTIVITY

An Overview of MNC Activity in Tax Havens

This section begins by describing some basic facts about MNC activity in tax havens, using the aggregate country-level data, provided by the BEA, on the foreign operations of U.S.-based MNCs.[3] The BEA dataset is based on surveys of U.S. multinational firms and collects extensive information about their affiliates abroad. Because firms can suffer legal penalties for failing to complete these surveys, it is generally thought that this dataset is highly reliable (although there are important problems of interpretation of aspects of this data, especially as it relates to havens). It has become a standard data source for scholars studying the behavior of U.S.-based MNCs. An extensive academic literature has developed using both this aggregate country-level data (for example, Hines and Rice (1994); Clausing (2016)) and the confidential affiliate-level microdata that are the basis of the aggregate data (for example, Desai, Foley, and Hines (2006); Dharmapala, Foley, and Forbes (2011)).

For 2016 (the most recent year for which the data are available), the BEA reports relevant measures for 201 separate countries and territories.[4] To determine which of these are havens, this chapter uses the list of havens reported in Dharmapala and Hines (2009, appendix A, 1067). Dharmapala and Hines (2009) begin with the list of jurisdictions in Hines and Rice (1994, appendix 2, 178), which is based primarily on various lists of havens produced by the U.S. Internal Revenue Service (IRS). They update this list and match it with countries and territories for which sufficient economic and institutional data were available in 2004.[5] This classification of havens has been widely used in the subsequent academic literature, and other existing classifications substantially overlap with this list.

Dharmapala and Hines (2009, 1058) define tax havens as "locations with very low tax rates and other tax attributes designed to appeal to foreign investors." There are about forty havens in their classification, typically small countries and territories that show a marked pattern of geographical clustering. Indeed, perhaps to a surprising degree, MNCs' use of havens appears to be influenced by geographical proximity.[6] This tendency may possibly reflect specialization by law and accounting firms. A deeper question is why havens are distinct geographical entities at all. A corporate tax haven is, in essence, a mechanism for imposing a low or zero tax rate on certain types of income earned by MNCs. In principle, non-haven countries could create domestic tax law vehicles to achieve this aim. However, the geographical separation of havens may offer advantages. One possibility is that small jurisdictions that rely on incorporation fees for raising government revenue, and that lack a political constituency for high tax rates (being small enough that there is no meaningful domestic corporate sector to tax) may be more credible in setting low tax rates.[7]

Of the 201 countries and territories for which the BEA reports data for 2016, thirty-five are havens using the definition described above. Table 11-1 reports the values of various measures of U.S. MNC activity in these thirty-five countries and territories, the corresponding values for all foreign affiliates, and the value of MNC activity in tax havens as a percentage of the value of their total foreign-affiliate activity.[8] The data pertain to majority-owned foreign affiliates (MOFAs) of U.S. parent firms in 2016. Figure 11-1 represents the same information in graphical form. The number of affiliates is included in table 11-1 because it is sometimes referred to in public discussions of havens. However, it is not particularly meaningful as a measure of MNC operations, as a given amount of economic activity in a country can be divided among an arbitrarily large or small number of legal entities.[9]

Indicators of real economic activity in havens—the number of employees, employee compensation, tangible assets in the form of plant, property, and equipment (PPE), research and development (R&D), and capital expenditures—suggest that approximately 5 percent to 15 percent of the foreign activity of U.S. MNCs is in havens. However, nearly half of a measure that the BEA terms the "net income" of the foreign affiliates of U.S. MNCs is reported in havens.[10] This naturally prompts the question of what is measured by "net income." To answer, it is helpful to begin with the BEA measure known as "total income" (which is rather more akin to gross receipts

TABLE 11-1. The Share of U.S. MNCs' Foreign Activity in Haven Jurisdictions *(Majority-owned foreign affiliates, 2016)*

Type of activity	All foreign countries	Havens	% of activity in havens
Number of affiliates	34,881	7,441	21.33%
Total assets (US$ millions)	25,226,581	8,636,399	34.24%
Net plant, property, and equipment (US$ millions)	1,367,094	184,686	13.51%
Capital expenditures (US$ millions)	199,478	28,261	14.17%
Sales (US$ millions)	5,781,264	1,420,096	24.56%
Net income (US$ millions)	1,015,559	503,302	49.56%
Value added (US$ millions)	1,300,419	231,136	17.77%
R&D activity (US$ millions)	53,451	7,423	13.89%
Employee compensation (US$ millions)	599,410	54,737	9.13%
Number of employees (thousands)	14,256.1	711	4.99%

Note: Author's calculations, using aggregate country-level data for 2016 on the foreign activities of U.S. MNCs from the U.S. Bureau of Economic Analysis (BEA), available at www.bea.gov. These calculations are based on the BEA's preliminary 2016 data, which may potentially change when revised by the BEA. Tax havens are defined using the classification in Dharmapala and Hines (2009), with some minor updates described in the text.

FIGURE 11-1. The Share of U.S. MNCs' Foreign Activity in Haven Jurisdictions
(Majority-owned foreign affiliates, 2016)

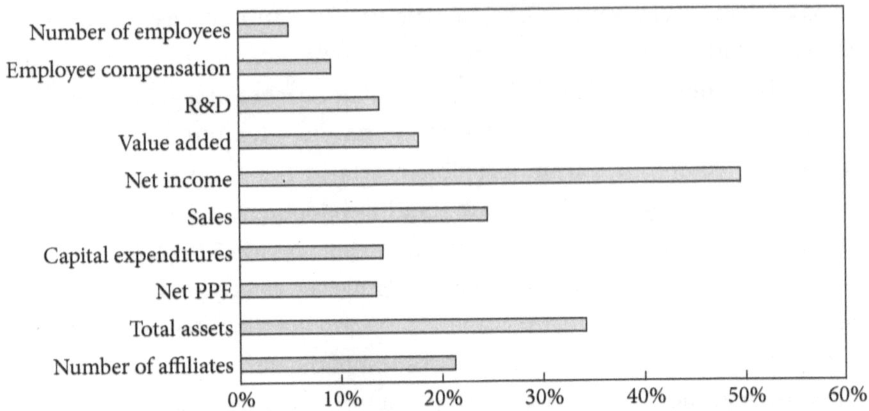

Note: Author's calculations, using aggregate country-level data for 2016 on the foreign activities of U.S. MNCs from the U.S. Bureau of Economic Analysis (BEA), available at www.bea.gov. These calculations are based on the BEA's preliminary 2016 data, which may potentially change when revised by the BEA. Tax havens are defined using the classification in Dharmapala and Hines (2009), with some minor updates described in the text.

than to income). Total income is the sum of sales revenue, capital gains or losses, certain other receipts, and a category known as "income from equity investments." This last element is a purely notional adjustment reflecting the affiliate's pro rata share of income earned by other foreign affiliates in which it holds equity (Blouin and Robinson (2019)). It is important to note that "income from equity investments" does not represent any dividend payments received by the affiliate from the lower-level affiliates that it owns, nor any realized capital gains from its ownership stake. Net income is obtained by subtracting from total income the cost of goods sold (COGS); selling, general, and administrative (SGA) expenses; certain other costs; and foreign tax payments. To be clear, net income includes "income from equity investments" (the purely notional adjustment described above) and is an after-tax concept as foreign tax payments are excluded.[11]

To illustrate the important role of "income from equity investments" in determining haven affiliates' share of net income, suppose (as illustrated in figure 11-2) that a U.S. parent firm owns 100 percent of a holding company in a haven (H), and that this holding company, in turn, owns 100 percent of an affiliate in a foreign non-haven country (F) with a 25 percent tax rate.

Holding companies are MNC affiliates that hold shares of other affiliates in the same MNC group, enabling the MNC parent to control the other affiliates indirectly via a chain of ownership rather than directly. Consider a scenario where the affiliate in F earns US$100, pays US$25 tax to the government of F, and retains the remaining US$75. The holding company in H would then be recorded in the BEA data as having "income from equity investments" of US$75 (Blouin and Robinson (2019)). Suppose that the H affiliate generates no profits and pays zero taxes. Nonetheless, because of its ownership of the F affiliate, it would be recorded in the BEA data as having net income of US$75 (and the F affiliate would also be recorded as having net income of US$75).

The BEA's accounting method is reasonable because it provides a clear picture of the economic position of each affiliate on a jurisdiction-by-jurisdiction basis (including its holdings of interests in other affiliates). However, when used without fully taking account of the definition of "income from equity investments," the BEA data may potentially exaggerate the fraction of income that is generated in jurisdictions that host holding

FIGURE 11-2. The BEA Definition of "Net Income": A Simple Example

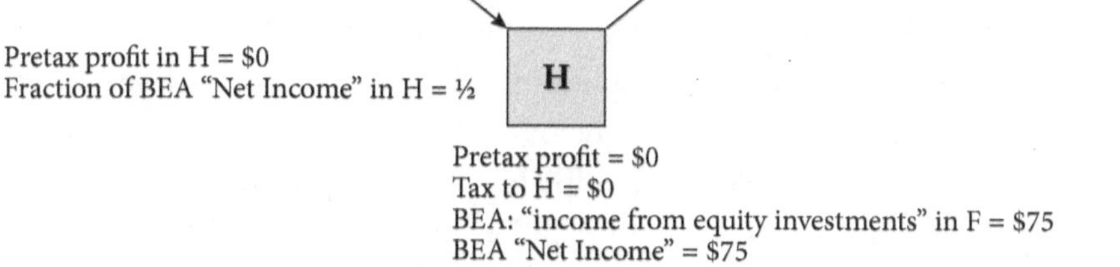

Note: This example illustrates the definition of the concept of "net income" reported by the Bureau of Economic Analysis (BEA), based on the discussion in Blouin and Robinson (2019). The U.S. parent firm owns a holding company in a haven (H), and this holding company, in turn, owns 100 percent of an affiliate in a foreign non-haven country (F) with a 25 percent tax rate. The affiliate in F earns US$100, pays US$25 tax to the government of F, and retains the remaining US$75. The H affiliate generates no profits and pays zero taxes. Nonetheless, it would be recorded in the BEA data as having "income from equity investments" of US$75, and therefore net income of US$75. The F affiliate would also be recorded as having net income of US$75.

companies. For the hypothetical U.S. MNC in figure 11-2, no foreign profit is actually generated or reported in the haven; however, the BEA's approach reports that 50 percent of the MNCs' worldwide foreign "net income" is in the haven affiliate. Moreover, all of the net income attributed to the haven affiliate has, in fact, been subject to tax in country F at a quite high tax rate.[12] The problem is potentially greatly magnified when an MNC uses chains of ownership that operate via holding companies in multiple havens (with the same US$75 of net income being attributed to several different haven affiliates).[13]

While the BEA data are not misleading, they are clearly susceptible to serious misunderstanding. It is quite common to point to descriptive statistics about net income to indicate the magnitude of profit shifting.[14] However, the location of relatively large numbers of holding companies in havens is likely to lead to an upward bias in the fraction of net income observed in havens due to the inclusion of "income from equity investments." It has long been thought that the apparently high fraction of income in havens may in part be a mechanical artifact of how the BEA data reflects MNCs' use of holding companies in havens (see, for example, Dharmapala (2014a, 444)). Recent work by Blouin and Robinson (2019) has clarified the central role of "income from equity investments" in producing this upward bias and suggests that the associated double counting problem may be far more pervasive and important than was previously recognized. There is, thus, arguably rather less to the approximately 50 percent share of net income in havens in table 11-1 and figure 11-1 than meets the eye.

While profit shifting may seem to be an obvious explanation for the patterns in table 11-1 and figure 11-1, this potential bias suggests extreme caution should be used in interpreting these patterns as being indicative of profit shifting. This caution applies in particular to the fraction of net income reported in havens, and to items such as royalties and interest that may pass through multiple haven affiliates in a chain of ownership (especially when they are reported in gross rather than net terms). The rather idiosyncratic definition and after-tax nature of the BEA concept of net income imply that it does not correspond to taxable income as defined by the tax laws of various jurisdictions. Hines (2010) argues that the share of "value added" (which equals sales minus the cost of inputs purchased, and excludes financial payments such as interest income or expense) may correspond more closely to taxable income, and provides a more meaningful measure of the role of havens, than does the share of net income. It is noteworthy that in table 11-1, the share of value added in havens (17.7 percent) is substantially smaller than the corresponding share of net income. Notwithstanding the potential mechanical upward bias in the BEA data, the differences between haven and non-haven affiliates are rather less pronounced than might be expected, as the discussion of tables 11-2 through 11-4 and figures 11-3 through 11-7 below suggests.

Commonly accepted accounts of MNCs' haven use stress the following functions of havens (as discussed, for instance, in Dharmapala (2008)). First, it is thought to be common to locate holding companies in havens. Second, haven affiliates are thought to be used in financing the activities of other (non-haven) affiliates. Debt finance provided by haven affiliates has clear tax advantages. For instance, when a haven affiliate receives an equity injection from its parent and lends to a high-tax affiliate, it generates interest deductions (subject to certain limitations) in the high-tax country and shifts income to the haven. Third, as has been widely discussed, MNCs may locate patents or other intellectual property in havens, with high-tax affiliates paying royalties to haven affiliates for the use of these assets.

The aggregate data on U.S. MNCs' haven activities tend to be consistent with each of these channels. To illustrate this, it is helpful to use the more extensive data provided in the BEA's benchmark surveys. These surveys are conducted every five years and provide a greater level of detail about the specific sources of affiliates' income (such as the categories highlighted in table 11-2 and figure 11-3 below). The most recent benchmark survey was conducted in 2014. However, the more extensive data are provided for a substantially smaller number of jurisdictions than the 2016 data used in table 11-1. In particular, table 11-2 is based on data for fifty-eight countries and territories, of which nine are havens under the definition described above.

Table 11-2 shows the shares of haven affiliates (relative to all foreign affiliates) for selected categories of income from the 2014 benchmark survey. Figure 11-3 depicts the same information in graphical form. First, note that "income from equity investments" is disproportionately (though by no means exclusively) concentrated in havens: about half of "income from equity investments" is reported in haven affiliates. This pattern indicates that holding companies are disproportionately located in havens, and that the double-counting problem described above is likely to bias upward the fraction of net income attributed to haven affiliates. Table 11-2 and figure 11-3 also show that 37 percent of dividends are received by haven affiliates (from other affiliates below them in the ownership chain). Capital gains and

TABLE 11-2. Haven Jurisdictions' Shares of Selected Types of Income *(Majority-owned foreign affiliates of U.S. MNCs, 2014 benchmark survey)*

Income category	All foreign countries	Havens	% reported in havens
Income from equity investments in foreign affiliates (US$ millions)	718,790	356,226	49.56%
Dividends or remitted profits (US$ millions)	519,039	193,667	37.31%
Capital gains/losses (US$ millions)	10,251	10,429	101.74%
Royalties and license fees (US$ millions)	67,786	44,129	65.10%
Royalties and license fees from U.S. sources (US$ millions)	6,040	1,736	28.74%
Royalties and license fees from non-U.S. sources (US$ millions)	61,746	38,666	62.62%
Interest receipts (US$ millions)	201,474	57,535	28.56%
Net income from finance and insurance activities (US$ millions)	161,243	84,077	52.14%

Note: Author's calculations, using aggregate country-level data for 2014 benchmark survey on the foreign activities of U.S. MNCs from the U.S. Bureau of Economic Analysis (BEA), available at www.bea.gov. The BEA's benchmark surveys provide more detailed information and more extensive coverage than its annual surveys. Tax havens are defined using the classification in Dharmapala and Hines (2009), with some minor updates described in the text.

FIGURE 11-3. Haven Jurisdictions' Shares of Selected Types of Income *(Majority-owned foreign affiliates of U.S. MNCs, 2014 benchmark survey)*

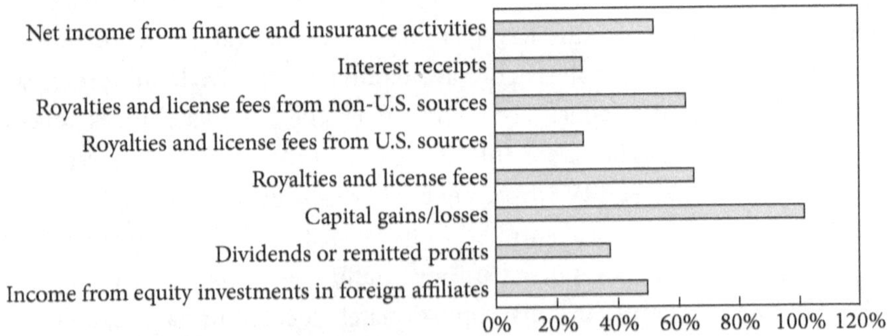

Note: Author's calculations, using aggregate country-level data for 2014 benchmark survey on the foreign activities of U.S. MNCs from the U.S. Bureau of Economic Analysis (BEA), available at www.bea.gov. The BEA's benchmark surveys provide more detailed information and more extensive coverage than its annual surveys. Tax havens are defined using the classification in Dharmapala and Hines (2009), with some minor updates described in the text.

losses similarly reflect equity ownership of other affiliates (and may also reflect portfolio investment in passive assets).[15] These measures are disproportionately large for haven affiliates relative to the benchmark of 5 percent to 15 percent for "real" activity, and support the inference that holding companies are disproportionately located in havens. At the same time, a substantial fraction of "income from equity investments" and dividends is in non-haven affiliates—an important piece of evidence regarding the role of nontax motivations and frictions in the location of holding companies.

Royalties and license fees indicate the holding of intellectual property. These types of receipts are also disproportionately received by haven affiliates. Haven affiliates earned about two-thirds of the royalty and license fee receipts of the foreign affiliates of U.S. MNCs in 2014. It is noteworthy that these receipts are driven almost entirely by royalties and license fees paid by foreign non-haven affiliates to haven affiliates, and not by royalty payments from the U.S. parent to haven affiliates. About 90 percent of haven affiliates' royalty and license fee receipts are from non-U.S. entities. U.S. tax law treats royalty income received by a foreign affiliate as U.S.-source income (subject to full and immediate U.S. taxation) if it is paid for property "located in the United States or . . . for the use of or for the privilege of using in the United States patents, copyrights, secret processes and formulas, goodwill, trademarks, trade brands, franchises, and other like property."[16] Royalty payments from the U.S. parent to haven affiliates are thus heavily taxed, and the disproportionate share of royalties received by haven affiliates (to the extent that it reflects profit shifting) reflects profit shifting *among* foreign countries rather than from the U.S. parent to haven affiliates.

Finally, interest receipts and the fraction of net income from the finance and insurance sectors point to havens' role as financial centers. About 29 percent of interest receipts by foreign affiliates are received by haven affiliates. While this is substantial, it is lower than the percentage of total assets in haven affiliates (reported in table 11-1 and figure 11-1). About half of the worldwide foreign net income of U.S. MNCs from finance and insurance activities is received by haven affiliates.

Table 11-3 and figure 11-4 report the corresponding measures using data from the prior benchmark survey in 2009. The patterns are similar to patterns in table 11-2 and figure 11-3. The main differences relate to "income from equity investments" and capital gains. Haven affiliates' share of "income from equity investments" was substantially smaller in 2009 (although the fraction of dividends was similar to the fraction in 2014). This difference may reflect growing complexity in the ownership structure of U.S. MNCs, and hence an increase in the double counting of net income. Possibly due to the economic environment in 2009, both haven and non-haven affiliates experienced capital losses.[17] Interest receipts and the share of net income from finance and insurance activities were modestly smaller in 2009 than in 2014, but not dramatically different. Overall, table 11-3 and figure 11-4 suggest that the patterns discussed earlier are fairly stable.

An alternative approach to understanding the same data is to compare the composition of the income of haven and non-haven affiliates, particularly the income categories that are highlighted in tables 11-2 and 11-3. Table 11-4 uses data from the BEA's benchmark surveys in 2014 and 2009 to compute the fraction of total income (the BEA concept defined above, roughly corresponding to receipts plus "income from equity investments") derived from "income from equity investments," capital gains or losses, interest receipts, and royalties for haven and non-haven affiliates. Sales constitute the bulk of the remainder of total income.[18] Figure 11-5 presents this composi-

TABLE 11-3. Haven Jurisdictions' Shares of Selected Types of Income *(Majority-owned foreign affiliates of U.S. MNCs, 2009 benchmark survey)*

Income category	All foreign countries	Havens	% reported in havens
Income from equity investments in foreign affiliates (US$ millions)	514,677	166,473	32.35%
Dividends or remitted profits (US$ millions)	467,399	173,455	37.11%
Capital gains/losses (US$ millions)	–29,140	–365	1.25%
Royalties and license fees from non-U.S. sources (US$ millions)	36,629	22,439	61.26%
Interest receipts (US$ millions)	224,282	52,678	23.49%
Net income from finance and insurance activities (US$ millions)	99,458	44,697	44.94%

Note: Author's calculations, using aggregate country-level data for 2014 benchmark survey on the foreign activities of U.S. MNCs from the U.S. Bureau of Economic Analysis (BEA), available at www.bea.gov. The BEA's benchmark surveys provide more detailed information and more extensive coverage than its annual surveys. Note that royalties and license fees from U.S. sources are not reported for 2009. Tax havens are defined using the classification in Dharmapala and Hines (2009), with some minor updates described in the text.

FIGURE 11-4. Haven Jurisdictions' Shares of Selected Types of Income *(Majority-owned foreign affiliates of U.S. MNCs, 2009 benchmark survey)*

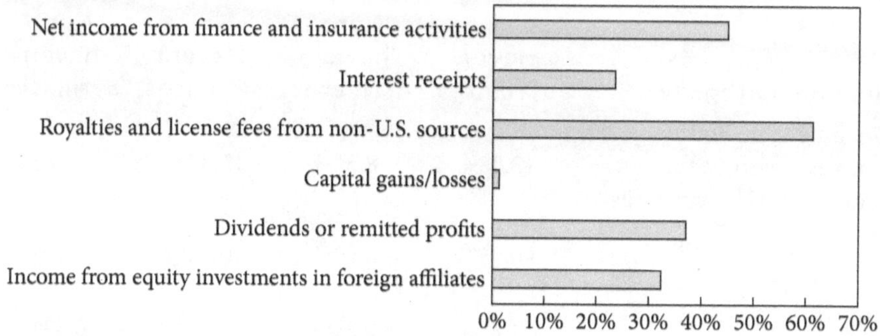

Note: Author's calculations, using aggregate country-level data for 2014 benchmark survey on the foreign activities of U.S. MNCs from the U.S. Bureau of Economic Analysis (BEA), available at www.bea.gov. The BEA's benchmark surveys provide more detailed information and more extensive coverage than its annual surveys. Note that royalties and license fees from non-U.S. sources are not reported for 2009. Tax havens are defined using the classification in Dharmapala and Hines (2009), with some minor updates described in the text.

tion in 2014, while figure 11-6 shows the composition in 2009. The notional adjustment for "income from equity investments" constitutes a substantially larger share of total income for haven affiliates than for non-haven affiliates (indicating the disproportionate location of holding companies in havens). The same is true of capital gains and losses (though the amounts involved are quite small in relation to total income). Royalties and license fees and interest receipts are also substantially higher for haven affiliates relative to non-haven affiliates. However, the differences across haven and non-haven affiliates are quite modest. The patterns for 2014 and 2009 are generally similar (though, as in tables 11-2 and 11-3, "income from equity investments" is larger for haven affiliates in 2014 than in 2009).

The overall picture that emerges from table 11-4 is that sales constitute the primary source of gross receipts for both haven and non-haven affiliates. This is somewhat less true for haven affiliates, but—notwithstanding the potential double counting problem noted earlier—the differences between haven and non-haven affiliates are less pronounced than might be expected if taxes were the only consideration driving MNCs' use of havens. This is reinforced by figure 11-7, which shows the fraction of net income derived from finance and insurance activities for haven and non-haven affiliates in 2014: the share for haven affiliates is 15.69 percent, while the share for non-

TABLE 11-4. Composition of the Total Income of Haven and Non-Haven Affiliates
(Majority-owned foreign affiliates of U.S. MNCs, 2009 and 2014 benchmark surveys)

	2009		2014	
Income category	Haven affiliates	Non-haven affiliates	Haven affiliates	Non-haven affiliates
Income from equity investments in foreign affiliates (US$ millions)	13.48%	8.31%	18.35%	6.58%
Capital gains/losses (US$ millions)	−0.03%	−0.69%	0.54%	0.00%
Royalties and license fees (US$ millions)	1.82%	0.34%	2.27%	0.43%
Interest receipts (US$ millions)	4.27%	4.09%	2.96%	2.61%

Note: Author's calculations, using aggregate country-level data for the 2009 and 2014 benchmark surveys on the foreign activities of U.S. MNCs from the U.S. Bureau of Economic Analysis (BEA), available at www.bea.gov. The BEA's benchmark surveys provide more detailed information and more extensive coverage than its annual surveys. Tax havens are defined using the classification in Dharmapala and Hines (2009), with some minor updates described in the text.

FIGURE 11-5. Composition of the Total Income of Haven and Non-Haven Affiliates
(Majority-owned foreign affiliates of U.S. MNCs, 2014 benchmark survey)

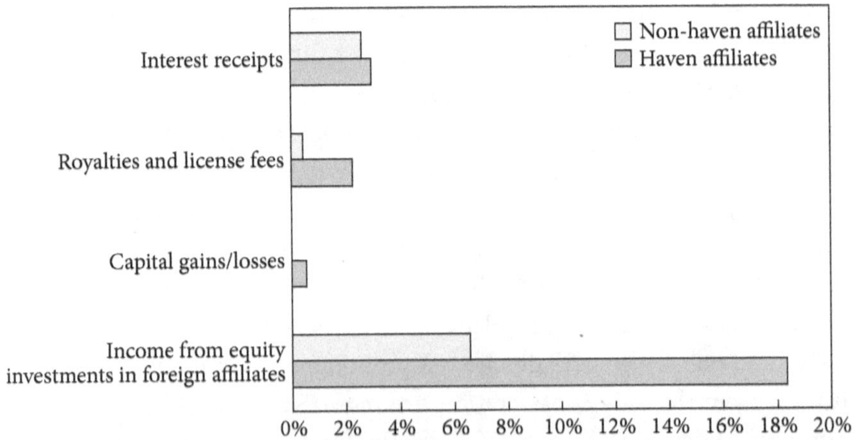

Note: Author's calculations, using aggregate country-level data for the 2014 benchmark survey on the foreign activities of U.S. MNCs from the U.S. Bureau of Economic Analysis (BEA), available at www.bea.gov. The BEA's benchmark surveys provide more detailed information and more extensive coverage than its annual surveys. Tax havens are defined using the classification in Dharmapala and Hines (2009), with some minor updates described in the text.

FIGURE 11-6. Composition of the Total Income of Haven and Non-Haven Affiliates

(Majority-owned foreign affiliates of U.S. MNCs, 2009 benchmark survey)

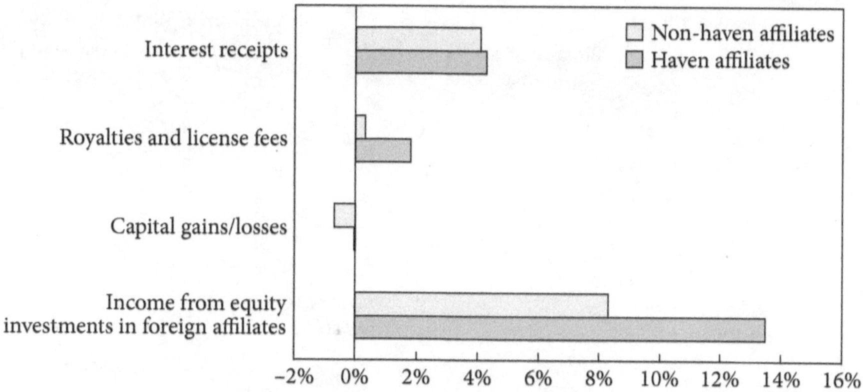

Note: Author's calculations, using aggregate country-level data for the 2009 benchmark survey on the foreign activities of U.S. MNCs from the U.S. Bureau of Economic Analysis (BEA), available at www.bea.gov. The BEA's benchmark surveys provide more detailed information and more extensive coverage than its annual surveys. Tax havens are defined using the classification in Dharmapala and Hines (2009), with some minor updates described in the text.

haven affiliates is 12.24 percent. While financial activities appear to be more important for haven affiliates than for non-haven affiliates, the difference is modest. This overall picture also suggests that in a world without havens—for instance, if a multilateral agreement were to require and enforce a relatively high minimum tax rate for all countries—MNCs may locate their holding companies, intellectual property, and financing activities somewhat differently, but not to the extent that some might expect.

Tax Avoidance and Other Motivations for MNCs' Tax-Haven Activity

It may seem strange to ask how much of MNCs' activity in havens is tax-motivated; this is, after all, tax-haven activity. However, the answer is by no means obvious. To explain why, it is helpful to pose another counterintuitive question, namely: Why is all MNC income not reported in havens? This is very different from the implicit premise of much public discourse that asks why any significant amount of income is reported in havens. However, it is, arguably, the more relevant question, given MNCs' presumed objective

FIGURE 11-7. The Share of Net Income from Finance and Insurance Activities for Haven and Non-Haven Affiliates
(Majority-owned foreign affiliates of U.S. MNCs, 2014 benchmark survey)

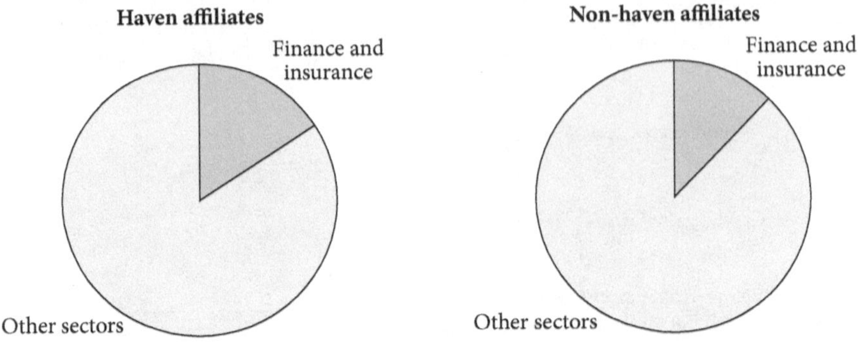

Note: Author's calculations, using aggregate country-level data for the 2014 benchmark survey on the foreign activities of U.S. MNCs from the U.S. Bureau of Economic Analysis (BEA), available at www.bea.gov. The BEA's benchmark surveys provide more detailed information and more extensive coverage than its annual surveys. Tax havens are defined using the classification in Dharmapala and Hines (2009), with some minor updates described in the text.

of maximizing (after-tax) value and the potentially large gains from cross-border tax planning. The answers can be classified into three categories. The first is that nontax business reasons ("nontax frictions") may limit profit shifting to havens. The second is that anti-avoidance tax rules in non-haven countries may limit profit shifting, while the third is that tax planning itself may be costly or subject to various frictions.

Profit shifting involves the relocation of reported profits from higher-tax to lower-tax jurisdictions. A classic and fairly simple example is when a haven affiliate receives an equity injection from the MNC parent and lends to a high-tax affiliate. This generates interest deductions (subject to certain limitations) in the high-tax country and straightforwardly shifts income from the high-tax country to the haven. Or, using slightly different terminology, it erodes the tax base of the high-tax country through what is known as "earnings stripping" or "interest stripping." Note, however, that interest deductions are available to both domestic firms and MNCs.[19] Moreover, these financing choices generate tax advantages without having any substantive effect on the real business operations of the MNC (apart from any resources used in the process of tax planning).[20]

The absence of real effects implies that profit shifting can be viewed as a particular form of tax avoidance that is relevant for the cross-border activities of MNCs. Tax avoidance is commonly defined as "the lawful reduction of tax obligations, while maintaining the same substantive economic outcome" (Dharmapala (2017, xv)). The absence of distortions to decisions about real economic activity distinguishes profit shifting (and tax avoidance, more generally) from real (or behavioral) responses to taxes. Real responses are exemplified, for instance, by an MNC's decision to locate more tangible assets (for example, build more factories) in a lower-tax location than in an otherwise identical higher-tax location. This decision (while it may be privately optimal for the MNC in after-tax terms) reduces social welfare by placing some of these assets in the wrong location (from a pretax perspective). The impact of taxes on such real decisions is constrained by nontax frictions. For instance, the physical infrastructure in the lower-tax location may be less suitable. In contrast, pure forms of tax avoidance (including profit shifting) are constrained instead by tax law and by the costs of tax planning (as, by assumption, there are no real distortions other than those associated with tax-planning costs).

The patterns in the data suggest that MNCs use tax havens as locations for holding companies and intangible assets, and for the internal financing of affiliates. Is the tendency to locate holding companies in havens a form of profit shifting (that is, does it have essentially no substantive economic effects)? This raises the question of what factors determine the optimal location of holding companies. While tax considerations are clearly important, some evidence suggests that both tax and nontax factors are relevant.[21] Nontax factors may include, for instance, the availability of local legal and business expertise relevant to managing the equity holdings of the affiliate. Desai, Foley, and Hines (2006) analyze the affiliate-level BEA data on U.S. MNCs. They find that 12 percent of U.S. MNCs' haven affiliates are holding companies, while 6 percent of non-haven affiliates are holding companies. In their dataset, about 24 percent of holding companies are in havens. This share is disproportionate to the measures of real activity described above, indicating that holding companies are more commonly located in havens. However, this is clearly not true to the extent that would be expected if holding companies' location reflected only tax considerations.

Even absent the detailed affiliate-level ownership data used by Desai, Foley, and Hines (2006), it is possible to draw some inferences about the distribution of holding companies across havens and non-havens using the aggregate BEA data on "income from equity investments" in foreign affiliates. As discussed, this measure reflects an affiliate's ownership of other affiliates, and so provides a strong indication of the presence of holding companies. Table 11-2 and figure 11-3 show that just under 50 percent of income from equity investments was attributed to haven affiliates in 2014. While this is clearly disproportionate, it indicates a substantial presence of holding companies in non-havens. However, favorable tax attributes of non-haven jurisdictions may well influence holding company location. In general, havens tend to match or outdo the favorable tax attributes of non-havens (such as territorial tax regimes and zero withholding taxes on royalties, interest, and dividends). However, the Netherlands is, arguably, a special case, in that it has a well-established special tax regime for foreign holding companies; it may also be preferred by MNCs to havens with similar regimes (for instance, because the Netherlands has a more extensive tax treaty network than many havens). Indeed, about 18 percent of "income from equity investments" was earned by Dutch affiliates of U.S. MNCs in 2014. While this is also disproportionate to measures of real activity, it leaves a significant fraction—nearly one-third—of "income from equity investments" in non-havens other than the Netherlands. For instance, about 7 percent is in the United Kingdom and 6 percent is in Canada.[22]

The evidence on holding companies is particularly significant in suggesting not merely that there are limits to tax planning, but specifically that they include substantial nontax frictions. If it were true that holding company structures are entirely tax-motivated, then anti-avoidance tax rules in non-haven countries and tax-planning frictions would reduce the prevalence of holding company structures. However, under the assumption of a pure tax motivation, these factors alone would not cause holding companies to sprout in non-haven jurisdictions. Yet a substantial fraction of holding companies are in non-havens. This implies that significant nontax considerations determine the location of holding companies. In other words, not all holding companies are in havens because these nontax business considerations presumably outweigh tax advantages in some (but not all) cases.

Nontax factors (which may include the jurisdiction's legal infrastructure and the availability of business expertise in managing royalty payments from other affiliates) are also likely to play a role in the location of intellectual property (IP). In general, the empirical evidence suggests that IP location is very sensitive to taxes. For instance, Dischinger and Riedel (2011) use the balance sheet item "intangible fixed assets" from the Amadeus database of European affiliates, compiled by the Bureau van Dijk, to test whether intangible asset holdings are disproportionately concentrated among affiliates in low-tax jurisdictions, controlling for unobserved affiliate effects that may influence the ownership of intangibles. They find a semi-elasticity of 1.7—that is, a tax rate in an affiliate 10 percentage points lower than the average for the MNC group leads to a 17 percent higher holding of intangible assets.[23] This is a substantial tax effect, but does not seem to indicate that IP location is solely determined by tax considerations. However, the evidence is less clear than for holding companies in ruling out anti-avoidance rules and tax-planning frictions as explanations for why not all IP is located in havens. Anti-avoidance rules and tax-planning costs (as well as nontax frictions) may potentially explain why higher-tax affiliates hold or retain IP (which, after all, must be held by one affiliate or another).

With respect to the role of havens as financing centers, the pure tax motivation underlying the interest-stripping example above is very clear. However, many tax havens are also (perhaps not entirely coincidentally) offshore financial centers (OFCs). They are thus the home of extensive financial expertise and infrastructure, which may reinforce the tax motivation to locate financial activities in havens.[24] Tax and nontax motivations are difficult to disentangle in this context, and the nontax financial advantages of havens may originally have arisen from agglomeration effects attributable to their tax advantages. However, figure 11-7 suggests that financial activities are, in aggregate, not that much more important to haven affiliates than to non-haven affiliates, and table 11-2 indicates that a substantial fraction of financial activities are carried out by non-haven affiliates.

The wider implications of these facts and the conceptual framework described above for how profit shifting should be understood and measured are taken up later in the chapter, following a review of the literature on the magnitude of profit shifting. For now, it is sufficient to bear in mind that the data suggest there are important frictions associated with MNCs' use of havens for tax avoidance. A particularly striking piece of evidence in the academic literature is that a substantial fraction of MNCs have no haven affiliates. Desai, Foley, and Hines (2006), using the affiliate-level BEA data, find that in 1999 only 59 percent of U.S. firms with significant foreign operations had affiliates in tax-haven countries. Dharmapala and Riedel (2013), using an Amadeus sample of European MNC affiliates from 1995 to 2005, report that only 58 percent of these affiliates belong to MNCs that include at least one affiliate in a non-European tax haven. More recent evidence comes from the German MNCs analyzed in Gumpert, Hines Jr., and Schnitzer (2016), using the Microdatabase Direct investment (MiDi) dataset provided by the German Bundesbank. Among these MNCs, only about 20 percent have any tax-haven affiliates. The ownership of haven affiliates appears responsive to tax motivations: among German manufacturing MNCs, higher foreign tax rates are associated with a higher likelihood of having tax-haven affiliates. However, on average, surprisingly few German MNCs use tax havens.

Why do more MNCs not use haven affiliates? The direct costs of establishing a haven affiliate—typically, incorporation fees paid to the haven government—are relatively modest, yet many MNCs manifestly do not find this cost worthwhile. One possibility is that there is a substantial fixed cost of tax planning (that is, of obtaining legal and accounting services and structuring the legal form of affiliates), so that many MNCs—especially those that are smaller—do not undertake any tax planning. Another possibility is that governments' anti-avoidance rules may be effective enough that many MNCs do not expect to derive tax benefits from establishing haven affiliates.

Tax Havens and Secrecy

In popular discussion, great emphasis is placed on the importance of secrecy in tax-haven jurisdictions (achieved, for instance, through laws related to the confidentiality of financial accounts). Havens are, indeed, sometimes described as "secrecy jurisdictions." However, secrecy plays at most a minor role in MNC haven activity. As the extensive data discussed suggest, the activities of MNCs in havens—including those involving tax avoidance—take place in the bright sunshine of academic, financial, and media scrutiny. On the other hand, secrecy has historically been important to tax evasion by individuals through financial accounts in tax havens.

Tax evasion (which is not to be confused with tax avoidance) is the "nonpayment of legally owed taxes, where it is assumed that the law clearly specifies the obligations of the taxpayer" (Dharmapala (2017, xv)). Individuals are typically subject to personal income tax in their country of tax residence. The laws of most countries with personal income taxation require that individuals report income generated in foreign financial accounts, and pay taxes on it, to their country of residence. Individuals who hold foreign financial accounts and fail to report to their home government the income these accounts generate are thus engaged in tax evasion. The confidentiality laws of some tax havens facilitated such evasion by reducing the likelihood of detection by the home government (although, until recently, there was quite-limited enforcement even for foreign financial accounts held in non-havens).

MNC activities in havens have essentially nothing in common with evasion by individuals. It is thus important to distinguish between MNCs' and individuals' use of havens (see, for example, Dharmapala (2008)). MNCs' activities in havens are generally lawful (although tax planning may involve taking more or less aggressive positions in the face of legal uncertainty). In contrast, individual evasion is typically unlawful and relies in part on secrecy. Moreover, the spread of information exchange among governments about individuals' foreign financial accounts (especially the introduction of the automatic exchange of information among governments) is, arguably, making individual evasion via tax-haven financial accounts (and foreign accounts more generally) largely a phenomenon of the past. In 2010, Congress enacted the Foreign Account Tax Compliance Act (FATCA), which essentially compels non-U.S. financial institutions to report accounts held by U.S. individuals to the U.S. government (see, for example, Dharmapala (2016)). This represents a unilateral approach by the United States, while the OECD and Group of Twenty (G-20) have developed a multilateral approach to information exchange known as the Common Reporting Standard (CRS).[25]

Some reasonable questions remain about whether the social welfare gains from reducing tax evasion—which depend on the incremental social value of the revenue collected when it is in government rather than private hands—exceed the compliance costs for financial institutions of reporting to a wide variety of foreign governments (see, for example, Dharmapala (2016)). Despite this caveat, the disappearance of individual evasion through offshore financial accounts is obviously welcome in terms of tax compliance, revenue generation, and the integrity of the world's personal income tax systems. There is some historical irony, though, in that this development has occurred in an era of what Ginsburg and Huq (2018) term "democratic retrogression"—a well-documented phenomenon in which democratic values and practices are in retreat globally in the face of the rise of elected leaders with authoritarian inclinations. Secrecy jurisdictions are thus disappearing at the same time that there may arguably be a greater need for individuals who reasonably fear persecution to protect their assets. However, Ginsburg and Huq (2018) also find that outright dictatorships have become less common in recent years, which may potentially reduce the need for secrecy jurisdictions.

While it has conventionally been thought that secrecy plays little or no role in MNCs' haven activity (see, for example, Dharmapala (2008)), there is an emerging body of evidence that adds some nuance to this picture. For instance, Braun and Weichenrieder (2015) analyze the effect on the foreign operations of German-based MNCs of Tax Information Exchange Agreements (TIEAs), which provide for enhanced exchange of information among governments. They find that the probability of a German MNC owning an affiliate in a haven falls after the signing of a TIEA between that haven and Germany. Bennedsen and Zeume (2017) analyze stock market reactions to the signing of TIEAs involving tax havens, using a dataset of 17,331 publicly listed firms in fifty-two countries. They find that the signing of a TIEA between a firm's residence country and a tax haven is associated with a 2.5 percent increase in firm value. They interpret this result as indicating that the insiders of firms with haven affiliates use these affiliates for activities involving the diversion of value from shareholders; these activities, they argue, are constrained by the greater transparency created by TIEAs.

O'Donovan, Wagner, and Zeume (2019) link previously secret offshore entities revealed by the "Panama Papers" leak, which occurred in 2015, to 338 publicly listed firms around the world. They find a negative market reaction of about 1 percent of firm value to the revelation of these entities. They interpret this result as indicating that activities undertaken through these secret entities (such as the bribery of foreign officials) are value-enhancing for shareholders; for instance, these firms reduced their subsequent activity in countries with higher levels of corruption. The negative reaction is less pronounced for firms with weaker corporate governance (suggesting that the secret activities of these firms were less likely to be value-enhancing for outside shareholders).

This new evidence suggests that havens' secrecy matters (or, rather, mattered while it existed) to certain peripheral MNC activities, such as the bribery of government officials. It does not imply that major MNCs use havens to engage in tax evasion per se (as defined above), something for which the literature has produced no evidence and that seems unlikely on conceptual grounds. Desai and Dharmapala (2006; 2008; 2009a, b; 2018) develop a framework, providing an agency perspective on tax avoidance, which can unify much of this new evidence. It highlights potential complementarities between tax avoidance (whether or not linked to havens) and managerial or insider opportunism. For instance, the complexity of transactions undertaken to avoid taxes may impede shareholder monitoring and thus reduce the cost of insider opportunism. Stronger corporate governance (increasing the alignment of interests between shareholders and insiders) then has a potentially ambiguous effect on tax avoidance activity. While stronger governance prompts insiders to increase firm value by engaging in tax avoidance, it may also dissuade insiders from engaging in opportunistic acts that are complementary with tax avoidance.

While some of the literature on corporate tax havens and secrecy alludes to this agency framework, its implications for the questions addressed in this chapter have not been explicitly articulated. Arguably, the agency perspective on corporate tax avoidance can be used to construct a theory of how havens may potentially reduce the welfare of non-havens. In this view, the existence of havens enables firms to engage in tax avoidance (at least to a greater degree than otherwise). When firms engage in tax avoidance, insiders of some firms (namely, those with weaker governance) will tend to also divert more value from shareholders. Shareholders (who are overwhelmingly resident in non-haven countries) will potentially be worse off if the amount diverted exceeds the increase in shareholder value from greater tax avoidance.

However, the underlying problem is not that tax havens exist, rather it is that corporate governance in non-haven jurisdictions is not as uniformly strong as it could be. If corporate governance were perfect, shareholders would be unambiguously better off with more tax avoidance opportunities (and therefore better off due to the existence of havens). Moreover, shareholders could, in principle, replicate firm behavior in a world without havens by forbidding or strongly disincentivizing the establishment of haven affiliates by managers. The Desai-Dharmapala theory presumes the imperfect observability of managerial actions (for example, whether a particular strategy is primarily for tax avoidance or for diversion); however, it should be feasible for shareholders to impose and enforce a simple bright-line rule such as forbidding all haven affiliates.

Separately, it is also possible to argue that havens that provide a domicile for secret entities make the (typically, developing) countries whose officials are bribed worse off by exacerbating corruption (if there would, counterfactually, be less bribery absent havens). Again, however, the fundamental problem is corruption in these countries rather than the existence of havens. Moreover, it is by no means obvious that in a second-best setting, where there are many other distortions, increased corruption would necessarily lower social welfare.

TAX HAVENS AND THE WELFARE OF NON-HAVEN COUNTRIES

This chapter examines the consequences of corporate tax havens for the welfare of non-haven countries, which, it should be emphasized, already have a powerful set of tools that can effectively neutralize the tax impact of havens. These include, among others, controlled foreign corporation (CFC) rules and thin capitalization rules (TCRs). Before proceeding, however, it is helpful to more explicitly define relevant international tax law concepts. In the terminology of international taxation, the country in which the MNC parent is domiciled (either incorporated or managed and controlled, depending on the country) is known as the "residence" country. A country in which MNC affiliates undertake business activity is known as a "source" country. Income generated by normal business operations in the source country is referred to as "active" income; income not associated with these business activities (such as interest and royalties) is referred to as "passive" income.

Controlled Foreign Corporation (CFC) Rules

Suppose that country A (in which an MNC known as firm A is resident) has a corporate tax rate of 20 percent. Firm A holds 100 percent ownership of affiliates in country B (a non-haven that also imposes a 20 percent corporate tax) and in country H (a haven with a zero tax rate). In the parlance of international taxation, the affiliates in B and H are known as "controlled foreign corporations" (CFCs). Most countries with significant outbound foreign direct investment (FDI) impose what are known as CFC rules. These rules specify a minimum tax rate and provide that if a resident MNC earns passive income in any jurisdiction with a tax rate below this minimum, it pays tax to the residence country at the residence country's tax rate. For example, suppose that country A imposes a CFC rule that specifies a minimum tax rate on foreign passive income of 10 percent. Then any passive income earned by firm A in country H will be subject to taxation by country A at its regular 20 percent tax rate (because the zero tax rate of the haven is less than the 10 percent threshold). Thus, a CFC rule taxes passive income earned in tax havens at the residence country rate. Such a rule clearly eliminates the incentive for firm A to shift profits from A to H. However, it also eliminates the incentive for firm A to shift profits from B to H. This latter effect increases the foreign tax payments made by firm A (to the government of country B). These increased foreign tax payments represent a reduction in the national welfare of country A.

A simple but useful characterization of national welfare in this context is to define it as the sum of the after-tax profits of a country's resident MNCs and the aggregate tax revenue collected by the country's government (see, for example, Dharmapala (2014b)). This is obviously a simplification, as funds in the hands of the government may be more socially valuable than those in the hands of the MNC's shareholders. However, it suffices for the purposes of this discussion of international tax policy and the strategic interactions among countries. For instance, it captures the idea that resident MNCs (despite growing global financial integration) often remain predominantly owned by shareholders who are also resident in the same country (a phenomenon sometimes termed "equity home bias"). It also highlights the contrast between foreign-to-foreign shifting (which unambiguously increases the residence country's national welfare) and the ambiguous effects of shifting from the residence country to havens. For instance, U.S.-to-haven shifting by U.S. MNCs reduces U.S. tax revenue, but this negative effect is entirely or partially offset by higher national welfare due to increased after-tax profits for U.S. MNCs. The discussion below emphasizes foreign-to-foreign shifting because of its clearer national welfare implications, but this does not deny the importance of shifting from the residence country to havens. Also, this simple framework is not suitable for analyzing the domestic effects of tax policy, where distributional considerations within a country play a significant role.

Consider first the outcomes in the absence of a CFC rule (as illustrated in figure 11-8), assuming that the costs of tax planning are US$2 per country from which profits are shifted. Suppose also that firm A earns US$50 in country A, US$50 in country B, and zero in the haven H, before taxes and prior to any profit shifting. When country A does not impose a CFC rule, firm A will find it worthwhile to shift all of its profits from both A and B to H (thereby saving US$10 of tax in each of A and B, and incurring a US$2 cost of tax planning in each country). Firm A's profits, taking account of the US$4 cost of profit shifting, will be US$96 and country A's revenue will be zero (so that the national welfare of country A is US$96).

Now consider the introduction of a CFC rule by country A (as illustrated in figure 11-9). Firm A will no longer shift profits from either A or B to the haven. Doing so would result in the income reported in H being taxed at

FIGURE 11-8. Residence Country (A's) National Welfare with no CFC Rule

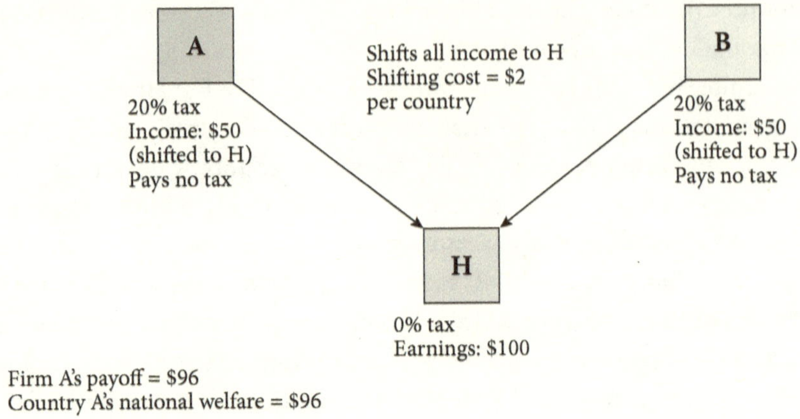

Note: When country A does not impose a CFC rule, Firm A will shift all of its profits from both A and B to the haven H (thereby saving US$10 of tax in each of A and B, and incurring a US$2 cost of tax planning in each country). Firm A's profits, taking account of the US$4 cost of profit shifting, will be US$96 and country A's revenue will be zero (so that the national welfare of country A is US$96).

country A's 20 percent tax rate, while firm A would also pointlessly incur a US$4 cost of tax planning. Thus, firm A would instead pay US$10 of tax to each of governments A and B and be left with after-tax profits of US$80. The government of country A now raises US$10 of revenue, so country A's national welfare is US$90. Country A's national welfare falls upon the introduction of the CFC rule because of the increased tax payments by firm A to country B. The higher revenue for foreign governments is not a loss from a global perspective, and so a CFC rule may be globally optimal (as in this example, though not necessarily in all circumstances). It generally increases the residence country's tax revenue. However, it may well reduce the national welfare of a country that introduces it, while generating positive revenue spillovers for other non-haven countries (for example, country B gains US$10 of revenue). As discussed below, residence countries thus face a collective action problem in introducing CFC rules and are likely to do so to a suboptimal extent (see, for example, Dharmapala (2014b); Haufler and others (2018)).

CFC rules were pioneered by the United States, in the form of what are known as the Subpart F provisions enacted in 1962. These rules made passive income earned in low-tax foreign jurisdictions subject to immediate taxation by the United States (whereas, otherwise, the U.S. taxation of for-

FIGURE 11-9. Residence Country (A's) National Welfare with a CFC Rule

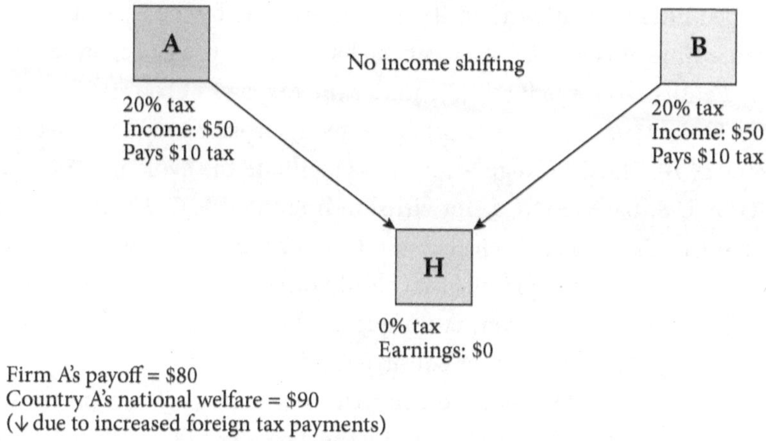

Note: Firm A no longer shifts profits from either A or B to the haven H, as doing so would result in the income reported in H being taxed at country A's 20 percent tax rate, while Firm A would also incur a US$4 cost of tax planning. Firm A pays US$10 of tax to each of governments A and B, and has after-tax profits of US$80. The government of country A raises US$10 of revenue, so country A's national welfare is US$90.

eign income was deferred until the repatriation of that income to the U.S. parent). Since then, even as CFC rules have spread around the world, U.S. CFC rules have undergone a significant transformation. In 1996, the U.S. Treasury issued what are known as the "check-the-box" (CTB) regulations. These regulations enable firms to choose their organizational form for tax purposes (for example, as a C-corporation or as a pass-through entity) by filing a simple form on which the appropriate box could be checked. The CTB (or "entity election") regime replaced a complex set of rules determining firms' tax status. However, it has also had the consequence of facilitating tax avoidance by U.S.-based MNCs using what are known as "hybrid entities" (see, for example, Altshuler and Grubert (2005)). Hybrid entities are classified in two distinct ways—as separately incorporated affiliates under the tax rules of a foreign country and as unincorporated branches for U.S. tax purposes.

Figure 11-10 illustrates the effect of the CTB regulations on the operation of the U.S. CFC rule. Suppose a U.S.-based MNC has affiliates in B and a haven H (with the same characteristics assumed above). The effect of the U.S. CFC rule can be avoided by using the CTB regulations as follows. Firm A can elect (for U.S. tax purposes) to have the haven affiliate treated as an unincorporated branch of the B affiliate. This makes the passive income received by the H affiliate invisible to the U.S. tax system. (The box outlined by dashed lines indicates the entity that is perceived by the United States.) At the same time, it is possible to treat the haven affiliate as a separately incorporated entity from the B affiliate under the tax laws of country B (thus enabling, for instance, interest or other payments from B to H to be deductible in country B). The CTB regulations thus facilitate the avoidance of country B's tax by U.S.-based MNCs, notwithstanding the U.S. CFC rule.[26] In effect, it makes the U.S. CFC rule elective, and can be viewed as a way to avoid the increased foreign tax payments that would otherwise be made under a CFC rule. This situation, however, is unique to the United States and does not apply to the CFC rules of other countries.

CFC rules provide residence countries with a very powerful means of eliminating profit shifting to havens by their resident MNCs. The empirical evidence suggests that CFC rules are highly effective. For instance, using a global dataset of MNCs, Markle and Robinson (2012) find that CFC rules imposed by the residence country reduce MNCs' use of tax havens. Using the MiDi dataset on German MNCs provided by the German Bundesbank, Ruf and Weichenrieder (2012) find that Germany's CFC rule is quite effec-

FIGURE 11-10. Entity Election and Tax Planning

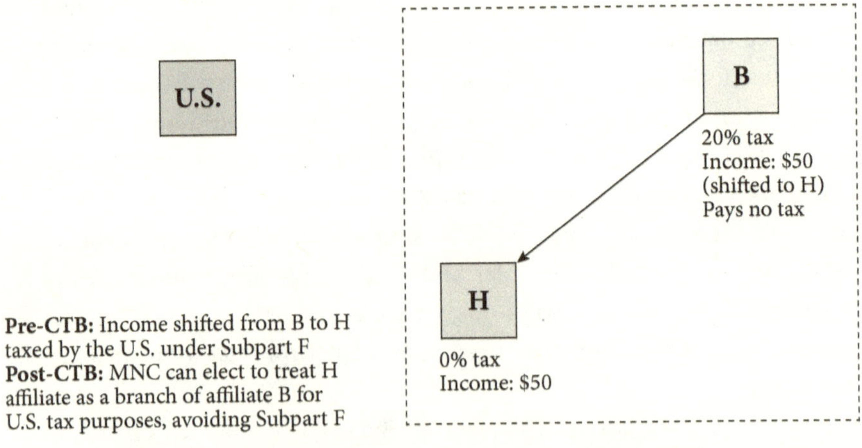

Note: Firm A elects (for U.S. tax purposes) to have the haven affiliate H treated as an unincorporated branch of the B affiliate. The passive income received by the H affiliate is invisible to the U.S. tax system (the box outlined by dashed lines indicates the entity that is perceived by the United States). At the same time, the haven affiliate is a separately incorporated entity from the B affiliate under the tax laws of country B (thus enabling, for instance, interest or other payments paid from B to H to be deductible in country B).

tive in limiting the amount of passive income located by German MNCs in low-tax countries.

Clifford (2019) uses a global dataset of MNC affiliates from 2003 to 2013 from the Orbis database compiled by the Bureau van Dijk, and codes the CFC rules (if any) applicable to each MNC affiliate in each of these years (based on the residence country of the MNC affiliate's parent and the tax characteristics of the source country). She finds evidence that MNCs reallocate profits from affiliates in countries with tax rates just below the tax rate threshold at which the CFC rule applies to countries with tax rates just above this threshold.[27] MNCs also tend to establish fewer affiliates in countries with tax rates below the CFC rule's threshold. She also estimates that a residence country introducing a CFC rule obtains about half of the resulting increase in tax revenue, with the other half accruing to other non-haven countries. The revenue spillovers of CFC rules illustrated by the simple example in figure 11-9 are thus empirically quite relevant.[28]

Thin Capitalization Rules (TCRs)

While CFC rules are imposed by residence countries, TCRs are an instrument of primary relevance to source countries. TCRs limit the use of internal debt within MNCs to erode the tax base of non-haven source countries. Such base erosion occurs most straightforwardly through the types of interest-stripping transactions described earlier in the chapter, in which a haven affiliate receives an equity injection from the MNC parent and lends to a high-tax affiliate. This generates interest deductions in the high-tax country and shifts income from the high-tax country to the haven. There are two main forms of TCRs (see, for example, Büttner and others (2012); Ruf and Schindler (2015)). The originally predominant type is based on safe harbor rules that set a maximum ratio of debt to total capital (the sum of debt and equity) and restrict the tax deductibility of interest payments (either for related-party interest or for all interest, depending on how a country's tax law specifies these restrictions) when this ratio is exceeded.[29]

More recently, many countries have adopted an alternative form of TCR, generally known as an earnings (or interest) stripping rule.[30] This involves specifying a limit to interest deductions as a fraction of pretax income. That is, an affiliate's interest deductions (either for inter-affiliate debt or for all debt) are restricted to some maximum fraction of some specified notion of income, typically earnings before interest and taxes (EBIT) or earnings before interest, taxes, depreciation, and amortization (EBITDA). Disallowed interest is usually carried forward and can potentially be used in a future year, but only in accordance with the TCR's limitations.

Consider a simple earnings-stripping rule adopted by country B in the example above. Suppose, in particular, that country B restricts interest deductions to 30 percent of EBIT, as illustrated in figure 11-11. Firm A (the MNC based in country A) injects US$100 of equity into its haven affiliate, which then lends this US$100 to firm A's affiliate in country B. Suppose that the (arm's-length) interest rate is 10 percent. In the absence of a TCR, affiliate B would be able to deduct US$10 of interest in country B. With B's TCR (as specified above), affiliate B's interest deductions are constrained. Assume that EBIT for affiliate B is US$12; then interest deductions are limited to US$3.60. Country B's TCR thus limits the profit shifted from B to H to US$3.60, rather than the US$10 that could be shifted absent the TCR.

TCRs are thus a powerful instrument for source countries to limit the erosion of their tax base by MNCs and neutralize the effect of havens. Indeed, a sufficiently strict TCR can, in principle, eliminate interest stripping to havens. Büttner and others (2012) use data on the foreign affiliates of German MNCs to show that the introduction and strengthening of TCRs reduces the use of inter-affiliate debt. However, while the adoption of TCRs

FIGURE 11-11. Thin Capitalization (Earnings Stripping) Rules

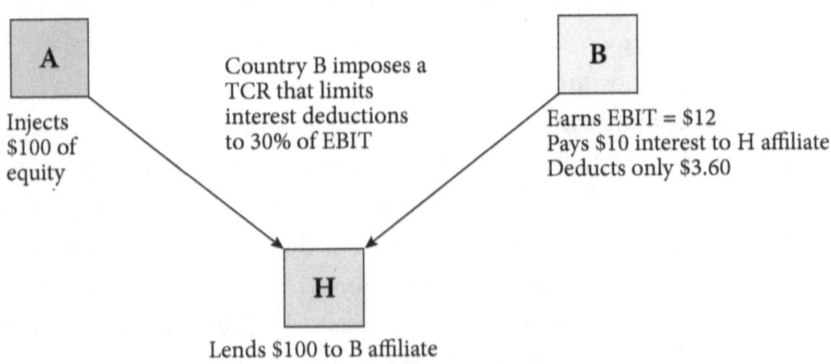

Note: Firm A injects US$100 of equity into its haven affiliate H, which then lends this US$100 to Firm A's affiliate in country B. Suppose that the (arm's length) interest rate is 10 percent. In the absence of a TCR, affiliate B would be able to deduct US$10 of interest in country B. With B's TCR, affiliate B's interest deductions are constrained. Assume that EBIT for affiliate B is US$12; then interest deductions are limited to US$3.60. Country B's TCR thus limits the profit shifted from B to H to US$3.60 rather than the US$10 that could be shifted absent the TCR.

by source countries prevents tax base erosion and generates tax revenue, it also increases effective tax rates on investment by MNCs (when taking account of the more limited possibilities for outbound profit shifting). Thus, TCRs have potential disadvantages, most notably that higher effective tax rates may discourage inbound investment by MNCs.

The Global Strengthening of Rules against Profit Shifting to Havens

The main implication of the preceding discussion is that non-haven countries have extremely powerful tax law provisions for neutralizing the advantages associated with MNCs' use of havens. Moreover, these tools have been increasingly widely adopted. Dharmapala (2019) constructs a dataset of CFC rules and TCRs for all OECD-member countries in 2000 and 2014.[31] This builds on the coding of these provisions by Haufler and others (2018), but is modified in certain respects to enable quantification. In particular, CFC rules can be characterized in a straightforward manner as establishing a minimum tax rate on foreign passive income earned by a country's resident MNCs. This is given by the foreign tax rate threshold for the CFC rule to apply. For example, in the earlier simple illustration, country A imposes a CFC rule with a tax rate threshold of 10 percent, implying that any foreign passive income earned by firm A that is taxed at less than 10 percent becomes subject to taxation by country A at its tax rate of 20 percent. This implies that firm A's foreign passive income can never be taxed at a rate less than 10 percent. If located in a haven with a tax rate below 10 percent, it will be taxed at 20 percent by country A; otherwise, it is taxed at the local tax rate, which cannot be below 10 percent without triggering the CFC rule. Note that the absence of a CFC rule (which was fairly common among OECD countries in 2000) means that the minimum tax rate on foreign passive income earned by a country's resident MNCs is zero: if passive income is earned in a zero tax jurisdiction, then it faces a zero tax rate.

As shown in figure 11-12, the median across OECD countries of this minimum tax rate on foreign passive income increased from zero to 12 percent. The corresponding mean increased more modestly from 10.8 percent to 10.9 percent (as also shown in figure 11-12). The strengthening of CFC rules among OECD countries is more marked if the minimum tax rate on foreign passive income is scaled by the country's corporate tax rate. Arguably, this scaling is sensible because many CFC rules specify the foreign tax rate threshold as a fraction of the country's corporate tax rate. Figure 11-13 shows that the mean across OECD countries of this ratio has increased from 0.34 to 0.42. The median across OECD countries of this ratio has increased more markedly, from 0 to 0.5. This implies that the median OECD country requires its resident MNCs to pay tax on their foreign passive income at a rate no less than half its regular corporate tax rate.

The particularly substantial increase in the median of the minimum tax rate on foreign passive income indicates that CFC rules have become sub-

FIGURE 11-12. Minimum Tax Rate on Foreign Passive Income Implied by the CFC Rules of OECD Countries, 2000 and 2014

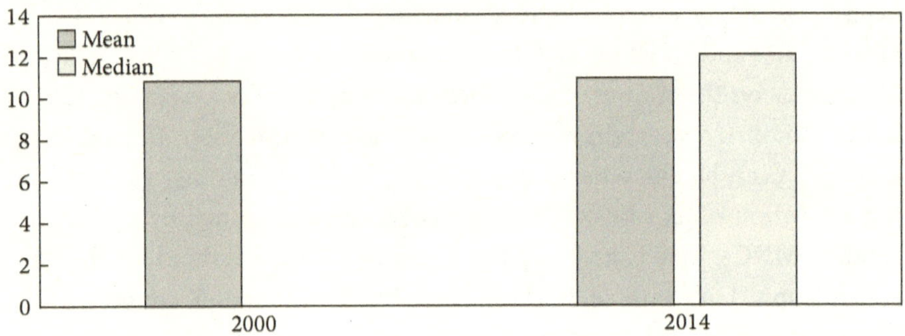

Source: Author's calculations, using the dataset on CFC rules constructed and described in Dharmapala (2019). Note that the median in 2000 was zero.

FIGURE 11-13. Ratio of the Minimum Tax Rate on Foreign Passive Income to the Corporate Income Tax Rate, as Implied by the CFC Rules of OECD Countries, 2000 and 2014

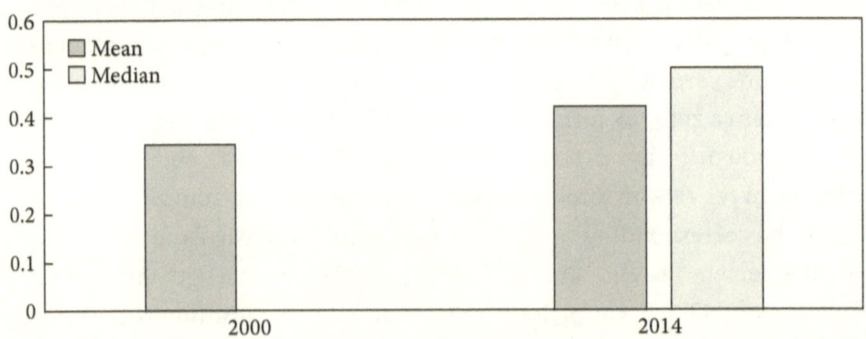

Source: Based on Dharmapala (2019, figure 1). Note that the median in 2000 was zero.

stantially more widespread among OECD countries. This development is illustrated in figure 11-14, which plots the minimum tax rate on foreign passive income (scaled by the corporate tax rate) for each country in the sample. A substantial number of countries that had zero minimum rates (that is, no CFC rules) in 2000 introduced CFC rules by 2014 (and hence have positive though relatively modest minimum tax rates on foreign passive income). On the other hand, countries that already had CFC rules in 2000 have fairly similar ratios of minimum tax rates on foreign passive income to their corporate tax rates in 2014 (albeit in an environment in which the average corporate tax rate has fallen). The widening of the distribution of CFC rules, however, is particularly important in practical terms, because even a CFC rule with a fairly low foreign tax threshold can completely deter profit shifting to zero tax havens.

TCRs of the safe harbor variety establish a maximum ratio of debt to equity above which interest deductions are disallowed. In comparing TCRs

FIGURE 11-14. Ratio of the Minimum Tax Rate on Foreign Passive Income to the Corporate Income Tax Rate, as Implied by the CFC Rules of OECD Countries, 2000 and 2014

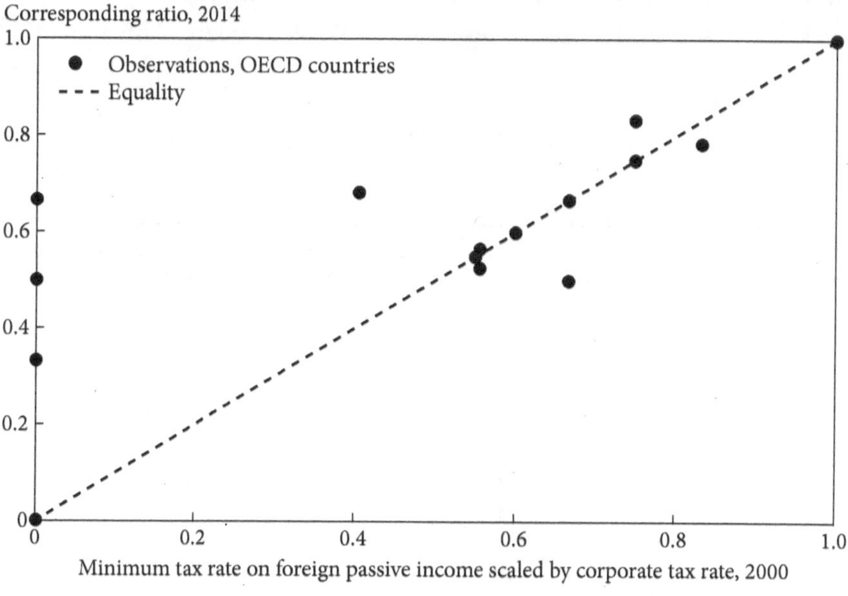

Source: Author's calculations, using the dataset on CFC rules constructed and described in Dharmapala (2019).

across countries and over time, it is convenient to recharacterize this as a minimum ratio of equity to total capital (equity plus debt), above which interest deductions are allowed. The absence of a TCR implies that this minimum fraction of equity is zero (so that interest payments are deductible without restrictions). TCRs of the earnings-stripping rule variety can be characterized straightforwardly by the fraction of pretax income that is specified as the maximum amount of deductible interest (30 percent of EBIT in the simple example above). Figure 11-15 shows that the mean fraction across OECD countries of equity in MNC affiliates required for interest deductibility has risen from 0.14 to 0.22. This indicates that safe harbor rules have been strengthened, thereby reducing opportunities for profit shifting. For earnings-stripping rules, the mean fraction of income that is subject to interest deductions has fallen across OECD countries from 1 to 0.65. Thus, only about two-thirds of MNC affiliates' income was potentially subject to interest deductions in 2014.

Why Are Rules against Profit Shifting Not Used (Even) More Extensively?

Rules against profit shifting (such as CFC rules and TCRs) are very powerful in principle, and, moreover, are increasingly being deployed by non-haven (residence and source) countries. Figures 11-12 through 11-15 show that

FIGURE 11-15. Thin Capitalization Rules in OECD Countries, 2000 and 2014

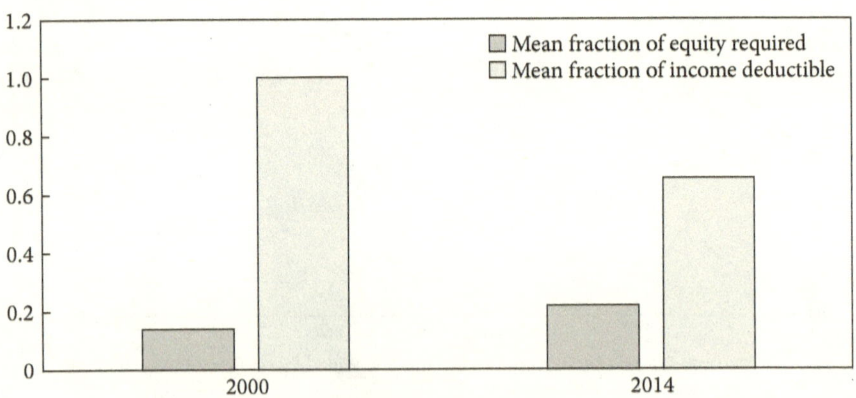

Source: Based on Dharmapala (2019, figure 2).

rules against profit shifting have been substantially strengthened among OECD countries in recent years.[32] Thus, it is arguable that MNCs' use of tax havens relies on the forbearance or even collusion of non-haven countries. Sufficiently strong CFC rules, TCRs, and other rules against profit shifting would eliminate the tax advantages of MNCs' use of havens. Arguably, the tax benefits to MNCs of havens thus exist only to the extent that non-haven (residence and source) countries refrain from imposing such rules.

There are potential alternative accounts in which non-haven countries are less complicit in MNCs' use of havens. In the course of the Base Erosion and Profit Shifting (BEPS) initiative, the OECD (2013) particularly emphasized unintended interactions among non-havens' tax laws that enable profit shifting to havens without deliberate facilitation by non-havens. If this were the entire explanation, governments committed to combating profit shifting could have quickly reformed the provisions responsible for these unintended interactions once they came to light, without the need for an extensive multilateral initiative. For example, it is very difficult to understand the persistence of the U.S. CTB provision within the OECD's conceptual framework, especially once its consequences for facilitating foreign tax avoidance should have become very clear to Congress.

The current discussions within the G-20 and OECD Inclusive Framework on a Global Anti-Base Erosion (GloBE) proposal (OECD (2019)) reflect this perspective. The GloBE proposal seeks to implement a global minimum tax by conferring additional powers (through changes to countries' domestic tax laws and to tax treaties) on residence and source countries to impose taxes on income that has been untaxed or lightly taxed by haven jurisdictions. This approach downplays the issue of whether countries have incentives to use their taxing powers. Conferring additional taxing powers is arguably superfluous, given that powerful tax law instruments to neutralize MNCs' use of havens are already available. In any event, the conferral of powers does not compel countries to use them, unless there is an effective enforcement mechanism for the global minimum tax.

It is also possible that non-havens' failure to fully neutralize MNCs' use of havens may represent a policymaking error or oversight. Governments' policymaking is hardly perfect. If the critics are correct that MNCs use havens excessively, however, this explanation would seem to require that errors are systematically in the direction of encouraging MNCs' use of havens, rather than being randomly distributed. It is also possible that governments favor limiting profit shifting to havens but have many other unrelated priorities that rank higher on their agendas. This would entail, however, that policymakers are failing to respond to what has become a highly salient public concern about MNCs' profit shifting. Such a failure might result from political dysfunction, or from the difficulty of mobilizing a sufficiently broad coalition in a political system with a large number of veto players (such as the U.S. system). However, the extent to which this type of explanation applies more widely among OECD countries (many of which have parliamentary systems with fewer veto players) is unclear.

As discussed, non-haven countries' rules against profit shifting are quite widespread and have become substantially stronger in recent years. Yet, they could, in principle, be even stronger. Why are such rules not used even more extensively, and how does MNCs' use of havens affect the welfare of non-haven countries? There are two main possible answers. One is that non-haven countries use the available tools suboptimally, due to a collective action problem. They would collectively be better off with stronger rules (and therefore less MNC use of havens), but no non-haven country has an incentive to strengthen their rules unilaterally. The other is that MNCs' haven activity serves the interests of non-haven countries, at least as those interests are construed by their political systems. Non-haven countries, therefore, have no reason (unilaterally or even collectively) to further reduce MNCs' haven activity. This subsection explores the first answer, while the next subsection addresses the second.

To illustrate the collective action problem that potentially affects the imposition of CFC rules, suppose that country B in the earlier example is the residence country of firm B, an MNC that is symmetric to firm A in that it earns US$50 of pretax (and pre-shifting) income in each of countries A and B and also has an affiliate in the haven H.[33] Recall that country B imposes a 20 percent tax, as does country A, while the haven H has a zero tax rate. National welfare for countries A and B is defined as the sum of tax revenue and the after-tax profits of its resident MNC. Profit shifting by firms A and B entails a cost of US$2 per country, from which profits are shifted to H. If neither country A nor country B imposes a CFC rule, firm A and firm B, each, generate US$100 of pretax profit, and each shifts all income out to H. As shown in table 11-5, each firm has after-tax profit of US$96 (US$100 minus the US$2 cost of profit-shifting at each affiliate). Tax revenue is zero for each country.

It is clear that neither country has an incentive to unilaterally introduce a CFC rule. For instance, if country A does so, firm A will no longer have an incentive to shift income to H. It would generate US$100 of pretax profit, incur zero tax-planning costs, and pay tax of US$10 to A and US$10 to B.[34] This tax payment to country B reduces country A's national welfare, without any offsetting increase in the revenue that country A derives from the local affiliate of firm B. As described above and shown in table 11-5, country A is clearly worse off by unilaterally introducing a CFC rule (with national welfare of US$90).[35]

However, in this example, both countries, in principle, could be better off if both simultaneously imposed CFC rules. Then each MNC would earn US$100 of pretax profit, incur zero tax-planning costs, and pay US$10 tax to each country. As shown in table 11-5, both countries are better off in this scenario, with national welfare of US$100 (US$80 of after-tax profit for its MNC, plus US$10 of revenue from its MNC, plus US$10 of revenue from the other country's MNC). The central reason is that while introducing a CFC involves giving up revenue to the other country, each country also collects more tax from the local affiliate of the other country's MNC due to the other country's CFC rule. In addition, global welfare is higher, because the deadweight costs of tax planning are not incurred. Such an outcome requires multilateral cooperation and a mechanism to enforce it.

The collective action problem is somewhat different for TCRs. It is closely related to the basic insight of the theory of tax competition (in which different jurisdictions noncooperatively set tax rates), namely that competition among jurisdictions to attract mobile capital entails that the tax rates chosen by these jurisdictions may be suboptimally low from the perspective of global welfare (see, for example, Wilson (1999)). For a source country seeking to attract FDI from MNCs, a stronger TCR, in effect, implies a higher tax rate. Thus, in a standard tax-competition framework that is extended to consider the choice of TCRs, countries' TCRs will be weaker than is globally optimal (see, for example, Haufler and others (2018)).

TABLE 11-5. Payoffs of Countries A and B

		Country B	
		CFC rule	No CFC rule
Country A	CFC rule	100, 100	90, 106
	No CFC rule	106, 90	96, 96

Source: Dharmapala (2014b)

The idea that rules against profit shifting are employed suboptimally because of collective action problems among residence countries (for instance, for CFC rules) and among source countries (for instance, for TCRs) is a conceptually coherent way to make sense of the notion that MNC activity in tax havens may decrease the (collective) welfare of non-havens, despite the existence in principle of tax law provisions that can neutralize the effect of havens. On the other hand, there are some reasons to doubt that this mechanism predominates. One is the substantial strengthening of CFCs and TCRs from 2000 to 2014. It is particularly noteworthy that this trend emerged before the implementation of the recent G-20 and OECD initiative to foster multilateral cooperation on the issue of base erosion and profit shifting (OECD (2015)). It appears that the collective action problems—while significant in principle—have in many instances been overcome. In more recent years and into the future, the inclusive framework arising from the BEPS initiative (for example, OECD (2019)) promises what may turn out to be a tectonic shift toward greater multilateral cooperation on profit shifting and tax havens. This implies that collective action problems may become even less significant over time. Moreover, while rules against profit shifting generate spillovers, a significant fraction of these spillovers affect only a relatively small number of major economies. These countries might be expected to develop mechanisms to implement collectively optimal policies. This is particularly the case for CFC rules, where a relatively small number of major residence countries are particularly important.

Does MNC Haven Activity Benefit Non-Havens?

The argument above is that non-haven countries want to restrict or eliminate MNCs' haven activity (presumably because it is detrimental to their welfare) and that they, in principle, have the legal instruments to achieve this aim, but that collective action problems prevent them from doing so. The major alternative view is that MNC activity in havens actually serves the interests of non-haven countries, at least as those interests are construed by their political systems. In this view, non-haven countries refrain from using legal instruments to fully eliminate MNCs' haven activity, because the activity is in the (individual and possibly collective) interests of non-havens.

How might MNCs' tax-haven activities benefit non-haven countries? A strand of theoretical literature in public finance (for example, Keen (2001); Peralta and others (2006); Hong and Smart (2010)) has specified conditions under which MNCs' tax-haven activities may generate such benefits (see also Hines (2007) and Dharmapala (2008) for discussions of this approach). Keen (2001) develops a model that is motivated by some non-haven countries' preferential tax regimes for foreign investors or specific sectors. While the model is not explicitly about tax havens, a non-haven country's decision to establish a preferential regime for foreign investors is analogous in some respects to, for instance, choosing a weak or nonexistent TCR to facilitate foreign MNCs' outbound profit shifting to havens. Keen (2001) introduces into a standard tax-competition model the assumption—which has proven to be important in this literature—that capital may be heterogeneous in its mobility across borders (that is, different firms may have differing ability or willingness to change the location of their activities in response to taxes). Preferential regimes, in principle, allow countries to impose lower tax rates for more mobile forms of capital and high tax rates on immobile capital. If preferential regimes are prohibited or infeasible, then countries are constrained to competing by setting a single tax rate for all forms of capital (regardless of mobility). This will result in an inefficiently low tax rate on immobile capital, and force countries to compete more broadly over the tax rate on all forms of capital. On the other hand, preferential regimes allow countries to tax immobile capital at high rates, while competing only over tax rates imposed on mobile capital. Preferential regimes can thus mitigate tax competition by restricting its effects to a subset of the tax base.

Hong and Smart (2010) develop a model of a small, open economy in which the corporate tax serves two functions: taxing the returns to inbound FDI and taxing the rents earned by domestic entrepreneurs (that is, the returns earned by these entrepreneurs in excess of the minimum return required to induce them to engage in their activities). If it were possible to decouple these functions, the country would set a zero tax on inbound FDI (as in a small, open economy, the burden of this tax is entirely shifted to domestic workers in the form of lower wages, as shown by Gordon (1986)), while imposing a relatively high tax rate on domestic entrepreneurs (as the government wishes to use the tax revenue generated from these entrepreneurs to make transfers to domestic workers or to reduce taxes on wages). When these functions cannot be decoupled, tax havens can increase the welfare of non-haven countries. In particular, a country can choose a weak or nonexistent TCR to facilitate foreign MNCs' outbound profit shifting to havens. This lowers foreign MNCs' effective tax rate and induces more inbound FDI (which makes domestic workers better off). It also allows the country to set a high (nominal) corporate tax rate, which does not (in practical terms) affect MNCs but enables more redistribution via the tax system from domestic entrepreneurs to domestic workers.

The crucial assumption in Hong and Smart (2010), which generates the result that tax havens raise welfare, is that the government cannot discriminate overtly between (immobile) domestic entrepreneurs and foreign investors in setting tax rates. While the details of the models in this literature differ, all assume that a political constraint prevents differential treatment or that there are limits to the observability of firms' mobility. These assumptions may be viewed by some as arguably ad hoc (although this does not necessarily imply that they lack real-world relevance). If this assumption is accepted, it follows that, in a wide range of circumstances, havens may increase the welfare of non-haven countries. The intuition underlying this result extends to a world with multiple non-haven countries. That is, the value of havens as a means of achieving de facto tax discrimination applies at both the individual and collective level for non-haven countries.

In this "differential mobility" theory, non-haven countries optimally use the tax law instruments at their disposal (where optimality means maximizing both national welfare and global welfare). While their chosen policies limit profit shifting to a significant degree, the countries facilitate some residual amount of profit shifting to havens, to the extent that it promotes their welfare. Indeed, tax havens are important in this view as a means of implementing optimal tax policies that are (by assumption) otherwise impossible to achieve. This view also implies that in a world without havens—for instance, if a multilateral agreement were to require and enforce a relatively high minimum tax rate for all countries—the welfare of non-havens would be lower, because they would be deprived of a means of taxing immobile capital more heavily. Moreover, tax competition may intensify, as tax rate differences across (non-haven) countries become more important when profit shifting to havens is not possible.

Recently, Weichenrieder and Xu (2019) have developed a critique of the differential mobility theory of havens using a model inspired, in part, by China's experience with "round-tripping" foreign investment. They argue, in effect, that tax-haven secrecy is a cause of, rather than the solution to, the difficulty of observing the degree of firms' mobility. In their framework, when a non-haven imposes lower effective taxes on foreign investment, domestic firms may masquerade as foreign (for instance, by round-tripping their investment via a foreign haven) and thereby obtain the preferential tax treatment intended for foreign MNCs. This makes it impossible to collect higher revenue from domestic firms and vitiates the benefit of havens implied by the differential mobility theory.

While the possibility that domestic firms will masquerade as foreign is real, the assumption in Weichenrieder and Xu (2019) that the high levels of FDI into China from havens represent tax-motivated round-tripping is questionable. At one time, China granted an explicit tax preference for foreign MNCs. This regime ended in 2008, yet havens such as the British Virgin Islands and the Cayman Islands have continued to be prominent sources of FDI into China. Sharman (2012) highlights this puzzle and argues that tax considerations do not adequately explain this type of round-tripping investment in China by Chinese entrepreneurs. Rather, Sharman (2012) developed an alternative explanation based on the idea that the use of havens in this context is driven by governance considerations and the institutional advantages of haven jurisdictions (especially the legal and financial infrastructure that they provide), rather than simply by tax considerations.

The differential mobility theory also assumes that investment is sensitive to the corporate tax rate (or, as an equivalent, that the corporate tax is an income tax that burdens the normal risk-free return to capital). Indeed, the theory tends to assume a small, open economy in which the burden of the corporate income tax is entirely shifted to domestic workers in the form of lower wages, as in Gordon (1986). Recently, it has been argued (for example, Fox (2020)) that the corporate tax has increasingly come to resemble a cash flow tax—a consumption-type tax that primarily burdens rents (that is, returns in excess of the rate required to compensate investors for the risk-free return and for bearing risk). Two primary reasons support this view. First, the risk-free rate of return is currently quite low. Second, investment in intangible assets is typically "expensed" (deducted immediately for tax purposes), which means that the risk-free return from investment in intangible assets is not burdened by the corporate tax. If the corporate tax is viewed as a cash-flow tax falling only on rents, then the implications of profit shifting and tax competition are quite different. In particular, profit shifting to havens would generate windfall gains for shareholders of MNCs, without inducing additional investment that could potentially benefit domestic workers.

Even in the scenario where the corporate tax approximates a tax on pure rents, however, it remains possible that non-haven countries may benefit from profit shifting to havens. Devereux and Griffith (1998, 2003) argue that

MNCs' decisions about discrete or "lumpy" investment decisions (such as whether to locate a new factory in country X or country Y) depend on the anticipated average tax rate (and hence on the taxation of pure rents). In contrast, decisions about incrementally increasing the level of investment in a country where the firm already has a factory depend on the marginal tax rate and are unaffected by the taxation of pure rents. For a non-haven country, allowing profit to be shifted to havens (thereby avoiding the tax on pure rents) will reduce the anticipated average tax rate and hence encourage MNCs to undertake discrete investment projects. Moreover, this effect may be substantial.[36] Admittedly, if the corporate tax were indeed a tax on pure rents—a claim that remains highly contested—profit shifting is less likely to generate collective (as opposed to individual) benefits for non-haven countries. However, the differential mobility theory of MNCs' haven use would retain some relevance.

Regardless of these theoretical considerations, does the evidence seem to favor the implications of the differential mobility theory? There is abundant empirical evidence that FDI is quite sensitive to taxes (see, for example, de Mooij and Ederveen (2003)). This is consistent with countries seeking to attract more FDI by either lowering their tax rates or limiting their measures against outward profit shifting to havens (although this evidence does not in itself establish that there are no alternative ways to achieve this objective). Especially relevant is that the empirical literature finds foreclosing profit-shifting opportunities to lead to reduced investment. For instance, Büttner, Overesch, and Wamser (2018) find that FDI becomes more sensitive to the tax rate, and FDI declines substantially when a country introduces a TCR, suggesting that profit-shifting opportunities may matter significantly for MNCs' real investment activity. De Mooij and Liu (2020) use a global dataset and find that stricter transfer-pricing regulations lead to substantial declines in investment by MNCs.

Suarez Serrato (2018) provides particularly striking evidence of this phenomenon. Until the relevant provision was repealed by Congress in 1996 (albeit with a ten-year transition period), U.S. tax law provided favorable treatment for the income reported by U.S. firms in Puerto Rico and other U.S. territories. Suarez Serrato (2018) uses establishment-level data to identify U.S. firms that had Puerto Rican establishments (and hence Puerto Rican affiliates to which profits were shifted from the U.S. mainland) and links these firms to their establishments located in the (mainland) United States. He finds that the repeal led to substantial declines in investment and employment in the (mainland) U.S. operations of U.S. firms that previously engaged in profit-shifting to Puerto Rico. These firms tended to be concentrated in certain local regions and labor markets within the United States, and Suarez Serrato (2018) finds a long-term decline in employment and wage growth in areas that were more exposed to these firms. These results suggest that provisions intended to limit MNCs' profit shifting may harm local communities and explain why non-haven governments may encourage MNCs to shift profits to havens.

This section has challenged the conventional view that MNC activity in tax havens reduces non-haven countries' welfare by eroding their tax base. As discussed above, the conventional view does not take full account of the fact that non-havens could use tax law provisions that effectively neutralize the tax consequences of havens. It is indeed true that MNCs' haven activity, among other things, erodes non-havens' tax bases. However, it arguably does so with the consent and encouragement of non-havens themselves, which seek, for example, to attract greater inbound investment or to encourage their resident MNCs to avoid foreign taxes. In this sense, MNCs' haven activity serves the interests of major non-haven countries; if it did not, the activity, presumably, would not be permitted. The real (and more difficult) questions concern whether MNCs' haven activity promotes non-havens' "true" welfare, or merely their interests as refracted through the prism of various political distortions (such as lobbying activity by MNCs). There are reasonable grounds for either view. However, conventional discourse tends to obscure the relevant questions that should be addressed.

HOW MUCH MNC PROFIT IS SHIFTED TO TAX HAVENS?

Estimates of the Magnitude of Profit Shifting

At the same time that MNCs' profit shifting activities have become the subject of increased public interest, a growing empirical literature has sought to estimate the magnitude of profit shifting. These studies can—broadly speaking—be divided into those using microeconometric techniques applied to affiliate-level microdata and those using aggregate (typically, country-level) data. Among the first category, a particularly influential approach is based on Hines and Rice (1994). Its basic premise is that the observed pretax profit of an MNC affiliate represents the sum of "true" profits (generated using capital and labor inputs, which are included in the regression analysis to predict the affiliate's counterfactual profit, absent shifting) and "shifted" profits. Differences between observed and counterfactual profits are attributed to profit shifting.[37]

The Hines-Rice approach is typically implemented using a log-linear specification that is used to estimate a semi-elasticity (that is, the percentage change in reported profit associated with a 1 percentage point change in the tax rate difference across countries), controlling for capital and labor inputs and using affiliate fixed effects to absorb unobserved heterogeneity at the affiliate level. Dharmapala (2014a) surveys the extensive literature that has used this approach. Recent estimates using affiliate-level data (such as the Amadeus and Orbis databases) have found the magnitude of profit shifting to be considerably smaller than found in earlier studies using country-level data. A representative consensus estimate from the literature is a semi-elasticity of reported profit with respect to the tax rate differential across countries of 0.8 (see, in particular, the meta-regression study of Heckemeyer and Overesch (2017)). This means that a 10 percentage point increase in the tax rate difference between an affiliate and its parent (for example, because the tax rate in the affiliate's country falls from 35 percent to 25 percent) would increase the pretax profit reported by the affiliate by 8 percent (for example, from US$100,000 to US$108,000). A more recent meta-regression analysis (Beer, de Mooij, and Liu (2020)) uses a larger number of underlying estimates (including those using aggregate data) and finds a somewhat higher—albeit comparable—semi-elasticity of 1. For studies using data for the most recent years, however, the semi-elasticity tends to be larger (as high as 1.5).

In general, the micro literature tends to find magnitudes of profit shifting that are substantially smaller than suggested by the aggregate data reviewed earlier, and this apparent disjuncture has generated a debate about how to best measure profit shifting.[38] As discussed, the aggregate data may be misleading in many respects; for instance, due to the double counting of the income of holding companies located in havens. On the other hand, critics of the microeconometric studies (for example, Clausing (2016)) highlight the limited coverage of tax-haven affiliates in the affiliate-level datasets.[39] Even when haven affiliate data exist, identification relies on within-affiliate changes in the tax rate (or in the tax differential relative to other affiliates). So, profit shifting to tax-haven affiliates with (unchanging) zero tax rates may not be fully captured by this approach. Profit shifting may also be relatively insensitive to small changes in the tax differential in the presence of the fixed costs of tax planning, even when the tax rate differential between the MNC parent's country and the haven changes due to reforms in the parent country. In essence, critics argue that part of the profit shifting phenomenon may be embedded in the affiliate fixed effect.

These concerns have led to a revival of studies using aggregate data, which generally find large magnitudes of profit shifting. For instance, Tørsløv, Wier, and Zucman (2018) used newly available macroeconomic data on tax havens (and, in particular, what are known as foreign affiliate statistics) to infer the specific non-haven countries from which income reported in havens has arguably been shifted. Their approach suggests that about 40 percent of the foreign profits of MNCs are shifted to havens.[40]

Micro versus Macro Approaches and the Conceptualization of Profit Shifting

Differences in data coverage of havens or the double counting of haven affiliates' income in aggregate datasets may account for some of the differences in the findings of the micro and macro literatures. However, it also appears that there are some fundamental conceptual differences between the notions of profit shifting underlying these approaches. In particular, by controlling for capital and labor inputs and other affiliate characteristics, micro estimates take as given the location of productive assets. Micro studies typically do not explicitly control for the location of intangible assets. However, to the extent that the location of these assets is time-invariant (for instance, always being located in lower-tax jurisdictions), the location of intangible assets would be largely absorbed by affiliate fixed effects. Given the location of productive assets, the micro approach seeks to estimate the extent of profit shifting, viewed as a form of tax avoidance (that is, a reduction in the worldwide tax burden of the MNC group, with little or no substantive economic effect on its operations).

The location of tangible capital (such as factories and machinery) is influenced by tax rate differences across countries, as suggested by the large empirical literature finding real investment by MNCs to be sensitive to taxes (for example, de Mooij and Ederveen (2003)). However, an MNC decision to build a factory in a lower-tax rather than higher-tax location is classified in the parlance of public finance theory as a behavioral (or real) response to taxation, rather than as tax avoidance. Recalling the definition of tax avoidance as "the lawful reduction of tax obligations, while maintaining the same substantive economic outcome" (Dharmapala (2017, xv)), it is clear that the MNC's substantive economic outcome is not the same when it makes a tax-motivated decision, whenever the higher-tax location is preferable on nontax grounds. For instance, the quality of physical infrastructure may be lower in the lower-tax location, and the MNC would have to trade off this disadvantage against the tax benefits of the lower-tax location. These nontax costs associated with the lower-tax location can be characterized as nontax frictions that limit the tax-optimality of the MNCs' real investment choices.

Behavioral responses to tax differences give rise to distortions—factories end up being located in the "wrong" place from the perspective of maximizing global (pretax) social welfare. Tax avoidance (including profit shifting) is fundamentally different because, by assumption, no nontax frictions change substantive economic outcomes. Consider, for instance, the interest-stripping strategy described earlier. The placement of debt in one affiliate rather than another has very limited substantive effects on the worldwide MNC group. This does not imply that tax avoidance does not have social costs, as resources may be used in tax planning. However, this social cost is quite different from the social costs of behavioral responses to taxation.[41] Figure 11-16 illustrates the difference between tax avoidance and behavioral responses to taxation, in terms of the importance of nontax frictions. When nontax frictions are minimal, as with interest stripping, (lawful) tax-motivated activities are best characterized as tax avoidance. When nontax frictions are substantial, as with the location of factories, tax-motivated choices are most usefully viewed not as tax avoidance but as behavioral responses to taxes.

FIGURE 11-16. Tax Avoidance versus Behavioral Responses

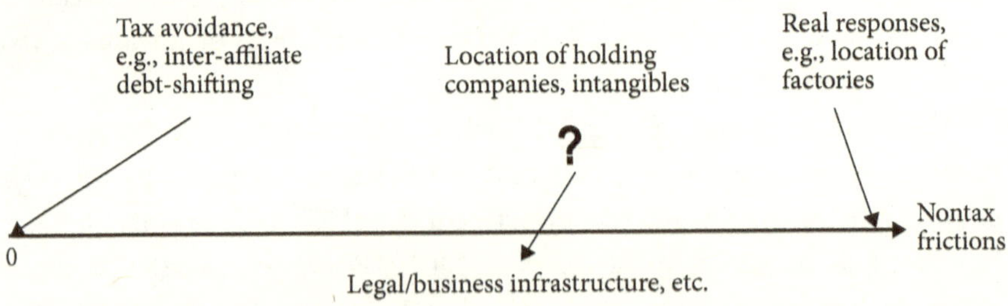

Note: This figure illustrates the difference between tax avoidance and behavioral responses to taxation. Nontax frictions are increasing along the axis toward the right. When nontax frictions do not exist, taxpayers' responses to taxes are classified as forms of tax avoidance. As nontax frictions become larger, taxpayers' responses to taxes are classified as behavioral (or real) responses.

In taking as given the location of productive assets, the micro approach seeks to isolate the amount of profit shifting per se (that is, of MNCs' cross-border tax avoidance via channels such as interest stripping and strategic transfer pricing). Properly understood, this approach does not aim to capture the disproportionate location of intangible assets and holding companies in havens (except to the extent that these change over time in response to tax differentials). That these effects are typically absorbed by the affiliate fixed effects is thus not a shortcoming of the approach. On the other hand, macro approaches that rely on aggregate data tend to presume that these locational choices are themselves a form of tax avoidance. An illustration is provided by Tørsløv, Wier, and Zucman (2018). They compare profit-to-wage ratios across local and foreign-owned firms in different countries, defining the relevant capital stock as consisting only of tangible assets. Thus, havens in which affiliates own substantial intangible assets appear in their analysis to have a dramatically inflated profit-to-wage ratio for foreign affiliates.[42]

This presumption may, however, be problematic. R&D is frequently financed by haven affiliates, for instance, under the cost-sharing arrangements that are important in U.S. transfer pricing law, even when researchers are located in non-haven countries. This implies that the profits from intangible assets (or some portion thereof) will appear in the profits-to-wages ratio of haven affiliates while the wages of the relevant R&D workers will not. Yet the haven affiliate quite legitimately owns a share of the intangible asset corresponding to its share of the cost. It is possible to critique such cost-sharing arrangements as being artificial. However, tax law in general tends to respect taxpayers' formal choices, and cost-sharing arrangements are blessed by the tax law of non-haven countries such as the United States. The arrangements are also consistent with basic income tax principles requiring the matching of the location of income and deductions (thereby ensuring alignment between the tax rates applicable to the income from intangible assets and to the deductions for their costs). For instance, if a haven affiliate finances 50 percent of the cost of an asset, 50 percent of its cost is deducted at the haven's tax rate, just as 50 percent of the income from that asset is taxed at the haven's tax rate.

This discussion raises a wider point about the extent to which MNCs' decisions about the location of IP and of holding companies are purely tax-motivated and whether nontax frictions are significant. In other words, where do these choices lie along the spectrum illustrated in figure 11-16? Ultimately, the extent of nontax frictions—and hence whether these types of locational choices should be viewed as tax avoidance or as behavioral responses to tax rate differences—is an empirical question. The evidence discussed above for holding companies (see, for example, Desai, Foley, and Hines (2006)) suggests that, while the location of holding companies may be highly tax motivated, the substantial fraction of holding companies in non-haven jurisdictions implies significant nontax frictions. Moreover, there is considerable direct evidence for nontax motivations in MNCs' use of haven affiliates.[43] In addition, MNCs' locational choices *among* zero-tax countries tend not to be random but to be influenced by nontax considerations. Better governance institutions are strongly associated with higher levels of MNC activity (for example, Wei (2000); Dharmapala and Hines (2009)), suggesting that nontax frictions of an institutional nature are significant.

These nontax frictions may include legal infrastructure and the availability of legal and business expertise in different locations. Historically, physical infrastructure has been emphasized as a determinant of FDI. More recently, legal and business infrastructure has grown in significance for MNC activity. If the conception of behavioral responses is limited to the location of tangible assets, it is possible that what is commonly viewed as profit shifting will tend to grow mechanically. Arguably, the notion of behavioral response should evolve to reflect the growing significance of legal and business (rather than physical) infrastructure in MNC activity. Of course, none of this is intended to suggest that MNCs' use of havens is not tax-motivated. The question here—highlighted by figure 11-16—is whether nontax frictions also exist that may make MNCs' locational choices for holding companies and IP more analogous to a behavioral response to taxation than is generally appreciated. This question is important for future analysis.

CONCLUSION

MNCs' use of tax havens has attracted increasing attention and scrutiny in recent years, and is now more relevant than ever in the light of policy initiatives such as the GloBE proposal for a global minimum tax rate on MNCs' profits (OECD (2019)). This chapter provides an overview of the current state of knowledge within the academic literature on this topic. The empirical evidence is consistent with MNCs' disproportionate use of havens as locations for holding companies, IP, and financial activities. However, there is also considerable evidence that frictions limit MNCs' use of havens. The standard view is that MNCs' use of havens harms non-haven countries by eroding their tax base. This chapter develops an alternative perspective based on the argument that MNCs' use of havens relies crucially on forbearance or active facilitation by non-havens, as non-havens can use a variety of powerful tax law instruments to neutralize the effect of MNCs' use of havens. The failure to deploy these instruments as fully as possible is arguably a deliberate policy choice, due either to collective action problems among non-havens or to the possibility that, in certain circumstances, MNCs' use of havens increases the welfare of non-haven countries. The chapter also discusses how the distinction commonly made in public finance theory between tax avoidance and behavioral responses to taxation can illuminate current debates about the magnitude and implications of MNCs' profit shifting to havens.

NOTES

I thank Fritz Foley, Jim Hines, David Wessel, and participants at the authors' conferences at the Brookings Institution (especially my discussant Kim Clausing) for helpful comments. I also thank participants at the 2019 American Economic Association meetings in Atlanta and the Loyola Law School Tax Policy Colloquium (especially my commentator Robert Peroni) for valuable comments on presentations of related ideas; Johannes Becker, Thiess Büttner, Clemens Fuest, Jim Hines, Tom Horst, Li Liu, Ray Mataloni, and Gabriel Zucman for helpful conversations; and Kelsey Nelson for outstanding research assistance. I acknowledge the financial support of the Lee and Brena Freeman Faculty Research Fund at the University of Chicago Law School. Any remaining errors or omissions are my own.

1. Dharmapala and Hines (2009) define tax havens as "locations with very low tax rates and other tax attributes designed to appeal to foreign investors": 1058.

2. It should be emphasized that the situation is quite different for individual evasion via havens: enforcement tools such as cross-border information exchange have not been available until recently, and there is no sense that non-havens necessarily facilitate individual evasion via havens.

3. These data are available at www.bea.gov/international/di1usdop.

4. The 2016 data were preliminary, and potentially subject to revision, at the time this analysis was conducted. However, as discussed below, their main features with respect to haven activity have generally been quite stable over time.

5. This chapter's data analysis involves further updating the list of havens with modifications to reflect subsequent (post-2004) changes in the political status of some jurisdictions. For instance, the Netherlands Antilles was dissolved in 2010. The jurisdictions that were formerly part of the erstwhile Netherlands Antilles (Curaçao, Sint Maarten, and what the BEA terms "Netherlands Islands, Caribbean") are classified here as havens (which is how the Netherlands Antilles was classified in Dharmapala and Hines (2009)). In addition, some geographical units used by the BEA do not correspond directly to jurisdictions in the Dharmapala and Hines (2009) classification. The most important of these is what the BEA terms "United Kingdom Islands, Carib-

bean." This is classified here as a haven, as it includes the Cayman Islands (in the view of many observers, perhaps the archetypal tax haven).

6. For instance, Caribbean havens appear to be particularly important for U.S. MNCs, while European and Mediterranean havens are important for European MNCs (although a partial exception is the prominence of Caribbean havens in foreign direct investment into China).

7. However, the recent rise of patent box regimes, which impose low tax rates on income derived from patents, in many putatively non-haven countries may indicate that this geographical separation is partially eroding.

8. This comparison of foreign havens and foreign non-havens follows naturally from the way that the aggregate BEA data are presented. To the extent that the income reported in foreign havens has been shifted from the U.S. parent, foreign havens' share of foreign income may not fully capture the effect of profit shifting on the U.S. parent and on U.S. revenues. Note, however, that (as explained below) the aim here is *not* to use these shares as measures of the magnitude of profit shifting, but rather to highlight the pitfalls of doing so.

9. Where the number of affiliates is particularly large, this is sometimes a legacy of mergers among MNCs (where the legal entities owned by each merging firm continue to survive).

10. The patterns revealed by table 11-1 are quite well established and have been generally similar for some time. For example, Dharmapala (2014a, table 2, 442) reports a similar set of calculations for 2011. These show that MOFAs of U.S.-based MNCs earned 42.6 percent of the net income of all foreign affiliates of U.S.-based MNCs in 2011. Thus, table 11-1 and figure 11-1 reflect a fairly stable pattern, although, as discussed in the text, the interpretation of these patterns is by no means self-evident.

11. In principle, it is possible to construct a pretax version of net income by adding back foreign tax payments. However, this can only be done for a more limited set of jurisdictions—those for which foreign tax payments are reported—than that used in table 11-1 and figure 11-1. Foreign tax-payment data are available for 2016 for fifty-eight countries, of which nine are havens. Haven affiliates' share of the pretax version of net income (that is, of net income plus foreign tax payments) is about 48 percent, and so is very similar to haven affiliates' share of net income in table 11-1 and figure 11-1.

12. The point that the income reported in havens has often been taxed by a higher-tax jurisdiction holds even absent the inclusion of "income from equity investments" in the BEA's income concept. For instance, if the US$75 of after-tax earnings of the F affiliate was not retained but rather repatriated to the haven holding company, then the haven holding company would have US$75 of (true rather than phantom) income. However, this would still represent income that has been subject to a 25 percent tax elsewhere.

13. This double counting (or multiple counting) problem can arguably be addressed using other BEA data series, such as the direct investment earnings series used by Clausing (2016). Blouin and Robinson (2019) propose using net income but subtracting "income from equity investments" to obtain a more meaningful income measure for affiliates.

14. See Dharmapala (2014a) for a description and critique of this practice.

15. Haven affiliates' share of capital gains slightly exceeds 100 percent because non-haven foreign affiliates of U.S. MNCs collectively made a (relatively small) capital loss in 2014, while haven affiliates collectively experienced a capital gain. Thus, haven affiliates' capital gain slightly exceeds the worldwide foreign capital gain of U.S. MNCs in 2014.

16. 26 U.S.C. § 861.

17. However, the capital losses of haven affiliates were disproportionately small (that is, their capital gains were more positive than those of non-haven affiliates, just as in 2014). In particular, 1.25 percent of all foreign capital losses were reported by haven affiliates.

18. There is insufficient information in the aggregate data to undertake these calculations for net income.

19. There are some conceptual difficulties in defining precisely what constitutes tax avoidance in the use of interest deductions, as interest deductibility is a (deliberately chosen) feature of tax law that is presumably intended to be used by firms. Desai and Dharmapala (2015) discuss these conceptual issues and describe how the distinctively cross-border elements of tax avoidance via interest deductions can be addressed without affecting the use of interest deductions by domestic firms.

20. It is worth noting that the welfare effects of profit shifting are more complex than may appear at first sight. Consider again the archetypal example above of interest stripping. Suppose that a U.S.-based MNC injects US$100 of equity into its Bahamas affiliate, which then lends the US$100 to the same MNC's German affiliate at an interest rate of 5 percent. The Bahamas affiliate will then receive US$5 of annual interest income. If the counterfactual (absent profit shifting) is that the U.S. affiliate would have directly injected US$100 of equity into the German affiliate (and assuming that the dividends paid by the German affiliate to the U.S. parent are not deductible in Germany, whereas the interest payments to the Bahamas affiliate are deductible), then the use of the Bahamas affiliate as a financing intermediary shifts profits from Germany to the Bahamas. The counterfactual is not necessarily obvious, however. For instance, if the U.S. parent would counterfactually have lent US$100 directly to the German affiliate and the interest payments are deductible in Germany regardless of whether they are paid to the U.S. parent or the Bahamas affiliate, then the use of the Bahamas affiliate as a financing intermediary could be viewed as shifting profits from the United States to the Bahamas.

21. For instance, for U.S. MNCs, holding companies helped avoid repatriation taxes under the worldwide tax system that prevailed until 2017.

22. In the 2014 BEA data, aggregate worldwide income from equity investments of U.S. MNCs' majority-owned foreign affiliates was US$718.79 billion. Of this amount, US$356.23 billion was in haven affiliates (using this chapter's classification of haven jurisdictions), US$128.45 billion in Dutch affiliates, US$52.49 billion in U.K. affiliates, and US$44.84 billion in Canadian affiliates.

23. To illustrate, suppose that an MNC group faces an average tax rate of 20 percent and that a typical affiliate of this MNC facing this tax rate holds US$100 worth of IP. Then, an affiliate in a zero-tax haven would hold US$134 worth of IP.

24. Rose and Spiegel (2007) find evidence suggesting that the presence of OFCs

may have some positive effects on nearby countries, for instance, because competition from OFCs potentially spurs financial development in neighboring countries.

25. Casi, Spengel, and Stage (2020) report evidence suggesting that the United States is emerging as, in effect, a major secrecy jurisdiction for tax evasion by non-U.S. individuals, because the United States does not participate meaningfully in the CRS.

26. Desai and Dharmapala (2009a) use this reform as a source of exogenous variation in U.S. firms' tax avoidance activities. Albertus (2018) offers evidence that the CTB regulations increased the after-tax return to innovation and increased innovative activity in the United States by U.S.-based MNCs.

27. For instance, in the example above, MNCs based in country A would reallocate profits from countries with tax rates below 10 percent to those with tax rates above 10 percent as passive income reported in the former would incur country A's 20 percent tax.

28. Prettl (2018) also uses Orbis data and finds evidence suggesting that CFC rules are associated with substantially lower reported financial income in haven affiliates. He also reports evidence of bunching at thresholds created by CFC rules.

29. A typical safe harbor rule applying only to related-party debt operates as follows (in somewhat stylized form). Suppose that a German MNC parent injects €100 into its Portuguese affiliate. Assume that (as reported by Büttner and others (2012, table 1, 932) for 2005 Portugal has a safe-harbor ratio of 2-to-1, pertaining only to related-party debt. This implies that interest payments from the Portuguese affiliate to other affiliates of the same MNC are fully deductible when the amount of debt owed by the Portuguese affiliate to external and related-party lenders is no higher than €200. If its debt exceeds €200, then interest deductions for related-party debt are partially disallowed. Specifically, a fraction of related-party interest corresponding to the ratio of excess debt (exceeding €200) to total debt is disallowed. It may seem that (if the choice of inter-affiliate debt is largely frictionless) the optimal strategy for an MNC would involve non-haven affiliates locating precisely at the safe harbor threshold to maximize interest deductions. Büttner, Overesch, and Wamser (2016), however, report evidence that the majority of affiliates locate below the threshold; in their data on foreign affiliates of German MNCs, about 25 percent of affiliate-year observations exceed the safe harbor threshold.

30. Mardan (2017) and Gresik, Schindler, and Schjelderup (2017) develop theoretical models of the choice between safe harbor rules and earnings-stripping rules. The 2017 U.S. tax legislation moved the United States from a safe harbor debt-equity ratio (of 1.5 to 1) to an earnings-stripping rule limiting interest deductions more broadly to 30 percent of income. See 26 U.S.C. § 163(j).

31. There are thirty-four countries in the sample (consisting of all member countries of the OECD as of 2014). One of these countries is the United States, for which it is difficult to characterize a CFC rule because of the CTB regulations described above. However, the findings are robust to either coding the United States as having or not having a CFC rule (bearing in mind that the CTB regime applied in both 2000 and 2014 and so does not affect the difference in rates between those two years).

32. Dharmapala (2019) shows that this change is statistically significant as well as meaningful in terms of magnitude.

33. This is a simplified version of the example developed in Dharmapala (2014b) and also discussed in Desai and Dharmapala (2018).

34. Because MNCs' residence is assumed to be fixed, it is not possible in the example for firm A to change its residence to country B. However, such an incentive would exist in reality.

35. Notwithstanding this incentive structure, the 2017 U.S. tax legislation—the Tax Cut and Jobs Act (TCJA)—unilaterally introduced a new residence-based minimum tax on U.S.-based MNCs, known as the Global Intangible Low-Taxed Income (GILTI) tax. This is not, however, a CFC rule (for instance, it potentially applies to active as well as passive income), and represents a rather idiosyncratic approach in many respects (see, for example, Dharmapala (2018)).

36. Devereux and Griffith (1998) study a sample of U.S. firms operating in Europe to analyze discrete choices of investment in different countries. They find that a one percentage point increase in a country's average tax rate reduces the probability of a U.S. firm producing in that country by 1.3 percentage points, suggesting that even a tax on pure rents may have sizeable effects on discrete location choices.

37. Several alternative microeconometric approaches have been developed to estimate profit shifting. For instance, Dharmapala and Riedel (2013) analyze the effect of industry-level shocks to MNC parents' income and compare how the reported earnings of high-tax and low-tax foreign affiliates reflect these shocks. Also, an emerging literature uses a bunching approach to examine the tendency of MNC affiliates—relative to domestic firms—to report zero profits (see, for example, Bilicka (2019); Dharmapala and Hebous (2017)). However, the Hines-Rice approach sketched above is the most widely used one to date.

38. For example, assuming that non-haven countries have a tax rate of 25 percent while havens have a zero tax rate, the 0.8 semi-elasticity discussed above implies that less than 20 percent of MNCs' foreign profits are shifted to tax havens (Dharmapala (2014a)).

39. Dowd, Landefeld, and Moore (2017) use U.S. corporate tax return data for 2002 to 2010, which include extensive information on tax haven (as well as other) CFCs of U.S.-based MNC groups. They also use an empirical specification that allows for nonlinearities in the effect of the tax variable on the log of profits. Using this approach, they find a substantially larger semi-elasticity of reported profits with respect to the tax variable for zero-tax jurisdictions. Note, however, the various limitations of this dataset. The consolidation of branches and CTB entities implies that profits of non-haven entities are attributed to haven affiliates. Financial data is often missing from the informational tax returns on which the analysis is based, and the sample is restricted to CFCs with positive profit (as is also true of much of the prior literature).

40. Blouin and Robinson (2019) discuss how the double-counting problem discussed above may bias these types of estimates upward when they use aggregate data on U.S. MNCs. Dyreng and Hanlon (chapter 10 in this volume) argue that the large estimates of MNCs' profit shifting found using aggregate data are implausible in the light of the effective foreign tax rates reported in firms' financial statements.

41. As discussed earlier, tax planning is also limited by anti-avoidance provisions in the tax law.

42. Their analysis also ignores the role of financial capital, but this issue is not emphasized here.

43. For example, as noted earlier, Sharman (2012) explains the prominent role of havens in FDI into China (even after the abolition of preferential tax treatment for foreign investment) by governance considerations and the legal and institutional advantages of the haven jurisdictions. Some Chinese entrepreneurs are believed to establish parent firms in jurisdictions such as the British Virgin Islands because they wish to issue dual-class stock (where voting rights differ across different classes of stock). It is unclear whether Chinese company law respects dual-class stock, and so firms can avoid this legal uncertainty by incorporating in a haven jurisdiction that clearly permits dual-class stock.

REFERENCES

Altshuler, Rosanne and Harry Grubert. 2005. "The Three Parties in the Race to the Bottom: Host Governments, Home Governments, and Multinational Companies," *Florida Tax Review*, 7: 137–209.

Beer, Sebastian, Ruud A. de Mooij, and Li Liu. 2020. "International Corporate Tax Avoidance: A Review of the Channels, Magnitudes, and Blind Spots," *Journal of Economic Surveys*, 34 (3): 660–88.

Bennedsen, Morten and Stefan Zeume. 2017. "Corporate Tax Havens and Transparency," *Review of Financial Studies*, 31 (4): 1221–64.

Bilicka, Katarzyna Anna. 2019. "Comparing U.K. Tax Returns of Foreign Multinationals to Matched Domestic Firms," *American Economic Review*, 109 (8): 2921–53.

Blouin, Jennifer and Leslie Robinson. 2019. "Double Counting Accounting: How Much Profit of Multinational Enterprises Is Really in Tax Havens?" Working paper, available at: https://papers.ssrn.com/sol3/papers.cfm?abstract_id=3491451.

Braun, Julia and Alfons J. Weichenrieder. 2015. "Does Exchange of Information between Tax Authorities Influence Multinationals' Use of Tax Havens?" ZEW-Centre for European Economic Research discussion paper 15-015.

Büttner, Thiess, Michael Overesch, Ulrich Schreiber, and Georg Wamser. 2012. "The Impact of Thin-Capitalization Rules on the Capital Structure of Multinational Firms," *Journal of Public Economics*, 96 (11–12): 930–38.

Büttner, Thiess, Michael Overesch, and Georg Wamser. 2016. "Restricted Interest Deductibility and Multinationals' Use of Internal Debt Finance," *International Tax and Public Finance*, 23 (5): 785–97.

Büttner, Thiess, Michael Overesch, and Georg Wamser. 2018. "Anti Profit-Shifting Rules and Foreign Direct Investment," *International Tax and Public Finance*, 25 (3): 553–80.

Casi, Elisa, Christoph Spengel, and Barbara Stage. 2020. "Cross-Border Tax Evasion after the Common Reporting Standard: Game Over?" *Journal of Public Economics*, forthcoming.

Clausing, Kimberly A. 2016. "The Effect of Profit Shifting on the Corporate Tax Base in the United States and Beyond," *National Tax Journal*, 69 (4): 905–34.

Clifford, Sarah. 2019. "Taxing Multinationals beyond Borders: Financial and Locational Responses to CFC Rules," *Journal of Public Economics*, 173: 44–71.

De Mooij, Ruud A. and Sjef Ederveen. 2003. "Taxation and Foreign Direct Investment: A Synthesis of Empirical Research," *International Tax and Public Finance*, 10 (6): 673–93.

De Mooij, Ruud A. and Li Liu. 2020. "At a Cost: The Real Effects of Transfer Pricing Regulations," *IMF Economic Review*, 68 (1): 268–306.

Desai, Mihir A. and Dhammika Dharmapala. 2006. "Corporate Tax Avoidance and High-Powered Incentives," *Journal of Financial Economics*, 79 (1): 145–79.

Desai, Mihir A. and Dhammika Dharmapala. 2008. "Tax and Corporate Governance: An Economic Approach," in *Tax and Corporate Governance*, edited by Wolfgang Schön (Berlin and Heidelberg: Springer): 13–30.

Desai, Mihir A. and Dhammika Dharmapala. 2009a. "Corporate Tax Avoidance and Firm Value," *Review of Economics and Statistics*, 91 (3): 537–46.

Desai, Mihir A. and Dhammika Dharmapala. 2009b. "Earnings Management, Corporate Tax Shelters, and Book-Tax Alignment," *National Tax Journal*, 62 (1): 169–86.

Desai, Mihir A. and Dhammika Dharmapala. 2015. "Interest Deductions in a Multijurisdictional World," *National Tax Journal*, 68 (3): 653–81.

Desai, Mihir A. and Dhammika Dharmapala. 2018. "Revisiting the Uneasy Case for Corporate Taxation in an Uneasy World," *Journal of the British Academy*, 6 (s1): 247–84.

Desai, Mihir A., C. Fritz Foley, and James R. Hines Jr. 2006. "The Demand for Tax Haven Operations," *Journal of Public Economics*, 90 (3): 513–31.

Devereux, Michael P. and Rachel Griffith. 1998. "Taxes and the Location of Production: Evidence from a Panel of U.S. Multinationals," *Journal of Public Economics*, 68 (3): 335–67.

Devereux, Michael P. and Rachel Griffith. 2003. "Evaluating Tax Policy for Location Decisions," *International Tax and Public Finance*, 10 (2): 107–26.

Dharmapala, Dhammika. 2008. "What Problems and Opportunities Are Created by Tax Havens?" *Oxford Review of Economic Policy*, 24 (4): 661–79.

Dharmapala, Dhammika. 2014a. "What Do We Know About Base Erosion and Profit Shifting? A Review of the Empirical Literature," *Fiscal Studies*, 35 (4): 421–48.

Dharmapala, Dhammika. 2014b. "Base Erosion and Profit Shifting: A Simple Conceptual Framework," *CESifo DICE Report*, 12 (4): 8–14.

Dharmapala, Dhammika. 2016. "Cross-Border Tax Evasion under a Unilateral FATCA Regime," *Journal of Public Economics*, 141: 29–37.

Dharmapala, Dhammika, ed. 2017. *The Economics of Tax Avoidance and Evasion* (Cheltenham, UK: Edward Elgar).

Dharmapala, Dhammika. 2018. "The Consequences of the Tax Cut and Jobs Act's International Provisions: Lessons from Existing Research," *National Tax Journal*, 71: 707–28.

Dharmapala, Dhammika. 2019. "Profit Shifting in a Globalized World," *American Economic Association Papers and Proceedings*, 109: 488–92.

Dharmapala, Dhammika, C. Fritz Foley, and Kristin J. Forbes. 2011. "Watch What I Do, Not What I Say: The Unintended Consequences of the Homeland Investment Act," *Journal of Finance*, 66 (3): 753–87.

Dharmapala, Dhammika and Shafik Hebous. 2017. "A Bunching Approach to Measuring Multinational Profit Shifting," working paper.

Dharmapala, Dhammika and James R. Hines Jr. 2009. "Which Countries Become Tax Havens?" *Journal of Public Economics*, 93 (9–10): 1058–68.

Dharmapala, Dhammika and Nadine Riedel. 2013. "Earnings Shocks and Tax-Motivated Income Shifting: Evidence from European Multinationals," *Journal of Public Economics*, 97: 95–107.

Dischinger, Matthias and Nadine Riedel. 2011. "Corporate Taxes and the Location of Intangible Assets within Multinational Firms," *Journal of Public Economics*, 95 (7–8): 691–707.

Dowd, Tim, Paul Landefeld, and Anne Moore. 2017. "Profit Shifting of U.S. Multinationals," *Journal of Public Economics*, 148: 1–13.

Dyreng, Scott and Michelle Hanlon. 2021. "Tax Avoidance and Multinational Firm Behavior," chapter 10 in *Global Goliaths: Multinational Corporations in the 21st Century Economy*, edited by C. Fritz Foley and others (Brookings Institution Press, 2021).

Fox, Edward G. 2020. "Does Capital Bear the U.S. Corporate Tax After All? New Evidence from Corporate Tax Returns," *Journal of Empirical Legal Studies*, 17 (1): 71–115.

Ginsburg, Tom and Aziz Huq. 2018. "How to Lose a Constitutional Democracy," *UCLA Law Review*, 65: 78–169.

Gordon, Roger H. 1986. "Taxation of Investment and Savings in a World Economy," *American Economic Review*, 76 (5): 1086–1102.

Gresik, Thomas A., Dirk Schindler, and Guttorm Schjelderup. 2017. "Immobilizing Corporate Income Shifting: Should It Be Safe to Strip in the Harbor?" *Journal of Public Economics*, 152: 68–78.

Gumpert, Anna, James R. Hines Jr., and Monika Schnitzer. 2016. "Multinational Firms and Tax Havens," *Review of Economics and Statistics*, 98 (4): 713–27.

Haufler, Andreas, Mohammed Mardan, and Dirk Schindler. 2018. "Double Tax Discrimination to Attract FDI and Fight Profit Shifting: The Role of CFC Rules," *Journal of International Economics*, 114: 25–43.

Heckemeyer, Jost H. and Michael Overesch. 2017. "Multinationals' Profit Response to Tax Differentials: Effect Size and Shifting Channels," *Canadian Journal of Economics*, 50 (4): 965–94.

Hong, Qing and Michael Smart. 2010. "In Praise of Tax Havens: International Tax Planning and Foreign Direct Investment," *European Economic Review*, 54 (1): 82–95.

Hines, James R. Jr. 2007. "Corporate Taxation and International Competition" in *Taxing Corporate Income in the Twenty-First Century*, edited by Alan J. Auerbach, James R. Hines Jr., and Joel Slemrod (Cambridge University Press).

Hines, James R. Jr. 2010. "Treasure Islands," *Journal of Economic Perspectives*, 24 (4): 103–25.

Hines, James R. Jr. and Eric M. Rice. 1994. "Fiscal Paradise: Foreign Tax Havens and American Business," *Quarterly Journal of Economics*, 109 (1): 149–82.

Keen, Michael. 2001. "Preferential Regimes Can Make Tax Competition Less Harmful," *National Tax Journal*, 54 (4): 757–62.

Mardan, Mohammed. 2017. "Why Countries Differ in Thin Capitalization Rules: The Role of Financial Development," *European Economic Review*, 91: 1–14.

Markle, Kevin and Leslie Robinson. 2012. "Tax Haven Use across International Tax Regimes," working paper.

O'Donovan, James, Hannes F. Wagner, and Stefan Zeume. 2019. "The Value of Offshore Secrets: Evidence from the Panama Papers," *Review of Financial Studies*, 32 (11): 4117–55.

OECD. 2013. *Addressing Base Erosion and Profit Shifting.* (Paris: OECD).

OECD. 2015. *Explanatory Statement.* OECD/G20 Base Erosion and Profit Shifting Project (Paris: OECD).

OECD. 2019. *Public Consultation Document: Global Anti-Base Erosion Proposal ("GloBE")—Pillar Two* (Paris: OECD).

Peralta, Susana, Xavier Wauthy, and Tanguy Van Ypersele. 2006. "Should Countries Control International Profit Shifting?" *Journal of International Economics*, 68 (1): 24–37.

Prettl, Axel. 2018. "Profit Shifting and Controlled Foreign Corporation Rules—The Thin Bridge between Corporate Tax Systems," working paper, available at https://papers.ssrn.com/sol3/papers.cfm?abstract_id=3102553.

Rose, Andrew K. and Mark M. Spiegel. 2007. "Offshore Financial Centers: Parasites or Symbionts?" *Economic Journal*, 117 (523): 1310–35.

Ruf, Martin and Dirk Schindler. 2015. "Debt Shifting and Thin-Capitalization Rules—German Experience and Alternative Approaches," *Nordic Tax Journal*, 1: 17–33.

Ruf, Martin and Alfons J. Weichenrieder. 2012. "The Taxation of Passive Foreign Investment: Lessons from German Experience," *Canadian Journal of Economics*, 45 (4): 1504–28.

Sharman, Jason Campbell. 2012. "Chinese Capital Flows and Offshore Financial Centers," *Pacific Review*, 25 (3): 317–37.

Serrato, Suarez and Juan Carlos. 2018. "Unintended Consequences of Eliminating Tax Havens," NBER Working Paper No. 24850.

Tørsløv, Thomas R., Ludvig S. Wier, and Gabriel Zucman. 2018. "The Missing Profits of Nations," NBER Working Paper No. 24701.

Wei, Shang-Jin. 2000. "How Taxing Is Corruption on International Investors?" *Review of Economics and Statistics*, 82 (1): 1–11.

Weichenrieder, Alfons J. and Fangying Xu. 2019. "Are Tax Havens Good? Implications of the Crackdown on Secrecy," *Journal of Economics* (previously *Zeitschrift für Nationalökonomie*), 127 (2): 147–60.

Wilson, John Douglas. 1999. "Theories of Tax Competition," *National Tax Journal*, 52 (2): 269–70.

12

Multinational Corporations and Their Influence through Lobbying on Foreign Policy

IN SONG KIM
HELEN V. MILNER

Multinational corporations (MNCs) play significant roles in shaping the global economy. For example, MNCs in the United States, the world's largest economy, make disproportionate contributions to the national economy. They represent a very small number of total American firms (less than 1 percent), but a large fraction of gross domestic product (GDP), exports, imports, research and development, and private sector employee compensation. Specifically, according to the Bureau of Economic Analysis (BEA), U.S. MNC parent companies in 2016 constituted more than 24 percent of private sector GDP (value added) and 26 percent of private sector employee compensation (BEA (2018a)). U.S. MNCs are engaged in more than half of all U.S. exports and more than 40 percent of U.S. imports (BEA (2018b)). Likewise, MNCs throughout the world dominate the global economy as well as their national economies. The Organization for Economic Cooperation and Development (OECD) estimates that MNCs account for half of global exports, nearly a third of world GDP (28 percent), and about a quarter of global employment (OECD (2018)). These firms all generate a significant share of their revenue from abroad as well.[1] It is important to note that their transnational activities have transformed the nature of international trade, investments, and technology transfers in the era of globalization. The extensive global value chains (GVCs) prevalent today have been driven by how MNCs structure their global operations through outsourcing and offshoring activities. In fact, their decisions have enormous implications for a wide range of policy issues—such as taxation, investment protection, and immigration—across many countries with different political and economic institutions. MNCs also may have strong political influence domestically. Indeed, their global economic dominance may go hand in hand with their powerful domestic political position.

Recent political developments bring multinational lobbying into stark relief. Multinational firms have vocally opposed the Trump administration's escalation of trade tensions, tightening of immigration restrictions, and disruption of global value chains. Intensive lobbying, however, does not always equate political power. While the Trump administration has largely rebuffed MNCs' efforts to preserve existing trade agreements, individual firms have lobbied successfully to win tariff exemptions. Pierce and Schott (2020, 51) also suggest the importance of MNCs in foreign policymaking. They discuss how multinational firms doing business in China—such as General Motors, Boeing, and Caterpillar—consistently expressed their concerns about the uncertainty surrounding the annual renewal of China's most-favored-nation status until the Congress passed a bill granting permanent normal trade relations (PNTR) status to China in 2000. In other policy domains, such as corporate taxation and the proposed Destination-Based Cash Flow Tax, multinationals have lobbied on both sides of the issues. Evidence suggests, however, that large American and Japanese multinational firms have been able to affect policy within the World Bank, successfully winning projects for themselves (Malik and Stone (2018)). Broz and Hawes (2006) show that multinational banks also exert powerful influence over U.S. policy toward the International Monetary Fund (IMF). Large international banks also have used campaign contributions to influence U.S. congressional voting on foreign loan bailouts (Broz (2005)). Jacobs and Page (2005) provide evidence that large international firms are the most important domestic influences on U.S. foreign policy. Despite the prevalence of MNCs' economic activities across the globe, few studies besides these examine their political influence on foreign policymaking.

This chapter investigates MNCs' distinct roles as political actors. We focus mostly on the United States and on one form of political activity: lobbying. However, we address several general questions. First, do MNCs' political activities differ from other firms? In particular, do these firms' global connections lead them to have policy preferences distinct from domestic firms? Second, do MNCs' political activities differ even from those of big domestic firms? Past research notes that big firms are different: they have more political activity generally and usually more of their activity is conducted individually. Are MNCs just global versions of these big firms? Third, do MNCs care about the same set of issues as all firms, or all big firms? We address these questions by reviewing much past research and then providing new empirical analyses.

We begin by pointing out MNCs' unique economic characteristics compared with other firms that compete primarily in domestic markets. In doing so, we relate our discussion to the theoretical framework of heterogeneous firms in international economics to describe MNCs' unique positions in the global economy. Specifically, we discuss how MNCs' engagement in international trade and foreign investment affects their policy preferences. We show that MNCs' preferences on foreign economic policy are likely to differ greatly from the preferences of purely domestic firms. This difference implies that these firms will differ from domestic firms, even big ones, in the issues they care about most. And it means their positions on many issues will diverge from the positions of the much more numerous domestic firms, who will be less likely to organize collectively for political action. In addition, because of their size, global reach, and leading role in the national economy, MNCs will have more means to affect politics and more reasons to do so.

This chapter's second contribution is to empirically examine MNCs' political activities in the United States. We introduce a new database of lobbying—LobbyView—to study MNCs' engagement in lobbying (Kim (2018)). This database, based on the lobbying reports filed under the Lobbying Disclosure Act of 1995, provides detailed data on lobbying that scholars and practitioners can use to evaluate special interest group politics. We merge this data with a firm-level finance database to investigate whether MNCs exhibit different political activities compared with purely domestic firms. To estimate the independent effect of the change in a firm's status from domestic to multinational, we employ a difference-in-differences identification strategy. Specifically, we compare the difference in lobbying expenditure of firms that became multinational against the spending of similarly sized domestic firms that previously engaged in similar lobbying. We find strong evidence for an increase in lobbying expenditures when firms become multinational. Furthermore, we find that MNCs tend to lobby on a more diverse set of foreign policy issues. To be sure, our study in this chapter is limited to the United States, recent years, and individual firms' lobbying activity. However, our findings lay an empirical foundation for future research of MNCs' political activities across various countries, in different periods, and their connections to lobbying through larger industry associations.

In sum, MNCs are distinct politically as well as economically. They act politically in ways that differ from those of domestic firms, and even from those of large domestic ones. Our findings suggest that MNCs are important political actors whose distinct interests should be incorporated into our understanding of foreign policymaking. While we cannot fully assess their political influence, we do note that many of the policy positions they alone have championed have become U.S. policy in recent decades and indeed have helped create the globalized world economy that we live in today.

THE POLITICAL INFLUENCE OF MULTINATIONAL CORPORATIONS

This section considers the roles that MNCs play in both economic and political marketplaces. To begin, we discuss their unique economic characteristics compared with those of other firms that primarily serve domestic markets, and how these differences affect MNCs' policy preferences. We then discuss MNCs' political efforts to affect foreign policymaking, which have been documented by many social scientists.

Firm-Level Heterogeneity and the Policy Preferences of MNCs

The first step in understanding the political influence of multinational corporations is to differentiate them from other firms.[2] Ample empirical evidence suggests that MNCs differ in important ways from purely domestic firms. They tend to be large and highly productive (see, for example, Bernard, Jensen, and Schott (2009)). They also tend to be the largest exporters, the most integrated into GVCs, employers of the highest-skilled workers, and the largest spenders on research and development (Autor and others (2017)). This makes them valuable in any economy.

MNCs' uniqueness has a close theoretical connection to the studies that examine firm-level heterogeneity in engagement in international trade. In earlier work, Bernard, Jensen, and Lawrence (1995) showed that exporters in manufacturing are very different from purely domestic firms.[3] While exports from the United States only account for about 12.2 percent of GDP, exporting firms overall play a large role in the U.S. economy. Exporting firms are larger, more productive, more capital-intensive, and they pay higher wages and employ many workers, especially the most productive ones.[4] Bernard and others (2007) point out that this evidence about exporting firms supports the new, new trade theory and its focus on productivity differences among firms.[5] As heterogeneous firm models predict, these firms benefit from trade and its liberalization; they tend to grow bigger and more productive, while less productive firms exit the market. That is, a very small number of firms within an economy dominate export markets and tend to export many different goods to many other markets. Moreover, roughly half of the firms that export also import, and thus are probably part of global value chains.

While not all importers or exporters are multinational firms, almost all MNCs export and import (Yeaple (2009)), accounting for more than 80 percent of U.S. trade (Bernard, Jensen, and Schott (2009)). These MNCs sit atop the productivity ladder of all firms. They are the largest, most capital- and skill-intensive, and the most innovative (Tomiura (2007); Bernard, Jensen, and Schott (2009); Doms and Jensen (1998); Slaughter (2004)). As theory implies, MNCs vary in where they invest and in how much. A pecking order arises where only the most productive firms invest in all types of foreign locations while the least productive firms invest in only the most productive locations (Yeaple (2009)). Although their numbers are small, these most productive firms have a large presence within any economy. And because of these characteristics, they have been viewed as powerful actors within any country where they operate, both host and home countries (Prakash and Potoski (2007); Luo (2001); Jensen and others (2012)).

A second important step is to identify MNCs' overall foreign policy preferences, and especially economic policies governing trade, foreign investment, immigration, and exchange rates. To understand if firms have political influence, researchers have studied what they want (especially ex ante) and whether it differs from what other groups want. In international relations, for example, a long-standing question has been whether business favored war or peace. Indeed, the so-called security preferences of business have been an important issue since Karl Marx's time, and many scholars saw business or capitalism itself as a driver of war and conflict, especially colonialism (Cohen (1973); Staley (1935)). The assertions about the military-industrial complex and its benefits from war are part of this tradition. On the other hand, more recent research has mostly cast doubt on this assertion. In particular, Brooks (2005) argues that business firms in the modern period are strong proponents of peace, not war. Building upon this, a literature now exists on the capitalist peace, arguing that capitalism and its agents are central to peace among countries (Gartzke (2007); Kirschner (2007); McDonald (2009)).

Others have studied firm-level preferences on policies such as trade, foreign investment, and immigration. In the trade area, it has long been recognized that firms will have different preferences, depending on their ties to the international economy. Domestic firms that face import competition will opt for protectionism, while big exporters and multinationals will want freer trade (Milner (1988); Gilligan (1997); Kim and Osgood (2019)). The preferences for freer trade at home and abroad are reinforced for multinationals if they are part of global value chains. In more recent work, Jensen, Quinn, and Weymouth (2015) predict that MNCs in GVCs will not use trade remedies like antidumping as much as domestic firms, and that there should be fewer trade disputes in their sectors. Many of the same divides are expected in foreign investment and financial markets. Small domestic banks and firms are expected to care most about protecting the domestic market and keeping large foreign firms and banks out. Big banks and multinationals, on the other hand, are expected to press for open capital markets, protection for foreign investments, and greater capital mobility (Frieden (1991)). Recent work also links firms' preferences to immigration. Peters (2017) argues that firms will press for open migration, especially if they face strong international competition and are limited to operating in their home country. Once firms can move production anywhere in the world, their concerns about immigration end, and they no longer press for open immigration policies.

Finally, MNCs are also the main proponents of preferential trade agreements and bilateral investment treaties, according to numerous studies (Manger (2009); Kim (2015)). And MNCs have been the main advocates of provisions in preferential trade agreements protecting investment and intellectual property rights and liberalizing services. The provisions help MNCs gain an edge over MNCs from other countries, which are excluded from the trade agreements (Baccini (2019); Dür, Baccini, and Elsig (2014); Rodrik (2018)). Baccini, Pinto, and Weymouth (2017) argue that intra-industry political divisions over preferential trade agreements exist, and they show that large and productive firms engaged in offshore production are the biggest beneficiaries of the agreements and the most ardent supporters. Some research also suggests that MNCs increasingly prefer that decisions be made at the supranational level—that is, in international institutions like the World Trade Organization (WTO) and IMF or at international tribunals like the International Centre for Settlement of Investment Disputes—where they may have even greater influence than they do domestically (Prakash and Hart (1999); Levy and Prakash (2003)). Other studies show that they are the most likely to lobby for national compliance in WTO Dispute Settlement rulings (Kim and Spilker (2019); Yildirim (2018)). Generally, much of the recent literature sees a large divide in foreign economic policy preferences between domestic firms and large global ones. Firms may also have significant preferences about domestic policies affecting taxes, regulation, and labor. Whether these preferences break down along domestic versus international lines seems less clear. The next question, however, is whether all firms pursue political influence to secure their preferences, and then, how the battle among firms and with other groups plays out.

Political Influence of MNCs

Channels of Political Influence

MNCs may employ different means of political influence from issue to issue and country to country. Scholars, as exemplified by Nye (1974), have identified three main channels through which firms may exert their influence over foreign policymaking: direct influence through lobbying, indirect influence through their role as instruments of the state, and unintentional influence via their agenda-setting power.

First, firms may directly engage in political activities such as lobbying and campaign contributions to affect policymaking or to press political leaders to address their demands. In doing so, they can also work with industry associations and political action committees to advance their interests. MNCs can leverage their bargaining power by offering both inducements (promises of new investment) and deprivations (threats of withdrawal of investment) (Nye (1974)). Grossman and Helpman (1994), in their famous "Protection for Sale" model, show how lobbying by interest groups may change trade policy. In addition to direct lobbying, firms can leverage informal ties to political leaders to provide information and apply persuasion (Bauer, Pool, and Dexter (1972); Denzau and Munger (1986)). While this is inside pressure (Culpepper (2011)), these influence attempts can also involve the public. Outside lobbying includes the use of public communication channels rather than exchanges with political elites, and involves tactics such as contacting journalists, issuing press releases, establishing public campaigns, and organizing protests (Kollman (1998); De Bruycker and Beyers (2018)).

Second, other scholars have argued that MNCs hold an unintended role in foreign policy as instruments of the state (Gilpin (1975)). In this view, governments have used MNCs to further the national interest by strengthening the effects of sanctions through MNC production networks, facilitating capital transfers through firms to strengthen monetary policy, or enabling MNCs' foreign affiliates to gather intelligence (Nye (1974, 157)).

Finally, firms can hold considerable agenda-setting power from their mere presence abroad. Firms' "privileged position" in the view of governments (Lindblom (1977)) assists political leaders in defining problems, devising policies, and prioritizing objectives. As Ray (1972, 82) noted long ago, "The influence of corporations on American foreign relations stems primarily from their ability to shape the external environment from which problems, conflicts, and crises grow, and their ability to define the axiomatic." While indirect and incidental lobbying are important avenues of influence, our empirical analyses below focus on the first type of political influence: lobbying.

The literature on firms' political influence points out that the most consistently interesting explanatory factors of political activity in home countries have been firm size, degree of government regulation, and the amount of firm or industry sales to the government (Mitchell, Hansen, and Jepsen (1997); Drope and Hansen (2006)). Countering the pressures of other groups that oppose their interests (so-called counter-mobilization) has also been an important reason for influence attempts by firms (Austen-Smith and Wright (1994)). The larger the firms the more they try to exercise political influence (Ansolabehere, de Figueiredo, and Snyder (2003); Hansen, Mitchell, and Drope (2004); Drope and Hansen (2006); Bombardini and Trebbi (2012); Naoi and Krauss (2009)). The more firms interact with the government and its regulations, the more political action they seem to take. These large firms also tend to act on their own and not in coalitions or industry associations (de Figueiredo and Richter (2014)).

The literature, at least for the United States, shows that spending on business lobbying far surpasses campaign contributions. Milyo, Primo, and

Groseclose (2000) demonstrate that lobbying expenditures at the U.S. federal level are five times as large as campaign contributions to political action committees. Firms of all sizes may suffer from collective action problems that deter political action, which is costly; however, large firms and hence MNCs may be less affected by this problem (Alt and others (1996)). Firms' political activities may lead to actual policy changes.[6] Gordon and Hafer (2005) and Blonigen and Figlio (1998) demonstrate that lobbying by firms can affect national policies and influence individual legislators. Fisman (2001) and Faccio (2006) also find that firms benefit economically from their political ties, and that larger firms, which are more likely to be MNCs, are more likely to have political connections. Furthermore, some additional evidence suggests that firms that lobby become bigger as a result, thus underscoring their successful influence (Huneeus and Kim (2018); Akcigit, Baslandze, and Lotti (2018)).

Scale Effect

A key finding of the research on business political activity is that large firms lobby the most. Numerous studies demonstrate that large firms spend the most on direct lobbying (Boies (1989); Grier, Munger, and Roberts (1994); Ansolabehere, de Figueiredo, and Snyder (2003); Hansen and Mitchell (2000); Hansen, Mitchell, and Drope (2004); Drope and Hansen (2006); Bombardini and Trebbi (2012); Naoi and Krauss (2009)). Several reasons explain why large firms lobby the most. First, they have the most resources. The size of the firm reduces the two primary costs of lobbying: the initial costs to establish a lobbying presence and the actual amount spent to influence policy (Kerr, Lincoln, and Mishra (2014); Hafner-Burton, Kousser, and Victor (2015, 10)). Bigger firms have a greater capacity to pay the upfront costs of establishing a lobbying presence (Bertrand, Bombardini, and Trebbi (2014); Kerr, Lincoln, and Mishra (2014); Kerr and others (2017)). Therefore, large firms select into lobbying whereas smaller firms cannot (Alt and others (1996); Aisbett and McAusland (2013); Blanga-Gubbay, Conconi, and Parenti (2020)).

Moreover, larger firms use their resources to spend more (Kim (2017); Dellis and Sondermann (2017); Igan, Mishra, and Tressel (2012)) and forge closer ties with politicians (Fisman (2001); Faccio (2006)). Bigger firms hold an advantage because they have more expendable resources to influence politicians, whereas policymakers are resource-poor (Drope and Hansen (2006)). The biggest firms are also able to leverage considerable informational advantages (for example, expert and technical information) that help to reduce uncertainty for policymakers (Helleiner (2011); Lall (2012); Young (2012)).

After a firm shoulders the initial upfront costs of lobbying, lobbying usually begets more lobbying. Kerr, Lincoln, and Mishra (2014, 166) "report a 92 percent probability that a firm will lobby in a given year conditional on lobbying in the prior year" (de Figueiredo and Richter (2014)). Bigger firms may also hold a first-mover advantage where regulators become more amicable to protecting the firm to preserve the reputations of the firm and the bureaucrats. This leads to "protection without capture" or consistently favorable treatment by regulators (Carpenter (2004)). That is, there are scale effects in which large firms see an increase in the marginal benefit of political engagement as they expand both domestically and internationally.

Regulatory Granularity

A second reason larger firms are more politically active is because policies are becoming increasingly granular (for example, product-specific trade policy), and therefore lobbying becomes a cost-benefit analysis for *individual* firms. In fact, scholars have consistently found that large firms and MNCs often choose to lobby alone and lobbying is becoming increasingly "particularistic" (Mizruchi (2013)). Gilligan (1997, 455) argued that since firms involved in "intra-industry trade are monopolists, lobbying essentially becomes a private good," and thus they are willing to lobby alone and bear the costs. Further, as Johns, Pelc, and Wellhausen (2019, 732) demonstrate, growing globalization has led to not "only an overall increase of lobbying, but more lobbying by individual firms rather than through industry associations, thus contributing to what Drutman (2015) has described as 'growing particularism' in corporate lobbying."

To be sure, lobbying through industry associations still serves as an important channel. However, there are other reasons why firms might choose to lobby alone. Large firms are more likely to have in-house lobbying offices, which reduces the importance of trade associations (Vogel (1996) as cited in Walker and Rea (2014, 11)). Finally, lobbying alone can be more effective than a coalition of strange bedfellows with a cacophony of voices diluting the overall message (Nelson and Yackee (2012)). Following these findings about the importance of lobbying by firms themselves, our research focuses on this aspect of political activity.

MNCs' lobbying preferences may differ from domestic firms, because they face diverse regulatory regimes from foreign activities. To be sure, many studies show that large global firms are significantly more likely to support trade liberalization and to lobby for it in a variety of countries, including the United States, Japan, and Costa Rica (Plouffe (2017), Osgood and others (2017)).[7] Osgood (2019) points out that the gains from trade are highly concentrated in a few firms in the United States and that these firms have GVCs that are specific to certain countries or regions. These facts mean that MNCs in the United States lobby extensively in favor of trade and strongly support trade agreements with the specific countries they deal with. These MNCs outweigh and out-lobby domestic firms that oppose trade, and they overcome collective action issues because each firm gains greatly from trade and lobbies on different agreements according to their GVC partners. Further, Kim (2017) shows that international firms lobby individually to reduce trade barriers on highly specific products, again because they anticipate large gains from liberalization on their products.

However, other research also shows that MNCs have preferences on policies that go beyond market access. Kim and others (2019) demonstrate that for many types of firms, the standard trade policy measures of the past (tariffs and subsidies) are no longer their most important concerns. Instead, the nature of firms' involvement in global value chains shapes their preferences so that other policy issues, such as the protection of foreign investments, are now most important for multinational corporations. These distinctive preferences and outsized resources mean that MNCs, even more than big domestic firms, may prefer to be very active and to operate individually in the political arena.

Influence over Host Countries and International Institutions

MNCs may play significant roles in shaping domestic policies of host countries. Lee (2018) studies foreign multinational corporations in the United States and shows that MNCs use their subsidiaries in the United States as local political agents that can influence the U.S. government. Using political action committee (PAC) contribution data, she finds that U.S. subsidiaries of foreign firms are more likely to sponsor a PAC compared with American firms of a similar size. They also give much greater amounts in campaign contributions. While this research is focused on the United States, it is very likely that MNCs play similar roles in other countries and perhaps exert even more influence because of their even greater presence in smaller economies.

A long literature examines MNC influence in the developing countries that host their investments. The dependency literature, as its name suggests, focused attention on how MNCs could realize their preferences and obtain better deals with these host countries because of their bargaining advantages (Biersteker (1978); Moran (1973, 1978); Evans (1979)). Other early research indicated that foreign investors could be at a disadvantage over time and that they faced an obsolescing bargain where the host country could expropriate their property once they had invested (Vernon (1971, 1980)).[8] Much evidence now suggests that the obsolescing bargain is not evident, and that firms have developed strategies to prevent it from occurring (Hillman, Zardkoohi, and Bierman (1999); Eden, Lenway, and Schuler (2005); Henisz and Zelner (2005)). The stress more recently has been on how MNCs protect their investments in host countries and what characteristics of host countries best safeguard them. The business literature notes that foreign firms can use alliances with domestic partners and host governments to mitigate risk (Malesky (2008); Eden and Molot (2002); Stopford and Strange (1991); Pinto (2013); Pinto and Pinto (2008)). Firms can also integrate into global supply chains (Johns and Wellhausen (2016)), build political ties with host state policymakers (Henisz and Zelner (2005)), ally with politically powerful multilateral institutions (Nose (2014)), and threaten and pursue investor-state arbitration using the global network of bilateral investment treaties (Salacuse (2010); Allee and Peinhardt (2011); Simmons (2014); Johns and Wellhausen (2016)).

Another branch of the literature focuses on choices MNCs make about which host country to invest in. This range of choice is often seen as giving MNCs great leeway to negotiate better deals with host countries and to influence their politics. In particular, the number of veto players in the government, the degree of private-property protection, and the extent of democracy all may affect whether MNCs can protect their investments and hence whether they invest in the first place (Jensen (2003); Li and Resnick (2003); Henisz and Williamson (1999); Henisz (2000)). First, more veto players, on the one hand, makes it harder for governments to change policies and thus reduce any ex post attempts to change their bargain with MNCs. However, more veto players may also mean more access points for MNCs and make it easier for them, especially in combination with other foreign and domestic firms, to influence policy (Ehrlich (2007, 2008); Pyle (2006), Gillespie (2006)). Second, more democracy and better private property protection, on the one hand, make it more likely MNCs can find allies in the host country. On the other hand, more political competition and more space for different interest groups in vigorous democracies seem to weaken

MNCs and lessen their influence (Jensen and others (2012)). Finally, MNCs can call on their home country government for assistance (Krasner (1978); Lipson (1985); Fisman (2001); Wellhausen (2014); Truex (2014); Lee (2019); Gertz (2018)). When political leaders desire foreign investment, the ability to choose locations enables MNCs to exercise important influence over the host country and its politics. The conditions that maximize MNC political influence are still much debated, however.

In particular, many studies have pointed out that MNCs have shaped the economic reform process in many developing host countries. They show that MNCs can affect local policy decisions in host countries by providing information and policy expertise about regulations in other countries; by lobbying officials, especially in alliance with local actors; by promising benefits such as more employment and access to new technology; by threatening to cut employment or withdraw; and by helping leaders overcome entrenched local interests by offering more revenue or employment (Li and Reuveny (2003); Rudra (2005); Mosley and Uno (2007); Malesky (2009); Jensen and others (2012)). Many of these influence techniques for host countries are the same as for home countries.

It is important to note that MNCs may influence international institutions as well as domestic governments. Hanegraaff and others (2015) point out that the most organized domestic interest groups, such as MNCs, are also the most potent actors in many international organizations, such as the WTO. In a series of papers, Broz (2005); Broz and Hawes (2006); and Broz, Frieden, and Weymouth (2008) show that large international financial firms can influence U.S. foreign policy as well as the IMF and World Bank. Indeed, some studies assert that MNCs are now more powerful than ever, due to globalization and the capital mobility it creates (Vernon and Spar (1989); Strange (1996); Levy and Prakash (2003)). These studies suggest that MNCs have a plethora of means to exert powerful influences over the countries they choose to operate in. These issues and forms of influence are very important to keep in mind when assessing the power of MNCs. But this chapter focuses on their political activity in the United States. In some ways, this is a difficult case for finding MNC influence, since the U.S. political system is highly institutionalized and filled with checks and balances.

The past research surveyed above leads us to focus on at least three key issues. First, does the type or level of political activities differ between MNCs and domestic firms? Second, are any differences in political activity among firms just due to differences in their size or are they due to the extent of their global ties? Third, do MNCs focus their political activity on different issues than domestic firms? These questions have been less systematically addressed in previous work.

DATA

Despite the significance of MNCs in foreign policymaking, quantitative studies of their political activities have been limited by the absence of direct measures of their economic and political activities. In this section, we describe two key firm-level variables that we develop for our analysis in the "Empirical Results" section: (1) multinationality and (2) lobbying activities.

Measuring Multinationality

We begin by measuring a firm's status as a multinational. This is key for our empirical analysis, since our goal is to examine whether firms' lobbying *changes* after they become multinational. We define an MNC as a corporation that owns or controls production of goods or services in at least one country other than its home country. We develop a binary measure of firms' multinationality based on the financial statements of all public firms available through Compustat database. Following Dyreng and others (2017), we begin by computing the ratio of a firm's pretax foreign income to its total pretax income in a given year. The use of this measure is justified by the section §210.4-08(h)(1), *Income Tax Expense*, of the U.S. Securities and Exchange Commission (SEC) rules, which mandates the disclosure of the components of income as either domestic or foreign.[9] It is still a noisy measure of firms' multinationality, because some foreign income might be generated by other activities, such as tax avoidance, that are not directly related to the production of goods or services.[10]

Thus, we further improve the measure by identifying a cutoff in the pretax-foreign-income-to-total-income ratio so that the resulting binary measure of multinationality approximates the distribution of some known statistics of multinational firms in the BEA data. Specifically, we compare the distribution of MNCs' sales against the corresponding numbers reported in Faulkender and Smith (2016), one of very few studies that directly measures multinationality based on the BEA data *and* calculates the aggregated characteristics of the MNCs using the Compustat dataset. This allows us to directly merge the economic data with the lobbying dataset. We use the numbers that appear in table 1 of their paper, where the authors report logged sales data separately for all Compustat firms, MNCs from the BEA data, and Compustat firms that aren't in the BEA data (that is, domestic firms).[11] This provides a valuable opportunity to match the sales distribution of MNCs in our data that approximates the distribution in the BEA data. We take the mean sales (logged) among Compustat firms, and then identify a cutoff in the continuous measure so that the mean sales of the firms above the cutoff matches exactly the number reported in the paper based on the direct measure of multinationality. Figure 12-1 shows the cutoff that we identified in the distribution of pretax foreign income to total income ratio—that is, 0.02139. Using this cutoff, we define firm i as multinational at year t if its pretax foreign income to total income ratio is above the cutoff and domestic otherwise.

FIGURE 12-1. Histogram of Continuous Multinationality Measure

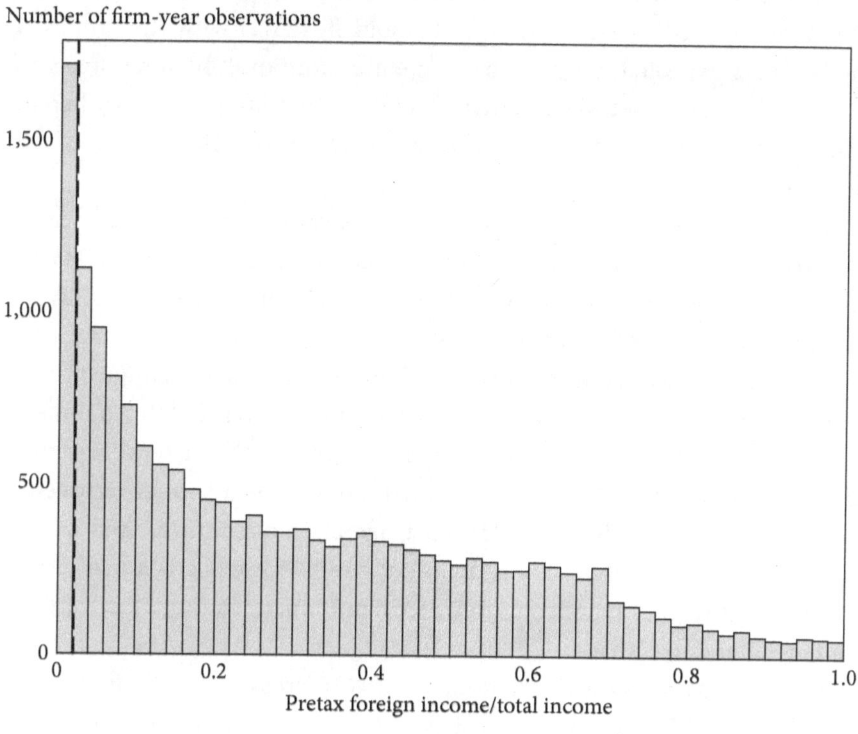

Note: This figure shows the distribution of the ratio of firms' pretax foreign income to its total pretax income. The vertical dotted line corresponds to the cutoff (= 0.02139) that we used to match the mean logged sales of MNCs reported based on the BEA data in Faulkender and Smith (2016). We code the firm-year as multinational if the ratio is above the cutoff and domestic otherwise.

We then carefully check the validity of our measure, both quantitatively and qualitatively. First, we compare the employment size of multinationals in the BEA employment numbers against the number computed by our own measure of multinationality.[12] According to the BEA, MNCs employed 28.0 million workers in the United States in 2016. Using the binary measure of multinationality that we developed, we find that MNCs employed 27.4 million people, which matches remarkably well with the number based on the BEA data. However, the numbers cannot be directly compared, because the BEA data include both private and public companies, whereas the Compustat data only include public entities.

Second, we perform another validity check by looking at the number of MNCs as reported in Barefoot and Mataloni Jr. (2011), who use the BEA data from 2009 to present some stylized facts about U.S. MNCs. In particular, in their table 6, they report the number of MNCs by employment size. Again, since they use all of the BEA data, their numbers include both private and public firms, and thus there will be more firms. Figure 12-2 compares the numbers reported in Barefoot and Mataloni Jr. (2011) with the proposed measure. As expected, we find that there are more multinational firms in the BEA data. However, we find that the overall distribution across different employment sizes based on our measure resembles the distribution of the BEA data.

Finally, we validate the accuracy of our measure manually. Specifically, we took a random sample of companies in the Compustat data for 2014 and checked whether we accurately code their multinationality status. Table 12-1 displays the list of firm names that we randomly sampled. To ensure the validity of our measure across firms with different sizes, we sampled firms based on their sales. We checked each firm online and verified that our measure indeed captures multinationality. For example, the Federal National Mortgage Association, also known as Fannie Mae, is a U.S. government-sponsored enterprise that provides mortgage-backed securities, and we accurately code it as domestic. On the other hand, Primerica is a marketing company with a 2017 net income of US$300 million, operating mostly in the United States and Canada.

Figure 12-3 shows the distribution of MNCs across various manufacturing industries.[13] On average, we find that 46 percent of Compustat firms are multinationals. This number is comparable to the one reported in Dyreng and others (2017), who find that about 40 percent of the same firms in their analysis are multinationals.[14] Having defined and identified public firms

TABLE 12-1. Sample of Companies Examined

Domestic	Multinational
Big companies	
Federal National Mortgage Association	Primerica Inc.
Cracker Barrel Old Country Store Inc.	Grainger (W. W.) Inc.
Saia Inc.	Outerwall Inc.
Heartland Payment Systems Inc.	II-VI Inc.
Denbury Resources Inc.	Tiffany & Co.
Time Warner Cable Inc.	Cabot Corp.
Neiman Marcus Inc.	PTC Inc.
Voya Retirement Insurance and Annuity Co.	Total System Services Inc.
Steel Dynamics Inc.	Invacare Corp.
MSC Industrial Direct Co. Inc.	Verizon Communications Inc.
Medium companies	
Griffin Industrial Realty Inc.	CUI Global Inc.
Capitol Federal Financial Inc.	Royal Gold Inc.
Entercom Communications Corp.	Powell Industries Inc.
Canterbury Park Holding Corp.	Zynga Inc.
Palmetto Bancshares Inc.	RealNetworks Inc.
Martha Stewart Living Omnimedia Inc.	FalconStor Software Inc.
Empire Resorts Inc.	RealD Inc.
Flagstar Bancorp Inc.	Daegis Inc.
AtriCure Inc.	PFSweb Inc.
Sequenom Inc.	Delta Apparel Inc.
Small companies	
Cellular Biomedicine Group Inc.	Success Holding Group International Inc.
International Barrier Technology Inc.	BeyondSpring Inc.
Notis Global Inc.	Histogenics Corp.
Alpha Network Alliance Ventures Inc.	EPIRUS Biopharmaceuticals Inc.
Ecosphere Technologies Inc.	Uranium Energy Corp.
Viaspace Inc.	Alimera Sciences Inc.
Anterios Inc.	Brainstorm Cell Therapeutics
Matinas BioPharma Holdings Inc.	SurePure Inc.
XZERES Corp.	Generex Biotechnology Corp.
Infinite Group Inc.	Midway Gold Corp.

FIGURE 12-2. Comparison of Number of Employees

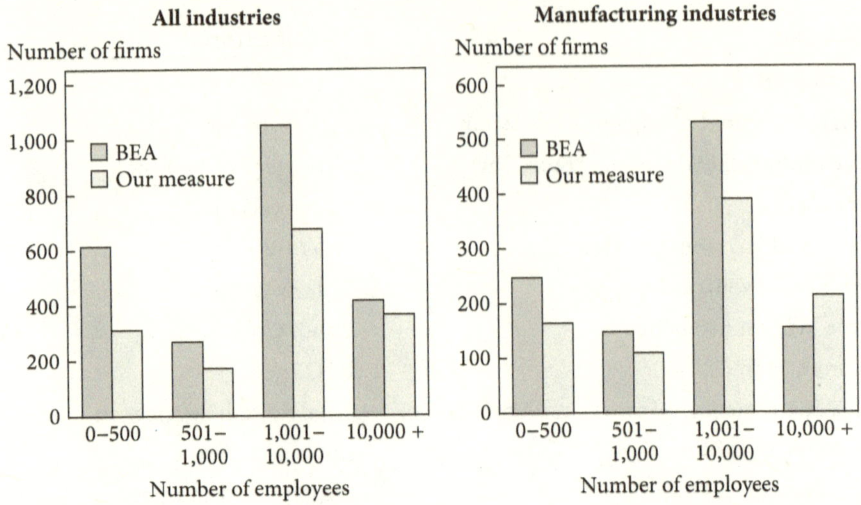

Note: This figure compares the distribution of MNCs based on four different size categories by number of employees. The left and right panels show the distribution across all industries and manufacturing industries, respectively. Dark gray bars represent the numbers reported in Barefoot and Mataloni Jr. (2011), who used the BEA data. The light gray bars on the right represent the number of MNCs in each category computed based on our measure of multinationality. It shows that we reasonably approximate the true distribution. The BEA data includes both public and private firms while we only consider public firms using the Compustat database.

in the United States that are multinational, and differentiating them from domestic firms, we can now compare the lobbying of MNCs and domestic firms within each industry in the "Empirical Results" section.

Measuring Lobbying Activities

The Lobbying Disclosure Act of 1995 (amended by the Honest Leadership and Open Government Act of 2007) requires lobbyists (for example, K Street lobbying firms) to file quarterly reports on behalf of their clients (for example, MNCs) describing their activities.[15] In doing so, they should report lobbying expenses (or their income), lobbied issues (for example, international trade), and lobbied congressional bills, among other items.

We use the LobbyView database that parses through the universe of 1.1 million lobbying reports filed from 1999 to 2019 (Kim (2018)). The primary benefit of using LobbyView is that it provides unique firm-level IDs linked to the Compustat data. Using the identifier, we can merge the lobbying data

FIGURE 12-3. Distribution of MNCs across Manufacturing Industries

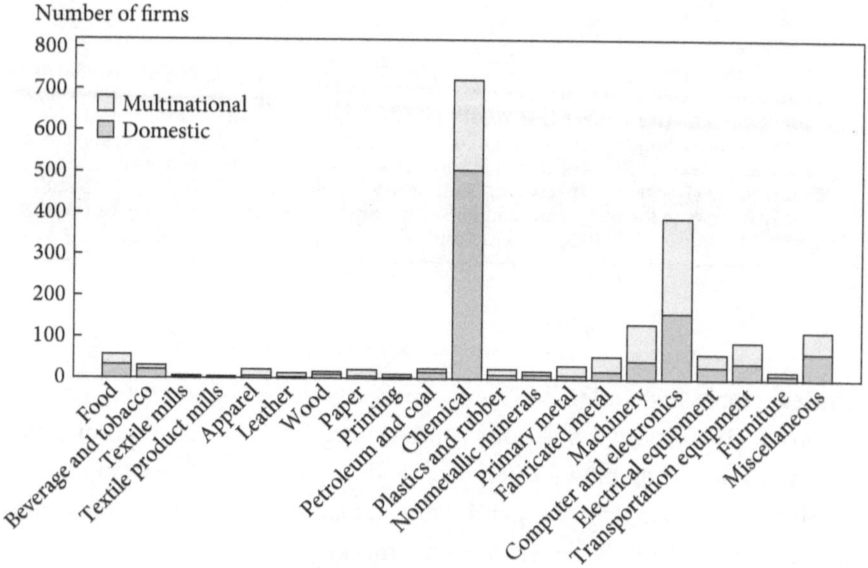

Note: This figure displays the distribution of MNCs across three-digit North American Industry Classification System (NAICS) industries in 2017. On average, 46 percent of Compustat firms are multinationals. The chemical industry has the largest number of firms while it accounts for about 17 percent of the total sales in manufacturing.

with Compustat so that we can use the multinationality measure that we developed in the previous section to examine the political activities of MNCs across time. The lobbying reports also contain detailed information about firms' political activities. There are seventy-nine issue categories specified in the Lobbying Disclosure Act of 1995, such as international trade (TRD), defense (DEF), and immigration (IMM).[16] For each issue category, lobbying firms are required to describe their activities on behalf of their clients. For example, figure 12-4 shows that Panasonic Corporation of North America actively engages in lobbying affecting various trade policies, such as the Rules of Origin in the North American Free Trade Agreement.[17]

EMPIRICAL RESULTS

In this section, we investigate whether firms tend to increase their lobbying expenses *after* they become multinational. We first compare the differences between MNCs' and domestic firms' economic and political activities at a given time. We find that MNCs are (1) larger and more productive, (2) spend

FIGURE 12-4. First Quarter Report by Panasonic Corporation of North America in 2018

Border Adjustment Tax (BAT) - Tax on imports with exemption on exports - Explain negative impact of BAT on company sales and U.S. employment Office of the United States Trade Representative Docket USTR-2017-0006 - Request for Comments on Negotiating Objectives Regarding Modernization of the North American Free Trade Agreement With Canada and Mexico - Rules of Origin for products manufactured in Canada and Mexico S. 2098, H.R. 4311 - Foreign Investment Risk Review Modernization Act of 2017 - National Security reviews of foreign investment or technology transfers H.R. 4170 - FARA (Foreign Agents Registration Act) Reform - Disclosing foreign influence requirements.

more on lobbying, and (3) lobby on a more diverse set of issues than domestic firms. To account for various confounding factors and selection bias in our analysis, we employ a difference-in-differences identification strategy. We find that a firm tends to spend more on lobbying when it becomes multinational than if it only serves the home market.

Differences Between MNCs and Domestic Firms

Many researchers find that MNCs' economic activities differ from domestic firms' activities (Tomiura (2007); Bernard, Jensen, and Schott (2009); Doms and Jensen (1998); Slaughter (2004)). Among other differences, MNCs are found to be larger, more productive, and more capital-intensive than domestic firms. We begin our analysis by checking the differences between MNCs and domestic firms based on the measure that we developed in the "Measuring Multinationality" section.

Figure 12-5 shows that MNCs are indeed larger and more productive than domestic firms, consistent with the literature. The figure also highlights that the size and productivity distributions of MNCs and domestic firms overlap enough to allow us to investigate the independent effect of multinationality on firms' political activities, while holding other factors that potentially drive firms' foreign policy preferences constant. Indeed, the new, new trade theory predicts that more productive firms are more likely to engage in exporting and benefit from trade liberalization. Figure 12-5 shows that there are highly productive domestic firms that are not multinational. To the extent that they do engage in international trade (not all exporters are MNCs), therefore, we can compare the differences in political activities between MNCs and domestic firms due to their differences in multinationality, while accounting for the fact that they both engage in international trade and are similar in size.

Next, we examine MNCs' lobbying. We construct two outcome variables. First, we compute the total lobbying expenditure by aggregating all the lobbying expenses across lobbying reports filed on behalf of each firm. Multiple reports are filed in a given year because each lobbying firm (both in-house lobbying departments and K Street lobbying firms) must file quarterly reports. Second, we identify the issues, out of the seventy-nine categories, that are reported to have been lobbied at least once in each report. This allows us to identify the differences in lobbying between MNCs and domestic firms.

Table 12-2 summarizes our analysis based on the ordinary least squares regression. In this analysis, we consider all publicly traded firms that have lobbied at least once between 2007 and 2017. Models (1)–(4) use lobbying expenditure, while models (5)–(8) consider the number of lobbied issues as the outcome variable. We find that MNCs tend to spend more on lobbying and that they lobby on more issues. To examine the differences between MNCs and domestic firms *within* industries (see figure 12-3, for example), we include the North American Industry Classification System (NAICS) three-digit, industry-level, fixed effects. Our finding suggests that firms' political activities differ even when they are in the same industry. This is in contrast to the existing studies of trade politics that tend to focus primarily on inter-

FIGURE 12-5. Overlaps in the Distribution of Sales and Productivity

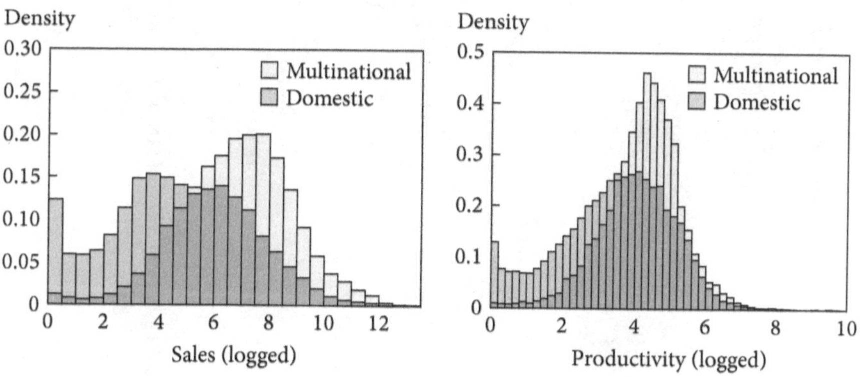

Note: This figure compares the distribution of firm size and productivity (measured as value-added per labor) between domestic and multinational firms. It confirms that multinational firms tend to be bigger and more productive, consistent with the findings in the literature. It also shows that there are sufficient overlaps in the two distributions. In our later analysis, we will match these firm-level characteristics to account for the possibility that these variables confound the relationship between multinationality and lobbying.

TABLE 12-2. Lobbying Expenditure and Number of Issues Lobbied by MNCs

	Lobbying expenditure				Number of issues lobbied			
	(1)	(2)	(3)	(4)	(5)	(6)	(7)	(8)
Multinational	0.899*** (0.061)	1.239*** (0.074)	1.203*** (0.074)	0.461*** (0.067)	1.649*** (0.072)	2.198*** (0.094)	2.182*** (0.095)	0.858*** (0.077)
Capital				3.035*** (0.063)				4.141*** (0.072)
In-house				0.0002*** (0.00002)				0.001*** (0.00002)
Constant	11.535*** (0.035)	12.316*** (0.557)	12.151*** (0.563)	11.128*** (0.487)	3.783*** (0.041)	4.432*** (0.710)	4.401*** (0.719)	2.838*** (0.559)
NAICS3 FE		✔	✔	✔		✔	✔	✔
Year FE			✔	✔			✔	✔
Observations	14,732	9,385	9,385	9,327	14,732	9,385	9,385	9,327
R^2	0.014	0.107	0.110	0.319	0.034	0.188	0.189	0.498
Adjusted R^2	0.014	0.100	0.101	0.313	0.034	0.181	0.181	0.494

Note: This table displays estimated effects of MNCs on lobbying expenditures and the number of lobbied issues by firms in all industries. We find that MNCs tend to (1) spend more on lobbying and (2) lobby on more issues than domestic firms, on average.

*** $p<0.01$, ** $p<0.05$, * $p<0.1$

industry differences (see, for example, Hiscox (2002)). We also control for year fixed effects to account for heterogeneity across time. Finally, we include capital size and the existence of an in-house lobbying department as firm-level controls.[18] In sum, MNCs are clearly different in their political activity from domestic firms; holding size and industry constant, they lobby more and do so on more issues.

Matching Analysis

Although the analysis in the previous section shows that MNCs exhibit different lobbying activities compared with domestic firms, many potential endogeneity problems prevent researchers from drawing causal inferences in observational studies, especially when firms are highly heterogeneous. For example, our focus on the firms that lobbied at least once (that is, intensive margin) may introduce a bias if firms have distinct organizational structures that determine the propensity of their lobbying (that is, extensive margin). Others may have distinct growth trends that might be correlated with their economic and political activities (see Meyer (1995), for an overview).

In this section, we apply a difference-in-differences estimator to investigate the causal effect of multinationality on lobbying behavior. We proceed in three steps. First, we identify a total of 210 companies whose multinationality status changed between 2007 and 2017. To ensure that they, indeed, turned from domestic to multinational, we then carefully investigate each one of them relying on public information from the media and online resources. We find that we correctly capture the treatment status as well as its timing for most of them using our measurement strategy described in the "Measuring Multinationality" section. For example, we find that ABM Industries became an MNC in 2014. In fact, the firm made several acquisitions around that period, including that of GBM Support Services Group Limited, a U.K. company. We also find that MetLife is measured as an MNC since 2010. It purchased American Life Insurance Company (ALICO), with operations in Japan and several European countries. Similarly, we found that Autozone became an MNC when the company opened its first store in Brazil. Also, a subsidiary, Autozone de Mexico, opened in 2003.[19] A majority of these companies became MNCs through purchases of, or mergers with, multinational or foreign companies.[20]

Second, for each "treated" firm i that became an MNC at year t (that is, $X_{it} = 1$), we find the set of all domestic firms that have an identical treatment history only up to year $t - 1$, that is, firms that remain to be domestic at t. Formally,

$$M_{it} = \{i' : i' \neq i, X_{i't} = 0, X_{i't'} = X_{it'} \text{ for all } t' = t-1, \ldots, t-L\} \quad (1)$$

where X_{it} denotes the MNC status for firm i at year t. Out of these domestic firms, we find the set of five closest "matched control" firms in the set M_{it} that are similar in terms of their pre-treatment observable characteristics including sales, productivity, employment size, presence of in-house lobbying department, and number of issues lobbied in years $t - 3$ to $t - 1$.[21] We compute the average Mahalanobis distance measure between the treated observation and each control observation over time.[22] Formally,

$$\frac{1}{3}\sum_{l=1}^{3}\sqrt{(\mathbf{V}_{i,t-l} - \mathbf{V}_{i',t-l})^T \Sigma_{i,t-l}^{-1}(\mathbf{V}_{i,t-l} - \mathbf{V}_{i',t-l})}$$

where $\mathbf{V}_{it'}$ is the pre-treatment observable covariates that we match (such as sales and productivity) and $\mathbf{\Sigma}_{it'}$ is the sample covariance matrix of $\mathbf{V}_{it'}$. Simply put, we find domestic firms that are comparable in their economic and political characteristics to the firms that turned into MNCs.

Finally, using these matched control firms, we compute the difference-in-differences estimate. Specifically, we compare the difference in lobbying expenses of the treated multinational firm i between year t and year $t + F$ against the mean difference in lobbying expenses during the same period among the matched control domestic firms. Under the parallel trends assumption, this gives an estimate of the effect on lobbying spending of the firm turning into an MNC. We then take the average of this estimate across all treated firms to gain our average treatment effect estimate. Formally, our quantity of interest is given by:

$$\hat{\beta} = \frac{1}{N}\sum_{i=1}^{N}\left\{(\mathbf{Y}_{i,t+F} - \mathbf{Y}_{i,t-l}) - \frac{1}{|M_{it}|}\sum_{i' \in M_{it}}(\mathbf{Y}_{i',t+F} - \mathbf{Y}_{i',t-l})\right\} \quad (2)$$

We use the bootstrap standard errors developed by Imai, Kim, and Wang (2019) for statistical inference.

In figure 12-6, we present our main finding based on the difference-in-differences estimator in equation (2): firms increase their lobbying spending after they become an MNC. The estimated effects are positive and become statistically different from zero (the horizontal dashed line) two years after the treatment status change (see $t + 2$ and $t + 3$). The effect size is substan-

FIGURE 12-6. Effects of Multinationality on Lobbying Expenditure

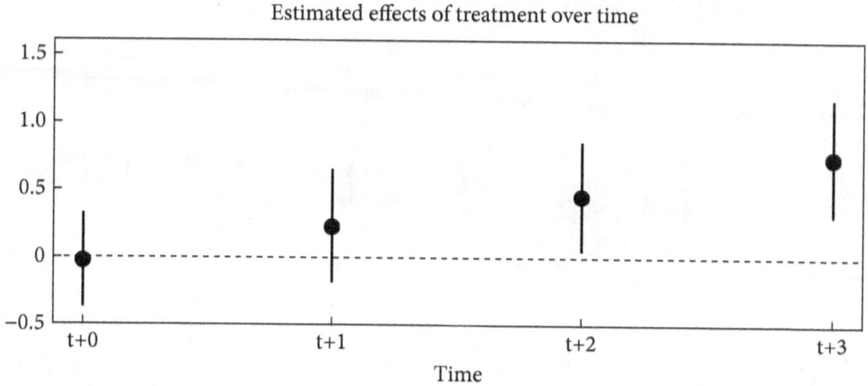

Note: This figure displays the estimated treatment effects of firm's turning to multinational corporation at time *t* on its lobbying expenditure from time *t* to *t* + 3. We find an increase in lobbying expenditure over time. We match firms based on their size, productivity, employment, number of lobbied issues, and the existence of in-house lobbying department.

tively significant as well: we find that firms increase their expenditure about 50 percent (≈ exp(0.4) – 1) two years after becoming a multinational.

Furthermore, we investigate the differences in lobbying for a few firms. We find that AAR Corp (a defense aviation firm) lobbied mostly on Department of Defense appropriations before it became an MNC, but started lobbying also on State Department appropriations in 2016 after becoming an MNC in 2014. Danaher lobbied on Title 1 of Senate bill S.2091 (112th Congress), which deals with tax exemptions for foreign dividends and income in 2012, one year after becoming an MNC. Sysco Corp (a company producing food products) reported that, two years after it became an MNC, it lobbied on the 2013 Farm Bill, H.R. 2393 (114th Congress), which would have repealed the requirement for meat products to be labeled with their country of origin. Similarly, Berkeley W. R. Corp (an insurance company) started lobbying the year it became an MNC in 2011 on "legislation related to tax treatment of underwriting and investment profits of foreign-owned insurance companies." Finally, Pandora Media (a music streaming firm) increased its lobbying spending after becoming an MNC in 2012. In addition to music licensing, it also began to lobby on intellectual property issues, including online copyright infringement and patent litigation. Our findings provide strong evidence that multinationals play important roles in foreign policymaking.

FIGURE 12-7. Effects of Multinationality on the Likelihood of Lobbying on Tariff- and Taxation-related Issues

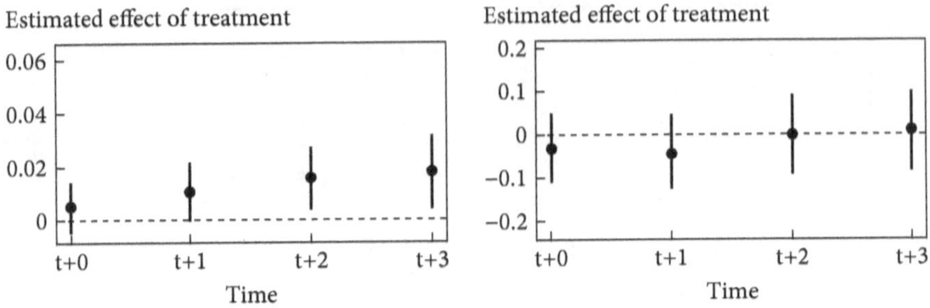

Note: This figure displays the estimated treatment effects of firm's becoming a multinational corporation at time *t* on the likelihood of lobbying on tariff (left panel) and taxation (right panel) policies. We find that multinational firms are more likely to lobby on tariff policies. However, we find limited evidence for an increase in lobbying related to taxation.

We conclude this section by investigating whether certain issues are more likely to be lobbied when firms become MNCs. Table 12-2 sheds light on the finding that MNCs tend to lobby on more issues. Specifically, for each firm that changed status from domestic to multinational, we check the set of *new* issues that are lobbied after firms became multinational. We find that energy/nuclear (ENG), budget/appropriations (BUD), defense (Defense), health issues (HCR), banking (BAN), and foreign relations (FOR) are the most-lobbied issues. This is expected, since the policy issues are related to firms' foreign operations.

To be sure, these issues may be as important for domestic firms as for multinationals. Furthermore, there might be various reasons why certain issues become more or less salient for both domestic and multinational firms in certain industries across time. Thus, we again rely on the difference-in-differences identification strategy to compare the changes in MNCs' lobbying against the changes of lobbying by similar domestic firms in terms of their size, productivity, and lobbying expenses. To minimize the difficulty in distinguishing foreign versus domestic policy, we focus on two specific policy domains that are comparable with each other with differences in their international and domestic focus: (1) tariffs and (2) taxation. Figure 12-7 displays the estimated effects. We find little evidence for any change in lobbying activities on taxation policies. However, we find that firms tended to lobby more on tariff policies once they became multinational, compared with similar domestic firms. In fact, Kim (2017) shows that large and productive firms tend to lobby more on trade-related issues; in addition, he finds that the differentiated products that they produce tend to have lower tariff rates on average. Our findings suggest that more attention should be paid to MNCs' political activities and their direct effects on foreign policymaking.

CONCLUSION

MNCs are economically different from other firms. But do they differ politically? Past research on this topic has been limited for various reasons, one being a lack of systematic data on political activity. Past research points out that MNCs are likely to have distinct preferences on foreign economic policy. As international actors who benefit from access to global markets, they are likely to favor policies that foster an open world economy. Furthermore, they may be more attuned to trying to harmonize regulations across borders. Reducing all costs for global activities is key for them. Moreover, being larger and more productive than most domestic firms, they have more means to try to influence politics. Studies of particular countries, firms, sectors, and issues often reveal the strong influence of MNCs (Vernon (1971); Strange (1991); Sampson (1973); Gereffi (1983); Manger (2012); Osgood (2017); Kim (2017)). But systematic evidence across firms, sectors, and issues has been harder to bring to bear.

This study tries to do this using new data. We first devise a method of identifying firms as multinational versus domestic. After validating this measure, we use it to show that, indeed, those we identify as MNCs have the particular characteristics that economists have noted MNCs should possess: they are larger, more productive, and more export-oriented. Then we show that MNCs spend more on lobbying, and lobby across a more diverse set of issues than do domestic firms. To more closely causally identify this, we also show that when a firm turns multinational, its political activity changes. It becomes more active, lobbying more and over more issues, compared with other firms. Past research has shown that big firms are different politically, but we show that MNCs are even distinct from big domestic firms. MNCs are politically different, as well as economically.

Our study has several important limitations. First, we focus on one form of political activity only: lobbying. As past research shows, firms have many means of exercising influence. We have touched on but one of many. Informal lobbying and connections, bribery, threats of exit or promises of new employment, and campaign contributions and PACs are all unexplored here. We assume that all these influence strategies are complements. But if they are substitutes, then our findings may not approximate the overall activity of MNCs. Second, we focus on individual firm activity and not trade associations. Past research suggests that this individual activity is most common among MNCs and thus more salient for our research. But more research about MNCs' use of industry-wide collective action would be useful. Finally, we focus on the United States alone. But we think that many of our findings are likely to carry over to other countries. As we stated, the U.S. case for MNC influence may be difficult to make, given the United States' well-institutionalized and very divided government. Other countries, smaller and poorer, faced with the resources and capabilities of these large global firms may be even more vulnerable to their pressures and hence more likely to generate MNC political activity.

Do MNCs have outsized influence over politics? And relative to whom? Domestic firms, the public and the median voter, or other interest groups? Our data cannot directly answer this critical question. We can say that MNCs have greater means and seem to use them to exert more influence than other firms, even big domestic ones. But are they more able to convert these means into political success? Again, our data cannot give a direct answer. But the direction of U.S. foreign economic policy in the past decades suggests they have been very powerful. MNCs have championed, and the U.S. government has actively pursued, lowering trade barriers via the General Agreement on Tariffs and Trade and the WTO and various preferential trade agreements, opening capital markets and signing bilateral investment treaties and economic agreements with investment protections, and harmonizing regulations in many areas. MNC preferences, versus those of purely domestic firms, seem to be very congruent with much of recent American foreign economic policy. Rodrik (2018) asserts, for example, that preferential trade agreements are tools for MNCs: "Trade agreements are shaped largely by rent-seeking, self-interested behavior on the export side. Rather than rein in protectionists, they empower another set of special interests and politically well-connected firms, such as international banks, pharmaceutical companies, and multinational corporations" (as cited in Blanga-Gubbay, Conconi, and Parenti (2020, 4)). Indeed, some have said that MNCs are ruling the world, as many nations have adopted similar policies fostering globalization. Notably, MNCs have expressed great concern about Trump administration policies that have rolled back America's support for globalization. Our research, then, may reveal one of the mechanisms for the powerful political influence of these global firms over the years.

NOTES

We thank Thomas Cunningham, Lukas Wolters, and Dominic De Sapio for their excellent research assistance. In Song Kim acknowledges financial support from the National Science Foundation (SES-1725235).

1. Manyika and others (2018) calculated that the top 1 percent of firms with annual revenue greater than US$1 billion source more than 42 percent of total sales from outside their home country.

2. We define an MNC as a corporation that owns or controls production of goods or services in at least two countries. Our definition stems from data availability using Compustat databases (see the subsection "Measuring Multinationality"). Other scholars use different definitions, often ones that focus on the percentage of ownership for subsidiaries abroad, which they obtain from the U.S. Bureau of Economic Analysis (BEA)'s confidential databases.

3. Almost all MNCs export but not all exporters are MNCs.

4. Entry into and exit from exporting is frequent. That is, exporting today is no guarantee of success for the firm in the future.

5. The new, new trade theory focuses on the decisions of individual firms in understanding the causes and consequences of international trade. This theoretical framework was motivated by consistent empirical findings that there exists substantial heterogeneity across firms in their productivity and engagement in trade.

6. See Baumgartner and others (2009) for a debate on this issue.

7. Moreover, workers may follow the preferences and political actions of their firms rather than their industry or union. The heterogeneous effects of globalization on firms in an industry produces heterogeneous effects on workers such that workers employed in larger and more globally competitive firms will more likely support trade, and those in small, uncompetitive firms will more likely oppose trade (Dancygier and Walter (2015)). However, offshoring may complicate this. Workers doing offshorable tasks may be especially opposed to trade if they work at large, globally engaged firms (Rommel and Walter (2018)).

8. Obsolescing bargaining refers to the bargaining between MNCs and a host country whereby the bargaining power of MNCs will be weaker once they have made fixed investment costs.

9. The U.S. Securities and Exchange Commission (SEC) defines foreign income as the income generated from operations outside of the United States that is more than 5 percent of the total income.

10. Dyreng and others (2017) proposes six alternative measures of multinationality.

11. We note two issues. First, the authors claim to report "the natural logarithm of sales," yet they report numbers of 5,000 and more. We suspect these numbers are not logged. Second, they report a total of 39,894 Compustat observations from 1995 to 2011. The Compustat data over that period, however, includes 172,425 observations. The authors report using only those observations for which "relevant variables are non-missing." Thus, we try to replicate their strategy by eliminating observations that have missing data for shareholders' equity (*teq*) and long-term debt (*dltt*), arriving at the comparable number of 41,265 observations.

12. See https://apps.bea.gov/scb/2018/09-september/0918-multinational-enterprises.htm#mnes.

13. Manufacturing accounts for about 37 percent of total sales of all public firms (about US$10 trillion) in the U.S. economy as of 2018. Out of this, about half of the sales are from MNCs.

14. They find that the number increases up to 70 percent in 2012.

15. Many firms either maintain their in-house government affairs offices or work with lobbying firms located on K Street NW in Washington DC.

16. The complete list of lobbying issues is available from https://lda.congress.gov/LD/help/default.htm?turl=Documents%2FAppCodes.htm.

17. The original report is available from https://soprweb.senate.gov/index.cfm?event=getFilingDetails&filingID=234D3211-32EA-4C8E-B4EC-01540AEE2036&filingTypeID=51. Panasonic Corporation of North America does not enter in our empirical analysis below, since we focus on public firms in the United States.

18. We include the existence of in-house lobbying department as a control, because organization expenses using the Lobbying Disclosure Act expense reporting method differs from lobbying firm income. See https://lobbyingdisclosure.house.gov/amended_lda_guide.html for details.

19. Other examples include: OneMain Holdings, formerly known as Springleaf Holdings, acquired OneMain Financial from Citi; Danaher Corp merged with Beckman Coulter, an American company that also operates in Japan. In 2012, it also acquired the British company Naveman Wireless; Jefferies Financial Group (then named Leucadia) merged with Jefferies Group, an American multinational investment bank with operations in Europe and Asia. In 2015, the company made an investment in FXCM, a British firm; Delcath Systems obtained authorization to market and sell one of their products in Europe; MannKind Corp is a pharmaceutical company that has products in clinical trials in the United States and Europe; Boulders Brands purchased Davies Bakery, a British company; InfuSystem Holdings is a medical devices company that currently sells its products and services in the United States and Canada.

20. Based on our measurement strategy, we do not find any firms reverting back to purely domestic.

21. We adjust for past outcomes because past outcomes may affect both the treatment and the current outcome.

22. Mahalanobis distance measures the distance in pretreatment observable characteristics between the treated and the control observations.

REFERENCES

Aisbett, Emma, and Carol McAusland. 2013. "Firm Characteristics and Influence on Government Rule-Making: Theory and Evidence," *European Journal of Political Economy* 29: 214–35.

Akcigit, Ufuk, Salomé Baslandze, and Francesca Lotti. 2018. "Connecting to Power: Political Connections, Innovation, and Firm Dynamics." NBER Working Paper No. 25136, October.

Allee, Todd, and Clint Peinhardt. 2011. "Contingent Credibility: The Impact of Investment Treaty Violations on Foreign Direct Investment." *International Organization*, 65 (3): 401–32.

Alt, James E., Jeffry A. Frieden, Michael J. Gilligan, Dani Rodrik, and Ronald Rogowski. 1996. "The Political Economy of International Trade: Enduring Puzzles and an Agenda for Inquiry," *Comparative Political Studies*, 29 (6): 689–717.

Ansolabehere, Stephen, John M. de Figueiredo, and James M. Snyder. 2003. "Why Is There So Little Money in U.S. Politics?" *Journal of Economic Perspectives*, 17 (February): 105–30.

Austen-Smith, David, and John R. Wright. 1994. "Counteractive Lobbying." *American Journal of Political Science*, 38 (1): 25–44.

Autor, David, David Dorn, Lawrence Katz, Christina Patterson, and John Van Reenen. 2020. "The Fall of the Labor Share and the Rise of Superstar Firms." *The Quarterly Journal of Economics*, 135 (2): 645–709.

Baccini, Leonardo. 2019. "The Economics and Politics of Preferential Trade Agreements," *Annual Review of Political Science*, 22: 75–92.

Baccini, Leonardo, Pablo M. Pinto, and Stephen Weymouth. 2017. "The Distributional Consequences of Preferential Trade Liberalization: Firm-Level Evidence," *International Organization*, 71 (April): 373–95.

Barefoot, Kevin B., and Raymond J. Mataloni Jr. 2011. "Operations of U.S. Multinational Companies in the United States and Abroad," *Survey of Current Business*, 91 (11): 29–48.

Bauer, Raymond Augustine, Ithiel de Sola Pool, and Lewis A. Dexter. 1972. *American Business and Public Policy: The Politics of Foreign Trade*, 2nd ed. (Chicago, Ill.: Aldine-Atherton).

Baumgartner, Frank R., Jeffrey M. Berry, Marie Hojnacki, David C. Kimball, and Beth L. Leech. 2009. *Lobbying and Policy Change: Who Wins, Who Loses, and Why* (University of Chicago Press).

Bernard, Andrew B., J. Bradford Jensen, and Jeffrey J. Schott. 2009. "Importers, Exporters, and Multinationals: A Portrait of Firms in the U.S. that Trade Goods," in *Producer Dynamics: New Evidence from Micro Data*, edited by Timothy Dunne, J. Bradford Jensen, and Mark J. Roberts (University of Chicago Press).

Bernard, Andrew B., J. Bradford Jensen, and Robert Z. Lawrence. 1995. "Exporters, Jobs, and Wages in U.S. Manufacturing: 1976–1987," *Brookings Papers on Economic Activity. Microeconomics* (1995): 67–119.

Bernard, Andrew B., J. Bradford Jensen, Stephen J. Redding, and Peter K. Schott. 2007. "Firms in International Trade," *Journal of Economic Perspectives*, 21 (3): 105–30.

Bertrand, Marianne, Matilde Bombardini, and Francesco Trebbi. 2014. "Is It Whom

You Know or What You Know? An Empirical Assessment of the Lobbying Process," *American Economic Review*, 104 (December): 3885–3920.

Biersteker, Thomas J. 1978. *Distortion of Development? Contending Perspectives on the Multinational Corporation* (MIT Press).

Blanga-Gubbay, Michael, Paola Conconi, and Mathieu Parenti. 2020. "Globalization for Sale," CEPR Discussion Paper No. 14597, Centre for Economic Policy Research, April.

Blonigen, Bruce A., and David N. Figlio. 1998. "Voting for Protection: Does Direct Foreign Investment Influence Legislator Behavior?" *American Economic Review*, 88 (4): 1002–1114.

Boies, John L. 1989. "Money, Business, and the State: Material Interests, Fortune 500 Corporations, and the Size of Political Action Committees," *American Sociological Review*, 54 (5): 821–33.

Bombardini, Matilde, and Francesco Trebbi. 2012. "Competition and Political Organization: Together or Alone in Lobbying for Trade Policy?" *Journal of International Economics*, 87 (1): 18–26.

Brooks, Stephen G. 2005. *Producing Security: Multinational Corporations, Globalization, and the Changing Calculus of Conflict* (Princeton University Press).

Broz, J. Lawrence. 2005. "Congressional Politics of International Financial Rescues," *American Journal of Political Science*, 49 (July): 479–96.

Broz, J. Lawrence, Jeffry Frieden, and Stephen Weymouth. 2008. "Exchange Rate Policy Attitudes: Direct Evidence from Survey Data," *IMF Economic Review*, 55 (3): 417–44.

Broz, J. Lawrence, and Michael Brewster Hawes. 2006. "Congressional Politics of Financing the International Monetary Fund," *International Organization*, 60 (2): 367–99.

Bureau of Economic Analysis. 2018a. "Activities of U.S. Multinational Enterprises: 2016," www.bea.gov/news/2018/activities-us-multinational-enterprises-2016.

Bureau of Economic Analysis. 2018b. "Activities of U.S. Multinational Enterprises: U.S. Parent Companies and Their Foreign Affiliates. Group H. U.S. Parents: U.S. Trade in Goods, Tables I.H 3 and I.H 11," www.bea.gov/international/usdia2016p.

Carpenter, Daniel P. 2004. "Protection without Capture: Product Approval by a Politically Responsive, Learning Regulator," *American Political Science Review*, 98 (4): 613–31.

Cohen, Benjamin J. 1973. *The Question of Imperialism: The Political Economy of Dominance and Dependence* (New York: Basic Books).

Culpepper, Pepper D. 2011. *Quiet Politics and Business Power: Corporate Control in Europe and Japan* (Cambridge University Press).

Dancygier, Rafaela M., and Stefanie Walter. 2015. "Globalization, Labor Market Risks, and Class Cleavages," in *The Politics of Advanced Capitalism*, edited by Pablo Beramendi, Silja Häusermann, Herbert Kitschelt, and Hanspeter Kriesi (Cambridge University Press).

De Bruycker, Iskander, and Jan Beyers. 2018. "Lobbying Makes (Strange) Bedfellows: Explaining the Formation and Composition of Lobbying Coalitions in EU Legislative Politics," *Political Studies*, 66 (4): 959–84.

de Figueiredo, John M., and Brian Kelleher Richter. 2014. "Advancing the Empirical Research on Lobbying," *Annual Review of Political Science*, 17 (May): 163–85.

Dellis, Konstantinos, and David Sondermann. 2017. "Lobbying in Europe: New Firm-Level Evidence," ECB Working Paper No. 2071, European Central Bank, June.

Denzau, Arthur T., and Michael C Munger. 1986. "Legislators and Interest Groups: How Unorganized Interests Get Represented," *American Political Science Review*, 80 (1): 89–106.

Doms, Mark E., and J. Bradford Jensen. 1998. "Comparing Wages, Skills, and Productivity between Domestically and Foreign-Owned Manufacturing Establishments in the United States," in *Geography and Ownership as Bases for Economic Accounting*, edited by Robert E. Baldwin, Robert E. Lipsey, and J. David Richards (University of Chicago Press).

Drope, Jeffrey M., and Wendy L. Hansen. 2006. "Does Firm Size Matter? Analyzing Business Lobbying in the United States," *Business and Politics*, 8 (August): 1–17.

Drutman, Lee. 2015. *The Business of America Is Lobbying: How Corporations Became Politicized and Politics Became More Corporate* (Oxford University Press).

Dür, Andreas, Leonardo Baccini, and Manfred Elsig. 2014. "The Design of International Trade Agreements: Introducing a New Dataset," *Review of International Organizations* 9 (3): 353–75.

Dyreng, Scott D., Michelle Hanlon, Edward L. Maydew, and Jacob R. Thornock. 2017. "Changes in Corporate Effective Tax Rates over the Past 25 Years," *Journal of Financial Economics*, 124 (3): 441–63.

Eden, Lorraine, and Maureen Appel Molot. 2002. "Insiders, Outsiders and Host Country Bargains," *Journal of International Management* 8 (4): 359–88.

Eden, Lorraine, Stefanie Lenway, and Douglas A. Schuler. 2005. "From the Obsolescing Bargain to the Political Bargaining Model," in *International Business and Government Relations in the Twenty-First Century*, edited by Robert Grosse (Cambridge University Press).

Ehrlich, Sean D. 2007. "Access to Protection: Domestic Institutions and Trade Policy in Democracies," *International Organization*, 61 (3): 571–605.

Ehrlich, Sean D. 2008. "The Tariff and the Lobbyist: Political Institutions, Interest Group Politics, and U.S. Trade Policy," *International Studies Quarterly*, 52 (June): 427–45.

Evans, Peter B. 1979. *Dependent Development: The Alliance of Multinational, State, and Local Capital in Brazil* (Princeton University Press).

Faccio, Mara. 2006. "Politically Connected Firms," *American Economic Review*, 96 (February): 369–86.

Faulkender, Michael, and Jason M. Smith. 2016. "Taxes and Leverage at Multinational Corporations," *Journal of Financial Economics*, 122 (1): 1–20.

Fisman, Raymond. 2001. "Estimating the Value of Political Connections," *American Economic Review*, 91 (4): 1095–1102.

Frieden, Jeffry A. 1991. *Debt, Development, and Democracy: Modern Political Economy and Latin America, 1965–1985* (Princeton University Press).

Gartzke, Erik. 2007. "The Capitalist Peace," *American Journal of Political Science*, 51 (1): 166–91.

Gereffi, Gary. 1983. *The Pharmaceutical Industry and Dependency in the Third World* (Princeton University Press).

Gertz, Geoffrey. 2018. "Commercial Diplomacy and Political Risk," *International Studies Quarterly*, 62: 107–15.

Gillespie, John S. 2006. *Transplanting Commercial Law Reform: Developing a "Rule of Law" in Vietnam* (Burlington, Vt.: Ashgate Publishing Company).

Gilligan, Michael J. 1997. "Lobbying as a Private Good with Intra-Industry Trade," *International Studies Quarterly*, 41 (September): 455–74.

Gilpin, Robert. 1975. *U.S. Power and the Multinational Corporation: The Political Economy of Foreign Direct Investment* (New York: Basic Books).

Gordon, Sanford C., and Catherine Hafer. 2005. "Flexing Muscle: Corporate Political Expenditures as Signals to the Bureaucracy," *American Political Science Review*, 99: 245–61.

Grier, Kevin B., Michael C. Munger, and Brian E. Roberts. 1994. "The Determinants of Industry Political Activity, 1978–1986," *American Political Science Review*, 88 (4): 911–26.

Grossman, Gene, and Elhanan Helpman. 1994. "Protection for Sale," *American Economic Review*, 84 (4): 833–50.

Hafner-Burton, Emilie M., Thad Kousser, and David G. Victor. 2015. "Lobbying at the Water's Edge: Corporations and Congressional Foreign Policy Lobbying," ILAR Working Paper No. 22, University of California, San Diego, Laboratory on International Law and Regulation, School of Global Policy and Strategy, July.

Hanegraaff, Marcel, Caelesta Braun, Dirk De Bièvre, and Jan Beyers. 2015. "The Domestic and Global Origins of Transnational Advocacy," *Comparative Political Studies*, 48 (October): 1591–1621.

Hansen, Wendy L., and Neil J. Mitchell. 2000. "Disaggregating and Explaining Corporate Political Activity: Domestic and Foreign Corporations in National Politics," *American Political Science Review*, 94 (December): 891–903.

Hansen, Wendy L., Neil J. Mitchell, and Jeffrey M. Drope. 2004. "Collective Action, Pluralism, and the Legitimacy Tariff: Corporate Activity or Inactivity in Politics," *Political Research Quarterly*, 57 (September): 421–29.

Helleiner, Eric. 2011. "Understanding the 2007–2008 Global Financial Crisis: Lessons for Scholars of International Political Economy," *Annual Review of Political Science*, 14: 67–87.

Henisz, Witold J. 2000. "The Institutional Environment for Multinational Investment," *Journal of Law, Economics, and Organization*, 16 (2): 334–64.

Henisz, Witold J., and Bennet A. Zelner. 2005. "Legitimacy, Interest Group Pressures, and Change in Emergent Institutions: The Case of Foreign Investors and Host Country Governments," *Academy of Management Review*, 30 (2): 361–82.

Henisz, Witold J., and Oliver E. Williamson. 1999. "Comparative Economic Organization—Within and Between Countries," *Business and Politics*, 1 (3): 261–77.

Hillman, Amy J., Asghar Zardkoohi, and Leonard Bierman. 1999. "Corporate Political Strategies and Firm Performance: Indications of Firm-Specific Benefits from Personal Service in the U.S. Government," *Strategic Management Journal*, 20 (January): 67–81.

Hiscox, Michael J. 2002. "Commerce, Coalitions, and Factor Mobility: Evidence from Congressional Votes on Trade Legislation," *American Political Science Review*, 96 (3): 593–608.

Huneeus, Federico, and In Song Kim. 2018. "The Effects of Firms' Lobbying on Resource Misallocation," University of Massachusetts, October 29, www.internationalpoliticaleconomysociety.org/sites/default/files/paper-uploads/2018-10-29-21_44_53-insong@mit.edu.pdf.

Igan, Deniz, Prachi Mishra, and Thierry Tressel. 2012. "A Fistful of Dollars: Lobbying and the Financial Crisis," *NBER Macroeconomics Annual*, 26 (January): 195–230.

Imai, Kosuke, In Song Kim, and Erik Wang. 2019. "Matching Methods for Causal Inference with Time-Series Cross-Section Data," Massachusetts Institute of Technology, March 3, http://web.mit.edu/ insong/www/pdf/tscs.pdf.

Jacobs, Lawrence R., and Benjamin I. Page. 2005. "Who Influences U.S. Foreign Policy?" *American Political Science Review*, 99 (1): 107–23.

Jensen, J. Bradford, Dennis P. Quinn, and Stephen Weymouth. 2015. "The Influence of Firm Global Supply Chains and Foreign Currency Undervaluations on U.S. Trade Disputes," *International Organization*, 69 (4): 913–47.

Jensen, Nathan, Glen Biglaiser, Quan Li, and Edmund Malesky. 2012. *Politics and Foreign Direct Investment* (University of Michigan Press).

Jensen, Nathan M. 2003. "Democratic Governance and Multinational Corporations: Political Regimes and Inflows of Foreign Direct Investment," *International Organization*, 57 (3): 587–616.

Johns, Leslie, Krzysztof J. Pelc, and Rachel L. Wellhausen. 2019. "How a Retreat from Global Economic Governance May Empower Business Interests," *Journal of Politics*, 81 (2): 731–38.

Johns, Leslie, and Rachel L. Wellhausen. 2016. "Under One Roof: Supply Chains and the Protection of Foreign Investment," *American Political Science Review*, 110 (1): 31–51.

Junk, Wiebke Marie. 2019. "When Diversity Works: The Effects of Coalition Composition on the Success of Lobbying Coalitions," *American Journal of Political Science*, 63: 660–74.

Kerr, Sari Pekkala, William Kerr, Çağlar Özden, and Christopher Parsons. 2017. "High-Skilled Migration and Agglomeration," *Annual Review of Economics*, 9 (August): 201–34.

Kerr, William R., William F. Lincoln, and Prachi Mishra. 2014. "The Dynamics of Firm Lobbying," *American Economic Journal: Economic Policy*, 6 (November): 343–79.

Kim, In Song. 2017. "Political Cleavages within Industry: Firm-Level Lobbying for Trade Liberalization," *American Political Science Review*, 111 (1): 1–20.

Kim, In Song. 2018. "LobbyView: Firm-Level Lobbying and Congressional Bills Database," Massachusetts Institute of Technology, August 30, http://web.mit.edu/insong/www/pdf/lobbyview.pdf.

Kim, In Song, Helen V. Milner, Thomas Bernauer, Iain Osgood, Gabriele Spilker, and Dustin Tingley. 2019. "The Charmed Life of Superstar Exporters: Survey Evidence on Firms and Trade Policy," *International Studies Quarterly*, 63 (1): 153–67.

Kim, In Song, and Iain Osgood. 2019. "Firms in Trade and Trade Politics," *Annual Review of Political Science*, 22: 399–417.

Kim, Soo Yeon. 2015. "Deep Integration and Regional Trade Agreements," in *The Oxford Handbook of the Political Economy of International Trade*, edited by Lisa L. Martin (Oxford University Press).

Kim, Soo Yeon, and Gabriele Spilker. 2019. "Global Value Chains and the Political Economy of WTO Disputes," *Review of International Organizations*, 14 (2): 239–60.

Kirschner, Jonathan. 2007. *Appeasing Bankers: Financial Caution on the Road to War* (Princeton University Press).

Kollman, Ken. 1998. *Outside Lobbying: Public Opinion and Interest Group Strategies* (Princeton University Press).

Krasner, Stephen D. 1978. *Defending the National Interest: Raw Materials Investments and U.S. Foreign Policy* (Princeton University Press).

Lall, Ranjit. 2012. "From Failure to Failure: The Politics of International Banking Regulation," *Review of International Political Economy*, 19 (4): 609–38.

Lee, Haillie Na-Kyung. 2019. "Why Arbitrate? The Role of State in Investor-State Arbitration," International Political Economy Society, November 15.

Lee, Jieun. 2018. "Foreign Direct Investment in Political Influence," International Political Economy Society, October 28.

Levy, David L., and Aseem Prakash. 2003. "Bargains Old and New: Multinational Corporations in Global Governance," *Business and Politics*, 5 (2): 131–50.

Li, Quan, and Adam Resnick. 2003. "Reversal of Fortunes: Democratic Institutions and Foreign Direct Investment to Developing Countries," *International Organization*, 57 (1): 175–211.

Li, Quan, and Rafael Reuveny. 2003. "Economic Globalization and Democracy: An Empirical Analysis," *British Journal of Political Science*, 33 (1): 29–54.

Lindblom, Charles E. 1977. *Politics and Markets: The World's Political-Economic Systems* (New York: Basic Books).

Lipson, Charles. 1985. *Standing Guard: Protecting Foreign Capital in the Nineteenth and Twentieth Centuries* (University of California Press).

Luo, Yadong. 2001. "Toward a Cooperative View of MNC-Host Government Relations: Building Blocks and Performance Implications," *Journal of International Business Studies*, 32 (3): 401–19.

Malesky, Edmund J. 2008. "Straight Ahead on Red: How Foreign Direct Investment Empowers Subnational Leaders," *Journal of Politics*, 70 (1): 97–119.

Malesky, Edmund J. 2009. "Foreign Direct Investors as Agents of Economic Transition: An Instrumental Variables Analysis," *Quarterly Journal of Political Science*, 4 (1): 59–85.

Malik, Rabia, and Randall W. Stone. 2018. "Corporate Influence in World Bank Lending," *Journal of Politics*, 80 (January): 103–18.

Manger, Mark S. 2009. *Investing in Protection: The Politics of Preferential Trade Agreements between North and South* (Cambridge University Press).

Manger, Mark S. 2012. "Vertical Trade Specialization and the Formation of North-South PTAs," *World Politics*, 64 (4): 622–58.

Manyika, James, Sree Ramaswamy, Jacques Bughin, Jonathan Woetzel, Michael Birshan, and Zubin Nagpal. 2018. "Superstars the Dynamics of Firms, Sectors, and Cities Leading the Global Economy," McKinsey Global Institute Discussion Paper, October.

McDonald, Patrick J. 2009. *The Invisible Hand of Peace: Capitalism, the War Machine, and International Relations* (Cambridge University Press).

Meyer, Breed D. 1995. "Natural and Quasi-Experiments in Economics," *Journal of Business & Economic Statistics*, 13 (2): 151–61.

Milner, Helen V. 1988. *Resisting Protectionism: Global Industries and the Politics of International Trade* (Princeton University Press).

Milyo, Jeffrey, David Primo, and Timothy Groseclose. 2000. "Corporate PAC Campaign Contributions in Perspective," *Business and Politics*, 2 (April): 75–88.

Mitchell, Neil J., Wendy L. Hansen, and Eric M. Jepsen. 1997. "The Determinants of Domestic and Foreign Corporate Political Activity," *Journal of Politics*, 59 (November): 1096–1113.

Mizruchi, Mark S. 2013. *The Fracturing of the American Corporate Elite* (Harvard University Press).

Moran, Theodore H. 1973. "Transnational Strategies of Protection and Defense by Multinational Corporations: Spreading the Risk and Raising the Cost for Nationalization in Natural Resources," *International Organization*, 27 (2): 273–87.

Moran, Theodore H. 1978. "Multinational Corporations and Dependency: A Dialogue for Dependentistas and Non-Dependentistas," *International Organization*, 32 (1): 79–100.

Mosley, Layna, and Saika Uno. 2007. "Racing to the Bottom or Climbing to the Top? Economic Globalization and Collective Labor Rights," *Comparative Political Studies*, 40 (8): 923–48.

Naoi, Megumi, and Ellis Krauss. 2009. "Who Lobbies Whom? Special Interest Politics under Alternative Electoral Systems," *American Journal of Political Science*, 53 (4): 874–92.

Nelson, David, and Susan Webb Yackee. 2012. "Lobbying Coalitions and Government Policy Change: An Analysis of Federal Agency Rulemaking," *Journal of Politics*, 74 (2): 339–53.

Nose, Manabu. 2014. "Triggers of Contract Breach: Contract Design, Shocks, or Institutions?" World Bank, Policy Research Working Paper. No. WPS6738, January.

Nye, Joseph S. 1974. "Multinational Corporations in World Politics," *Foreign Affairs*, 53 (1): 153–75.

OECD. 2018. "Multinational Enterprises in the Global Economy: Heavily Debated but Hardly Measured," policy note (May). Available from www.oecd.org/industry/ind/MNEs-in- the-global-economy-policy-note.pdf.

Osgood, Iain. 2017. "The Breakdown of Industrial Opposition to Trade: Firms, Product Variety, and Reciprocal Liberalization," *World Politics*, 69 (January): 184–231.

Osgood, Iain. 2019. "Vanguards of Globalization: Attitudes and Political Action among America's Pro-Trade Firms," *Business and Politics*, 1–35.

Osgood, Iain, Dustin Tingley, Thomas Bernauer, In Song Kim, Helen V. Milner, and Gabriele Spilker. 2017. "The Charmed Life of Superstar Exporters: Survey Evidence on Firms and Trade Policy," *Journal of Politics*, 79 (January): 133–52.

Peters, Margaret E. 2017. *Trading Barriers: Immigration and the Remaking of Globalization* (Princeton University Press).

Pierce, Justin R., and Peter K. Schott. 2020. "Trade Liberalization and Mortality: Evidence from U.S. Counties," *American Economic Review: Insights*, 2 (March): 47–64.

Pinto, Pablo. 2013. *Partisan Investment in the Global Economy: Why the Left Loves Foreign Direct Investment and FDI Loves the Left* (Cambridge University Press).

Pinto, Pablo M., and Santiago M. Pinto. 2008. "The Politics of Investment Partisanship: And the Sectoral Allocation of Foreign Direct Investment," *Economics and Politics*, 20 (2): 216–54.

Plouffe, Michael. 2017. "Firm Heterogeneity and Trade-Policy Stances: Evidence from a Survey of Japanese Producers," *Business and Politics*, 19 (March): 1–40.

Prakash, Aseem, and Jeffrey A. Hart. 1999. "Globalization and Governance: An Introduction," in *Globalization and Governance*, edited by Aseem Prakash and Jeffrey A. Hart (London: Routledge).

Prakash, Aseem, and Matthew Potoski. 2007. "Investing Up: FDI and the Cross-Country Diffusion of ISO 14001 Management Systems," *International Studies Quarterly*, 51 (3): 723–44.

Pyle, William. 2006. "Collective Action and Post-Communist Enterprise: The Economic Logic of Russia's Business Associations," *Europe-Asia Studies*, 58 (June): 491–521.

Ray, Dennis M. 1972. "Corporations and American Foreign Relations," *Annals of the American Academy of Political and Social Science*, 403 (1): 80–92.

Rodrik, Dani. 2018. "What Do Trade Agreements Really Do?" *Journal of Economic Perspectives*, 32 (May): 73–90.

Rommel, Tobias, and Stefanie Walter. 2018. "The Electoral Consequences of Offshoring: How the Globalization of Production Shapes Party Preferences," *Comparative Political Studies*, 51 (5): 621–58.

Rudra, Nita. 2005. "Globalization and the Strengthening of Democracy in the Developing World," *American Journal of Political Science*, 49 (4): 704–30.

Salacuse, Jeswald W. 2010. "The Emerging Global Regime for Investment," *Harvard International Law Journal*, 51: 427–74.

Sampson, Anthony. 1973. *The Sovereign State of ITT* (New York: Stein and Day).

Simmons, Beth A. 2014. "Bargaining over BITs, Arbitrating Awards: The Regime for Protection and Promotion of International Investment," *World Politics*, 66 (1): 12–16.

Slaughter, Matthew J. 2004. "Skill Upgrading in Developing Countries: Has Inward Foreign Direct Investment Played a Role?" in *Labor and the Globalization of Production*, edited by William Milberg (London: Palgrave Macmillan U.K.).

Staley, Eugene. 1935. *War and the Private Investor: A Study in the Relations of International Politics and International Private Investment* (Garden City, N.J.: Doubleday, Doran & Co.).

Stopford, John M., and Susan Strange. 1991. *Rival States, Rival Firms: Competition for World Market Shares* (Cambridge University Press).

Strange, Susan. 1991. "Big Business and the State," *Millennium*, 20 (2): 245–50.

Strange, Susan. 1996. *The Retreat of the State: The Diffusion of Power in the World Economy* (Cambridge University Press).

Tomiura, Eiichi. 2007. "Foreign Outsourcing, Exporting, and FDI: A Productivity Comparison at the Firm Level," *Journal of International Economics*, 72 (May): 113–27.

Truex, Rory. 2014. "The Returns to Office in a 'Rubber Stamp' Parliament," *American Political Science Review*, 108 (2): 235–51.

Vernon, Raymond. 1971. *Sovereignty at Bay* (New York: Basic Books).

Vernon, Raymond. 1980. "The Obsolescing Bargain: A Key Factor in Political Risk," in *The International Essays for Business Decisionmakers*, edited by Mark B. Winchester, vol. 5 (Houston, Tex.: Center for International Business).

Vernon, Raymond, and Deborah Spar. 1989. *Beyond Globalism: Remaking American Foreign Economic Policy* (New York: Free Press).

Vogel, David J. 1996. "The Study of Business and Politics," *California Management Review*, 38 (3): 146–65.

Walker, Edward T., and Christopher M. Rea. 2014. "The Political Mobilization of Firms and Industries," *Annual Review of Sociology*, 40 (July): 281–304.

Wellhausen, Rachel L. 2014. *The Shield of Nationality: When Governments Break Contracts with Foreign Firms* (Cambridge University Press).

Yeaple, Stephen Ross. 2009. "Firm Heterogeneity and the Structure of U.S. Multinational Activity," *Journal of International Economics*, 78 (July): 206–15.

Yildirim, Aydin B. 2018. "Firms' Integration into Value Chains and Compliance with Adverse WTO Panel Rulings," *World Trade Review*, 17 (1): 1–31.

Young, Kevin L. 2012. "Transnational Regulatory Capture? An Empirical Examination of the Transnational Lobbying of the Basel Committee on Banking Supervision," *Review of International Political Economy*, 19 (4): 663–88.

13

Principles for Policymakers

C. FRITZ FOLEY
JAMES R. HINES JR.
DAVID WESSEL

Multinational corporations are global goliaths, but they have not conquered the world, nor are they responsible for every economic ill, as is sometimes alleged. These firms contribute to global prosperity by improving productivity and efficiency, innovating, and creating jobs—mostly good jobs—in both home and host countries. Governments lavish attention on multinational corporations, seeking the good that accompanies their investments even as policymakers worry about the influence multinational firms have on the local environment, social conditions, and politics. In this regard, governments face the tradeoffs that commonly afflict economic policymaking. Efforts to control the actions of multinational firms typically come at the cost of reduced investment, thereby reducing the contributions of these firms to local economies. This tradeoff is particularly stark when, as is often the case, governments compete with each other to attract multinational firms.

Multinational corporations also have substantial market and political power that they can, and often do, use to reduce their tax bills, thwart competitors, and influence regulation, legislation, and trade agreements to their particular advantage. To promote the general welfare, governments should and do monitor their activities and, when appropriate, regulate them by national rules and laws and by international agreements. Drawing from the available evidence in this volume and elsewhere, this chapter offers several principles for public policy toward multinational corporations. Our objective is to encourage policymakers to protect and, indeed, encourage those activities of multinational corporations that contribute to rising living standards around the world while restraining activities that thwart competition or exacerbate social ills and inequities. This chapter represents the views only of its three authors, not other contributors to this volume—although it does draw on their work.

PRINCIPLE 1: Governments should avoid erecting barriers to realizing benefits that multinational corporations offer modern economies. They should avoid tariffs, punitive regulations, and taxes directed at foreigners, and other restrictions on the movement of goods, people, investment, and data across borders.

Multinational corporations contribute to investment, innovation, employment, productivity, and other dimensions of economic performance by integrating their operations throughout the world. The economic benefits created by these firms accrue to countries rich and poor, notwithstanding certain multinational practices in low-income countries and the economic harm suffered by some workers and communities in high-income countries.

The prosperity of high-income economies relies on multinational firms, whose international operations enhance capital and labor productivity. Much multinational production still occurs in high-income countries, belying the caricature of the modern multinational as choosing only the lowest-cost production locations. As colorfully described by Davies and Markusen in chapter 2 in this volume, typical multinational production is less like a snake that moves production along a value chain from one low-cost location to another and more like an octopus, reaching out to perform similar activities in multiple locations across the globe, often to serve local markets. Evidence offered in chapter 6 in this volume by Oldenski shows that when a U.S. multinational expands its employment abroad, it typically, though not always, expands employment in the United States. Consequently, efforts by governments to prevent their resident multinational firms from investing abroad are unlikely to improve economic conditions either at home or abroad.

Multinational corporations depend on the free movement of goods, services, ideas, people, and data. International operations function most smoothly when firms can draw on resources available elsewhere. The multinational business model, which relies on deploying firm-specific capital and internal transactions to create value in multiple locations simultaneously, is impossible to implement properly without fluid movement. Governments that create barriers at their borders throw sand in the gears of this otherwise highly functioning economic machine, and in the process do their economies significant harm. Governments often are tempted to limit the penetration of foreign multinational firms in their economies, in efforts to preserve the competitive positions of domestic companies to maintain their employment and as bulwarks against monopoly; in fact, openness to foreign direct investment may be the best way to create good jobs, spread innovation, and spur market competition.

Claims that national security concerns justify imposing limits on multinational investment and restrictions on research activities of multinational firms, including whom they employ, require careful and skeptical scrutiny. Multinationals creating particularly advanced technologies in certain strategic sectors, such as communications and defense, could face situations in which their commercial interests conflict with national security interests, and these situations create needs for policies and processes that would then limit the actions of multinational firms. But these are unusual situations, whereas there are apt to be many such claims by those seeking to limit market competition in order to benefit from protection.

For all of the employment, investment, R&D, and other economic contributions that multinationals make, many countries have not fully realized the potential economic benefits of multinational operations. Lower-income countries, in particular, do not currently attract the investment and employment levels of higher-income economies. Yet it is in less affluent economies that multinational firms have the greatest ability to contribute to economic welfare, since the employment opportunities, economic openness, and exposure to the rest of the world that they foster can be extremely valuable if properly managed.

PRINCIPLE 2: Governments and multinational corporations should adopt policies and practices that ensure that all segments of society benefit from the activities of multinational corporations and from globalization more generally.

While the net effects of the activities of multinational corporations, and globalization more generally, are positive, there are costs. These costs are disproportionately borne, at least in developed countries, by less educated workers, particularly those who perform routine tasks that are easily moved offshore or automated. Within countries, this has contributed to a worrisome increase in inequality in recent decades. At the same time, labor's share of income—both in the United States and globally—has declined, and many measures of median income and wages have stagnated. Globalization and the activities of multinational corporations are not the only factors driving these trends, but they have played a role. For all the discussion of "compensating the losers," efforts that have been made in the United States through Trade Adjustment Assistance and worker training programs have been inadequate. The regional economic dislocation associated with abrupt plant closures or imports of low-cost foreign goods can be severe, even if more than offset by gains elsewhere in the economy.

The solutions involve spending more money and spending it more wisely and creatively, and in experimenting with such programs as wage insurance, flexible training subsidies, and other measures targeted at individuals and communities who have not enjoyed the benefits of globalization. Multinational corporations and their executives should support—and be willing to pay taxes to help finance—such public efforts. Moreover, multinational corporations need to invest more in training to better equip their employees to cope with a rapidly changing economy.

The pain borne by individuals, families, and entire communities is reason enough to pursue different policies, but it also threatens the post–World War II political consensus that produced decades of peace and rising living standards around the world. Governments that stand idle in the face of such severe economic pain risk popular backlash. Multinational corporations that do not assume responsibility for their actions—that do not identify and remedy the unwelcome side effects of their actions—not only betray the standards they publicly proclaim for themselves and risk vilification, but also undermine support for economic policies from which they benefit, fuel the rise of populist politicians, and put their future prosperity at risk. As the Business Roundtable noted in updating its "statement on the purpose of a corporation," the stakeholders of a corporation are not only their shareholders, but also their customers, employees, suppliers, and communities.[1]

Public opinion plays an important role in determining economic policies in democratic societies. Over time, public attitudes about multinational corporations have soured. In the United States, the Gallup Organization's annual survey finds that in the 1970s, an average of 31 percent of respondents reported having either a "great deal" or "quite a lot" of confidence in big business. By the 2010s, the fraction reporting these favorable opinions had fallen to an average of 21 percent. In this environment, it can be challenging for democratic governments to strike arrangements conducive to extensive multinational investment, notwithstanding the economic benefits such investment may bring. Multinational corporations that ignore this deterioration of public trust put themselves at risk of policies that will not only hurt their profits but restrain their capacity to innovate and improve global productivity.

In developing countries, as Aisbett and others note in chapter 7 in this volume, there is evidence that multinational corporations violate workers' rights, including discriminating by gender and preventing workers from organizing unions. This suggests that managements of multinational corporations everywhere need to address the conditions of those they employ around the world and those who work for companies on whose labor they depend, and that governments need to consider working conditions when they strike global trade agreements.

PRINCIPLE 3: Governments should cooperate to formulate consistent, cohesive policy frameworks because what happens in one place influences what happens elsewhere. These policy frameworks should respect the right of sovereign nations to reflect the preferences and needs of their people.

To this end, policymakers should strengthen multilateral institutions that regulate international trade and investment, fixing their shortcomings and adapting them to the evolving global economy. Trade and investment disputes should be resolved more quickly. Trade rules should be extended to cover a broader set of services, and policies should be written to account for the growth of e-commerce. Guidelines on the appropriate role of government in promoting and supporting businesses should be negotiated. International investment and trade regulations that serve favored corporate interests but do not promote general economic welfare should be removed.

Because they span country borders, multinational firms can transmit economic shocks from one part of the world to others. National regulators must, therefore, remain aware of their country's exposure to policy actions and economic conditions elsewhere. For example, lax financial regulation in one country can increase the fragility of the banking systems of others. Policymakers should incorporate insights related to these transmission mechanisms and coordinate efforts to make global systems more robust.

There is also a need for greater coordination of antitrust policy. Many large firms that face accusations of engaging in anticompetitive practices are multinational firms. But antitrust authorities in different jurisdictions have divergent regulations and objectives. This diversity is further complicated when governments choose to support and subsidize national champions in some industries. Authorities should cooperate when collecting and analyzing evidence of anticompetitive behavior. Basic questions regarding how to define the boundaries of a relevant market are complicated in an international context, because even just the threat of foreign competition can affect behavior. Antitrust issues are particularly nettlesome in parts of the technology sector that are subject to large economies of scale and network externalities that make a network more valuable if more people are connected to it. Furthermore, many offerings in this sector can be accessed from anywhere. These features require a coordinated approach to determine what regulations should be applied and what constitutes evidence of inappropriate behavior.

Climate change presents an enormous challenge. No matter how much one company or one country does to reduce emissions, it cannot effectively reduce the dangers of climate change unless other companies and other countries join in the effort. Public policy can and should find ways to make private actors shoulder the cost of their contributions to greenhouse gas emissions; the obvious options include carbon taxes and cap-and-trade permit systems. Multinational corporations, many of which have announced climate-related goals, can and should support and help design such government efforts. National governments—and multilateral organizations—should use their leverage to get other governments to cooperate in what must be a global effort.

PRINCIPLE 4: Innovation is an important contributor to prosperity, so governments should pursue policies that encourage multinational corporations to pursue innovations and share the benefits with the world.

Innovation is a critical driver of economic growth and the accompanying rising living standards around the world. The process of innovation has become more global over recent decades. Multinational corporations are major innovators, and their efforts are the products of contributions by the best minds from every part of the world, rich and poor countries alike. As chapter 8 in this volume, by Branstetter, Glennon, and Jensen, illustrates, the rise of economic nationalism, the aggressive use of tariffs, the opposition to immigration, and new restrictions on cross-border flows of data all threaten to limit rates of innovation and adoption of new goods and ideas. Therefore, policies that enable the general operations of multinationals—policies that support the free flow of goods, services, human capital, and data—also are essential to supporting innovative activity. Innovations are often embodied in goods like new scientific equipment, and trade in these goods allows innovations to spread, facilitating further innovation. Immigration of highly educated foreign nationals, many of whom came to the United States for college or graduate school, plays a significant role in innovation that occurs within the United States; other countries have similar experiences. This role of immigration calls for legislation making it easier for foreign students to obtain work visas upon graduation. Policies that make it harder for foreign individuals to stay in the United States would impede research and, in turn, induce U.S. multinationals to locate more of their innovative activity abroad.

Strong and strictly enforced intellectual property rights are essential to provide incentives for multinationals to invest in innovation. Such rights also give multinationals comfort in transferring technology to their foreign affiliates and in shifting research and development efforts abroad. While governments should commit to defending intellectual property rights, there are limits to how far these rights should extend. Corporations can abuse the patent system, protecting monopoly profits far beyond the period of exclusivity required to provide incentives for innovation. Governments should limit the ability of patent trolls to obtain intellectual property rights in a manner that limits innovation. And policy should ensure that innovations such as life-saving drugs are widely accessible even in markets where income levels might limit their availability.

PRINCIPLE 5: Governments should forge consensus on principles governing the taxation of multinational corporations.

Governments struggle in their efforts to craft appropriate taxes on multinational corporations amid widespread concern that multinational corporations pay very little in taxes, manipulate their accounting to exploit tax havens, and thereby starve governments of badly needed revenue. As chapter 10, by Dyreng and Hanlon, and chapter 11, by Dharmapala, in this volume indicate, firms do structure their affairs in ways that reduce their tax liabilities, but the more spectacular claims of lost tax revenue have flimsy empirical support and are inconsistent with the reality that multinational firms collectively pay considerable taxes. Both chapters note that self-help is not the only source of multinational tax reduction. Over time, governments have reduced their tax rates and enacted other tax provisions designed to make their countries attractive locations for multinational firms, including by a reluctance to adopt measures that would diminish the impact of tax-haven operations.

Governments need tax revenue and feel pressure from reform advocates and domestic business and labor lobbies, all of which argue for heavier taxation of multinationals; but they are also lobbied by multinational corporations and are loath to risk losing the employment, productivity, and other benefits that multinationals bring. Furthermore, there is conflict between governments, which frequently disagree over which country has the right to tax profits made by firms whose operations lie in many countries—and whether certain types of taxes are legitimate under international agreements. The governments of multinational home countries often bristle at taxes imposed by countries where their multinationals have operations, the most recent prominent example being the U.S. reaction to digital taxes imposed by several other countries that are alarmed by the rising presence of U.S. digital firms described by Edelman in chapter 9 in this volume.

All countries stand to benefit from establishing agreement over principles that govern the taxation of multinational corporations. These principles should identify the types of taxes covered and identify in which countries, and under what circumstances, governments have rights to tax income. This does not entail agreement over tax rates but instead over taxing authority—and, in particular, the extent to which income is appropriately subject to taxation by the countries in which multinationals are based and the countries in which they have foreign operations. In the present environment, it is often unclear whether and to what extent firms earn income, and when they do, where the income was earned and to what extent it may have been taxed. Too frequently, countries feel that they are missing out on tax revenue that is legitimately theirs, which puts them in conflict with taxpayers and other governments, and drives them to consider expedients that do not represent sound policy. With agreed-upon principles, each country can better understand the scope of its legitimate taxing authority, cooperate with other governments in enforcing its taxes, and make reasoned choices over appropriate levels of taxation, given all the tradeoffs that taxing business income inevitably entails.

PRINCIPLE 6: Governments should invest in collecting more and better data about the activities of multinational corporations.

The availability of reliable and robust data is a necessary, albeit not sufficient, condition for good policy and for informing a public debate that is too often influenced by anecdotes. This volume relies heavily on data compiled by the U.S. Commerce Department's Bureau of Economic Analysis. These data are unique in their coverage of the financial and operating activities of multinational parent firms as well as each of their foreign affiliates. They cover U.S.-based multinationals and foreign-based multinationals with interests in the United States. Very few countries dedicate resources to conducting surveys of multinationals operating within their borders, making it hard to understand these firms, never mind regulate them. U.S. data collection efforts face threats of budget cuts that would raise reporting thresholds and reduce the extensiveness of reporting. It is imperative that statistical agencies receive the resources they need to measure the activities of multinationals; policy makers, business managers, and the general public depend on it.

In response to the OECD Base Erosion and Profit Shifting Project, many countries are introducing legislation that requires firms to provide tax authorities with country-by-country reports of financial tax data. These data have the potential to increase transparency regarding basic measures of economic activity as well as tax payments in different jurisdictions. Governments should create opportunities for researchers to access and analyze the data that are collected as a part of this and other efforts.

Private sector organizations have emerged as providers of data on multinationals. The Orbis dataset compiled by Bureau van Dijk provides some income statement and balance sheet information covering the operations of parents and affiliates based in more than 30 developed and developing countries. The WorldBase data compiled by Dun & Bradstreet cover establishments in more than 205 countries and territories, providing basic information about the industries of multinational affiliates and the scales of their activities. Private data can supplement and improve the accuracy of government-collected data, but they cannot substitute for the breadth, historical continuity, and integrity of publicly gathered and distributed data.

Additional effort should also be dedicated to tracking more extensively forms of multinational activity that have likely grown in recent decades and present distinctive policy considerations. For example, anecdotal evidence suggests that a considerable fraction of international activity occurs on a long-term contractual basis that is distinct from an ownership relationship or a spot market transaction. Under these relationships, a multinational parent might contract for manufacturing to occur in one location at an establishment it does not own, while distribution occurs in a separate set of owned wholesale or retail locations. More and better data on such global supply chains that stretch between unrelated firms would improve our understanding of these production processes and inform relevant public policies.

CONCLUSION

The benefits and risks of the activities of multinational corporations call for thoughtful and rigorous regulation. Multinationals can have enormous impacts on real income levels, the products and services that people consume, and on quality of life. However, the size and scale of these firms position them to take advantage of aspects of the global economic system in a manner that promotes narrow corporate self-interests. Well-designed policies are required to allow the free movement of economic factors so that multinationals can operate efficiently while at the same time protecting those who lose out when efficiency gains are realized. The cross-border nature of multinational firm activity necessitates that policies be coordinated across jurisdictions, particularly policies related to innovation and taxes. And the formulation of well-designed policies depends on our understanding the activities of these firms, an understanding that can only be obtained with extensive financial and operating data that characterize their behaviors. Given the extent of public skepticism about multinationals despite the benefits they create, it is imperative that regulators take further action to address the risks posed by multinationals now.

NOTES

1. Business Roundtable, *Statement on the Purpose of the Corporation,* August 19, 2019, https://opportunity.businessroundtable.org/ourcommitment/.

CONTRIBUTORS

EMMA AISBETT is a fellow at the School of Regulation and Global Governance, and associate director (research) of the Zero-Carbon Energy for the Asia-Pacific Grand Challenge at the Australian National University. She has published widely on the interaction between globalization (particularly multinational enterprises) and social and environmental policy and outcomes. With a PhD in agricultural and resource economics (Berkeley), an MSc in environmental change and management (Oxon.), and a bachelor's in chemical engineering (UNSW), she brings a transdisciplinary approach to complex global problems and regularly collaborates with scholars from disciplines including law, political science, and engineering.

ANDREW B. BERNARD is the Kadas T'90 Distinguished Professor at the Tuck School of Business at Dartmouth College. He received his AB from Harvard and his PhD from Stanford. Professor Bernard is affiliated with the National Bureau of Economic Research (NBER), the Centre for Economic Policy Research (CEPR), the Centre for Economic Performance (CEP) at the LSE, and CESIfo. He has been named by Thompson Reuters as one of the most highly cited researchers each year since 2014 and is among the one hundred most cited economists. Professor Bernard is an expert in international trade and investment and specializes in firm responses to globalization and global production networks.

LEE BRANSTETTER is a professor of economics and public policy at the Heinz College of Information Systems and Public Policy at Carnegie Mellon University, a nonresident senior fellow at the Peterson Institute for International Economics, and a research associate of the National Bureau of Economic Research. In 2011 and 2012, Branstetter served as a senior economist on the staff of President Barack Obama's Council of Economic Advisers. Branstetter holds a BA in economics and mathematical methods in the social sciences from Northwestern University and a PhD in economics from Harvard University.

ANUSHA CHARI is a professor of economics and finance at the University of North Carolina at Chapel Hill and a research associate in the NBER's International Finance and Macroeconomics Program. Her research interests lie in international finance, with a specific focus on emerging market economies. She received a PhD in business economics from the Anderson School at UCLA and holds a BA in philosophy, politics, and economics from Balliol College at Oxford, where she was the recipient of a Radhakrishnan Scholarship, and a BA in economics from Delhi University. She has held faculty positions at the University of Chicago, Michigan, and Berkeley. She served as a special adviser to the prime minister of India's Economic Advisory Council and a member of an Advisory Group of Eminent Persons on G20 Issues.

RONALD B. DAVIES has been a professor of economics at University College Dublin since 2008. After earning his PhD at the Pennsylvania State University in 1999, he joined the University of Oregon faculty, where he remained until relocating to Dublin. Specializing in trade and foreign direct investment, he has a particular focus on the tax and trade policies that affect globalization. In addition to his primary affiliation with UCD, professor Davies is a fellow with the Oxford University Centre for Business Taxation, the CESIfo, and a founder of the Society of International Trade Theory.

DHAMMIKA DHARMAPALA is the Julius Kreeger Professor at the University of Chicago Law School, co-editor of the *Journal of Law and Economics*, a member of the advisory board of the Urban-Brookings Tax Policy Center, an international research fellow at the Oxford University Centre for Business Taxation, and a fellow of the CESifo Research Network. He received an undergraduate degree from the University of Western Australia and a PhD in economics from the University of California at Berkeley. His PhD thesis was awarded the National Tax Association's Outstanding Doctoral Dissertation Award. His research has been published in scholarly journals in law, economics, and finance and has been cited in various media outlets, including the *New York Times*, the *Washington Post*, *Bloomberg Businessweek*, and *The Economist*.

SCOTT DYRENG is professor of accounting at Duke University. His research interests are in corporate tax avoidance, international taxation, and accounting for income taxes. He has published in *The Accounting Review*, *Journal of Accounting Research*, *Journal of Accounting and Economics*, and *Journal of Financial Economics*, among others. He teaches managerial accounting to graduate students, and has received the Excellence in Teaching Award in the Duke MBA and MMS programs. He received his PhD at the University of North Carolina at Chapel Hill in 2008. He holds a master's and bachelor's in accounting from Brigham Young University.

BENJAMIN EDELMAN is an economist at Microsoft, where he writes—and advises the company—about a variety of questions at the intersection of software, strategy, economics, and public policy. His article is based on his research while serving as an associate professor at the Harvard Business School.

ISIL EREL is the David A. Rismiller Chair in Finance and the academic director of the Risk Institute at the Ohio State University. She is also a research associate at the NBER's corporate finance program. Her research focuses on mergers and acquisitions, corporate governance, and financial institutions, and has been published in the *Journal of Finance*, *Journal of Financial Economics*, and *Review of Financial Studies*. She is currently an editor of the *Review of Corporate Finance Studies*. She is the recipient of the Pace Setters Faculty Research Award, the Distinguished Faculty Award, and the Recognition Award at the Fisher College of Business. Erel holds a PhD in financial economics from MIT Sloan School of Management. She serves on the boards of FARFE and the Risk Institute.

C. FRITZ FOLEY is the André R. Jakurski Professor and senior associate dean for strategic financial planning at Harvard Business School. His research focuses on corporate finance and international trade and investment.

BRITTA GLENNON is an assistant professor at the Wharton School at the University of Pennsylvania and a faculty research fellow of the National Bureau of Economic Research. Her research sits at the intersection of innovation, immigration, and international economics, with a particular focus on the changing structure of the high-skilled activities of multinational firms. Glennon holds a BA in economics and East Asian studies (Chinese) from Cornell University, an MPP from the University of Chicago, and a PhD in public policy and management from Carnegie Mellon University.

MICHELLE HANLON is the Howard W. Johnson Professor at the MIT Sloan School of Management. Her research focuses on taxation and the intersection of taxation and financial accounting. She has published in each of the top accounting and finance journals, among others. She is an editor at the *Journal of Accounting and Economics*, has won awards for her research and for her teaching, and was named a 2020 Presidential Scholar by the American Accounting Association. She has testified in front of House and Senate congressional committees and worked as an academic fellow at the U.S. House Ways and Means Committee. She is currently on a tax commission for Massachusetts. She earned her PhD at the University of Washington.

ANN E. HARRISON is dean of the Haas School of Business at the University of California, Berkeley. Harrison came to Haas from the University of Pennsylvania's Wharton School, where she was a professor of multinational management and business economics and public policy. Before joining Wharton, she was the director of development policy at the World Bank. She is the author of dozens of journal articles and the editor of three books, including *Globalization and Poverty* and *The Factory-Free Economy: Outsourcing, Servitization, and the Future of Industry*. Harrison earned her PhD in economics from Princeton University. She also holds a DEUG (diplôme d'études universitaires générales) from the University of Paris.

JAMES R. HINES JR. teaches at the University of Michigan, where he is Richard A. Musgrave Collegiate Professor of Economics in the department of economics, L. Hart Wright Collegiate Professor of Law in the law school, and research director of the business school's Office of Tax Policy Research. He is the 2017 recipient of the National Tax Association's Daniel M. Holland Medal for lifetime achievement in the study of public finance.

YEEJIN JANG is a senior lecturer (assistant professor) in the School of Banking and Finance, University of New South Wales. She worked as an assistant professor at Purdue University from 2013 to 2018. Her research focuses on empirical corporate finance with special interests in mergers and acquisitions, capital raising in global markets, multinational firms, and international banking. She holds a PhD in finance from the Ohio State University, as well as a BAA and an MS in business administration from Korea University.

J. BRADFORD JENSEN is McCrane/Shaker Chair of International Business at the McDonough School of Business at Georgetown University, a nonresident senior fellow at the Peterson Institute for International Economics, and a research associate at the National Bureau of Economic Research. Prior to joining Georgetown, Jensen had served as deputy director at the Peterson Institute for International Economics and director of the Center for Economic Studies at the U.S. Census Bureau. Jensen received a PhD in economics from Stanford University and a BA from Kalamazoo College.

IN SONG KIM is the Class of 1956 Career Development associate professor of political science at the Massachusetts Institute of Technology. He completed his PhD in politics at Princeton University. His research interests include international political economy and formal and quantitative methodology. His research focuses on the political economy of lobbying and campaign donation, estimation of political preferences, and causal inference with panel data. He conducts big data analysis of international trade, developing methods for dimension reduction and visualization to investigate how the structure of international trade around the globe has evolved over time. His work has appeared in various academic journals, including the *American Political Science Review*, *American Journal of Political Science*, *International Organization*, *Political Analysis*, and *The Journal of Politics*.

DAVID I. LEVINE is the Eugene E. and Catherine M. Trefethen Professor of Business Administration at Berkeley Haas, where he chairs the economic analysis and policy group. He is past chair of the university's Center for Health Research, and of the advisory board for the Center for Effective Global Action (CEGA). Levine was an undergraduate at Berkeley. He has taught at the Haas School since receiving his PhD in economics from Harvard University. Levine has also had visiting positions at the Sloan School of Management at MIT, the U.S. Department of Labor, and the President's Council of Economic Advisers.

JAMES R. MARKUSEN earned his BA and PhD degrees in economics from Boston College. He holds the rank of University Distinguished Professor at the University of Colorado, Boulder. Much of Markusen's research has concentrated on the location, production, and welfare effects of multinational corporations. He developed the knowledge-capital model of multinational firms, which focuses on the non-rivaled and non-excludable properties of knowledge-based assets. Markusen is particularly known for advancing the idea and finding that multinationals are primarily horizontal structures; the replication of firm activities in many countries better characterizes multinationals than vertical models based on production fragmentation.

RAYMOND J. MATALONI JR. is chief of the Research and Methodology Group of the International Economics Directorate of the U.S. Bureau of Economic Analysis. He has more than thirty years of experience at the bureau in measuring and analyzing the U.S. economy, with a primary focus on international economics, particularly foreign direct investment and trade in services. He is a member of the NBER Conference on Research in Income and Wealth and a bureau member of the OECD Working Group on International Investment Statistics. He (and his co-authors) have published in journals such as *Journal of World Business*, *Journal of International Management*, and *Review of Economics and Statistics*. He holds a PhD in economics from American University.

HELEN V. MILNER is the B.C. Forbes Professor of Politics and International Affairs at Princeton University and the director of the Niehaus Center for Globalization and Governance at Princeton's School of Public and International Affairs. She is a member of the National Academy of Sciences, the American Academy of Arts and Sciences, and the Council on Foreign Relations. She has written extensively on issues related to international and comparative political economy, the connections between domestic politics and foreign policy, and the impact of globalization on domestic politics. She is currently working on issues related to globalization and the rise of extreme right parties in democracies, the political economy of foreign aid and trade, and the resource curse and democracy in developing countries.

LINDSAY OLDENSKI is an associate professor at Georgetown University's School of Foreign Service. She received her PhD in economics from the University of California, San Diego, and her master's in public policy from the

Harvard University Kennedy School of Government. Prior to joining the Georgetown faculty, Dr. Oldenski taught at the Johns Hopkins University School of Advanced International Studies and California State University, San Marcos. She has also worked as an economist at the U.S. Department of Treasury, an analyst at the Federal Reserve Bank of Boston, and a consultant in the biotech industry. She has been awarded research fellowships from the Federal Reserve Board of Governors, the Center on Pacific Economies, and the Institute on Global Conflict and Cooperation.

JASON SCORSE completed his PhD in agricultural and natural resource economics at UC-Berkeley with a focus on environmental economics and policy, international development, and behavioral economics. Upon graduation, he became a full-time faculty member of the Middlebury Institute of International Studies at Monterey. He teaches courses in environmental and natural resource economics, ocean and coastal economics, and behavioral economics. In 2009 he was promoted to chair of the International Environmental Policy Program, and in 2011 he became the director of the Center for the Blue Economy, which provides "leadership in research, education, and analysis to promote a sustainable ocean and coastal economy."

JED SILVER is a PhD student in agricultural and resource economics at UC-Berkeley. His research focuses on the relationship between household savings and consumption smoothing, particularly for agricultural households and small firm owners in developing countries. Prior to Berkeley, he was a research assistant in IFPRI's Development Strategy and Governance Division.

CATHERINE THOMAS is an associate professor of managerial economics and strategy at the London School of Economics. She is the director of the Centre for Economic Performance (CEP) International Trade Programme and is a research fellow at the Centre for Economic Policy Research (CEPR) and the CESifo Research Network. She was formerly an assistant professor of economics at Columbia Business School, her PhD is from Harvard University, and she has an MA from the University of Edinburgh. Her research fields are industrial organization, trade, and organizational economics. She has published papers in economics and management journals and also serves on several editorial boards. She worked at McKinsey and Company before starting her PhD.

MICHAEL S. WEISBACH is the Ralph W. Kurtz Chair in finance at the Ohio State University, as well as a research associate at the National Bureau of Economic Research. Professor Weisbach has a broad range of research and teaching interests in finance and economics, with specialties in corporate finance, corporate governance, and private equity. He has fifty-eight publications on these and related topics. These papers have won a number of major awards, including the Brattle Group Prize (twice), the Jensen Prize, the Fama/DFA Prize, and the Wharton/WRDS award. His papers, written with fifty-five different co-authors, have been cited more than 40,000 times according to Google Scholar, and have been downloaded from SSRN.com more than 79,000 times.

DAVID WESSEL is a senior fellow in the Economic Studies program at the Brookings Institution and director of the Hutchins Center on Fiscal and Monetary Policy. Before joining Brookings, he spent thirty years at the *Wall Street Journal*. He is the author of *In Fed We Trust: Ben Bernanke's War on the Great Panic* (2009), and *Red Ink: Inside the High Stakes Politics of the Federal Budget* (2012). His book on opportunity zones, *The Zero Tax Zone*, will be published in October 2021. He has shared two Pulitzer Prizes, one for a *Boston Globe* series on the persistence of racism in Boston and the other for *Wall Street Journal* stories on corporate scandals. David is a graduate of Haverford College.

INDEX

Page numbers followed by b, f, or t represent boxes, figures, or tables, respectively.

content.com/pod-product-compliance
urce LLC

4210926
'00001B/20
0 8 1 5 7 3 8 5 5 8 *